Athenian Potters
and Painters
Volume III

This volume is dedicated to H. A. Shapiro

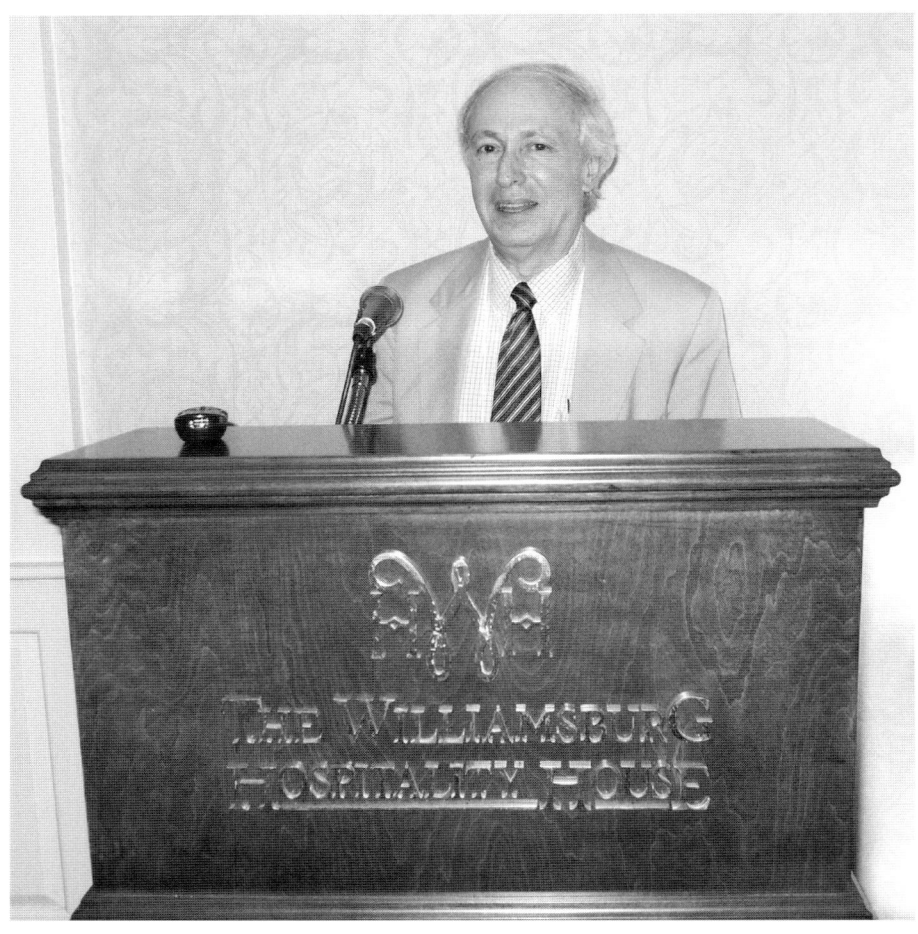

The honoree at the conference
(Photo: William Kahlenberg)

Athenian Potters and Painters
Volume III

EDITED BY
JOHN H. OAKLEY

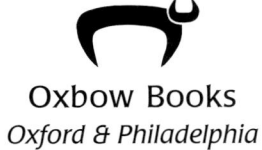

Oxbow Books
Oxford & Philadelphia

Published in the United Kingdom in 2014 by
OXBOW BOOKS
10 Hythe Bridge Street, Oxford OX1 2EW

and in the United States by
OXBOW BOOKS
908 Darby Road, Havertown, PA 19083

© Oxbow Books and the individual authors 2014

Hardcover Edition: ISBN 978-1-78297-663-9
Digital Edition: ISBN 978-1-78297-664-6

A CIP record for this book is available from the British Library

Library of Congress Control Number: 2010290514

All rights reserved. No part of this book may be reproduced or transmitted in any form or by any means, electronic or mechanical including photocopying, recording or by any information storage and retrieval system, without permission from the publisher in writing.

Printed in the United Kingdom by Short Run Press, Exeter

For a complete list of Oxbow titles, please contact:

UNITED KINGDOM
Oxbow Books
Telephone (01865) 241249, Fax (01865) 794449
Email: oxbow@oxbowbooks.com
www.oxbowbooks.com

UNITED STATES OF AMERICA
Oxbow Books
Telephone (800) 791-9354, Fax (610) 853-9146
Email: queries@casemateacademic.com
www.casemateacademic.com/oxbow

Oxbow Books is part of the Casemate Group

Front cover: Attic black-figure amphora, Berlin F1685. Photo: bpk, Berlin/ Antikensammlung, Staatliche Museen, Berlin, Germany/Ingrid Gesk /Art Resource, NY.
Back cover: Attic white-ground lekythos attributed to the Thanatos Painter. Boston, Museum of Fine Arts 01.8080, Henry Lillie Pierce Fund. Photo: © 2013 Museum of Fine Arts, Boston.

Contents

Foreword vii

1 Fallen Vessels and Risen Spirits: Conveying the Presence of the Dead on White-ground Lekythoi
   Nathan T. Arrington 1

2 Under the Tuscan Soil: Reuniting Attic Vases with an Etruscan Tomb
   Sheramy D. Bundrick 11

3 Regional Variation: Pelops and Chrysippos in Apulia
   T. H. Carpenter 22

4 Baskets, Nets and Cages: Indicia of Spatial Illusionism in Athenian Vase-painting
   Beth Cohen 30

5 Red-figured Cups in the Kerameikos
   Heide Frielinghaus 40

6 Smikros and Epilykos: Two Comic Inventions in Athenian Vase-painting
   Guy Hedreen 49

7 Facing West: Athenian Influence on Isolated Heads in Italian Red-figure Vase-painting
   Keely Elizabeth Heuer 63

8 The Gigantomachy in Attic and Apulian Vase-Painting. A New Look at Similarities, Differences and Origins
   Frank Hildebrandt 72

9 Plates by Pasteas
   Mario Iozzo 80

10 Some Greek Vases in the Museum of Mediterranean Archaeology at Nir David (Gan Hashlosha) Israel
    Sonia Klinger 98

11 Trade of Athenian Figured Pottery and the Effects of Connectivity
    Kathleen Lynch and Stephen Matter 107

12 Beautiful Men on Vases for the Dead
    Thomas Mannack 116

13 The View from Behind the Kline: Symposial Space and Beyond
    Timothy McNiven 125

14 Chariots in Black-figure Attic Vase-painting: Antecedents and Ramifications
    Joan R. Mertens 134

15 "Whom are You Calling a Barbarian?" A Column Krater by the Suessula Painter
    J. Michael Padgett 146

16 Good Dog, Bad Dog: A Cup by the Triptolemos Painter and Aspects of Canine Behavior on Athenian Vases
    Seth D. Pevnick 155

17 A Scorpion and a Smile: Two Vases in the Kemper Museum of Art in St. Louis
    Susan I. Rotroff 165

18 Demographics and Productivity in the Ancient Athenian Pottery Industry
    Philip Saperstein 175

19 An Amazonomachy Attributed to the Syleus Painter
    David Saunders 187

20 Democratic Vessels? The Changing Shape of Athenian Vases in Late Archaic and Early Classical Times
    Stefan Schmidt 197

21 A Kantharos in the Museum of Fine Arts, Boston and the Reception of Athenian Red-figure in Boeotia
    Phoebe Segal 206

22 Oikos and Hetairoi: Black-figure Departure Scenes Reconsidered
    Martina Seifert 215

23 The Robinson Group of Panathenaic Amphorae
    H. A. Shapiro 221

24 Guess Who's Coming to Dinner? Red-figure Komasts and the Performance Culture of Athens
    Tyler Jo Smith 231

25 Menelaos and Helen in Attic Vase Painting
    Mark D. Stansbury-O'Donnell 242

26 Attic Black-figure and Red-figure Fragments from the Sanctuary of Apollo at Mandra on Despotiko
    *Robert F. Sutton and Yannos Kourayo*s 253

27 The Attic Phiale in Context. The Late Archaic Red-figure and Coral-red Workshops
    Athena Tsingarida 263

Color Plates 1–32 273

Foreword

This volume contains the papers presented at the international conference *Athenian Potters and Painters III* held at the College of William and Mary in Virginia on September 11–14, 2012 (http://www.wm.edu/as/classicalstudies/athenian-conference/). The study of Athenian pottery, the most important fine ware in the Mediterranean during the Greek Archaic and Classical periods, is a rich subject, and this is the third conference devoted to it, the first in the USA. The two previous ones were held in Athens, Greece at the American School of Classical Studies at Athens in 1994 and 2007.

Joan Mertens, Curator of Greek and Roman Art at the Metropolitan Museum of Art in New York, gave the Keynote Address which also served as the Department of Classical Studies' tenth annual Virginia Northcutt Brinkley Lecture on Ancient Greece and Egypt. Twenty-four other scholars presented papers, and three others came prepared to present should some emergency prevent one of the twenty-four from coming, which turned out to be the case in one instance. All twenty-seven papers are included here. The cast was international, as were the over one hundred participants, and representatives from thirteen countries were present (Austria, Belgium, Canada, Germany, Greece, Israel, Italy, Japan, Russia, Spain, Switzerland, United Kingdom, United States).

Accompanying the conference was an exhibit at the College's Muscarelle Museum of Art, *Greek Vases from Virginia Collections* (http://www.wm.edu/news/stories/2012/wm-hosts-international-conference-on-ancient-athenian-pottery-123.php). I thank Aaron De Groft the Director, John Spike the Chief Curator, and the rest of the museum's staff for all their help, assistance, and good humor in planning and running this exhibit, as well as our lenders, which included the Virginia Museum of Fine Arts, the Chrysler Museum, and private collectors in the State. All of the vases in the exhibit met the Archaeological Institute of America's (AIA) guidelines for antiquities. The exhibit was co-curatored by me and one of my students, Alex Endres. The labels for the exhibit were penned by students in my course on Greek Vase-Painting.

The conference was sponsored by the Department of Classical Studies, The Reves Center for International Studies, the Provost's Office, the Office of Research Funds, the Williamsburg Chapter of the AIA, the Muscarelle Museum of Art and a Joseph J. Plumeri Award. Particular thanks for their help and generosity are due to Michael R. Halleran (Provost), Stephen E. Hanson (Vice Provost), Dennis M. Manos (Vice Provost), the faculty of the Department of Classical Studies, Joyce Holmes, Maura Brennan, Greg Callaghan, Peter Schertz, and Paul Hasse.

Professor Erika Simon, was the honorary guest. The Proceedings of the first conference were dedicated to her and Sir John Boardman, and the second to Professor Michalis Tiverios. This third volume is dedicated to my long-time friend and colleague, Professor Alan Shapiro, for he, as the earlier dedacatees, has contributed greatly to the field of Greek vase-painting, not only by his numerous influential and innovative publications, but also by the students that he has trained and the generosity that he has shown to us all. He, as the other dedacatees before him, set an example that is rarely found.

The abbreviations for archeological publications are those of the Deutsches Archäologisches Institut (http://www.dainst.org/tr/node/28771?ft=all). The format is that used in the earlier volume, which I retain here for continuity and simplicity. I did not standardize spellings or transliterations of Greek, but allowed the authors to use what they preferred. Abbreviations for the ancient literary sources are those of the *Oxford Classical Dictionary*^{3} (1996) xxix–liv. In addition, the following abbreviations are used:

ABL	C. H. E. Haspels, Attic Black-figured Lekythoi (1936).
ABV	J. D. Beazley, Attic Black-figure Vase-painters (1956).
Agora XII	B. A. Sparkes – L. Talcott, Black and Plain Pottery of the 6th, 5th, and 4th Centuries B.C., The Athenian Agora vol. XII (1970).
Agora XXIII	M. B. Moore – M. Z. P. Philippides, Attic Black-figured Pottery, The Athenian Agora vol. XXIII (1986).
Agora XXX	M. B. Moore, Attic Red-figured and White-ground Pottery, The Athenian Agora vol. XXX (1997).
ARV^2	J. D. Beazley, Attic Red-figure Vase-painters, 2nd ed. (1963).
APP	J. H. Oakley – O. Palagia – W. D. E. Coulson (eds.), Athenian Potters and Painters (1997).
APP II	J. H. Oakley – O. Palagia (eds.), Athenian Potters and Painters, Volume II (2009).

BAdd²	T. H. Carpenter, Beazley Addenda, 2nd ed. (1989).	Para	J. D. Beazley, Paralipomena (1971)
BAPD	Beazley Archive Pottery Database (http://www.beazley.ox.ac.uk/pottery/default.htm).	RH	G. M. A. Richter – L. F. Hall, Red-figured Athenian Vases in the Metropolitan Museum of Art (1936).
CAVI	H. Immerwahr, Corpus of Attic Vase Inscriptions (http://www2.lib.unc.edu/dc/attic/).	RVAp	A. D. Trendall – A. Cambitoglou, The Red-figured Vases of Apulia (1978–1982).
CB	L. D. Caskey – J. D. Beazley, Attic Vase Paintings in the Museum of Fine Arts, Boston (1931–1963).	Tsingarida, Shapes	A. Tsingarida (ed.), Shapes and Uses of Greek Vases (7th–4th Centuries BC) (2009).

John H. Oakley

1 Fallen Vessels and Risen Spirits: Conveying the Presence of the Dead on White-ground Lekythoi

Nathan T. Arrington

The Bosanquet Painter decorated two white-ground lekythoi with scenes that, at first glance, appear to be nearly identical. On both, a lekythos in the Metropolitan Museum of Art (Fig. 1)[1] and another in the Antikenmuseum und Sammlung Ludwig in Basel (Fig. 2; Color Pl. 1A),[2] a woman and a young, beardless man flank grave monuments. The grave stelai are wrapped with fillets, and vessels, wreaths, and fillets adorn the monuments' steps. So the women are visiting the graves at some unspecified period after burial.[3] They carry oinochoai in their left hands and hold out phialai in their right hands to make libations (probably of wine) in honor of the dead. The young men at the grave look intently at the women. In short, the New York and Basel lekythoi both display typical scenes of a visit to a grave. Such images became quite common around the middle of the fifth century, when lekythoi had a predominantly funerary function.[4] Deposited with the dead or at their tombs, when decorated they bore imagery appropriate for the grave, with women often depicted bringing wreaths, fillets, and vessels (including lekythoi) to honor the dead. And yet one detail on the Basel lekythos is rather unusual within the corpus of white-ground lekythoi: among the grave offerings on the steps of the tomb, a lekythos lies fallen on its side. Is there any significance to this small sign? Is the Basel lekythos semantically any different from the New York lekythos?

A fallen vessel, often a lekythos, occurs on only ten white-ground lekythoi. Six are similar in composition to the Basel lekythos – a man and a woman flank a decorated grave with one or more fallen vessels on its steps – and are chronologically close.[5] The Sabouroff Painter provides one image;[6] the Bosanquet Painter depicts four in addition to Fig. 2;[7] and the Thanatos Painter one.[8] The three other examples differ. The Beldam Painter represents a fallen vessel at the bottom of the image's field (i.e., not on the tomb steps) in one of the earliest scenes of a visit to the grave, where two women with baskets of offerings flank the tomb.[9] An artist near the Quadrate Painter depicts two women flanking a grave monument, a child on its steps touching the stele, and a hydria split in two tumbling off the steps.[10] An unattributed lekythos in the Louvre

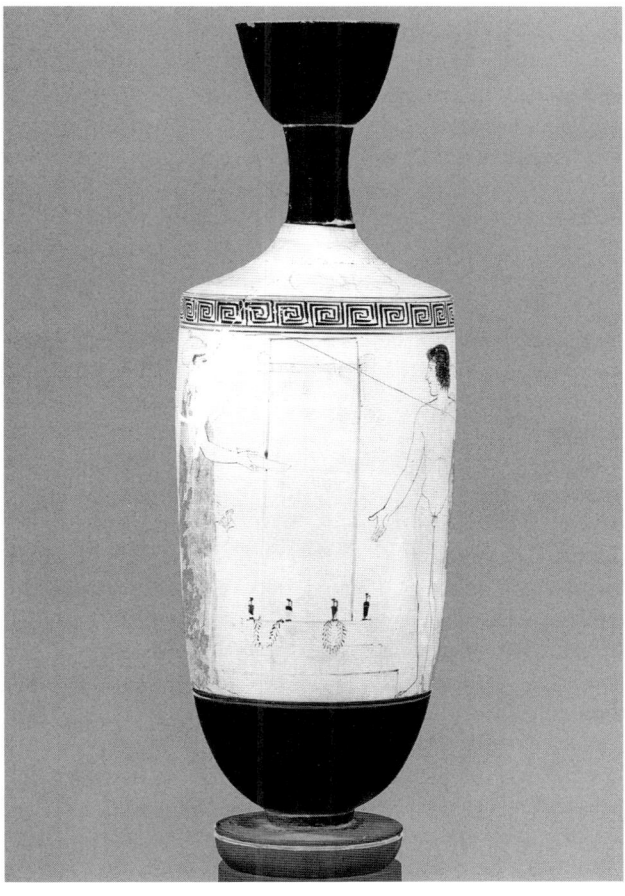

Fig. 1 Attic white-ground lekythos attributed to the Bosanquet Painter. New York, Metropolitan Museum of Art 23.160.39. Photo: © The Metropolitan Museum of Art. Image source: Art Resource, New York.

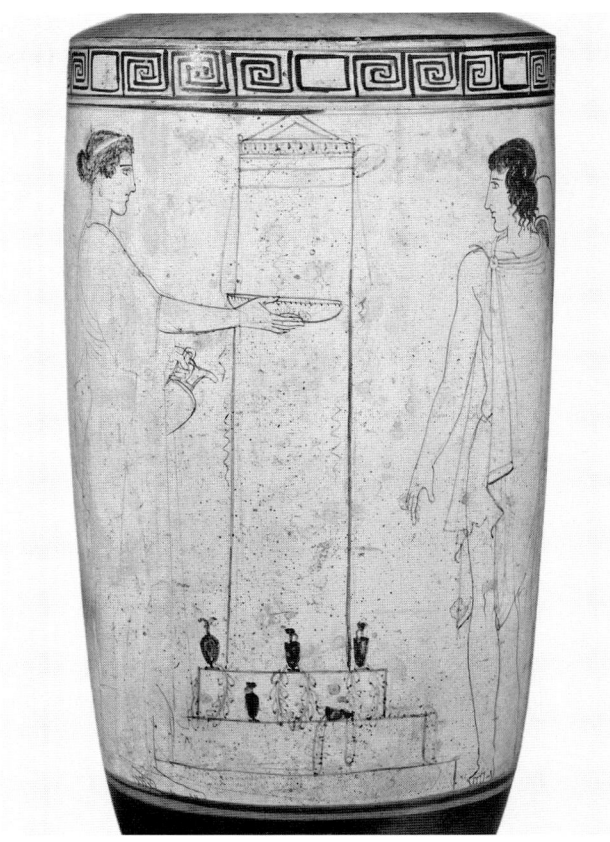

Fig. 2 Attic white-ground lekythos attributed to the Bosanquet Painter. Basel, Antikenmuseum und Sammlung Ludwig, Kä 402. Photo: Antikenmuseum und Sammlung Ludwig/A. Voegelin.

focalizes the steps of the grave and reveals several fallen vessels, but no persons are at the grave.[11] Fallen vessels on tomb steps also appear on a monumental red-figure loutrophoros in the manner of the Talos Painter,[12] where a group visits a grave decorated with an equestrian monument, and on a red-figure pelike attributed to the Jena Painter, where Orestes leaves a lock of hair at the tomb of Agamemnon.[13] The sign of the fallen vessel need not have the same significance in all these examples. In this essay I will first focus on the white-ground lekythoi with a composition similar to the Basel lekythos, for which sufficient comparanda exist for a productive, semiotic approach. I will then consider the red-figure vessels and the unusual lekythos in the Louvre.

Fallen vessels in Attic vase-painting usually index motion and surprise. A fallen and sometimes broken hydria, for instance, accompanies many scenes of Achilles pursuing Troilus, representing the haste of Polyxena's flight and perhaps also foreshadowing the youth's death.[14] Dropping a vase became a standard device to show women rushing from their pursuers,[15] and non-ceramic fallen objects could perform similar narrative functions. Menelaos, for instance, may drop his sword as he runs toward Helen.[16] The fallen weapon signals his change of intent while also conveying his swift motion. Armor and weapons can lie on battle grounds, indexing the movement of figures and the disarray of war.[17] Centaurs and Lapiths topple vases to the ground in their strife as they battle indoors.[18]

The hydria depicted in the process of tumbling off the steps of the grave monument on the lekythos by an artist near the Quadrate Painter similarly indexes motion, although it is difficult to identify with confidence what caused the vessel to fall (Fig. 3).[19] Some scholars have thought that the broken hydria on our lekythos stems from a ritual act,[20] but since both women are depicted in the process of going to the tomb with offerings in their hands, this is an unlikely scenario. The images on other lekythoi demonstrate that hydriai could rest on the steps of the tomb or serve as grave markers,[21] and so the child on the Quadrate Painter's lekythos probably broke a hydria placed on the grave steps as he ran from the left up to the stele. The vessel tumbles to the right, and traces of the child's right leg suggest that it was raised off the ground in a running motion. Although this fallen hydria seems to conform to the general function of fallen vessels in Attic vase-painting by indexing movement, the other fallen vessels do not fit the mold. The vessels are not in the process of falling, and the scenes in which they appear are quiet and nearly motionless.[22] The lekythos near the Quadrate Painter only makes the other lekythoi in need of further explication.

Fallen vessels on lekythoi have not gone unnoticed, nor have they received any sustained discussion. Interpretations generally may be divided into two views, although usually they were not advanced to explain every example. The first, advocated by Ernst Buschor, Donna Kurtz, Christoph Clairmont, and Erika Kunze-Götte, sees the vessels as efforts to represent the actual appearance of the grave.[23] They represent the detritus from rituals where vessels were broken at the tomb, or they simply fell over in the course of time. These images, the scholars contend (to varying degrees), reveal the artists' interest in reality. A second view adopts a more semiotic approach. For Stefan Schmidt, at least some of the vessels serve to demonstrate the consequences of not tending the grave.[24] John Oakley argues that they mark the passage of time.[25] A third view, of course, might be that these fallen vessels are meaningless variations to repetitive, stock scenes of a visit to the grave.

Painted *broken* lekythoi by the Beldam Painter, in the manner of the Talos Painter (Fig. 9), and possibly by the Bosanquet Painter[26] may stem from rituals, but the others are simply fallen rather than smashed. For instance, in the example by the Sabouroff Painter (Figs. 4–5) the lekythos clearly has fallen from the space between vessels two steps above.[27] So the view that the lekythoi transcribe a ritual moment can only explain a few of the examples, if any. And although some tombs may indeed have resembled the paintings of graves with fallen vessels, the interpretation that these objects were details serving to increase a painting's realism faces the difficulty that realism was not

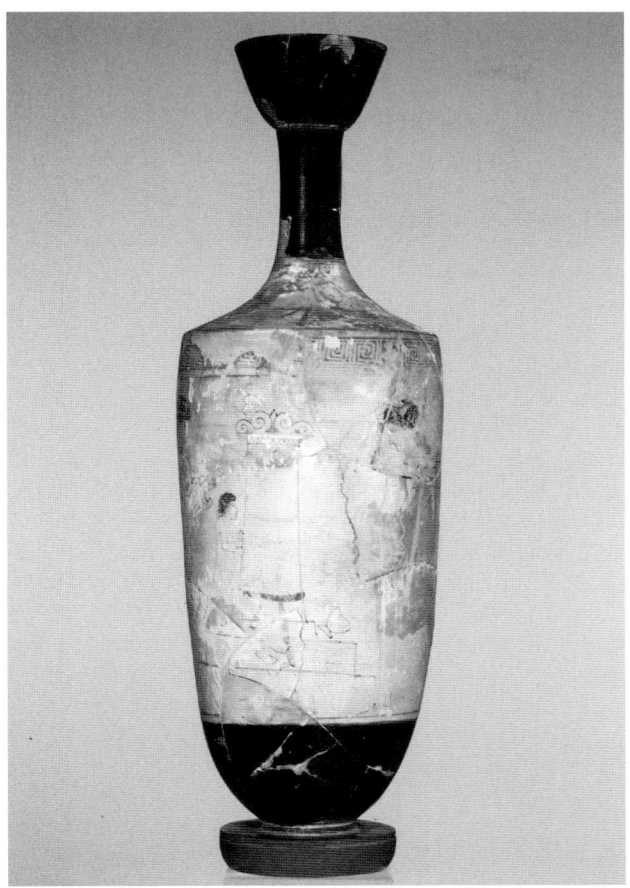

Fig. 3 Attic white-ground lekythos by an artist near the Quadrate Painter. Munich, Staatliche Antikensammlungen und Glyptothek, 2779. Photo: Renate Kühling.

the primary concern of Classical painters of white lekythoi such as the Sabouroff, Bosanquet, and Thanatos Painters. They conflate home and grave, with items such as vessels and mirrors impossibly suspended in midair by the tomb.

Moreover, there is reasonable doubt whether or not the grave monuments in the paintings are real, for few stone monuments survive from Classical Athens until they start to be made again ca. 430. While it is possible that some of these painted monuments imitate wooden ones erected at Athens that do not survive in the archaeological record – or reflect gravestones erected outside of Athens – or, after ca. 430, actual Athenian gravestones – in the end, the connection between the depicted image and reality remains remarkably loose.[28] There is little indication that painters strove to make any reliance on a model explicit. If the painters copied wooden stelai, they made them look like stone. If they copied real tymboi, they painted many with an improbable egg-shaped form. At the end of the century, when stone grave markers reappeared and when we might expect to find some consistency between depicted and real monuments, the painters reveal their hand, shunning the emerging sculpted forms of naiskoi or rosette stelai.

Find contexts further disassociate the images on the lekythoi from the intent of representing actual gravestones, for there is no consistency in appearance among the painted tomb monuments on various lekythoi deposited in the same grave. Considering the dearth of private stone monuments in the archaeological record, Christoph Clairmont postulated that painted monuments represented the state graves for the war dead.[29] This also is an unlikely explanation for the majority of the lekythoi. A few lekythoi that do seem to represent the public graves indicate what we could expect: multiple graves in one image, and a multitude of fillets wrapped around the stelai, which commemorated many persons.[30] In sum, lekythos painters strove not after realism but to present the idea of a grave and the concept of a grave visit.

The interaction between the persons and the tomb on Figs. 1–5 could occur at any grave, be it a public grave, a private grave, or a private cenotaph, with or without a large monument at the grave. The painted scenes have a basis in reality, but the painters did not aim to transcribe reality. The fallen vessels do not just heighten the realistic appearance of the grave, but participate in a constructed and imaginary picture. This does not necessarily imply, of course, that the painted fallen vessels have any significance. They might just be the quick work of a painter bored at the end of the day with making one grave visit after another. For a productive reading, we will have to look closer at the images of a man and woman at a tomb with one or more fallen vessels as a group to analyze them systematically in relation to each other and to their painters' output.

The fallen vessels on these lekythoi are signs within a larger semantic field that denotes a visit to a grave. To determine if these signs carry any connotations, we can assess to what extent they accompany other shifts in the semantic field of grave visit scenes.[31] Since this field functions according to its own inner, coherent logic as a signifying system composed of different elements working in relationship with one another, a meaningful change in the sign of the grave (i.e., the addition of the sign of a fallen lekythos) may entail a perceptible shift elsewhere in the field. Admittedly, such an examination of the relationship of the signs to one another produces a closed, syntactical reading of the image. By no means is this the only valid approach to the fallen vessels. Assessments of their paradigmatic significance (such as allusions to the detritus in battles), their metaphorical connotations (such as references to emptiness and absence),[32] or their manifestation of the image-in-image phenomenon[33] certainly are possible.

I have discussed elsewhere more broadly the implications of the fallen vessels for Athenian views on the role of objects in the commemoration of the war dead.[34] Here my aim is narrower: to assess the function and signification (if any) of the fallen vessel on lekythoi as a sign within a coherent system. This closed approach places more weight on artistic intent within a particular cultural setting than on viewer comprehension, especially when applied to such a small item as a fallen vessel on a grave monument, but is not inappropriate for these creative and talented artists who were masters of composition and detail. Indeed, the visits to a grave shown on white-ground lekythoi invite a semiotic approach, with a *sēma* front and center, small signs like vessels in mid-air signifying the home, and single attributes like aryballoi indicating a person's status. This is an image field in which details matter, but the detail of the fallen vessel has not been sufficiently addressed in scholarship.

Before considering anew the lekythos in Basel attributed to the Bosanquet Painter (Fig. 2; Color Pl. 1A), let us first look at the two examples of a fallen vessel by the hands of the Sabouroff Painter and the Thanatos Painter. As the Bosanquet Painter's predilection for the fallen vessel might be considered an idiosyncrasy (occurring on five out of a total fifteen white-ground lekythoi attributed to his hand), the Sabouroff Painter's and Thanatos Painter's single examples might be considered meaningless variations on an otherwise common subject of a visit to a grave. Let us first assess these one-offs within the repertoire of their work to determine what other shifts in the semantic field they may accompany.

On the lekythos by the Sabouroff Painter (Figs. 4–5) a woman approaches the grave, carrying a fillet in her hands which now has faded away.[35] Across from her, a man stands with his body frontal, hand on his hip, looking at the woman. The Sabouroff Painter depicted no small number of grave visits, and yet the frontal, hand-on-hip stance of the man in Figs. 4–5 reappears on only three other grave visits attributed to this painter.[36] The connotation of the pose for the Sabouroff Painter can be deduced from a lekythos where Hermes waits for the deceased with his hand on his hip.[37] Similarly, the youth on a Nolan amphora adopts the pose as he waits to be crowned by Nike.[38] The youth on a red-figure lekythos strikes the same stance, waiting to be crowned by a woman.[39] So the Sabouroff Painter consistently deploys this pose to show that a figure stands still and waits attentively.[40] He underscores the immobility and solidity of the man in Figs. 4–5 by placing his legs and feet close together, creating a strong vertical line. Thus, the fallen vessel accompanies a shift in the semantic field. The image denotes not just a man at the grave, but more particularly a man who has been waiting at the grave. In this context, the fallen vessel intensifies the value of the man's posture. Both the sign of the vessel and the posture of the man connote the passage of time and work in tandem to qualify the presence of the man.

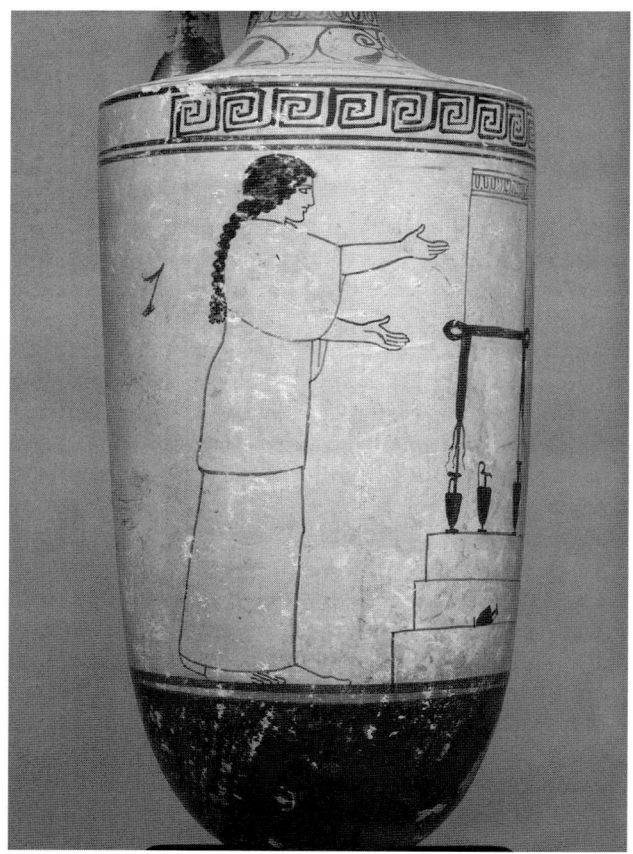
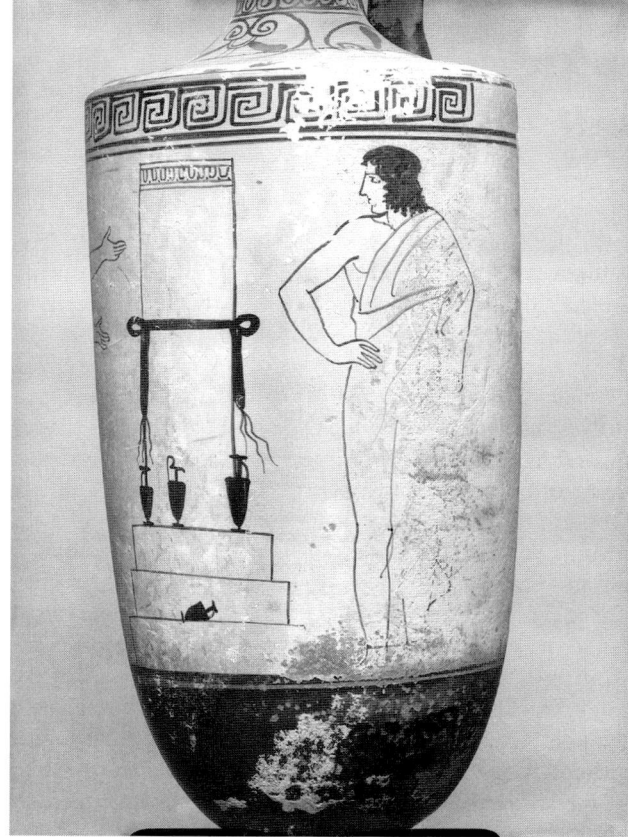

Figs. 4–5 Attic white-ground lekythos attributed to the Sabouroff Painter. Athens, National Museum 12739. Photo: © Hellenic Ministry of Education and Religions, Culture and Athletics/Archaeological Receipts Fund.

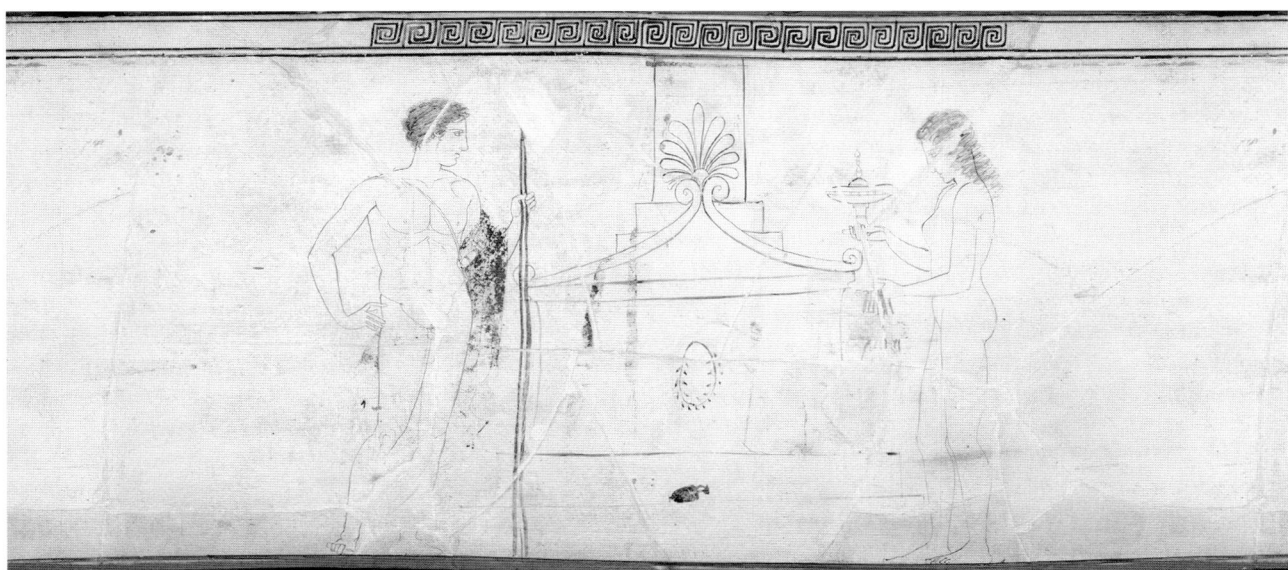

Fig. 6 Attic white-ground lekythos attributed to the Thanatos Painter. Boston, Museum of Fine Arts 00.359, Henry Lillie Pierce Fund. Photo: © 2013 Museum of Fine Arts, Boston.

On the lekythos attributed to the Thanatos Painter with a fallen vessel (Fig. 6) a woman approaches the tomb monument with an exaleiptron and writing tablets in her hands.[41] Across from her stands a man naked except for a chlamys draped over his left arm and a baldric with sword slung over his chest; one foot faces out of the image field and the other is turned toward the grave. He rests his right hand on his hip, has placed the butts of his spears on the ground, and motionlessly watches the woman approach the tomb.

There are no exact parallels for this posture among figures that flank grave monuments in the Thanatos Painter's repertoire, but there are comparanda among the statues that he depicted. On one lekythos, a statuette of a naked youth with his left hand on his hip stands atop a grave stele.[42] On another lekythos, one of the two statuettes depicted on a sarcophagus assumes a stance very close to the man in Fig. 6, with one foot facing out of the image field and the other turned toward the center of the grave, his left hand on his hip, and his right hand holding spears that rest on the sarcophagus lid (Fig. 7; Color Pl. 2A).[43] Often, instead, the Thanatos Painter shows men moving toward the tomb monument. On a lekythos in Athens, for instance, a soldier approaches a grave with both feet facing the monument. He carries a spear that does not touch the ground, and he raises his right arm to greet the woman at the other side of the monument.[44] Similarly, on a lekythos in Saarbrücken, a young male walks toward the tomb with both feet facing the monument and with his spear elevated off the ground.[45] In contrast, the positions of the spear and of the feet of the man in Fig. 6 convey his motionless presence. In sum, although the man in Fig. 6 adopts a slightly different stance than the man in Figs. 4–5, an overview of both painters' iconography

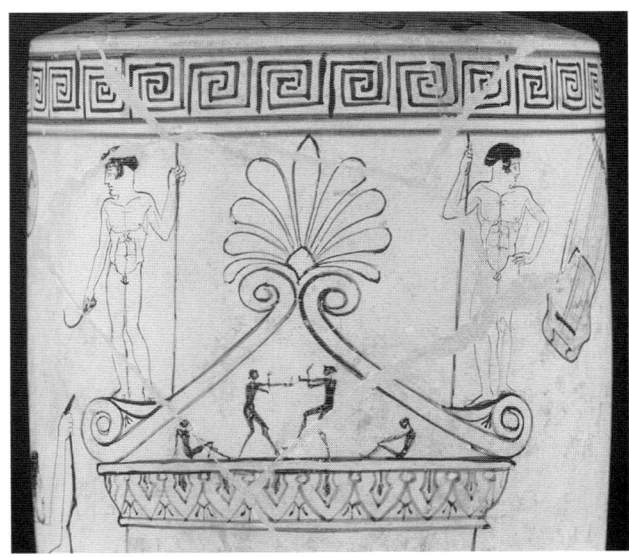

Fig. 7 Attic white-ground lekythos attributed to the Thanatos Painter. Boston, Museum of Fine Arts 01.8080, Henry Lillie Pierce Fund. Photo: © 2013 Museum of Fine Arts, Boston.

demonstrates that in each case the men assume postures that signify motionless and attentive waiting at the tomb. In this semantic field, the fallen vessels emphasize the temporal aspect of the men's presence that was also conveyed by their stance.

If we now return to the two lekythoi by the Bosanquet Painter (Figs. 1–2), we see that here, too, the fallen vessel accompanies a temporal difference in the images. In Fig. 1, the man is arriving at the tomb. His feet face the grave and his right hand gestures in greeting toward the woman.[46] In Fig. 2, in contrast, the man does not walk toward the grave or make a sign of salutation, but faces out of the field like the men in Figs. 4–6. His spears rest on the ground, emphasizing his immobility. His posture indicates that he has been waiting at the tomb, and the fallen vessel marks the considerable passage of time during which he waits.

The temporal coloring in Figs. 2, 4, 5, and 6 conveyed by posture and by the sign of the fallen vessel is significant because the men represent the spirit or *eidōlon* of the deceased. The dead in Homer, such as Patroclus and Elpenor, may appear to the living to seek proper burial.[47] By the Classical period, the border to the underworld had become more porous and the dead were less interested in seeking propitiation, being more keen on providing comfort and guidance.[48] The lines of tragedy contain many references to visions of the deceased. The dead might appear themselves on stage, such as Darius in Aeschylus' *Persians*, Polydorus in Euripides' *Hecuba*, or Achilles in Sophocles' *Polyxena*.[49] During the annual festival of the Anthesteria, the dead ranged through Athens.[50] They also could appear in dreams and visions: Admetus in Euripides' *Alcestis* voices the hope that he will see his dead wife when he sleeps.[51] The spirits of the dead were depicted in art.[52] In Archaic vase-painting, they could be represented as small, under-lifesize beings. On white-ground lekythoi, the dead may appear as miniature winged figures, but more often in the same guise as the living.

This ambiguous representational mode renders problematic the labeling of the dead in scenes of a visit to the grave, where both the living and the dead may appear at the tomb.[53] There are no strict guidelines for identification. A small stick-figure poised above the head of a figure can indicate his deceased status.[54] If a figure points down at the ground[55] or sits on the steps of the tomb,[56] he or she is probably the deceased. On a few occasions, the dark color of the dead conveys their phantom appearance.[57] If one of the figures visiting the tomb reacts emotionally to the sight of the other, then it is likely that the second figure is deceased, although it is also possible that the first figure only reacts to the sight of the grave.[58] Finally, the nudity or military apparel of a man at a grave usually indicates that he is dead, since people did not customarily dress this way when visiting tombs. Based upon their military attire and/or nudity, the men accompanying the fallen vessels in Figs. 2 and 6 are ghosts or *eidōla* of the deceased. On one other lekythos with fallen vessels from the hand of the Bosanquet Painter, a man similarly appears at the tomb naked, both feet facing forward, hand on hip, and spear resting on the ground; he is the deceased.[59] The emotional reactions of the visitors to the grave on two of the three comparanda for the man's posture in Figs. 4–5 suggest that the Sabouroff Painter used this stance to depict the dead,[60] and it recurs on a lekythos attributed to the Bosanquet Painter with a fallen vessel.[61] A pattern emerges: with the exception of the early lekythos attributed to the Beldam Painter and the lekythos near the Quadrate Painter, fallen vessels accompany visits to the grave in which the dead wait at the tomb.[62]

Of course, the dead can be present without a fallen vessel at the tomb. In Fig. 1, for instance, the man's nakedness indicates that he represents the deceased. But he is present in a different way than the *eidōlon* in Fig. 2: he walks toward the grave and greets the woman. In Fig. 2, in contrast, he has been waiting. There is also a temporal element at work in Fig. 1, since the woman visits an already decorated grave, but the fallen vessel in Fig. 2 increases the temporal span: it has been erected so long that it has tumbled.[63] These different modes of presentification accompany different moments of ritual at the tomb on these two lekythoi. In Fig. 1, the woman bends her arm down and dips the phiale slightly but visibly; she has begun to pour. In Fig. 2, in contrast, the phiale is still horizontal; she has not made a libation yet. In the first example, the libation triggers the appearance of the dead, who responds to the honor given to his tomb and perhaps to the invocation of his name. In the second, the dead is conceived as always present at his grave, waiting for mourners to tend the tomb. This attentive presence could be a warning to the living to care for the tomb and remember the deceased, but also could constitute a comforting message that the dead resided at the grave and perceived their honors.

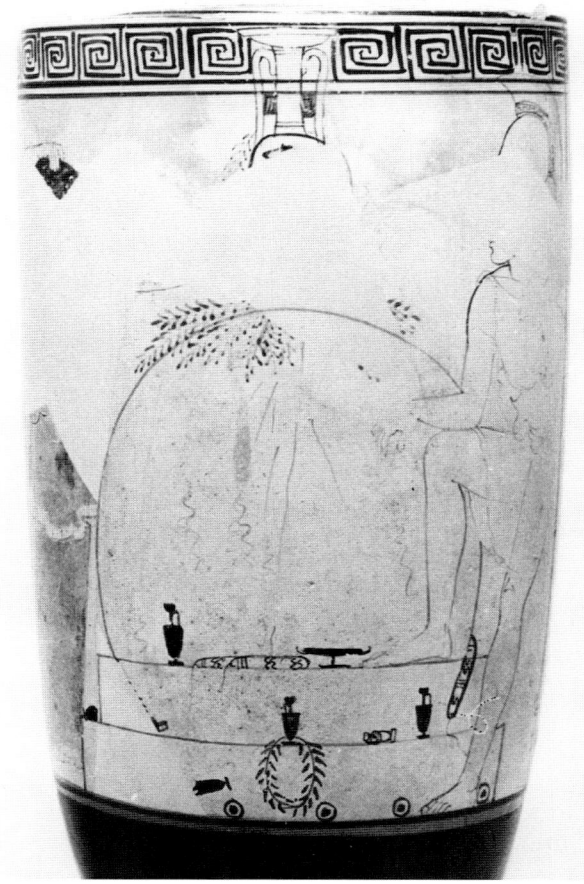

Fig. 8 Attic white-ground lekythos attributed to the Bosanquet Painter. Ticino, private K 315. Photo: Owner.

While the vessels were tipped and broken, the dead were conceived as assertive, permanent, and solid. We have seen that the Thanatos Painter used a posture for the deceased he normally reserved on lekythoi for statues. The frontal, hand-on-hip stance used by the Sabouroff Painter and also on two lekythoi by the Bosanquet Painter lends a stable mien to the dead. On a third example by the Bosanquet Painter, the deceased rests one leg on the steps of the tomb, invading the space of the grave monument and forcefully, albeit quietly, asserting his presence (Fig. 8).[64] He becomes assimilated to the site of ritual designated by the monumental tomb marker. On the loutrophoros in the manner of the Talos Painter, the deceased appears at his grave along with living visitors (Fig. 9).[65] He stands motionless, his spears cradled in his left arm, their ends resting on the ground. Juxtaposition with an equine bronze statue further conveys his statuesque presence. Working in tandem with the posture of the man to convey the passage of time, the sign of the fallen vessel also invites a comparison between the fragility of objects and the stable presence of the deceased.

For all the construction of the attentive and assertive presence of the dead in these images, for all their permanence heightened through contrast with the fallen vessels and assimilation to stone stelai and bronze statues, these *eidōla* were not always seen by the visitors to the tomb. On the loutrophoros, a large group processes to the tomb, but there is no indication that any of the living figures perceives the dead. The woman behind him looks down, and the position of her right foot indicates that she walks in front of the deceased. On the lekythos by the Thanatos Painter (Fig. 6), the woman who approaches the tomb also looks down and does not notice the dead. Whether or not the man in Fig. 2 is visible to mourners remains ambiguous; unlike the deceased in Fig. 1, he does not gesture toward the woman, but merely looks at her as she performs her ritual act. In Figs. 4–5, the woman continues her task of decorating the stele under the deceased's watchful eye. These present, but not necessarily visible dead witness the rituals performed at their grave like gods on Attic vases who view the sacrifices made in their honor.[66] The lekythoi suggest that an encounter with dead who perceived them was possible – as ghosts, visions, or dreams, all of which were forms of *eidōla* – but not certain.

The fallen vessel, then, becomes the visible and tangible sign of the presence of the dead, the reminder

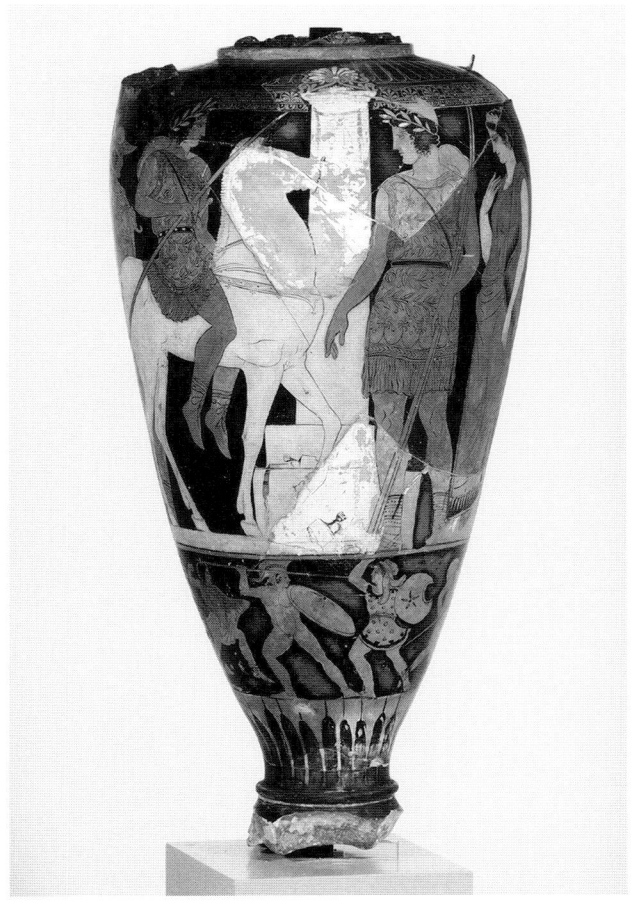

Fig. 9 Attic red-figure loutrophoros in the manner of the Talos Painter. Berlin, Staatliche Museen, Antikensammlung Inv. V.I. 3209. Photo: Johannes Laurentius. Photo: Art Resource, New York.

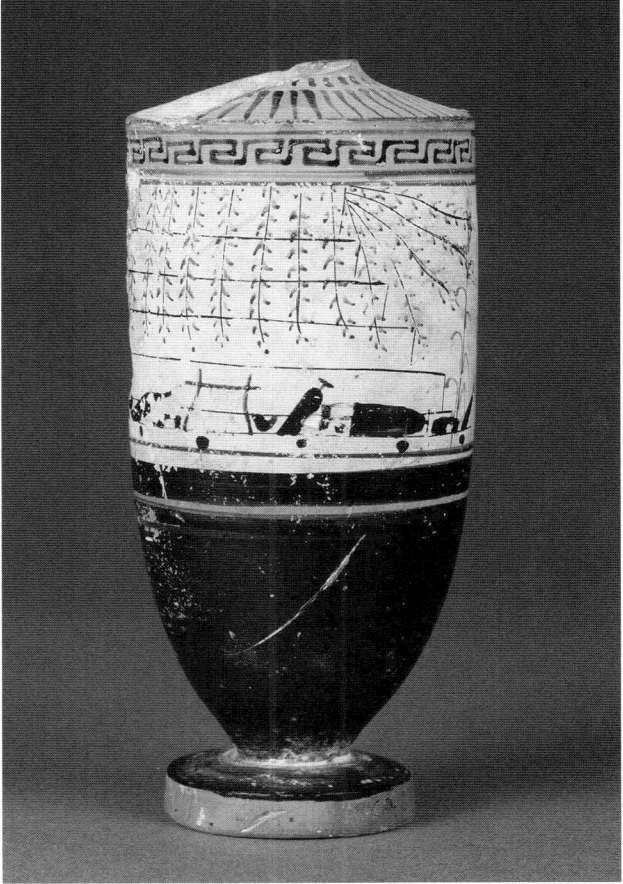

Fig. 10 Unattributed Attic white-ground lekythos. Paris, Musée du Louvre CA 3758. Photo: Hervé Lewandowski, © RMN-Grand Palais/Art Resource, New York.

that as time passes, the tomb persists as a site of memory, and the dead remain at their tomb. Perhaps the fallen vessel could even convey the presence of the dead without the sign of the man occurring in the image field. On the early-fourth century pelike with the tomb of Agamemnon and a fallen vessel,[67] the dead does not appear, but the viewer knows Agamemnon hears the prayers of Orestes and Electra who meet at his grave. The presence of Agamemnon is conveyed only by his name written on the tomb steps, accompanied by a fallen vessel. The dead also was not depicted on an unusual, unattributed lekythos that focuses on the steps of the tomb (Fig. 10; Color Pl. 1B).[68] Lekythoi and alabastra stand askew or lie on their side, and to the right of the tomb monument two stalks of grain have grown tall. This image precludes the vision of the dead even from the viewer of the lekythos. The fallen vessels and shoots of grain show that time has passed and may suggest that the dead is present, even if he remains unseen.

White-ground lekythoi preserve diverse modes of conceiving of the dead as present at sites of ritual and memory. While some Athenians pictured the dead coming to the tomb in response to rituals, others pictured the dead as always there, waiting to be remembered. The fallen vessels on a small group of white-ground lekythoi qualify and comment on the presence of the dead at the tomb, showing the passage of time in which the dead were present, although not necessarily visible, and inviting a contrast between fleeting objects and persistent *eidōla*. Mourners could be comforted by the thought that somehow, even if they were not visible, the dead were as present at the tomb as solid statues.

Acknowledgments

I thank John Oakley for the invitation to speak at *Athenian Potters and Painters III* and all the participants for their helpful comments, particularly Mark Stansbury-O'Donnell and Tim McNiven. Michael Padgett and Michael Koortbojian provided valuable feedback on earlier versions of this paper.

Abbreviations

Boardman, Classical	J. Boardman, Athenian Red Figure Vases, The Classical Period (1989)
Kavvadias, Sabouroff	G. G. Kavvadias, Ο Ζωγράφος του Sabouroff (2000)
Kurtz, AWL	D. C. Kurtz, Athenian White Lekythoi: Patterns and Painters (1975)
Oakley, Picturing Death	J. H. Oakley, Picturing Death in Classical Athens: The Evidence of the White Lekythoi (2004)

Notes

1 New York, Metropolitan Museum of Art 23.160.39; BAPD 216332; ARV^2 1227,4; $BAdd^2$ 350; Kurtz, AWL 209–210 pl. 30, 2.
2 Basel, Antikenmuseum und Sammlung Ludwig, Kä 402; BAPD 216331; ARV^2 1227,3; Para 466; $BAdd^2$ 174; Kurtz, AWL 37 n. 6; 38 n. 2; CVA Basel 3 76–77 pls. 47, 5–6. 50, 1–6.
3 Perhaps they visit the grave on the third or ninth days after burial, or on the occasion of the Genesia festival.
4 For the development and iconography of white-ground lekythoi, see the comprehensive treatment in Oakley, Picturing Death.
5 F. Felten, Thanatos- und Kleophonmaler (1971) identified the early phase of the Thanatos Painter as the Bosanquet Painter. Contra: J. H. Oakley, in: APP 243–244. 247, with further references. J. Mertens, GettyMusJ 2, 1975, 27–36 compares and contrasts the Bosanquet and Sabouroff Painters.
6 Infra n. 27 Figs. 4–5.
7 Supra n. 2 Fig. 2; infra n. 64 Fig. 8; infra ns. 26. 59. 61. Note also the dropped top on a red-figure lekythos attributed to the Bosanquet Painter: Oakley (supra n. 5) figs. 11–14.
8 Infra n. 41 Fig. 6.
9 Athens, National Museum 1982; BAPD 209259; ARV^2 751,1; $BAdd^2$ 285; ABL pls. 51,4; 52,1; Kurtz AWL 202 pl. 18, 2.
10 Infra n. 19 Fig. 3.
11 Infra n. 68 Fig. 10.
12 Infra n. 65, Fig. 9.
13 Exeter University; BAPD 231036; ARV^2 1516, 80; $BAdd^2$ 384; Boardman, Classical fig. 361.
14 E.g. the François Vase; BAPD 300000; ABV 76, 1; 682; Para 29; $BAdd^2$ 21; J. Boardman, *Athenian Black Figure Vases* (1991) fig. 46, 5.
15 E.g. Ferrara, Museo Nazionale di Spina; BAPD 213441; ARV^2 1032,58; 1679; Para 442; $BAdd^2$ 155; Boardman, Classical fig. 137.
16 E.g. Vatican, Museo Gregoriano Etrusco Vaticano 16535; BAPD 215554; ARV^2 1173; Para 460; $BAdd^2$ 339; Boardman, Classical fig. 309.
17 E.g. Geneva, Musée d'Art et d'Histoire MF238; BAPD 207115; ARV^2 615,1; Para 397; $BAdd^2$ 269; Boardman, Classical fig. 17.
18 E.g. Vienna, Kunsthistorisches Museum 1026; BAPD 214586; ARV^2 1087,2; $BAdd^2$ 327; Boardman, Classical fig. 185.
19 Munich, Antikensammlungen 2779; BAPD 9024399; CVA Munich 15 Germany 87 88–90 pl. 53.
20 W. Riezler, Weissgrundige attische Lekythen (1914) 108 n. 47.
21 On steps: G. Pellegrini, Catalogo dei vasi antichi dipinti delle Collezione Palagi ed universitaria (1900) no. 364 pl. IV. As grave marker: Harvard University, Arthur M. Sackler Museum 60.341; BAPD 207134; ARV^2 617,13 – London, British Museum E186; BAPD 207218; ARV^2 623,64 – Munich, Antikensammlungen 7663 (bronze hydria as grave marker); BAPD 215874; ARV^2 1200,40. Hydria brought to tomb: Bayonne, Musée Bonnat 223; BAPD 212333; ARV^2 846,185; Kavvadias, Sabouroff 198

no. 193 pls. 130–131 – London Market; BAPD 212337; ARV² 846,189 – Lausanne, Private; BAPD 212393; ARV² 849,244; 1672; Kavvadias, Sabouroff 203 no. 254 pl. 161 – Berlin, Antikensammlung 3964; BAPD 216383; ARV² 1230,42 – Athens, National Museum 1760; BAPD 216691; ARV² 1238,37 – Paris, Musée du Petit Palais 337; BAPD 217886; ARV² 1388,2 – Athens, National Museum 19335; BAPD 275502; ARV² 1687,2 – Athens, Third Ephoreia; Kavvadias, Sabouroff 207 no. 292 pl. 182. Libation: Karlsruhe, Badisches Landesmuseum 234; BAPD 217616; ARV² 1372,17; Aesch. *Pers.* 613. Washing stelai: Plut. *Arist.* 21.5. Cf. filling hydriai at fountains on lekythoi, e.g. Berlin, Antikensammlung 2338; BAPD 208160; ARV² 686,202. Sepulchral use of hydriai: E. Diehl, Die Hydria: Formgeschichte und Verwendung im Kult des Altertums (1964) 65–146.

22 The lekythos depicted on the bottom step of a lekythos in Ticino (Fig. 8) may be in the process of falling, but the full image is not preserved.

23 E. Buschor, MüJb 2, 1925, 168–170; Kurtz, AWL 38. 202. 210; C. W. Clairmont, Patrios Nomos: Public Burial in Athens during the Fifth and Fourth Centuries B.C. (1983) 79; D. C. Kurtz, in: H. A. G. Brijder (ed.), Ancient Greek and Related Pottery (1984) 328; E. Kunze-Götte, in: CVA Munich 15 Germany 87 90 (in reference to the broken hydria of Fig. 3).

24 S. Schmidt, Rhetorische Bilder auf attischen Vasen: visuelle Kommunikation im 5. Jahrhundert v. Chr. (2005) 46.

25 Oakley, Picturing Death 205.

26 The whole vessel is not preserved: Amsterdam, Allard Pierson Museum 2703; BAPD 42147; CVA Amsterdam 4 Netherlands 87 65–66 pl. 210, 6.

27 Athens, National Museum 12739; BAPD 212315; ARV² 845, 167; Kavvadias, Sabouroff 196 no. 174.

28 On the debate, see Oakley, Picturing Death 195. 198–199.

29 Clairmont (supra n. 23) 84–85.

30 A few vessels which probably do represent public graves conform to this pattern: New York, Metropolitan Museum of Art 35.11.5 (lekythos); BAPD 209194; ARV² 744,1; Para 413; BAdd² 284; Oakley, Picturing Death Color pl. 7 – Athens, National Museum 1700 (loutrophoros); BAPD 215190; ARV² 1146,50; Para 456; BAdd² 335; Boardman, Classical fig. 176 – Amsterdam, Allard Pierson Museum 2455 (loutrophoros); BAPD 42150; Clairmont (supra n. 23) pl. 3c – Athens, Third Ephoreia 6437 (lekythos); BAPD 45400; O. Tzachou-Alexandri, in: V. Ch. Petrakou (ed.), Ἔπαινος Ἰωάννου Κ. Παπαδημητρίου (1997) figs. 1–11.

31 Cf. C. Sourvinou-Inwood, 'Reading' Greek Culture: Texts and Images, Rituals and Myths (1991) 27–98.

32 Cf. the interpretation of tipped aryballoi in seduction scenes in J. Davidson, The Greeks and Greek Love: A Bold New Exploration of the Ancient World (2007) 540–543.

33 On the phenomenon: S. J. Gasiorowski, Le motif du vase dans l'art monumental de l'antiquité (1929); H. Gericke, Gefässdarstellungen auf griechischen Vasen (1970); W. Oenbrink, Hephaistos 14, 1996, 82–134.

34 Forthcoming monograph on the presence and memory of the war dead in fifth-century Athens.

35 For the fillet, cf. Athens, National Museum 2019; BAPD 212365; ARV² 848,216; Kavvadias, Sabouroff 201 no. 226 pl. 6.

36 Athens, Akropolis Museum; BAPD 212370; ARV² 848,221. 1672; Kavvadias, Sabouroff no. 231 pl. 154 – New York, Metropolitan Museum of Art 06.1021.132; BAPD 212394; ARV² 849,245; Kavvadias, Sabouroff 203 no. 255 pl. 162 – Athens, National Museum 17314; BAPD 212396; ARV² 849,247; Kavvadias, Sabouroff 204 no. 257.

37 Berlin, Staatliche Museen F 2455; BAPD 212344; ARV² 846,196; BAdd² 297; Kavvadias, Sabouroff 199 no. 204 pl. 139.

38 Amsterdam, Allard Pierson Museum L 1002; Kavvadias, Sabouroff 191 no. 131 pl. 95.

39 Laon, Musée Archéologique Municipal 37.957; BAPD 212300; ARV² 844,152; Kavvadias, Sabouroff 194 no. 158 pl. 110. Cf. Ferrara, Museo Nazionale Archeologico di Spina 9465; BAPD 212235; ARV² 840,56; Kavvadias 183 no. 56 pls. 56–57.

40 For the connotations of the pose, see T. J. McNiven, Gestures in Attic Vase Painting: Use and Meaning, 550–450 B.C. (1982) 97–100.

41 Boston, Museum of Fine Arts 00.359; BAPD 216364; ARV² 1229,23; BAdd² 351; Kurtz, AWL 210–211 pl. 32,1; Oakley, Picturing Death 196–197 figs. 158–159.

42 Bonn, Akademisches Kunstmuseum 66; BAPD 216356; ARV² 1229, 15; CVA Bonn 1 Germany 1 50 pls. 43,2.4; 44,2.4.

43 Boston, Museum of Fine Arts 01.8080; BAPD 216394; ARV² 1231; Oakley, Picturing Death 195 figs. 156–157.

44 Athens, National Museum 1761; BAPD 216358; ARV² 1229,17; BAdd² 351; Riezler (supra n. 20) pl. 31.

45 Saarbrücken, Institut für Klassische Archäologie 14; BAPD 22843; K. Braun, Katalog der Antikensammlung des Instituts für Klassische Archäologie der Universität des Saarlandes (1998) pl. 9.

46 For the significance of the gesture, see McNiven (supra n. 40) 128–131.

47 Hom. *Il.* 23.65–101; Hom. *Od.* 11.51–80.

48 On the appearance of ghosts, see S. I. Johnston, Restless Dead: Encounters Between the Living and the Dead in Ancient Greece (1999). In contrast, J. D. Mikalson, Honor thy Gods: Popular Religion in Greek Tragedy (1991) 114–121 argues that there was a pervasive belief that the dead did not perceive the actions of the living.

49 Aesch. *Pers.* 681–842; Eur. *Hec.* 1–58; Soph. *Polyxena* fr. 523 (Loeb).

50 Anthesteria: R. Parker, Polytheism and Society at Athens (2005) 290–316. See also Plato's reference to the popular belief that the dead could be seen at the grave: Pl. *Phd.* 81c–d.

51 Eur. *Alc.* 348–356.

52 On *eidōla*: G. Siebert, in: idem (ed.), Méthodologie iconographique: actes du Colloque de Strasbourg, 27–28 avril 1979 (1981) 4–63; E. Peifer, *Eidola* und andere mit dem Sterben verbundene Flügelwesen in der attischen Vasenmalerei in spätarchaischer und klassischer Zeit (1989); Sourvinou-Inwood (supra n. 31) 335–337; LIMC VIII (1997) 566–570 s.v. Eidōla (R. Vollkommer); D. Steiner, Images in Mind: Statues in Archaic and Classical Greek Literature and Thought (2001) 5–6; Oakley, Picturing Death 212–213.

53 Identification of the dead: J. Thimme, AntK 7 (1964) 24–26; D. C. Kurtz – J. Boardman, Greek Burial Customs (1971) 104–105 (skeptical about identifying the dead

and living together); J. Bažant, in: L. Kahil – C. Augé – P. Linant de Bellefonds (eds.), Iconographie classique et identités regionales, BCH Supp. 14 (1986) 37–44 (ambiguity was deliberate); Sourvinou-Inwood (supra n. 31) 324–325 n. 99; J. H. Oakley, The Achilles Painter (1997) 66–69; Oakley, Picturing Death 148. 165 (men in armor are the deceased); E. Kunze-Götte, in: S. Schmidt – J. H. Oakley (eds.), Hermeneutik der Bilder: Beiträge zur Ikonographie und Interpretation griechischer Vasenmalerei (2009) 53–64; eadem, CVA Munich 15 (2010). Kunze-Götte interprets too many grave scenes as epiphanies of the deceased; see the review of her CVA volume by T. J. McNiven, AJA 115, 4 (2011) on-line at: http://www.ajaonline.org/sites/default/files/1154_McNiven.pdf.

54 E.g. New York, Metropolitan Museum of Art 1989.281.72; BAPD 1140; Oakley, Picturing Death Color pl. 8.

55 E.g. supra n. 54 – New York, Metropolitan Museum of Art 08.258.18; BAPD 214001; ARV^2 999,180; Para 438; Oakley (supra n. 53) pl. 129A.

56 E.g. Athens, National Museum 1816; BAPD 217813; ARV^2 1383,12. 1692; Para 486; $BAdd^2$ 372; Boardman, Classical fig. 281.

57 E.g. Athens, National Museum 1942; BAPD 216368; ARV^2 1229,27; $BAdd^2$ 251; Oakley, Picturing Death 166 fig. 125.

58 E.g. Munich, Antikensammlungen 6044; BAPD 9024397; CVA Munich 15 Germany 87 83–85 pls. 49,1–4. 50,1–3.

59 New York, Metropolitan Museum of Art 23.160.38; BAPD 216333; ARV^2 1227,5; Para 466; $BAdd^2$ 350; Kurtz, AWL 209–210 pl. 30,1; Mertens (supra n. 5) 34 fig. 7.

60 Supra n. 36, the vessels in the Metropolitan Museum of Art and the National Museum.

61 Athens, private; BAPD 21582; Oakley (supra n. 5) 243 figs. 5–6; M. Pipili, in: APP II Color pl. 19A.

62 On fragments in Amsterdam (supra n. 26), the one figure visible is a mourner, for he holds a fillet in his hand. Presumably the deceased stood on the other side of the grave marker.

63 It is unlikely that the dead knocked over the vessels when they made their appearance. Fallen vessels are not usually the ones closest to the *eidōla*, nor do they fall in a uniform direction that could indicate the movement of the dead. The only exception may be the lekythos in Munich (Fig. 3) with a child at the grave monument and a hydria tumbling off the steps, although I maintain that the child is not dead.

64 Ticino, private; BAPD 21581; Oakley (supra n. 5) 241–243 figs. 1–3; Oakley, Picturing Death 207 fig. 168.

65 Berlin, Antikensammlung V.I. 3209 and Athens National Museum 26821; BAPD 5280; G. Bakalakis, AntK 14, 1971, 74–83; R. Mösch-Klingele, Braut ohne Bräutigam: Schwarz- und rotfigurige Lutrophoren als Spiegel gesellschaftlicher Veränderungen in Athen (2010) 58 figs. 23A–B; P. Hannah, in: D. M. Pritchard (ed.), War, Democracy and Culture in Classical Athens (2010) 289 fig. 11,5; A. Schwarzmaier, in: O. Pilz – M. Vonderstein (eds.), Keraunia: Beiträge zu Mythos, Kult und Heiligtum in der Antike (2011) 115–130; CVA Berlin 15 Germany 95 pls. 66–70; Beilage 12,4; 13.

66 E.g. Boston, Museum of Fine Arts 95.24; BAPD 215345; ARV^2 1159; Para 458; $BAdd^2$ 337; Boardman, Classical fig. 183.

67 Supra n. 13.

68 Paris, Musée du Louvre CA 3758; BAPD 3032; Kurtz, AWL 205–206 pl. 23, 3; M. Blech, Studien zum Kranz bei den Griechen (1982) 99; H. Froning, AA, 1985, 224–225; Schmidt (supra n. 24) 46 fig. 10.

2 Under the Tuscan Soil: Reuniting Attic Vases with an Etruscan Tomb

Sheramy D. Bundrick

In 1879, Giuseppe Cappannelli of Cortona and Giacomo Tempora of Bettolle conducted excavations of an Etruscan necropolis near the church of San Francesco in Foiano della Chiana in Tuscany, on land belonging to Alfonso del Soldato. In the course of their work, they were visited by Wolfgang Helbig, who published a brief report in that year's *Bullettino dell'Instituto di Corrispondenza Archeologica*.[1] By the time Helbig arrived at Foiano, sixty chamber tombs had already been uncovered and their contents dispersed, some still visible at Soldato's villa; Helbig could only observe that the finds were dominated by black- and red-figured vases of Greek manufacture, presumably Athenian. He was, however, present for the discovery of two *tombe vergini*, as he called them, and he noted their contents in the *Bullettino*. These finds, too, were scattered with only some of the pieces identified even today, but Helbig's report nonetheless provides critical evidence for burial practices in this area of Tuscany, the Valdichiana. It also provides critical evidence for the use of Attic vases as cineraria in Etruria, for in both of these *tombe vergini*, vessels of assorted shapes were employed as ossuaries.

This paper focuses on the first tomb that Helbig discusses, 100 steps from the façade of San Francesco, which was carved from the tufa and had two chambers. The inner chamber featured a single inhumation burial, while the outer included six cremation burials along the right-hand wall. Two of the latter were kept in local Etruscan containers, an urn of *pietra fetida* and bronze *secchia*, but the other four were placed in Athenian vases converted into cineraria, with a fifth vase used as a lid. Helbig describes each in great detail and provides measurements; the styles of the vases suggest that the burials proceeded chronologically from the inner chamber through the outer, with the entire tomb containing at least three generations of presumably a single family. Aside from the ossuaries, the finds in the outer chamber were few and placed along the left-hand wall. These included fragmentary impasto vessels and bronze implements that Helbig records as being in bad condition, namely a strigil, two ladles, and what might have been a meat spit or *thymiaterion*.

The five Athenian vases present a striking combination of shapes and imagery that prove appropriate for a tomb context. Moreover, they raise questions about the reception of Greek vases among the Etruscans. I argue that in evaluating such reception, one must consider the regional customs of the specific area of Etruria involved and not simply lump the Etruscans into a single cultural entity. In the case of the Foiano tombs, the funerary customs of Chiusi prove essential to understanding why these vases were chosen for deposition and what their meaning may have been, the Valdichiana lying within that city's sphere of influence in this period. More than reflecting any particular "hellenization" in this part of Etruria, the primary value of Athenian vases lay in their appropriation and manipulation to suit local, traditional mortuary practice and belief.[2]

Before turning to the vases, one must begin with the innermost and older chamber, which Helbig said contained a single skeleton along the righthand wall, male it seems, resting upon a bench carved from the tufa.[3] Likely the deceased was a patriarch and honored ancestor of this Foiano family.[4] His remains were surrounded by bucchero vessels, including a footed cup, two jars, three chalices adorned with horse protomes, and "un piatto con quattro teste di donna sporgenti sopra l'orlo," whose description corresponds to a *focolare*, or offering tray typical of the Chiusine region.[5] Helbig emphasizes that some of the vessels contained eggshells, likely remains of the mortuary feast.[6] None of these objects are identified today, but all were surely examples of sixth-century Chiusine *bucchero pesante*. Helbig records no foreign objects in this inner chamber.

The outer chamber, as already noted, included six ossuaries. Inhumation and cremation coexisted in many parts of Archaic Etruria, so their juxtaposition is not unusual, even in a single tomb; the second tomb Helbig describes at Foiano contained one inhumation and one cremation burial, so the practice may have been common here. Noteworthy, though, is the marked preference for cremation in the Valdichiana and Chiusine region, compared to areas where inhumation was more common by this point. Funerary practices that can be traced to the Villanovan period, namely the production and usage of cinerary urns, persisted more strongly at Chiusi than sites like Vulci, Tarquinia, or Orvieto. Indeed, the oldest cremation burial in this Foiano tomb was housed in a stone urn of almost certainly Chiusine manufacture, with a roof-like cover and sculpted triglyphs on its long side. It was broken when Helbig saw it and has never been identified.

The next burial featured the first two Athenian vases placed in the tomb. Helbig details at length "un'anfora colossale...con manichi a volute," adding that "sopra l'anfora piena di cenere era posta a guisa di coperchio una grande tazza a figure nere di stile piuttosto avanzato".[7] Thanks to his descriptions and the measurements he provides, both vessels can be identified. The eye cup, with a diameter of sixty centimeters (seventy-four centimeters including the handles), was acquired by the Museo Archeologico Nazionale in Florence from a private collection in 1892, when its provenience was erroneously given as Bettolle (Figs. 1–4; Color Pl. 4A).[8] It was later recognized as coming from this Foiano tomb, namely in Caskey and Beazley's *Attic Vase Paintings in the Museum of Fine Arts, Boston*.[9]

Attributed by Beazley to the manner of the Lysippides Painter and dating to the last third of the sixth century BC, the exceptionally large cup features on each side a trio of divine figures between the pair of eyes. Herakles, Athena, and Hermes form one of these groups in what is likely an abbreviated version of the hero's arrival on Olympos (Figs. 1–2; Color Pl. 4A): Herakles stands before the two deities as Hermes raises his hand in greeting.[10] The inscription *Heraspos kalos* appears above Herakles and further draws attention to him. The figure of Hermes repeats on the opposite and more fragmentary side, together with Dionysos and a satyr, grapevines surrounding this trio to accentuate the Dionysian theme. Around each handle appear scenes of combat (Fig. 3) with hoplites and so-called Scythian archers, while the cup's interior features a leering gorgoneion.

Where the eye cup's connection to the Foiano tomb has long been known, its companion has only more recently been recognized.[11] What Helbig called *un'anfora con manichi a volute dipinti* with a height of fifty-six centimeters cannot be an amphora, and his detailed report confirms that it is an unattributed, black-bodied volute krater today in the Walters Art Museum (Figs. 5–7; Color Pl. 4B).[12] Henry Walters purchased this vase in 1902 from Don Marcello Massarenti in Rome and immediately shipped it to the United States with the rest of Massarenti's collection, the arrival noted in the *New York Times* of 13 July.[13] Massarenti had earlier published the krater in an 1897 catalogue of his collection but had given no information about its acquisition or provenience and, indeed, had misidentified its scenes as "les jeux olympiques".[14] Rather, both friezes explore the theme of combat. Herakles wrestles the Nemean Lion in the center of the obverse side (Figs. 5–6; Color Pl. 4B), watched by Iolaos, a female figure, and the seated Athena.[15] Framing this central vignette are a pair of chariots with drivers, plus seated and standing men with staffs. A trio of hoplites

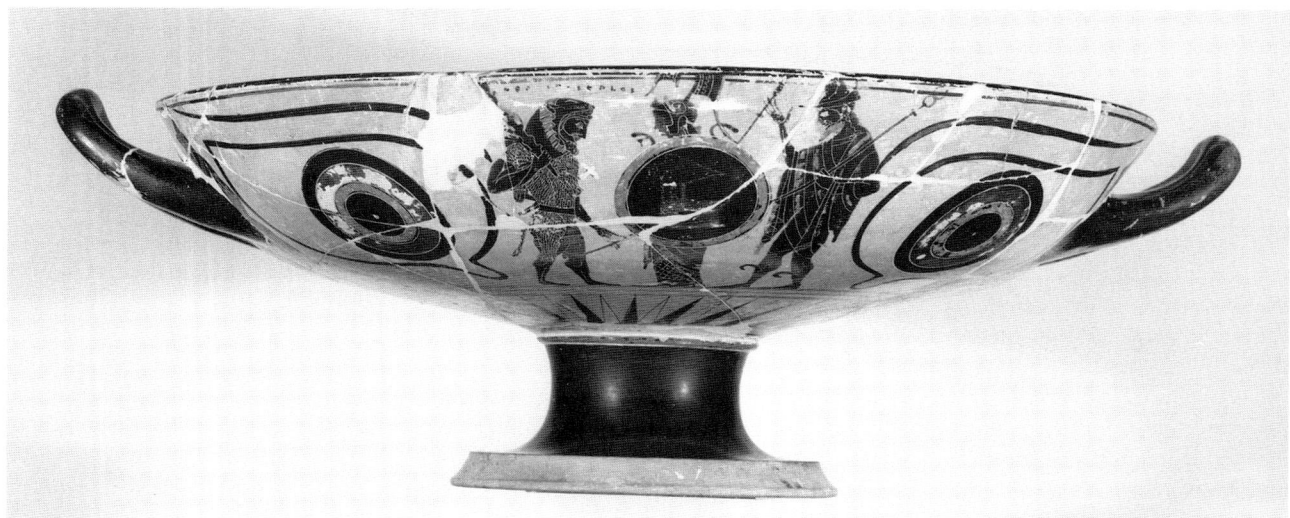

Fig. 1 Eye cup attributed to the Lysippides Painter, Florence, Museo Archeologico Nazionale 74624, on loan to the Museo dell'Accademia Etrusca e della Città di Cortona. Photo courtesy of the Ministero per i Beni e le Attività Culturali – Soprintendenza per i Beni Archeologici della Toscana.

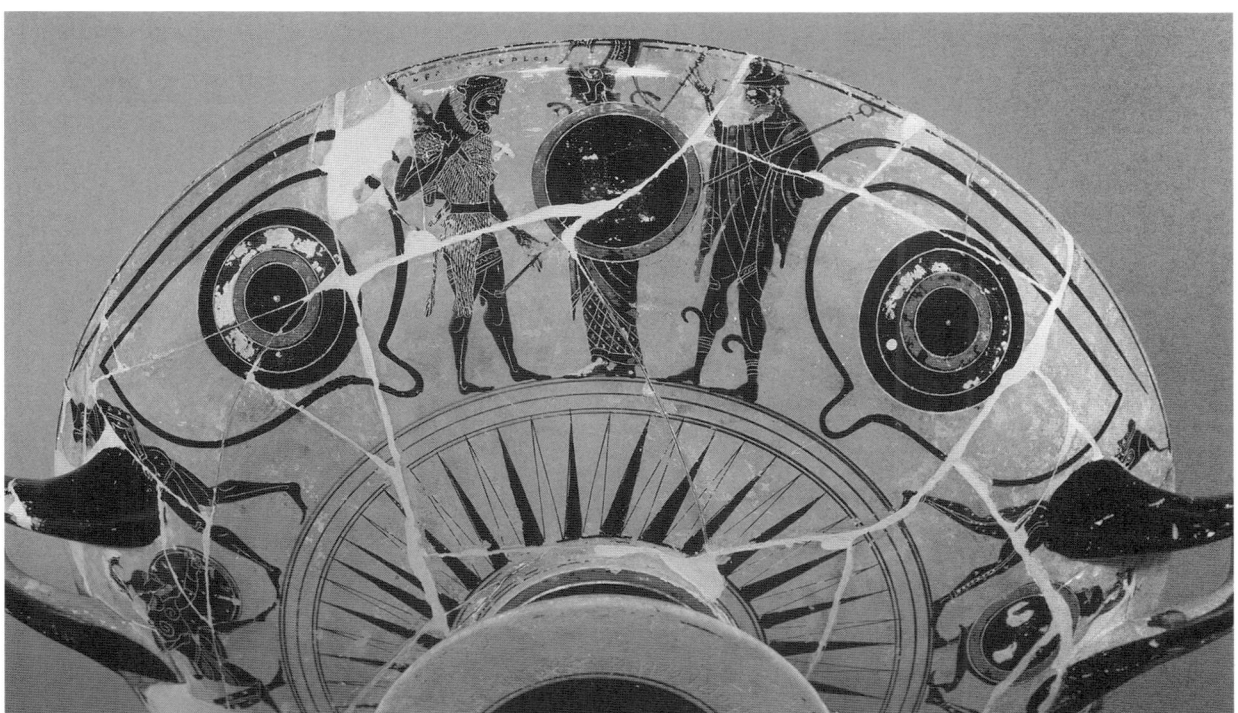

Fig. 2 Detail of Fig. 1 with the apotheosis of Herakles. Photo courtesy of the Ministero per i Beni e le Attività Culturali – Soprintendenza per i Beni Archeologici della Toscana.

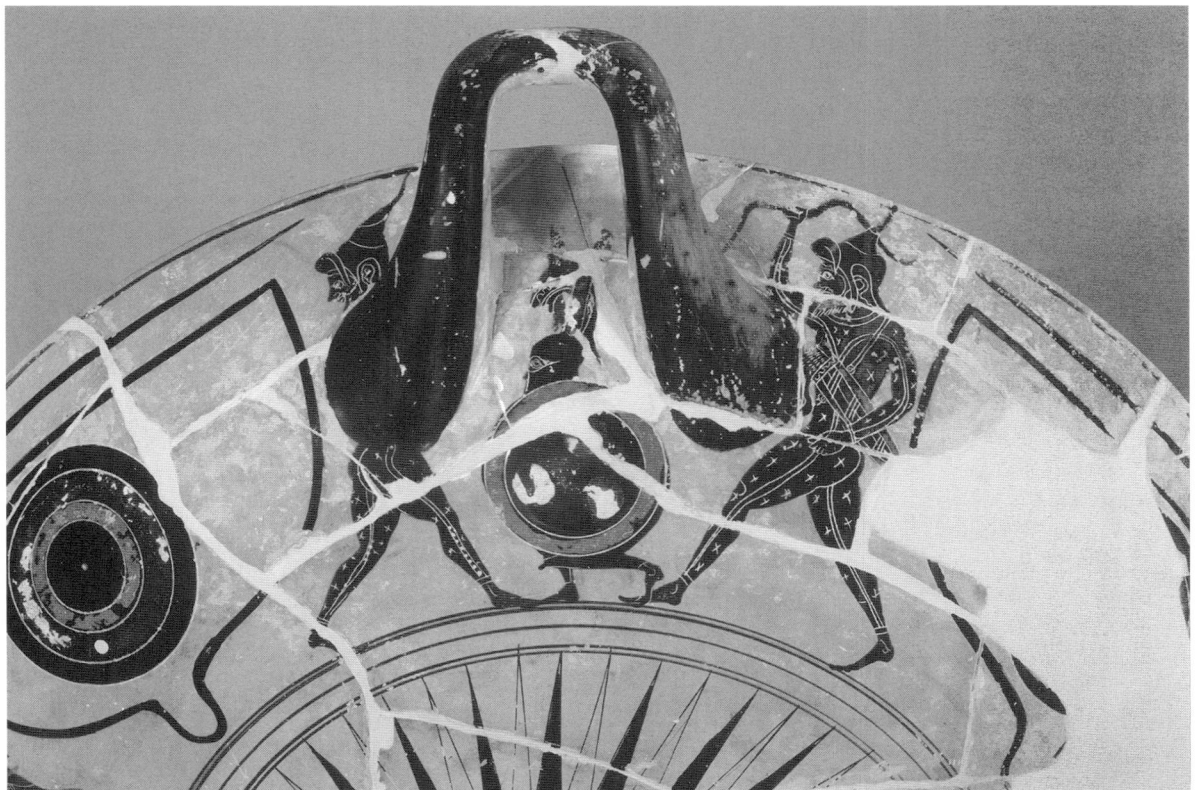

Fig. 3 Detail of Fig. 1 with combat scene. Photo courtesy of the Ministero per i Beni e le Attività Culturali – Soprintendenza per i Beni Archeologici della Toscana.

fight in the center of the reverse frieze (Fig. 7), flanked by standing female figures, while male figures in various poses occupy the rest of the space, including one with a horse and another mounting a chariot.

The confluence of shape, size, and imagery suggests that the choice to place cup and krater together was thoughtfully made by the deceased's relatives, not a random decision based on what was handy. Not only do Herakles and Athena appear on both, but if the cup shows the hero's apotheosis (Fig. 2; Color Pl. 4A), then his first labor is paired with his happy ending. The three fighters surrounding each handle of the cup (Fig. 3) similarly echo the central trio of the krater's battle scene (Fig. 7). Even the ivy spiralling around the krater's handles complements that framing Dionysos on the cup. The Gorgon's face, meanwhile, stared down into the krater and provided protection for the deceased's remains, while the eyes on the exterior further repelled evil forces. An Etruscan inscription of over sixty characters appears on the eye cup's foot (Fig. 4), possibly added at the time of burial.[16] This, too, faced upward from the ossuary and may have contained information about the deceased, perhaps wishes for protection. Unfortunately, although the inscription can be transcribed, it cannot be read. Etruscologist Rex Wallace reports that "there are no recognizable names, nouns, or verbs," and adds "at this point there is no hope for an interpretation of any sort".[17]

Recent scholarship has asserted that Greek vases found in Etruscan tombs may have been valued possessions in homes prior to their deposition; perhaps this krater served as a centerpiece for banquets, its owner the head of the household at that time.[18] The eye cup, in contrast, seems impossible to drink from with such a large diameter. It may have been a display piece in a *kylikeion*, like those rendered in the Tomba della Nave and Tomba dei Vasi Dipinti at Tarquinia, used only for ritual or special occasions. The painted *kylikeion* of the Tomba dei Vasi Dipinti features a volute krater – almost certainly metal, not ceramic – and what might be a black-figured eye cup underneath.[19] Lisa Pieraccini and Athena Tsingarida have each discussed the use of wine and kylikes in Etruscan ritual, with Tsingarida noting the particular popularity of oversized cups in Etruria; the Foiano eye cup may have served a ceremonial purpose and been used for offerings at the burial.[20] Taken all together, shape and iconography proclaim the importance of banqueting in both life and death, while suggesting the deceased's status and protection. The apotheosis of Herakles on the eye cup, if that is indeed the subject, further implies passage into the afterworld. The Etruscan viewer may have read Dionysos/Fufluns on the opposite side in a similar eschatological way.[21]

The eye cup placed atop the volute krater, although upside down, has the further, curious effect of anthropomorphizing

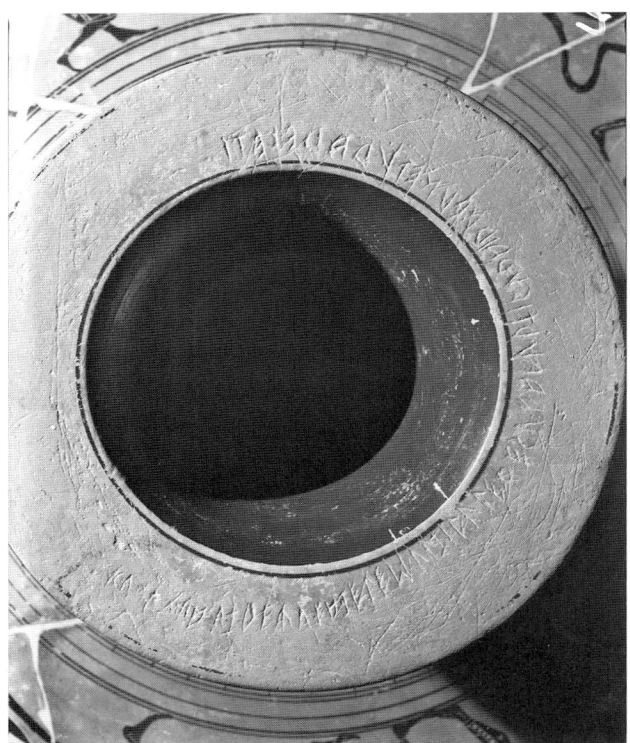

Fig. 4 Detail of Fig. 1 with Etruscan inscription. Photo courtesy of the Ministero per i Beni e le Attività Culturali – Soprintendenza per i Beni Archeologici della Toscana.

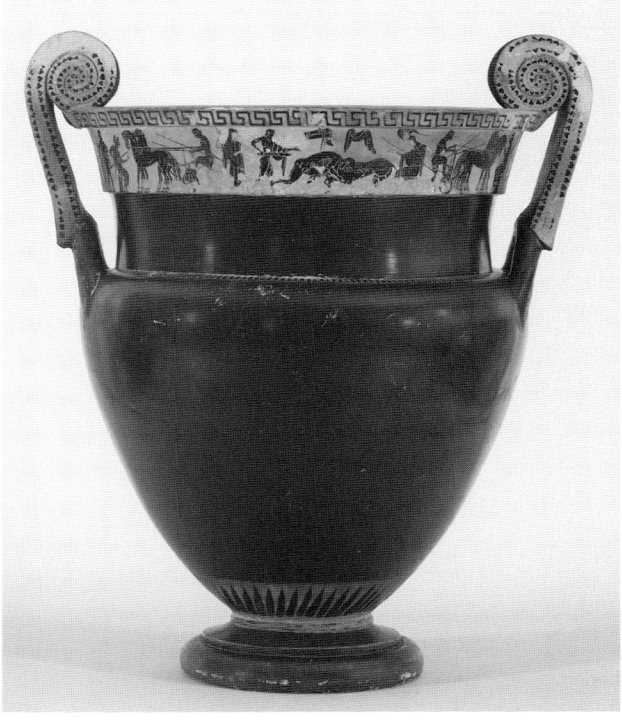

Fig. 5 Black-figured volute krater, Baltimore, Walters Art Museum 48.29. Photo: © Walters Art Museum.

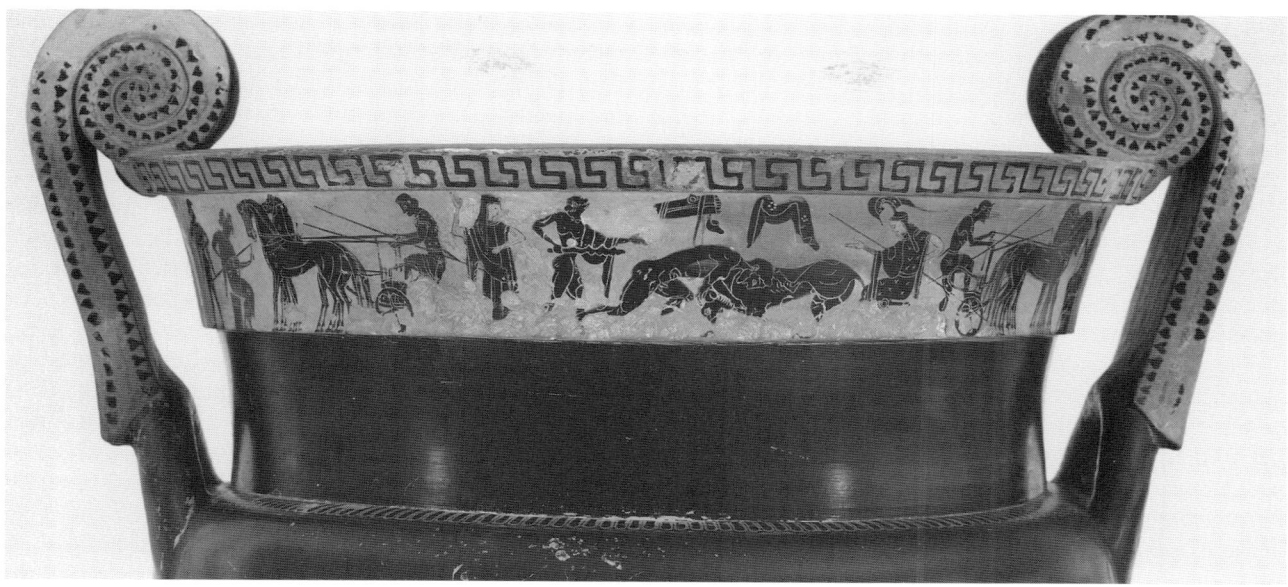

Fig. 6 Detail of Fig. 5 with scene of Herakles. Photo: © Walters Art Museum.

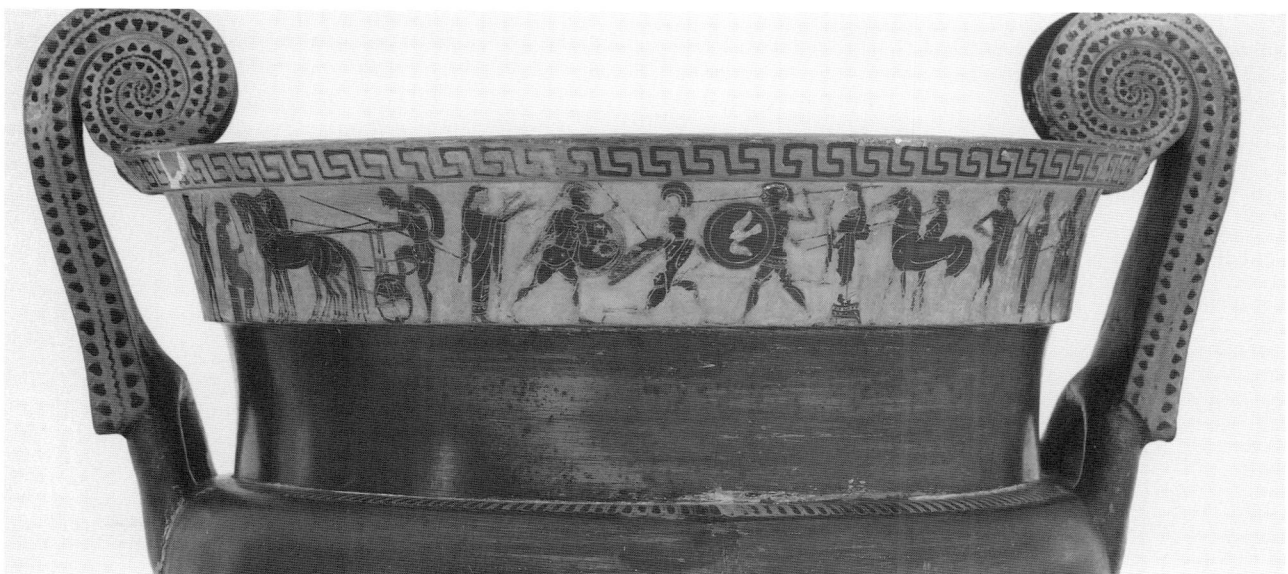

Fig. 7 Detail of frieze on reverse side of krater in Fig. 5. Photo: © Walters Art Museum.

the whole. One is reminded of terracotta and bronze cinerary urns from late seventh- and early sixth-century Chiusi, the so-called canopic urns, in which the deceased's remains were given cursory human form by adding a head and sometimes arms.[22] Striking variations on this custom exist: in a pair of late seventh-century burials, one discovered at Poggio alla Sala in 1876 and the second just outside Chianciano Terme in 1994, thin sheets of gold were placed over the openings of the bronze cremation urns, pairs of bone eyes then laid on top.[23] Perhaps the relatives of the Foiano deceased chose the Athenian eye cup for the ossuary not only because of its size, shape, and imagery, but because its juxtaposition with the krater paid homage to local funerary tradition and revitalized the dead.[24]

The next cremation burial in the chamber was kept in a now-lost, very fragmentary "secchia di bronzo" of surely Chiusine manufacture, while the last three were placed in Attic vases. Helbig calls the next ossuary "un'anfora a figure nere di stile avanzato" and gives the height as thirty-seven centimeters. Using the lengthy description that follows, Anna Rastrelli identified the vase in 1998 as an unpublished black-figured pelike by the Eucharides Painter, residing at that time in the Villa Passerini near Bettolle.[25] The Italian

State has recently purchased the pelike together with the remaining Passerini collection, for display in the Museo Archeologico Nazionale di Chiusi.[26] One side depicts a seated woman in the center, a swan head decorating her chair with a bird standing underneath; she is flanked by two standing men with staffs, both wreathed and bearded, hands raised in conversation. Birds were considered auspicious creatures by the Etruscans, while seated women were prominent in Chiusine funerary art: in Archaic funerary relief sculpture, as Classical cinerary statues, and in fifth-century painted tombs like the Tomba della Scimmia.

The opposite scene places the pelike into a group of similar Attic vases depicting musical concerts or contests. Helbig's description reads: "Nel centro si scorge un uomo barbato, vestito di lungo chitone e mantello, in piedi, suonando la cetra. Egli è attorniato da due uomini barbati, ignudi salvo l'himation, ognuno con un bastone in mano, che sentono la musica, l'uno seduto e l'altro in piedi".[27] The *cetra* in question is the flat-bottomed concert kithara, instrument of choice for professional musicians in Athens, used in the most prestigious *mousikoi agones* for the kitharode who sang as well as played.[28] Seven other Attic black-figured pelikai with kithara players are known, including another by the Eucharides Painter from Samothrace, and three with Etruscan provenience by other painters.[29] The subject is also known in red figure for this shape. No two of the black-figured examples are alike, but compositionally, the best comparisons for the Foiano vase are two pelikai both found at Cerveteri – one by the Leagros Group now in Kassel, another by the Nikoxenos Painter now in Bologna – although each features two seated listeners rather than one seated and one standing.[30] The shape of the concert kithara as depicted by vase painters complements the shape of the pelike, the vessel's sagging belly reversing the curves of the instrument's soundbox. The costume of the kitharode on the Eucharides Painter's pelike, a long, ungirt chiton, grants this musician a monumentality that further accentuates his grand instrument.

Musical subjects are frequent throughout Etruscan funerary art, from Tarquinian tomb paintings to contemporary Chiusine stone urns and cippi.[31] One thinks again of banquets in life and death, and music in general as emblematic of celebration.[32] The square-based concert kithara shown on the pelike, however, was not common in Etruscan art nor presumably in Etruscan practice, although it was familiar from imported Athenian vases.[33] Better known in Chiusine and other Etruscan funerary art was the round-based, so-called cradle or cylinder kithara, also known in modern scholarship as the phorminx.[34] The figures with long staffs on the pelike – staffs being a symbol of power in local art – would have been interpreted as important characters, especially the man seated on the *diphros*, which likewise appears on Chiusine funerary reliefs.[35] As for the shape, although other documented examples of Attic pelikai serving as Etruscan ossuaries are few, they do exist, for example at Cerveteri and Tarquinia.[36]

The next Attic vase used as an ossuary in the Foiano tomb, called by Helbig "un'anfora a figure rosse di stile piuttosto severo" with a height of 38.5 centimeters, has yet to be identified. The obverse features a scene of so-called erotic pursuit: a bearded man with chiton, himation, and scepter, taenia around his head, pursuing a long-haired woman with long robes. The man grasps the shoulder of the woman, who looks back even as she runs away.[37] The reverse depicts a wreathed youth enveloped in his himation, flanked by two seated, bearded men who each wear a himation and carry a staff. Given Helbig's use of the word *anfora* to describe any two-handled storage vessel, the piece could instead be another pelike or a stamnos.[38] As for the key male figure, Helbig's mention of a scepter implies the scene shows Zeus chasing Aigina; however, if he misread the object in the vase's newly excavated condition, the male figure could instead be Poseidon with trident or Dionysos with thyrsos.[39]

Examination of the findspots of Athenian red-figured vases with erotic pursuit scenes – whether hetero- or homosexual, with either mortals or deities doing the chasing – reveals that a large concentration of those with known proveniences come from Italian contexts.[40] Among Etruscan sites, this includes southern coastal cities like Vulci and Cerveteri, as well as northerly sites like Bologna and Spina. Three red-figured vessels with pursuit scenes, for instance, all with male gods chasing women and all by the same painter, come from the main chamber of the early fifth-century Tomba dei Vasi Greci in the Banditaccia necropolis at Cerveteri.[41] Vases with pursuit scenes likewise derive from Campanian sites like Capua and Nola, where the patrons could be either Etruscan or Greek in this period, and Sicilian Greek cemeteries like those of Gela and Agrigento. A calyx krater by the Achilles Painter with a scene of Zeus chasing a woman held cremated remains at the necropolis of Suessula.[42] The mortuary context of these images demonstrates that Etruscans and western Greeks saw in them references to death, perhaps premature death, a theme that attained even greater poignancy when the vase was used as an ossuary.[43]

Premature death, verging on human sacrifice, is certainly the subject of the last Attic vase in the Foiano chamber, long since identified as coming from this tomb: a red-figured hydria attributed to the Niobid Painter with a scene of the death of Orpheus (Figs. 8–9).[44] The hydria was acquired by Edward Perry Warren in Rome in 1890 and is in the Museum of Fine Arts, Boston. The hapless Orpheus, clad in chitoniskos, boots, and laurel wreath and identified by inscription, falls to the ground at the attack of the Thracian women, holding his chelys lyre above his head in vain.[45] Three women surge from the left and two from the right, the former bearing meat spits (*oboloi*), the latter carrying a sword and sickle (*harpe*) respectively. The two nearest Orpheus grab him by his long hair as the sword-wielding woman prepares to strike the death blow. Unusually for this motif, probably because the painter has room, two male Thracian soldiers stand at the edges of the composition. One of the mythological traditions surrounding Orpheus says that the Thracian women were furious because the poet had distracted their husbands with his music; Athenian vase painters were just beginning to depict Orpheus playing his lyre for the Thracian soldiers at the time this hydria was made.[46] Perhaps here the soldiers have been enchanted to the point of inactivity, for they do nothing to stop the murder unfolding before them.[47]

The death of Orpheus as a subject on Athenian red-figured vases first appeared early in the fifth century and remained popular until its last quarter. Among vases with the scene that have a known provenience three examples are from Vulci, one from Chiusi, one from Adria, three from Spina, and this hydria comes from Foiano.[48] Etruscan viewers would surely have known the story of Orpheus, although the earliest appearances of *Urphe* in Etruscan art date from the following century. The theme of untimely death would make the scene appropriate for an ossuary or for placement in a tomb generally; however, one can also speculate upon locally relevant meanings. Representations of Orpheus/Urphe on late fourth-century Etruscan bronze mirrors depict his head speaking prophecy; this divinatory aspect of the poet seems to have been important to the Etruscans.[49] On the Foiano hydria, the women grabbing Orpheus' hair and the woman with sickle show that decapitation is imminent. Rather than the poet's death being seen as a hopeless act and the story's end, perhaps the Etruscan viewer understood that it led to a continued existence of another sort. For this ossuary, one can be confident that the deceased was male, for Helbig mentions a carnelian scarab "tra la cenere deposta in cosifatta idria".[50] Such an object was associated with Etruscan men and was worn by the deceased at the time of cremation. Helbig says it was "tante scomposto dal fuoco" to the degree that its incised decoration was unrecognizable.

When the Foiano tomb group is considered as a whole, significant points and questions can be raised. First, of the seven burials in the tomb, the remains of four individuals were placed in Athenian vases. Does this imply that the family was itself Greek? There is no reason to think so. Not only are the other cremated individuals interred in Chiusine containers, but the likely ancestor of the entire family was buried in local style, and at some point, an Etruscan inscription was added to the eye cup. Nor must one suggest any particular affinity with Greek culture and customs. Cremation had long been preferred in this part of Etruria, and as Helbig noted, Athenian vessels were common among the dozens of other Foiano graves.[51] In both this tomb and the other he described intact, Attic vases were but one part of an assemblage that also included Chiusine ware and bronzes, and thus cannot be considered in isolation. Once acquired by their local owners, the vases had been given new life as Etruscan objects used in Etruscan funerary practices, not becoming Athenian again until their discovery and dispersal on the art market.

One can suggest, by extension, that the family members who selected these vases for the tomb may have done so for reasons beyond their "Greekness". With the likely exception of the volute krater, whose shape was particularly distinctive and size particularly noteworthy, image as much or more than shape seems to have inspired the choice for each ossuary.[52] Whereas neck amphorae of either Attic or Etruscan manufacture were preferred at Tarquinia and other contemporary sites with cremation burials, any vessel of good size seems to have been suitable for this tomb, as long as its images spoke to the status of the deceased and/or reflected funerary belief.[53] Quality as defined in modern terms seems less important; today the Niobid Painter's hydria (Fig. 8), with its fine draftsmanship and attribution to a significant painter, would fetch a higher price than the Eucharides Painter's pelike, and yet both functioned equally well for their Foiano owners. Indeed, while the tomb's terracotta vases have been privileged since 1879 by modern collectors and scholars, in ancient times they may have been considered less prestigious in this area than stone or bronze containers, relatively plain examples of the latter being included here and Attic vases seeming to be well available. Perhaps the family would have preferred Chiusine stone urns with images in relief but could not afford them, turning instead to pots already in their possession and making careful selections based on iconography.

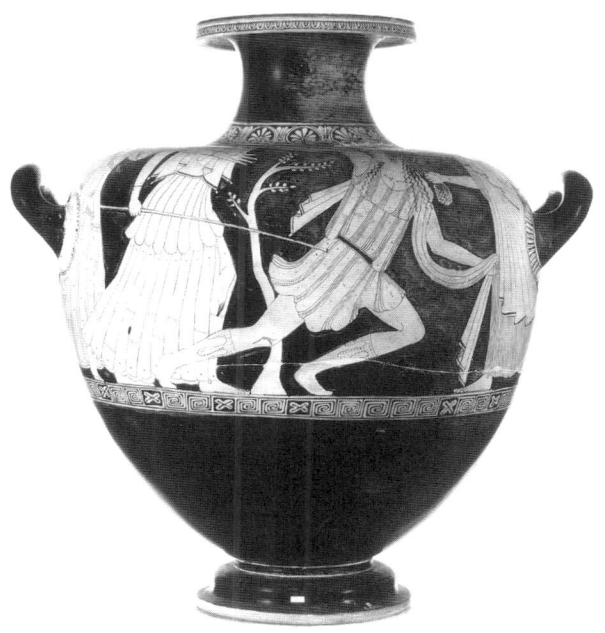

Fig. 8 Hydria attributed to the Niobid Painter, Boston, Museum of Fine Arts, Gift of Edward Perry Warren, 90.156. Photo: © 2014 Museum of Fine Arts, Boston.

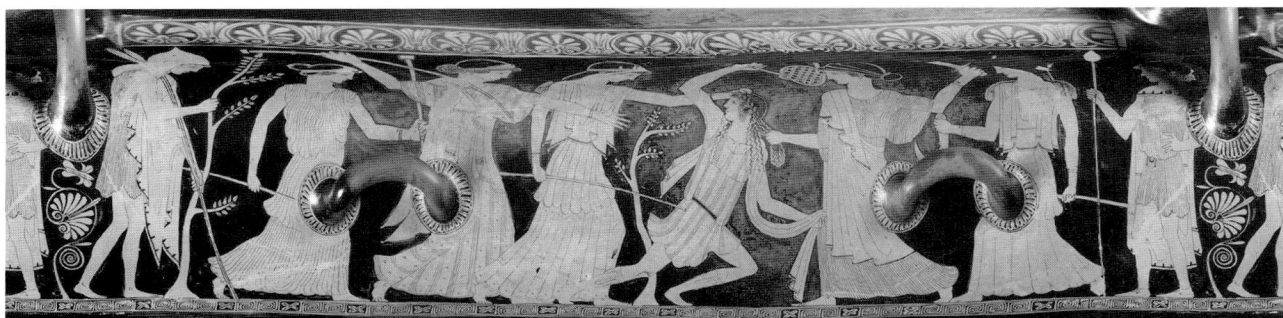

Fig. 9 Rollout photograph of scene in Fig. 8. Photo: © 2014 Museum of Fine Arts, Boston.

The images on all five Athenian vases attain new meaning when considered in an Etruscan funerary context. In the tomb are mythological and so-called genre scenes that evoke status, celebration, and protection, from the combat against the Nemean Lion on the krater (Fig. 6) to the musical concert on the pelike. To an Etruscan viewer, other scenes – the apotheosis of Herakles (Fig. 2), death of Orpheus (Fig. 9), and Zeus's erotic pursuit – would suggest premature death and the passage of the *hinthial* (soul or shade). All these themes echo images found on sixth- and fifth-century funerary art from Chiusi, which although eschewing mythological narrative, privileged the status of the dead and their mortuary rites.[54] The Foiano tomb further reflects belief in ancestor cult: that the deceased's remains should be placed in containers evoking themselves and their lifestyles, and that family members will be reunited after death.[55] The Athenian vases thus serve a triple function: to keep the deceased safe, say something about them, and provide for their eternal feast in the afterworld.

Acknowledgements

Special thanks are due to John Oakley for the invitation to participate in *Athenian Potters and Painters III*, and for his kindness and support through the years. Thanks also to fellow speakers and audience members for their helpful comments. For assistance with photographs and permissions, I thank Sue Bell from the Museum of Fine Arts, Boston; Ruth Bowler of the Walters Art Museum; and Mariacristina Guidotti of the Soprintendenza per i Beni Archeologici della Toscana. The College of Arts and Sciences of the University of South Florida St. Petersburg provided funds for the acquisition of images.

Notes

1 W. Helbig, BdI, 1879, 242–249. See too P. Giulierini, AnnAcEtr 39, 1999–2001, 51–88, especially 57–62; also M. Giuman, in: S. Fortunelli (ed.), Il Museo della Città Etrusca e Romana di Cortona: Catalogo delle collezioni (2005) 246.

2 Cf. D. Paleothodoros, in: V. Nørskov – L. Hannestad – C. Isler-Kerényi – S. Lewis (eds.), The World of Greek Vases (2009) 58–59; also V. Izzet, The Archaeology of Etruscan Society (2007) 211–225. Compare too principles of object biography, which suggest that the meaning(s) of an object is/are transformed as it changes context: e.g., C. Gosden – Y. Marshall, WorldA 31, 1999, 169–178.

3 The other tomb Helbig discusses contained a similar inhumation burial in its single chamber, with that figure holding a piece of *aes rude* in his (?) right hand. This tomb contained a cremation burial as well, placed inside "un'anfora a figure rosse" with symposion scene. Helbig (supra n. 1) 248.

4 Despite the interment of this figure in a separate chamber from the cremation burials, there is no reason to doubt that all the individuals belonged to a single, multigenerational family. In the second *tomba vergine* cited in the previous note, an inhumation and cremation burial separated by decades according to Helbig's descriptions of the styles of the objects were placed together in a single room. It seems unlikely that a second family would impose upon the burial of an earlier individual in either tomb. There would be no need to do so, for as Helbig says, the necropolis was large, and room for new tombs clearly existed (for discussion of the specific location of the necropolis using archival evidence, see Giulierini [supra n. 2] 61–63 and figures C–D). One can speculate that the inhumation technique of burial, less common locally compared to cremation, was used to distinguish important individuals like the family patriarch, but without the evidence of the sixty unrecorded tombs, it is impossible to be certain.

5 Cf. e.g., Florence 3122–31 and London 1851,812.1, and see generally L. Donati, StEtr 36, 1968, 319–355.

6 Compare finds of eggs in Etruscan tombs elsewhere, e.g., tomb III of the Maroi Tumulus in the Banditaccia necropolis of Cerveteri, and their representation in tomb paintings, e.g., the banquet scene of the Tomba dei Leopardi at Tarquinia. See L. Pieraccini, EtrSt 7, 2000, 35–49, especially 43–44 for eggs.

7 Helbig (supra n. 1) 245–247.

8 Florence 74624, currently on loan to the Museo dell' Accademia Etrusca e della Città di Cortona: ABV 262,46; Para 117; BAdd² 68; BAPD 302278; A. M. Esposito – G. De Tommaso, Museo Archeologico Nazionale di Firenze, Antiquarium, Vasi Attici (1993) 41–42 figs. 50–51; Giulierini (supra n. 1) 71–73 figs. 8–11; M. Giuman, in:

9 Fortunelli (supra n. 1) 248 cat. VI.112; M. Iozzo, in: J. de la Genière (ed.), Les clients de la céramique grecque, Actes du colloque de l'Académie des Inscriptions et Belles-Lettres, Paris, 30–31 janvier 2004 (2006) 125. 234 fig. IV.4; A. Tsingarida, in: T. Mannack – R. R. R. Smith – D. Williams (eds.), Greek Pots Abroad (forthcoming). I thank Athena Tsingarida for sharing her paper with me in advance of publication.
9 CB II (1954) 76.
10 A similar schema appears on a black-figured amphora in the manner of the Lysippides Painter: a standing Herakles greets Athena, clasping hands with her as Hermes and a female figure (Hebe?) observe. The clasped-hands gesture, coupled with the appearance of the fight with the Nemean Lion on the amphora's other side, suggests the arrival of Herakles on Olympos. Munich 1556/J270, BAPD 1493, CVA Munich 8 Germany 37 pls. 392, 1; 393, 1–2.
11 A. Rastrelli, in: G. Capecchi et al. (eds.), In memoria di Enrico Paribeni (1998) 351, focusing on Attic imports to Chiusi as reflected in the Foiano tomb rather than the tomb's complete assemblage as here; Iozzo (supra n. 8) 112; Tsingarida (supra n. 8).
12 Baltimore 48.29, BAPD 16188; F. Brommer, Vasenlisten zur griechischen Heldensage, 3rd ed. (1973) 118 cat. 14; J. Gaunt, The Attic Volute Krater, Ph.D. diss. (New York University, 2002) 453 cat. 42; Iozzo (supra n. 8) 125. 234 fig. IV.3; H. A. Coccagna, in: S. Albersmeier, (ed.), Heroes: Mortals and Myths in Ancient Greece (2009) 276 cat. 83; all with further references. Neither Gaunt nor Coccagna seem to have been aware of Rastrelli's 1998 identification; Gaunt gives the provenience as "presumably from Italy". An unpublished CVA entry gives the krater's measurements as follows: height at rim, 51.2–5 cm; height at handle 57.9 cm; diameter at mouth 44.0–3 cm; greatest width 52.7 cm. I thank John Oakley for sharing his CVA entry with me.
13 See W. R. Johnston, William and Henry Walters, The Reticent Collectors (1999) 153–163.
14 M. Massarenti, Catalogue du Musée de peinture, sculpture, et archéologie au Palais Accoramboni, vol. 2 (1897) 45–46 cat. 209.
15 Herakles wrestling the lion appears on an Athenian black-figured amphora used as an ossuary in the Monterozzi necropolis at Tarquinia: Tarquinia RC7453, A. Palmieri, Mediterranea 8, 2011, 132, fig. 30; BAPD 320071.
16 Transcriptions can be found in M. Pallottino, Testimonia Linguae Etruscae, 2nd ed. (1968) 88 cat. 673 and Guiman (supra n. 8) 248 cat. VI.112.
17 Personal communication, 14 October 2011. I thank Nancy de Grummond for contacting Prof. Wallace on my behalf and Prof. Wallace for his assistance.
18 E.g., C. Reusser, Vasen für Etrurien. Verbreitung und Funktionen attischer Keramik im Etrurien des 6. und 5. Jahrhunderts vor Christus (2002) and D. Paleothodoros, EtCl 70, 2002, 143. For kraters in Etruria, see e.g., N. Spivey, GaR 54, 2007, 229–253, especially 237–244.
19 D. Paleothodoros, Mediterranea 8, 2011, 47, likewise believes this to be an Attic eye cup.
20 Tsingarida (supra n. 8); L. Pieraccini, in: N. T. de Grummond – I. Edlund-Berry (eds.), The Archaeology of Sanctuaries and Ritual in Etruria, JRA Supplement 81 (2011) 127–137.

21 For the apotheosis of Herakles on Attic vases in tombs at Bologna, see A. M. Brizzolara – V. Baldoni, Bollettino di Archeologia Online 1, 2010, especially 10–12, and for Etruscan reception of scenes of the hero's apotheosis by chariot, W. G. Moon, in: W. G. Moon (ed.), Ancient Greek Art and Iconography (1983) 106–109. For eschatological implications of Dionysos on Attic vases in Etruria, see e.g., Paleothodoros (supra n. 18) 151–153; Paleotodoros (supra n. 2) 50–51; C. Pizzirani, Bollettino di Archeologia Online, 1, 2010, 29–35; and Palmieri (supra n. 15) 123–128.
22 See R. Gempeler, Die etruskischen Kanopen. Herstellung, Typologie, Entwicklungsgeschichte (1974); G. Paolucci, ScAnt 16, 2010, 109–118; and H. Damgaard Andersen, AnalRom 21, 1993, 7–66.
23 Poggio alla Sala tomb: A. Rastrelli, AnnFaina 7, 2000, 159–184; and for its original discovery, Helbig, BdI, 1883 193–196. For the urn in the Chianciano Terme tomb, see G. Paolucci – A. Rastrelli, La tomba principesca di Chianciano Terme (2006) 18–21.
24 Eye cups may have been used as ossuary lids more frequently than we can now recognize. The other example known to me is an Attic black-figured eye cup with scenes of Dionysian *thiasos* (diam. 28.5 cm) that covered an Attic black-figured column krater in a *tomba a pozzo* of the Poggio della Mina–Palazzetta necropolis near Bisenzio. Cup: Chiusi P300, BAPD 6841, krater: Chiusi P270, BAPD 32292 (both formerly Paolozzi collection). See W. Helbig, RM 1, 1886, 23–24, and C. Reusser, Prospettiva 70, 1993, 75–86.
25 Rastrelli (supra n. 11) 350–351.
26 I thank Mario Iozzo for information about the vase's whereabouts and providing photographs to use in research and the conference presentation.
27 Helbig (supra n. 1) 245.
28 For *mousikoi agones*: H. Kotsidu, Die musischen Agöne der Panathenäen in archaischer und klassischer Zeit (1991); H. A. Shapiro, in: J. Neils (ed.), Goddess and Polis: The Panathenaic Festival in Ancient Athens (1992) 53–75; and S. D. Bundrick, Music and Image in Classical Athens (2005) 160–174. For the concert kithara in Greece, see M. Maas – J. M. Snyder, Stringed Instruments of Ancient Greece (1989) 53–78, and Bundrick, ibid. 18–21.
29 Adapted from H. A. Shapiro, in: APP 70 n. 52: a) Bologna G10 (PU199), from Cerveteri, attributed to the Nikoxenos Painter, ABV 393,14; D. von Bothmer, JHS 71, 1951, 42 cat. 4; Kotsidu (supra n. 28) cat. 28; BAPD 302930; b) Florence, no inv. no., from Populonia, NSc 1934, 423 fig. 78a; von Bothmer (supra n. 29) 44 cat. 55; Kotsidu (supra n. 28) cat. 20; c) Samothrace 57.565, attributed to the Eucharides Painter, from Samothrace, ARV² 232,1; AJA 75, 1971, pl. 94 fig. 7; Kotsidu (supra n. 28) cat. 26; BAPD 202274; d) Kassel T675, attributed to the Leagros Group, from Cerveteri, CVA Kassel 1 Germany 35 pl. 24, 1; Kotsidu (supra n. 28) cat. 10; Shapiro (supra n. 28) 69 fig. 47; BAPD 351233; e) once New York market, Kotsidu (supra n. 28) cat. 13; BAPD 12323; f) New York 07.286.72, von Bothmer (supra n. 29) 46 cat. 5 pl. 22; Kotsidu (supra n. 28) cat. 22; BAPD 4093; g) Sydney, Nicholson Museum 47.7, von Bothmer (supra n. 29) cat. 60 [erroneously stating that both sides show aulos players]; Kotsidu (supra n. 28) cat. 24; photographs unpublished but available on the museum's website.

30 A better comparison for the one seated, one standing spectator is a black-figured pelike with scene of rhapsode, Dunedin, Otago Museum 48.226, Shapiro (supra n. 29) 66 fig. 7.

31 S. Steingräber, in: M. Carrese – E. di Castro – M. Martinelli (eds.), La musica in Etruria: Atti del convegno internazionale Tarquinia 18/20 settembre 2009 (2010) 37 provides statistics for musical instruments in tomb paintings from Tarquinia, Chiusi, and Orvieto in the period ca. 550–300 BC: five tombs with barbitos players, 21 with kithara (concert kitharas and so-called cylinder kitharas or phorminxes), 12 with chelys lyre, 52 with aulos, nine with players of cornu and trumpet-lituus, and 11 with dancers holding krotala. J.-R. Jannot, AntCl 48, 1979, 469–507 discusses stringed instruments and provides a catalogue of selected representations.

32 For music in Etruscan culture: J.-R. Jannot, CRAI, 1988, 311–334.

33 As noted in Jannot (supra n. 32) 481; B. Lawergren, EtrSt 10, 2004–2007, 122. 127–128; S. Sarti, in: Carrese – Castro – Martinelli (supra n. 31) 185–187.

34 See Jannot (supra n. 32) 481–489 and Lawergren (supra n. 33) 127. For musicians with this instrument on Chiusine cippi and urns, see Jannot (supra n. 32) 482–486 cat. 33. 38–41. 43–54 all dating between ca. 510–470 BC.

35 See J.-R. Jannot, in: La civiltà di Chiusi e del suo territorio (1993) 217–237.

36 Cerveteri: red-figured pelike from tomb 20 *a pozzetto* in the Banditaccia necropolis, Villa Giulia 46942; J. de la Genière, in: M. Bonghi Jovino – C. Chiaramonte Treré (eds.), Tarquinia: Richerche, scavi, e prospettive (1987) 207 pl. 57; BAPD 17982. From a *tomba a buca* at Tarquinia: black-figured pelike, RC1063, W. Helbig, BdI, 1878, 178; C. Tronchetti, Ceramica attica a figure nere. Grandi vasi. Anfore, pelikai, crateri. Materiali del Museo Archeologico Nazionale di Tarquinia 5 (1983) cat. 44; BAPD 8235.

37 Helbig's description reads (supra n. 1) 244: "Un uomo con lunga barba aguzza, vestito di chitone lungo e mantello, il capo cinto di una tenia, ed una donna ch'ha i capelli sciolti, vestita di chitone e mantello, stanno in piedi, l'uno dirimpetto all'altra. L'uomo, chi tiene colla sin. uno scettro, pene la mano d. sulla spalla della donna, la quale stende la d., quasi se cercasse calmare l'uomo e scusarsi con esso".

38 It would not be a column krater, also popular for these scenes, because Helbig elsewhere uses the word *cratere* for that shape, e.g., BdI, 1878, 179, referencing Tarquinia RC968. Nor would it be a hydria, for he uses *idria* in reference to the Orpheus vase in the Foiano tomb, discussed below.

39 For pursuit scenes with Zeus, see S. Kaempf-Dimitriadou, Der Liebe der Götter in der attischen Kunst des 5. Jahrhunderts v. Chr. (1979) 22–26 with catalogue at 93–97; and K. W. Arafat, Classical Zeus: A Study in Art and Literature (1990) 77–86 with catalogue at 191–195. The Foiano vase does not appear in either study.

40 As revealed through searches on the BAPD.

41 All by the Painter of the Birth of Athena: a) pelike with Poseidon pursuing Amymone on the obverse, together with Aphrodite (?) and Eros, and Zeus chasing a woman on the reverse, Villa Giulia 20846, ARV[2] 494,2; BAdd[2] 250; BAPD 205561; b) a second pelike, nearly identical, Villa Giulia 20847, ARV[2] 494,3; BAdd[2] 250; BAPD 205562; c) stamnos with Zeus pursuing a woman on both sides, Villa Giulia 20844–5, ARV[2] 495,6; 1656; BAdd[2] 250; BAPD 205565.

42 Boston 03.817: ARV[2] 991,59; BAPD 213880; J. H. Oakley, The Achilles Painter (1997) 125 cat. 80. Cf. also the appearance of three vases with erotic pursuit scenes, all including Eos chasing a youth, in the so-called Brygos Tomb (Tomb II) at Capua: D. Williams, AJA 96, 1992, 624–636.

43 Williams (supra n. 42) 633–634 for this reading as applied to the vases in the Brygos Tomb, and see S. Lewis, The Athenian Woman: An Iconographic Handbook (2002) 201–202.

44 Boston 90.156, ARV[2] 605,62; BAdd[2] 267; BAPD 207002; CB II cat. 107. Death of Orpheus: LIMC VII (1994) 85–87 cats. 28–59 s.v. Orpheus (M.-X. Garezou) and Bundrick (supra n. 28) 118–121.

45 Unlike the concert kithara, the chelys lyre was well known to the Etruscans: Jannot (supra n. 32) 473–481.

46 See Bundrick (supra n. 28) 121–125, with further references.

47 Cf. F. Lissarrague, Musica e storia 2, 1994, 277.

48 Vulci: amphora by the Painter of the Berlin Hydria (Vatican 16534, ARV[2] 616,7; 1662; BAdd[2] 269; BAPD 207127), stamnos by the Dokimasia Painter (Basel BS1411, Para 373, 34ter; BAdd[2] 234; BAPD 275231), and amphora by the Niobid Painter (Brooklyn 59.34, ARV[2] 604,57; 1701; BAdd[2] 267; BAPD 206996). Chiusi: stamnos attributed to the Group of Polygnotos (now lost, ARV[2] 1050,1; 1679; BAdd[2] 321; BAPD 213632). Spina: unattributed cup (San Simeon 5546); column krater by the Painter of the Florence Centauromachy (Ferrara 2795, ARV[2] 541,7; BAdd[2] 256, BAPD 206135), and oinochoe by the Schuwalow Painter (Zurich, Univ. 3637, BAPD 16089). Adria: fragmentary cup by the Briseis Painter (Adria 22110/B496, ARV[2] 409,44; BAdd[2] 233; BAPD 204442).

49 Five such mirrors are known, four with central Italian findspots (Chiusi, Orvieto, and Castelgiorgio). See R. D. De Puma, Record of the Princeton University Art Museum 60, 2001, 18–29, and N. de Grummond, in: M. D. Gentili (ed.), Aspetti e problemi della produzione degli specchi etruschi figurati (2000) 27–67, further speculating that mirrors could be used for divinatory purposes. The oracular head of Orpheus appears on three red-figured Athenian vases: Bundrick (supra n. 28) 125–126.

50 Helbig (supra n. 1) 244, and for Etruscan scarabs generally, P. Zazoff, Etruskische Skarabaen (1968). Hydriai are associated with male inhumation burials elsewhere, e.g., the recently excavated Tomba del Kottabos (A9/1998) in the Osteria necropolis of Vulci: A. M. Moretti Sgubini (ed.), Veio, Cerveteri, Vulci: Città d'Etruria a confronto (2001) 220–221. 230–239.

51 Surely reflecting the role of Chiusi in the diffusion of Athenian vases in central Italy, cf. Rastrelli (supra n. 11) and Iozzo (supra n. 8).

52 Cf. Paleothodoros (supra n. 2), especially 47–48, *contra* those believing shape was the primary consideration, e.g., H. Blinkenberg, in: C.-M. Villaneuva-Puig – F. Lissarrague – P. Rouillard – A. Rouveret (eds.), Céramique et peinture grecques. Modes d'emploi. Actes du colloque international. École du Louvre, 26–27–28 avril 1995 (1999) 439–444.

53 Etruscan and Attic vases used as ossuaries at Tarquinia and elsewhere: Palmieri (supra n. 15) 83–150. Paleothodoros (supra n. 19) stresses the interchangeability of Attic and Etruscan vases in tombs, whether used as ossuaries or as part of a *corredo*, opposing the notion that Athenian vases were considered superior.

54 J.-R. Jannot, Les reliefs archaïques de Chiusi (1984) for catalogue and discussion.

55 For Etruscan ancestor cult, see e.g., Damgaard Andersen (supra n. 22); S. Steingräber, in: J. M. Højte (ed.), Images of Ancestors (2002) 127–158; and G. Camporeale, in: S. Bell – H. Nagy (eds.), New Perspectives on Etruria and Early Rome: In Honor of Richard Daniel De Puma (2009) 220–250.

3 Regional Variation: Pelops and Chrysippos in Apulia

T. H. Carpenter

To broaden the discussion of Attic vases, my focus here is on the offspring of Athenian potters and painters in Apulia. For iconographic studies it would be short sighted to restrict our discussion to the parents and to ignore successful offspring whose brilliance can shed light back on their progenitors.

In the Greek world an artisan creating an image on a vase had to believe there was a market for it, and it follows that images aimed at a particular market can reflect interests and concerns of the clients. When the image is a depiction of a myth we should assume that the reason for the artisan's choice goes beyond the liveliness of the implied narrative and may have political, psychological, cultural or ethnic implications. Not surprisingly the choices of myths often differ from region to region as well as over time. Thus, surviving images, by their very nature, may allow us to access ancient regional perspectives that are otherwise lost. Too little attention has been paid to this phenomenon.

The depiction of the suicide of Ajax is a case in point and demonstrates well regional preferences. The earliest certain depiction of that subject is on an early seventh-century BC Protocorinthian aryballos where Ajax falls on his sword.[1] On a gem from Perachora of the second half of the seventh century, his name is inscribed as it is on several Corinthian vases from the first quarter of the sixth-century.[2] His suicide was also the subject of a relief on an ivory comb from Sparta, dated to the first quarter of the sixth century,[3] as well as on many shield bands from the second quarter of that century.[4] The occurrences of the scene are almost entirely from the Peloponnesus, while the subject rarely appears on Attic vases of any period, with a couple of very notable exceptions. One scholar has even interpreted this as reflecting "partisan [anti-Ionic] sympathy for Ajax".[5]

Imagery on South Italian vases provides more complex examples of regional differences (Fig. 1). The earliest South Italian workshops, Lucanian and Apulian, may well have been established by Athenian potters; the technique they used and many of the shapes they painted were based on Attic models. Greek myths were often used as sources for imagery, but many of the myths the South Italian painters chose were never depicted by Attic vase-painters. A careful look at imagery also shows that when they do use traditional Greek myths, they often reshape them to express new meanings, which might have been incomprehensible to Athenian audiences.

A significant difference between Attic and South Italian pottery has to do with their markets, and I can't stress enough how important this is. Apulian red-figure is usually said to have been made in Taranto, which was the only Greek city in all of Apulia, though there is reason to think that it may have been made at other sites in Apulia as well. All of the rest of Apulia was occupied by non-Greek, Italic people. As with Attic pottery, we know little or nothing about the people who produced the pots. But the difference is that Apulian pots were made for local markets, while Attic pots, the majority of which have been found outside of Attica, were usually export commodities. For Apulian pottery, Trendall estimated that only about one percent of known vases were found outside of Apulia, which means that the production centers, wherever they were, could not have been more than 100km from their find spots.[6]

A quick glance at large Apulian vases with complex imagery on them makes it clear that they could not have been mass produced. These were prestigious vases, some more than a meter and a half tall, designed for the tomb, and it is unlikely that they were made on spec; rather, it makes sense to assume they were made for specific clients. The imagery was not a whimsical choice, but was determined by the market. An extensive series of Apulian column kraters with depictions of Italic warriors in distinctive local costumes illustrates this point (Fig. 2). None of these has ever been found in a Greek context, and the Italic people on them are the protagonists.[7] Beyond this specific case, the Italic people of Apulia rather than Greek

3 Regional Variation: Pelops and Chrysippos in Apulia

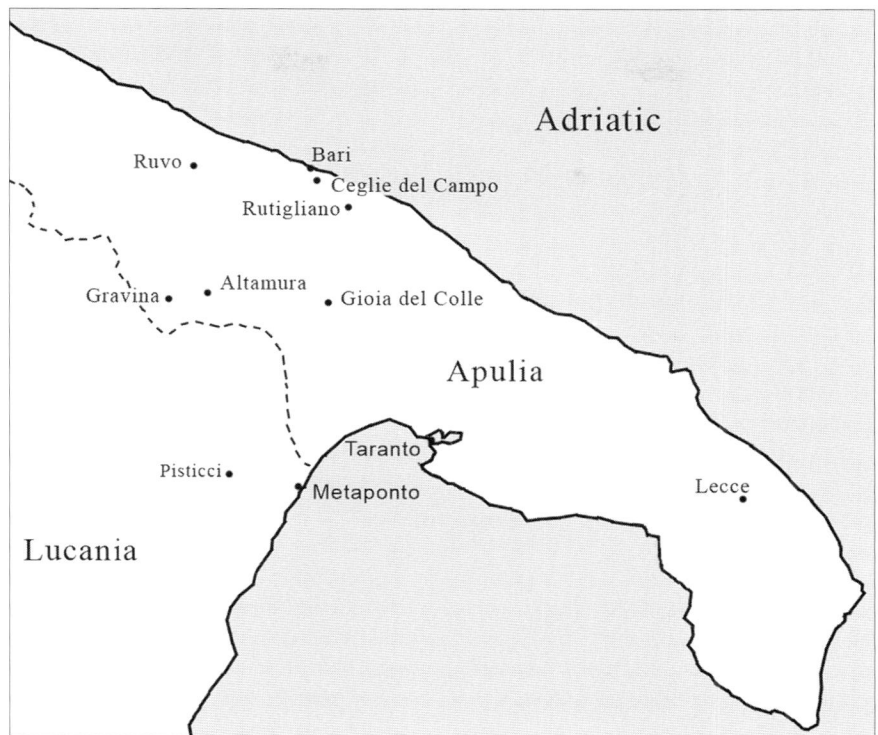

Fig. 1 Map of Apulia (author).

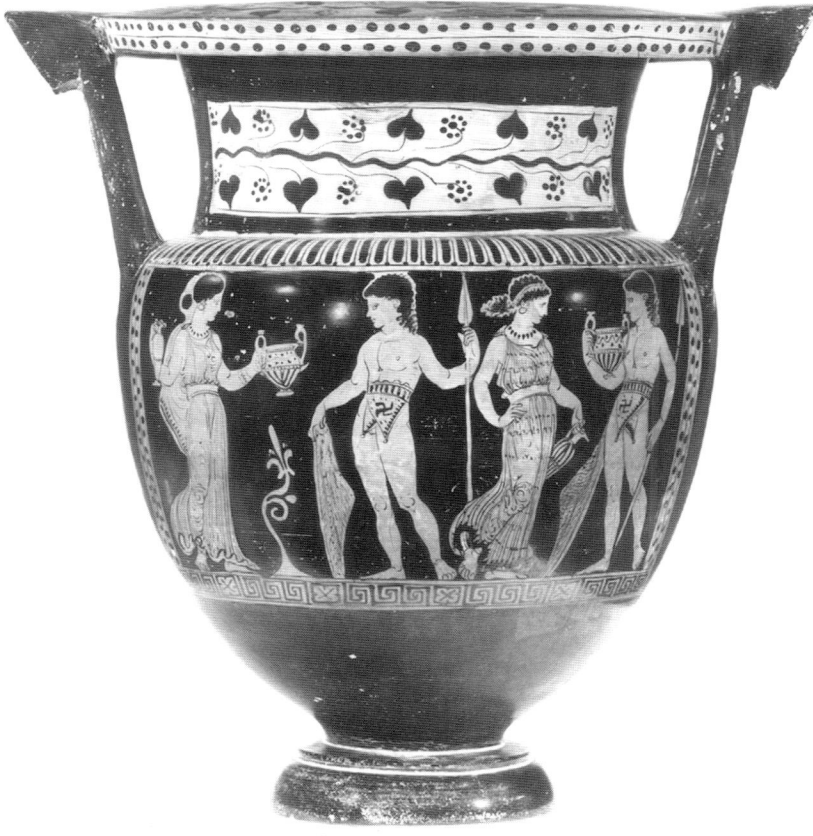

Fig. 2 Apulian red-figure column krater. New York, Metropolitan Museum of Art 17.120.241. Photo: Metropolitan Museum of Art.

colonists provided principal markets for large Apulian red-figure pots with complex images from myth, so we should assume that the imagery in some way reflected the interests and concerns of these people.

My focus in what follows here is on one Apulian painter, the Darius Painter, and on two related subjects that he painted several times for Italic markets. Pelops figures in both: one, the abduction of his son Chrysippos by Laius of Thebes never appears in Attic imagery, and the other, his chariot race with Oinomaos for the hand of his daughter Hippodameia, appears there only rarely.[8] Both stories were used by Attic tragedians who seemed to have focused on the curses provoked by the activities of Laius and Pelops and the dire consequences for later generations. The imagery used to depict these stories on Apulian pots suggests that the meanings they carried for the Italic people who obtained them may have been quite different from the traditional Greek view.

Images depicting the rape of Chrysippos only appear in Italic contexts. It is a subject on nine Apulian vases, three of them by the Darius Painter ca. 340–330 BC and the others from a decade or so later.[9] I should mention that it is also the subject on a Faliscan volute krater, probably near the middle of the fourth-century BC,[10] and on a Praeneste cista of ca. 320 BC.[11] There are no known Attic depictions of it.[12]

In the standard version of the scene, a beardless Laius, with his left arm around a naked boy, drives a chariot to the left. In five of the six Apulian depictions, Pelops, Chrysippos' father, pursues the chariot on foot. He is dressed in eastern garb including a Phrygian cap, indicating his foreign origin as son of Tantalos from Sipylos in Asia Minor (Fig. 3).

Euripides wrote a tragedy about Chrysippos from which only half a dozen fragments survive, but attempts to reconstruct it have tended to dominate discussions of the Chrysippos myth, and have unduly influenced interpretations of the imagery on the vases.[13] According to the now commonly accepted reconstruction of the lost tragedy, a young, exiled Laius of Thebes was offered hospitality by Pelops at Pisa in Elis, and while there he fell in love with Pelops' young son, Chrysippos. While teaching the boy how to drive a chariot, he abducted him. In this version, Chrysippos died possibly by his own hand; Pelops then cursed Laius.[14] Some scholars suggest that Euripides may have invented this version of the Chrysippos story.[15]

The Darius Painter, one of the most creative of Apulian painters from the middle of the fourth century BC puts the scene on three vases, each a variation on the theme. Two of the vases have known Italic provenances, one from Ruvo di Puglia and one from nearby Ceglie del Campo. In the upper band on an amphora from Ceglie (Fig. 3), an Italic settlement near modern Bari, a naked youth in front of the chariot holds two spears with one hand and reaches out to grab the bridle of one of the horses with the other.[16] Eros, with a wreath and ribbon flies in from the right toward the couple in the chariot, and Chrysippos reaches back toward his father's outstretched hand. Youths in front of the chariot, apparently trying to stop it, appear on another depiction by the Darius Painter and in each of the scenes by the Baltimore Painter a decade later. In this scene from Ceglie the boy is clearly distressed as he reaches out to his father for help, but Eros flying above them seems to give divine encouragement for the deed.

The subject appears on another amphora of similar size (ht. 101cm) by the same painter (Fig. 4). It was found with four other large vases in Tomb 163 at Ruvo di Puglia, an Italic site ca. 30 km northwest of Cegli.[17]

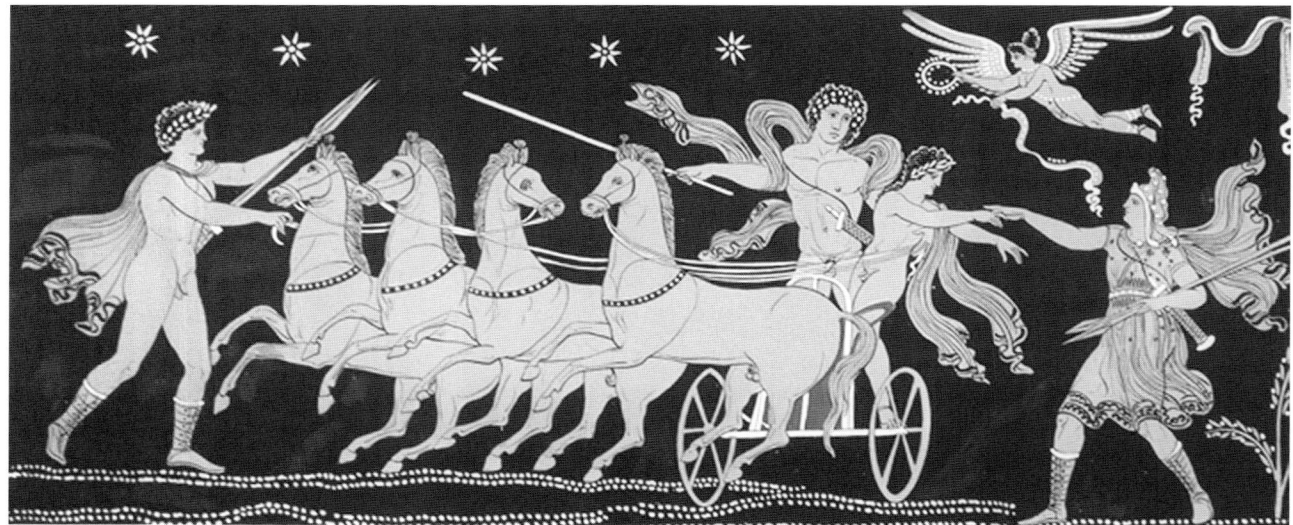

Fig. 3 Apulian red-figure amphora. Berlin, Antikensammlung F 3239 from Ceglie del Campo. Photo: after E. Gerhard, Apulische Vasenbilder des Königlichen Museums zu Berlin (1845) pl. 6.

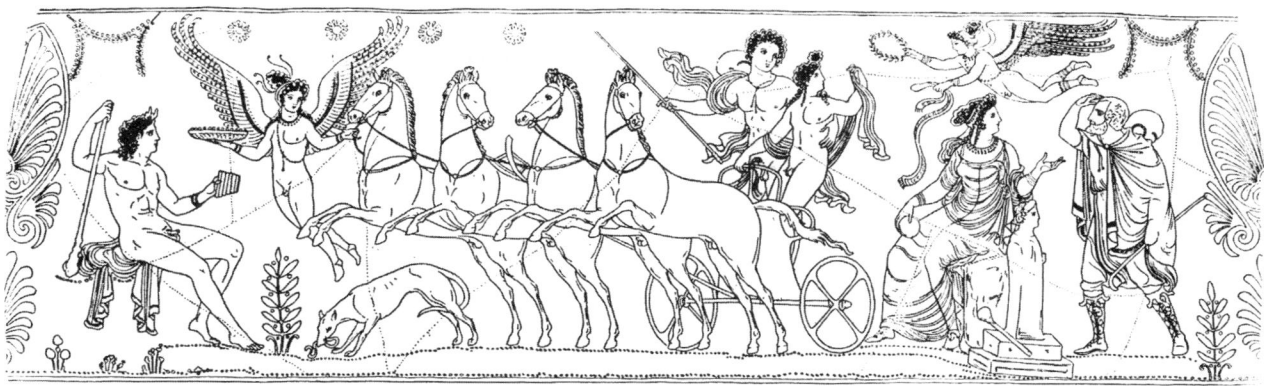

Fig. 4 Apulian red-figure amphora. Naples, Museo Archeologico Nazionale 81942 (H 1769) from Ruvo di Puglia. Photo: after C. Robert, JdI 29, 1914, pl.11.

In the scene, Eros, with a phiale, leads the galloping horses toward a seated Pan who holds a syrinx and a lagobolon. To the right of the chariot another Eros, holding out a wreath, flies toward it. A seated woman, usually identified as Aphrodite, leans on a herm while looking back and gesturing at an old paidagogos who watches the departing chariot, his right hand shielding his eyes. Chrysippos looks back toward Eros and raises his left arm as if saluting him. Pelops does not appear. There is something almost celebratory about this scene, and it is hard to conclude that something terrible is happening. The subject is the same as on the Ceglie vase, but the emphasis is very different.

It is also difficult to believe that the differences between the two scenes are expressions of the painter's whimsy and not the choice of the client. Séchan, noting the differences in the imagery on the Ceglie and Ruvo vases, wrote that they should not be attributed to different sources but rather to the fantasies of the individual painters. Since both are now understood to be by the same painter, the more likely explanation for the differences has to do with the client's desires.

An idiosyncratic detail on two of the vases from the Ruvo tomb supports this assumption and suggests a personal dimension to the scene. Below the horses in the Chrysippos scene, the painter has put a dog with a snake in its mouth that seems to have nothing to do with the scene itself. The same dog appears on a companion piece, an amphora of precisely the same size (ht. 101cm) also by the Darius Painter, found in the same tomb.[18] In that scene Helios drives a chariot to the right toward a seated Poseidon to whom Nike presents a ribbon. The dog, below the horses, approaches the snake but has not yet taken it in his mouth (Fig. 5). Again, the dog seems to have nothing to do with the scene, but his inclusion on the two vases from the same tomb undoubtedly meant something to the client who obtained them.

A third version of the subject by the Darius Painter, on a bell krater, surfaced in 1968.[19] In the lower part of

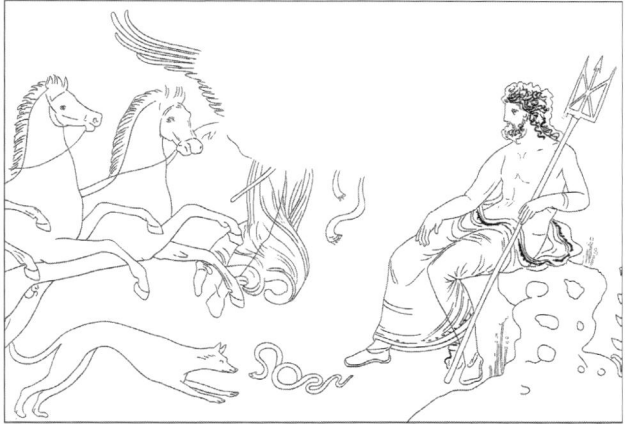

Fig. 5 Apulian red-figure amphora. Naples, Museo Archeologico Nazionale 81953 (H 3219) from Ruvo di Puglia. Photo: after MonInst IV, 1845, pl. 16.

the scene Chrysippos in the chariot reaches back with both hands toward Pelops, who is in eastern dress (Fig. 6). Two youths with spears in front of the horse try to stop it. Pan and three deities are seated in the upper part of the scene along with a paidagogos who stands with his hand raised to his head as on the Ruvo vase. One of the deities is Aphrodite with a phiale, who sits directly above the couple in the chariot, attended by Eros. Suspended below Aphrodite and right over the couple in the chariot is a iynx wheel, a magical love charm invented by Aphrodite.[20]

A comment by Aelian (NA 6.15) that Euripides presented Laius in his *Chrysippos* "as the first among the Greeks to inaugurate the love of boys" has led some to look for a social critique in Euripides' play, and one scholar has argued that the play was a reaction against the pederastic tradition of Athenian upper class males "concomitant with the growing democratization of Athenian culture".[21] While this may have been true for the tragedy, the imagery on the vases does not seem to support such a view.

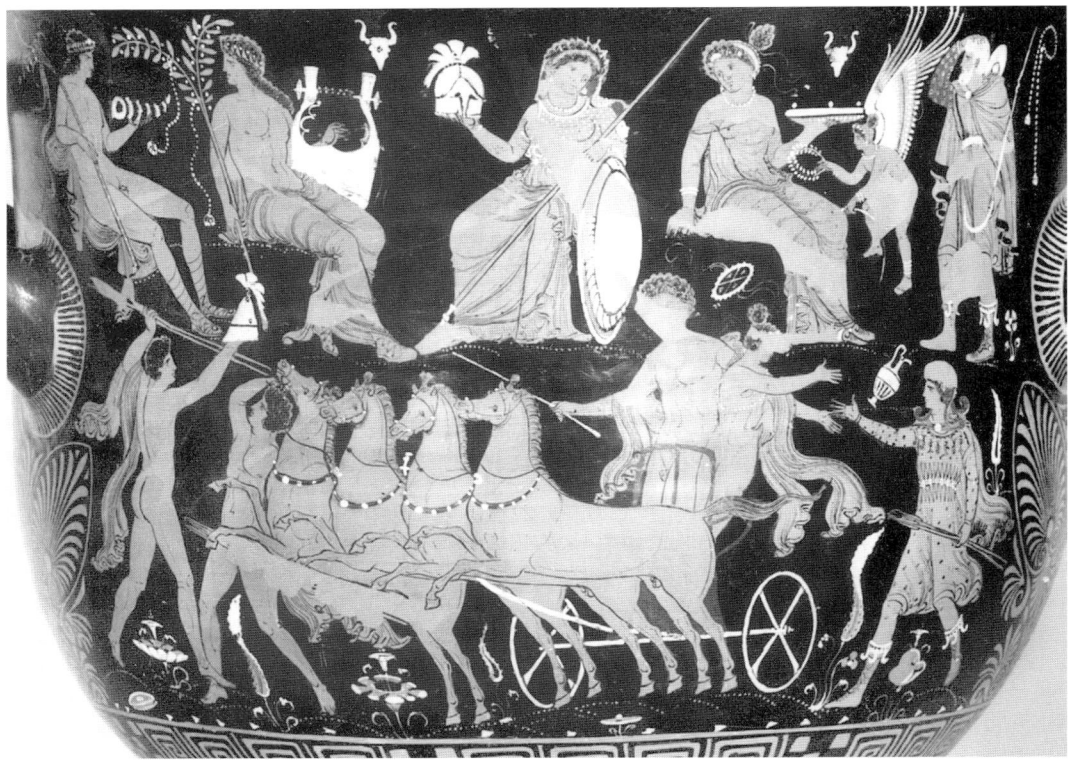

Fig. 6 Apulian red-figure bell krater. Berlin, Antikensammlung 1968.12. Photo: Ingrid Geske-Heiden.

In fact, there were other versions of the death of Chrysippos current in Athens when Euripides wrote his tragedy. Thucydides (1.9.2) writes that Atreus was banished by his father for the death of Chrysippos, and Plato (*Cra* 395B) also assigns the murder of Chrysippos to Atreus. Hellanicus [*FGrH* 1.50 (42)] writes that both Atreus and Thyestes participated in the murder at the urging of their mother, Hippodameia. The motive was jealously of Pelops' fondness for the boy and worries about their inheritance. Plutarch (*Mor* 313 D–E), citing a Dositheos as his source, writes that Atreus and Thyestes stopped Laius as he attempted to carry off Chrysippos and that Pelops forgave him because he was motivated by love. He continues that Hippodamia then urged Atreus and Thyestes to kill Chrysippos, and because of her involvement in the death, Pelops banished her. In exile she ultimately killed herself.[22] Plutarch's version has been dubbed a "Hellenistic concoction",[23] which it may be, but Pausanias (6.20.7) seems to refer to that version when he describes the Hippodameium at Olympia and writes that Hippodamia "withdrew to Midea in Argolis because Pelops was very angry with her over the death of Chrysippos". Later her bones were brought back from Midea and buried at Olympia.[24]

It is not possible to know which version of the myth was current in fourth-century Apulia, but the images hint that the painter was aware of elements of the story that make it more complex than the plot of the Euripidean tragedy. Five of the six depictions of the subject show a youth or youths stopping the chariot.[25] If we identify those youths as Atreus and Thyestes, which seems plausible, the likelihood of Euripides' play as the principal inspiration for the imagery diminishes. Since literary sources are of limited use in understanding the imagery on the Darius Painter's vases here, we turn to comparisons with related scenes which do shed some light for a possible interpretation of them.

While the story of the abduction of Chrysippos by Laius may have been a fifth-century invention, Pelops' race with Oinomaos has an ancient pedigree that goes back at least to the late seventh or early sixth century BC when it was depicted on the Chest of Kypselos, which Pausanias (5.17.7) saw in the temple of Hera at Olympia. It was, as Pausanias tells us (5.10.6–7), also the subject of the East pediment of the Temple of Zeus at Olympia.

Rare in Attic imagery, it appears on more than twenty fourth-century BC Apulian vases.[26] For our purposes here its appearance on four vases by the Darius Painter found in Italic tombs at Ruvo – including the Chrysippos tomb discussed earlier – is of particular interest.

In the version of the story depicted by Apulian painters, Oinomaos, king of Pisa, had promised the hand of his daughter Hippodameia to any suitor who could defeat him in a chariot race, with the understanding that the suitor who lost the race would be killed. Myrtilos, the king's charioteer, bribed by Pelops or Hippodameia, agreed to sabotage Oinomaos' chariot thus guaranteeing Pelops' victory. Later, when Myrtilos attempted to claim promised sexual favors from Hippodameia, Pelops threw him into the sea where he drowned, but not before Myrtilos placed a curse on the house of Pelops. Both Sophocles and Euripides wrote tragedies titled *Oinomaos*, about which we know almost nothing, but elsewhere both playwrights refer to the death of Myrtilos and his curse on the house of Pelops.[27]

Pelops is the quintessential Peloponnesian hero; as one scholar has written, "if Athens had Theseus, the Peloponnese had Pelops. As founding father of the Atreidai, he was genealogically ancestor of all Peloponnesians";[28] this may help to explain why he rarely appears on Attic vases, where he can be identified with certainty on only three.[29] Although central to Peloponnesian cult, Pelops' role in Greek myth is limited to the Oinomaos story. In depictions of the chariot race, as in the Chrysippos scenes, Pelops almost always wears distinctly eastern garments, alluding to his Phrygian/Lydian origins. Thus, while his Peloponnesian connection may help explain his absence from Attic vases, it does not seem to be a factor in the choice to depict him on South Italian vases.

Pelops' success in obtaining the hand of Hippodameia depended on multiple betrayals. As one scholar has recently noted, "There is nothing admirable in Myrtilos, who betrays Oinomaos; nor in Hippodameia, who betrays her father, and least of all in Pelops who wins the race by sabotage and then, having won, kills his helper".[30] For both Sophocles and Euripides, Pelops was clearly blameworthy. But this is not the conclusion suggested by the Apulian images. I should note that the Darius Painter seems to have been well versed in Attic tragedies, as demonstrated well on his Hypsippyle vase, which I have discussed elsewhere.[31] Thus, we should see the decision to alter the focus of the stories as an informed choice.

The Darius Painter's depiction of the scene on the neck of the krater also from Tomb 163 at Ruvo is revealing (Fig. 7).[32] The chariots race to the right, Pelops with Hippodameia in the lead followed by Oinomaos and Myrtilos. Eros flies above the lead chariot, while an eagle with a snake in its beak flies above the second. Between the two chariots is a Fury brandishing her torches at Oinomaos and Myrtilos.[33] Here, as in the Chrysippos scenes, the focus is on the triumph of Eros. This is supported by another of the Darius Painter's images from another tomb at Ruvo (Fig. 8).[34] The scene depicts the preparation for the race. Pelops and Hippodameia stand on either side of an altar and reach across it to touch hands as Oinomaos looks on. Myrtilos approaches from the right carrying a ram. Aphrodite and Eros stand behind Pelops, while a Fury, to the right, watches Myrtilos. The Fury in both of these scenes focuses her attention on Myrtilos and Oinomaos, not on Pelops, as Sophocles and Euripides would have it. Rather, as on the Chrysippos vases where Aphrodite and Eros support and even celebrate the actions of Laius, here they support the victory of Pelops and Hippodameia.

The tragedians' uses of the Chrysippus and Oinomaos stories seems to have been turned on their heads by the Darius Painter, particularly in his depictions on vases from the same tomb at Ruvo di Puglia. Laius' abduction of Chrysippos is celebrated, not derided, as is Pelops' victory over Oinomaos, in spite of the betrayals involved. The central deity in each of the scenes is Aphrodite or her agent Eros, and this is most likely the key to an understanding of this imagery designed for the tomb. Her power is in some way a consoling factor in facing death. Abductions are positive events. So, on the opposite side of the krater with Pelops and Oinomaos, is another chariot

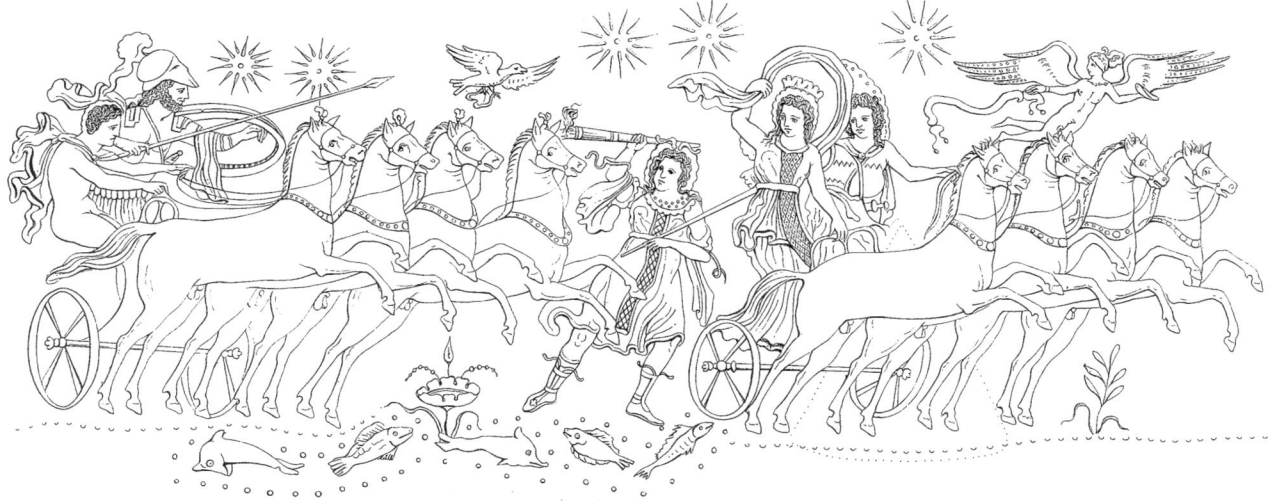

Fig. 7 Apulian red-figure volute krater. Naples, Museo Archeologico Nazionale 81667 (H 3256) from Ruvo di Puglia. Photo: after MonInst II, 1836, pl. 32.

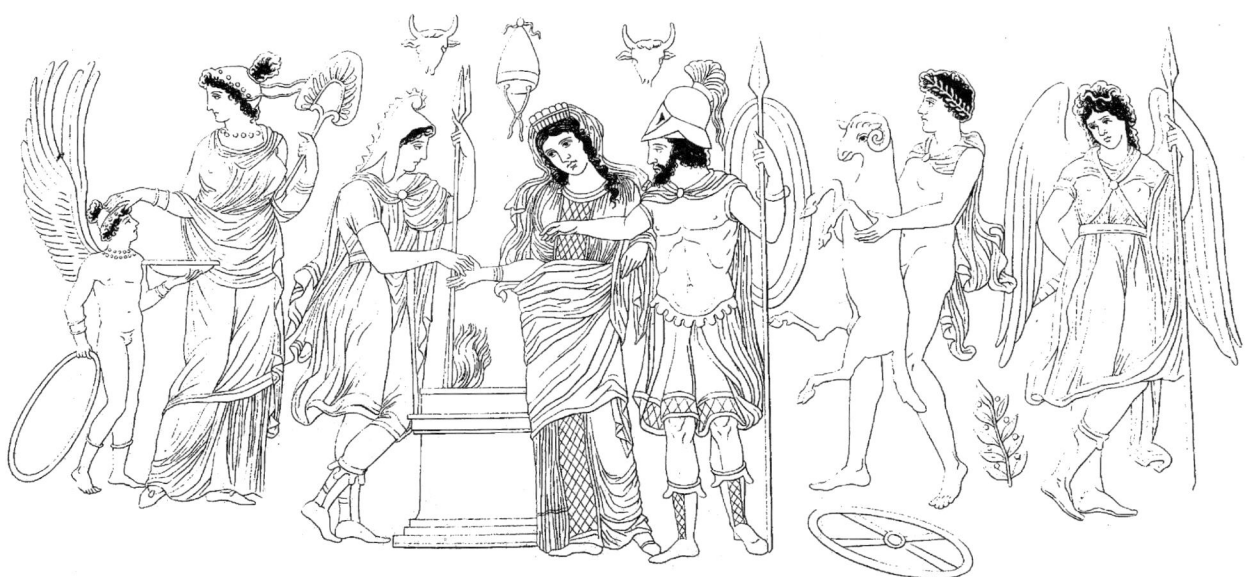

Fig. 8 Apulian red-figure column krater. St. Petersburg, State Hermitage Museum 4323 from Ruvo di Puglia. Photo: after AdI 23, 1851, pl. Q,R.

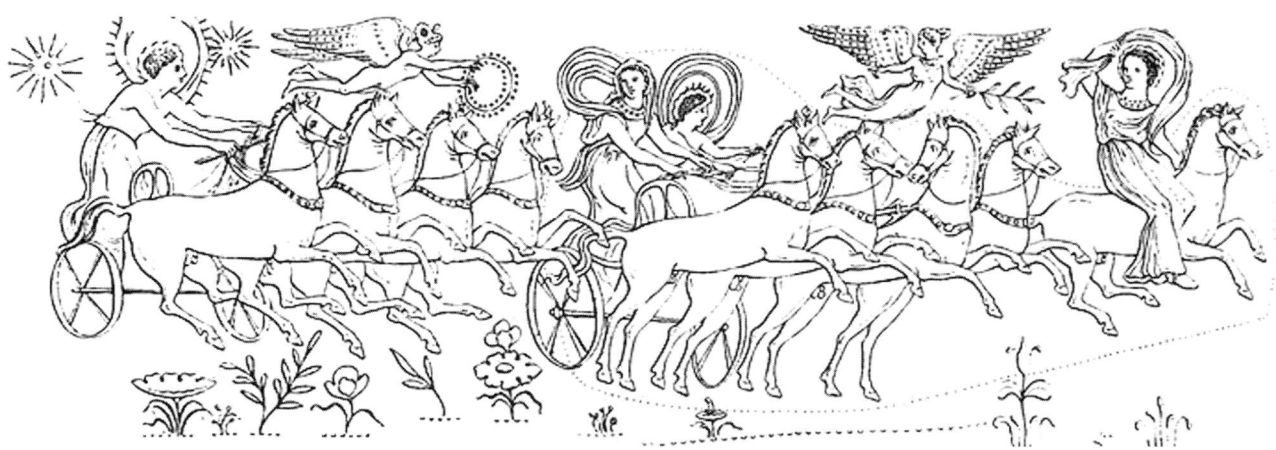

Fig. 9 Naples 81667 (see Fig. 7).

scene, plausibly Eos abducting Tithonos, preceded by Selene and followed by Helios. Eros and Nike fly above the chariot (Fig. 9).

The Italic people of Apulia were not Greeks, and while they adopted aspects of Greek culture, including imagery, they modified what they borrowed so that it fit their own needs. They used images from myth as vehicles to express their own ideas, which often may have been only tangentially related to the corpus of Greek literature. We can only speculate on the meaning these scenes had for the client who obtained them, but I think we should conclude that the choice of the images was not accidental, and that the meaning was local and personal – and distinctly not Attic.

Notes

1   Berlin, Antikensammlung 3319. I. Jenkins, in: A. Clark et al. (eds.), Essays in Honor of Dietrich von Bothmer (2002) 153–156 has identified a bronze in the British Museum (1865.11–18.230) from the last quarter of the eighth century as the earliest representation of the death of Ajax; see 154 n. 5 for Berlin 3319.

2   Gem: New York, Metropolitan Museum of Art 42.11.13: LIMC 1 (1981) 329 no. 110 s.v. Aias I (O. Touchefeu). Vases: Berlin, Antikensammlung 3182; Paris, Louvre E 635; Basel, Antikenmuseum und Sammlung Ludwig BS 1404: idem, 330 nos. 119. 120. 122.

3   Athens, NM 15522, L. Marangou (ed.), Lakonische Elfenbein- und Beinschnitzereien (1969) 94 no. 40 fig. 69a.

4   E. Kunze, Archaische Schildbänder (1950) 154–157.

5   A famous Attic exception is the amphora by Exekias in Boulogne, Musée Communal 558, ABV 145,18; Touchefeu (supra n. 2) 329 no. 104. See R. Kannicht, ClAnt 1, 1982, 81–82 for speculation on the popularity of the subject in the Peloponnese and its absence from Attica.
6   RVAp xlviii.
7   T. H. Carpenter, MemAmAc 48, 2003, 1–24. H. Frielinghaus, Einheimische in der apulischen Vasenmalerei: Ikonographie im Spannungsfeld zwischen Produzenten und Rezipienten (1995).
8   For the Rape of Chrysippos see LIMC III (1986) 286–289 s.v. Chrysippos I (K. Schefold); for Pelops' contest with Oinomaos, see LIMC VII (1994) 19–23 s.v. Oinomaos (I. Triantis) and 282–287 s.v. Pelops (I. Triantis).
9   Darius Painter: Berlin, Antikensammlung F 3239, RVAp 18/22; Naples, Museo Nazionale H 1769 (81942), RVAp 18/48; Berlin, Antikensammlung 1968.12, RVAp 18/66. Baltimore Painter: Malibu, J. Paul Getty Museum 77.AE.14, RVAp 27/26; Naples, Private RVAp 27/27; Fiesole, Costantini 153, RVAp 18/55. White Saccos-Kantharos Group: Bari, Loiudice Collection, RVAp (second supplement) 29/D3; Once New York Market, RVAp (second supplement) 29/D4. M. Gualtiere has recently published an oinochoe with a depiction of the rape found at Roccagloriosa in Lucania with two other vases attributed to the circle of the Darius Painter in S. Schierup – B. Bundgaard Rasmusen (eds.), Red-figure Pottery in its Ancient Setting (2012) 59–68.
10 Melbourne D87/1969, A. D.Trendall, JbBerlMus 12, 1970, 159. For images, see F. Gilotta, Prospettiva 45, 1986, 4–5.
11 Villa Giulia 13199, G. Bordenache Battaglia, Le ciste prenestine (1990) no. 69.
12 For a recent discussion of the myth and its imagery, see Z. Parthene, Οι απεικονίσεις του Χρύσιππου στην σπουλική αγγειογραφία: παραστηρήσεις στην εικονογροφία τους in: E. Kephalidou, et al. (eds.), Αντίδωρο στον Καθηγητή Μιχάλη Τιβέριο από τους μαθητές του (2012) 219–228.
13 See L. Séchan, Études sur la tragédie grecque dans ses rapports avec la céramique (1926) 311–318 for a review of earlier interpretations.
14 C. Collard – M. Cropp (eds.), Euripides VIII, Fragments (2008) 459–471; D. Mastronarde, in: Euripides, Phoenissae (1994) 31–38.
15 T. Gantz, Early Greek Myth (1993) 488; H. Lloyd-Jones, The Justice of Zeus (1971) 121 argues that Aeschylus used the rape of Chrysippus in his Labdacid trilogy. M. L. West, in: J. Griffin (ed.), Sophocles Revisited. Essays Presented to Sir Hugh Lloyd-Jones (1999) 42–43 strongly disagrees.
16 Berlin, Antikensammlung F 3239, RVAp 18/22. In Berlin since at least 1834.
17 Naples, Museo Nazionale 81942 (H 1769), RVAp 18/48. A. Montanaro, Ruvo di Puglia e il suo territorio (2007) 707–717.
18 Naples, Museo Nazionale 81953 (H 3219), RVAp 18/45.
19 Berlin, Antikensammlung 1968.12, RVAp 18.66. A. D. Trendall, JbBerlMus 12, 1970, 153–161.
20 For the iynx wheel see C. Faraone, Ancient Greek Love Magic (1999) 56–57.
21 T. Hubbard, in: J. Davidson et al. (eds.), Greek Drama III. Essays in Honour of Kevin Lee (2006) 223.
22 See also Hyginus, Fab. 85.
23 Collard – Cropp (supra n. 14) 460–461.
24 B. McCauley, ClJ 93, 1998, 236 dates the return of the bones to 420 BC.
25 The youths appear on all three of the Baltimore Painter's depictions.
26 Quite remarkably, three versions of the subject by three different Apulian painters were found in one tomb at Ruvo; see A. Montanaro, Ruvo di Puglia e il suo territorio (2007) 883–888, T 321. On a volute krater by the Baltimore Painter without a known provenance, both the abduction of Chrysippos and the chariot race are included: Naples, Private 370, RVAp 27/27.
27 Soph. El. 505–515; Eur. Or. 988–996. Pherekydes is known to have included the role of Myrtilos in the sixth century. Cf. Pind. Oly.1.
28 H. Kyrieleis, in: D. Buitron (ed.), The Interpretation of Architectural Sculpture in Greece and Rome (1997) 24.
29 Athens, National Museum 595, ABL 96, a black-figure lekythos of ca. 500 BC is usually said to show Oinomaos sacrificing and Pelops in his winged chariot, but Haspels, ABL 98, rightly questioned this identification. Ferrara, Museo Nazionale 3058, ARV^2 1032,58, a hydria from Spina, has a named Pelops in a chariot as Peleus pursues Thetis. Beazley, ARV^2 1679, wrote "I do not understand the collocation of Peleus and Pelops" and Robertson (Gnomon 39, 1967, 822) calls it "a very odd picture altogether", On Arezzo, Museo Civico 1460, ARV^2 1157,25, ca. 410 BC Pelops and Hippodameia, both named, ride in a quadriga to the right. A dolphin below the chariot would seem to indicate the sea, and as Shefton notes in P. E. Arias – M. Hirmer – B. Shefton, A History of 1000 Years of Greek Vase Painting (1962) 375, the version here may be one that connects the hero with Lesbos. Naples, Museo Nazionale 2200, ARV^2 1440, ca. 370 BC depicts the start of the race.
30 W. Hansen, The Winning of Hippodameia, TransactAmPhilAss 130, 2006, 25.
31 T. Carpenter, The Darius Painter: Text and Context in: S. Schmidt – J. H. Oakley (eds.), Hermeneutik der Bilder – Beiträge zu Ikonograpie und Interpretation griechischer Vasenmalerei (2009) 153–159.
32 Naples 81667 (H 3656), RVAp 18/40.
33 For a similar use of a Fury see Naples, Museo Nazionale Stg. 697, RVAp 18/236.
34 St. Petersburg, Hermitage 4323, RVAp 18/18.

4 Baskets, Nets and Cages: Indicia of Spatial Illusionism in Athenian Vase-painting

Dedicated to the Memory of Ellen N. Davis

Beth Cohen

The baskets, nets and cages employed in ancient Greek daily life have generally not come down to us because they were made from ephemeral, organic materials such as rushes, hemp, rope, cord, lightweight wood, and wicker.[1] Athenian vase-paintings thus provide a visual record of these lost utilitarian objects,[2] which were used by nearly everyone: from the elite man or youth (e.g., Fig. 1), to the maiden serving in a festival procession as a *kanephoros* (basket bearer),[3] the child at play,[4] and the town or country worker.[5]

Reflections in ancient art underscore that these once-ubiquitous objects had served as containers for inanimate things or for capturing, or confining living creatures since prehistoric times.[6] And several of their functions depended upon their fabrication as sometimes flexible, openwork constructions whose spaces allowed the passage of light and air, or liquid, and enabled visibility of their contents.

In Athenian vase-painting, depicting openwork objects presented a challenge for the standard technical vocabularies. Both black- and red-figure canonically show forms as detailed silhouettes against a contrasting background.[7] And, early on, white-ground normally relied on black-figure silhouettes as well, before transitioning to outline drawing with dilute glaze and/or color.[8] But, as we shall see, vase-painters' visualizations of objects whose forms are not solid and opaque result in technically unconventional renditions that occasionally suggest spatial depth.

Tightly-woven baskets, commonly depicted in Athenian vase painting using standard technical vocabulary, can serve as a contrasting reference point. For example: On an Exekian black-figure amphora in Boston of ca. 540–530 BC showing Dionysos drinking during the vintage, diagonally hatched lines incised on curved black-glazed silhouettes describe the woven harvesting baskets.[9] On a fragmentary tondo from a red-figure cup of ca. 500–490 BC in Brussels inscribed *hopais [k]alos* (Fig. 1),[10] an athlete using a pick straddles a densely woven opaque basket shown as a curved reserved form covered with cross-hatched black lines. And on a white-ground pyxis of ca. 460, attributed to the Painter of London D 12, women juggle over a flaring wool basket or *kalathos*, which is painted on the engobe with lines of glaze and dilute.[11]

In black-figure, before the advent of red-figure, the Amasis Painter is known for employing technically unconventional black-glaze outlines and reserve for the flesh of certain females (e.g., Fig. 2, right) instead of the standard white color applied over the black.[12] His technical handling of baskets is equally memorable. On the amphorae in Würzburg[13] and Basel[14] (Fig. 2. Color Pl. 2B) of ca. 540 BC, showing the vintage in Dionysos' vineyard, satyrs tread grapes in woven baskets, set on

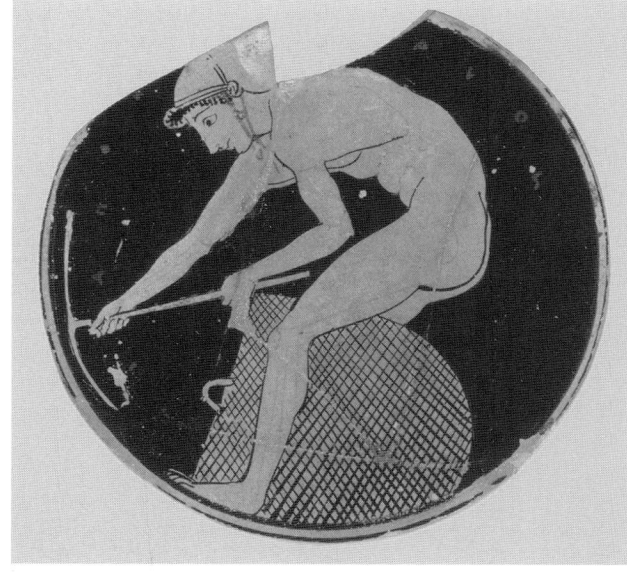

Fig. 1 Athlete using a pick straddling a basket, fragmentary tondo from Athenian red-figure cup, unattributed, ca. 500–490 BC, Brussels, Musées Royaux d'Art et d'Histoire R 347 (Photo: Museum).

legged troughs, which siphon the escaping juice into sunken storage vessels. These baskets' weave is indicated by broad cross-hatched strokes of black painted on reserve instead of the standard incised hatching on black. In black-figure's technical vocabulary, the reserve that the Amasis Painter employs in these distinctive baskets suggests the background of the vase-painting peeping through their openwork structure. But this technically implied translucency is not realized, and perhaps not intended, because neither the satyrs' lower legs nor harvested grape bunches can be glimpsed through these baskets' seemingly open weave. Black-figure wine-making scenes by other painters show grapes trod in solid black-glazed baskets, whose weave is incised.[15]

Significantly, spatial layering suggesting translucency is achieved in black-figure employing a non-canonical technical execution similar to the Amasis Painter's baskets on the Princeton Painter's amphora of ca. 540 BC in Brussels depicting the sale of oil and/or wine (Fig. 3).[16] On side B, a pointed amphora is propped up in an openwork basket, or stand, rendered with cross-hatched strokes of black glaze upon the reserved ground. Remarkably, the amphora's pointed bottom is shown inside this openwork object and against the scene's reserved background, which is visible through the grid along with the (partially preserved) foot of the man at the right.

The venerable technology of knotting fibrous material for hunting and fishing nets can be observed in preserved ancient fragments.[17] Nets are and were effective because their translucency enables them to blend invisibly with the environment, and dying makes them even more difficult for quarry to see.[18] However, depictions of hunting and fishing nets in Athenian vase-painting of the late sixth century largely avoid these objects' illusionistic artistic potential as openwork constructions of flexible meshed fabric. Inside an early black-figure on white-ground phiale at the British Museum of ca. 520 BC, hounds chase a hare toward a hunter's trap consisting of a net stretched over a frame.[19] Here, black-figure silhouette and incision have been abandoned for the net, which is drawn with cross-hatched lines of diluted glaze on the engobe.[20] Interestingly, on several late sixth-century purely black-figure vases, net traps approached by hunted hares are likewise described by the non-black-figure shorthand of cross-hatched black lines on the vessels' pale ground.[21] In their technical vocabulary, these net traps, which recall the Amasis Painter's basketry (Fig. 2. Color Pl. 2B), seem to be translucent although nothing is ever shown trapped inside them.

The same moment in the chase, with the pursued hare approaching a net trap, is spotlighted on a red-figure askos of ca. 470–460 BC (Fig. 4), attributed to the Pan Painter.[22] Here the net trap is a reserved form articulated

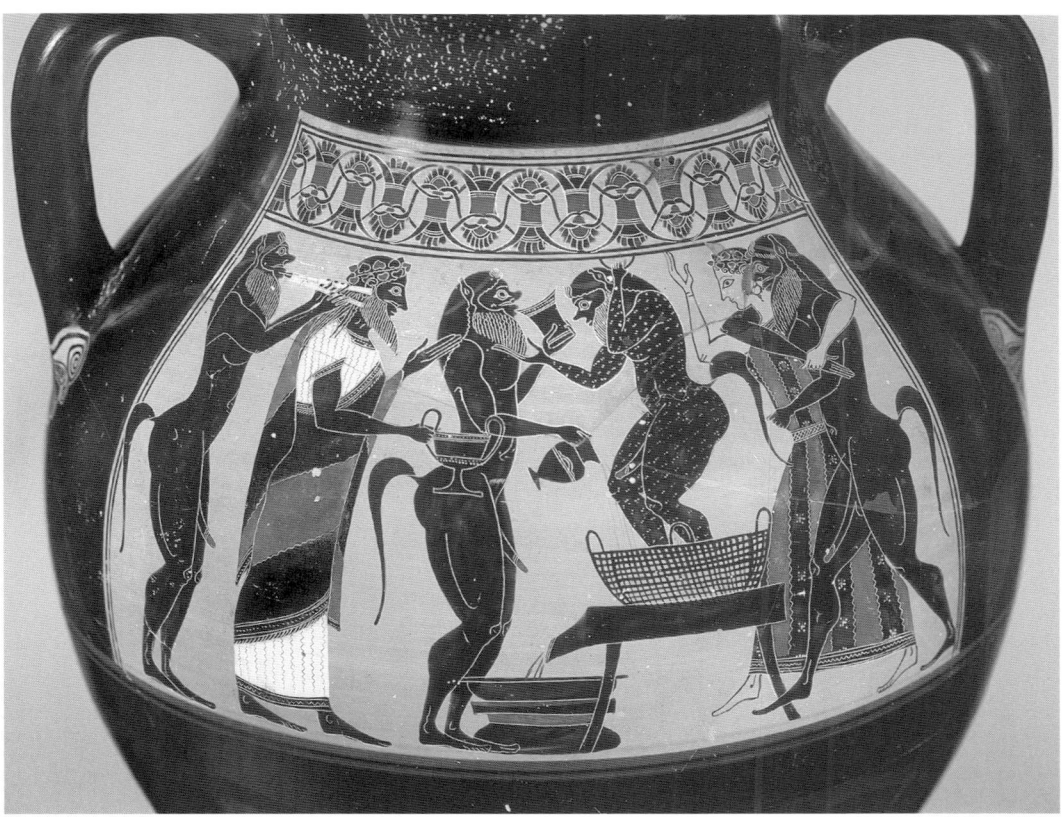

Fig. 2 Dionysos with satyrs at the vintage: one satyr treads grapes in a basket, another dances with a maenad, panel on side A of Athenian black-figure amphora of type B, attributed to the Amasis Painter, ca. 540 BC, Basel, Antikenmuseum Basel und Sammlung Ludwig Kä 420 (Photo: Museum).

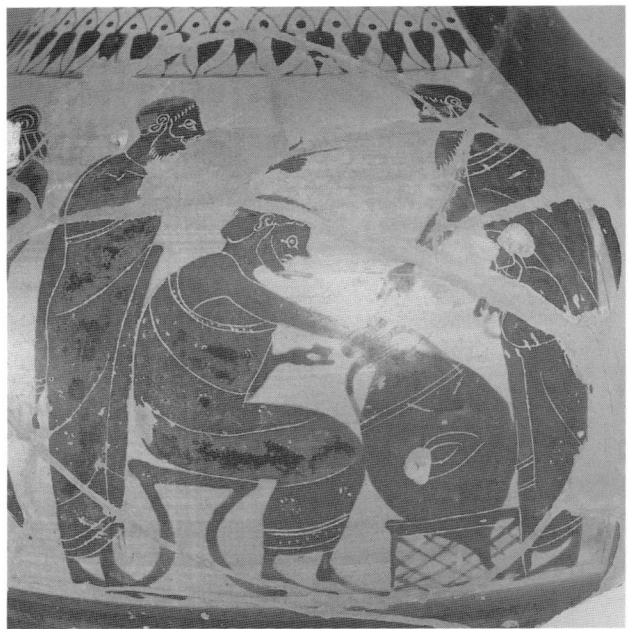

Fig. 3 The sale of oil or wine with a pointed amphora propped up in a basket or stand, detail, panel on side B of Athenian black-figure amphora of type B, attributed to the Princeton Painter, ca. 540 BC, Brussels, Musées Royaux d'Art et d'Histoire R 279 (Photo: Museum).

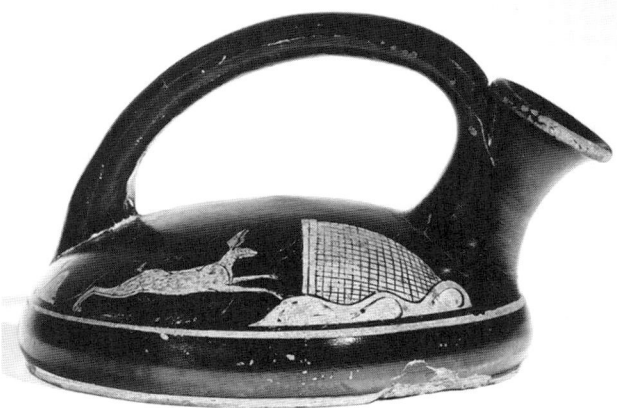

Fig. 4 Running hare (pursued by a Laconian hound on side A) approaching a net trap, side B of Athenian red-figure askos, attributed to the Pan Painter, ca. 470–460 BC, Ashmolean Museum, University of Oxford, AN1979.20 (Photo: Museum).

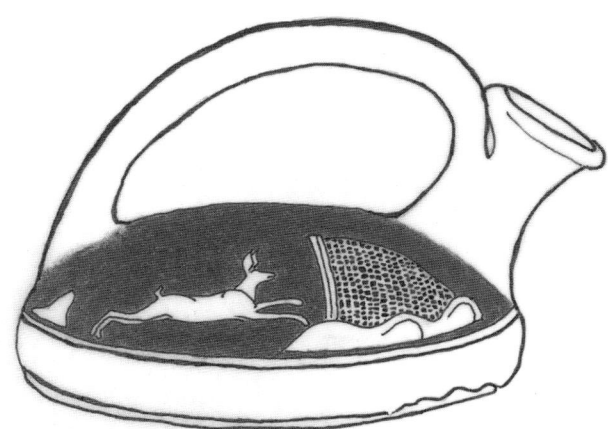

Fig. 5 Running hare approaching a net trap, hypothetical reconstruction of standard red-figure technique for the Athenian askos in Fig. 4 (Drawing: Author).

with cross-hatched black lines. This facile rendering, recalling the Brussels athlete's opaque, tightly-woven basket (Fig. 1), does not suggest the translucency of the net's openwork structure in a manner consistent with red-figure's technical vocabulary, which, as may be demonstrated in a hypothetical reconstruction (Fig. 5), ought to depict a trap with reserved netting and black openwork spaces. While the photo-negative shorthand employed instead in red-figure may not describe a translucent extended net illusionistically (cf. Figs. 4. 5), it is effective for the remarkable piled up fishermen's hauling nets depicted on a late-sixth-century psykter attributed to Smikros (Fig. 6),[23] which may be compared visually to the piled-up nets in the foreground of a New York Times photograph of a Maine fisherman.[24]

Some earlier red-figure baskets, nets and cages can have a confusing visual affinity since all may be shown as reserved forms, and a certain representational reticence inhibits depiction of contents inside openwork objects. For example: On the unusual tondo inside the red-figure cup in Boston of ca. 510–500 BC, attributed to the Ambrosios Painter,[25] a fisherboy holds at the ready – to bag his imminent catch – what appears to be a sagging net (though it lacks overall crosshatching) rather than the rounded basket employed by the fisherman on the Pan Painter's red-figure pelike in Vienna[26] of ca. 470 BC. According to experts on ancient fishing, the male figure standing opposite the pelike's fisherman carries suspended from a pole – not a basket – but a dipnet or handnet; although its surface articulation is lost, this object may display a sagging contour.[27] The reserved oblong form, detailed with vertical and horizontal lines, and topped by a cone, hanging amid the energetic, heterosexual love-making scene on side B of Nikosthenes' late-sixth-century red-figure kantharos in Boston,[28] has generally been called a cage by modern scholars,[29] and a cage would be an appropriate prop here since cages held live birds and hares given as love gifts. Elke Böhr suggests instead that this object is a basket,[30] and, indeed, red-figure cages, extending down to the one depicted on a mid-fourth century Kerch-style lekanis lid, attributed to the Eleusinian Painter,[31] have small hanging loops rather than this object's large curved basketry handle.

On the Boston fisherboy cup,[32] the underwater realm is boldly suggested by means of outline drawing on a special reserved ground. Here the large openwork object, surrounded by outlined fish and itself drawn with black relief lines on the reserved water, has been called a trap but may be a cagelike device used to keep caught fish fresh underwater. Since this openwork container is empty, however, a detailed illusion of layered spatial depth has been avoided, though here the reserved watery background appears to be visible through its outlined form.

Small net bags, like those accompanying boys playing knucklebones on a late fifth-century chous in the British Museum, are now generally identified as the phormiskos or knucklebone bag.[33] According to red-figure's technical conventions, these net bags have reserved surfaces articulated with black lines, drawn either crosshatched as on the chous or in a carefully observed true net pattern as on a cup of ca. 480 BC by Douris in Malibu.[34] And they are commonly depicted as opaque entities, i.e., solid reserved forms that do not reveal the vase-painting's black background or anything else behind them. Net bags, which might also have held treats such as fruit or nuts for love gifts, are an accouterment of elite male social gatherings in red-figure vase-painting: in the courting scene on the exterior of Douris' cup an example is shown on each side, hanging alongside a sponge and an aryballos.

A degree of spatial illusionism is achieved for such openwork objects in red-figure by depicting something inside them. In the homoerotic encounter on the tondo of a cup in Oxford of ca. 490 BC, attributed to the Brygos Painter, for example, the boy's reserved net bag contains small, round black objects.[35] Reserved net bags likewise containing round black objects commonly appear in male scenes on cups by Makron.[36]

A more sophisticated rendering of the reserved net appears on a cup of ca. 480 BC once in a London private collection,[37] perhaps associated with the Brygos Painter's circle.[38] Here, beneath a hanging, bulging net bag, a young bird seller crouches beside a large rounded net shown containing two captive birds, perhaps ducks,[39] visible through its cross-hatched mesh fabric. These birds are drawn in outline on the net's reserved ground and shaded with dilute. In addition, the youth's left hand is likewise drawn in outline and visible through the netting.

An extant occupied cage first appeared on the poorly preserved red-figure tondo of the Euphronian Gotha cup (Fig. 7),[40] from the late-sixth-century. Here a youth embraces a boy beside possible love gifts – a white hunting dog excited by a captured hare crouching inside the cage hanging at the left.[41] This conical domed cage – with no depicted door – is a space capsule reserved against the vase-painting's black background; its vertical bars, indicated by lines of dilute glaze, extend over the tightly confined hare delineated in outline and originally toned with dilute – a predecessor of the London birds in the net.[42] For the caged hare, the painter features in red-figure the outline drawing newly characteristic of contemporary white ground like the frieze with reclining symposiasts that encircles the Gotha cup's own exterior.[43]

A spatially illusionistic, detailed rendering of an empty hare cage appears on the tondo of a red-figure cup by Douris (Fig. 8. Color Pl. 3A)[44] of ca. 490 BC where a tethered captured brown hare – presumably a now-somewhat-domesticated love-gift – crouches on a

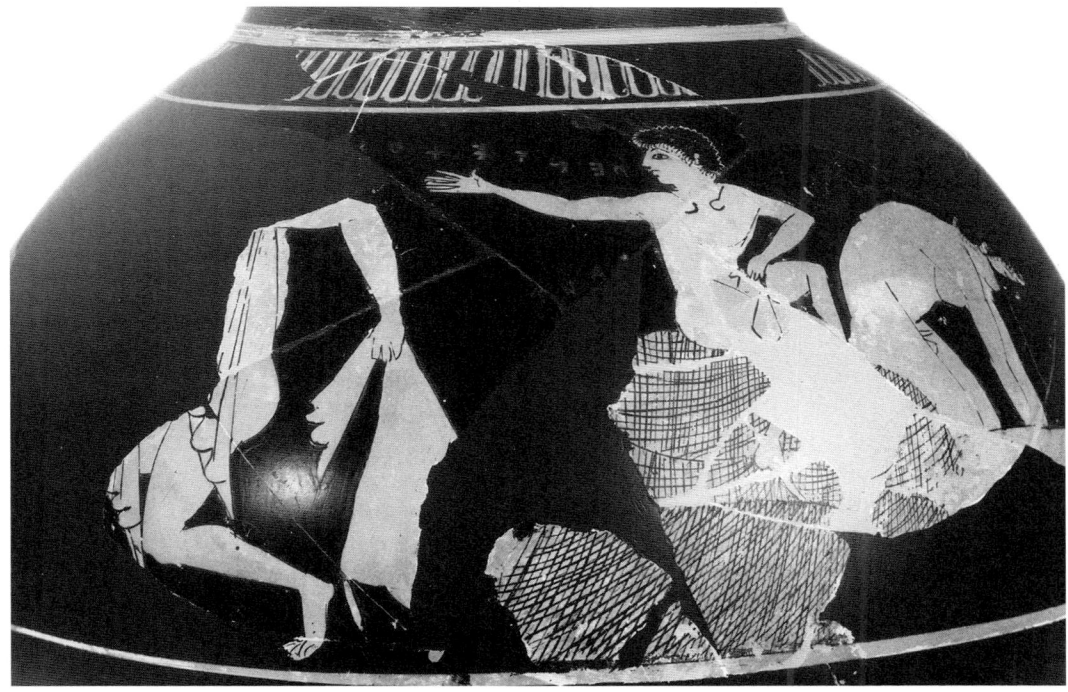

Fig. 6 Male figures (fishermen?) with piled-up fishing nets, detail, Athenian red-figure psykter, attributed to Smikros, ca. 510–500 BC, The J. Paul Getty Museum, Villa Collection, Malibu, California, Gift of Herbert L. Lucas, 83.AE.285 (Photo: Museum).

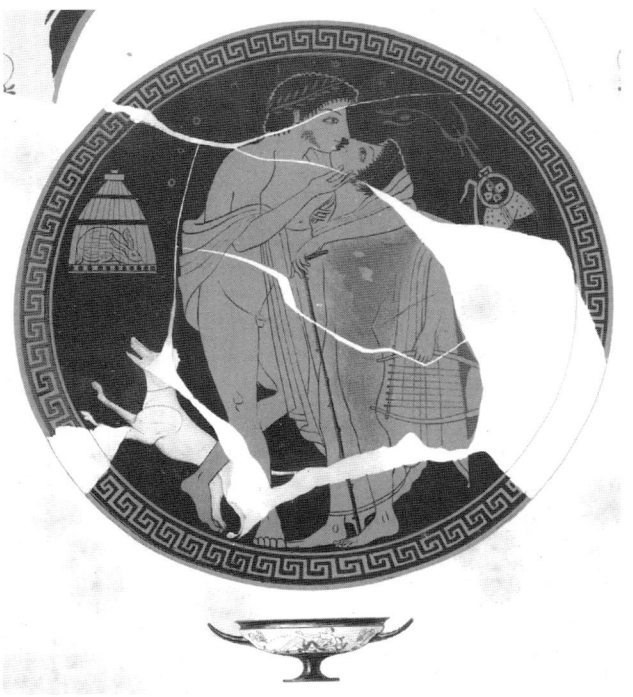

Fig. 7 Youth courting boy beside hound and caged hare, red-figure tondo of Athenian cup with white-ground symposium on exterior, influenced by Euphronios, ca. 510–500 BC, Gotha, Schlossmuseum 48 (After MonInst 10, 1877, pl. 37A).

handsome youth's lap.[45] The creature's reserved domed cage hangs at the right. Each of the bars in the grid on the front of this openwork cage is a slender reserved form bounded by outlines. This cage's door is depicted: it is wide open, and, remarkably, the part of the door shown against the black background is painted as a red-figure grid. Within the cage's open doorway, moreover, the far side of its interior's reserved space capsule is detailed with a grid of bars indicated by lines of dilute glaze. Shading with dilute washes further enhances the depiction. And it is relevant here that early Douris had displayed his technical mastery of outline and dilute in white-ground.[46]

In addition to hare cages, several depictions of occupied birdcages further illuminate Athenian representational conventions. As we have seen for the net, a solution other than outlining for depicting a form within a space capsule like a bird cage, is to paint it black whether or not the form would actually have been black. On a cup fragment of the early fifth century from the Athenian Agora with a draped youth and attributed to the Colmar Painter, part of a black bird inside a reserved footed cage with black bars is preserved at the break.[47] On a red-figure lekythos of ca. 480–470 BC, near the Pan Painter, in Oxford (Mannack Fig. 1. Color Pl. 11B),[48] in a summary or cutaway rendering, no bars or door are indicated on the reserved cage hanging at the left, which nonetheless contains a black-painted bird whose silhouette resembles

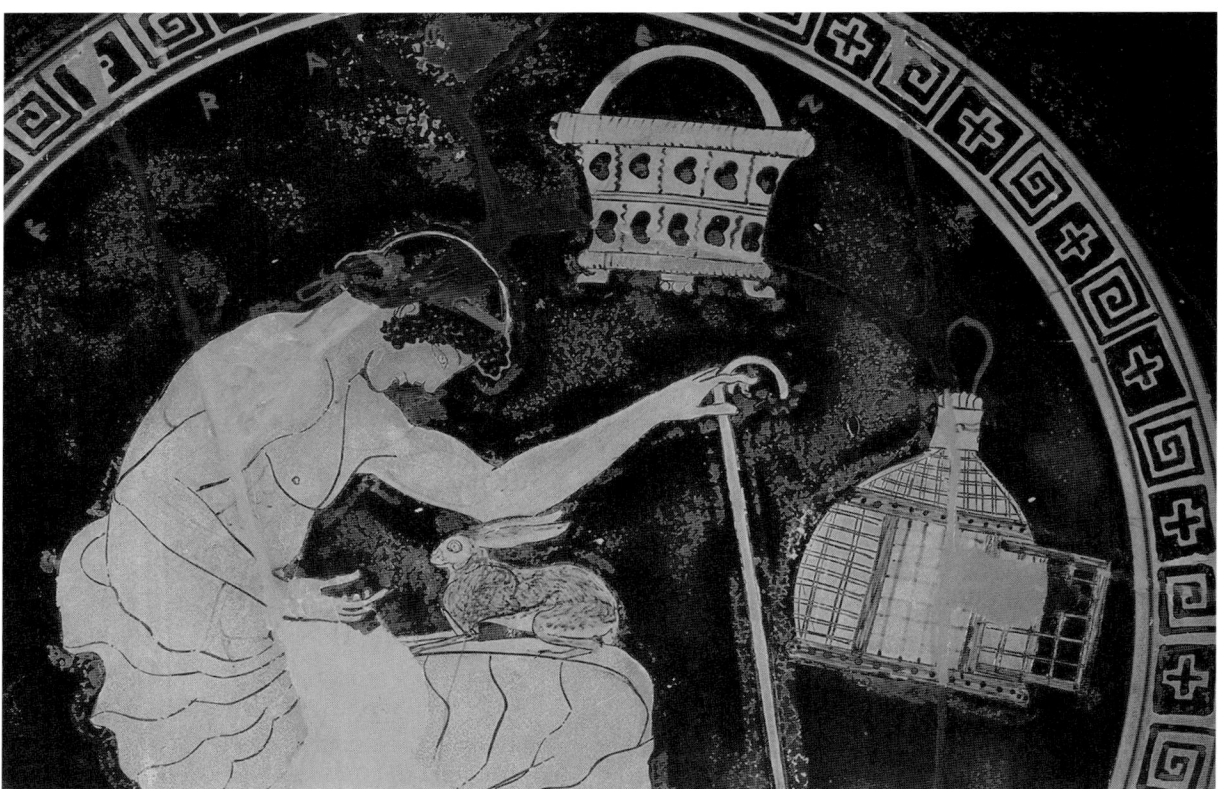

Fig. 8 Youth with a hare on his lap and the animal's cage hanging at the right, detail, tondo of Athenian red-figure cup, by Douris, ca. 490 BC, private collection (Photo: private collection).

a quail.⁴⁹ And black-painted creatures need not be birds: on an often misinterpreted contemporaneous lekythos at Harvard,⁵⁰ with a man selling a red-figure snake to an old woman, two black-painted snakes are visible inside an artistically cutaway reserved basket or chest before the woman's feet.

The Oxford lekythos' simplified birdcage's shape, with a cylindrical base and peaked upper portion that is rounded at the top, differs from the dome-shaped cage employed for a hare (cf. Figs. 7–8. Color Pl. 3A). Its silhouette recalls the most famous birdcage in Athenian vase-painting on the tondo of a red-figure cup from ca. 485–480 BC in the British Museum – the name-vase of Beazley's Cage Painter.⁵¹ Here, a handsome seated youth has set upon his knees a reserved cage, containing a black bird with reserved wing markings,⁵² and he is perhaps endeavoring to open the cage's invisible door. The Cage Painter's birdcage is shown as a mesh of black cross-hatched lines; this mesh, together with the slightly curved horizontal cross-bands, suggests the three-dimensionality of the cage's rounded form.

A cross-hatched mesh cage containing a large black bird is likewise depicted on an unpublished white-ground rim from a lost head-vase of ca. 470 BC on the New York Market, attributed by J. Michael Padgett to the Syriskos Painter.⁵³ Shown hanging in a rare heterosexual context, this cage with a conical top is drawn with heavy black outlines – i.e., in white-ground technique – on the engobe. Thus delineated in black on a continuous pale white ground, should this cage be read as semi-opaque like red-figure cages reserved against a black ground (cf. Figs. 7–8 and Color Plate 3A) or as entirely translucent?

Another hanging cage containing a large black bird is suspended between two standing draped youths on side B of a red-figure pelike at Stanford (Fig. 9), whose drawing is related to the Villa Giulia Painter.⁵⁴ Interestingly, this small reserved cage is shown with several summarily indicated dilute-glaze bars radiating from its elongated top section, some of which fail to extend down to its bottom edge. Böhr would associate the Stanford black bird with "a jackdaw, crow or raven – the holy bird of Apollo, who appears on side A".⁵⁵

A black-painted bird is shown inside a large, reserved cylindrical cage that rests on the ground before a seated woman juggling in a red-figure women's scene on a pyxis lid in the British Museum.⁵⁶ This semi-opaque cage is likewise described with vertical, rather than crosshatched, black bars, though they are more carefully rendered. A rectangular object articulated with cross-hatching held by a running female figure on the pyxis lid is a loom for making a woman's sprang hairnet⁵⁷ – another type of ancient Athenian net represented in vase-painting,⁵⁸ but not examined here in the context of spatial illusionism.

The name-vase of the Bird Painter, a white-ground funerary lekythos of ca. 430 BC in Athens, depicts a youth visiting a tomb carrying a little birdcage containing a plump quail.⁵⁹ Winged birds symbolized the soul,

and, according to John Oakley, "bird bones…have been found in Athenian burials, so what the lekythoi suggest, namely that the birds accompany the deceased to the grave, is confirmed by the archaeological evidence".⁶⁰ Here both the doomed bird and the cage are drawn in outline, and this summary or cutaway cage has no bars; however, painted color might originally have further enhanced this white-ground depiction as it would have the contemporaneous marble grave stele, probably from Salamis, whose deceased youth holds a bird in his left hand while reaching toward a hanging cage with his right.⁶¹

The occupied cage or net in vase-painting perhaps visualizes in microcosm grander spatial constructions surely achieved in monumental Classical pictorial art and occasionally reflected on pottery. A unique signal example of the last appears on the white-ground interior of a cup with wishbone handles of ca. 460 BC, attributed to the Sotades Painter, that shows King Minos' deceased son Glaukos, the seer Polyeidos, and the snakes that inspired the boy's revivification within the cutaway space capsule of Glaukos' tomb mound. The last is suggested by an arc painted in dilute glaze on the engobe covering the shallow curved inner surface of this cup's bowl.⁶²

A widely employed indicium of spatial recession in Classical Athenian vase-painting, which may likewise parallel free painting, is the doorway or window shown opening into the picture field; this motif is handled in two ways. In one, as exemplified in red-figure wedding imagery of ca. 430 BC attributed to the Marlay Painter, the standard black-glazed ground of the vase-painting represents the

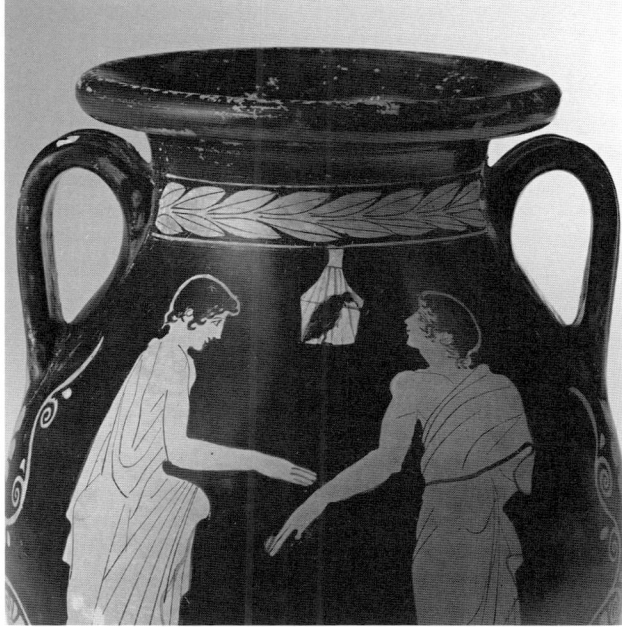

Fig. 9 Two standing draped youths flanking a bird in a hanging cage, detail, side B of Athenian red-figure pelike, related to the Villa Giulia Painter, ca. 475–450 BC, Stanford, Iris & B. Gerald Cantor Center for Visual Arts at Stanford University, Hazel D. Hansen Fund, 1977.13 (Photo: Center).

deeper space revealed by half-open doorways, and the forms shown in that recessed space are rendered in red-figure, such as the woman and the bridal chamber depicted in the doorways on the painter's well-known pyxis in the British Museum[63] and fragmentary loutrophoros-hydria in the Benaki Museum.[64] In the other, as on a pyxis in the British Museum of ca. 475–470 BC, attributed to a follower of Douris, a house's half-open doorway reveals a reserved recessed interior realm, where a female figure, inscribed Iphigeneia, is depicted with outline.[65] The reserved, recessed realm is embraced later in red-figure, as in depictions showing the *epaulia* after the wedding of Alkestis on side A of the Eretria Painter's eponymous epinetron[66] of ca. 430–420 BC and Herakles with his wife Deianeira and son Hyllos on a bell-krater of ca. 380 BC in Munich attributed to the Pourtalès Painter.[67] This technically aberrant use of reserve and outline drawing to suggest spatial recession in red-figure vase-painting may be related to the reserved space capsule employed in the depiction of nets and cages since Late Archaic times.

In Greek myth and legend, beyond the commonplace use of nets in capturing or confining animals, they were also employed for human figures. According to Homer's *Odyssey* (8.266ff), the gods laughed when Hephaistos trapped his wife Aphrodite with her lover Ares in an invisible net. While this myth is not in the repertory of Athenian vase-painting, an eighteenth-century ceiling painting by Costantino Cedini (1741–1811) in the Palazzo Emo Capodilista, Padua, shows flying putti lowering a translucent golden net over the unsuspecting illicit couple.[68] A net is also employed in the tragic legendary scene associated with cuckoldry depicted on side A of the red-figure calyx-krater of ca. 470 BC in Boston perhaps by the Domkimasia Painter.[69] Here, upon his return to Mycenae from Troy, King Agamemnon has been caught in a net, while his unfaithful wife Kleitaimestra's lover, Aegisthos, inflicts the death blow. Most of Agamemnon's body is visible through the net, which is conceived as a reserved gossamer cloth detailed in dilute with wavy lines and a delicate pattern. However, this net is not fully illusionistic spatially because it does not reveal any of the black background through the fabric surrounding Agamemnon's body.

On side B, a spatially layered rendering contrasts with Agamemnon's semi-opaque reserved net. Here, Aegisthos, about to be killed by Orestes, is shown still holding his barbitos.[70] This instrument's row of black strings overlaps and reveals behind it both the black background and the reserved skirt of the woman at the right.

Historically, the rendering of musical-instrument strings tends to be spatially translucent. In black-figure, these strings, are normally incised, and, as in the symposium of Dionysos with a satyr playing a kithara on a hydria in the British Museum in the Manner of the Lysippides Painter,[71] when a musician faces right, the instrument's incised strings overlap his left playing hand before the reserved background. In red-figure, after some experimentation, relief lines are commonly used for strings, as on the Berlin Painter's black-bodied amphora of ca. 490 BC depicting a kitharode in the Metropolitan Museum of Art.[72] Here, the instrument's three-dimensional black strings overlap the kitharode's reserved hand and the black background,[73] enhancing the spatial illusion of layered depth.

Alongside the observant handling of instrument strings, the *kaunon*, or offering basket, is described in translucent renderings on Athenian vases that reveal the background through its openwork, even in the black-figure technique.[74] The *kaunon* is sometimes shown overlapping the far arm of the figure carrying it.[75] And this elaborate basket, moreover, enjoys notable treatment on late Kerch-style vases where drawing its delicate looping structure against the black background is facilitated by the use of originally gilded extruded added clay,[76] which makes the *kaunon* a tangible object. On the famous lebes gamikos of ca. 360 BC attributed to the Marsyas Painter (Fig. 10. Color Pl. 3B),[77] the originally gilded, extruded added-clay *kaunon* both projects forward from the picture plane and recedes into space.

As we have seen, Archaic and some earlier Classical representations of openwork baskets, nets, and cages generally achieve a balance between foregrounding a vessel's surface decoration and suggesting pictorial spatial recession. But exploration of these openwork objects also contributes to Athenian vase-painting's ultimate emphatic embrace of indicia of spatial illusionism.

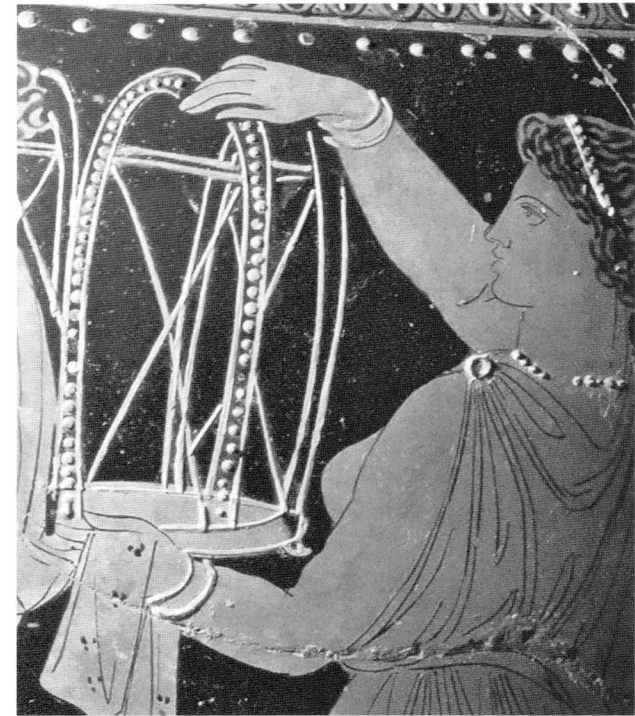

Fig. 10 Woman carrying kaunon, detail, Athenian red-figure lebes gamikos (H. 46 cm), attributed to the Marsyas Painter, ca. 360 BC, The State Hermitage Museum, St. Petersburg, P 1906.175 (Photo: Author).

Acknowledgements

I would like to thank John Oakley for inviting me to speak at the Williamsburg conference. For help with images, I am grateful to: Natacha Massar and Greet Van Deuren (Brussels), Vera Slehofer (Basel), Amy Taylor and Anja Ulbrich (Oxford), Jacklyn Burns, Claire L. Lyons, and David Saunders (Malibu), a private collection, Allison Akbay (Stanford), Vladimir Matveyev (St. Petersburg); Julia Ilina, Alexander Kruglov, Thomas L. Mannack and Athéna Tsingarida also provided assistance.

Abbreviations

Böhr 1999   E. Böhr, in: R. F. Docter – E. M. Moormann (eds.), Proceedings of the XVth International Congress of Classical Archaeology, Amsterdam, July12–17, 1998 (1999) 78–79

Calder 2011   L. Calder, Cruelty and Sentimentality: Greek Attitudes to Animals, 600–300 BC (2011)

Cohen 2006   B. Cohen, The Colors of Clay: Special Techniques in Athenian Vases (2006)

Williams 1993   CVA, British Museum 9 Great Britain 17 29–30 no. 16 pl. 20a–b

Notes

1. See A. Abetel, Aspects de l'artisanat attique: La vannerie un exemple de comptage (1982) esp. I, 4–8; see also D. A. Amyx, Hesperia 27, 1958, esp. 264; H. H. Bobart, Basketwork through the Ages (1936) 27–45; C. A. Giner, in: T. Bekker-Nielsen – D. B. Casasola (eds.), Ancient Nets and Fishing Gear: Proceedings of the International Workshop on "Nets and Fishing Gear in Classical Antiquity: A First Approach", Cádiz, November 15–17, 2007 (2010) 55–81. esp. 58. 65–66.

2. For depictions of baskets, see Abetel (supra n. 1); Amyx (supra n. 1) 264–275 pl. 51; see also for baskets and nets, N. Malagardis, AEphem 127, 1988, esp. 114–131; for cages and nets see Williams 1993 and Böhr 1999 78–79 pl. 7.

3. E.g., the maiden carrying a wicker offering basket (restored) on her head, red-figure oinochoe, ca. 480 BC, attributed to the Triptolemos Painter, Berlin, Antikensammlung – F 2189: ARV² 363,27; BAPD 203818; N. Kaltsas – A. Shapiro (eds.), Worshipping Women: Ritual and Reality in Classical Athens (2008) 216–217 no. 94.

4. E.g., the male child training a bird let out of its cage, late fifth-century red-figure chous: BAPD 11560; Masterpieces of Greek Vase Painting: 7th to 5th century B.C.: André Emmerich Gallery, New York, April 22 to May 30, 1964 (1964) no. 37; Williams 1993 30.

5. In domestic scenes, women working wool employ a *kalathos* (wool basket): e.g., red-figure lekythos, ca. 480–470 BC, attributed to the Brygos Painter, Boston, Museum of Fine Arts 13.189: ARV² 384,214; BAdd² 228; BAPD 204114; CB I 25–26 no. 29 pl. 10. In agricultural scenes, baskets commonly appear, e.g., carried by a sower on the zone inside the black-figure cup, ca. 520 BC, signed by Nikosthenes as potter, attributed to Painter N, Berlin, Antikensammlung F1806: ABV 223,66; Para 104; BAdd² 58; BAPD 301815; Malagardis (supra n. 2) 118 fig. 8B; and the harvesting basket carried by a woman on her head while other women pick fruit, black-figure hydria, ca. 510–500 BC, attributed to the Priam Painter, Munich, Antikensammlungen 1702A: ABV 334,6; 677. 694; Para 147; BAdd² 91; BAPD 301819; H. Rühfel, Begleitet von Baum und Strauch: Griechische Vasenbilder (2003) 96 fig. 59; 97.

6. E.g., Amyx (supra n. 1); from early Greece, see the "violent" gold cup with a bull trapped in a net from the Vapheio tholos tomb, 15th cent. BC, Athens, National Archaeological Museum 1759: J. G. Pedley, Greek Art and Archaeology, 4th ed. (2007) 75 fig. 3.17.

7. As is apparent on bilingual vases: e.g., amphora of type A, attributed to the Andokides and Lysippides Painters, Boston, Museum of Fine Arts 99.538: ABV 255,6; ARV² 4,12; Para 113; BAdd² 66; BAPD 200012; Cohen 2006 29–32 no. 2.

8. Cf., e.g., Cohen 2006 199–200 no. 52 (black-figure white-ground plate, attributed to Psiax, 520–510 BC, Basel, Antikenmuseum und Sammlung Ludwig Kä 421; ABV 294,21; ARV² 11,30; Para 128; BAdd² 77; BAPD 320367) and 211–212 no. 57 ca. 510–500 BC (outline white-ground alabastron, Pasiades potter, Pasiades Painter, London, British Museum GR 1887.7–801.61; ARV² 98,1; 102,top,2; 1626; Para 330; BAdd² 172; BAPD 200859).

9. Boston, Museum of Fine Arts 63.952, side B: Para 62. 317; BAdd² 41; BAPD 350462.

10. Brussels, Musées Royaux d'Art et d'Histoire R 347: ARV² 334; Para 361; BAPD 203435.

11. Toledo, Toledo Museum of Art 63.29: ARV² 1675,94bis; Para 434; BAdd² 308; BAPD 275416; J. Neils – J. H. Oakley (eds.), Coming of Age in Ancient Greece: Images of Childhood from the Classical Past (2003) 273 no. 81.

12. Cohen 2006 154–155.

13. Würzburg, Universität, Martin-von-Wagner Museum 265, side A: ABV151, 22; Para 63; BAdd² 43; BAPD 310451; D. von Bothmer, The Amasis Painter and His World: Vase-Painting in Sixth-Century B.C. Athens (1985) 61, color plate; 113–118 no. 19.

14. Basel, Antikenmuseum Basel und Sammlung Ludwig Kä 420, side A: Para 65; BAdd² 43; BAPD 350468; Cohen 2006 167–170 no. 43.

15. For grape-treading depictions see B. Sparkes, BABesch 51, 1976, 47–64. On an earlier black-figure Deianeira lekythos, ca. 560–550 BC, considered Euboean by Sparkes, ibid. 64 fig. 2, incised cross-hatching describes the basket's weave: Tampa Museum of Art, Joseph Veach Noble Collection 1986.015 was related to the Painter of Munich 1842 by Beazley, Para 198; BAPD 351459, and, according to S. Pevnick (Tampa), it might be Athenian rather than Euboean.

16. Musées Royaux d'Art et d'Histoire R279: ABV 299,20; BAdd² 78; BAPD 320419.

17. For examples from fourth-century BC Iberia and Roman times, see Giner (supra n. 1) 70 fig. 6; 75 figs. 12–13.

18. On ancient nets being dyed see Giner (supra n. 1) 57.

19. London, British Museum GR 1873.8–20.388 (B 678): BAPD 4566. See M. Bouvier, Le Lièvre dans L'Antiquité (2000) 81–82 no. 785, 125.

20 Cohen 2006 194–195 no. 50.
21 E.g., Black-figure band cup, ca. 525 BC, London, British Museum B386: BAPD 13235; J. M. Barringer, The Hunt in Ancient Greece (2001) 96. 98 fig. 58; black-figure lekythos, ca. 500 BC, Boston, Museum of Fine Arts 08.291, attributed to the Painter of Boston 08.291: ABV 92; Para 34; BAdd² 25; Barringer, ibid. 96–97. figs. 55–57; black-figure mastoid, ca. 500 BC, Brussels, Musées Royaux d'Art et d'Histoire R 343: BAPD 10555; A. Schnapp, Le chasseur et la cité: Chasse et érotique dans la Grèce ancienne (1997) 215. 486 no. 80, and a net appears earlier in the Proto-Corinthian hare hunt, 179 fig. 3; 477 no. 3 (Paris, Louvre E 415, ovoid aryballos, ca. 640–625BC).
22 Oxford, Ashmolean Museum AN1979.20: BAPD 7414. For the net signifying a human rather than a purely animal hunt see Schnapp (supra n. 21) 404–405. 523 no. 449.
23 Malibu, J. Paul Getty Museum, Villa Collection 83.AE.285: BAPD 13369. See Malagardis (supra n. 2) 114. 115 fig. 4.
24 Photograph by H. Swanson for A. Sabar, The New York Times, Wednesday, February 28, 2007, A11.
25 Museum of Fine Arts 01.8024: ARV² 173,9; BAdd² 184; BAPD 201573; Cohen 2006 171–172 no. 44.
26 Vienna, Kunsthistorisches Museum 3727: ARV² 555,88; BAdd² 258; BAPD 206331.
27 See esp. A. Bernhard-Walcher – J. Lehner, Alltag, Feste, Religion: antikes Leben auf griechischen Vasen: Tiroler Landesmuseum Ferdinandeum Innsbruck, 14. Mai–30. Juni 1991 (1992) 89 no. 35; color pl. 86 for side A; D. B. Casasola, in: Nielsen – Casasola (supra n. 1) 126. 127 fig. 26 (B), and see fig. 26(A) for a now-unclear net or basket on the red-figure cup, attributed to the Group of Acropolis 96, Gela, Museo Archeologico 8719: ARV² 105,7; BAPD 200915.
28 Museum of Fine Arts 95.61: ARV² 123,132; BAdd² 177; BAPD 201063; E. Vermeule, AntK 12, 1969, 12–13 no. 11 pl. 9,3.
29 See esp. Vermeule (supra n. 28) and Williams 1993 30.
30 Böhr 1999 79 n. 18.
31 St. Petersburg, State Hermitage Museum ST1791: ARV² 1476,3; Para 496; BAdd² 381; BAPD 230433; J. H. Oakley – R. H. Sinos, The Wedding in Ancient Athens (1993) 76 fig. 44.
32 Supra n. 25.
33 London, British Museum E 537: BAPD 4184; E. Hatzivassiliou, BICS 45, 2001, 118 pl. 5 (caption switched with pl. 4); 119.
34 J. Paul Getty Museum, Villa Collection 86.AE.290: Para 375,51bis; BAdd² 237; BAPD 275972; D. Buitron-Oliver, Douris: A Master-Painter of Athenian Red-figure Vases (1995) 25. 78 no. 93 pl. 61; Neils – Oakley (supra n. 11) 101–102 (color). 246–247 no. 45.
35 Ashmolean Museum 1967.304: ARV² 378,137; BAdd² 226; BAPD 204034; Barringer (supra n. 21) 85. 86 fig. 50, considers the net bag a hunting net.
36 Paris, Louvre G 149, side A: ARV² 473,212; BAPD 204895: N. Kunish, Makron (1997) 184 no. 233 pl. 77.
37 Once London, private collection: BAPD 41875; Hesperia Arts Auction Ltd., Egyptian, Near Eastern and Classical Greek and Roman Antiquities, Part I November 27, 1990, New York, no. 121.
38 Williams 1993 30.
39 For Böhr 1999 78, these are "ducks," "probably on the way to the kitchen," pl. 7a; for Calder 2011 91, the context is purchasing birds as pets.
40 Gotha, Schlossmuseum 48: ARV² 20; Para 322; BAdd² 153; BAPD 200100.
41 See Bouvier (supra n. 19) 107 no. 1146; 133; Barringer (supra n. 21) 83. 105. 230 n.112; Calder 2011 107. 191 no. 231.
42 Supra ns. 37–39. A quail (or partridge), confined in a small birdcage with vertical bars held by a youth, is shown in outline with black internal markings on a red-figure neck-amphora (published only in a nineteenth-century drawing), name-vase Nikon Painter, ca. 450 BC, Paris, Cabinet des Médailles 361: ARV² 651,16; 1602; BAPD 207582; H. T. P. J. Luynes, Description de quelques vases peints, étrusques, italiotes, siciliens et grecs (1840) pl. 37; Williams 1993 30.
43 Cf., however, J. R. Mertens, Attic White-Ground: Its Development on Shapes Other Than Lekythoi (1977) 162 no. 2; 165–166.
44 BAdd² 396; BAPD 7242; Buitron-Oliver (supra n. 34) 24. 78 no. 89; pl. 59 see also A. Lezzi-Hafter, in: H. Bloesch (ed.), Greek Vases from The Hirschmann Collection (1982) 68–69 no. 33.
45 For the iconography, see esp., Schnapp (supra n. 21) 330–331 no. 335; 512 no. 335; Barringer (supra n. 21) 77. 107–108. 230 n. 112 and Calder 2011 80. 86. 187 no. 201; 96 on hare cages suffering from gnawing.
46 Cf., e.g., the white-ground lekythos, ca. 500–490 BC, Malibu, J. Paul Getty Museum 84.AE.770: BAdd² 398; BAPD 16229; Buitron-Oliver (supra n. 34) 18. 78 no. 45; pls. 28–29; Cohen 2006 213–215 no. 58; 214 fig. 58.2.
47 Athens, Agora Museum P 17531: ARV² 355,50; BAPD 203733; H. A. Thompson, Hesperia 17, 1948, 189 with n. 113, "dilute glaze" for the bird, pl. 68, 2.
48 Ashmolean Museum V 321: ARV² 561,9, 1586; Para 388; BAPD 206412.
49 Böhr 1999, 78; J. D. Beazley in CVA Oxford 1 Great Britian 3 29 no. 5; Williams 1993 30.
50 Cambridge, Mass., Harvard University Art Museums 2236: BAPD 13462; CVA Fogg Museum and Gallatin Collections USA 8 34 pl. 17,5.
51 London 1901.5–14.1: ARV² 348,2; 1647; BAdd² 220; BAPD 203642; CVA British Museum 9 Great Britain 17 29–30 no. 16 pl. 20a–b.
52 Böhr 1999, 78, "…the diagonal stripes in the plumage indicate that it is a rock partridge;" Calder 2011 91, "or a quail," 193 no. 256.
53 I would like to thank J. Michael Padgett for adding this white-ground birdcage.
54 Iris and Gerald Cantor Center for Visual Arts at Stanford University 1977.13; BAPD 8957. According to the curator, B. Barrtye, the pelike, acquired as Circle of the Niobid Painter, was attributed to the Villa Giulia Painter by D. von Bothmer in 1979 (museum correspondence), but an attribution to the painter himself was not accepted by D. C. Kurtz and M. Robertson in 1982 (museum correspondence).
55 Böhr 1999 78. See also Williams 1993 30.
56 London, British Museum, GR 1907.5–19.1, ca. 470 BC: BAPD 2089; H. B. Walters, JHS 41, 1921, 145–146 no.16 pl. 3, V. 16. Cf. St. Petersburg, Hermitage ST 1791 (supra n. 31).

57 I. Jenkins – D. Williams, AJA 89, 1985, 411–418 pls. 44–46; for the sprang frame on the pyxis lid (supra n. 56) see 417 no 8; pl. 45, fig. 6.
58 For a female figure's hairnet with black cross-hatching on reserve see side B, black-figure lip-cup (head-cup), signed by Epitimos as potter, New York, Metropolitan Museum of Art 25.78.4: ABV 119, 9; Para 48; BAPD 310289; CVA Metropolitan Museum of Art 2 USA 11 pl. 10.12d–e.
59 National Archaeological Museum 1769: ARV² 1232,9; BAdd² 352; BAPD 216406; for the iconography see J. H. Oakley, Picturing Death in Classical Athens: The Evidence of the White Lekythoi (2004) 209 fig. 171. 210 List 21 no. 4 and Calder 2011 85. 190 no. 225.
60 Oakley (supra n. 59) 212.
61 Athens, National Archaeological Museum 715: N. Kaltsas, Sculpture in the National Archaeological Museum, Athens (2002) 148–149 no. 287, "found on Salamis or Aegina." See also Oakley (supra n. 59) 209–210.
62 London, British Museum GR 1892.7–18.2 (D 5): ARV² 763,2; 772β; BAdd² 286; BAPD 209459; see Cohen 2006 304–305 no. 92.
63 London 1920.12–21.1: ARV² 1277,23; 1282,1; 1689; BAdd² 357; BAPD 216210; Oakley and Sinos (supra n. 31) 92 fig. 75.
64 Athens, Benaki Museum 35495: ARV² 1277,17; BAPD 216204; Kaltsas – Shapiro (supra n. 3) 320 no. 143; color fig. on right.
65 London GR 1873.1–11.7 (E 773): ARV² 805,89; 1670; Para 420; BAdd² 291; BAPD 209970; see Cohen 2006 158. 180–181 no. 48.
66 Athens, National Archaeological Museum 1629: ARV² 1250,34; 1688; Para 469; BAdd² 354; BAPD 216971; see Cohen 2006 158. color fig. 8.
67 Munich, Antikensammlungen 2398: ARV² 1446,3; Para 492; BAPD 218150; H. A. Shapiro, in: Neils – Oakley (supra n. 11) 93 for the setting; 94 fig. 8.
68 G. Pavanello, Bollettino del Museo Civico di Padova 61, nos. 1–2, 1972, 202–203. 224; color image: http://it.wikipedia.org/wiki/File:Costantino_Cedini_-_Venus_und_Mars_werdem_im_Netz_überrascht.jpg.
69 Museum of Fine Arts 63.1246: ARV² 1652; Para 373; BAdd² 235; BAPD 275233; T. H. Carpenter, Art and Myth in Ancient Greece (1991) fig. 351. Herakles is shown trapped in a net and perhaps inside a cave on an Athenian red-figure jug found in Bulgaria: see G. Kitov, Archaeologia Bulgarica 9, 2005, no. 3, 33 fig. 19. 35. According to John Oakley, who kindly brought this vase to my attention, the now-faded net was originally painted in added-white. Another unique mythological depiction shows the chest that bore Danae and Perseus to Seriphos as hauled ashore in a black cross-hatched fishing net: red-figure pyxis, attributed to the Wedding Painter, ca. 450 BC, Bern, Historisches Museum, Leihgabe Clairmont; ARV² 924,35; BAdd² 305; BAPD 211249; K. Schefold – F. Jung, Die Urkönige: Perseus, Bellerophon, Herakles und Theseus in der klassischen und hellenistischen Kunst (1988) 99 figs. 114–117.
70 Supra n. 69; S. D. Bundrick, Music and Image in Classical Athens (2005) 25 fig. 13.
71 London GR 1837.6–9.35 (B302): ABV 261,40. 691; Para 115; BAdd² 68; BAPD 302272; Carpenter (supra n. 69) fig. 16.
72 New York 56.171.38: ARV² 197,3; 1633; Para 342; BAdd² 190; BAPD 201811; Carlos A. Picón et al., Art of the Classical World in the Metropolitan Museum of Art: Greece, Cyprus, Etruria, Rome (2007) 108 fig. 118; 428–429 no. 118.
73 J. V. Noble, the Techniques of Painted Attic Pottery, rev. ed. (1988) 116 fig. 205.
74 E.g., on the fragmentary black-figure lekythos attributed to the Edinburgh Painter, Athens, National Archaeological Museum, Akropolis Collection 2298, the openwork kaunon held by a priest overlaps the vessel's upper meander border: BAPD 32454; ABL 216, no. 8; B. Graef, Die antiken Vasen von der Akropolis zu Athen (1925–1933) pl. 96 no. 2298; E. Hatzivassiliou, Athenian Black Figure Iconography between 510 and 475 B.C. (2010) 61. 115 no. 80 pl. 3,4.
75 E.g., the overlapped left arm of the flying Nike carrying a *kaunon*, red-figure neck-amphora, attributed to the Alkimachos Painter, Palermo, Museo Archeologico Regionale 2078 (V745): ARV² 530,14; BAPD 205986; CVA Palermo 1 Italy 14 pl. 28,1.
76 For well-preserved gilding see the *kaunon* on the Kerch-style red-figure skyphos, ca. 350 BC, New York, Metropolitan Museum of Art 06.1021.181: BAPD 15218; J. R. Mertens, How to Read Greek Vases (2010) 144–146 no. 29.
77 St. Petersburg, State Hermitage Museum P 1906.175: ARV² 1475,1; Para 495; BAdd² 381; BAPD 230419; Cohen 2006 334–336 no. 103. On equating the Eleusinian Painter (supra n. 31) with the late Marsyas Painter, e.g., M. Robertson, in: G. R. Tsetskhladze – A. J. N. W. Prag – A. M. Snodgrass (eds.), Periplous: Papers on Classical Art and Archaeology Presented to Sir John Boardman (2000) 244.

5 Red-figured Cups in the Kerameikos

Heide Frielinghaus

Form and iconographic evidence as well as the distribution, use and significance of cups in different geographic areas and in different contexts have been dealt with quite extensively, but not exhaustively. This paper, inspired by an ongoing study of stray finds of red-figured cups in the Kerameikos, will focus on a single question: the use of cups in a specific geographical area, the Kerameikos of Athens.[1]

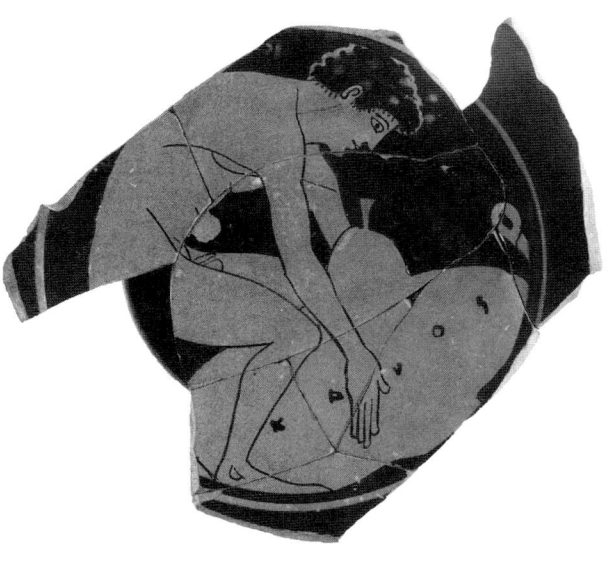

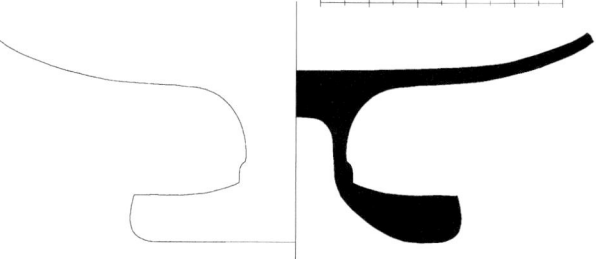

Figs. 1–2 Kerameikos, Inv. 3193 (C. Graml).

The Stray Finds: Comments on the Material

Among the stray finds in the Kerameikos there are parts of about 240 Attic red-figured cups. While a modest number of these are quite well preserved, although put together from many fragments, the largest part of the material is mere scraps. Many of the fragments have been roughly handled, so the glaze is abraded or flaked in places, or there are deep scratches. Most of this damage does not come from normal usage, but has been inflicted after the cups were discarded.

Not every variant of shape of Attic red-figured cups has been found in the Kerameikos, but it needs to be kept in mind that many of the fragments cannot be assigned with certainty to a specific variant. Of the three major types of stemmed cups only two are represented for certain in the material. While examples of Type A cannot be identified, at least two fragments belong to cups of Type C (Figs. 1–2; Color Pl. 5A).[2] Both of them date to the last decade of the sixth century. About twenty fragments can be assigned to cups of Type B,[3] and forty others come from stemmed cups, most probably Types B or C. These range in date from the end of the sixth until the beginning of the fourth century BC. Of the minor types of stemmed cups at least one fragment is from an Acrocup.[4]

A large portion of these 240 cups, about fifty fragments, can be recognized as being from stemless cups,[5] the ring bases of which are molded in a large variety of forms. They range in date from the second quarter of the fifth century until about the middle of the fourth century. Within this group some pieces can be identified as belonging to sub-groups. One quite well-preserved delicate cup is close in kind to the black-glazed cups with bevelled foot (Fig. 3; Color Pl. 5B).[6] Six fragments belong to a type which is called saucer-foot by Beazley; the form is close to that of the black-glazed Rheneia cups.[7]

The earliest fragments are datable to the last decade of the sixth century,[8] but the vast majority is quite evenly spread throughout the fifth century. A score of fragments belong to the fourth century. Some of the latest pieces are cups decorated with youths wrapped in a himation, as for example the part of one stemless cup that probably belongs to the second quarter of the fourth century (Fig. 4).[9] A more elaborate specimen shows Athena sitting beside a Panathenaic prize amphora in the tondo.[10] The distinctive shape of this prize amphora helps us to date the cup to about 340/30 BC.

The spectrum of subjects shown on the cups can be differentiated only approximately because of the fragmentary condition of the material, but the range of themes seems to be rather limited (Fig. 5). Most of the depictions are connected with men in one way or another, including pictures of sport, war or the symposion. Many fragments show only a small part of a male figure, and it is not possible to determine exactly what subject is depicted. Women are relatively rarely depicted, and when they are, once again, because of the fragmentary condition of the cups, it is uncertain if they are shown alone or with men. Another small part of the depictions belongs to the world of Dionysos; even less is the number of fragments which show gods or worship at an altar. On about 16% of the fragments there is nothing left of the figural decoration.

As for the size of the cups, there is a wide range represented in the material. One of the smallest is a stemless cup with bevelled foot whose rim diameter is 12.5cm (Fig. 3).[11] Roughly of the same size must have been the stemmed cup, Kerameikos 9508,[12] that preserves about 9 cm from one broken side to the other (Figs. 6–7). The largest specimen is the late cup, Kerameikos Inv. 1941, whose diameter can be reconstructed at about 35–40 cm.[13]

Cups in Context

The Kerameikos presents several contexts in which the use of cups in classical times can be studied, including a private house (the so-called 'Bau Z'), a public building (Pompeion) and a wide stretch of the classical cemetery.

'Bau Z'[14] is not a typical Athenian house of classical times because of its size, about 600 square meters, but thanks to the circumstances of its destruction, it offers the opportunity to get an idea of how the objects found in a house of rather large dimensions were used. In the classical period there are three phases of occupation: two short-lived phases in the last quarter of the fifth century and a third phase that took place after a period of no occupation around the middle of the fourth century.[15] During the two earliest phases (Z1, Z2) the building seems to have been a private house, whereas changes in the room-division and in the range of objects discovered led the excavator, U. Knigge, to interpret the fourth-century building (Z3) as a guest house and weaving mill.[16]

Within the building a large number of objects are preserved. Quite a large proportion of these were found along the walls of the rooms, presumably having dropped down from above when the house was destroyed by a catastrophe.[17] Pottery connected with the household and the symposion was prominent among the objects. Actually, it was largely the number of vases associated with the symposion that led U. Knigge to interpret the first building's rooms O1 and P1 as dining-rooms.[18]

Among these finds, however, there were only a rather modest number of cups. From phase Z1[19] quite a large

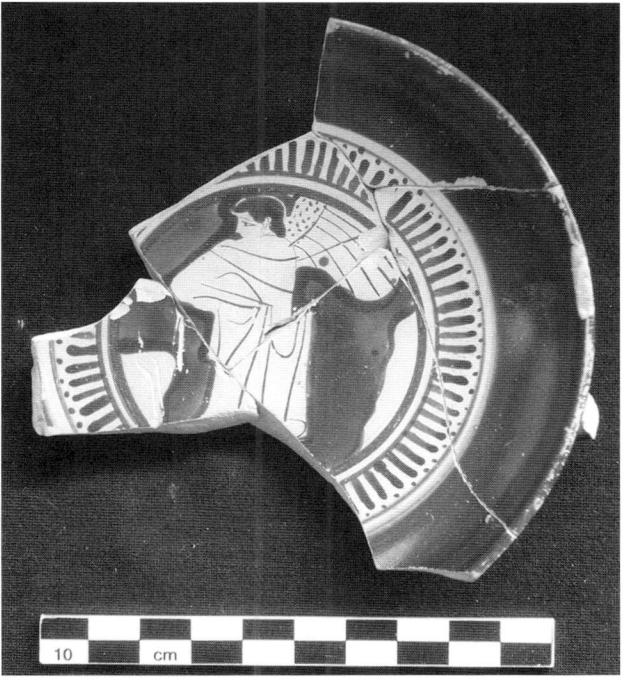

Fig. 3 Kerameikos, Inv. 4847 (author).

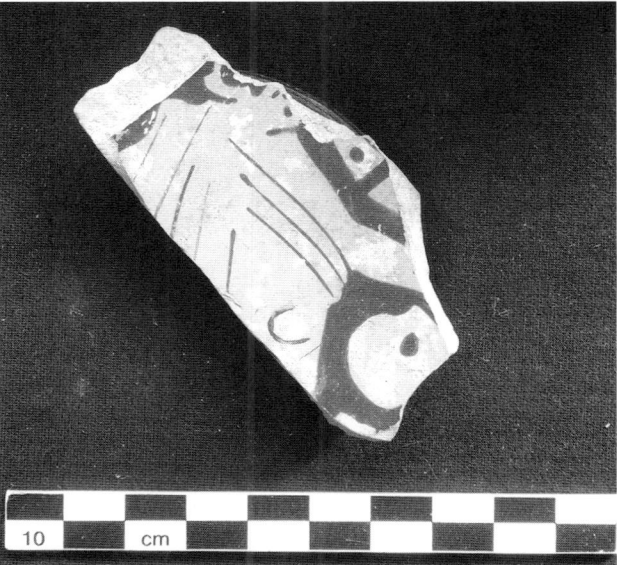

Fig. 4 Kerameikos, Inv. 9594 (author).

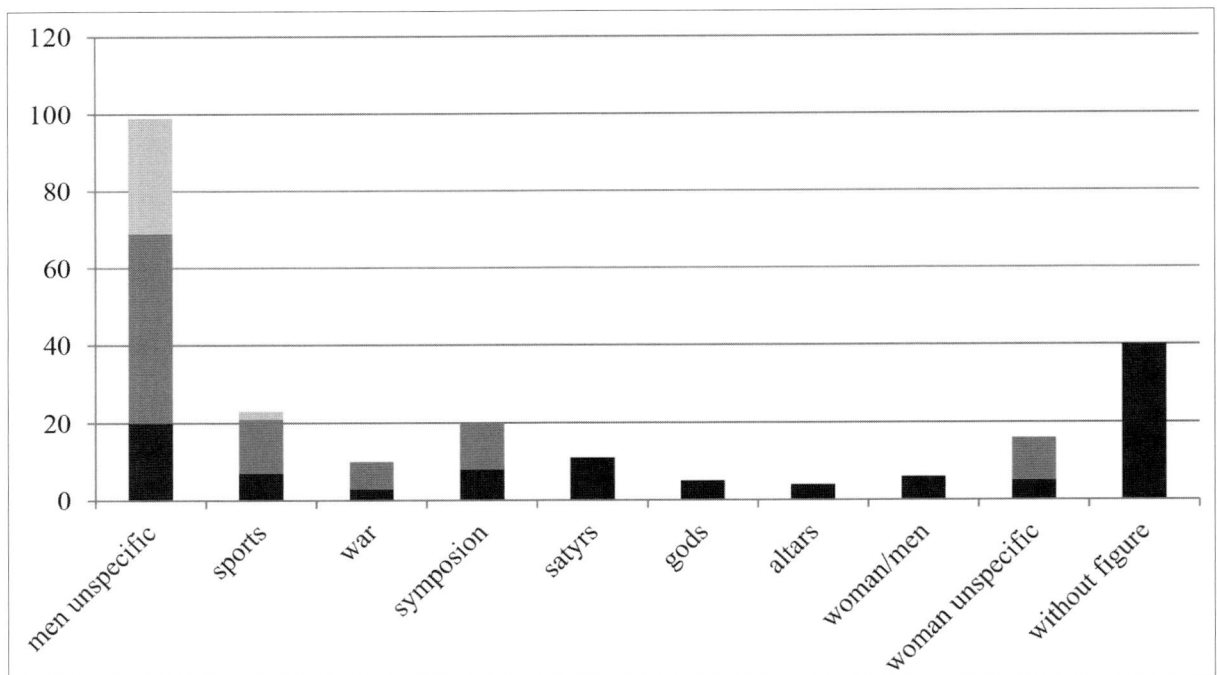

Fig. 5 Stray Finds of Red-figure Cups: Their Themes (author).

number of drinking vessels are preserved, but there are only five (fragmentary) red-figured cups.[20] One of these was found in the dining-room O1, while the rest of the red-figured pieces, as well as two black-glazed cups, were dumped in the central court a1, either in the well or in the layer of household-debris. The rest of the drinking vessels – skyphoi, bolsals[21] and one-handler[22] – were spread among six rooms: the kitchen K1, the dining-room P1, the open multipurpose spaces G1 and Q1, as well as two rooms, which were interpreted as belonging to the gynaikonitis (R1, B1).

From phase Z2[23] there is a considerably larger number of drinking vessels, but with three specimens the red-figured cups are fewer than in the previous phase.[24] The find spots of the latter were rooms L2 and R2, both of which contained several drinking-vessels of other types (cup-skyphoi, skyphoi, bolsals, and one-handler) as well. While the first 'room' served as a cistern, meaning that the cups were not found at the place where they had been used but where they had been discarded, the second room probably was the oikos (cup fragment part of an offering pit?). The five black-glazed cups were found at two places of waste disposal (courtyard Q2 and well 13), in the 'oikos' R2, in the Room K2 and in the Room Wb2 (part of the gynaikonitis? room for servants?). Several of them contained drinking vessels of other types also. The kitchen (?) Aa2 and the room O2 did not contain cups, but only drinking vessels of other types (bolsals, cup-skyphoi, and skyphoi).[25]

Just to complete the picture, it should be mentioned that in phase Z3,[26] at a time when the building presumably served as a guest-house and weaving mill, not only is the number of drinking vessels conspicuously fewer than before, but obviously none of the very latest, very few examples of red-figured or black-glazed cups found their way into the building. Serving as drinking vessels were mainly black-glazed cup-skyphoi, skyphoi and one-handler.[27] These were spread about the courtyard a3 and six different rooms of non-definable role (Aa3, B3, F3, J3, K3, and U3).

The finds from the house give the impression that generally the stouter drinking vessels – as skyphoi, cup-skyphoi, bolsals and one-handler – were preferred to the more finely made cups which were specifically designed for communal drinking.[28] The preference for stouter forms is even more obvious when the forms of the cups are given a closer look. Only three (probably four) out of the five red-figured specimens in Z1, and one out of three pieces in Z2 are of the stemmed variety, while all the black-glazed cups that have been found in Z1 and Z2 are of the stemless variety.

The difference in number probably represents the distinction between vessels which were used in the occasional symposion and vessels which could play a role in symposia as well as in daily use. The layout of Z1 seems to support this point of view. As we have seen, there is a concentration of stemmed as well as stemless cups in one room and in a place used for waste disposal, while drinking vessels in general are distributed among six rooms with presumably different uses. Less clear is the picture in building Z2: while the stemmed kylix has been found in a rubbish dump, there is a combination of

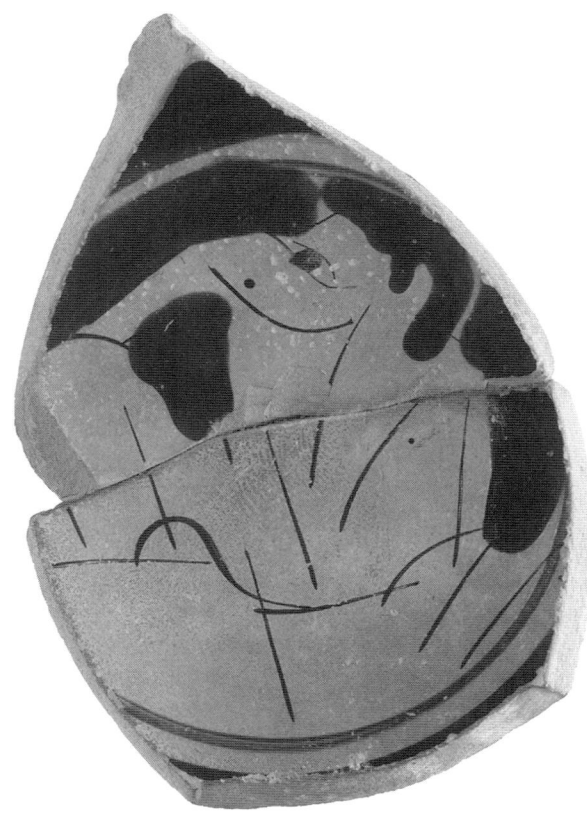

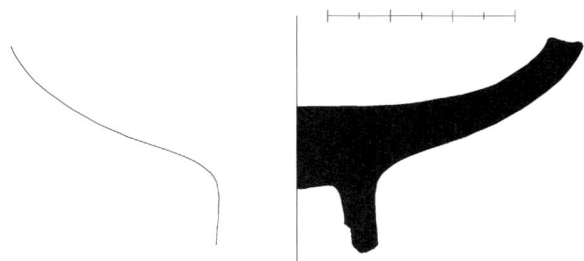

Figs. 6–7 Kerameikos, Inv. 9508 (C. Graml).

stemless cups and several drinking vessels of other types spread about no less than five rooms of different purposes (two of them used for waste-disposal); two further rooms contained only drinking vessels of other types.

On the basis of the very few contexts available, one may hazard to think that in Athenian private houses of this area the interest in cups declined in the course of the fifth century.[29] A domestic context with data comparable to 'Bau Z' is a Late Archaic house near the Agora of which only the eastern part with four rooms (about 30–40 m²) has been excavated. Within the house is a well that was filled with the 'Persian destruction cleanup debris' shortly after 479 BC.[30] Part of this debris is the remnants of up to 17 red-figured cups, at least nine of which are of the stemmed type; in addition, up to 17 stemmed cups were of the black-figured or black-glazed variety.[31] In this house, too, there is a difference between the number of cups and stouter forms of drinking vessels – cup-skyphoi (up to 26), skyphoi (up to 24) and one-handler (1), of varying type of decoration – but the difference is not as considerable as it is in the first two phases of 'Bau Z'. Just looking at the Late Archaic house near the Agora, the building Z1 of the years 430/20 BC and the building Z2 of the end of the fifth century, there seems to be a remarkable decline on several levels. Generally, there is a decline in the absolute number of cups used in a private house, corresponding with an increasing difference between the number of cups and the number of stouter drinking vessels. More specifically, there is a decline in the number of red-figured cups – 17 pieces in the Late Archaic house, 5 pieces in Z1, 3 pieces in Z2 – as well as a decline in the number of stemmed cups, red-figured as well as black glazed – at least 9 red-figured and 17 black-glazed specimens in the Late Archaic house, 3 or 4 red-figured specimens in Z1, 1 red-figured specimen in Z2. The available data does indicate that – at least as far as ceramic vessels were concerned – in private Athenian houses of our limited area forms made exclusively for use during the symposion in the course of the fifth century were increasingly 'replaced' by multi-purpose drinking vessels which could play a role during the symposion as well as in daily use.

It is very difficult to assess the 'social and economic value'[32] of the red-figured and black-glazed cups[33] in their domestic contexts in the Kerameikos. This is due to the general scarcity of house-contexts still containing a sufficient part of their former equipment and even more to the lack of several contemporary house-contexts which could give a clearer idea of the average number of red-figured and black-glazed cups to be found in houses of different sizes at the same time. It can be pointed out, however, that because of the house's size and the number of objects found in it, the owner(s) of both phases of Bau Z very probably was (were) economically well off, but among the household-equipment neither the cup in general nor the red-figured cup (or more specifically the red-figured stemmed cup connected especially with the symposion) played a conspicuous role. As the size of the house did not diminish from phase Z1 to phase Z2, and as the number of objects found in the house did increase considerably in phase Z2, the declining numbers of red-figured stemmed cups do give a comparatively reliable indication of the lessening significance of those cups as reference to the symposion.

The Pompeion,[34] which has been erected about 400 BC, is an outstanding example of a public building. The fact that within the building there are six rooms which are interpreted with good reason as dining-rooms[35] leads one to expect that quite a large number of drinking vessels connected with the area would have been found. Unfortunately, however, there are no deposits in the form of dumping pits which can be associated for certain with the Pompeion. In so far as there is a more or less exact find spot recorded for the red-figured fragments coming out of the area (they came out of the fills of the building, many from pits belonging to Late Antique walls)[36] there is good reason to assume that those fragments are remains from the use of the building, rather than from fills having been brought there from elsewhere – so much the more so as quite a large number of fragments from Panathenaic prize amphorae have also been found in those contexts.[37] Considering the published material, however, it becomes obvious that, although a number of red-figured and black-glazed symposion-related vessels have been discovered here, there were only a very modest number of cups among them, none of them red-figured.[38]

Among the extensive cemeteries having a large number of Late Archaic and Classical graves, it is the area west-northwest of the Tritopatreion[39], the so-called South Hill[40] and the so-called Corner-Terrace,[41] which are almost completely published. I, therefore, restrict myself to these. It is noteworthy that the red-figured cups found in these areas of the necropolis are very few, as until now only two specimens have been discovered in graves there: a kylix of type C and a stemless cup.[42] If one considers other types of cups, however, the picture is different. In the graves of the late sixth century there were found five (probably six) black-figured cups,[43] in those of the sixth and fifth centuries forty black-glazed cups, thirteen of them of the stemmed type.[44] All in all, though, cups do not play a very important role in the graves of these necropoleis in classical times: out of the 779 graves containing offerings[45] only about 6% has been equipped with cups of some sort; in the case of the stemmed cups only about 2.5% of the graves have one. The very small proportion of graves provided with cups does not mean that drinking vessels in general are rare among the offerings in Athenian graves of classical times. The number of (mostly black-glazed) skyphoi, for instance, amounts to nearly 200. It is obvious, therefore, that even if drinking vessels in general are not one of the regular grave-offerings, they are by no means rare either.[46]

Looking at a diachronic distribution of cups and cup-related drinking vessels, it is obvious that cups were used as grave-offerings mainly at the end of the sixth century and in the first half of the fifth century.[47] Obviously, there was no 'replacement' of the cups by stouter forms after the middle of the fifth century, as skyphoi and related forms, too, served as grave-offerings, mostly in the first half of the fifth century.[48] The percentage of reduction seems to be quite similar in the case of cups and drinking vessels of other types. After the middle of the fifth century, therefore, the whole spectrum of drinking vessels seems to play only a marginal role in the 'sets' of grave-offerings; furthermore, it can be observed that stemmed cups disappeared completely.

The two red-figured cups, made and used at different times, come from the same area: both were found in the Eridanos-Necropolis, the first in the south-eastern area, the second at the place where at a later time the grave precinct of a family from the deme Potamos was erected. While the stemmed cup dates to the beginning of the fifth century, a time when cups comparably often served as grave-offerings, the stemless specimen is one of the rather few pieces dated to about 430/20 BC. In both of the graves with a red-figure cup there were found several other vessels that can be understood as part of symposion-equipment.[49]

All in all then, drinking vessels were not regularly part of the 'sets' of grave-offerings in the classical graves of this area. In the cases in which drinking vessels formed a part of the 'set', there was a clear preference for stouter, multi-purpose forms, while the stemmed cups with their close connection to the symposion were quite rare; even rarer was the use of red-figured specimens. Noticeably, several of the graves containing stemmed cups were those of children, as were also a large proportion of the graves containing stemless cups.[50] To date, though, no red-figured drinking cup can be connected with a child's grave.

The Stray Finds and their Contexts

Unfortunately, for most of the material the term 'stray find' is most appropriate, although for a dozen pieces there is at least some sort of general area recorded as a find spot. The stray finds contribute in only a very limited way to the picture painted above. Many of them can be traced back to older excavations by way of photographs in the Kerameikos Archive, and even when the exact find spot cannot be determined, it seems very unlikely that some of them could have come from the only recently excavated Bau Z. Therefore, alterations of our picture of domestic use are not to be expected by the stray finds. As for the Pompeion, the publication of the pottery has been admittedly selective.[51] Furthermore, the long history of the excavation[52] – starting in 1872, progressing further in the 1920/30ies, and commencing once again anew in the 1950ies – makes it quite probable that many of the fragments pictured in old photographs in the Kerameikos Archive had indeed come out of that area. Therefore, judgment on the use of red-figured cups in the Pompeion must be reserved. Similar reasoning can be put forward for the area of the necropoleis, even more so as several fragments of red-figured cups have been found for certain in that area in the fillings of graves or in layers covering parts of the area. Working on the assumption that fills and layers for the most part were not brought in from the outside but were made from what had been available in the immediate surroundings, it seems not too farfetched to suppose that such fragments formerly had been part of the grave-offerings in one way or other. But even so, the percentage of graves equipped with red-figured cups remains quite small.

As for other contexts that could have served as possible find spots for the stray finds, due to incomplete publication no conclusions can be made concerning sanctuaries as a possible source, but we do have a better picture in respect to red-figure pottery workshops. Outside the area of the German excavations, but surely within the ancient Kerameikos, deposits of red-figured pottery have been found which can be associated with the workshops of three red-figure vase-painters.[53] Inside the area of the Kerameikos excavations an even greater number of pottery workshops has been found than outside the excavation area.[54] Only one of these, however, can be associated for certain with pieces of red-figured pottery, but none of them with cups. This picture does not change considerably because of the stray finds. Only a rather small number of the fragments are misfired red in places and only on just a very few pieces are larger parts of the surface affected by misfiring, as for example on the fragment Kerameikos 12306 (Fig. 8). But because many partially misfired vessels are known to have been in use,[55] none of these pieces can be taken as debris from a workshop for certain. The same is true of trial-pieces. Although at first it seems possible that some fragments of stemless cups, such as Kerameikos 9574 (Figs. 9–10), served as trial-pieces, a closer examination shows that this is unlikely. Even if the female head of 9574 is only outlined with a few strokes and the background is not filled with black glaze, the underside of the foot has been completed; the outer and inner sides of the molded ring base are covered with glaze, and the underside of the foot is fully decorated with bands and concentric circles. There is no indication, therefore, that a major part of the stray finds were part of the debris from a pottery workshop.

On the other hand, there remains a good possibility that a considerable part of the stray finds comes from street layers, building fills, or the strata caused by the leveling of an area (outside of the necropoleis), so much the more so as most of the (few) pieces whose find 'spots' have been recorded come from 'open contexts' of this type.

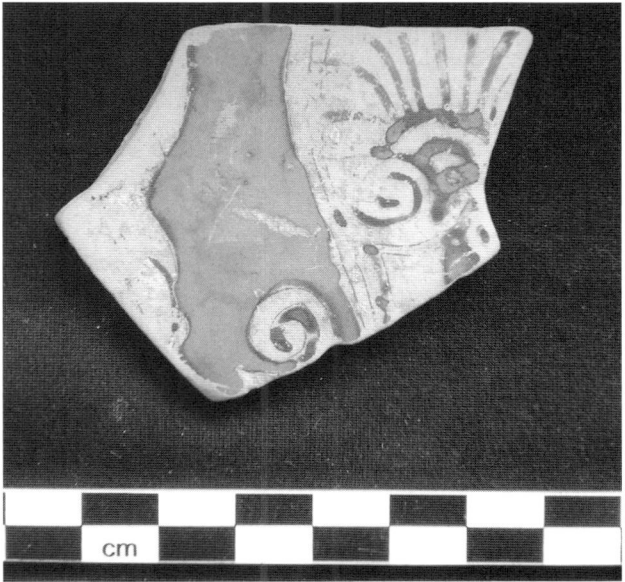

Fig. 8 Kerameikos, Inv. 21306 (author).

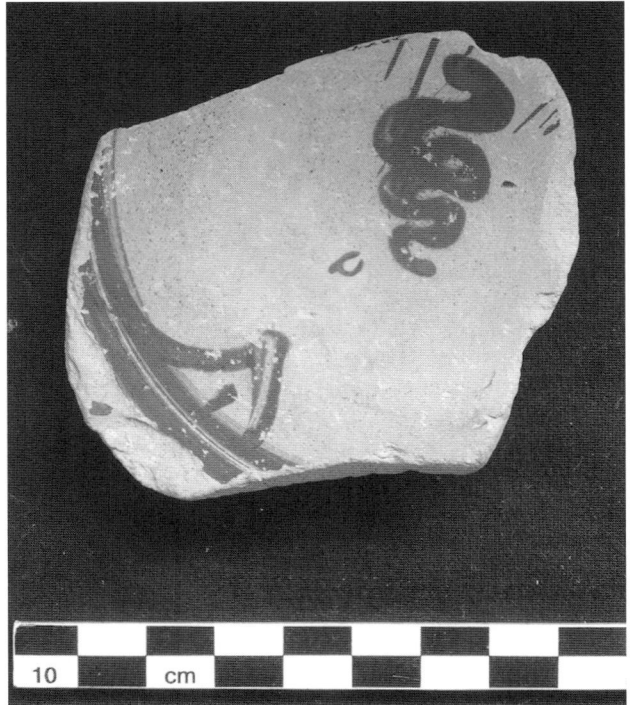

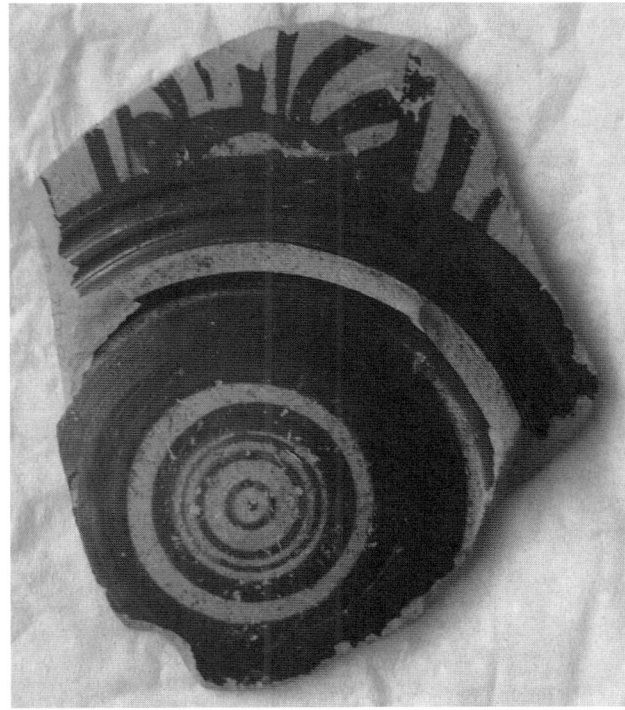

Figs. 9–10 Kerameikos, Inv. 9574 (author).

Cups in the Kerameikos

The stray finds do illustrate that red-figured cups were not as scarce in the area of the Kerameikos as the published contexts seem to indicate, but nevertheless their number is rather modest. In contrast to what we saw to be the situation in house- and grave-contexts, there is no remarkable decline in the number of stray-finds during the fifth century. It is only in the fourth century that we see a reduction in numbers. This is probably due to the different types of use to which some of the cups were put as it is possible that quite a large number of the stray finds have come from the Pompeion or some of the open context layers and fills.

Acknowledgements

I am indebted to J. Stroszeck who entrusted me with the publication of the stray finds of red-figured cup-fragments, and I am grateful to J. Oakley who invited me to present a part of the work at the congress. Several pieces of the stray finds have been studied in the course of a university project by C. Graml and N. Nappert who also drew most of the profiles.

Abbreviations

Eridanos-Nekropole	B. Schlörb-Viernesel – U. Knigge, AM 81, 1966, 1–135
Kerameikos VII,2	E. Kunze-Goette – K. Tancke – K. Vierneisel, Die Nekropole von der Mitte des 6. bis zum Ende des 5.Jhs.: Die Beigaben. Kerameikos, Ergebnisse der Ausgrabungen Bd. VII,2 (1999)
Kerameikos IX	U. Knigge, Der Südhügel. Kerameikos, Ergebnisse der Ausgrabungen Bd. IX (1976)
Kerameikos X	W. Höpfner, Das Pompeion und seine Nachfolgerbauten. Kerameikos, Ergebnisse der Ausgrabungen Bd. X (1976)
Kerameikos XIV	W. A. Kovacsovics, Die Eckterrasse an der Gräberstraße Kerameikos. Kerameikos, Ergebnisse der Ausgrabungen Bd. XIV (1990)
Kerameikos XVII	U. Knigge, Der Bau Z. Kerameikos, Ergebnisse der Ausgrabungen Bd. XVII (2005)
Lynch, Hesperia Suppl. 46	K. M. Lynch, The Symposium in Context. Pottery from a Late Archaic House near the Classical Athenian Agora, Hesperia Suppl. 46 (2011)

Notes

1. Only the part of the Kerameikos is considered that is situated within the limits of the German excavations.
2. Kerameikos, Inv. 3193. Fragment studied by C. Graml. For type C generally see Agora XXX 71–73.
3. For type B see H. Bloesch, Formen attischer Schalen von Exekias bis zum Ende des strengen Stils (1940) 41–109; Agora XXX 68–71.
4. Kerameikos, Inv. 1941. H. Frielinghaus, in: M. Bentz – N. Eschbach (eds.), Panathenaika. Symposion zu den Panathenäischen Preisamphoren 25.11.–29.11.1998 (2001) 147–159, profile 147 fig. 1. – For acrocups see Agora XII 93–97. Bloesch (supra n. 3) 141–144, esp. pl. 39,4.
5. For stemless cups see Agora XII 98–104; Agora XXX 66–67.
6. Kerameikos 4847. Profile in: H. Frielinghaus, AM 114, 1999, 174 figs. 1,7. For cups with bevelled foot see Agora XII 98–99, especially fig. 4 cat. 449.
7. Profiles in: Frielinghaus (supra n. 6) 174 fig. 1,1–6. For the term 'saucer-foot' see Beazley ARV² 398,2. For Rheneia-cups see Agora XII 100–101.
8. See for example Kerameikos IX 113 cat. 98 pl. 28,1. See also footnote 2 above.
9. Kerameikos, Inv. 9594. – For example, B. Sabattini, in: B. Sabattini (ed.), Le céramique du IVe siècle en mediterranée occidentale (2000) 62 fig. 26; 60 fig. 20. CVA British Museum 4 Great Britain 5 pl. 31,5a/b. CVA Turin 2 Italy 40 pl. 14,6–7.
10. Frielinghaus (supra n. 4) esp. 148–150.
11. Kerameikos, Inv. 4847 (see n. 6 above). For the probable uses of small cups see Lynch, Hesperia Suppl. 46 92, with references to earlier suggestions.
12. Fragment studied by C. Graml.
13. Frielinghaus (supra n. 4) 147 n. 7.
14. Kerameikos XVII.
15. Kerameikos XVII 96.
16. Kerameikos XVII 78.
17. As for the destruction see Kerameikos XVII 6. 28. 49. For objects found along the walls see for example Kerameikos XVII 11.
18. Kerameikos XVII 18.
19. For a map of the building in phase Z1 see Kerameikos XVII Beil. 3.
20. Red-figured cups/cup-fragments: Kerameikos XVII cat. 179. 247. 248. 249. 250. – Black-glazed cups: – Kerameikos XVII cat. 240. 269. – Black-glazed bolsals: Kerameikos XVII cat. 255. 263. – Red-figured skyphoi: Kerameikos XVII cat. 207. 251. – Black-glazed skyphoi: Kerameikos XVII cat. 123. 145. – Black-glazed one-handler: Kerameikos XVII cat. 146. 168 (miniature). 181 (miniature). 182 (miniature). 208. 224.
21. As regards the form and use of bolsals see Agora XII 107–108.
22. As regards the form and use of one-handlers see Agora XII 109–112. Lynch, Hesperia Suppl. 46 148 argues against a 'primary function of drinking cup', but doesn't term it improbable.
23. For a map of the building in phase Z2 see Kerameikos XVII Beil. 4.
24. Red-figured cups/cup fragments: Kerameikos XVII cat. 279. 353. 398. – Black-glazed cups: Kerameikos XVII cat. 280. 334. 400. 409. 427. – Black-figured cup-skyphos:

Kerameikos XVII cat. 302. – Red-figured cup-skyphos: Kerameikos XVII cat. 351. – Black-glazed cup-skyphoi: Kerameikos XVII cat. 299. 303. 304. 352. 411. – Black-glazed bolsals: Kerameikos XVII cat. 281. 339. 356. 357. 358. 359. 416. 417. – Red-figured skyphoi: Kerameikos XVII cat. 278. 300. 349. 350. – Black-glazed skyphoi: Kerameikos XVII cat. 301. 399. 410. 426. – Black-glazed one-handler: Kerameikos XVII cat. 360. 361. 362. 363. 364. 412. 413. 414. 415.

25 For room R2 see Kerameikos XVII 32–33; for room L2 see Kerameikos XVII 41–42; for room K2 see Kerameikos XVII 38–39; for room Wb2 see Kerameikos XVII 41. For room Aa2 see Kerameikos XVII 33. For room O2 see Kerameikos XVII 39.

26 For a map of the building in phase Z3 see Kerameikos XVII Beil. 5.

27 Black-glazed cup-skyphoi: Kerameikos XVII cat. 989. – Black-glazed skyphoi: Kerameikos XVII cat. 465. 666. 667. 857. 858. 884. 885. – Plain skyphoi: Kerameikos XVII cat. 665. – Black-glazed one-handler: Kerameikos XVII cat. 466. 564. 565. 668. 669. 670. 671. 672. – As for red-figured stemmed cups from the middle of the fourth century or shortly after see n. 4 above. For stemless red-figured cups of the middle of the fourth century see, for example, Agora XXX cat. 1357. 1358.

28 For the close relationship of kylix and symposion see A. Schäfer. Unterhaltung beim griechischen Symposion (1997) 46–47; Lynch, Hesperia Suppl. 46 78–80.

29 In the course of the congress I was informed by K. Lynch that she had come to a similar conclusion that she will publish in the near future.

30 Lynch, Hesperia Suppl. 46. For the excavated structures of the house see Lynch, Hesperia Suppl. 46 29–30. For the size of two of the rooms see Lynch, Hesperia Suppl. 46 35. 168. For the well and the contents of its fill see Lynch, Hesperia Suppl. 46 15.

31 Unlike Lynch, Hesperia Suppl. 46 who distinguishes between several levels of the well's contents as probably representing different fills, and who (p. 169) counts only 6 red-figured, 2 coral-red and 8 black-glazed kylikes as part of one strata, I did count complete vessels and fragments alike (that goes for cups as well as drinking vessels of other types). Since I did the same in the case of Bau Z1 and Bau Z2, there is no problem in comparing the numbers. But even if one were to take Lynch's lowest estimation of numbers, there would still be the visible decline that is described in the following paragraph in my text.

32 See Lynch, Hesperia Suppl. 46 76. 168.

33 As for the combination of red-figured and black-glazed cups in a 'flexible set' serving groups having different numbers of participants in the house-context see Lynch, Hesperia Suppl. 46 99.

34 Kerameikos X.

35 Kerameikos X 55.

36 Kerameikos X 196–197. 221. Find spots of Panathanaic prize amphorae: Kerameikos X 239.

37 Kerameikos X 238–239.

38 In the catalogue there are listed only black-glazed cups, apparently all of them of the stemless type: Kerameikos X 203–205. The number of cups is even fewer than indicated, as at least a part of the specimens listed as 'cups' (Kerameikos X 203 K 28–41) have to be classified as 'bowls'. – Red-figured skyphoi: Kerameikos X 198 K 4. 220 K 12. Cf. skyphoi Kerameikos X 205.

39 Kerameikos VII,2; Eridanos-Nekropole.

40 Kerameikos IX.

41 Kerameikos XIV.

42 Kerameikos VII,2 cat. 221,4 (type C). 443,4 (stemless). – In addition a fragment that was part of the fill of a grave may be mentioned: Kerameikos IX cat. 98.

43 Kylix: Kerameikos VII,2 cat. 234,3. 33,1. 472,11 (miniature). 21,1 (miniature). 470,4 (miniature). – Additionally, a fragment (type B) that was found in the fill of a grave can be mentioned: Kerameikos IX cat. 85.

44 Kerameikos VII,2 cat. 9,5. 234,4. 472,9. 18,2. 221,5. 298,3. 147,4. Kerameikos IX cat. 10. 12. 48 (miniature). 145. 197. 200. – Stemless cup: Kerameikos VII,2 cat. 27,2. 46,3. 39,5. 208. 142,5. 179,3. 161,1. 437,2. 437,3. Kerameikos IX cat. 106. 151 (miniature). 160. 162. 241. 249. 263 (miniature). 279. 281 (miniature). Eridanos-Nekropole: Kat. 58. 87. 90. Kerameikos XIV cat. 40 (probably a bowl?). Not to be included are cat. 104 (bolsal). 148 (cup-skyphos). 152 (bowl). – Omphalos-cup: Kerameikos VII,2 cat. 454,2. 73,18. 77,1. – Additionally, some ‚cups' may be mentioned that have not been identified in the material and which, therefore, cannot be classified: Kerameikos VII,2 8 Schachtgrab 8. cat. 21.

45 Eridanos-Necropoleis: 330 (Kerameikos VII,2) + 112 (Eridanos-Nekropole) graves with offerings. South Hill: 262 graves with offerings. Corner-Terrace: 75 graves with offerings.

46 Skyphoi: 7 black-figured, 133 black-glazed, 46 with other types of decoration. – Cup-skyphoi: 1 black-figured, 8 black-glazed. – Bolsals: 8 black-glazed. – One-handler: 43 black-glazed or plain.

47 Out of the about 50 cups only 6 (probably 7) specimens date later than 450 BC; all of them are stemless cups. Specimens dating after the middle of the fifth century: Kerameikos VII,2 cat. 443,4. 437,2. 437,3. Eridanos-Nekropole cat. 58. 87. 90. Kerameikos XIV cat. 40 (probably a bowl).

48 Out of about 190 skyphoi only thirty-four date later than 450 BC. For specimens dating after the middle of the fifth century see Kerameikos VII,2 cat. 86,2. 111,4. 114,2. 149,7. 149,8. 205,2. 323,1. 409,4. 409,5. 409,6. 437,4. 440,3. 440,4. 443,10. 528,3. 566,2. 595. 622,1. Eridanos-Nekropole cat. 59. 77. 106. 107. Kerameikos IX cat. 282. 284. 289. 292 (2x). 295. 297 (2x). 301. 302. 303 (2x). – The number of 'stouter drinking vessels' can be slightly augmented by incorporating contemporary cup-skyphoi and bolsals. Cup-skyphoi: Kerameikos IX cat. 298. Kerameikos XIV cat. 1. Bolsals: Kerameikos VII,2 cat. 95,1. 393,6. 442,2. 443,9. 489,12. 515. 625,2. Kerameikos XIV cat. 22. 56. – One-handler dating later than 450 BC: Kerameikos VII,2 cat. 95. 107. 112. 383. 437. 443. 445. 498. 526. 529. Kerameikos IX cat. 278. 290. 298. Eridanos-Nekropole cat. 58. 175.

49 Grave 39 HTR 15 contained 1 red-figured kylix, 1 black-glazed kylix, 1 black-glazed 'kelch', 1 black-figured pelike, 2 black-figured lekythoi (see Kerameikos VII,2 60–61). – Grabbau o contained 1 red-figured stemless cup, 1 black-glazed cup-skyphos, 1 black-glazed skyphos, 1 black-glazed bolsal, 1 black-glazed one-handler, 1 red-figured lebes (miniature), 3 black-glazed pyxides, 3 lekythoi (see Kerameikos VII,2 111–113).

50 Children's graves with kylikes: Kerameikos VII,2 cat. 21a. 33. 298. Kerameikos IX cat. 48 (miniature). Cf. Kerameikos IX 56f. – Children's graves with stemless cups: Kerameikos VII,2 cat. 27. 39. 46. 142. 161. 179. Eridanos-Nekropole cat. 58. 104. Kerameikos IX cat. 160. 241. 249. 263. 279.
51 Kerameikos X 196.
52 Kerameikos X 3–6.
53 M. C. Monaco, Ergasteria. Impianti artigianali ceramic ad Atene ed in Attica dal protogeometrico alle soglie dell'ellenistico (2000). – 1. Deposit near the street to the Kolonos Hippios, about 200 fragments of kylikes which have been decorated by the Brygos Painter and his colleagues (59. 211–213). 2. Deposit presumably found in the area of the Metro station 'Theseion', with mainly craters which have been decorated by the Painter of the Athens Dinos (59–60. 196–201). 3. Deposit presumably found in the area of Ermou Street, containing mainly cups and cup-fragments decorated by the Jena Painter (63–67).
54 1. Remnants of three kilns of the fifth and fourth centuries underneath the Museum (Monaco [supra n. 53] 70–71). 2. Three kilns of the second half of the fifth century, a red-figured skyphos and a trial-piece (part of an amphora) underneath the Monument of the Third Horos (Monaco [supra n. 53] 72–74). 3. Three kilns of the second half of the fourth century or the third century in the area northwest of the Round Bath (Monaco [supra n. 53] 76–78).
55 See Lynch, Hesperia Suppl. 46 99 with cat. 123. 128. 133. 134. Cf. also cat. 121. 191.

6 Smikros and Epilykos: Two Comic Inventions in Athenian Vase-painting

In memory of Frederick A. Cooper

Guy Hedreen

The possible meanings of the vase-paintings we study are suggested to us in part by the images themselves and in part by what we know – or think we know – about the roles that the imagery played within society. Many Athenian vases appear to have been made and painted for use in symposia, but what sort of expectations did the painters and users bring to sympotic imagery?[1] Archaic monody and recitative poetry that re-circulated as traditional sympotic entertainment offers one means of developing models for the interpretation of sympotic imagery. The verses of the seventh-century poet Archilochos and the sixth-century poet Hipponax, which the ancients categorized as *iambos*, appear to have circulated widely within symposia as well as through public rhapsodic performance. They were well-known to fifth-century Athenian comic playwrights and presumably to their audiences as well.[2] One characteristic of Archaic iambic poetry offers a new way of looking at several old problems concerning Athenian potters and painters.

This characteristic is the manner in which the iambic poet fictionalizes his own identity. Archilochos and Hipponax attribute to themselves names, actions, or character traits that contradict their probable social origins or status. The fifth century aristocratic apologist Kritias expressed displeasure in noting that Archilochos publicly claimed that he was an impoverished, lecherous, adulterous, quarrelsome poet, the son of a slave girl who threw away his own shield out of cowardice.[3] Those claims are at odds with other testimonia, which suggest that the family of Archilochos was prominent socially.[4] Hipponax repeatedly describes himself as an impoverished thief although his name bespeaks an aristocratic background.[5] In a game-changing essay, Kenneth Dover called attention to a testimonium of Aristotle. Aristotle claims that Archilochos regularly represented someone else as the speaker of his first-person narratives, such as Charon the lowly carpenter in the poem beginning, "The possessions of Gyges are of no concern to me".[6] Aristotle suggests that Archilochos employed pseudonyms in order to avoid jealousy or controversy, but scholars have recently and rightly recognized that iambic poets fictionalized the claims of their poet-narrators for the sake of artistic competition, originality, and humor.[7] One proof of that is the extent to which both Archilochos and Hipponax modeled their own literary personae after the epic hero Odysseus.[8] Another is the fact that historical contemporaries of the poets can occasionally be identified in the poetry, but the representations of the individuals often strain credulity.[9]

In a recent paper, I argued that the Athenian vase-paintings signed *Smikros egraphsen* are pictorial manifestations or equivalents of the iambic practice of fictitious autobiography and authorial self-assertion.[10] The present paper advances the initial argument in two ways. First, I address the history of the scholarship on the vase-painter known as Smikros and the arguments that the vases signed *Smikros egraphsen* represent the work of a distinctive hand. Second, I reexamine several anomalous artists' signatures within the oeuvre of Skythes in the light of new evidence. I reopen the cold case of the erstwhile artist Epilykos.

Smikros and Euphronios

The initial argument is easily summarized. The name "Σμίκρος," "Smikros," or "Shorty" occurs as part of a vase-painter's signature on at least three, very likely four, and possibly five vases.[11] The name may occur as well as part of a potter's signature on a large, ambitious, now fragmentary phiale signed by the painter Douris.[12] The vase-painting signed *Smikros egraphsen* has always been recognized as extremely close in style to the vase-painting of Euphronios. Because it was signed by a different name, however, the stylistic similarities between it and the work of Euphronios have been accounted for according to a hypothesis that the vase-painter who called himself

Smikros was an imitator of Euphronios. That hypothesis was given an authorative stamp by J. D. Beazley in 1925, in the memorable epithet, "kümmerlicher Nachahmer des Euphronios".[13] Discoveries made since then, however, have made the imitator-hypothesis harder to sustain. In 2005, Dyfri Williams acknowledged that "Smikros began to be able to imitate his master so closely that it is sometimes difficult to tell them apart...The armed dancing satyr on the [Berlin amphora] is very powerful and matches almost line for line what one would expect of Euphronios at his height. Nevertheless, there is beside him the signature of Smikros as painter".[14] The last sentence of the quotation is telling: the chief argument for believing that Smikros was an actual, historical vase-painter is not a generally agreed upon set of stylistic differences between the vase-painting signed *Smikros egraphsen* and the vase-painting of Euphronios, but rather the existence of a handful of signatures containing the name of Smikros. Today, the question in need of answer is not whether the vases bearing the signature of Smikros are stylistically distinguishable from those signed by Euphronios, but rather the problem is how to explain the fact that vases seemingly identical in style bear the signatures of two different artists. I argue that Smikros was not a real vase-painter at all but a fictional, pictorial creation of Euphronios.

Iambic poetry plays an important role in the argument, because it expands our understanding of what was conceptually possible or comprehensible for vase-painters decorating pottery for symposia, and for patrons examining the pottery in a sympotic context. Iambic poetry grounds the practices of writing under an assumed name, and creating fictitious artisans, within the very sympotic culture for which, it appears, the vases were created. The hypothesis that Euphronios painted the vases signed *Smikros egraphsen* has the merit of not only accounting for the stylistic similarities between the vase-paintings bearing the two different signatures, but also of clarifying several features within the inscriptions that call critical attention to the identity of Smikros. The presence of clues calling into question the reality of Smikros makes sense, if the purpose of signing under a pseudonym was not to fool the patron like an art forger, but rather, like the inventions of the iambic poets, to call attention to the cleverness of Euphronios himself.

Let us consider briefly the vases bearing the signature *Smikros egraphsen* and the distinctions drawn between those vase-paintings and the painting of Euphronios. The best-known vase is a stamnos in Brussels (Fig. 1; Color Pl. 5C).[15] It is conceptually extraordinary because it contains, alongside the signature, a symposiast identified through an inscription as Smikros himself. The vase-painting purports to be a very rare type of picture in Greek art, a self-portrait. When he published the vase in 1902, Camille Gaspar believed that the same painter was responsible for the great volute krater in Arezzo depicting Herakles and the Amazons (Fig. 2).[16] The chief argument was that the figures of Herakles and the Amazon Teisipyle on the krater were clearly painted by the same artist who was responsible for the Amazon Barkida and the statue of Herakles on an amphora in the Louvre (Fig. 3).[17] The amphora bears a tantalizing inscription, *dokei Smik<r>oi <e>inai*, which Gaspar interpreted ("it seems to be by

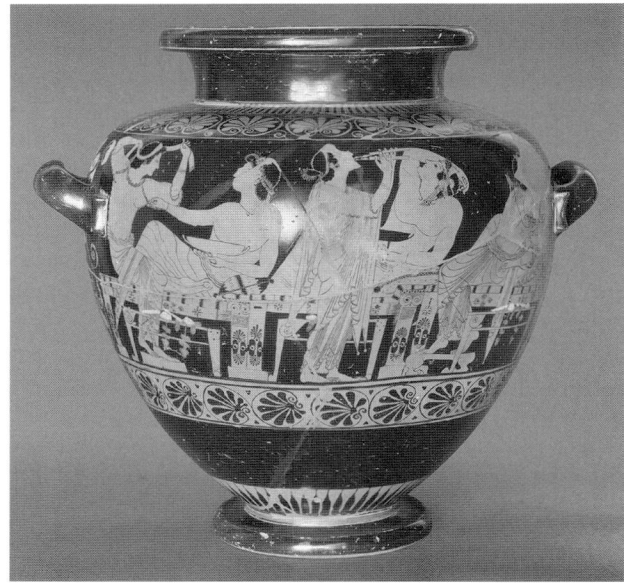

Fig. 1 Brussels, Musées Royaux A717. Photo: Courtesy of the Musées Royaux, Brussels.

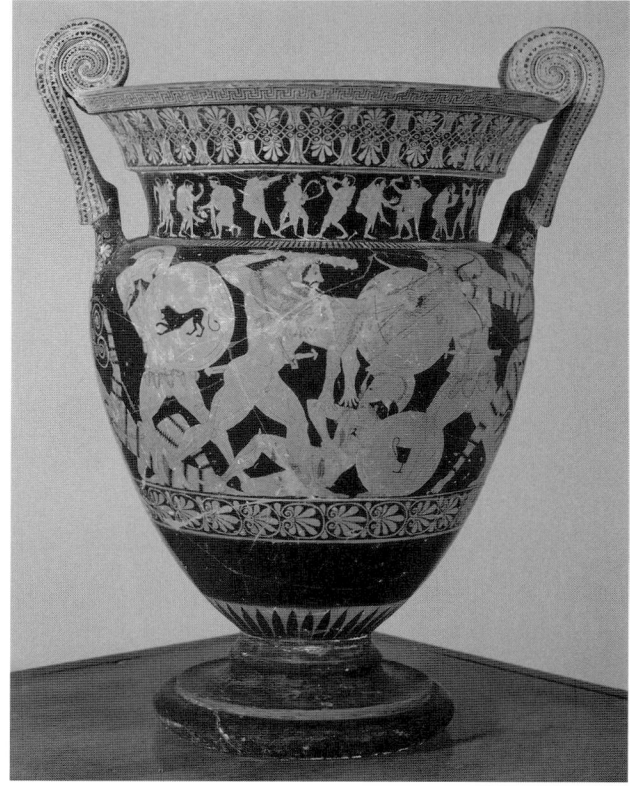

Fig. 2 Arezzo, Museo Civico 1465. Photo: Courtesy Scala/Art Resource NY.

Smikros") as indicating that Smikros was responsible for the design of the figures. Adolf Furtwängler subsequently recognized the principal vase-painting on the krater as the work of the same hand who signed several vases *Euphronios egraphsen*. He believed that the mysterious statement on the amphora in Paris necessarily implies ("how does it seem to Smikros?") that someone *other* than Smikros wrote it. And he distanced the stamnos in Brussels from the artistic hand responsible for the painting of the krater without going into any detailed comparisons. He simply noted that the vase in Arezzo was a much better and more significant work of art; that it was stylistically a little further developed; that the profiles of the heads are drawn better, the drapery is more graceful, and the ornament is different.[18] Beginning with Furtwängler, the principal criterion for distinguishing the vase-painting of Euphronios from that of Smikros has been quality, rather than a consistent set of stylistic traits.

Our understanding of the stamnos in Brussels (Fig. 1; Color Pl. 5C) was fundamentally altered by the publication in 1965 of a fragmentary krater in Munich convincingly attributed to Euphronios (Fig. 4).[19] The similarities between the two unusual vase-paintings are extensive enough to make one confident that the painter of one vase had actually seen the other. That is an extraordinarily rare circumstance in view of the fact that neither vase would have been visible to an imitator once the pot had been exported to Etruria, where it was, most likely, found.[20] Among the many compositional or programmatic similarities, the one that highlights the uniqueness of this pair of vase-paintings is the presence in both of a symposiast identified by name as Smikros. There are differences between the two vase-paintings. Perhaps the most obvious is the treatment of the hair and eyes. On the vase in Brussels, the hair of Smikros is a homogeneous mass of black gloss and the pupil of his eye is solid black. On the vase in Munich, the hair of Smikros, like the hair of every figure on the obverse, is fashioned out of individual brush strokes of dilute gloss – a lighter look. The eye is also lighter in appearance, having a small black dot surrounded by a black ring with a reserved ring in between. In hair and eyes, the choices made in painting the stamnos in Brussels, both on the obverse and reverse, resemble the hair and eyes that Euphronios usually reserves for figures of secondary importance. On the signed krater in the Villa Giulia depicting the deceased Sarpedon, for example, dilute gloss is used for the hair of Sarpedon and Thanatos, and Thanatos and Hypnos have light-colored eyes, but solid black masses are employed for the hair and pupils of all the other figures on the vase.[21]

For my purposes, what is important is the fact that the extensive similarities between the stamnos in Brussels (Fig. 1; Color Pl. 5C) and the krater in Munich (Fig. 4) go beyond compositional details. Martha Ohly-Dumm, who has offered the most extensive comparison of the two vase-paintings, acknowledged that the inner muscular detail of the "self-representation" of Smikros is entirely Euphronian. One may compare the single gentle, W-like relief line for the pectorals, and the line in dilute gloss encompassing the abdominal muscles and curving back on itself. Ohly-Dumm reasserted nevertheless the hypothesis that Smikros was an imitator of Euphronios. She singled out two details that, she believed, signal the inability of the imitator to follow the master. First, the fingers of the *aulētris* on the stamnos are stiff in comparison with the dynamism of the accompanist's hands on the krater. Second, the attachment of the foreshortened left leg to the torso of the drinker Pheidiades is not concealed by drapery, as it is on an amphora in the Louvre attributed to Euphronios.[22] Dietrich von Bothmer also identified two features on the stamnos in Brussels indicative, he argued, of Smikros' failure to keep up with the model provided by Euphronios. Smikros forgot to depict himself with an open mouth, even though he is meant to be singing, like Ekphantides on the krater, and Autonomes has two left hands.[23]

The weakness in all of those claims is that the alleged deficiencies in the painting abilities of Smikros can be found within the painting of Euphronios. The Euphronian krater in Munich, like the stamnos in Brussels, depicts

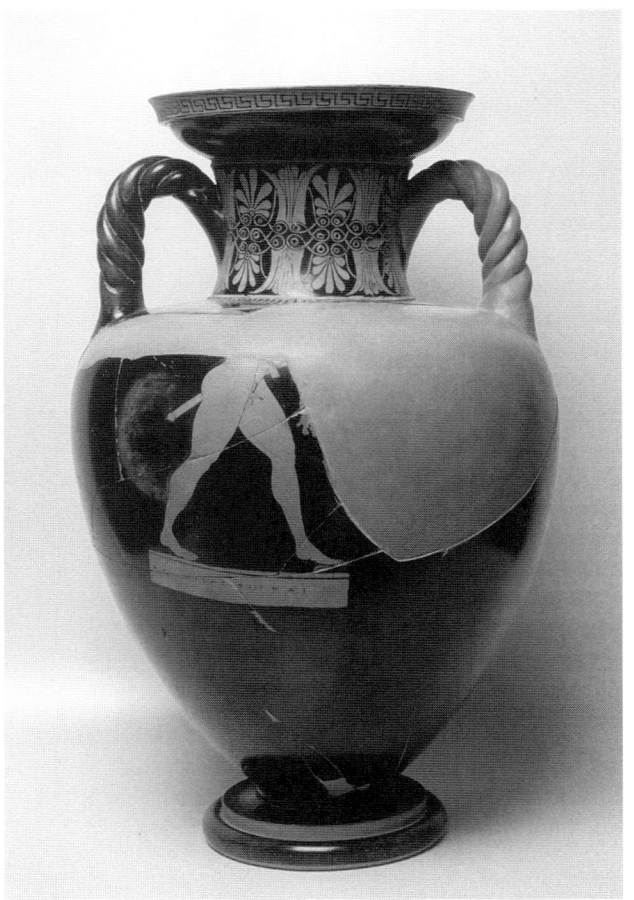

Fig. 3 Paris, Musée du Louvre G107. Photo: Claude Gaspari. Réunion des Musées Nationaux/Art Resource NY.

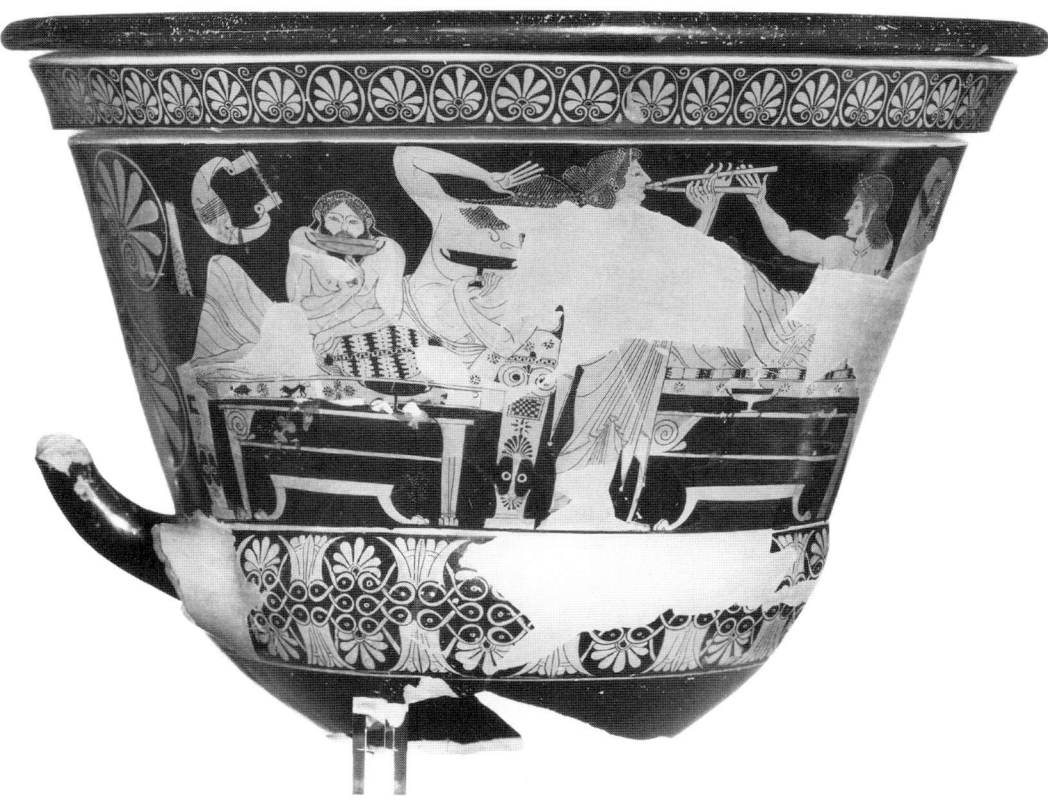

Fig. 4 Munich, Antikensammlungen 8935. Photo: Renate Kühling. Courtesy of the Staatliche Antikensammlungen und Glyptothek München.

a drinker (named Thodemos) with a foreshortened left leg. A fragment is missing from the critical area, but it is still possible to see that the drawing of the himation around the waist and above the knee of Thodemos is more similar to the handling of the clothing of Pheidiades on the stamnos than to what is drawn on the Euphronian amphora in Paris. On the krater, Thodemos also has two left hands, as Richard Neer perceptively noted.[24] On the Euphronian amphora in Paris, one symposiast is depicted with his lips pressed together in spite of the fact that he is obviously singing to his own lyric accompaniment, because the words of his song are written on the vase. The fingers of flute-players vary considerably within the oeuvre of Euphronios, and those of the accompanist on the hydria in Dresden, for example, are closer to those on the stamnos in Brussels than to those on the krater in Munich.[25] As Ingeborg Peschel persuasively argued, the vase-painting in Brussels represents a different, more meditative sort of musical experience, in keeping with its emphasis on sensuality (imagine Barry White playing in the background), compared to the lively sing-along depicted on the krater in Munich.[26]

The publication in 1967 of an amphora in Berlin (Fig. 5; Color Pl. 6) signed *Smikros egraphsen* forced scholars to acknowledge that the affinities between Smikros and Euphronios were even closer than hitherto thought.[27] The shape of the vase, the "spot-light" decorative scheme, and even the subject matter are attested in the work of Euphronios.[28] Most significantly, the muscular silen dancing the pyrrhic is virtually indistinguishable in terms of anatomical detail from Euphronian strong-men such as Herakles on the krater in Arezzo (Fig. 2). One may compare the breast bone or pectoral contour, the serratus anterior muscles, the naval, and the systems of lines articulating the muscles and tendons of the arms and legs. The comparison reveals not only a virtually identical set of anatomical markings, but, significantly, no difference in the sureness of the line. Williams acknowledged, in the quotation given earlier, that it is not easy to distinguish the painting of the silen on this vase from the painting of Euphronios.[29] In attempting to single out what is *not* Euphronian about the style of the amphora in Berlin, Ohly-Dumm relied in part on a fragmentary neck amphora in Paris depicting athletes (Fig. 6). The neck amphora has been accepted by Beazley and many others as a fine work of Euphronios.[30] Although the anatomical forms are closely comparable, there is, she suggested, a lack of power and proportion in the silen compared to the athlete. In 2002, however, Neer reported that a significant portion of the inscription *Smikros egraphsen* could be read on the fragmentary Parisian neck amphora.[31] The signature documents within the work of Smikros not only a range of capability in painting the human body equal perhaps to anything in the signed work of Euphronios, but also light-colored hair.[32]

In her 1974 study, Martha Ohly-Dumm attributed to Smikros an additional vase that has played an important role in recent writing about the artist. The vase, a psykter now in Malibu, depicts five pairs of men courting boys.[33] Many of the figures are identified by name. The notoriety of the psykter stems from the fact that one of the men courting a boy is named Euphronios. "Euphronios" is the young man, confidently leaning on a stick as if he did that sort of thing all the time, reaching for the chin of the boy identified by an inscription as *Leagros kalos*.[34] In making the attribution to Smikros, Ohly-Dumm offered but a single comparison, to an unsigned psykter attributed to Smikros by Beazley.[35] Subsequently, two additional psykters have been assigned to Smikros.[36] On the basis in part of comparison with the pyskter in Malibu, there is even speculation that Smikros painted some or all of the figures on the neck of the krater in Arezzo (Fig. 2).[37] What I wish to emphasize is that the attribution of this psykter to Smikros, which is not based, so far as I can tell, primarily on comparisons with the vase-paintings signed *Smikros egraphsen*, is far from uncontroversial. Although the psykter has been attributed to Smikros by several scholars, the attribution has been contested by several others.[38] The eyelashes of Leagros, back-view of Ambrosios, and "portrait" of the artist suggest that the painter of the psykter was intimately familiar with the vase-painting of Euphronios.[39] But other aspects of the painting are difficult to parallel in vase-painting signed by Euphronios, and the impression they give is of incompetence. Robertson suggested that the painting is perhaps even a parody of Pioneer style.

The figures on the krater in Arezzo epitomize the methodological problem of recognizing the range or limitation of what was possible stylistically for the artist who signed as Euphronios. Of course, it is possible that more than one vase-painter worked on the krater, as it appears that vase-painters collaborated on other vases.[40] It is generally accepted, however, that the majority of vases were decorated by a single artist, and that the quality of the painting of even a single vase could vary

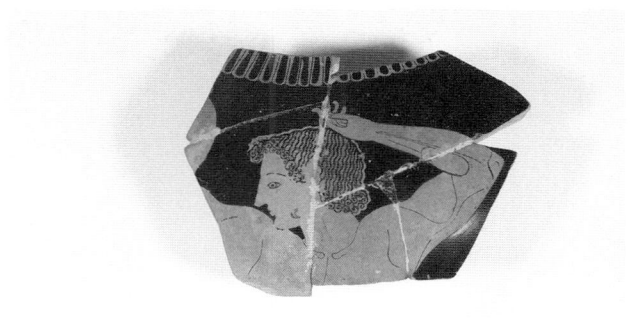

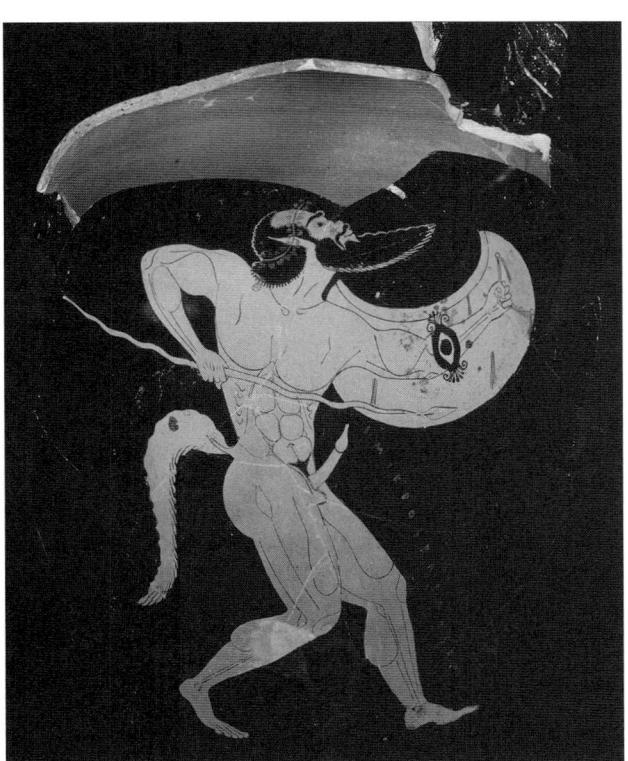

Fig. 5 Berlin, Antikensammlung 1966.19. Photo: Johannes Laurentius. Courtesy bpk, Berlin/Antikensammlung/Art Resource NY.

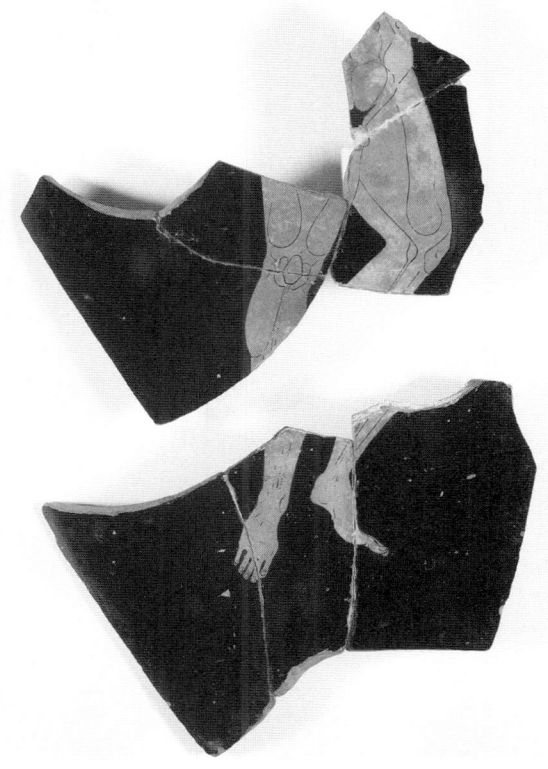

Fig. 6 Paris, Musée du Louvre C 11071. Photo: Les frères Chuzeville. Courtesy Réunion des Musées Nationaux/Art Resource NY.

markedly.⁴¹ More importantly, the pictures on one side of vases signed by or attributed to Euphronios are often less complex, ornate, detailed, or challenging than the main pictures. It is surprising to note how staid, simply drawn, and physiologically homogeneous is the rat-pack on the reverse of the well-known "Antaios" krater in Paris, given the monumental, physiognomically varied, and compositionally experimental knot of hero and anti-hero on the obverse. "The picture is a programme piece of the new style, but the artist has put everything into the two principals. The little figures of women running in the background... are quite traditional in treatment; and the charming picture on the back... puts little emphasis on the new concerns".⁴²

Noticeable stylistic variation is arguably a self-conscious feature of at least one Euphronian vase-painting. On the obverse of a beautiful, sadly fragmentary krater in the Louvre (Fig. 7) is an ambitious picture of Herakles fighting the Nemean lion easily attributable to the painter of the Antaios vase.⁴³ The picture on the reverse depicts young men dancing, drinking, making music, and playing with an inflated wineskin. Between two gymnastic dancers are the letters ευφρον. Below, and at a forty-five degree angle to them, are the letters γικος and, immediately below and at the same forty-five degree orientation, εγρ[α]φσεντᾳδε, *egraphsen tade*, "painted these," *tade* being understood as the neuter plural demonstrative adjective.⁴⁴ It has always been assumed that the letters "Euphron" were completed with "ios" on the other side of the dancer whose raised right arm nearly touches the top border of the picture (even though it is unprecedented for Euphronios to divide his name). The full signature is imagined to read *Euphronios egraphsen tade*, "Euphronios painted these," and the letters "nikos," to have been part of a personal name of one of the dancers, perhaps [Elpi]nikos. Daniele Maras has rightly questioned, however, whether the letters "Euphron" are not too far removed from the verb *egraphsen* to be taken as its grammatical subject. Maras also noted that the letters immediately above and parallel to the verb *egraphsen* can be restored as]*mikos* just as well as]*nikos*. He suggested that the letters formed the name "[S]mik<r>os," and were part of a painter's signature, *[S]mik<r>os egraphsen tade*: "Smikros painted *these*".⁴⁵ Maras understood the demonstrative adjective as limiting the claim of the painter's signature to the figures on the back of the vase: Smikros painted *these* figures of komasts, but not the figures of Herakles and the Nemean Lion on the obverse. It is fair to assume that the signature *Euphronios egraphsen* would have been written above the scene of Herakles, as it is above the principal picture on other calyx kraters signed by this artist. Maras took the inscription at face value, to mean that two different painters, Smikros and Euphronios, actually worked on the same vase. But no one, so far as I know, has ever doubted that the style of the komasts is the style of the painter Euphronios.⁴⁶

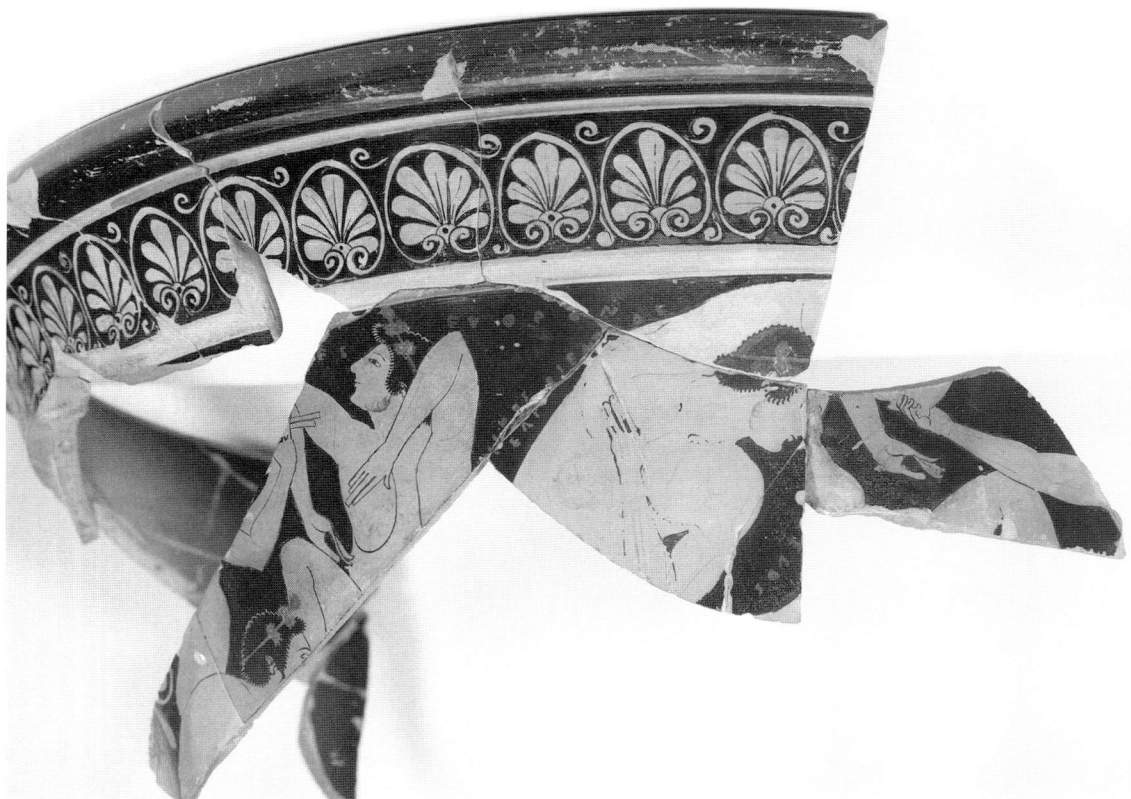

Fig. 7 Paris, Musée du Louvre G110. Photo: Les frères Chuzeville. Courtesy Réunion des Musées Nationaux/Art Resource NY.

The signature *[S]mik<r>os egraphsen tade* arguably serves several purposes. One is to question the distinctiveness of the artist who signs *Smikros egraphsen*. Modern scholars may not have been the only beholders to doubt that any artist other than Euphronios actually painted part of this vase, in spite of what the signature claims.[47] In that respect, the fictitious signature is comparable to the inscription on the amphora in Paris (Fig. 3), *dokei Smik<r>oi <e>inai*, "it *seems* to be by (or belong to) Smikros". The significance of the latter inscription rests in part on a distinction implicit in certain usages of the verb *dokeō* between appearance and reality.[48] The second effect of the signature, *[S]mik<r>os egraphsen tade*, is to highlight the visible differences between the pictures on the front and the back of the vase. The painter has arguably capitalized in the inscription precisely on the possibility that a beholder might take the compositionally simpler, less detailed, and thematically more frivolous picture of wrestling with a greased pigskin to be the work of a "lesser" artist than the more heroic picture of Herakles' deadly struggle with the impermeably skinned lion. The idea of lesser stature is nicely captured in the name of the artist to whom Euphronios has attributed the painting of the party-boys. Through the fictitious signature, the reverse of the krater acquires a conceptual originality every bit as great as the stylistic originality of the obverse. If such stylistic self-awareness and conceptual complexity is evidenced by the writing on the fragmentary Parisian krater, then perhaps even self-parody is not outside the range of possible explanations of the [self-?] "portrait" of Euphronios on the Malibu psykter.[49]

In short, the presence of the signatures containing distinct names has made it seemingly unnecessary to identify descriptive, as opposed to qualitative, differences between the styles of the vase-paintings signed *Smikros* and *Euphronios egraphsen*.[50] As a result, the existence of a stylistically distinct hand behind the vase-painting signed by Smikros has not been subjected to systematic scrutiny. More significantly, in positing the existence of a distinct historical vase-painter, Smikros, and attributing to him Euphronian vase-painting that does not correspond to our notions of what the master was capable of painting, a significant portion of the creativity of Euphronios may have been overlooked.

Epilykos and Skythes:

Smikros is perhaps not an isolated pictorial proposition parallel to the iambic poetic conception of the fictitious narrator or artist. Let us exhume a long-buried corpse from the scholarly graveyard. Five late-sixth-century red-figure cups bear the signature *Skythes egraphsen*, "[the] Scythian painted [this]" (e.g., Fig. 8).[51] One cup also bears the signature *Skythes epoiesen*.[52] On the basis of the signed vases, it has been possible for Beazley and others to identify several dozens of vases (mostly cups) as the work of the painter who signed as Skythes. Martin Schulz' 2001 dissertation lists sixty vases signed by or attributed to the painter. It appears that Skythes was an innovative and versatile artist. To him is attributed one bilingual eye-cup that may have been potted by Amasis.[53] Several cups assigned to him employ red-figure and black-figure decoration on a coral-red ground, an unusual technique.[54] Several fragmentary black-figure plaques, dedications from the Athenian Acropolis, bear the signature *Skythes (or ho Skythes) egraphsen* and are very likely the work of the red-figure painter.[55] Skythes appears to have potted his own cups, and, on the basis of close similarities in form, to have worked closely with Kachrylion.[56] In the workshop of Kachrylion, Skythes presumably encountered the contemporary vase-painter Euphronios.

One of the cups in Paris attributed to Skythes (Fig. 9) bears a more complicated signature: Ἐπίλυκο[ς ἔγραφ]σεν καλός, "Epilykos painted [this] well" (or "Epilykos the beautiful painted [this]," an ambiguity considered below).[57] A second cup attributed to Skythes, very fragmentary and mostly in the Villa Giulia, appears to have exhibited a closely related signature: [Ἐπίλυκο]ς καλός ἔγ[ραφ]σεν.[58] The pair of signatures, taken together, suggests that one should read *egraphsen*, rather than *epoiēsen*, on the cup in Paris, and Epilykos, rather than Skythes, on the cup in the Villa Giulia. The name Epilykos appears on over two dozen cups attributed to or signed by Skythes, but otherwise always (when the inscriptions are complete) as the name of a man described as *kalos*, "good looking".[59] In earlier scholarship, several vase-paintings were identified as the work of a vase-painter who signed as Epilykos. Two vase-painters, Skythes and Epilykos, were envisioned as

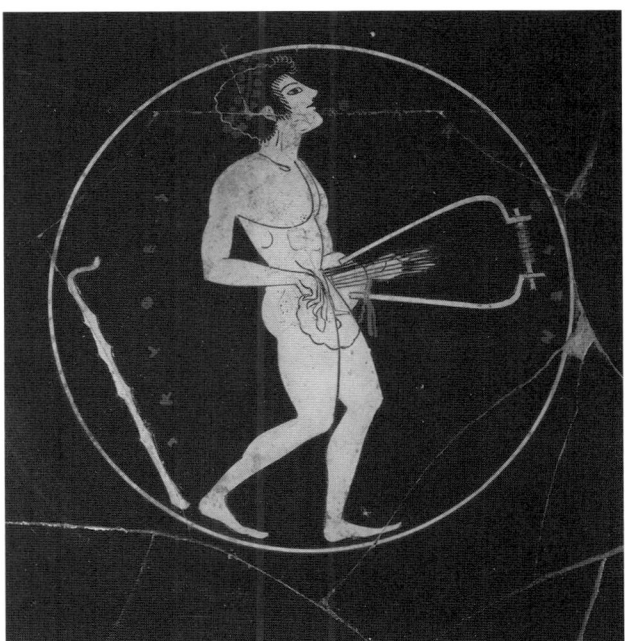

Fig. 8 Rome, Museo Nazionale di Villa Giulia 20760. Photo: Courtesy Scala/Art Resource NY.

working together in the same shop, and engaging in mutual admiration in their *kalos*-inscriptions.⁶⁰ The attempt to identify a group of vase-paintings as the work of a real artist named Epilykos failed, however, because all of the vases in question ultimately were persuasively attributed to Skythes. The inscription *Epilykos egraphsen kalos* was explained away as an error. Epilykos was understood to be nothing more than a *kalos*-name.⁶¹

In 2008, however, Alexandra Zampitē and Vibē Vasilopoúlou published a late-sixth-century red-figure cup dedicated to a nymph from a cave in Boiotia (Fig. 10).⁶² In decoration, the cup is special, because it features three images that appear to be representations of the choruses of satyr-play. For the moment, however, the most important feature of the cup for us is the painted signature in the tondo: Ἐπίλυκο[ς] ἐπο[ίεσεν], "Epilykos made [it]." In this signature, there is no trace of, or room for, the word *kalos*, and no ambiguity about the verb. The cup from the cave of the nymphs, with the unambiguous inscription *Epilykos epoiesen*, necessitates a reassessment of the inscription on the cup in Paris, *Epilykos egraphsen kalos*. The new cup establishes beyond reasonable doubt that the inscriptions *Epilykos egraphsen* or *Epilykos epoiesen* are intentional and not the result of error. Both cups, however, the one in Paris and (according to the excavators) the new cup, appear to have been painted by the artist who signs as Skythes; and with the exception of a few very early pieces, Skythes appears to have painted cups potted by no one other than himself.

The oeuvre attributable to Skythes appears to manifest the same peculiarity as that of Euphronios. Many of the vases are signed by one artist as painter, but a few bear the name of a different artist. Those few vases are neither persuasively attributable to a different hand; nor are the signatures explicable as errors. I suggest that the function of those signatures is the creation of propositions that are amusing due to their contrary-to-factness. The factitiousness is amusing in part because the vase-painters are commandeering for themselves a model of creativity associated with literary characters such as Odysseus, and in part because it is not completely undetectable but subtly hinted at.

The inscriptions on the cups in Paris and, perhaps, the Villa Giulia, contain one suggestive clue that Epilykos is not the artist he claims to be. That clue is the word *kalos*, which is meaningful, ambiguously, either as the adverb *kalōs*, "Epilykos painted [this] very well," or as an adjective modifying the personal name, "Epilykos the handsome painted this." It is unusual to find any boastful language in ceramic artists' signatures, and therefore the self-congratulatory signatures of Epilykos ought to have raised an eyebrow.⁶³ The presence of the word *kalos* within the signature of Epilykos ought to have attracted attention as well because the inscription *Epilykos kalos* occurs so frequently (and almost exclusively) on vases attributable to Skythes.⁶⁴ One is accustomed to think that the men who signed vases as potters or painters, and the men who are frequently praised on vases as *kalos*, belonged to two distinct social classes in Athens. On the one hand, a relatively large number of names of potters and painters correspond to the names of foreign regions or places. Strabo claims that it was an Athenian custom to name slaves after their place of origin, and the practice is confirmed by manumission inscriptions.⁶⁵ The ethnic character of the names of potters and painters has encouraged the hypothesis that some of the artisans were (or formerly were) enslaved.⁶⁶ On the other hand, a relatively large number of the names in *kalos*-inscriptions

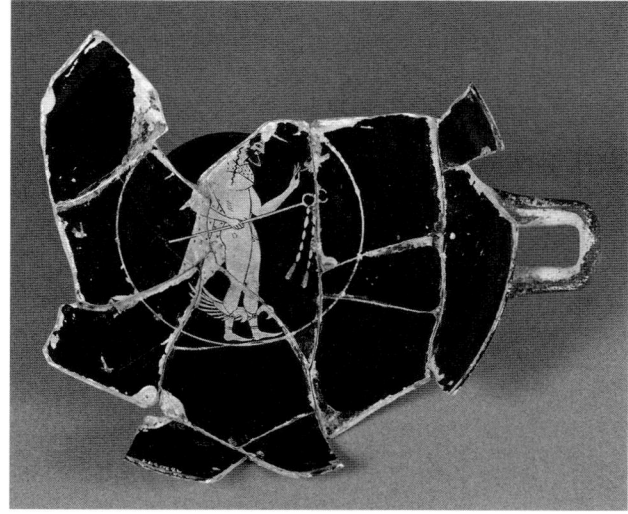

Fig. 9 Paris, Musée du Louvre G10. Photo: Stephane Marechalle. Courtesy Réunion des Musées Nationaux/Art Resource NY.

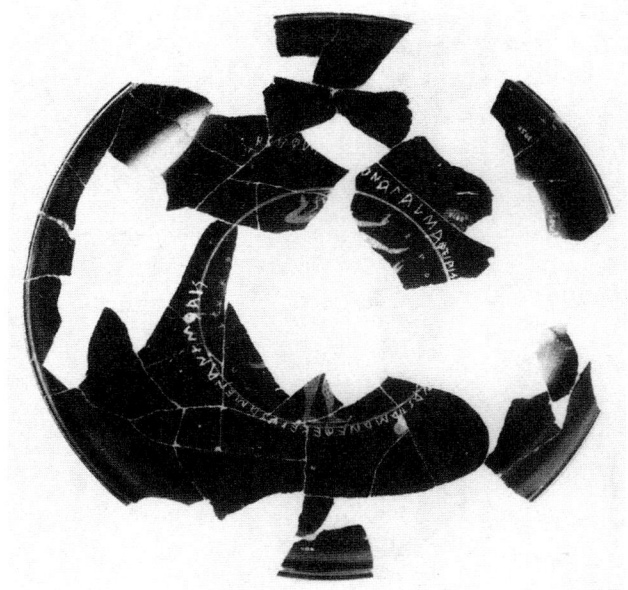

Fig. 10 Unknown collection, from the cave of the nymph Koronia in Boiotia. Photo: after A. Zampitē – V. Vasilopoúlou, in: V. Aravantinos (ed.), Epetēris tēs etaireias Boiōtikōn meletōn vol. 4A (2008) 471 fig. 30.

can be correlated with the names of persons important politically, socially, or economically.[67] Epilykos appears to oscillate mysteriously between those two theoretically distinct social categories.

It is true that the names of potters and painters are occasionally the subjects of *kalos*-inscriptions.[68] A red-figure hydria in Berlin painted by Euphronios or in his manner features the inscription, *Smikros kalos*, which appears to be uttered by one of the two naked bathing girls in the picture.[69] In pictorial conception, the vase is comparable to a contemporary red-figure hydria in Munich attributed to Phintias.[70] On the shoulder of the vase, two female figures, nude from the waist up, reclining on cushions, prepare to play the drinking game of kottabos. The one says to the other, σοὶ τηνδί Εὐθυμίδη καλῷ, "this (toss) is for you, beautiful Euthymides." The reference is presumably to the vase-painter familiar from contemporary signatures. The case of Epilykos is different. Whereas any given artist is generally named more frequently as potter or painter than as *kalos*, Epilykos is much better attested as *kalos* than as an artist. The case of Epilykos is also different because, at Athens, the personal name is fairly well attested, the men who bore it were of some prominence, and the family was wealthy. The grandfather of Perikles' daughter-in-law was named Epilykos, and a much earlier figure so-named was prominent in Athenian politics.[71] Is it possible that a good-looking young man from a prominent Athenian family also worked as a ceramic artist? Or is this an instance of the creative practice, familiar from iambic poetry, of adapting an historical name for humorous fictional purposes?[72]

Girlie Men: Epilykē, Smikra, and Comic Invention in Onomastics

In favor of the hypothesis that the artist-signature of Epilykos is fiction is additional evidence suggesting that the personal name Epilykos, like the name Smikros, was in play, so to speak, among contemporary vase-painters. On the hydria in Berlin is not only the inscription *Smikros kalos* but also the inscription *Epilykē kalē*. The writing of the feminine name runs parallel to the back of the girl on the left, the adjective, outward from her abdomen; the placement of the words suggests that the depicted figure is to be understood as the beautiful Epilykē. This figure is publicly praised for her female beauty and depicted buck naked. Given the importance placed on modesty and anonymity in the Athenian conception of proper womanhood, it seems unlikely, to say the least, that she was understood as a straightforward representation of a bona fide member of a prominent Athenian family, in which the name Epilykos and its feminine counterpart were traditional. Of course, it is possible to imagine that the name refers to a woman unrelated to the seemingly important family, a woman for whom a reputation for modesty might have been of no concern. There is no evidence that the name was actually used by an historical individual, though an argument from silence is not conclusive.[73] In short, the possibility that the inscription *Epilykē kalē* refers to a real woman cannot be ruled out, but the presence of the name within red-figure vase-painting can also be accounted for – and better accounted for – on the hypothesis that it is an invention, a transposition of gender of the name Epilykos, which had already been extracted, so to speak, from the prosopography of the Athenian aristocracy, and transformed into a fictional potter and painter in the vase-painting of Skythes.

For a parallel example of such a reversal of gender, one arguably needs to look no further than the signed work of Euphronios. On a psykter in the Hermitage signed *Euphronios egraphsen*, four female figures recline on mattresses, sip wine, and play drinking games in the manner of men.[74] All four of the women have personal names, written on the vase. Three of the names are transparently appropriate to the imagery and unusual as historical names. Ἀγάπē, Agapē, "love," is the earliest occurrence of a word that would play an important role much later in Christian writing. In LGPN, there are no attestations of this personal name prior to the Byzantine period. Παλαιστό, Palaistō, means "wrestler." It is unattested as a personal name but the erotic connotations of wrestling are obvious.[75] The third party-girl is Σέκλινē, Seklinē, an imaginary Greek word formed out of the word *klinē*, "couch," and meaning perhaps "[I'll] couch you." The name is unattested outside of vase-painting, in which it occurs on this vase as well as a contemporary hydria attributed to the Dikaios Painter, where it is the name of a girl making love to a man.[76] The three names are easily understood as inventions, created on the model of inscriptions identifying figures in vase-painting (gods, heroes, mortals), but toying with the model by defying reference to anyone outside of the imaginary world of the imagery. The name of the fourth female figure in the group, the one who provocatively offers a kottabos-toast to Leagros – τὶν τάνδε λατάσσō Λέαγρε, "I toss these dregs for you, Leagros" – fits that model especially well. Like the naked bathing girl on the hydria in Berlin, who bears a gender-inverted form of the name of the fictitious, (pseudo-?) aristocratic vase-painter and potter Epilykos, the fourth girl on the pyskter in St. Petersburg bears a gender-inverted form of the name of the mysterious vase-painter Smikros. Her name is Smikra.

The personal name Smikra is not entirely unattested, and its occurrence elsewhere in vase-painting supports the hypothesis that a comic pictorial conception informs the vase-painting we have been examining. In the tondo of an infamous cup in Berlin (Fig. 11), two men and a girl crowded onto a single couch engage in an orgy of intercourse, masturbation, and spanking.[77] Lying beneath the couch is a girl with head turned away from the action, eyes closed, and left hand on the top of her head. She is completely self-absorbed. Perhaps she is asleep. But the position of her right hand, immediately before her pudenda, suggests that she is absorbed in clitoral stimulation, a seemingly unparalleled act in Greek art.[78] The name of this eye-catching orgiast is Σμίκα.[79] It is either a feminine spelling of the name "Smikos," which occurs on two vases attributed to Euphronios discussed earlier, or an abbreviated spelling of the name "Smikra".[80]

Curiously, the cup in Berlin also features the name of the other fictionalized artist of interest in this paper. On one exterior surface, a bearded male figure, ithyphallic, a flute-case hanging carelessly from his erect penis, pursues, it appears, the naked girl before him. Beginning at the tip of his penis is the inscription *Epilykos*.[81] Because the cup in Berlin dates to approximately the same moment in time as the cups by Skythes, the figure labelled Epilykos – much advanced in age, to judge from his full beard, from the time when he might reasonably be thought of as *kalos* in the sense of homoerotically desirable – has been taken to represent another member of the same family, such as a debauched uncle.[82] There is much to said, however, in favor of the hypothesis that the imagery and writing on the cup in Berlin operates in a satiric or parodic mode, rather than an historical, documentary one. The cup's general pictorial program or conception encourages one to understand the inscriptions as intentionally toying with reality.

To begin with the figure of Epilykos himself, the use of the erect penis as a means of transporting a flute-case is noteworthy not only for its inherent improbability (don't try this at home) but also for its parallels within Athenian vase-painting. Silens or satyrs, endowed with superhuman sexuality and omnipotent penises – not humans – are depicted as transporting flute-cases in this way.[83] Consider also the boy in the tondo (Fig. 11). As he watches an older man screw a girl, the boy grips his own erect penis. It is exceedingly rare to see mortal men masturbating in Athenian vase-painting, but very common to see silens resorting to this practice. The implied comparison between Epilykos and his jauntily turbaned mates, on the one hand, and the uncultured silens, on the other, is not flattering. Silens epitomize the absence of self-control, modesty, and authority, which are integral to the Greek conception of masculinity. The frequency with which silens engage in masturbation, for example, is partly an expression of the superhuman scope of their sexual desire. It is an expression equally, however, of their lack of authority to compel females (within the imaginary realm inhabited by silens, the females in question are nymphs) to accept their sexual desire.[84] In vase-painting, the relative powerlessness of the silens to force themselves sexually on the nymphs is epitomized in the image of one or more silens discovering a sleeping nymph. The silens are depicted most often both as mightily desirous of intercourse with the nymph, but also as never successfully consummating their desire. One fragmentary hydria in Malibu makes explicit the link between masturbation and powerlessness: a silen resorts to onanism as a nymph sleeps unmolested beside him.[85] In an intensification of the logic informing such a vase-painting, the boy in the tondo of the cup in Berlin masturbates while the girl, Smika, theoretically available to him as a sexual partner, chooses to satisfy herself instead.

In the pictorial program of the cup in Berlin, unprecedented sexual initiative, authority, and freedom are accorded to the girls, and subordinate status is given to most of the men, in an inversion of expectation. In the tondo, in addition to the unprecedented image of dual male and female masturbation, there is a highly unusual image of female-on-male sadism. The girl on the couch allows a man to penetrate her, but she is hardly a passive figure. Entwined with the man in a virtuoso performance of Kama-Sutric contortion, this girl has twisted her way on top of her partner, so that she can beat him on the buttocks with a shoe. Spanking with a sandal is a well-attested if rare motif in Greek art. Its earliest occurrences appear to be in scenes of the disciplining of children. The motif begins to appear in erotic situations around the time of this cup. It is unprecedented, however, to see a woman threatening a man in this way.[86] On the outside of the cup, a similar pattern of inversion of expectations is evident. The female figures initiate erotic intimacy with the male figures or at least appear to be equal partners. One girl leads a man off by his erect penis, gripping it in her hand. Another girl balances on one leg, lifting the other, making her pudenda available visually to the spectator and physically to a young man. He rests on the ground, touches the girl's upper thigh with one hand, reaches for the pudenda with the other, and positions his face so close to the erogenous zone as to preclude any interpretation other than that he intends to stimulate the woman orally, a sexual practice unparalleled in vase-painting.[87]

The names inscribed beside several of the figures contribute to the impression that the decoration of the cup in its entirety is conceived as comically inventive fiction. One provocatively dancing girl bears the name *Aphros*, historically unattested in Attica as a personal name, and transparently related to the name of the goddess presiding over the erotic escapades on this cup. The figure which carries the big club is named *Megas*, "mighty, big, giant".[88] Megas is a common adjective or epithet, and exceedingly rare as a personal name. It seems ideally ironically suited to the visual image of a mighty-club-wielding man who nevertheless seems unable to dominate a girl. Finally, the name of the girl pursued by Epilykos, Κορονε, Korōnē, reappears in an ambitious pictorial joke in contemporary Athenian vase-painting. On the obverse of an amphora attributed to Euthymides, Theseus carries off a girl who is labelled Korōnē.[89] In pursuit of the couple, hoping to prevent the elopement is a female figure named Helen. On the reverse is another female figure formerly beloved by Theseus, now abandoned, the Amazon Antiope, also in hot pursuit: *eidon the<o>men*, "I see them, let's go!" she says. The pictorial proposition is a humorous inversion of traditional mythology, in which Theseus carries off Helen or Antiope.[90] The humor is based in part on the fact that the mythological heroines themselves seem to understand, out of a kind of meta-fictional awareness of their own role within the tradition, that they are the ones whom Theseus should be carrying off. The humor also rests on the idea that Korōnē belongs not to heroic mythology, but rather to the literature of prostitution. Jiří Frel and others have suggested that Korōnē was an historical courtesan at Athens in the late sixth century, to whom the vase-painter Euthymides is paying a supreme complement.[91] Within Attica, a half-dozen occurrences of the name are attested, but virtually all occur within works of art or literature.[92] Korōnē appears to have been a stock name for a prostitute within Comedy and later Classical belles-lettres. It is uncertain that any real historical figure lies behind those literary elaborations.[93] It is even possible that the word *korōnē* was already associated with prostitution within the iambic poetry of Archilochos.[94]

To conclude, pictorial and onomastic considerations suggest that the two names on the cup in Berlin (Fig. 11), Smika and Epilykos, are part of a complex web of comic ceramic invention. The inversion of the expected, conventional balance of gender power, and the occurrence of sexual practices otherwise unattested in art, signal that the vase-painting should not be taken either as a document of actual customs or as a male fantasy. They point instead to the sort of inversion of gender power attested in Old Comedy such as Lysistrata or Ekklesiazousai.

The reoccurrence on contemporary vases of the names, as well as gender-inverted forms of the names, provides one indication of the specific nature of the comic invention. The people referred to exist primarily within the collective pictorial imagination of the Pioneer Group of vase-painters, even if the names can occasionally be identified outside of the world of vase-inscriptions. Smika, the girl in the tondo of the Berlin cup, is related to Smikra, one of the naked girls on Euphronios' pyskter. Numerous other features of the cup (raised black clay dots for curly hair in the tondo, the pose of the girl dancing on one foot, the lamp stand, the Kachrylion-esque potter-work) suggest that the name Smika is one of the cup's many features indebted to the work of Euphronios. The presence on the cup of the name of Epilykos brings the vase-painting of Skythes into the same orbit. Two of the names on the cup, Smika and Epilykos, appear in gender-inverted form as Epilykē and Smikros, on the contemporary Euphronian hydria in Berlin. The names Epilykos and Smikros occur as artists' signatures on contemporary vases attributable to two artists, Euphronios and Skythes, associated through potting with a common workshop. This network of artistic interconnections supports the hypothesis that the names of Smikros and Epilykos (as well as the names of their twin sisters) are familiar and attractive to the artists thanks to each other's vase-painting. Smikros and Epilykos are products of pictorial creativity, painterly competition, and cross-media emulation and rivalry.

Notes

1   On this question, see now M. Catoni, Bere vino puro. Immagini del simposio (2010) 111–215 and passim. For the invitation to participate in Athenian Potters and Painters III, I warmly thank John Oakley.
2   For evidence of sympotic context, see Archil. fr. 124W and 215W; Ar. Pax. 1298–1299; Arist. *Pol.* 1336 b 20–22; Hymn.Hom.Merc. 54–56; Theognis 309–312; adesp. eleg. 27 West, together with G. Nagy, Poetry as Performance. Homer and Beyond (1996) 218; I. Kantzios, in: D. Katsonopoulou – I. Petropoulos – S. Katsarou (eds.), Paros 2. Archilochos and His Age. Proceedings of the Second International Conference on the Archaeology of Paros and the Cyclades, Paroikia, Paros, 7–9 October 2005 (2008) 38–40; A. Rotstein, The Idea of Iambos (2010) 151–166. For rhapsodic re-performance, see D. Lavigne, Iambic Configurations. Iambos from Archilochus to Horace, Ph.D. diss. (Stanford University, 2005) 12–57.
3   Archil. test. 33 in Douglas E. Gerber, Greek Iambic Poetry. From the Seventh to the Fifth Centuries BC (1999). On this important testimonium, see R. Rosen, Making Mockery. The Poetics of Ancient Satire (2007) 243–255; Rotstein (supra n. 2) 305–317.
4   See M. West, Studies in Greek Elegy and Iambus (1974) 24–25 on the family's alleged involvement in cult.
5   Hippon. fr. 32, 36, 37W and C. Carey, in: F. Budelmann (ed.), The Cambridge Companion to Greek Lyric (2009) 162–165.
6   Arist. *Rh.* 1418 b 23–33. See K. J. Dover, in: Archiloque. Entretiens sur l'Antiquité Classique, 10 (1964) 206–208.
7   E.g. D. Lavigne, in: Paros 2 (supra n. 2) 91.
8   B. Seidensticker, GrRomByzSt 19, 1978, 5–22; R. Rosen, Eikasmos 1, 1990, 11–25.
9   E.g., Archil. test. 167 Gerber with fr. 168W on Charilaos, and test. 1 with fr. 117W on Glaukos son of Leptines.

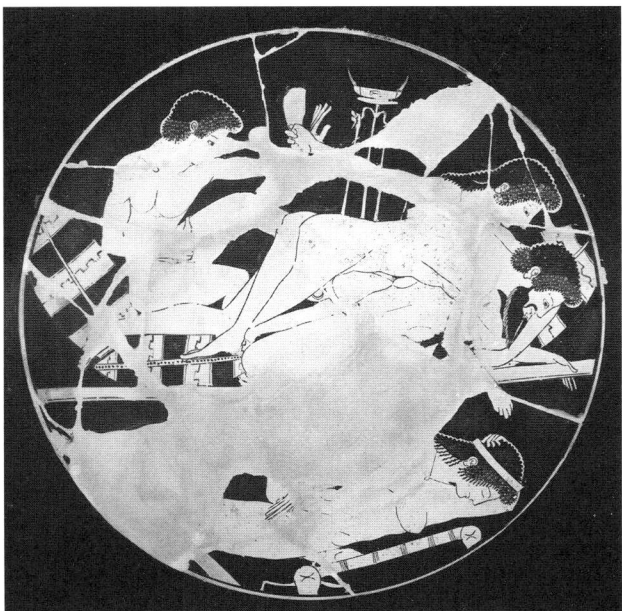

Fig. 11 Berlin, Antikensammlung V.I. 3251. Photo: Courtesy bpk Berlin/Antikensammlung/Art Resource NY.

10 G. Hedreen, in: V. Cazatto – D. Obbink – E. Prodi (eds.), The Cup of Song. Ancient Greek Poetry and the Symposion (forthcoming).
11 All of the signed vases are considered below except London E438, ARV² 20,3, BAPD 200104, which is too poorly preserved to provide useful information on the style of the painting. In shape, patternwork, and pictorial composition, however, it has good parallels within the work of Euphronios.
12 Once Malibu 81.AE.213, now Rome, Villa Giulia, BAPD 15527. For the signature, see below.
13 J. D. Beazley, Attische Vasenmalerei des rotfigurigen Stils (1925) 62.
14 D. Williams, in: V. Strocka (ed.), Meisterwerke. Internationales Symposion anläßlich des 150. Geburtstag von Adolf Furtwängler, Freiburg im Breisgau 30. Juni–3. Juli 2003 (2005) 281.
15 Brussels A717, ARV² 20,1, BAPD 200102.
16 C. Gaspar, MonPiot 9, 1902, 14–41. Arezzo 1465, ARV² 15,6, BAPD 200068.
17 Louvre G107, ARV² 18,1, BAPD 200088.
18 A. Furtwängler – K. Reichhold, Griechische Vasenmalerei (1900–1925) 2:6–13.
19 Munich 8935, ARV² 1619,3 bis, BAPD 275007.
20 On this point, and the many similarities, see D. Ohly, MüJb 22, 1971, 234.
21 Rome, Villa Giulia L.2006.10, BAPD 187. For the selective use of light-colored hair and eyes, as well as eyelashes, within the painting of Euphronios, see D. von Bothmer, in: Διαλέξεις 1986–1989 (1990) 34–35.
22 M. Ohly-Dumm, MüJb 24, 1974, 17–18. Amphora: Louvre G30, ARV² 15,9, BAPD 200071.
23 Bothmer (supra n. 21) 35–36.
24 R. Neer, Style and Politics in Athenian Vase-Painting. The Craft of Democracy, ca. 530–460 B.C.E. (2002) 116. Notice also the right hand attached to the left arm of the dancer looking to the left on the reverse of the vase in Paris (Louvre G110, Fig. 7) discussed below.
25 Dresden 295, ARV² 16,13, BAPD 200075.
26 I. Peschel, Die Hetäre bei Symposion und Komos in der attisch-rotfigurigen Vasenmalerei des 6.–4. Jahrhunderts vor Christus (1987) 376 n. 43.
27 Berlin 1966.19, Para 323,3bis, BAPD 352401.
28 On the parallels in shape, scheme of decoration, and subject matter, see L. Giuliani, in: E. Goemann et al. (eds.), Euphronios der Maler. Eine Ausstellung in der Sonderausstellungshalle der Staatlichen Museen Preußischer Kulturbesitz Berlin-Dahlem 20.3–26.5.1991 (1991) 254. For the silens, see New York 2001.563, BAPD 9017837, which provides a very close parallel for the drawing of the faces of the silens on the amphora in Berlin, apart from the eyelashes, which are an optional feature in Euphronian vase-painting.
29 See also A. Greifenhagen, JbBerlMus 9, 1967, 22: "on the Berlin amphora, 'the imitator' Smikros has caught especially well, with good understanding, the manner of Euphronios." Beazley, Para 323,3bis: "the drawing is very like Euphronios."
30 Louvre C11071, ARV² 15,10, BAPD 200072.
31 Neer (supra n. 24) 229 n. 109: S[mikro]s [e]graphse[n]. The reading is noted by Williams (supra n. 14) 281.
32 The light colored eye was already attested on the girl named Chorō on the stamnos in Brussels.
33 Malibu 82.AE.53, BAPD 30685.
34 The pertinence to the identification of the boy of the inscription Leagros kalos is persuasively argued by J. Boardman, in: M. Cygielman et al. (eds.), Euphronios. Atti del seminario internazionale di studi, Arezzo 27–28 Maggio 1990 (1992) 45–50.
35 Louvre G68, ARV² 21,6, BAPD 200107.
36 Malibu 83.AE.285, BAPD 13369; Rome, Villa Giulia, BAPD 28197. On the additions to the oeuvre of Smikros, see D. Williams, in: M. Denoyelle (ed), Euphronios peintre. Actes de la journée d'étude organisée par l'Ecole du Louvre et le départment des Antiquités grecques, étrusques et romaines du Musée du Louvre 10 octobre 1990 (1992) 87–90.
37 See P. Mingazzini, ASAtene 45–46, 1967, 336–337, who made this suggestion without, it seems, knowledge of the psykter. More refined attributions were made by Williams (supra n. 36) 92; Williams (supra n. 14) 280. See also B. Cohen, The Colors of Clay. Special Techniques in Athenian Vases (2006) 53 n. 40, who suggested that the Hegesiboulos Painter may have been responsible for the figures on the reserve.
38 For the attribution, see J. Frel, in: W. Moon (ed), Ancient Greek Art and Iconography (1983) 150. Against the attribution, see M. Robertson, Greek Vases in the J. Paul Getty Museum 5, 1991, 96; L. Giuliani (supra n. 28) 16.
39 For the back-view, cf. Berlin F2180, ARV² 13,1, BAPD 200063.
40 See J. D. Beazley, in: D. Kurtz (ed.), Greek Vases. Lectures by J. D. Beazley (1989) 51–54.
41 On the question of quality, cf. M. Robertson, The Art of Vase-Painting in Classical Athens (1992) 3–6.
42 Robertson (supra n. 41) 24. Louvre G103, ARV² 14,2, BAPD 200064.
43 Louvre G110, calyx krater, ARV² 14,3, BAPD 200065.
44 For the demonstrative adjective, see M. Denoyelle, in: Alain Pasquier et al. (eds.), Euphronios. Peintre à Athènes au VIe siècle avant J.-C. (1990) 60–66. There are precedents for the use of the demonstrative adjective: cf. the virtuoso verbosity of Neandros on Boston 61.1073, Para 69,3, BAPD 350341.
45 D. Maras, RdA 29, 2005, 149–154. Here, as on the neck amphora in Paris (Louvre G107 above, Fig. 3), the "rho" has been omitted from the name "Smikros." In both cases, the name appears to be spelled along the lines of the several well-attested variant spellings of the word smikros, such as mikos.
46 When Beazley first attributed the vase to Euphronios, in (supra n. 13) 59,3, all that existed was one of the komasts, plus part of the name Leag[ros]. The scene of Herakles and the Lion, which compares so readily with the signed painting of Euphronios, was not then known to Beazley, yet he saw the painter's hand in the komast alone (and perhaps in the kalos-name).
47 On the fragmentary phiale once in Malibu, signed by Douris as painter and listed above n. 12, the potter's signature was reported by D. Buitron-Oliver, Douris. A Master-Painter of Athenian Red-Figure Vases (1995) 74 no. 29, to read: [..]κρος [επο]ιεσεν ...ο]δε (with the possibility that the kappa is a chi). Robertson (supra n. 38) 92–93 restored the name as [Smi]kros. If Buitron-Oliver's reading is correct, the phiale offers another example of the use of

the demonstrative adjective to flag the signature as worthy of scrutiny. In the explicitness of the reference to this vase is the idea that Smikros did not make some (or any?) other vase. Although Robertson did not note the presence of the adjective, he seems to have entertained suspicions nevertheless. If Smikros actually made this phiale with his own hands "then Smikros shows himself a more talented potter than painter: the phiale fragments are of very fine technique indeed." C. Cardon, J. Paul Getty Museum Journal 6/7, 1978/1979, 137, has argued that phialai of this sort, which are very rare, originated in the workshop of the potter Euphronios. Is it plausible that an "imitator" of Euphronios might have perfectly acquired not only the master's style of painting but also the master's manner of potting a shape of such rarity, size, and delicacy? (See also Tsingarida in this volume).

48 See further in Hedreen (supra n. 10).
49 That would not be the only self-representation of Euphronios. On the fragmentary krater in Paris (Fig. 7), following the letters "Euphron," there was room to write the three letters, "ios," if "Euphronios" was what the artist wished to write. See Hedreen (supra n. 10) for details. The best explanation of the spacing and arrangement of all the letters in this area of the vase is that the name "Euphron" is complete as such and is the personal name of the wildly gyrating dancer. The vase-painter has identified himself as a figure within his own vase-painting – but only partially.
50 To my knowledge, only two significant descriptive differences between the styles of the vase-paintings signed by the two artists have been noted, the renderings of trochanters and pubic hair. See Williams (supra n. 36) 95 n. 58. I confess that I am unable to see those distinctions. I cannot see, for example, that the pubic hair of the silen on the amphora in Berlin (Fig. 5; Color Pl. 6) possesses less fluffy lightness than that of the figure of Sarpedon on the krater in the Villa Giulia signed by Euphronios.
51 Rome, Villa Giulia, ARV² 82,1, BAPD 200663; Paris, Louvre S1335+, ARV² 83,4, BAPD 200666; Rome, Villa Giulia 20760, ARV² 83,14, BAPD 200674; Paris, Louvre G12+, ARV² 84,17, BAPD 200677; New York, market, BAPD 41871, Hesperia Arts Auction, Ltd., Antiquities, New York, November 27, 1990, no. 115. There was a signature on Berlin 4041.1, ARV² 83,10, BAPD 200671, but the name is missing.
52 Brussels A1377, ARV² 134,2, wider circle of the Nikosthenes Painter, BAPD 201117. Though not mentioned by Beazley, the signature is recorded in CVA Brussels 2 Belgium 2, on pl. 10,2. See M. Schulz, Skythes und Pedieus-Maler. Zwei attische Vasenmaler im Werkstattzusammenhang, Ph.D. diss. (Ludwig Maximilians Universität München, 2001) 106.
53 Florence A B 1, ARV² 160, AMA Group, BAPD 200056. For the attribution, see J. Mertens, in: Papers on the Amasis Painter and His World (1987) 174.
54 Louvre F129, ARV² 84,20, BAPD 200430; Palermo V651, ARV² 85,21, BAPD 200431; Basel BS 458, BAPD 4473. On these cups, see B. Cohen, Attic Bilingual Vases and Their Painters, Ph.D. diss. (New York University, 1977) 513–519.
55 Athens, NM Acrop. 2557, ABV 352,1, BAPD 301989; Athens, NM Acrop. 2586, ABV 352,2, BAPD 301990. See also Athens, NM Acrop. 2556, ABV 352, BAPD 301991, with the dedication Σχύθες μ'ἀν[έθεκεν]. For the attribution of the plaques to the red-figure vase-painter Skythes, see Schulz (supra n. 52) 26–27.
56 For Skythes as potter, see Schulz (supra n. 52) 105–17.
57 Louvre G10, ARV² 83,3, BAPD 200665. Schulz (supra n. 52) 159, S19, reads the inscription [SKYTHES EGRAPH]SEN KALOS EPILYKO[S], but there is simply not room between the letters "Epilyko" and "sen" for all the letters needed to complete his reading. On this point, see S. Pevnick, Foreign Creations of the Athenian Kerameikos. Images and Identities in the Work of Pistoxenos-Syriskos, Ph.D. diss. (University of California at Los Angeles, 2011) 211–213, who includes a drawing of the inscription based on personal inspection.
58 Rome, Villa Giulia plus Toronto 923.13.11, ARV² 83,8, BAPD 200669.
59 ARV² 1578,1–14, plus nos. S10. 13. 37. 42. 43. 45. 47–49. 51. 56 in Schulz (supra n. 52).
60 On Epilykos the vase-painter, see E. Pottier, MonPiot 9, 1902, 135–178; G. Rizzo, MonPiot 20, 1913, 101–153.
61 See G. Rodenwaldt, AA, 1914, 87–90 and especially E. Buschor, JdI 30, 1915, 37–38. Beazley (ARV² 82–85) reviewed the entire problem and attributed all of the vases in question to Skythes. For the history of the scholarship, see Schulz (supra n. 52) 8–10.
62 Present location unknown, BAPD 9026229. A. Zampitē – V. Vasilopoulou, in: V. Aravantinos (ed.), Epetēris tēs etaireias Boiōtikōn meletōn, 4A, (2008) 453–455.
63 Perhaps the closest parallel in diction and in date is Florence 91456, a red-figure cup with coral-red ground, ARV² 108,27, BAPD 200931: Χαχρυλιον [επ]οεσεν καλος. The inscription was recently discussed by M. Iozzo, AntK, 55, 2012, 57–58. As can be seen in the excellent photograph in that essay, the word kalos is close enough in proximity to the verb epo<i>esen that someone might have taken the word kalos as an adverb modifying the verb: "Kachrylion painted this very well." Compare Athens, NM, Acrop. 833, black-gloss olpe fragment, ABV 170,2, BAPD 301083: Πρίαπος ἐποίεσεν καλōς, "Priapos made this very well." Similar inscriptions employing the word εὖ encourage reading kalos as an adverb: e.g., Civitavecchia, lip cup fragment, ABV 83, BAPD 300773: Νέαρχος [ἐποίεσε]ν εὖ, [Νέαρχος ἐπ]οίεσε[ν εὖ], "Nearchos made me well." Cf. Torlonia, lip cup, ABV 161,1, BAPD 310536; Boston 61.1073, band cup, Para 69–70,1, Neandros, BAPD 350341; Louvre F54, lip-cup, ABV 146,2, BAPD 310406. See also Basel, Herbert Cahn collection, HC 695 and 696, BAPD 45604 and 45603, two red-figure cup fragments that probably come from the same cup, Mertens (supra n. 53) 173 figs. 4a. b. On the latter fragment are the letters [A]ΜΑΣΙΣ. Schulz (supra n. 52) 157, S6 reads all of the letters on the former fragment [KA]LO[S] [AMASI]S EPOIE[SEN]. Perhaps significantly, the cup has been attributed to Skythes.
64 Aside from the two dozen vases attributed to Skythes, the kalos-name Epilykos occurs on two vases attributed to the Pedieus Painter, cups that Beazley considered to be so close in style to those of Skythes as to be perhaps the late work of the latter. Apart from those, there are just two vases bearing the kalos-name of Epilykos not attributable to Skythes or a follower: Louvre G11, fragmentary cup, ARV² 180, manner of the Carpenter Painter, BAPD

201649, which Beazley thought may have been shaped in the workshop of Skythes; Philadelphia, University Museum 3499, cup, ARV² 134,10, wider circle of the Nikosthenes Painter, BAPD 201125: *Eppilykos kalos* (not in CAVI: see G. Ferrari – B. Ridgway (eds.), Aspects of Ancient Greece [1979] 70).

65   See P. Fraser, in: S. Hornblower – E. Matthews (eds.), Greek Personal Names. Their Value as Evidence (2000) 152–153.

66   E.g., see D. Williams, in: A. Verbanck-Piérard – D. Viviers (eds.), Culture et cité. L'avènement d'Athènes à l'époque archaïque (1995) 139–160.

67   See, e.g., the survey in D. Robinson – E. Fluck, A Study of the Greek Love-Names (1937) 66–191.

68   A short list was provided by Buschor (supra n. 61) 39–40. He believed that praise of a painter or potter actually occurred only on Palermo V655, ARV² 113,3, Thalia Painter, BAPD 200960: ΧΑ[ΧΡΥΛ]ΙΟΝ ΚΑΛ[Ο]Σ. But there are other possibilities, such as Andokides (ABV 664 + ARV² 1), Nikosthenes (ABV 671 + ARV² 122), and Megakles (ARV² 1555. 1598–1599).

69   Berlin 1966.20, Para 508, BAPD 340207. For the attribution to Euphronios, see Ohly-Dumm (supra n. 22) 25 n. 55.

70   Munich 2421, ARV² 23,7, BAPD 200126.

71   See J. K. Davies, Athenian Propertied Families: 600–300 B. C. (1971) 296–298; H. A. Shapiro, Hesperia 52, 1983, 305–310.

72   It is perhaps worth noting that the root-word *lykos*, "wolf," is also the root-word of one of the best known antagonists in Archilochean iambic poetry, Lykambes, the "wolf-walker."

73   The name "Epilykē" is unattested in LGPN apart from this one vase inscription.

74   St. Petersburg 644, ARV² 16,15, BAPD 200078.

75   See Ar. Pax 896–904 and Peschel (supra n. 26) 78.

76   Brussels R351, ARV² 31,7, BAPD 200192. On the occasional suggestion that *Seklinē* is an abbreviation of Σηκυλίνη, an ethnic name, see J. Frel, RdA 20, 1996, 51 n. 24.

77   Berlin 3251, ARV² 113,7, Thalia Painter, BAPD 200964. In addition to the cup in Berlin, there is an inscription σμικρὰ ἱερά on the handle of a merrythought cup, IG I³ 577. It is not certain, however, that σμικρὰ is a noun and not an adjective. If it is a proper noun, the woman would be a priestess and presumably not a party-girl. There is also a dedicatory inscription, Σμίκρα ἀνέθηκεν, on a fourth-century votive plaque from Pikermi, IG II² 4926.

78   For the identification of the girl's activity, see Greifenhagen (supra n. 29) 25 n. 82; O. Brendel, in: T. Bowie – C. Christenson (eds.), Studies in Erotic Art (1970) 24 n. 22; Peschel (supra n. 26) 52; L. Kurke, ClAnt 16, 1997, 134.

79   For the reading, see ARV² 113.

80   Σμίκκη is attested in a third-century list of dedications to Asklepios (IG II² 1534B) according to LGPN. Μίκα is a well-attested Attic name, e.g., Ar. Thesm. 760.

81   For the restoration of the inscription, see J. Frel, RivArch 20, 1996, 48 n. 6. He reports that Robert Guy identified a fragment in the Villa Giulia (ARV² 440,169, BAPD 205214) as completing the retrograde letters E[...]κος on the Berlin cup. The fragment is reported to contain the letters]ILL[(retrograde), and the name of the male figure was thus restored by Guy as Epilykos. Judging from the photograph available at BAPD, the sherd corresponds in outline to the appropriate lacuna. The sherd shows that Epilykos carried a short knobby stick, and the girl in front of him, a kylix.

82   Frel (supra n. 81) 38. The name Epilykos also appears to identify a bearded trainer on a psykter attributed to Phintias: Boston 01.8019, ARV² 24,11, BAPD 200134. For the problem of identifying the bearded figures labelled Epilykos, and the Epilykos praised as *kalos*, with a single historical individual, see Beazley, CB II 3–4; Shapiro (supra n. 71) 308.

83   E.g., Paris, Cab. Méd. 509, plate, ARV² 77,91, signed by Epiktetos, BAPD 200618. On the association of this sort of utilitarian modification of the penis with silens rather than mortal men, see F. Lissarrague, in: D. Halperin – J. Winkler – F. Zeitlin (eds.), Before Sexuality. The Construction of Erotic Experience in the Ancient Greek World (1990) 58.

84   See G. Hedreen, ClAnt, 25, 2006, 277–284.

85   Malibu 85.AE.188, Kleophrades Painter, BAPD 43417.

86   For a list of occurrences of the motif in Athenian vase-painting, see J. Boardman, AA, 1976, 286–287.

87   For the interpretation of the action, see Brendel (supra n. 78) 23–24; Peschel (supra n. 26) 53. The reservations of K. Dover, Greek Homosexuality (1978) 102 seem motivated by the idea that the practice was held in such contempt in Old Comedy that its occurrence in art is inherently unlikely; but he does not offer any alternative explanation of what the man is doing to the woman.

88   For the reading, see Greifenhagen, CVA Berlin 2 Germany 21 14.

89   Munich 2309, ARV² 27,4, BAPD 200157.

90   See L. Giuliani, in: I. Wehgartner (ed.), Euphronios und Seine Zeit. Kolloquium in Berlin 19./20. April 1991 (1992) 118–119 with further references.

91   Frel (supra n. 81) 38–39.

92   The exception is the inscription Κορώνη on a stele of the fourth century BC (IG II² 11893). The name Korōnē occurs on two other Athenian vases of this period: New York 1971.258.2, ABV 677,1, BAPD 306481, related in style perhaps to the work of Euphronios: Frel (supra n. 81) 48 n. 9; Lyon 75, ABL 229,2, ABV 677,2, BAPD 305516: goddess mounting a chariot, Apollo, a fawn, and the inscription *Koro(n)ē kalē philō*, "I love beautiful Korōnē." In the former, the placement of the inscription suggests that it identifies one of the Amazons by name. In the latter, the inscription occurs in a zone under the picture, and therefore may be unrelated to the image. It is worth recalling, however, that Apollo once loved a beautiful girl named Koronis.

93   E.g., the Chreiai of the Hellenistic writer Machon, in which courtesans exchange witty remarks with their partners and each other (Ath. 583a =Machon 435 Gow). Or the Peri hetairōn of the fourth-century writer Antiphanes of Thrace (Ath. 587b). See also Menander's Kolaki (Ath. 587e).

94   Archil. fr. 331 West, quoted in Ath. 594c–d: "[l]ike a fig tree on rocky ground that feeds many crows (κορώνας), good-natured Pasiphilē [lit., loved by all] takes on strangers." The fragment is listed as dubious by West (supra n. 4) 139–140, partly because of its style and partly because Athenaios connects the reference to a fourth-century courtesan named Plangon. But see Dover (supra n. 6) 185 n. 1: "I suspect that κορώνη must be added to Archilochos's numerous terms for 'prostitute'."

7 Facing West: Athenian Influence on Isolated Heads in Italian Red-Figure Vase-painting

Keely Elizabeth Heuer

During the fourth century BC the isolated head was the predominant decorative motif in South Italian, Etruscan, and Alto-Adriatic vase-painting (Fig. 1; Color Pl. 7).[1] Serving as primary and secondary decoration, most heads are female, but those of youths, mature males, satyrs, Pan, winged figures, and individuals wearing Phrygian caps occur. The motif's flowering is part of a predilection in the region for isolated heads starting in the late tenth century BC[2] and was manifested in various media, including gold jewelry, carved amber heads, as well as terracotta antefixes and votive protomes. In contrast, heads represented apart from the body, with the exception of the gorgoneion, are not prominent in mainland Greek art. However, painted and plastic isolated heads began to occur on Attic vases as early as ca. 600–575 BC (Fig. 2). The motif, relatively uncommon on the products of the Athenian Kerameikos, is usually concentrated in specific workshops and often applied to particular shapes. Furthermore, it appears to have been intentionally selected for export goods,[3] especially to Italy, where roughly half of the Attic vases decorated with heads of known provenience were found.[4] The earliest pieces were uncovered in the vicinity of Greek settlements, such as Paestum and Taranto,[5] but nearly three-quarters come from Italic and Etruscan contexts, attesting to the particular resonance of the image with the indigenous population.[6] Native interest in the motif is further supported by the fact that the majority of red-figure vases decorated with heads produced on the Italian peninsula and Sicily during the fourth century BC were made and consumed in areas not under Greek control. This paper explores the question of imported Attic vases as the inspiration for the use of the isolated head in South Italian, Etruscan and Alto-Adriatic vase-painting.

For centuries, Greek settlers and native peoples of Italy imported most of their painted vases from the Greek mainland, particularly from Athens. Local production was limited in scale and duration.[7] However, in the mid fifth century BC, the red-figure technique was transferred from Athens to southern Italy, the earliest evidence of which comes from kilns at Metaponto.[8] Within a generation, pottery workshops were likely established in Taranto,[9] and by the end of the century red-figure vases were created on Sicily and at Vulci and Falerii in Etruria. Shifting trade relations due to the Peloponnesian War resulted in a steady decrease of Athenian vases to southern Italy, Sicily, and Etruria during the latter part of the fifth century BC.[10] In fact, Attic vases decorated with heads dating after ca. 430 BC are concentrated in ports along the Adriatic coast, particularly Spina, an Etruscan trade emporium.[11]

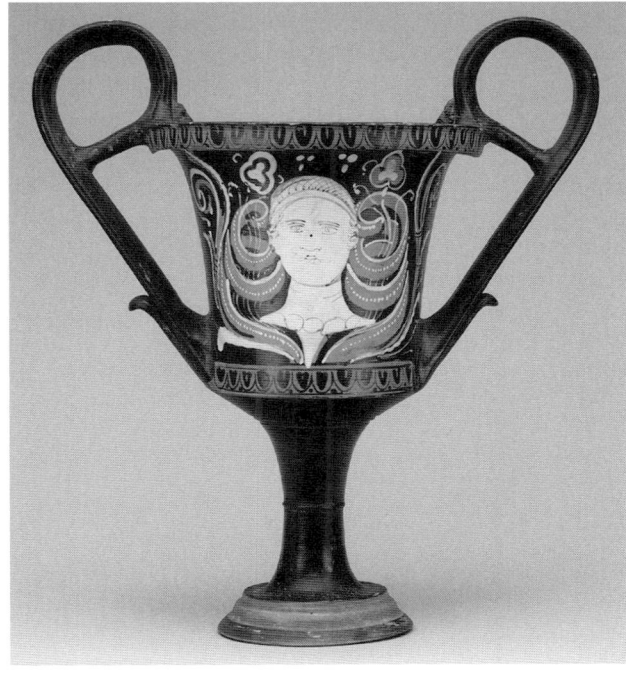

Fig. 1 New York, Metropolitan Museum of Art 06.1021.233, Apulian kantharos, Painter of Bari 5981, ca. 325–300 BC, from Canosa (Image © The Metropolitan Museum of Art).

The limited availability of Attic vases greatly spurred the growth of South Italian and Etruscan red-figure workshops, whose products were increasingly viewed as viable replacements for Athenian imports.

The earliest South Italian vases exhibit strong ties with contemporary Athenian workshops in their shape, iconography, and style of drawing.[12] But at the turn of the century, South Italian vase-painting began to diverge from its Attic models, resulting in the development of its innovative imagery and distinctive iconographic preferences. Isolated heads on South Italian vases are part of this phenomenon, with the earliest examples dating to the last decade of the fifth century. One is a fragmentary Apulian kylix from Gioia del Colle featuring a female head in three-quarter view to left with striking cat-like eyes (Fig. 3).[13] Heads occur on Athenian cups, but they generally appear on the exterior and date to the second half of the sixth century BC.[14] Rare in the tondi of Attic cups, heads are first seen on Siana cups of the second quarter of the sixth century.[15] An elegant female head drawn in outline decorates the tondo of a kylix (ca. 500 BC) discovered at Orvieto,[16] and heads are seen again in the interior of Attic cups only after 440 BC, when they were sometimes painted in profile in the tondi of stemless cups. Three such cups were found in Italy: two at Spina[17] and one in Etruria,[18] neither in close proximity to Apulia, where the Gioia del Colle cup was made. Heads within a circular ornamental frame were common on a type of Attic stemmed plate produced in the last third of the fifth century BC,[19] likely created by a single workshop in imitation of similar shapes in Etruscan bucchero and impasto (Fig. 4).[20] Like the stemless cups, these plates decorated with profile heads have not been uncovered in southern Italy. Rather, they were exported exclusively to the northern Adriatic coast, especially Spina.[21] Another early South Italian vase decorated with an isolated head is a barrel discovered at Locri with a female head in profile on one of its round ends.[22] The vase's low, elongated shape is unusual in South Italian vase-painting and is without an equivalent in Attica. Perhaps the closest counterpart in Athenian vase-painting to the barrel's female head set in a small round space are the occasional heads of women on the lids of Type B and D pyxides,[23] none of which have Italian provenance.

It was not until 380 BC that heads began to repeatedly appear on South Italian vases, when the very low number of Attic imports to the region makes it unlikely that South Italian vase-painters had access to contemporary Athenian vases decorated with the motif. Earlier Attic vases kept as

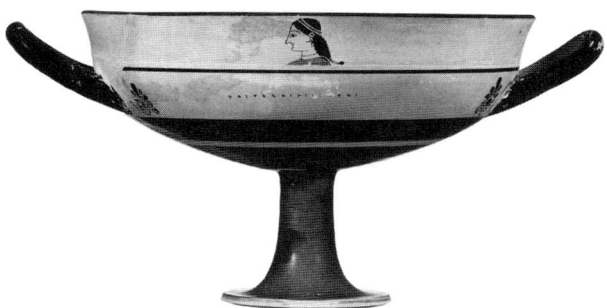

Fig. 2 Munich, Staatliche Antikensammlungen 2165, Attic lip cup, Sakonides, ca. 550–530 BC, from Vulci (photograph provided by the Staatliche Antikensammlungen und Glyptothek München)

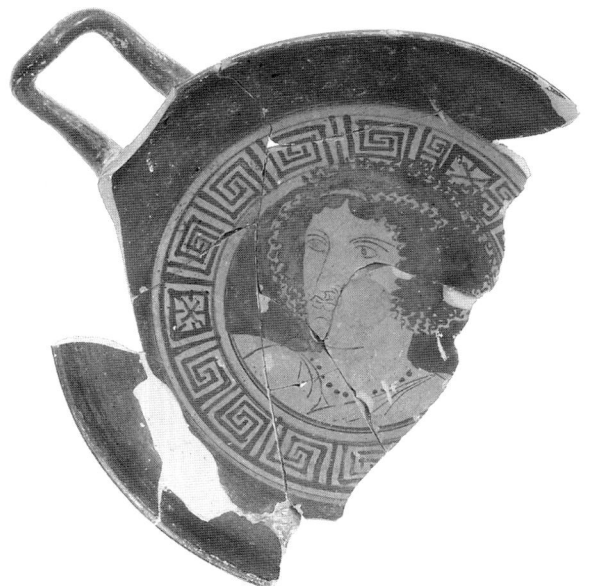

Fig. 3 Gioia del Colle, Museo Archeologico Nazionale MG 337–338. 340. 355, Apulian type B kylix, Sisyphus Painter, ca. 410–400 BC, from tomb 104–108 at Monte Sannace (image courtesy of the Trendall Research Centre for Ancient Mediterranean Studies, La Trobe University)

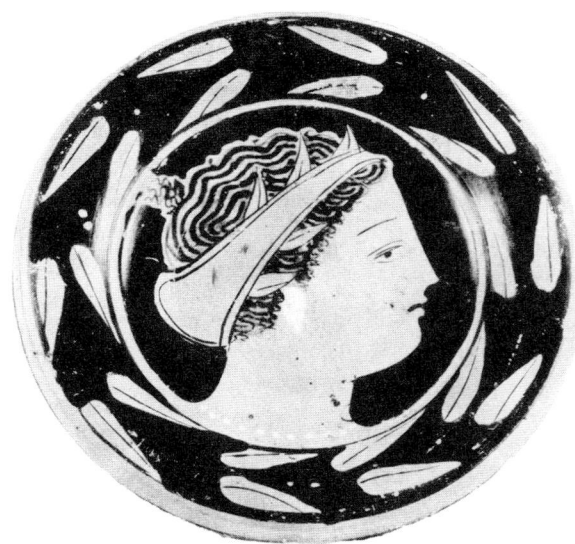

Fig. 4 Ferrara, Museo Nazionale di Spina VP 143A, Attic stemmed plate, late fifth century BC, from Spina (image after CVA Ferrara 1 Italy 37 pl. 44,4)

heirlooms or circulated via the secondhand market might have served as models. No clear stylistic similarities between heads on South Italian vases and the work of Athenian painters can be found, but such ties do exist for heads painted on Etruscan vases. The earliest examples of the motif in Etruscan red-figure date to the second quarter of the fourth century BC,[24] and, as on Attic vases, heads are most frequently painted on particular shapes, such as Genucilia plates,[25] Torcop oinochoai, Clusium Group duck askoi,[26] and Volterran kelebai.[27]

The heads on the earliest Genucilia plates, painted by the Berkeley Genucilia Painter, have details that resemble the facial features, profiles, and headdresses of full-length females in the work of the Meidias and Jena Painters.[28] For example, compare the head on Berkeley 8/992[29] (Fig. 5) to the heads of the full-length women on the Meidias Painter's name vase in London[30] or the head of Aphrodite on Jena 0477 by the Jena Painter.[31] The Jena Painter included isolated heads in his iconographic corpus, namely in the tondi of four stemless cups, two of which are in Jena and were found in Athens.[32] Even the shape of the Genucilia plate vaguely resembles the Attic stemmed plates decorated with heads with their high stems and encircling groove that frames the flaring rim. However, the Spina plates are larger and lack the heavy, overhanging lip of the Genucilia plates.[33] Del Chiaro initially attempted to connect the Attic stemmed plates of the late fifth century with the Faliscan branch of the Genucilia Group, a tie that consequently proved to be untenable when he reassessed the chronology of the Genucilia plates and assigned them to the last third of the fourth century BC,[34] nearly three-quarters of a century later than the Attic vases with which they bear stylistic similarities. In addition, no Attic stemmed plates decorated with a head has been found further west than Bologna, well over 200 miles from either center of Genucilia plate production.

A similar chronological and geographic divide can be found between the oinochoai of the Torcop Group and an oinochoe from Spina by the Makaria Painter, an associate of the Meidias Painter (Fig. 6).[35] The Makaria Painter's oinochoe bears affinity to the Torcop Group in its shape (oinochoe, shape VII) and the placement of a female head in profile on the neck.[36] Torcop oinochoai typically feature three female heads wearing kekryphaloi and a multi-rayed diadem – one in profile on the neck and two confronting heads on the body, between which are objects, such as the so-called "suspended wreath," a patera, a vertical floral

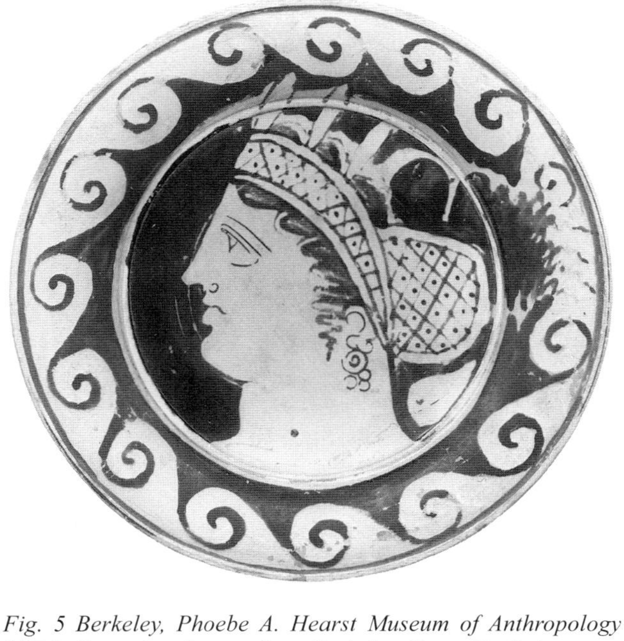

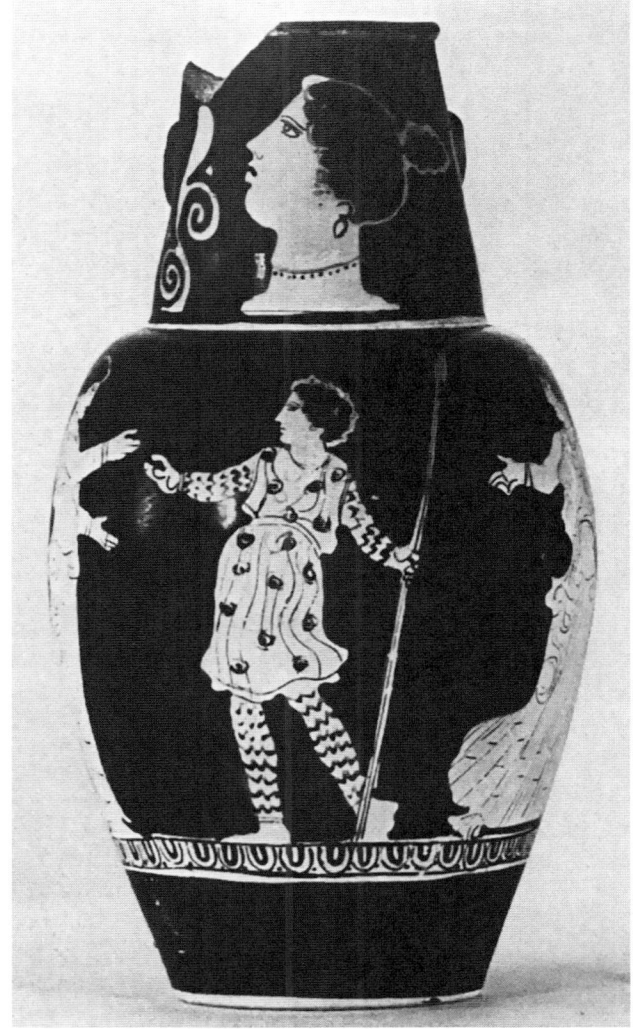

Fig. 5 Berkeley, Phoebe A. Hearst Museum of Anthropology 8/992, Genucilia Group plate, Berkeley Genucilia Painter, ca. 330 BC (Image © Phoebe A. Hearst Museum of Anthropology and the Regents of the University of California)

Fig. 6 Ferrara, Museo Nazionale di Spina 2497, Attic oinochoe (type VII), Makaria Painter, late fifth century BC, from tomb 652 Valle Trebba, Spina (Image after A. Lezzi-Hafter, Der Schuwalow-Maler. Eine Kannenwerkstatt der Parthenonzeit [1976] pl. 157b) tendril, a palmette, or even an altar (Fig. 7).[37] The Torcop Group postdates the Attic piece by at least seventy years, and there is no evidence of trade between Caere, the site of Torcop Group production, and Spina. Confronted heads are found on a variety of fourth-century Attic shapes including squat lekythoi, askoi, oinochoai (shape 2) and lekanides, but none have been discovered in the vicinity of Caere.[38]

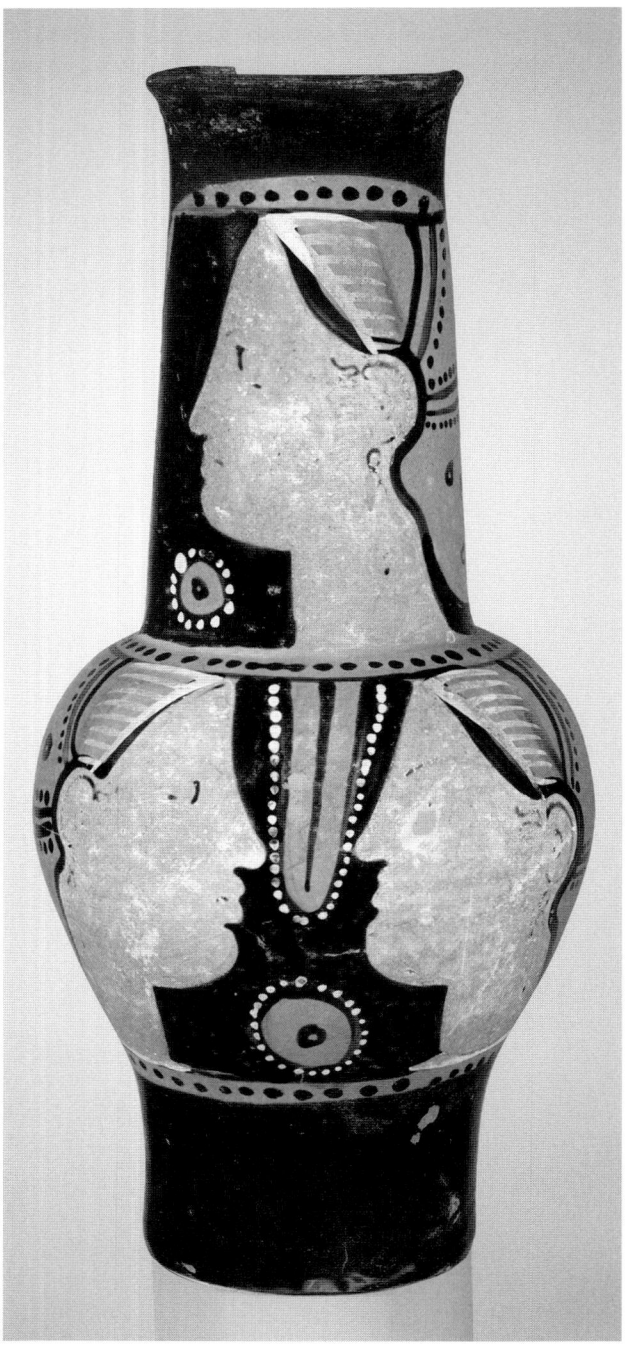

Fig. 7 New York, Metropolitan Museum of Art 91.1.465, Torcop Group oinochoe, ca. 300 BC (Image © The Metropolitan Museum of Art)

Importation of Attic vases to Spina and Adria continued during the mid-fourth century, when Alto-Adriatic workshops were established at both sites.[39] Nevertheless, heads on Alto-Adriatic calyx-kraters,[40] bell-kraters,[41] lekanides,[42] oinochoai,[43] and skyphoi[44] of the second half of the fourth century BC lack definitive links to specific Attic vase-painters or workshops to my knowledge. The painting of heads on stemmed plates made exclusively at Numana may have been inspired by similar Attic pieces, a few of which have been uncovered there, but they are at least fifty years apart in date.[45]

Based on the current chronologies for South Italian, Etruscan, and Alto-Adriatic vase-painting and known proveniences of Attic vases with heads, red-figure vase-painters working on the Italian peninsula and Sicily do not appear to have ever directly copied their heads from Athenian vases. They may have borrowed the motif's concept from earlier Attic vases still accessible to them, which could explain the chronological gaps for Etruscan vases decorated with painted heads that have stylistic resemblances to fifth-century Attic pieces. Most likely the use of the motif on South Italian vases facilitated its acceptance into Etruscan and Alto-Adriatic vase iconography during the second half of the fourth century BC. Few South Italian vases decorated with heads have been uncovered in Etruscan and Adriatic contexts, but two Apulian kantharoi of the late fourth century with a female head on each side were discovered in tomb 505C in Valle Pega at Spina.[46]

Apulian, Campanian, and Paestan influences have been noted in Etruscan and Alto-Adriatic vase-painting, such as Beazley's "Campanianizing Group,"[47] which may be due to the northward migration of vase-painters and potters from these southern Italian regions. Striking parallels may be found between vases decorated with heads in southern Italy and those of Etruria and the Adriatic coast. For example, the female head in three quarter view in the tondo of the Gioia delle Colle cup, discussed previously (Fig. 3), bears a striking resemblance to that found on Tarquinia Inv. RC 3391, a Faliscan kylix dated to ca. 380–370 BC (Fig. 8).[48] Similar heads rising from acanthus calyxes and surrounded by floral tendrils appear on both Apulian and Chiusine vases.[49] Confronted heads on Campanian and Sicilian vases find parallels in the Etruscan Torcop and Barbano Groups.[50] The motif's likely point of transference between the southern and northern halves of the Italian peninsula is Campania, which was once partially settled by Etruscans, such as at Capua and Nola.[51] By the late fifth century BC, the region fell to the Oscan-speaking Samnites, but Etruscan elements survived, particularly at Pontecagnano. Two of the Campanian vase-painting schools defined by Trendall were located in Capua, which produced hundreds of vases decorated with heads found in the city's tombs and the necropoleis of nearby sites with Etruscan roots.[52] Another northward route possibly taken by the motif from southern Italy and Sicily was along the eastern coastline of the Italian peninsula after the policies of Dionysius I of Syracuse brought the Adriatic into the Italiote and Sicilian

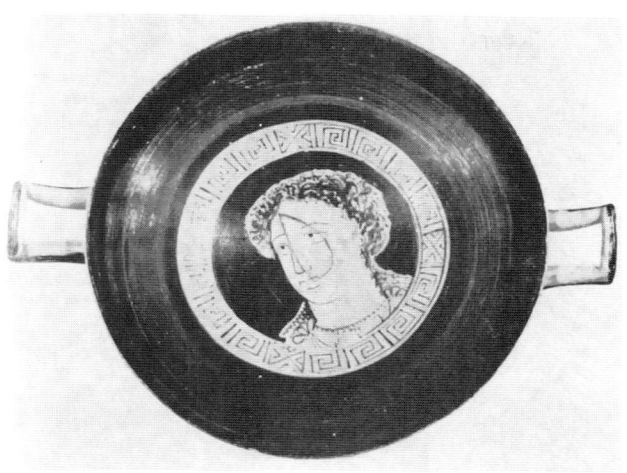

Fig. 8 Tarquinia, Museo Archeologico Nazionale Tarquiniense Inv. RC 3391, Faliscan kylix, ca. 370–360 BC, from Tarquinia (photograph provided by the Soprintendenza per i Beni Archeologici dell'Etruria meridionale, Archivo fotografico, Roma)

sphere of interest.[53] Additionally, the Etruscan presence on the Adriatic coastline at Spina may have made Etruscan vases with heads available to Alto-Adriatic vase-painters.[54]

Attic plastic head vases, exported to the west between ca. 520 and 390 BC, more directly influenced their Italian counterparts.[55] In the early fifth century BC, local imitations of contemporary Attic plastic head vases (e.g. the London and Marseilles Classes) were produced in the Etruscan settlements of Campania, where large numbers of Attic plastic head vases have been found.[56] In southern Italy, the earliest plastic head vases were made in Apulia ca. 370–355 BC in the workshop of the Iliupersis Painter.[57] These Apulian kantharoi, often janiform heads of women and satyrs (a common pairing on Attic plastic vases), have strong stylistic and technical similarities to the Athenian Spetia and Persian Classes,[58] which are only a decade or two older and have been found in Apulia at Ruvo as well as in the Basilicata and at Nola in Campania (Figs. 9. 10; Color Pl. 8).[59] The faces of both the Attic and Apulian pieces are painted white, on top of which polychromy was

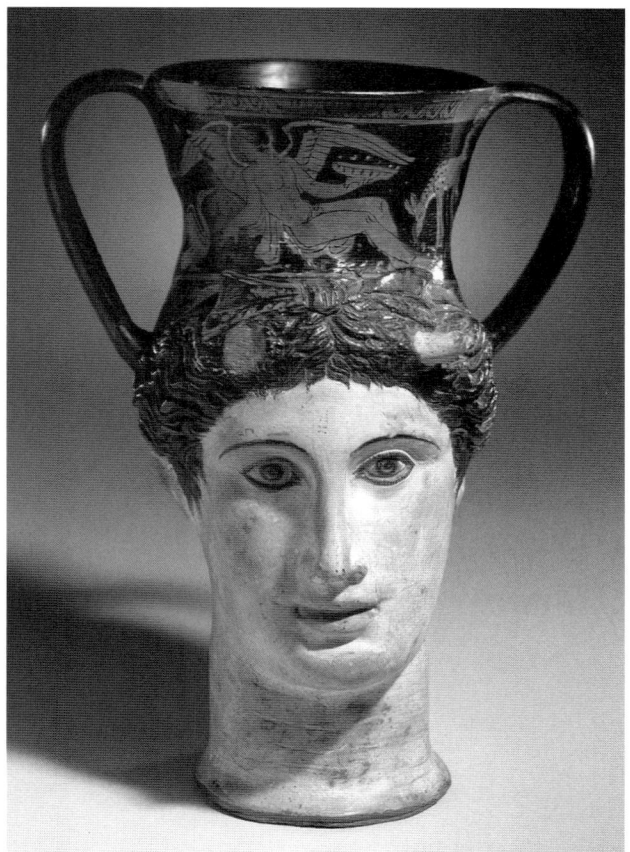

Fig. 9 Los Angeles, Los Angeles County Museum of Art 50.8.25, Apulian plastic head kantharos of a female faun or Io, Iliupersis Painter, ca. 370–355 BC (Photograph: © Los Angeles County Museum of Art)

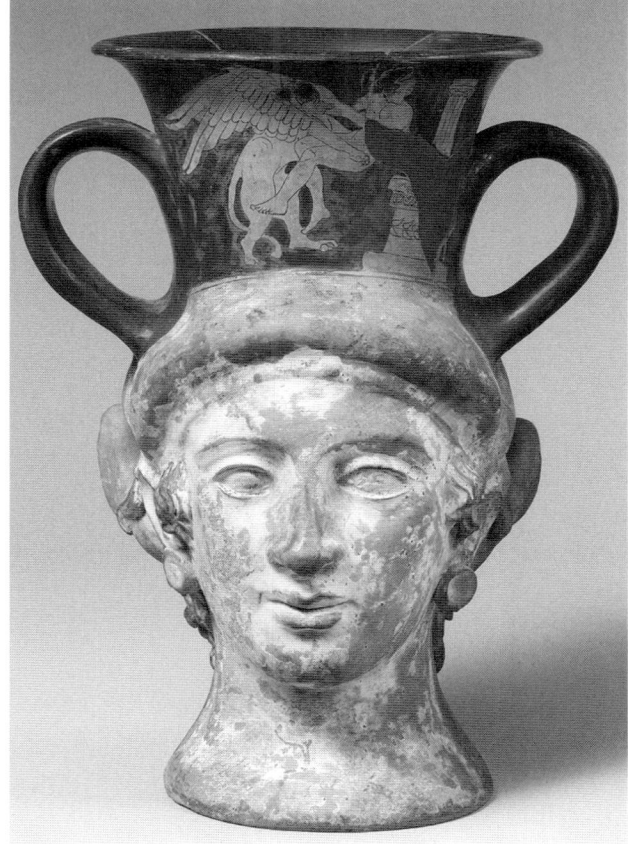

Fig. 10 New York, Metropolitan Museum of Art 21.88.64, Attic plastic janiform head kantharos of a satyr and woman, Class W (Persian Class) of Head Vases, late fifth century BC, said to be from Anzi, Basilicata (Image © The Metropolitan Museum of Art)

applied. The vases of the Iliupersis Painter's workshop were the forerunners of the later Apulian polychrome head vases, usually in the form of oinochoai, that were made throughout the second half of the fourth century and enjoyed particular popularity in Canosa until the early decades of the third.[60] Beazley noted that satyr heads, like that of the Attic janiform kantharoi New York 27.122.9 of the Spetia Group and New York 21.88.64 of the Persian Group, found particular favor with Apulian potters after 350 BC.[61] Etruscan plastic head vases of the second half of the fourth century BC produced in Chiusi and Falerii have satyr and female heads clearly related to those of late Attic plastic head vases,[62] but this Athenian influence probably was transmitted via southern Italy as Attic plastic head vases of the late fifth and early fourth centuries have not been found in Etruria. Other parallels in physiognomic features exist between Attic plastic head vases and their South Italian and Etruscan counterparts, such as vases in the form of African heads[63] or the Sotades mug found at Spina and the Etruscan Charun vase in Munich,[64] but the significant time gap between their manufacture (at least 50–100 years) has yet to be explained.[65]

The heavy concentration of Attic vases decorated with painted and plastic isolated heads dating between ca. 575 and 400 BC on the Italian peninsula and Sicily suggests that use of the image was, at least in part, fueled by the Athenian Kerameikos' awareness of Etruscan and Italic interest in the subject. The earliest Etruscan plastic head vases of the early fifth century and South Italian plastic head vases of the second quarter of the fourth century are clearly inspired by slightly earlier or contemporary Attic products. Less straightforward is the extent of Attic influence on the practice of painting isolated heads on South Italian, Etruscan, and Alto-Adriatic vases of the fourth century BC due to geographic and chronological discontinuities in the surviving archaeological record. The first South Italian vase-painters did not paint isolated heads on vases. Rather, the motif first appears during the late fifth century BC, coinciding with dwindling exports of Attic vases to Magna Graecia and Etruria. If South Italian vases with painted heads were originally intended to replace Attic products, it is noteworthy that western vase-painters chose to apply the motif to new shapes and did not stylistically copy their Attic predecessors. Instead, by the second quarter of the fourth century BC, they created new iconographic meaning for the image by combining it with funerary imagery.[66] In turn, the frequent use of the motif by Apulian, Campanian, and Paestan workshops likely led to its adoption by Etruscan and Alto-Adriatic painters in the mid fourth century.

Notes

1 For example, painted heads appear on over one-third of the surviving corpus of South Italian vases, more than 7,400 published examples. For further information, see K. E. Heuer, The Development and Significance of the Isolated Head in South Italian Vase-Painting, Ph.D. diss. (New York University, 2011).

2 Heads carved of local stone were placed on top of tombs in Daunia (northern Apulia) from the late tenth through the eight centuries BC: E. M. De Juliis, La rappresentazione figurata in Daunia (2009) 61–64; E. M. De Juliis, in: M. Mazzei (ed.), La Daunia antica: dalla preistoria all'altomedioevo (1984) 142–145.

3 Eighty-four percent of the 810 Attic vases featuring a painted or plastic head with known provenience were uncovered outside of Attica. Note that all statistics in this paper regarding Attic vases are based upon the contents of the BADB as of July 31 2012.

4 379 pieces (47%).

5 E.g. the black-figure oinochoe Taranto 6504 (ABV 10,2).

6 278 Attic vases with heads were discovered in non-Greek settlements in Italy and Sicily, 73% of the total found in the region. This number increases to 282 pieces if one includes the pieces found at Cumae that date after the Oscan conquest in 421 BC. Etruscan contexts include not only Etruria, but also the Etruscan settlements in Campania (e.g. Capua) and in the Po River valley (Bologna, Spina, etc.). For Attic vases at Etruscan sites, refer to M. Bentz – C. Reusser (eds.), Attische Vasen in etruskischem Kontext. Funde aus Häusern und Heiligtümern (2004); C. Reusser, Vasen für Etrurien (2002); A. Nilsson, Analecta Romana 26, 1999, 7–23; F. Curti, in: Studi sulla necropoli di Spina in Valle Trebba, Convegno 15 ottobre 1992 (1993) 133–154; L. Hannestad, Acta Archaeologica 59, 1999, 113–130.

7 For Etruscan painted vases prior to the late fifth century BC, turn to J. D. Beazley, Etruscan Vase Painting (1947) 11–24; L. Hannestad, The Paris Painter: An Etruscan Vase-Painter (1974); L. Hannestad, The Followers of the Paris Painter (1976); N. J. Spivey, The Micali Painter and His Followers (1987), J. G. Szilágyi, La ceramica etrusco-corinzia figurata Vol. 1 630–580 a.C. (1992); M. Micozzi, "White on Red": Una produzione vascolare dell'orientalizzante etrusco (1994); and J. G. Szilágyi, La ceramica etrusco-corinzia figurate, vol. 2 590/580–550 a.C. (1998). For locally produced black-figure vases in southern Italy and Sicily, refer to M. Denoyelle – M. Iozzo, La céramique grecque d'Italie méridionale et de Sicile (2009) 33–95 and A. Rumpf, Chalkidische Vasen (1927).

8 Theories regarding the origins of South Italian vase-painting are discussed in: A. Furtwängler, Meisterwerke der griechischen Plastik (1893) 149–152; LCS 3; RVAp I 16; M. Denoyelle, in: APP 395–405; F. Guidice – S. Barresi, in: B. Schmaltz – M. Söldner (eds.), Griechische Keramik im kulturellen Kontext. Akten des Internationalen Vasen-Symposions in Kiel vom 24.–28.9.2001 (2003) 280–286; and F. Guidice – I. G. Rizzo, in: G. Sena Chiesa – E. A. Arslan (eds.), Miti Greci: archeologia e pittura dalla Magna Grecia al collezionismo (2004) 137–141.

9 Thomas Carpenter points out that the lack of early Apulian vases associated with kilns in Taranto suggests that production might have been elsewhere, such as in Peucetia, where there were strong trade connections between Italic settlements and Athens throughout the fifth century BC (AJA 113, 2009, 29–31). The assumption of early Apulian vase production based in Taranto is also discussed by Jed Thorn (Antiquity 83, 2009, 174–183).

10 For the decline in Attic vase exports to southern Italy and Sicily: F. Guidice, in: N. Bonacasa – L. Braccesi – E. De Miro (eds.), La Sicilia dei due Dionisi, Atti della settimana di studio, Agrigento 24–28 febbraio 1999 (2002) 107; F. Giudice – S. Barresi, in: Schmaltz – Söldner (supra n. 8) 283; W. Johannowsky, in: Adriatico tra IV e III sec. a.C. Vasi alto-adriatici tra Piceno, Spina e Adria. Atti del convegno di studi Ancona, 20–21 giugno 1997 (Rome) 150–152.

11 Ancient sources give conflicting origins for Spina, some stating that it was a Greek foundation, either settled by the Pelasgians or by the Homeric hero Diomedes, while others emphasize the site's Etruscan roots. The discovery of an oblong stone incised with a cross and the Etruscan inscription *mi tular* ("I [am] the boundary") at the intersection of two roads, suggests Etruscan rites were used in the foundation of the settlement. Refer to D. Baldoni, Museo archeologico nazionale di Ferrara (2001) 93–95; S. Haynes, Etruscan Civilization (2000) 193. A few fourth-century Attic vases decorated with heads made their way to Campania and Basilicata, such as an oinochoe now in the National Museum in Warsaw (CVA Goluchow 1 Poland 1 pl. 41,6; ARV² 1493,20) and the bell-krater Naples 82753 by the Painter of Rodin 966 (ARV² 1449,4).

12 Trendall points out ties between the Pisticci and Amykos Painters, the earliest Lucanian vase-painters, and some of the followers of the Achilles Painter as well as members of the Polygnotan Group, such as the Christie Painter, the Cassel Painter, and the Painter of the Louvre Centauromachy (LCS 3–5). He further notes the close parallels between the earliest Apulian vases and works of the Polygnotan school, the Kleophon Painter, and the Dinos Painter. (RVAp I 4) See also A. D. Trendall, in: J.-P. Descoeudres – A. D. Trendall (eds.), Greek Colonists and Native Populations. Proceedings of the First Australian Congress of Classical Archaeology, Sydney 9–14 July 1985 (1990) 218–219.

13 Gioia del Colle, Museo Archeologico Nazionale MG 337–338, 340, 355 from tomb 104–108 at Monte Sannace – CVA Gioia del Colle 1 Italy 68 pl. 38,1–3.

14 Heads occur on the exterior of Attic Siana cups of the second quarter of the sixth century BC (e.g. New York 12.234.2 – CVA Metropolitan Museum of Art 2 USA 11 pl. 4). Soon after, Sakonides began to paint outline profile heads on Little Master lip cups, and similar heads are found on cups potted by Hermogenes and Phrynos. Examples include: Munich 2165 by Sakonides (ABV 171,1; BAdd² 48; CVA Munich 10 Germany 56 pls. 22,3. 5–6; 23, 1–2) and New York 25.78.4 attributed to Phrynos (ABV 119,9; Para 48; CVA Metropolitan Museum of Art 2 USA 11 pls. 10. 12a–f). Profile heads executed in outline and in black-figure, often of warriors and divinities, appear on the exteriors of contemporary and slightly later proto-Type A cups and eye-cups. More than one head may be on each side of the cup, either facing one another, such as on Naples Stg. 172 (ABV 203,1; CVA Naples 1 Italy 20 pls. 21–22) or overlapping and facing the same direction, as on Vatican 456 (ABV 235). A number of eye-cups with heads are attributed to the Painter of Villa Giulia 63613, and two of his pieces are signed by Nikosthenes as potter: Munich 2029 (ABV 230,4; CVA Munich 13 Germany 77 pl. 9,3–9) and Malibu 86.AE.170 (CVA Malibu 2 USA 25 pls. 110–113). Since other products of the Nikosthenic workshop were export goods to Etruria, it is not implausible that these cups were intended to cater to Etruscan tastes.

15 See Taranto 20273 (ABV 112,69; Para 44; CVA Taranto 3 Italy 35 pl. 19,3–4) and Taranto I.G. 4492 (ABV 113,73; Para 45; CVA Taranto 3 Italy 35 pl. 19,1–2), both attributed to Lydos.

16 Bonn 63 – ARV² 119,1; J. D. Beazley, review of CVA Bonn 1 Germany 1, JHS 59, 1939, 150.

17 Ferrara, by the Painter of Florence 4217 (ARV² 1223,6) and Ferrara T782 by the Painter of Ferrara T 101 (ARV² 1306,9). A female head in profile is in each tondo.

18 Villa Giulia 50639 (head of a youth) – P. Mingazzini, Vasi della Collezione Castellani, vol. 2 (1971) pl. 177,1–2, no. 704.

19 The most common heads are those of a woman or youth, as on Ferrara T. 28 (ARV² 1308,2; CVA Ferrara 1 Italy 37 pl. 43,3 – female head) or Milan 3643.13 (ARV² 1306,2; CVA Milan 1 Italy 49 pl. 17,6–7 – head of youth). Heads of mythological figures like Dionysos (Ferrara T. 1027 – ARV² 1307,8; CVA Ferrara 1 Italy 37 pl. 43,5) and Athena (Ferrara T. 1158 – ARV² 1307,6; CVA Ferrara 1 Italy 37 pl. 43,2) occur as do heads of foreigners including Africans (Bologna old no. 570 – ARV² 1310,11) and those wearing Phrygian caps (Ferrara T. 1142 – ARV² 1310,7). The plates may also be decorated with an incised four-spoked wheel or occasionally with a full length figure or animal.

20 E.g. Erlangen I 510C, a Faliscan stemmed plate dated to the last third of the seventh century BC (CVA Erlangen 1 Germany 67 pl. 43,1–2). For the influence of locally made stemmed plates at Spina on the Attic shape, see A. Parrini, in: Studi sulla necropolis di Spina in Valle Trebba. Convegno 15 ottobre 1992 (1993) 68–69; Nilsson (supra n. 6) 17–18.

21 J. D. Beazley, in: D. Kurtz (ed.), Greek Vases, Lectures by J. D. Beazley (1989) 61; T. B. L. Webster, Potter and Patron in Classical Athens (1972) 292–293.

22 Reggio Calabria 4794, an early Sicilian vase found in a child's burial (grave 884) of the Lucifero Necropolis at Reggio Calabria, attributed to the Locri Painter – LCS p. 75, no. 378; Denoyelle – Iozzo (supra n. 7) 167. 169.

23 For example, once Marseilles, Ravel collection attributed to the Painter of London D 12 (ARV² 964,8) and Bonn 769 by the Painter of Florence 4217 (ARV² 1222,1; CVA Bonn 1 Germany 1 pl. 27,4–5).

24 Such as Tarquinia Inv. nos. RC 3391 and RC 3390 (G. Pianu, Ceramiche etrusche a figure rosse [1980] 12–14 pls. 5–6), which date to the late second quarter of the fourth century BC.

25 The Genucilia plates, produced first at Falerii and then at Caere, were decorated with either a red-figure female head in profile or an abstract pattern in black glaze: M. Del Chiaro, The Genucilia Group: A Class of Etruscan Red-Figured Plates (1957); M. del Chiaro, Etruscan Red-Figured Vase-Painting at Caere (1974) 64–68.

26 M. del Chiaro, Expedition 26, 1984, 15–20; M. Harari, StEtr 48, 1980, 101–120.

27 P. Bocci, StEtr 32, 1964, 89–103; M. M. Pasquinucci, Le kelebai volterrane (1968); E. Mangani, StEtr 58, 1992, 115–143.

28 Del Chiaro (supra n. 25) 308–310.

29 Del Chiaro (supra n. 25) 252–253 pl. 18b.

30 London E 224 – ARV² 1313,5; Para 477; CVA London 6 Great Britain 8 pls. 91–92; L. Burn, The Meidias Painter (1987) 15–25 pls. 1–9.

31 ARV² 1511,1; 1704; Para 499; BAdd² 383.

32 Bonn 128 (ARV² 1514,48; CVA Bonn 1 Germany 1 pl. 11,3–4); London F 134 (ARV² 1514,49); Jena 500 (ARV² 1515,77); and Jena 0410 (ARV² 1515,78). For information on the Jena Painter, see V. Paul-Zinserling, Der Jena-Maler und sein Kreis: zur Ikonologie einer attischen Schalenwerkstatt um 400 v. Chr. (1994); Der Jenaer Maler. Eine Töpferwerkstatt im klassischen Athen (1996).

33 The Genucilia plates tend to be 13.5–15.5 cm. in diameter and 4.5–6 cm. in height, while those from Spina are ca. 18 cm in diameter and 6.2 cm in height (del Chiaro [supra n. 25] 8–9).

34 Del Chiaro (supra n. 25) 129–143. A small cluster of stemmed plates from Caere has affinity with the Spina plates in shape and decoration, including female heads, a running hare, and a bird executed in added white. The dating of the Caere plates is inconclusive (del Chiaro [supra n. 25] 9 n. 8). For more information, see F. Gilotta, in: In memoria di Enrico Paribeni vol. I (1998) 202.

35 Found in Tomb 652 in Valle Trebba, ca. 410–400 BC – ARV² 1330,2; BAdd² 365; A. Lezzi-Hafter, Der Schuwalov-Maler. Eine Kannenwerkstatt der Parthenonzeit (1976) 35. 38. 47 pl. 157b–d; L. Puritani. Die Oinochoe des Typus VII. Produktion und Rezeption im Spannungsfeld zwischen Attika und Etrurien (2009) 69–74. 249–250 no. A 26 fig. 5; pls. 24–25.

36 Beazley (supra n. 7) 168–169; M. del Chiaro, StEtr 28, 1960, 137–164; M. del Chiaro, AJA 74, 1970, 292–294; del Chiaro (supra n. 25) 16–18. 68–72.

37 For example: Lille inv. Ant. 2 (CVA Lille 1 France 40 pl. 39,1–6); Lille Ant. 46 (CVA Lille 1 France 40 pl. 38,1–6); and Limoges 78.93 (CVA Limoges and Vannes 1 France 24 pl. 20,5–7).

38 Examples of Attic vases with confronted heads found on the Italian peninsula: an oinochoe in Warsaw from Basilicata (CVA Goluchow 1 Poland 1 pl. 41,6; ARV² 1493,20) and the oinochoe from tomb 371B at Valle Pega at Spina (ARV² 1493,21).

39 Alto-Adriatic vases with figural imagery come from contexts dating from the second half of the fourth century to the early third century BC. Recent studies argue for lowering the lower end of the chronology: C. M. Dräger, in: Adriatico tra IV e III sec. a.C. Vasi alto-adriatici tra Piceno, Spina e Adria. Atti del convegno di studi Ancona, 20–21 giugno 1997 (2000) 105.

40 Such as Ferrara 2207 from Tomb 1078 at Spina (G. Riccioni, StEtr 58, 1992, 152–153 pl. 54).

41 E.g. Ferrara 2094 from tomb 779 at Spina (F. Berti – P. Desantis, in: Adriatico tra IV e III sec. a.C. Vasi alto-adriatici tra Piceno, Spina e Adria. Atti del convegno di studi Ancona, 20–21 giugno 1997 (2000) 100–102; N. Alfieri – P. E. Arias, Spina. Guida al museo archeologico in Ferrara [1960] 86) and Ferrara 2264 from tomb 369 (Dräger [supra n. 39] 107; Alfieri – Arias [supra n. 41] 87). Refer also to G. Riccioni, StEtr 56, 1989–1990, 85–97.

42 See Adria IG AD 9783 from tomb 20 (1995) of Necropoli di Ca'Cima (S. Bonomi – N. Camerin – K. Tamassia, in: Adriatico tra IV e III sec. a.C. Vasi alto-adriatici tra Piceno, Spina e Adria. Atti del convegno di studi Ancona, 20–21 giugno 1997 [2000] 51 pl. IV,2) and Ferrara Inv. 2224 from tomb 613 (Dräger [supra n. 39] 106).

43 For example, Adria IG AD 9781 from tomb 20 (1995) Necropoli di Ca'Cima (Bonomi – Camerin – Tamassia [supra n. 42] 51, pl. IV,1) and Numana-Sirolo inv. N. 27045 (M. Landolfi, Vasi Alto-Adriatici del Picino, in: Adriatico tra IV e III sec [2000] 125–126 pl. VIII,3–4).

44 Such as Ferrara 27994 from tomb 1189 at Spina (F. Berti – S. Bonomi – M. Landolfi, Classico e Anticlassico. Vasi alto-adriatici tra Piceno, Spina e Adria [1996] 122–123) and Numana 31418 from Camerano, tomb 96 (Berti – Bonomi – Landolfi [supra] 74. 131).

45 Late fifth century Attic plates decorated with heads were discovered at Numana and other Picene centers such as S. Angelo in Lizzola and Pitino di S. Severino Marche, such as the plate with a female head in tomb 178 at Numana now in Ancona (Landolfi [supra n. 43] 121–122 pl. I.1, II.1). It is noteworthy that Lucanian workshops at the end of the fifth century BC also exported red-figure high-stemmed plates to Picenum (albeit not decorated with heads).

46 Both are attributed to the Painter of Sèvres 1, a follower of the Patera and Baltimore Painters: Mostra dell'Etruria padana e della città di Spina Vol. I (1960) 363; Alfieri – Arias (supra n. 41) 176; RVAp Suppl. 1 28/281a–b p. 178.

47 For connections between South Italian and Etruscan vase-painting, refer to: Beazley (supra n. 7) 63–67; del Chiaro (supra n. 25) 114–127; B. Adembri, in: J. Christiansen – T. Melander (eds.), Proceedings of the Third Symposium on Ancient Greek and Related Pottery, Copenhagen, August 31–September 4 1987 (1988) 10. 12. 14; E. Mangani, in: Populonia in eta ellenistica. I materali dalle necropolis (1992) 48–51. For the links between South Italian and Alto-Adriatic vase painting, see: F. Gilotta, in: Adriatico tra IV e III sec. a.C. Vasi alto-adriatici tra Piceno, Spina e Adria. Atti del convegno di studi Ancona, 20–21 giugno 1997 (2000) 153–154 and M. Harari, in: Adriatico tra IV e III sec. a.C. Vasi alto-adriatici tra Piceno, Spina e Adria. Atti del convegno di studi Ancona, 20–21 giugno 1997 (2000) 164–166.

48 Pianu (supra n. 24) 12–13 pl. 5a–c.

49 Compare the neck of Boston 1970.235, an Apulian volute-krater attributed to the Iliupersis Painter dated to ca. 365–355 BC (RVAp I 8/11, p. 194), and the Chiusine glaux New York 07.286.33, attributed to the Tondo Group, ca. 325–300 BC.

50 E.g. the Sicilian oinochoe Agrigento AG 3061 of the Lentini-Hydriai Group ca. 330–310 BC (LCS 618 no. 219; LCS Suppl. 3 282 no. 219; CVA Agrigento 2 Italy 72 pl. 62) and the contemporary Tarquinian oinochoe Tarquinia Inv. RC 5343 by the Painter of Geneva MF 142 (Pianu [supra n. 24] 41 pl. 22a–c; del Chiaro [supra n. 36] 157–158). For confronted heads in South Italian and Etruscan vase-painting, see del Chiaro (supra n. 25) 122–127; Heuer (supra n. 1) 202–204.

51 For Etruscan expansion and influence in Campania, see M. B. Jovino, in: M. Torelli (ed.), The Etruscans (2000) 157–167; Haynes (supra n. 11) 197–199.

52 LCS 196–446. Examples include Capua 7554 (LCS 225 no. 1; CVA Capua 1 Italy 11 pl. 22); London F 194 from Nola (LCS 430 no. 495; CVA British Museum 2 Great Britain 2 pl. 10,5); and Salerno 170 from Pontecagnano (LCS 324 no. 730).

53 Diod. Sic. 15.13.1–4; Strabo 5.4.2.241. Maurizio Landolfi proposes that Syracusan intervention in the Adriatic facilitated the importation of Attic and South Italian red-figure along the western Adriatic coast leading to the establishment of Alto-Adriatic pottery workshops as well as that on the island of Vis off the Albanian coast. See Landolfi (supra n. 43) 117–120; Haynes (supra n. 11) 262; T. A. Tonini, in: L. Braccesi – M. Luni (eds.), I Greci in Adriatico I (2002) 211–216.

54 Gilotta (supra n. 47) 156–158; Harari (supra n. 47) 166–167; F. Gilotta, Prospettiva 87–88, 1987, 91–99. B. M. Felletti Maj, who constructed a chronological-topographical sequence of Alto-Adriatic vase-painting projecting from Numana to Spina and Adria, believed that vases produced in the latter two were more "Etruscan" in their development and under South Italian influence (StEtr 14, 1940, 43–87).

55 Eighty-six plastic head vases have been found in Etruscan contexts and another fifty-seven were discovered elsewhere in Italy and Sicily. Only eighteen have provenance within Attica. For chronology of these vases, refer to J. D. Beazley, JHS 49, 1929, 37–78 and I. Richter, Das Kopfgefäss. Zur Typologie einer Gefässform, MA Thesis (Universität zu Köln, 1969).

56 Beazley (supra n. 7) 187. 305. For example, compare New York 06.1021.45 to London 1856,12–26.61 from Nola (CVA British Museum 4 Great Britain 5 pl. 10) and London E 784 from Capua (CVA British Museum 4 Great Britain pl. 36,1; 38,1)

57 A slightly earlier example may be Ruvo 1521 (RVAp II 612–613) dated to the beginning of the fourth century BC, but it is unclear whether it is of Attic or Apulian origin.

58 Compare the head of Io of the Apulian kantharos Los Angeles 50.8.25 (CVA Los Angeles 1 USA 18 pl. 43,1–4) to the female head of the Attic mug London E 790 from Nola (ARV^2 1550,1; BAdd^2 388; Beazley [supra n. 55] 75; CVA British Museum 4 Great Britian 5 pl. 37,5).

59 From Ruvo: Ruvo 1509 (ARV^2 1550,5; Beazley [supra n. 55] 75), Ruvo 1515 (ARV^2 1550,4; Beazley [supra n. 55] 75), and Naples Stg. 57 (Beazley [supra n. 55] 72). From Basilicata: London E 792 (ARV^2 1550,7; Para 505; BAdd^2 388; Beazley [supra n. 55] 75; CVA British Museum 4 Great Britian 5 pls. 36,3; 38,2) and New York 21.88.64 (ARV^2 1550,6; BAdd^2 388). From Nola: London E 790 (ARV^2 1550,1; BAdd^2 388; Beazley [supra n. 55] 75; CVA British Museum 4 Great Britain 5 pl. 37,5) and London E 791 (ARV^2 1550,3; Beazley [supra n. 55] 75; CVA British Museum 4 Great Britian 5 pls. 37,6; 38,4).

60 RVAp II 613.

61 Such as the plastic kantharoi London F 436 (RVAp II 26/508, p. 851) and Matera 11013 (RVAp II 21/92, pp. 616–617); Beazley (supra n. 55) 74.

62 E.g. Taranto Inv. RC 6220 (Pianu [supra n. 24] 146–147); Petit Palais 356 (CVA Paris, Petit Palais 1 France 15 pl. 42,1–2); and Petit Palais 398 (CVA Paris, Petit Palais 1 France 15 pl. 43,3–5).

63 Attic African plastic head vases have been found in southern Italy and Sicily as well as Etruria. Compare the Attic oinochoe London 1836,2–24.359 (CVA British Museum 4 Great Britain 5 pl. 44,2) found at Vulci (ca. 450 BC) to the Etruscan mug Tarquinia Inv. N. 453 (Pianu [supra n. 24] 147–148 pl. CXIa–b) and the Apulian mug Cabinet des Médailles 1238, both dating to mid fourth century BC.

64 Beazley (supra n. 7) 188–189 pl. 40,1–2.

65 Ferrara 20401, dated to ca. 470–460 BC – H. Hoffmann, OxfJA 3, 1984, 65–69; ARV^2 766,5; BAdd^2 286.

66 Heuer (supra n. 1) 230–256.

8 The Gigantomachy in Attic and Apulian Vase-painting. A New Look at Similarities, Differences and Origins

Frank Hildebrandt

Introduction

Greek art depicts some extensive fights that center on, in an almost canonical manner, a small number of mostly mythological subjects. These are the Amazonomachy, Centauromachy, Ilioupersis and Gigantomachy.[1] Only in the case of the Gigantomachy are the Olympian gods themselves depicted as being part of the action, and unlike the other mythological fights, the Gigantomachy appears already in literature in the late seventh century BC, but not in art until the sixth century BC.

Two new vases with depictions of the Gigantomachy have recently become known: an Attic red-figure pelike from Tragilos and an Apulian red-figure volute krater in Hamburg (Figs. 1–4). They allow us to consider the questions of whether late South Italian vase painters were directly influenced by Athens and what the similarities and the differences are between the works of the two schools of vase-painting at this time, as well as whether there was a clear evolution in the depiction of the Gigantomachy; and if so, what was the impetus for this?

During archeological excavations in the necropolis of Tragilos in Macedonia in 1989 an Attic red-figure pelike was discovered that was almost complete.[2] In the same year a short report of the find was made, and later in 2011 a more thorough publication of the vase was penned by Maria Nikolaïdou-Patera.[3] The pelike is dated to the end of the fifth century BC and comes from the workshop of the Pronomos Painter. On both sides are multi-figure scenes. On side A the figures are arranged on two levels and as pairs in combat. The giants appear to be young, naked men. As weapons they use tree trunks and clubs. Over the left arm are hung animal skins in the manner of a shield. The gods are dressed in himations; the goddesses wear long chitons. The characters are identifiable by their attributes or details of clothing. Side A shows Zeus in the center with Athena, Apollo and Artemis around him in semicircular fashion; on side B there are two more combatant pairs, one featuring Dionysos, the other a satyr.

The giants are depicted in the same manner: They retreat back with a large step, raise their right arms and hold up their weapons protectively. Scene A is more detailed and has a greater complexity and dynamism. The individual fights take place on two levels; only Zeus fights from the top down.

In 2003 the Museum für Kunst und Gewerbe in Hamburg bought some fragments from a German private collecter. From the over 150 shards of Apulian pottery stylistically attributable to the Darius Painter,[4] sixty-six fragments belong to a volute krater whose entire body is depicted with a Gigantomachy.[5] Thirty-four gods and giants are preserved; three more giants are lost. The number of figures, including animals and other creatures, adds up to a total of sixty-seven figures. Dotted lines, plants, and two trees beneath the handles integrate the battle into a landscape and give it spatial depth. The composition can be divided into four separate parts with the structuring elements on the front (Fig. 1) and back (Fig. 2; Color Pl. 10) being the quadrigae of Zeus and Hera, and on the sides in the area of each handle a tree (Figs. 3, 4; Color Pl. 11). Through the interconnections between the figures to one another, and their movements the painter has managed to create a successfully interwoven picture, not just an image of a large number of individual fights. This volute krater by the Darius Painter has to be added to the list of the most complex, multi-figure depictions in South Italian vase painting that we have, while also being a special among Gigantomachies.

Literary Sources

Can the literary sources provide any insight into understanding the development of the iconography of the Gigantomachy from the sixth to the fourth centuries BC? Although giants are mentioned by Homer in the Odyssey[6] and by Hesiod in the Theogony,[7] there is no

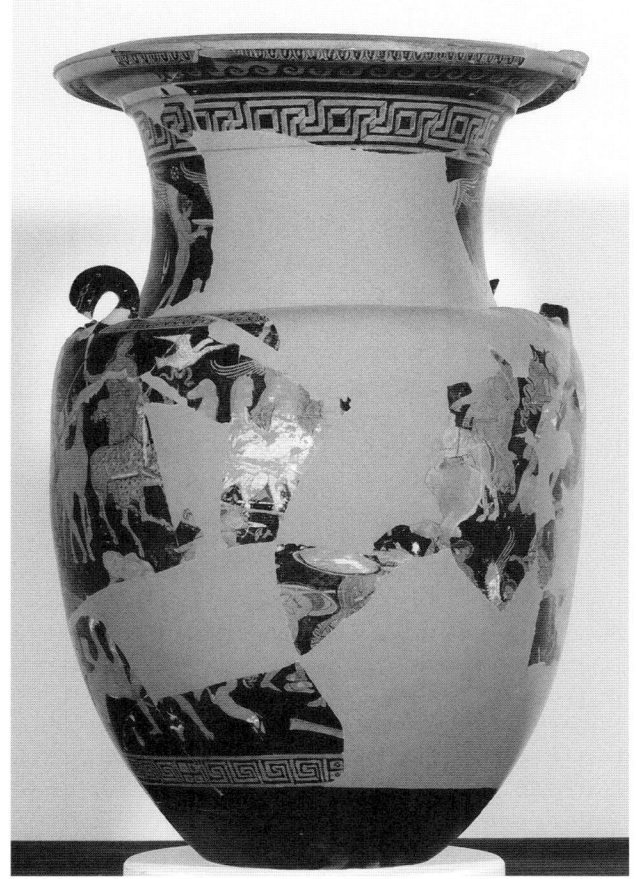

Fig. 1 Hamburg, Museum für Kunst und Gewerbe 2003.130, Side A.

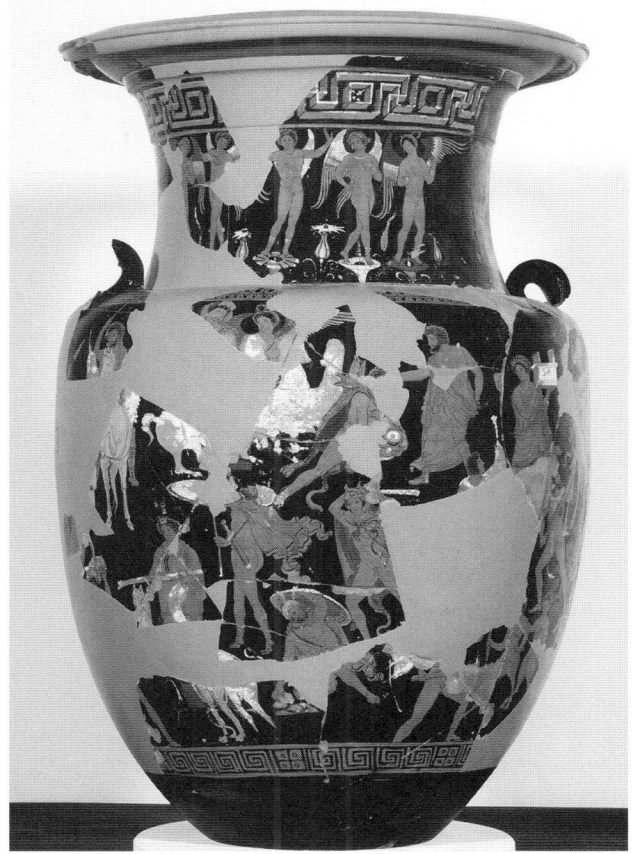

Fig. 2 Hamburg, Museum für Kunst und Gewerbe 2003.130, Side B.

reference to a battle between the Olympian gods and the giants in their works. It is likely, therefore, that the myth was not developed before the late seventh or early sixth century BC, for in the time of Solon apparently a poem of a battle between the gods and giants was created.[8] Certain is that in the sixth century BC the story of a battle was refered to by Ibykos,[9] Xenophanes,[10] and Alcman.[11] Notes by later authors, especially Apollonios Rhodes[12] and Athenaeus,[13] suggest that an epic poem, which has been forgotten, was the source of the story.[14] The most complete version of the epic Gigantomachy is that narrated by Apollodoros,[15] who in the second half of the second century BC probably created his version by compiling other narrations available to him.

An important concept behind the Gigantomachy was to have a stringent structure and order to the community of gods in the way it was presented by Hesiod. This social and political order of the pantheon served as an orientation for the people, and in addition to the Greek language, it provided a linking and unifying element for the Greeks. The loss of this divine order would have had a direct impact on people's daily life; that is why the preservation and security of it was of the utmost importance.

In the fifth century BC the Gigantomachy became an even more prominent issue, especially in the theater in plays by Aeschylos,[16] Euripides,[17] and Aristophanes.[18] Even the poets Bacchylides[19] and Pindar[20] mention the battle. Unfortunately, a complete, coherent narrative from this period does not survive.

In the fourth century BC the older story lines were continued but were supplemented by three factors: First, the identification of the topography mentioned in the myth is connected with real landscapes. The giants were believed to have lived under high mountains[21] and in volcanoes,[22] especially in the Chalcidice and the Phlegrean Fields. Second, there were a growing number of giant names that were place names – the battle served as an explanation for these topographical features and locations. Third, new participants appear on the side of the Olympian gods, e.g. the Dioscuri. This expansion of the story allowed for a stronger identification with the myth for all Greeks.

In short, the literary sources are of limited value for understanding this vase, which leaves only the images to answer the question of similarities and differences between the depictions of the story.[23]

Representations in Attic Vase Painting and their Development

The Gigantomachy had a special importance in Attic vase painting, and in total over 652 black- and red-figure vase paintings with this myth survive, all created between 560–380 BC.[24] The oldest iconographic source is an image on a pinax from Eleusis, dated around 570 BC.[25] The other early depictions are on vases which were offerings on the Athenian Acropolis. A good example is the large dinos of Lydos dating soon after 560 BC.[26] Shown on it are groups of fighters, each consisting of a deity and one or two giants – and sometimes of several deities against several giants. The real character of the battle, the self-defense of the gods, is not underscored in these early scenes: Who attacks and who defends her- or himself is not really clear. They seem to show a balance of power that emphasizes the power and strength of the giants and their threat. The gods are identified by their attributes or by their specific kind of fighting. The giants are shown – as described by Hesiod[27] – wearing the armor of hoplites with spears, helmets, and breastplates.

The immediate appearance of the Gigantomachy in the decade after 570 BC is generally associated with the re-organization of the Greater Panathenaia in 566 BC by the tyrant Peisistratos.[28] The highlight of the festival was the procession in honor of Athena, in which the richly embroidered peplos of the goddess was brought to the Acropolis.[29] For each Greater Panathenaia a new peplos decorated with a Gigantomachy was woven. Beforehand, a specially appointed commission examined and approved the plan for the new garment. Although frequently mentioned, depictions of this part of the festival do not exist.

The depictions on the so-called Acropolis vases dating to ca. 560–550 BC have, as Luca Giuliani has observed, "vielfigurige Komposition im Format eines langgestreckten Frieses auf und stimmen sowohl in den Hauptmotiven als auch in zahlreichen Einzelheiten überein".[30] The content and form of complexity found in the vase paintings of this period and in the following depictions have no parallels. The frieze on the peplos of Athena is commonly considered to be a model for these early paintings.[31] This led Karl Schefold to suggest that the Panathenaia be regarded as the birthday of Athena/Athens and a celebration of the victory over the giants restoring the just order of the Olympian gods.[32] The myth is even more, for it is a story of guilt and atonement. Gaia is guilty by fighting the divine order first with the Titans, later with the giants.

The appropriation of this subject in Athens was used not only to represent the superiority of the Olympian gods and their order, but also to emphasize the special role of the goddess Athena and to imply the supremacy of the polis Athens. This can be seen as the beginning of Athenian hegemonic thinking long before the Persian Wars. One wonders whether this can be connected with the increasing importance of Athenian pottery which replaced Corinthian as the leading figured ceramic fabric in the Meditarranean.

Characteristic of the early images is the depiction of the three main protagonists: Zeus, Athena and Herakles as, for example, on a pseudo-Panathenaic amphora in London.[33] Here Zeus as ruler of the Olympians is the target of the giants' attack. According to the myth a mortal was needed to fight alongside the gods, and Athena succeeed in persuading Herakles to do so. She herself kills the leader of the giants, a requirement for their defeat.

From about 540 BC on the individual participants in the battle become the subject. There are scenes with Athena, Dionysos, and Poseidon. The extensive friezes of the first decades are followed by small groups of usually two or three gods in a fight against an equal number of giants who are armed identically with helmet, breastplate, lance and shield.

After the building of the Temple of Athena on the Acropolis around 520 BC the giants lose their hoplite-like look and display athletic nudity. Bleeding wounds increase the drama and also point to the oncoming defeat of the giants.

At the turn from the sixth to the fifth century BC the images change fundamentally. Characterized first by their arms as hoplites, and later with naked, muscular bodies displaying an athletic, heroic ideal, their connection to the wilderness becomes obvious. They are now dressed in furs and animal skins. Rocks, stones, tree trunks, and later torches replace the conventional weapons. Two types of giants can be found. Thomas Carpenter calls them "civilized and barbarian giants".[34] He sees the Greeks experiences with barbarians in the context of the Persian Wars as responsible. Luca Giuliani prefers to connect the change with the reforms of Cleisthenes[35] which led to the new ideal of the Athenian citizen as a hoplite; the iconographic result was a clear demarcation of the giants. At the same time the iconography of the battle changed: the contrast between powerful victors and powerless defeated was now shown.[36]

The images of the Gigantomachy on Attic black-figure vases continue until the first decades of the fifth century BC. Early Attic red-figure vases start ca. 530–525 BC, but the theme of Gigantomachy was taken up very rarely.[37] Of the 652 images of the Gigantomachy only 128 are red-figured.[38] But this is not due to reduced interest. Instead, the explanation lies in the continuing high appreciation of the black-figure vases: the Gigantomachy as a tradition that expressed itself in adherence to a traditional technique – quite similar to the Panathenaic prize-amphorae. In contrast to the early fifth century BC when the depictions show tremendous and violent power,[39] around 470/460 BC a greater tranquility and peace occurs in the scenes.[40] A new subject to appear is the retreating giant.[41] From here on out there is a continuous loss of iconographic complexity. The images are limited to the fragmentary repetition of the same models and variations, and differences occur only in the change of the giants from hoplites over to naked fighters with skins, stones, torches, etc.

A fundamental reassessment of the theme is made by Pheidias: The Gigantomachy was now shown on the throne of Zeus in Olympia as a Pan-Hellenic memorial, but also – and this is more remarkable – three times on the Parthenon: on the metopes on the east side, on the peplos of Athena, and painted on the inside of the shield of the goddess. The depiction on a krater in Naples by the Pronomos Painter[42] is often said to be a representation of the scene on this shield. The arch separating gods and giants, the presence of Helios and Selene – as in the pediment of the Parthenon – and the figures on the outside of the shield link the iconography with works by Pheidias. Even the composition with different levels can be attributed most likely to Pheidias, since it is also employed in the Amazonomachy on this shield.[43]

Around the middle of the fifth century BC other friezes with extensive depictions of the Gigantomachy can be found. Quite unusual is the image on a calyx krater in Ferrara.[44] Twelve gods fight against only nine giants! Were one not to assume that the equilibrium is dissolved in a rather less honorable way for the gods or that the vase painter has committed an error in his planning of the frieze, this depiction could be inspired or influenced by another image. This might have been a large *Schlachtengemälde* or – more probably – the frieze on the peplos of Athena. Iconographically remarkable is that for the first time even a goddess, Artemis, fights with torches. The clear contrast between gods and giants is now varied and individualized. Another calyx krater in Basel,[45] which clearly uses the same template as the krater in Ferrara, confirms the hypothesis of an important model for the image. The depiction on another calyx krater in Ferrara[46] shows two important features: The goddess Athena becomes the central figure, and – for the first time – one of the three key players, Herakles, is missing.

In the second half of the fifth century BC the scenes become dramatic and display pathos again. At the same time the scheme of fighting next to each other changes fundamentally: the battle area employs landscape-lines and is divided into 'top' and 'bottom'. This innovation leads to a fundamental restructuring of the iconography by the end of the fifth century BC. The giants fight on the lower level and are thus characterized already in a simple, visual way as the losers. The painters do not attempt to show the power and near equality of the giants nor the threat they present. This leads to a 'devaluation' of the giants as opponents and as a consequence even to a 'devaluation' of the gods. This is a general trend of the late fifth century BC, which can also be seen in other monuments, along with a greater interest in the human individual. In the last decades of the fifth century BC the images become open to new influences. On an amphora in Paris[47] the Eleusinian deities are represented, and a pelike in Athens shows the Dioscuri.[48] By the second quarter of the fourth century BC Gigantomachies play no role anymore in Athenian vase painting.[49]

Representations in South-Italian Vase Painting

There are only twenty-two vessels from southern Italy (twenty from Apulia, two from Campania) that show a Gigantomachy – a very small number in comparison to the 652 images on Athenian vases. Although the subject appears on several different shapes,[50] the most popular are the twelve examples on calyx and volute kraters. Of particular significance are the multi-figured images on the kraters, which can be iconographically divided into two types.[51] The earliest is found on a calyx krater in Taranto.[52] On it the combatants are strictly divided into two hierarchical levels. On the top are the gods – Zeus in the center with Nike on a quadriga, flanked on the left by Athena, and on the right by Artemis and Apollo. On the bottom are four giants. Three turn to the gods above, while one fights Herakles on the lower level. Nearly identical is the image on a volute krater in St. Petersburg,[53] although Apollo is missing. The giants rise from the meander and are thus characterized as earth-born. Likewise related is a depiction on a volute krater in New York[54] where the composition is again based on two levels: the upper with the gods, the lower with the giants. In the center is the quadriga of Zeus with Nike. As in the Athenian images, the major characters – Zeus, Athena and Herakles – are represented. This very simple composition can be directly connected with that on the shield of Athena Parthenos as shown on the calyx krater in Naples,[55] although it lacks the astral deities and the clear dividing line.

This simple composition is replaced by the second type, which was used between 340–320 BC and is found on three volute kraters. The first is in Berlin.[56] On it pairs of fighters are arranged in a semicircle around Zeus with Nike in a quadriga. This same composition is also employed on a volute krater in Bochum,[57] but wounded and dead giants also appear. On the third, a volute krater from the Deletaille collection,[58] a giant with legs in the form of snakes appears for the first time.

Luca Giuliani summarized this as follows:

Die Ikonographie wurde von attischen Vasenbildern übernommen und ein ganzes Jahrhundert lang weitergebildet, durch immer neue Erfindungen bereichert und variiert. Die Familienähnlichkeit aller apulischen Gigantomachien findet ihre naheliegende Erklärung darin, daß keiner der Maler sein Bild je vollständig neu erfunden hat: die allgemeinen Prinzipien der Komposition sowie einzelne Figuren und Motive wurden immer zum Teil aus der Werkstatt-Tradition übernommen: doch immer mit dem Ziel, ein neues, so noch nie dagewesenes Bild zu schaffen.[59]

In light of the vases known at that time, this was a logical conclusion, but the new Apulian volute krater in Hamburg now has to be considered in this context.

It is an exceptional vase, created and painted by the Darius Painter around 340 BC. On it is a Gigantomachy that goes around the entire body. Thirty-four deities and giants fight each other. Including the animals and other creatures that are shown, there are sixty-seven figures in total. Side A (Fig. 1) show Zeus with Nike in a quadriga and B (Fig. 2; Color Pl. 10) Hera with Iris in another quadriga. The majority of the Olympians fight from bigai drawn by various creatures and animals that participate actively in the combat. Others, such as Ares, Herakles, and Hephaistos fight on foot; one of the Dioscuri has dismounted from his horse. Compared with the other Apulian images, this picture gives much more detail.[60] One example (Fig. 3; Color Pl. 11) is the calmly standing Hestia who prepares to fling the altar she holds above, while to the left below strides a wild giant who raises a stone over his head. But this is not just a simple stone, it is an island with plants and buildings; this emphasizes the blasphemy of the giants. This theme is taken up again on the other side and remains unique in vase painting. Artistic novelties are the riding Poseidon in a frontal view and Apollo with a griffin biga. The giants often wear furs; some are shown with helmets, shields and weapons. The helmets and armor represent South Italian types that are known from Daunian tombs and from the Lucanians.

With the multitude of deities in action it is difficult to gain an understanding of all the details of the battle quickly. Nevertheless, it is striking that the most important participant is missing: the goddess Athena.[61] Why is she absent? And why does this Gigantomachy differ so clearly from the other Apulian depictions? It is probably not due solely to the genius of the Darius Painter.[62] Rather the scene's complexity and attention to detail suggests that it was inspired by some lost source, be it a lost painting, literary description, etc. There must have been a visual template available to the painter. One possibility might be that the vase-painting is somehow connected with images on a recent peplos for the statue of Athena Polias. The absence of the goddess in the picture could be explained by the fact that as the wearer of the garment she was there anyway.

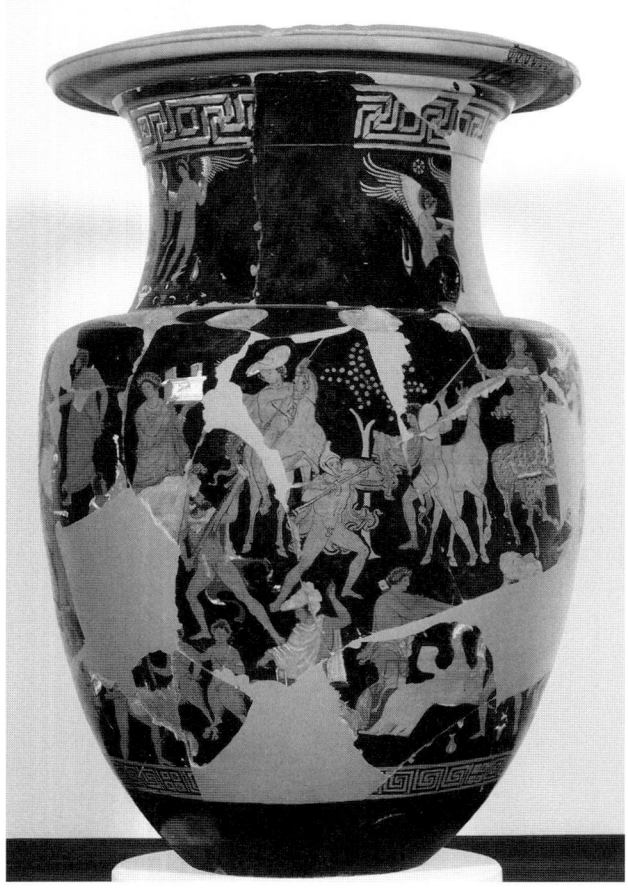

Fig. 3 Hamburg, Museum für Kunst und Gewerbe 2003.130, Side B/A.

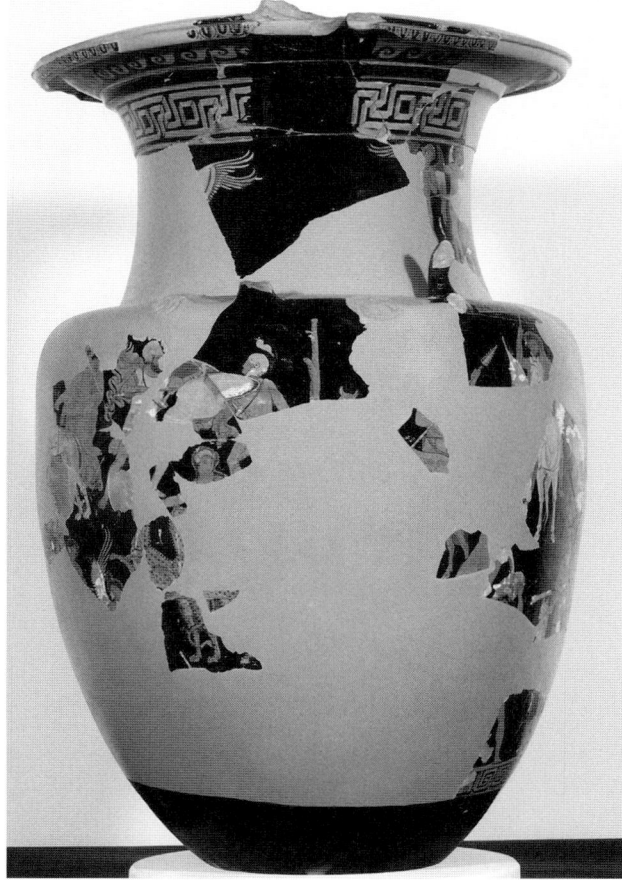

Fig. 4 Hamburg, Museum für Kunst und Gewerbe 2003.130, Side A/B.

Conclusion

More than 674 Attic and South Italian vases with a depiction of the Gigantomachy are known, and they all date between 560 and 310 BC. Three main steps in the development of the scene can be identified:

1. The subject of the Gigantomachy is first shown on vases about 570/560 BC. The beginning is generally associated with the reorganization of the Panathenaia in 566 BC. At the pageant the newly woven peplos of Athena decorated with the Gigantomachy was shown to the public. Fragments of large-scale vases from the Athenian Acropolis are the earliest evidence of these Gigantomachies, for these complex images were adopted from the robe of Athena[63] and are an expression of the hegemonial thinking in archaic Athens.

    In the following decades, the iconography of the giants changed, reflecting contemporary taste – first they are warriors in hoplite armor, then athleticly naked, at the end wild with furs, trees and torches. At the same time the mass combat was replaced by a small number of groups or individual gods fighting giants. Gigantomachies continued to be painted in the red-figure technique until ca. 480 BC.

2. A new development that can be associated with Pheidias takes place around 450 to 430 BC. The Gigantomachy is more strongly anchored in state ideology and connected with the representations shown on the peplos of Athena, on the shield of Athena Parthenos, and on the Parthenon metopes. For Athenians, as well as foreigners, the most important location was the Acropolis of Athens. Several extensive friezes on vases show a renewed interest in this subject. Images with an unequal number of gods and giants suggest that their model was most probably the frieze on the peplos of Athena.

3. The Gigantomachy makes a final developmental step around 350/340 BC in Apulia. Here the theme, no longer depicted on Athenian pottery, is picked up again and displayed on monumental vases. There are two main types of compositions: gods and giants fighting from the top down and pairs of opponents in a semicircle around Zeus and Nike in a quadriga. It is assumed that the latest images from Athens mark the starting point for the Apulian depictions, which developed slight new nuances.[64] The volute krater in Hamburg does not fit with this, and the complexity and scope of the scene on it suggests a model that might be the peplos of Athena as well. This vase then would be the latest testimony for the images on the peplos that we have.

As already pointed out by Karl Schefold, the Gigantomachy as a reflection of 'good order' legitimizes the Greek pantheon.[65] Athena and Herakles – goddess and hero – are significantly important for the victory of the Olympians over their wild, earth-born enemies. For this reason, it is not surprising that Athens adopted and stylized this story to a state-supporting myth in a time when its first major hegemonic aspirations take place. In the fifth century BC, under Pericles, this idea was apparently renewed. The emphasis then was primarily on the victory over the Persians and the non-Greeks. With the defeat of Athens in the Peloponnesian War, the loss of leadership, the conflicts with Sparta and the Macedonians, a stronger focus on domestic issues and the rise of individualism in the fourth century BC, the topos of the Gigantomachy was not appropriate for Athenians anymore.

In contrast, however, was the situation in southern Italy. Although the Italic indigenous populations were trading partners with the Greeks and consumers of ceramics and metalworks, strong competition and occasional conflicts beween them and their Greek neighbors arose in the fourth century BC.[66] The South Italian ceramic workshops, where the Gigantomachies were produced, were located mainly in Canosa, a place of contact for the Greeks with Daunians, Messapians, and Peucetians. The Darius Painter's giants wear Italic armor,[67] not without reason. Against this background, the extensive images of the Gigantomachy in Apulia have a new, previously overlooked importance.

Abbreviations

Giuliani, Bildervasen	L. Giuliani, Tragik, Trauer und Trost. Bildervasen für eine apulische Totenfeier (1995)
LIMC IV	LIMC IV (1988) 196–236 s.v. Gigantes (F. Vian – M. B. Moore)
Muth, Gewalt	S. Muth, Gewalt im Bild. Das Phänomen der medialen Gewalt im Athen des 6. und 5. Jahrhunderts v.Chr. (2008)
Schefold, SB II	K. Schefold, Götter- und Heldensagen der Griechen in der spätarchaischen Kunst (1978)

Notes

1. For literature see RE Suppl. III (1918) 655–759. 1305–1306 s.v. Giganten (O. Waser); LIMC IV 196; Muth, Gewalt 268–328. 700–710; L. Giuliani, in: T. Hölscher (ed.), Gegenwelten zu den Kulturen Griechenlands und Roms in der Antike (2000) 263–286; LIMC Suppl. 1 (2009) 220–221 s.v. Gigantes (Chr. Ioannitis – P. Linant de Bellefonds); R. Hurschmann, in: CVA Hamburg 2 Germany 91 pl. 17.
2. N. Nikolaïdou-Patera, AEMTH 3, 1989, 483–498.
3. N. Nikolaïdou-Patera, in: S. Pigniatoglou – Th. Stephanidou-Tiveriou (eds.), Νάματα. Τιμητικος τομος γιά τον καθηγητη Δημητριο Παντερμαλή (2011) 303–310 pls. 7–9.
4. K. Schauenburg, Studien zur Unteritalischen Vasenmalerei IV/V (2002) 39–55; CVA Hamburg 2 Germany 91 pls. 14–23. 46–49 [with literature].

5 See note 3. Four other vases were reconstructed: volute krater Inv. 2003.129, lekythos Inv. 2003.131, fragment of a lekythos Inv. 2009.7, fragment of a volute krater Inv. 2010.18.
6 Hom. *Od.* 7.56–60; 7.204–206; 10.120–122.
7 Hes. *Theog.* 50–52. 183–186.
8 K. Schefold, Götter- und Heldensagen der Griechen in der Früh- und Hocharchaischen Kunst (1993) 200; DNP 4 (1998) 1069 s.v. Gigantomachie (J. Latacz). It seems to be part of a mythological cycle of the titanomachy.
9 Page, *SLG* S 192.2.
10 Diels – Kranz, *Vorsokr.* 21 B 1, 21.
11 Page, *PMG* fr. 1.30–32; see D. L. Page, Alcman. The Partheneion (1951) 42–43.
12 Schol. Ap. Rhod. 1.559.
13 Ath. 9.462 F.
14 Schefold, SB II 55.
15 Apollod. *Peri Theon* 1.6.1–2.
16 Aesch. *Eum.* 295–297.
17 Eur. *Cyc.* 5–9; *Hec.* 473; *Heracl.* 177–179. 906–909. 1192–1194. 1272; *Ion* 205–218. 987–997. 1528–1529; *IT* 222–224; *Phoen.* 127–130. 1130–1133.
18 Ar. *Av.* 823–825. 1205–1207. 1242–1256. 1633. 1763–1765.
19 Bacchyl. 15.62–63.
20 Pind. *Isthm.* 6.32–35; *Nem.* 1.67–72. 4.25–30. 7.90; *Pyth.* 8.12–18.
21 Pseudo-Apollod. *Bibliotheca* 1.37; Strabo 10.5.16; Paus. 1.2.4: Poseidon buried a giant with the island of Nisyros.
22 Callim. *Hymn 4* 141–147: The giant Enceladus was buried under Mount Etna in Sicily.
23 K. Schefold, Die Göttersage in der klassischen und hellenistischen Kunst (1981) 92: "Auf den Vasen können wir verfolgen, wie die Auffassung des Gigantenkampfes sich unaufhörlich verändert, wenn auch in Athen einige Grundmotive bleiben, so die zentrale Stellung von Zeus, Athena und Herakles."
24 These numbers are taken from the BAPD: 524 Attic black-figure, 128 Attic red-figure vases.
25 Schefold, SB II 54; LIMC IV 215 no. 99. It is not considered to be an Attic work, but it is also not attributable to the workshops of Corinth, from which in the second quarter of the sixth century BC at least five pinakes with fighting giants are known.
26 Athens, Acropolis Museum Inv. 607: ABV 107,1. 684; BAdd² 12; LIMC IV 215 no. 105; Muth, Gewalt 271–277 fig. 174 A–G; BAPD 310147.
27 Hes. *Theog.* 186: "the radiant splendor of the weapons, the mighty spears in their hands". The earliest depictions show the giants in this way, e. g. the dinos, Malibu, J. P. Getty Museum Inv. 81.AE.211 (Kylennios, ca. 560 BC): LIMC IV 220 no. 171; Muth, Gewalt 702 n. 24; BAPD 10047.
28 M. Rekow, Die Panathenäen zur Zeit der Tyrannis der Peisistratiden – Soziale Identität und Herrschaftslegitimation (2005) 6: Under the Archon Hippokleides foreign poleis participated for the first time in the celebrations. In this context s. P. Siewert, in: M. Bentz – N. Eschbach (eds.), Panathenaika. Symposion zu den Panathenäischen Preisamphoren (2001) 4–5.
29 The saffron-colored robe was displayed on a movable frame in the shape of a ship, carried through the city to the Acropolis, where the statue of a deity was clothed. – Schefold, SB II 55; LIMC IV 210 no. 32; G. Nick, Die Athena Parthenos. Studien zum griechischen Kultbild und seiner Rezeption, 19. Beih. AM (2002) 147–148 with further literature.
30 Giuliani, Bildervasen 115.
31 Muth, Gewalt 700 n. 7 with further literature.
32 Schefold, SB II 55. Muth, Gewalt 270, describes the battle as "mythisches Sinnbild für die Verteidigung politischer Macht".
33 London, British Museum B 208 (manner of the Lysippides Painter, ca. 530–520 BC): ABV 260,69; Para 14; BAdd² 34; LIMC IV 217 no. 120; BAPD 302261.
34 T. H. Carpenter, Dionysian Imagery in Fifth-century Athens (2003) 23–24.
35 Giuliani (supra n. 1) 277–281.
36 Muth, Gewalt 312, rightly points out that the defeated giants are further characertized as dangerous opponents. While dying they hold their weapons and do not turn their heads away from their enemies.
37 Reggio di Calabria, Museo Nazionale Inv. C 1143 (Fragments of a cup, Epiktetos): ARV² 72,19; LIMC IV 228 no. 298; BAPD 200463. – Athens, Acropolismuseum Inv. 211 (Fragments of a cup, Euthymides): ARV² 29,20; LIMC IV 228 no. 299; Muth, Gewalt 292–293 fig. 192; BAPD 200125.
38 These numbers are taken from the BAPD (see n. 25). LIMC IV lists the following: 194 Attic black-figure, 107 Attic red-figure, 14 South Italian / LIMC Suppl. 1 (Düsseldorf 2009) 221–223 s. v. Gigantes (P. Linant de Bellefonds) lists 1 Attic red-figure and 6 South Italian vases.
39 E.g. cup Berlin, Antikensammlung SMPK F 2293 (Brygos Painter, ca. 485 BC): ARV² 370, 10; Para 365,10; BAdd² 111; LIMC IV 228 no. 303; Muth, Gewalt 298 fig. 197.
40 E.g. volute krater London, British Museum E 469 (Altamura Painter): ARV² 589,1; LIMC IV 229 no. 309; Muth, Gewalt 314 fig. 215; BAPD 207137. – stamnos, Museum of Fine Arts, Boston Inv. 00.342 (Blenheim Painter): ARV² 598,4. 1661; Para 394; LIMC IV 234 no. 379; BAPD 206906.
41 Muth, Gewalt 311.
42 Naples, Museo Archeologico Nazionale Inv. 2045 [H 2883] (ca. 430/420 BC): ARV² 1338; Para 481; BAdd² 183; LIMC IV 230 no. 316; BAPD 217517.
43 V. M. Strocka, Piräusreliefs und Parthenosschild. Versuch einer Wiederherstellung der Amazonomachie des Phidias (1967); id., in: E. Berger (ed.), Parthenon-Kongreß Basel, 4.–8. April 1982 I (1984) 188–196.
44 Ferrara, Museo Archeologico Nazionale Inv. 2891 [T 313 VT] (Niobid Painter, ca. 460–450 BC): ARV² 602,24. 1661; Para 395; BAdd² 130; LIMC IV 229 no. 311; Muth, Gewalt 316–319 fig. 218 A–E; BAPD 206956.
45 Basel, Antikenmuseum und Sammlung Ludwig Lu 51 (manner of the Niobid Painter, ca. 450 BC): ARV² 609,7. 1661; Para 396; BAdd² 130; LIMC IV 229 no. 312; Muth, Gewalt 319 f. fig. 219 A–B; BAPD 275292.
46 Ferrara, Museo Archeologico Nazionale Inv. 44893 (Group of Polygnotus?, ca. 440–430 BC): ARV² 1680; Para 446; BAdd² 158; LIMC IV 229 no. 313; Muth, Gewalt 319–321 fig. 220; BAPD 275447.
47 Paris, Musée du Louvre Inv. S 1677 (Suessula Painter, ca. 400/390 BC): ARV² 1344,1. 1691; Para 482; BAdd² 183; LIMC IV 230 no. 322; Muth, Gewalt 323. 326–327 fig. 224 A–C; BAPD 217568.

48 Athens, Nationalmuseum Inv. 1333 (Pronomos Painter, ca. 420–400 BC): ARV² 1337,8; Para 481; BAdd² 183; LIMC IV 230 no. 319; BAPD 217512.
49 From the group of the Kertsch vases is known only one fragmentary pelike in Odessa: LIMC IV 236 no. 404.
50 Lekythos, plate, lekanis, amphora, askos, oinochoe, and cup.
51 Not categorizable are the krater Bari, Museo Archeologico Nazionale Inv. 4399 (Circle of Lykurgos Painter, ca. 360/350 BC): RVAp I 421.44; LIMC IV 235 no. 392; Giuliani, Bildervasen 116 no. D; fragment, New York, Metropolitan Museum of Art 1919.192.81 frr. 4. 5. 7. 10. 11. 19 (Baltimore Painter, ca. 320 BC): RVAp II 867.31; LIMC IV 236 no. 399; Giuliani, Bildervasen 116 no. H.
52 Tarento, Museo Archeologico Nazionale Inv. 52265 (Workshop of the Painter of the Birth of Dionysus, first quarter of the fourth century BC): RVAp I 39.24; K. Schauenburg, AntK 5, 1962, pl. 18,2; J.–M. Moret, L'Ilioupersis dans la ceramique italiote. Les mythes et leur expression figuree au IVᵉ siècle (1975) pl. 60.1 [dates the krater to around 360/350 BC]; LIMC IV 234 no. 390; Giuliani, Bildervasen 115 no. A.
53 St. Petersburg, Hermitage Inv. 1714 (Lycurgos Painter, ca. 360–340 BC): RVAp I 416.12; LIMC IV 235 no. 391; Giuliani, Bildervasen 116 no. B.
54 Private collection (De Schulthess Painter, ca. 340 BC): RVAp Suppl. 2 135.17/18; A. D. Trendall, Red Figure Vases of South Italy and Sicily (1989) 88 fig. 199; D. von Bothmer (ed.), Glories of the Past. Ancient Art from the Shelby White and Leon Levy Collection (1990) 176–178 no. 126; Giuliani, Bildervasen 116 no. E.
55 See note 41.
56 Berlin, Antikensammlung SMPK Inv. 1984.44 (Darius Painter, ca. 340 BC): LIMC IV 235 no. 397; Giuliani, Bildervasen 111–118 pl. 2,2.

57 Bochum, Kunstsammlung der Universität Inv. S 993 (Underworld Painter, ca. 320/310 BC): RVAp II 534.287; LIMC IV 235 no. 396; Giuliani, Bildervasen 116 no. G.
58 Former Brussels art market, Collection Deletaille (Baltimore Painter, ca. 320 BC): RVAp Suppl. I 152.23b; LIMC IV 235–236 no. 398; Giuliani, Bildervasen 116 no. I.
59 Giuliani, Bildervasen 118.
60 E.g. for the inside of the animal skins of the giants Hom. Il. 10.21–24.
61 A fragment of a volute krater acquired by the museum shows Athena killing the giant Enkelados (Hamburg, Museum für Kunst und Gewerbe Inv. 2010.18: CVA Hamburg 2 Germany 91 pl. 23,2.). Contrary to the LIMC Supplementum I (Düsseldorf 2009) 222–223 s.v. Gigantes add. 10 (Chr. Ioannitis) the fragment belongs to another volute krater for different reasons: thickness of the shards, turning groves, diameter, lack of space for fitting, and the iconography of the giants.
62 T. H. Carpenter, in: St. Schmidt – J. H. Oakley (eds.) Hermeneutik der Bilder – Beiträge zur Ikonographie und Interpretation griechischer Vasenmalerei, 4. Beih. CVA (2009) 153–160; R. Hurschmann, in: CVA Hamburg 2 Germany 91 pl. 14 p. 34 [with literature].
63 Schefold, SB II 57; M. B. Moore, AJA 83, 1979, 79–99.
64 Giuliani, Bildervasen 118.
65 Schefold, SB II 55.
66 The tombs of the 3rd century BC in Paestum give indications of the changes, which tell of a local elite with Italian roots. B. Andreae et al. (eds.), Malerei für die Ewigkeit. Die Gräber von Paestum (2007) 28–39.
67 Especially the helmet with plume forms and the abdominal belts; see CVA Hamburg 2 Gemany 91 pl. 14 p. 34.

9 Plates by Paseas

Mario Iozzo

In the last quarter of the sixth century BC, some Athenian *ergasteria* specializing in cups also began to produce red-figured plates,[1] a simple shape to paint, and impressive in terms of its ornament. The earliest known examples are datable to 520–500 BC and today number not more than about sixty.[2] Almost all of them belong to Type B in D. Callipolitis-Feytmans' classification, that is, the kind with the larger and more squarish tondos inside, and with a foot smaller in diameter than in the earlier types. Derived from old Sub-Geometric shapes, plates of Type B were made in Athens in particular (none are known from Corinth, for example), where the painters of the *Kerameikos* applied to plates the formats and patterns usually painted on the inside of their cups, leading Callipolitis-Feytmans herself to put forward the intriguing hypothesis that the small-sized plates of Types B II and B III were themselves created to go with the cups used in Athenian banquets and symposia.[3]

Among the red-figure painters of the early Archaic who decorated plates were Psiax, Euthymides, Euphronios, Oltos, Apollodoros,[4] the Ambrosios Painter, the Painter of Acropolis 24, and the Painter of the Acropolis Plates; but above all Epiktetos[5] and Paseas were dedicated to the production of plates, often reaching high levels of compositional balance and style. It even seems that this same Psiax, who was the teacher of Epiktetos, painted black-figured plates inspired by the red-figured ones made by his student.[6] According to Mary B. Moore, the entire series of red-figured plates was started by Epiktetos.[7]

In Greece,[8] the red-figure examples have been found, for the most part, in sanctuaries: from the Acropolis of Athens, with at least fifteen examples, but also from the Telesterion of Eleusis, the Heraion of Delos, and the Heroon of Iphigenia at Brauron. The same is true at Cyrene, where the extramural sanctuary of Demeter and Persephone has yielded two plates by Epiktetos and the Heraion Painter respectively.[9] Far rarer are the examples from funerary contexts, such as the tombs at Vari and in the Athenian *Kerameikos*,[10] or, even less meaningful, from deposits such as the ones in the Agora[11] or the fill on the Pnyx.

In all of Magna Graecia and Sicily the shape seems to have been almost totally ignored, and the few red-figured plates from Taranto (Paseas), Cuma (manner of Euthymides and the Briseis Painter), and Gela (Altamura Painter)[12] probably came from tombs.[13] The final destination of the majority of red-figured plates was undoubtedly Etruria, especially Vulci and Chiusi, but also Cerveteri and Tarquinia. Here, clearly, the plates – whether singly, in pairs, or in groups – were intentionally chosen, above all, as *kterismata* for the rich tombs of the highest social classes.[14] This is so for at least the first three or four "generations" of plates, from the beginning of their production to about the middle of the fifth century BC. In the Classical and the Late Classical periods, in fact, there is a definite increase in production, as shown by both the greater number of examples, found by the dozen in the Athenian Agora,[15] and by the hundreds found along the Adriatic coast of Etruria, chiefly at Spina. A search in the Beazley Archive Pottery Database (BAPD) is enough to determine the fact that there are many plates, of various types (even with a high foot), repeatedly coming from a limited number of workshops and exported in groups.

In Etruscan funerary culture, the plate has a specific role, unquestionably both ritual and symbolic, well-attested throughout the sixth and fifth centuries BC. This is shown by the enormous quantity of small plates in bucchero – black and grey –, plain, painted, and even of bronze, that were buried in sets of ten, twelve, or twenty. A case in point is the service of ten plates painted by the Micali Painter, presumably discovered in the same tomb, sold at auction by Sotheby's in 1982 and now in an American private collection.[16] With regard to the Attic imports, perhaps the most striking example is that of the six plates, all signed by Epiktetos and discovered in one tomb in Vulci, that D. Paleothodoros reasonably has proposed to call the "Tomb of Epiktetos," and to reconstruct the original number of the set as including, possibly, another four plates. That set, then, made by Epiktetos at the beginning of his career, about 520–515 BC, would have consisted of ten very beautiful and elegant plates, today divided between Paris, London, and New York.[17]

Recently, the overall picture has been augmented by the twenty plates attributed to the Bryn Mawr Painter discovered by the Italian Carabinieri in the infamous Corridor 17, Giacomo Medici's secret deposit of looted antiquities in the Free Port of Geneva. Offered to the Getty Museum in 1987 for two million dollars, they were returned to Medici one and one-half years later because the price was too high. These plates, the largest set of Attic plates ever known, were found together in the same grave in southern Etruria, very likely in Cerveteri.[18]

Plates also have a long tradition of use at Chiusi, which, in the second half of the sixth century BC, probably received the latest arrivals from Athens direct from Vulci.[19] The predilection of the local clientele for this shape is shown by the purchase (from one shipment or more than one?) of at least thirteen examples of various sizes and different kinds, all produced by the workshop of Lydos, painted either by the man himself in his latest period or by his pupils, colleagues, or imitators.[20] With these also may go the black-figured plate in Glasgow with Peleus and Thetis, attributed to a painter working in the manner of Psiax and not far from Paseas. It almost certainly also comes from the area of Chiusi, where Alessandro François discovered it in 1850, since today it is still the only known black-figured plate with the subject of the "love-fight" between the future parents of Achilles, except for the Cretan one, from Praisos, and one from Boeotia, perhaps local or Attic peripheral, in the Louvre.[21]

The series continues in red-figure with a group of seven plates painted by Paseas,[22] which probably should be eight if one also takes into account the plate with white ground rim painted in his manner (Fig. 9), representing a man leading a horse and with the problematic signature of the potter Soklees who, if the inscription is authentic (as I firmly believe), worked in the same *ergasterion*.[23]

The well-known examples are: 1) the one in Boston (01.8025) with Herakles and Cerberus[24] (Fig. 1), which gave the painter one of his initial names, the Cerberus Painter, before J. Boardman associated him with the one who painted the singular inscription [*to*]*n Paseou gram(m)aton* ("one of the paintings by Paseas")[25] on a white-ground *pinax* with Athena and a worshipper, dedicated on the Acropolis;[26] this plate shows also an elegant floral exergue, a special pattern that Paseas shares with the Sosias Painter,[27] Douris,[28] and in a different way with Epiktetos;[29] 2) The one at Yale (1913.170),[30] with Dionysos and a rude dancing satyr in the gesture of the *aposkopein* (Fig. 2), who covers his eyes before the bedazzling epiphany of the *Diosphos*;[31] 3) The very famous one in Oxford[32] with the inscription *Miltiades kalos* (Fig. 3; Color Pl. 9A). This is the only occurrence of the name on Attic vases and probably celebrates Miltiades the Younger, the eponymous archon in Athens in 524/523 BC, who was sent by the sons of Peisistratos, around 516 BC, to take over the rule of his family's domain in the Thracian Chersonese, as Herodotus informs us.[33] He was the hero celebrated by Pherekydes of Athens for having repelled, together with the Scythians, the first attack of Darius in 513 BC. Representing him as an archer and

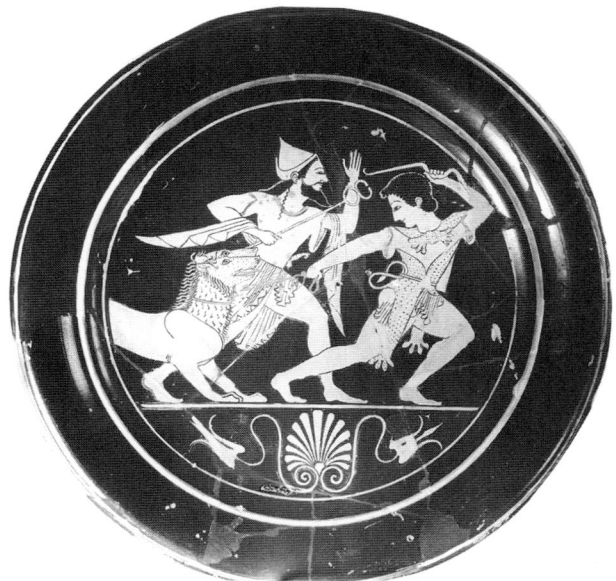

Fig. 1 Plate attributed to Paseas (formerly Cerberus Painter, namepiece): Herakles and Cerberus. Museum of Fine Arts, Boston 01.8025. From Chiusi.

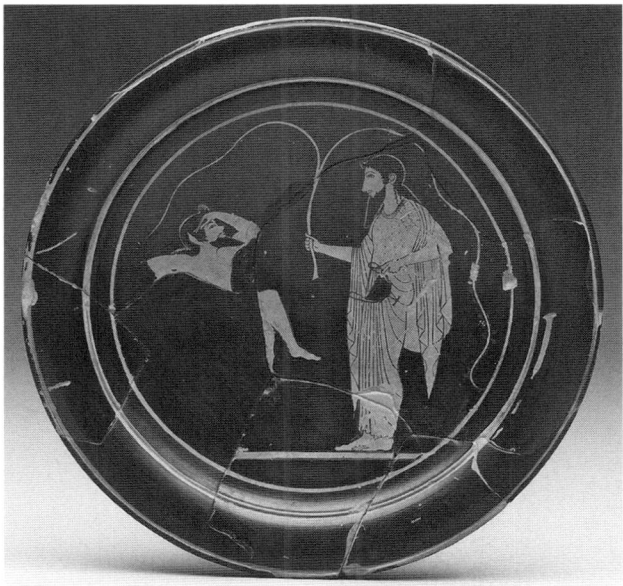

Fig. 2 Plate attributed to Paseas: Dionysus's epiphany in front of a satyr. New Haven, Yale Museum 1913.170. From Chiusi.

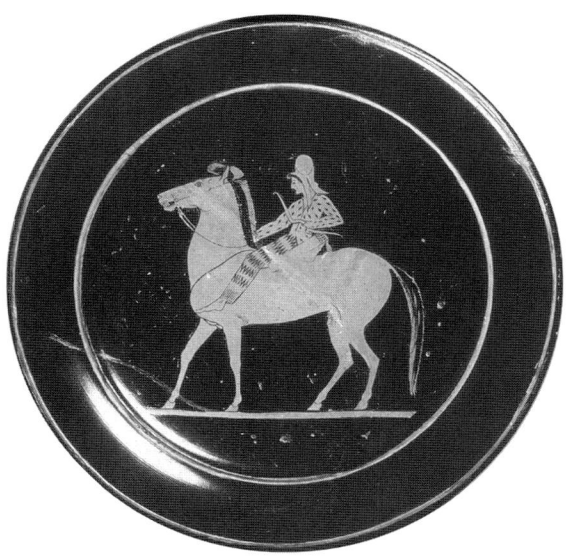

Fig. 3 Plate attributed to Paseas: horseman in Scythian costume, inscription Miltiades kalos. Oxford, Ashmolean Museum 310. From Chiusi.

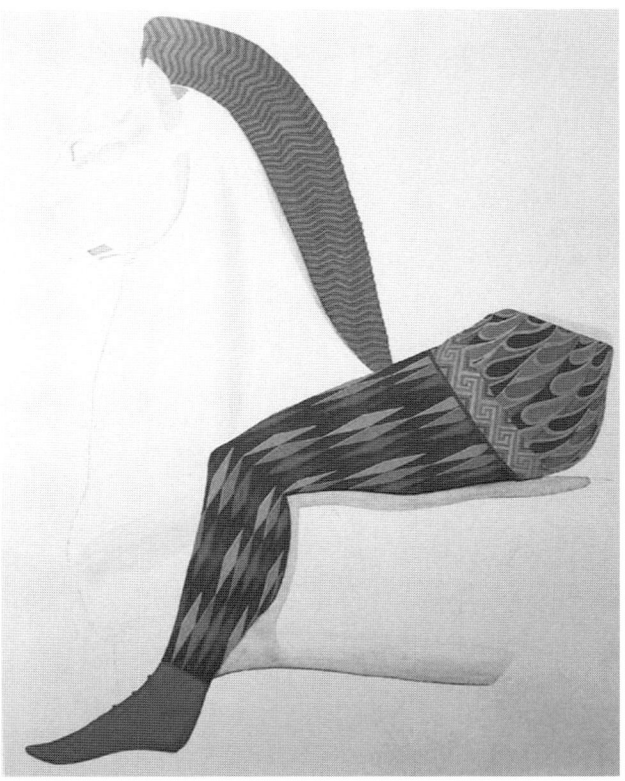

Fig. 4 The Scythian costume of the horseman Acr. 606, reconstruction of the colors (after V. Brinckmann – R. Wünsche, Gods in Color. Painted Sculpture of Classical Antiquity [2007] 80 fig. 126).

definitely in Scythian dress (not Thracian), on the small terracotta plate that found its way to Chiusi, Paseas seems to have copied faithfully the statue of the Scythian rider dedicated (perhaps by Miltiades himself?) on the Acropolis of Athens (Fig. 4), which probably celebrated the humiliating defeat suffered by the King of Persia;[34] 4) The plate once in the Pizzati collection in Florence, then in the Hull collection at Blaydes House in England, and subsequently lost (Fig. 5). It depicts *Io apotauromene* whom Hermes liberates from her torment by killing Argos.[35] Hera's avenger is depicted normally, with only one eye, a conceit which we can still find in the same Pherekydes. This is not, therefore, the version of Argos with two eyes in front and two in back recorded in the epic poem *Aigimios*, perhaps by Hesiod or by Kekrops of Miletus, which was the inspiration for Exekias' amphora from Bomarzo in London;[36] nor is he the Argos with the body covered with eyes, as later described by Aeschylus, who, in the *Prometheus*,[37] defines him as *myriopos*, "with a myriad of eyes," and in the *Suppliants*[38] as *panoptes*, "the one who sees all".[39] The Argos plate was found in the same Chiusine tomb as another plate; 5) in Boston (03.785), depicting the athletes Dorotheos and Chsenophon with a discus (Fig. 6; Color Pl. 9B);[40] 6) Another one of these plates, less well-known, comes from the necropolis associated with the Etruscan settlement of Bettolle, in the area of ancient *Camars* or *Clevsie* – today Chiusi, and more precisely from a group of not more than seven or eight tombs excavated by Count Napoleone Passerini, a senator of the Italian Kingdom in 1905, in the park south of his villa.[41] The plate (Figs. 7, 14, 19 and Color Pl. 9C), which was previously mentioned only in passing,[42] depicts an *auletris* playing while a youth with Negroid

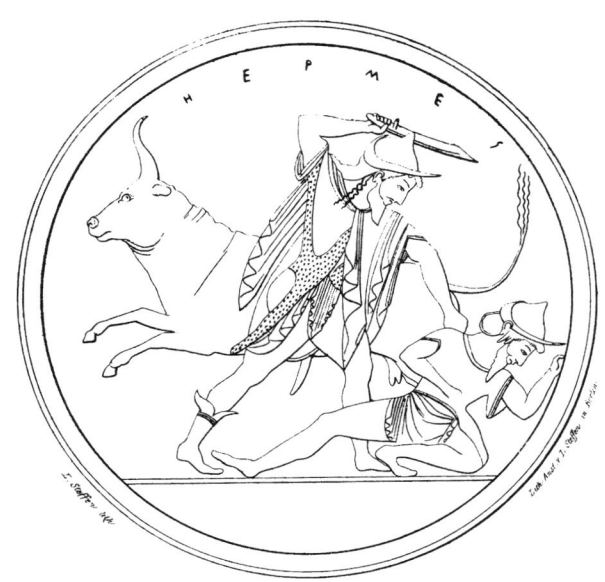

Fig. 5 Drawing of a lost plate attributed to Paseas: Io apotauromene and Hermes killing Argos. Once Florence, Pizzati Collection; then Blaydes House, Hull Collection (after AZ 5, 1847, pl. II). From Chiusi, discovered with Fig. 6.

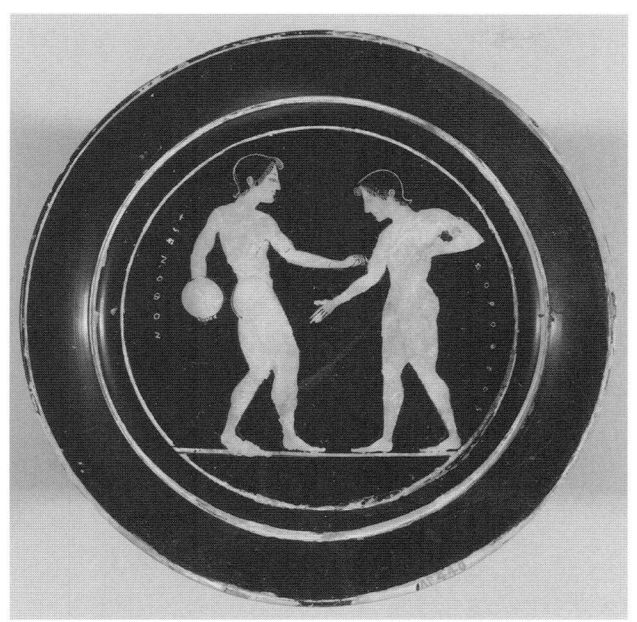

Fig. 6 Plate attributed to Paseas: Dorotheos and Chsenophon with a discus. Museum of Fine Arts, Boston 03.785. From Chiusi, discovered with Fig. 5.

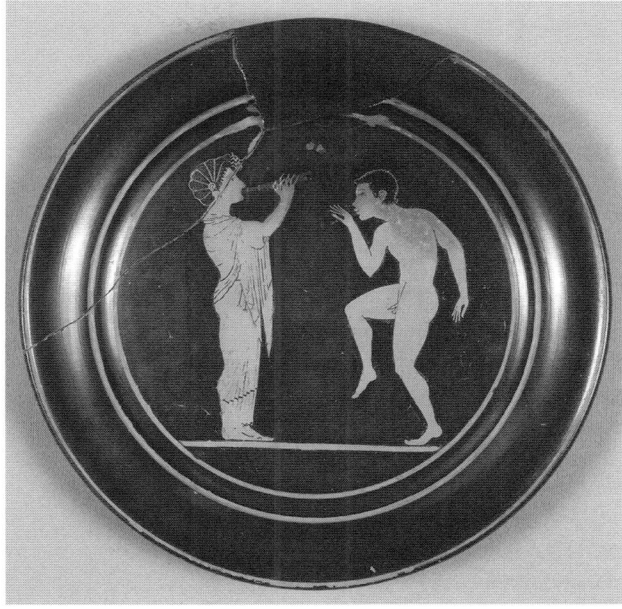

Fig. 7 Plate attributed to Paseas: auletris and negro dancer. Chiusi, National Archaeological Museum 252138 (formerly Bettolle, Passerini Collection). From Bettolle, discovered with Fig. 22.

features dances. The girl, who differs somewhat from the one painted by Psiax on his Anacreontic plate in Basle,[43] stands dressed in a fine *chiton*, its hem at mid-leg, and with a *himation* over her shoulders. She is adorned with a beribboned *mitra*, elegant headwear of oriental origin,[44] and with disc-shaped earrings as well as a *hormos* around her neck. The youth is nude, crowned by a floral wreath which is not easily seen today. The *aulos*, too, which the girl plays by puffing out her cheeks, is nearly gone, and the added color is only a ghost.[45] The luxurious costume[46] of the flute-player shows that she is a *megalomisthos*, an elite professional, who, together with her partner, an exotic African dancer probably also of servile status,[47] gladdens a symposium in Peisistratid Athens. In this period an *auletris* still had not become synonymous with a prostitute costing two drachmas a night (the maximum price allowed by law for flute-girls), as will be the case in the time of Aristophanes, Xenophon, Epikrates, and Aristotle.[48] Pairs of performers recall those later described by Xenophon in his *Symposium*, when a good flute-girl, a dancer who could do amazing tricks, and a very attractive boy who danced beautifully arrived in the *andron* of Kallias' house.[49] The association of a beautiful courtesan and a black youth brings to mind the janiform *aryballos* of the Epilykos Class in the Louvre.[50] Paseas already had created a two-figure composition, a musician and a beautiful girl at a symposium, on a true masterpiece in miniature, the squat *lekythos* in Berlin, which is, perhaps, from Cerveteri (Fig. 8);[51] 7) Another plate from Chiusi is the one with the man holding a horse by the reins, potted by Soklees and painted by a potter who worked in Paseas' manner (Fig. 9).

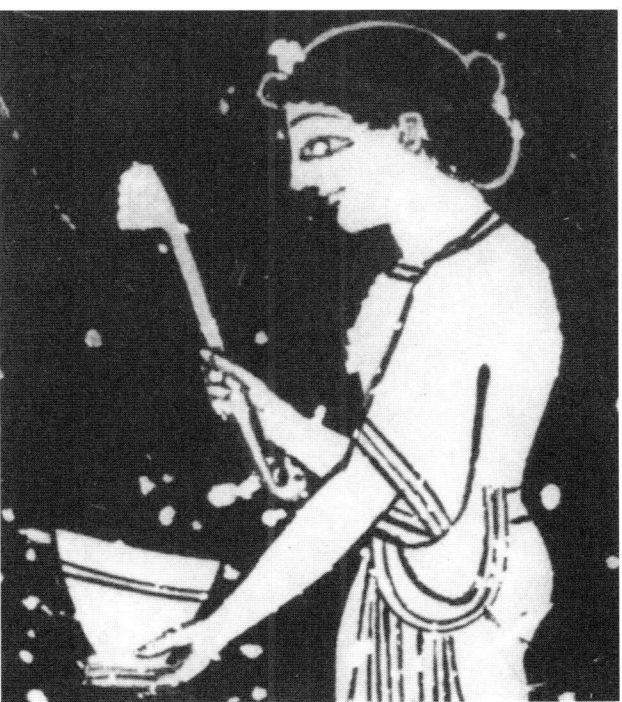

Fig. 8 Drawing of a squat lekythos attributed to Paseas: girl at a symposium (detail after CVA Berlin 8 Germany 62 pl. 38,7). Berlin, Antikensammlung 1960.32. From Cerveteri?

The style of Paseas[52] may be recognized by his carefully-drawn and usually rather vigorous figures who, nevertheless, move gracefully. Their bodies are generally quite well proportioned, but in some cases the torso is too short, with hardly a hint of foreshortening, yet their heads can be rather large and the legs very thin, especially the calves. The eyes, narrow and elongated, are set very high, near the bridge of the nose, with the upper eyelid sharply arched while the lower is straight. They frequently show a distinction between the iris and the pupil, as in our example and as one can see on the fragments of a kantharoid vase from the Athenian Acropolis (Fig. 10).[53] As so often among the Late Archaic painters, and as Paseas himself also does on his black-figured vases, the hair is rendered three-dimensionally by slightly raised, glazed dots of clay that indicate the individual curly locks,[54] here more visible in the young girl's hair; an invention that, in the realm of figured Attic vases, can be credited to the great Exekias,[55] and which Paseas probably inherited from Psiax through the Andokides Painter. His garments are sometimes a little stiff, especially the *himatia*, like, for instance, in the fragment of a Type C cup from Populonia (Fig. 11);[56] but the painter has a sure hand when drawing the delicate, undulating folds of *chitons*, and in general his garments are correctly drawn and richly detailed.

In a number of pictures by Paseas, some figures have reduced proportions, namely, those figures upon which the dramatic effect of the scene is focused. On one of the plates at Yale (Fig. 12) is the oldest red-figure representation of Kassandra clinging to the statue of Athena Polias. The adolescent body of Cassandra underscores how defenseless the Trojan princess is in the face of the violent Ajax, who towers over her and who is hardly any smaller than the statue of Athena, behind which the young girl hides and which she holds onto with one arm.[57] The diminutive size of Cassandra takes its place in a well-established iconographic tradition,[58] yet on the Louvre plate with the killing of the Minotaur (Fig. 13; Color Pl. 9D), this terrible adversary, who very often is even larger than Theseus, has become a small, monstrous boy whom the hero greatly surpasses in height.[59] Perhaps Paseas wanted to magnify the glory of the Athenian hero, but it seems to me that here the result is otherwise, in this almost lopsided fight between the two.[60] The plate,

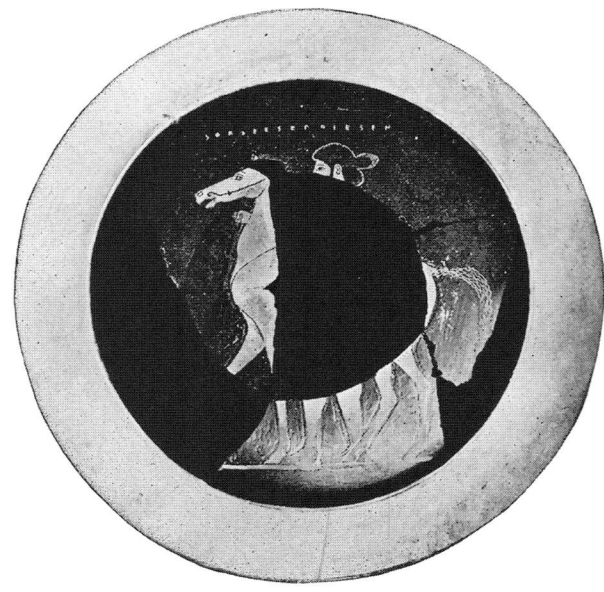

Fig. 9 Plate attributed to Paseas, with the potter's signature Soklees: man leading a horse. Paris, Louvre CA 2181. From Chiusi.

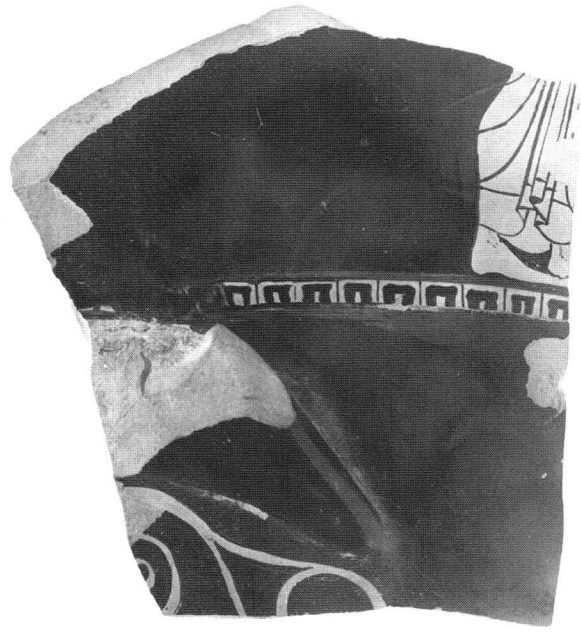
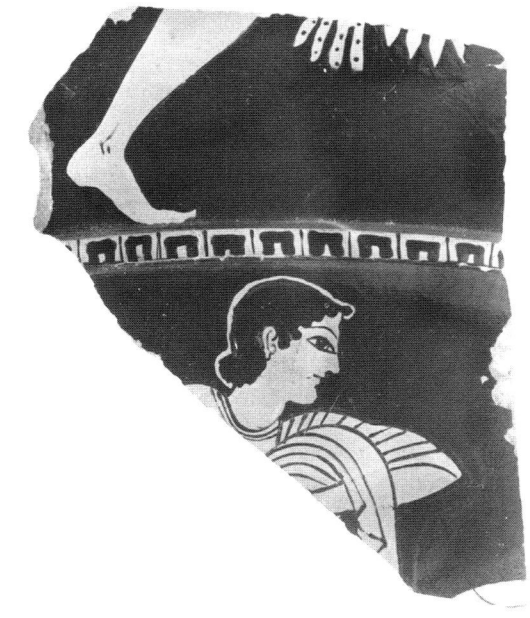

Fig. 10 Frs. of a kantharoid vase attributed to Paseas: above an adventure of Herakles, a youth below. Athens, National Archaeological Museum Acr 551. From the Acropolis of Athens.

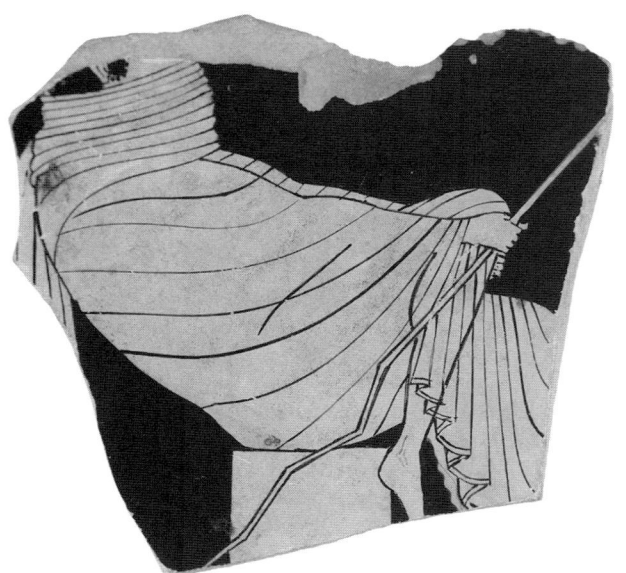

Fig. 11 Fr. of a cup attributed to Paseas. I: mantled youth seated, with stick. Florence, National Archaeological Museum 153086 (formerly PD 147). From Populonia.

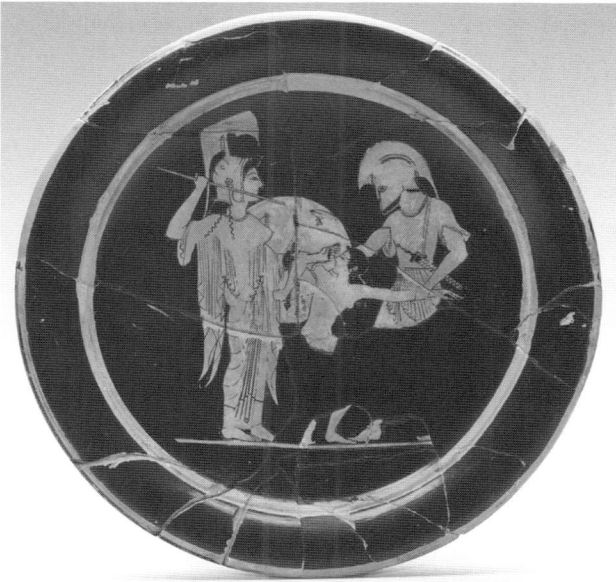

Fig. 12 Plate attributed to Paseas: Ajax and Kassandra at the Palladion. New Haven, Yale University Art Gallery 1913.169.

then, belongs in that iconographic tradition developed in Athens a few decades earlier (just after the middle of the century), that tended to represent the Minotaur as a helpless victim, already defeated; a tradition that will find its full realization in Euripides' lost tragedy *Kretes* and that will lead, over time, to the Etruscan iconography of a childish monster that shows all his weakness, as a being who suffers the mistakes made by others before him.[61]

The tondo of our plate is framed by a reserved double line which marks the offset of the sides and which is also found on the examples in Yale, with Dionysos and a satyr, and in the Metropolitan Museum of Art, where, however, the band on the offset is reserved. The two-figured composition, the one favored by Paseas, is balanced and symmetrical; the ground-line, occasionally short and placed rather high, is of a type which he shares with Euthymides and Oltos, with some plates by Epiktetos, as well as with Psiax.[62]

The undersides of the plates by Paseas are quite varied (Fig. 14). The arrangement and depth of the small circles in relief are different in each example and are placed in different locations; the black bands painted on the outside surfaces vary like this, too. If one considers how even the rims are not exactly the same, it is clear that Paseas painted for a potter who did not create his plates with an existing mold, but turned them freely by hand and varied the profile from time to time.[63] According to Callipolitis-Feytmans, in fact, almost all the plates by Paseas were the work of a single potter, who could be the one who also made the Chalcidizing cup now in the Villa Giulia, Heidelberg and probably Amsterdam also (Fig. 15), with Herakles and Geryon on one side and a puzzling scene on the other, perhaps an assembly of gods that include at least

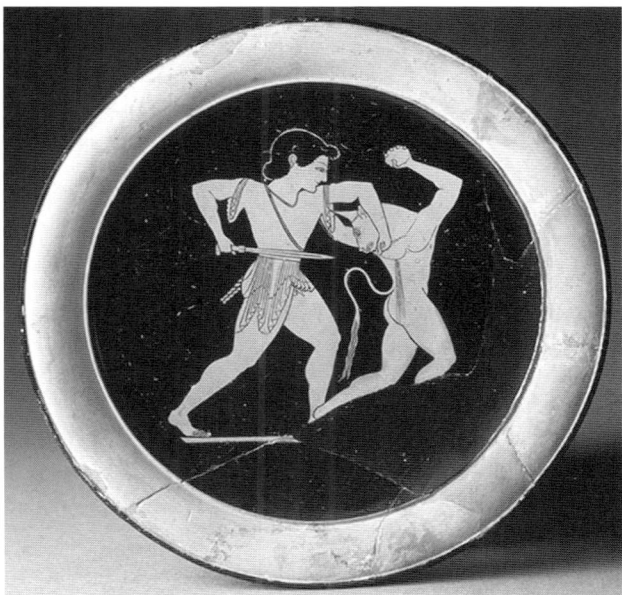

Fig. 13 Plate attributed to Paseas: Theseus and the Minotaur. Paris, Louvre G 67.

Apollo and Artemis.[64] The plate from Bettolle also belongs to this group, as shown especially by its similarities with the ones in Boston and the Metropolitan Museum of Art.

From the series of plates by Paseas, D. von Bothmer has separated out the one from Taranto, now in Amsterdam (Fig. 16) as probably by a different *poietes*.[65] Here, Paseas has left us a rare example of a figured plate decorated on both sides: in the tondo are part of an athlete with his seated trainer, and on the underside are the legs of a male running and the inscription (EPI)DROMOS. This makes

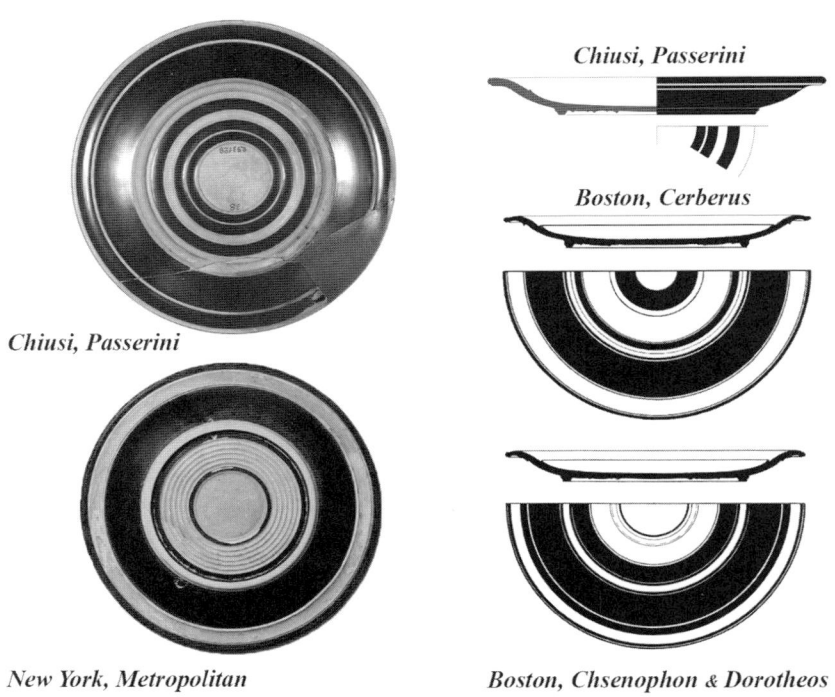

Fig. 14 Undersides of some plates painted by Paseas.

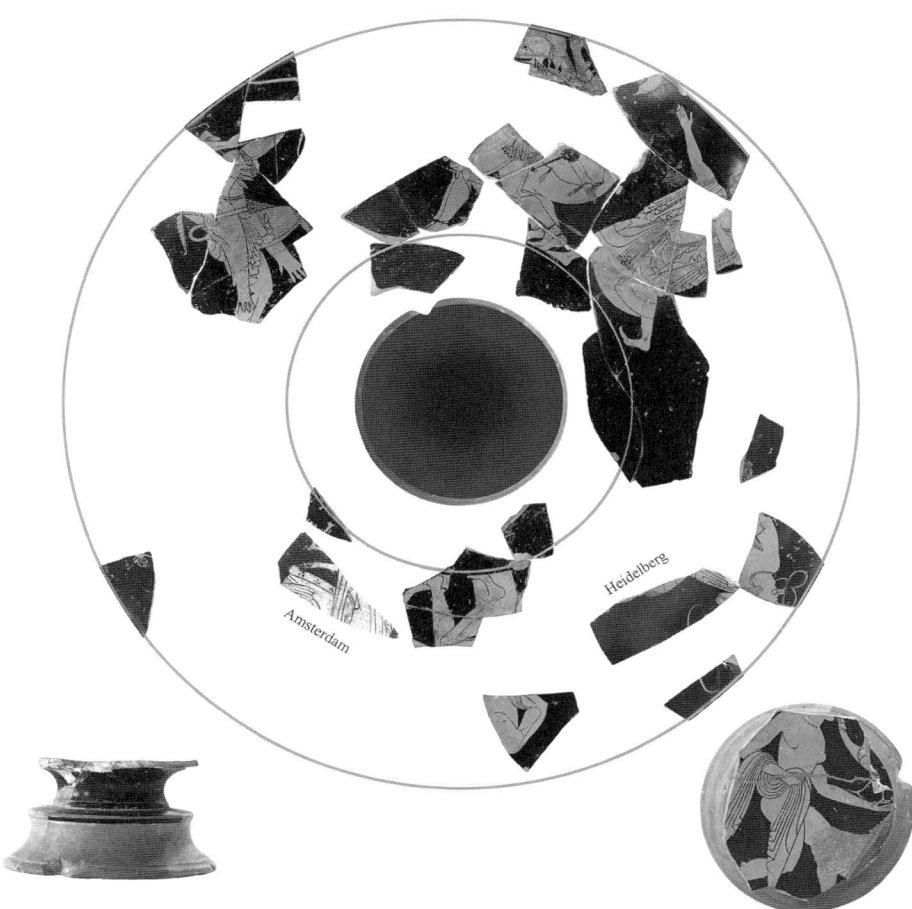

Fig. 15 Chalcidizing cup attributed to Paseas. I: hetaira with phallus-bird; A: Herakles and Geryon, with Ge; B: assembly of gods. Rome, Villa Giulia (no inv.) + Heidelberg, Univ. B 25 (Kr. 20) + Amsterdam, Allard Pierson 2892. Hypothetical photomontage by the author.

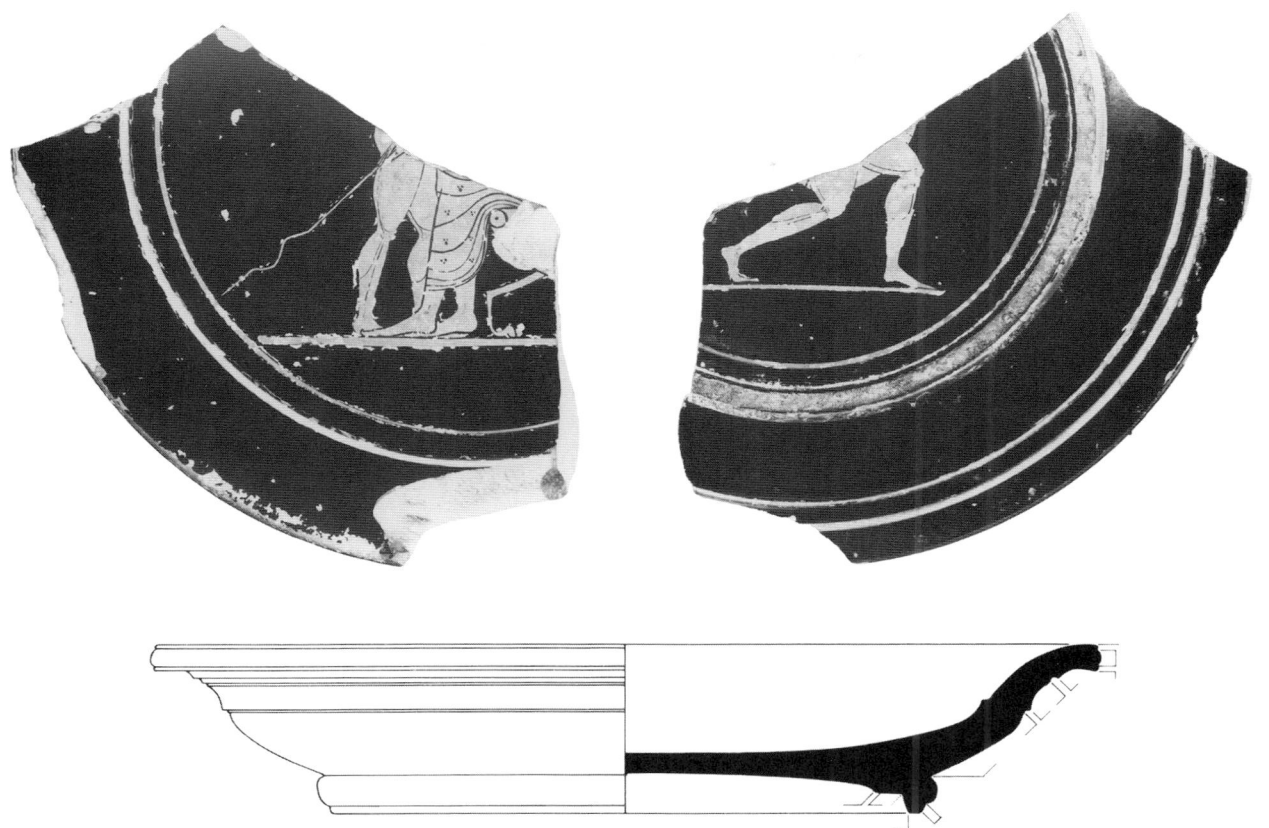

Fig. 16 Fr. of a plate attributed to Paseas, figured on both faces. Amsterdam, Allard Pierson 2474. From Taranto.

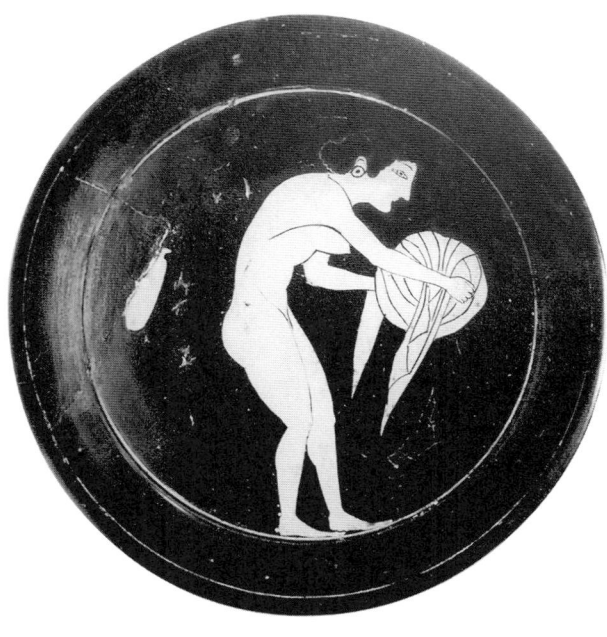

Fig. 17 Unattributed plate, namepiece of the Class of Berkeley 8/5: nude woman preparing for her bath. Berkeley, Phoebe Apperson Hearst Museum 8/5.

perfect sense as an object which must have been hung up, as shown by the drilled holes for suspension that all the examples probably had. The plate in Berkeley (Fig. 17) has a different and simpler shape, for which Callipolitis-Feytmans put together a separate class (the Class of Berkeley 8/5). This plate, one of the oldest depictions of a nude woman preparing for her bath, had first been attributed by H. R. W. Smith to Paseas, but according to Beazley[66] it recalled early works of Oltos; over time, however, he changed his opinion and excluded the plate from ARV². On the other hand, the fragment in Tübingen (Fig. 18) is close to some of the plates by Paseas, and in fact it must have been made by the same potter as the main group of plates by Paseas and the Chalcidizing cup; however, owing to its style of drawing it must be considered as near Oltos.[67]

The Passerini plate, mentioned once at the end of the nineteenth century, was published recently in a thumbnail-sized photo, and even I placed a small picture of it in an article on the importation of Greek ceramics into Chiusi;[68] until now, however, its inscriptions had eluded all of us. In connection with preparing this paper, though, I actually was able to identify them:[69] painted in those thin red characters typical of Paseas,[70] the letters (Fig. 19) are

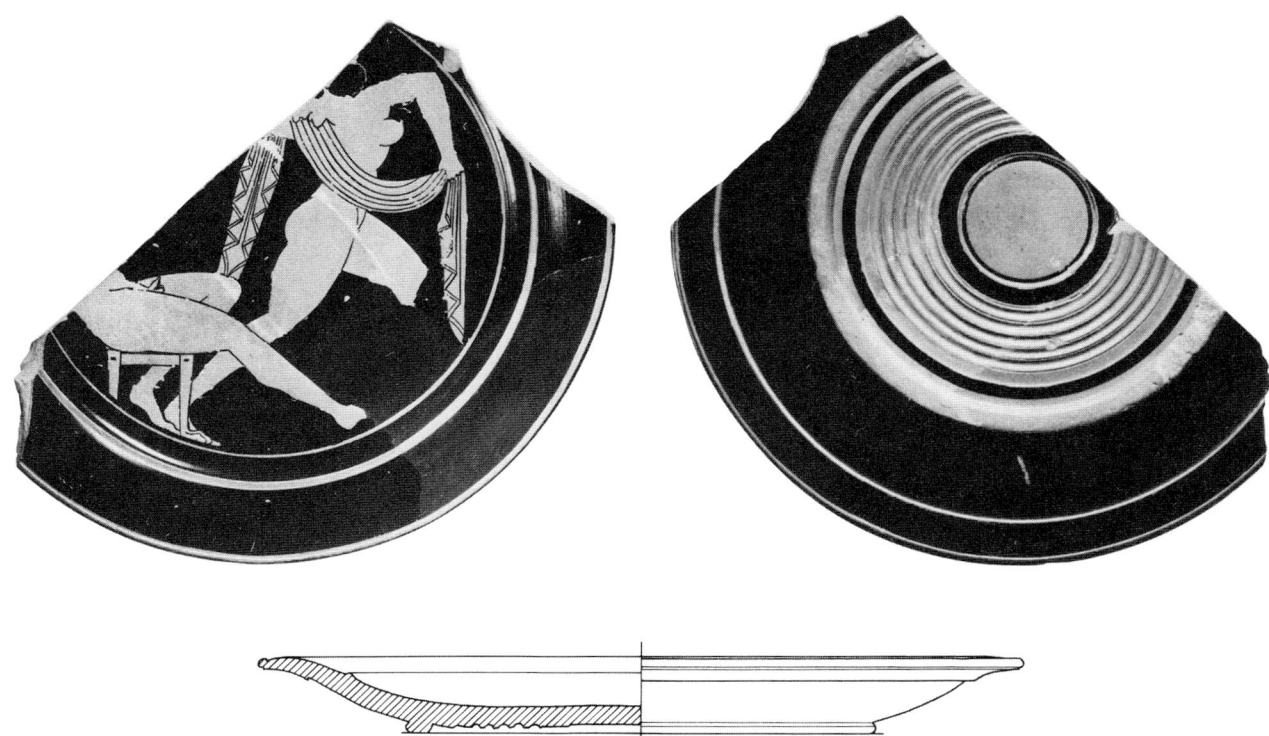

Fig. 18 Fr. of a plate near Oltos: naked youth seated (playing the flute?) and hetaira dancing. Tübingen, Univ. S./10 1539.

evenly spaced and symmetrically disposed around the tondo for Hippotia, the name of the *auletris*, and vertically between the two figures, for Amasis, the dancer. The effect of symmetry like this is striking, because without a doubt the inscriptions are an integral part of the syntax of the overall decoration.

The name Hippotia, "she who rides a horse,"[71] is not attested elsewhere, yet seems to be appropriate for a courtesan, if one considers the well-known association of "riding" in the sexual realm, as also recently examined on the linguistic level by K. Kapparis, and which spread rapidly, starting with Menander, and earlier, perhaps, with Aristophanes, and ending with *Hippopornos* or *Hippoporne* meaning "a horse-whore, a giant whore".[72] Analogous feminine names are found elsewhere, such as Hippotima and especially Hippotis, the depraved mother who abandons her son Staphylos in a vineyard, according to a fragment of a romance, perhaps with a Dionysiac subject, set in the milieu of Miletus or Sardis, and preserved on a papyrus fragment from Oxyrhynchus of the late second century AD in Florence.[73] Hippotia, on the other hand, remains a *hapax*.

By contrast, the name Amasis is attested in archaic Attica and still in late classical Elis.[74] In addition, the name has a number of possible relationships with the philhellene Egyptian pharaoh Ahmoses (Ahmes) of Dynasty 26 (570/569-526 BC).[75] According to Herodotus, Solon visited him and even was inspired by his legislation to enact a law in Athens, although there is a chronological problem with this. Polykrates of Samos made a pact of hospitality with Ahmoses, and he was the one who granted Naukratis to the Greeks, where they maintained what was basically a monopoly of trade with their mother-cities in Greece, and where they set up the Hellenion sanctuary.[76] It is very likely that already by the time of Exekias the name of this famous African king had become a formulaic name for any black. The great Exekias was the first to use the name, and he did so twice, once in the nominative as Amasis (London B 209), and once as Amasos (Philadelphia MS 3442).[77] Recently, the latter has been interpreted as being in the genitive, with Amasos as the shortened form of Amaseos, even though we know that the genitive of Amasis was Amasidos, as used in an inscription naming Amasis as the father of Kleophrades. In fact, the same name, Amasos, appears in a list of nominatives on a fourth-century BC funerary slab from Megara.[78] And then there is the possibility that Exekias was making a joke about his rival Amasis, with whom he might have worked very closely in the small world of the Athenian *Kerameikos*; a kind of joke in which – if it really existed – Paseas also plays a role. This seems to be confirmed by a *lekythos* (Fig. 20) once in a German private collection at Bad Nauheim, later sold at Christie's in 1996, and now in a private collection in New England. It depicts a *komos* of three youths, with music and dancing, and on the topside of the mouth (Fig. 21) one reads the unique inscription of a new potter, which has been interpreted as [Theidiadi]*s epoiesen*.[79] However, I propose to read it

9 Plates by Paseas

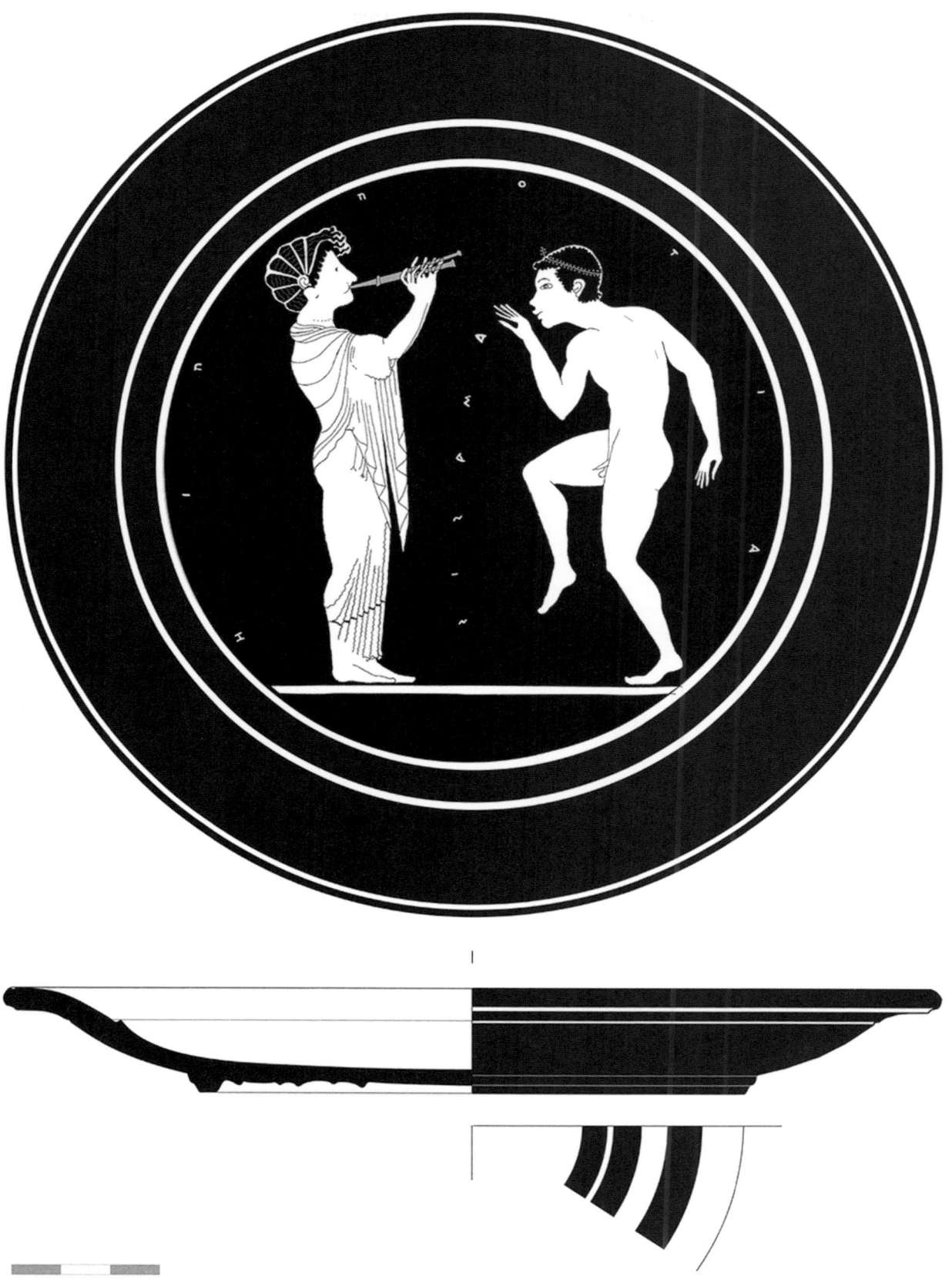

Fig. 19 Drawing of the Passerini plate (see Fig. 7).

as [Pheidiade]s (or Pheidiadis) *epoiesen*, which I believe more probable because it seems to me that the first letter is more likely to be a *phi*. In that case we would have the same name which is praised as *kalos* on two vases by Smikros, and there is the possibility that the one depicted by Smikros as a symposiast is that of another of the artisans of the Athenian *Kerameikos*, one of Smikros' and Paseas' contemporary companions. Consequently, we can recognize this new potter as another one of the leading figures in the ironic and humorous dialogue between the Pioneers, examined most recently by G. Hedreen; a dialogue into which Paseas rightly enters at this point.[80]

In 1879 Wolfgang Helbig, during his travels in Etruria, called on Count Passerini, and in the *Bullettino dell'Instituto di Corrispondenza Archeologica* for that year[81] he gave a brief account of what he had found in the park of Passerini's villa. He records the discovery of two "matching" red-figured plates, both 19 cm in diameter, and gives a detailed enough description so that C. Reusser, in late 2004, could recognize that the second plate (Fig. 22) is the one 8) that was once in the collection of Heinz Hoek in Riehen (Basle), and is now in the Metropolitan Museum of Art, which acquired it in 2010.[82]

So our plate, the one with the *auletris* who plays and the black youth who dances, was a pair with that one, of the same size, which shows a young *auletes* (his beard is just hinted at) and a dancing komast with his *skyphos*. This pair of plates (6 and 8), therefore, shows how music and the *mousourgoi*,[83] the music-makers and especially the professional flute-players, could entertain the symposiasts with the rhythmic sounds of their *auloi*; not only inside, in the *andron*, but also outside, during a *komos* out in the open: this reflects the dualism between the domestic interior of the *oikos* and the civic exterior of the *polis*, that has been pointed out recently by S. Corner.[84]

As is the case with the plate depicting Argos and the one in Boston with the young athletes, the plates once in the Passerini and Hoek collections also arrived in pairs (if they were not part of a set as a matter of course) from the port of Athens to one in Etruria, probably Vulci. From there, they were sent to the wealthy inland city of Chiusi, around the time of Lucumo Porsenna, and then went on to the surrounding area, ending up in the satellite settlement of Bettolle, where they were deposited as *kterismata* in the necropolis of a high-ranking clan, very likely in the

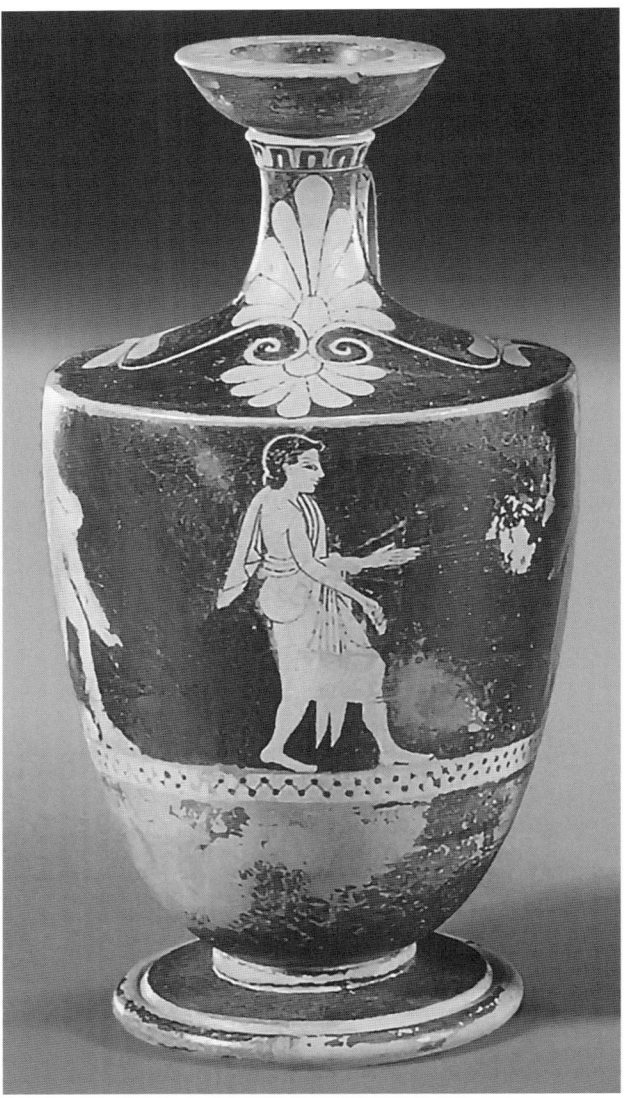

Fig. 20 Lekythos attributed to Paseas, signed [Pheidiade]s epoiesen: komos of three youths, New England, private collection (after Christie's Catalogue 1996).

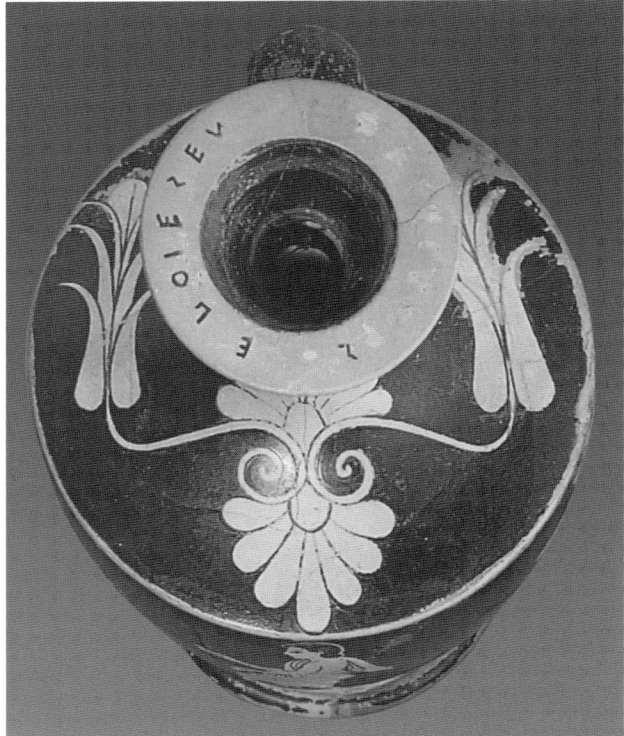

Fig. 21 Lekythos attributed to Paseas (see Fig. 20): detail of the potter's signature on the mouth. New England, private collection (after Christie's, London, 3 July 1996, 54–55 lot 65).

same tomb. Thus, they are part of the phenomenon of paired vases; vases that are twins or closely related in shape and iconography, whose connection with each other is sometimes confirmed by the same Etruscan graffito, and which were deposited in the same funerary context.[85] Here I mention only a few examples: the well-known stands, formerly in the Schimmel Collection, with sphinxes and Iris, attributed to the potter Nikosthenes and the Euergides Painter;[86] two *pyxides* of Nikosthenic shape from the same grave in Poggio Gaiella at Chiusi;[87] the two *hydriai* by the Meidias Painter from Populonia with the myths of Adonis and Phaon;[88] a pair of *lebetes gamikoi* from a late fifth century BC grave of a female in the *Kerameikos* of Athens;[89] two Chalcidian neck-amphorae with riders by the Group of the Phineus Cup, both from the same grave at Metauros, plus two others that ended up in Tampa and Copenhagen;[90] two *kylikes* by Douris with the *hoplon krysis* in the Astarita Collection;[91] two *pelikai* by the Syleus Painter in that same collection, now in the Vatican;[92] and likely even the François Vase with its "younger brother," a large *dinos* by the Painter of London B 76 – two *megala poteria* for the symposium that depict the very same subject, the Thessalian Wedding, and which, perhaps, were exported together to Chiusi and deposited in the same necropolis at Fonte Rotella.[93] This is just to cite the most prominent instances of funerary contexts, but there are many others, and this is without even considering dedications in sanctuaries, about which one can only occasionally be certain about pairs destined for one place, such as, for example, the two Chalcidian neck-amphorae by the Group of the Phineus Cup discovered a few years ago in a votive pit at Pyrgi.[94]

One final issue. In total we have eight plates produced by Paseas and his *ergasterion* that reached the area of Chiusi: the one in Boston with Cerberus (Fig. 1); the one in Yale with Dionysos and a satyr (Fig. 2); the Oxford Miltiades (Fig. 3); the lost one with the killing of Argos (Fig. 5), which formed a pair with the one in Boston depicting athletes (Fig. 6); the one perhaps signed by Soklees with the man and the horse (Fig. 9); and the pair comprising the Passerini (Figs. 7. 19) and Metropolitan Museum of Art (Fig. 22) plates, both with *komos/symposion* scenes. According to Callipolitis-Feytmans,[95] these plates are all different in shape but were all potted by the same *poietes*. They all belong to Paseas' early

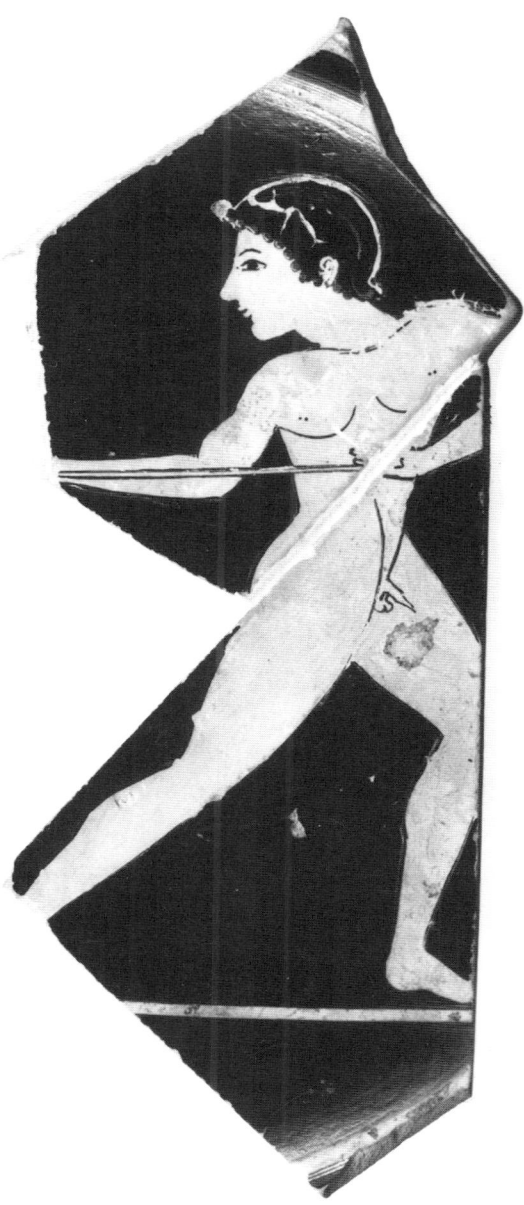

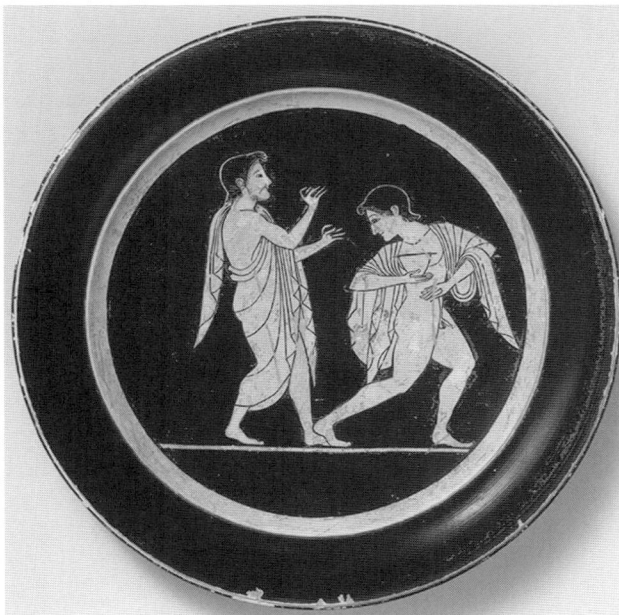

Fig. 22 Plate attributed to Paseas: young auletes and a dancing komast. New York, Metropolitan Museum of Art 2010.64. From Bettolle, discovered with the Passerini plate (Fig. 7).

Fig. 23 Frs. of a plate attributed to Paseas: akontist. London, British Museum E 138 (the lower part formerly Parma, National Archaeological Museum 74).

phase, yet follow a clear development: the oldest is the one with the athletes, with its less concave inner surface, and it goes with a fragment in London with an akontist (and another figure), to which D. von Bothmer added a part formerly in Parma (Fig. 23);[96] the plates with a more concave interior are later, such as the one with the Minotaur and the one depicting Miltiades. And so, if we suppose that the Miltiades plate could date to 516 BC, then we have a possible absolute date for the end of Paseas' early phase.[97]

Now, if these plates were painted at varying intervals of days, months, or even years, yet were found together at Chiusi, then were they all shipped together too? Packed and dispatched to Italy in one shipment that included newly-finished plates along with those that had remained unsold in the workshop? Or did they arrive separately, in several shipments? If we knew, then we will have identified the actual behavior of a group of high-ranking Etruscans who lived in the area of Chiusi, and who had liked Paseas' plates enough to buy several, at different times, and to use them in pairs in a funerary ritual, at least twice. So then, some coastal merchant, probably at Vulci, who had kept in mind the preferences of his clients in inland Etruria, sent plates by Paseas to Chiusi, which from there were sent on to the surrounding area, at least sometimes.

In closing, I ask myself this question: Is it not possible that the development of shape and style that we put together here might be the product of those seven or eight months of work, during which the Athenian potters and painters patiently crafted their vases, and who then waited until the late winter (when Pleiades raised again at sunset) for the resumption (on the occasion of the Great Dionysia, then under the auspices of Dionysus)[98] of sea-voyages to the west and, consequently, for the sale of their products, which in the meantime had accumulated on the shelves? I ask the question, but I have no answer.

Acknowledgements

With many thanks to Enrico Benelli, Ida Caruso and Giulia Rocco (Rome); Elke Böhr (Wiesbaden); Luca Cappuccini (Florence); Jasper Gaunt (Atlanta); Robert Guy (Basle); Michael Halleran (Williamsburg); Giorgos Kavvadias (Athens); Susan Matheson (New Haven); Michael Padgett (Princeton); Dimitris Paleothodoros (Volos); Aaron Paul (Washington D.C.); Hermann Pflug (Heidelberg); Alexandra Villing (London). I am especially grateful to Andrew J. Clark (Los Angeles) for helping me with the translation of this paper.

Abbreviations

Callipolitis-Feytmans   D. Callipolitis-Feytmans, Les plats attiques à figures noires (1974)

Iozzo 2006   M. Iozzo, in: J. de La Genière (ed.), Les clients de la céramique grecque. Actes du Colloque de l'Académie des Inscriptions et Belles-Lettres, Paris, 2004. Cahiers du CVA France 1 (2006) 107–132

Paléothodoros 2004   D. Paléothodoros, Épictétos (2004)

Notes

1   I prefer not to use the ancient word *pinakes* in order to avoid confusion with the clay plaques also painted by Paseas.
2   Callipolitis-Feytmans 211–223; Paléothodoros 2004 13–14.
3   Callipolitis-Feytmans 201. 211–212.
4   For a long time known as a painter of cups only; in 1999 a plate from Gravisca was correctly attributed to him, a work of his later phase (500–490 BC): K. Huber, Gravisca. Scavi nel santuario greco, 6. Le ceramiche attiche a figure rosse (1999) 145 no. 808.
5   For plates by Epiktetos, which belong almost exclusively to the first phase of his activity (520–515 BC), see recently Paléothodoros 2004 13–14. 147–150 nos. 17–28 pls. VII,3–5; VIII–IX; so far only two have been attributed to his third phase (510–500/495 BC): Paléothodoros 2004 40. 166 nos. 139–140 fig. 16 pl. XXXVIII,3.
6   The hypothesis proposed by M. Robertson, A History of Greek Art (1975) 219 was accepted by Paléothodoros 2004 13; Callipolitis-Feytmans 225 held the opposite opinion.
7   Agora XXX 88.
8   On the provenance, see Callipolitis-Feytmans 211 n. 1; 371–377.
9   I. McPhee, in: D. White (ed.), The Extramural Sanctuary of Demeter and Persephone at Cyrene, Libya. Final Reports, VI (1997) 73. 97 nos. 110–112 pl. 42; for those by Epiktetos, see now Paléothodoros 2004 149–150 no. 26 pl. IX,3, with earlier bibliography.
10   Besides the one in Callipolitis-Feytmans 373 n. 21, see also U. Knigge, AA 1983, 215 fig. 15; W. Oenbrink, Hephaistos 14, 1996, 103. 109. 132 no. B 15 fig. 20.
11   To the red-figured plates, add one painted in Six's technique: Agora XXIII 270 no. 1411 pl. 96.
12   Taranto: J. M. Hemelrijk, CVA Amsterdam 1 Netherlands 6 32 pl. 21,4. 6 fig. 64, to which may be added the white-ground examples in the Group of the Negro Alabastra: G. Giboni, in: A. D'Amicis et al., Catalogo del Museo Nazionale Archeologico di Taranto. I,3: Atleti e guerrieri. Tradizioni aristocratiche a Taranto tra VI e V sec. a.C., exh. cat. Taranto 1994 (1994) 316–317 no. 99,1; J. Neils, AntK 23, 1980, 15 no. 4 pl. 3,5 (Group A). Cuma: ARV²

29,3 (manner of Euthymides); 410,67 (Briseis Painter); M. Denoyelle: Vasi antichi. Museo Archeologico Nazionale di Napoli (2009) 57. Gela: G. Giudice – R. Panvini – F. Giudice (eds.), TA ATTIKA. Veder greco a Gela. Ceramiche attiche figurate dall'antica colonia, exh. cat. Gela, Syracuse, and Rhodes, 2004 (2003) 473 no. pl6 (Altamura Painter).

13 Unlike Etruria and Magna Graecia, in Sicily the Attic plates were preceded by several of Corinthian manufacture, already since the Early Protocorinthian period; see D. Callipolitis-Feytmans, BCH 86, 1962: Syrakousai (143 no. 7; 145 no. 10; 155 no. 75; 161 nos. 42–43 a pair in the same grave), Megara Hyblaia (147 no. 1; 148 no. 5), Gela (149 no. 8; 150 no. 16; 151 no. 24; 152 no. 38), Katane (152 no. 34; 155 no. 81), Selinous (152 no. 43; 154 no. 69; 155 no. 74; 156 nos. 101–102); one plate *originis incertae* (but very likely from Sicily) is in the Archaeological Museum of Palermo (154 no. 62); moreover, there is one from Italy in the Bibliothéque Nationale, Paris (154 no. 71).

14 C. Reusser, Vasen für Etrurien. Verbreitung und Funktionen attischer Keramik im Etrurien des 6. und 5. Jahrhunderts vor Christus (2002) passim; C. Reusser, in: H.A. Shapiro – M. Iozzo – A. Lezzi-Hafter (eds.), The François Vase: New Perspectives. Papers of the International Symposium – Villa Spelman, Florence 2003 (2013) 33–51. For the distribution of the Attic red-figured plates see also M. Morandi, StEtr 64, 1998 (2001) 370–374 no. 33; D. Paleothodoros, in: V. Nørskov – L. Hannestad – C. Isler-Kerényi (eds.), The World of Greek Vases, AnalRom Supplementum 41, 2009, 51–54, esp. 54 n. 68. Although scarce, there is also evidence from Etruscan sanctuaries, so it is possible that the figure depends upon the particular type of documentation we have, even though the selection of plates chosen by the Etruscans for their tombs remains unequivocal.

15 The finds from the Agora demonstrate a more intense type of production from the late Classical onwards: Agora XII 14; Agora XXX 143 nos. 57–59 pl. 13; 124. 292–295 nos. 1187–1222 pls. 112–115; Iozzo 2006 115 n. 53.

16 Paleothodoros (supra n. 14) 54 n. 69, with bibliography.

17 Paléothodoros 2004 125–126. 148–150 nos. 17–24. 28 pls. VII,3–5 ; VIII–IX,1–2 fig. 21; Paleothodoros (supra n. 14) 51–54 figs. 4–7. The idea of ten plates is based on the fact that on the underside of another contemporary example, painted by Epiktetos and from Vulci, the graffito "X" appears, which Paleothodoros interprets as the Etruscan numeral ten. In reality this is not the case, as also deduced by A. W. Johnston, Trademarks on Greek Vases (1979) 121 no. 50 Type VIID ii, especially because similar marks (which very often are more like a cross than an X) and analogous non-alphabetical marks are extremely common on Etruscan ceramics; so, as with other marks of uncertain significance (the bar: one or two simple scratched lines; the asterisk: perhaps 100; and the arrow: perhaps 50), and even the "X" are still excluded from the Thesaurus Linguae Etruscae and are not considered numbers. Bear in mind, however, that the marks VIII and XII are thought to be numbers (eight and twelve), and so Paleothodoros' idea cannot be rejected *a priori*.

18 The plates are now in Rome, Museum of Villa Giulia: P. Watson – C. Todeschini, The Medici Conspiracy. The Illicit Journey of Looted Antiquities, from Italy's Tomb Raiders to the World's Greatest Museums (2006) 21. 96. 205; see also The crack down on looted artefacts in museums, Elginism (periodical on line), no. 1801 (December 31, 2005). An image of two of these plates appeared in F. Isman, I predatori dell'arte perduta (2009) 107–109 pl. XXVI, 44–45.

19 Some bibliographic sources on this question are collected in Iozzo 2006 108 (n. 3). 117; for the same opinion, see Reusser, Vasen für Etrurien (supra n. 14) 22, and Reusser, The François Vase (supra n. 14). The shape of plates undoubtedly was very much appreciated in Vulci, where a specialized local production developed, probably by the Group of the Dot-circles: J. G. Szilágyi, in: F. Buranelli (ed.), La raccolta Giacinto Guglielmi, I. La ceramica (1997) 280–282. 287–296; V. Jolivet, in: ibid.: 352–358. The tradition of the use of plates in Etruria is much more ancient: M. Cascianelli, La Tomba Giulimondi di Cerveteri (2003) 42–47.

20 Iozzo 2006 115–116. 131–132 pls. XI,3–4. Another black-figure plate from Chiusi (now whereabouts unknown) is listed among the results of the excavations conducted by A. François in 1851, in a document kept in the Archive of the German Archaeological Institute in Rome (kind information of G. Paolucci). It depicted a hunter and a woman ("*Un cacciatore ed una donna con un Cornopotorio. Fondo rosso e figure nere. Diametro soldi 8*"): could it be the one perhaps by Antimenes Painter, formerly Ludwig and today Basel, LU24 (Callipolitis-Feytmans 156. 339 no. 19, pl. 54; BAPD 5550, with other bibliography, with a little misunderstanding of some details?

21 Iozzo 2006 116 pl. XI,5. The idea of Chiusi as a possible provenance, that goes back to Callipolitis-Feytmans 224 n. 43; 377 no. 6; especially 229 with n. 55, is considered certain in BAPD 7908, but does not appear in E. Moignard, CVA Glasgow 1 Great Britain 18 18–19 pl. 21,4. For the discovery, see G. Henzen, in: BullInst 1851, 171. The Praisos plate is in LIMC VII (1994) 257–258 no. 78 s.v. Peleus (R. Vollkomer); the one from Boeotia, in the Louvre (CA 2569), considered Attic by Vollkommer (258 no. 79), was attributed by Callipolitis-Feytmans 306 no. A I, 67, to an Attic workshop active outside of Athens, but there is the possibility that it is a Boeotian product very much atticizing, as was stated by A. Waiblinger, in CVA Louvre 17 France 26 33–34 pls. 26,2; 31,4 fig. 11. X. Krieger, Der Kampf zwischen Peleus und Thetis in der griechischen Vasenmalerei: eine typologische Untersuchung (1973) 18–20. 22. 174 no. 167 pl. 2b, is in doubt whether the plate is Attic or Euboean, while it is Attic for E. Grabow, Schlangenbilder in der griechischen schwarzfigurigen Vasenkunst (1978) 209. 308 no. 148 pl. 27; it was not included in J. D. Beazley's or in K. Kilinsky's *corpora*.

22 For all of them, see Iozzo 2006 116 ns. 55–56 pls. XI,6–8; XII,1–2. On the painter, see K. Karoglou, Attic Pinakes. Votive Images in Clay (2010) 84–85. 118–119 nos. 69. 207 figs. 35. 96.

23 Iozzo 2006 116 n. 56; R. Blatter, in: R. Vollkommer (ed.), Künstlerlexikon der Antike (2001–2004) 840 s.v. Sokles (I); J. D. Beazley's doubts about the authenticity of the signature still remain unresolved. See: L. Threatte, The Grammar of Attic Inscriptions, II: Morphology (1980) 184. 186; B. Cohen, MetrMusJ 26, 1991, 61. 90 n. 73 fig. 21; H. R. Immerwahr – R. Wachter, A Corpus of Attic Vase

Inscriptions (online, 1998–) no. 6672; M. F. Kilmer – R. Develin, Phoenix 55, 2001, 20. For an opposing view, see Callipolitis-Feytmans 217 n. 23. The inscription is still considered problematic, but this seems to me very unlikely: the fragments of the plate were found by Alessandro François in 1850 and immediately published by G. Henzen, in: BdI for the year 1851, 171, with the signature; it appears to be almost impossible that someone at that time could make such a forgery. We should accept its authenticity, with Cohen as the final word. Moreover, although I personally did not see the plate, thanks to modern technology, by scanning and enlarging the image from J. C. Hoppin, A Handbook of Attic Red-figured Vases II (1919) 420, I see an additional *chi* in the lower right of the signature.

24 BAPD 201524; Iozzo 2006 116 n. 55 no. 2.

25 According to J. Neils, in: J. Neils (ed.), Goddess and Polis. The Panathenaic Festival in Ancient Athens, exh. cat., Hanover, NH – Princeton, NJ 1992 (1992) 147 no. 3, the phrase seems to be an imitation of the official inscriptions on Panathenaic amphorae and, in any case, a type of publicity that Paseas made for himself. For the alternative name of Io-Meister see note 35.

26 Karoglou (supra n. 22) 84–85 no. 69 fig. 35.

27 Berlin F 2278: ARV² 21,1; Para 323; BAdd² 154.

28 Vatican City, Gregorian Etruscan Museum 35091, formerly Astarita collection 132a–b: M. Iozzo, in: G. Rocco – J. Gaunt – M. Iozzo – A. J. Paul, Vasi Antichi Dipinti del Vaticano. La Collezione Astarita nel Museo Gregoriano Etrusco, II,2. Ceramica attica a figure rosse (2014) in press.

29 Paléothodoros 2004 37–38. 166 no. 138 fig. 15 pls. XL–XLI,1.

30 BAPD 201521; Iozzo 2006 116 n. 55 no. 3; CVA Yale 1 USA 38 45–46 pls. 46. 47,2 no. 38.

31 I am uncertain about the interpretation of the satyr as *aposkopōn* as proposed by D. M. Buitron, Attic Vase Painting in New England Collections, exh. cat., Harvard, Fogg Art Museum 1972 (1972) 71 no. 32; in fact, it could be a simple movement in a coarse, energetic dance, or – more probably – connected with the epiphany of Dionysos, against the light of which the satyr shields himself; indeed, the god is praised as kalos Diosphos, "Light of Zeus," on the well-known neck-amphora from S. Maria Capua Vetere, today in Paris (Cabinet des Médailles 219: ABV, 509,120; BAdd² 127), yet even if this epithet seems to be validated by the two torches that the youth holds up to the god, alternative interpretations of the inscription have been proposed: RE 9 (1903) 1144 s.v. Διὸς φώς (O. Kern); F. Lissarrague, Greek Vases. The Athenians and Their Images (2001) 201–202 fig. 158. For the meaning of *aposkopein*, always a sign of bedazzlement, see I. Jucker, Der Gestus des Aposkopein (1956); F. Lissarrague, in: T. H. Carpenter – C. Faraone (eds.), Masks of Dionysus (1993) 219. As reported by Matheson (supra n. 21) 46; M. L. Catoni, Schemata. Comunicazione non verbale nella Grecia antica (2005) 166–170; J. Neils has noted that pictures of the god with a single satyr are rare, but in this case I think it is mainly due to the two-figured composition that suits perfectly the tondo.

32 BAPD 201526; Iozzo 2006 116 n. 55 no. 4.

33 6.40. For another, only theoretical representation of Miltiades see. G. Ferrari, ClAnt 22, 2003, 41. 43.

34 A. Shapiro, in: D. Yatromanolakis (ed.), An Archaeology of Representations. Ancient Greek Vase-Painting and Contemporary Methodologies (2009) 336–340 fig. 9. Still, the possibility remains that there is no relationship between the painted figure and the name praised, as recently maintained, for example, by H. R. Immerwahr, Attic Script. A Survey (1990) 62 n. 21; R. Osborne, Greece in the Making 1200–479 BC (2009) 312–313 with fig. 84. For a reconstruction of the Scythian costume and weapons see L. Bonfante (ed.), The Barbarians of Ancient Europe. Realities and Interactions (2001) pl. VI.

35 BAPD 201523; Iozzo 2006 116 n. 55 no. 7 (with an incorrect LIMC citation: it should be LIMC V (1990) 665 no. 3 s.v. Io I [N. Yalouris]); Threatte (supra n. 23) 76. For the reference to the Florentine collection of Dr. Pizzati see E. Curtius, AZ 5, 1847, 17–19 with pl. II. This was the plate that had given the first name to Paseas, originally called the Io-Meister by E. Pfuhl, Malerei und Zeichnung der Griechen (1923) 433, but the name was replaced with the one proposed a little later by J. D. Beazley, Attische Vasenmaler des rotfigurigen Stils (1925) 29 (Cerberus Painter), definitively confirmed in ARV¹ 55.

36 ABV 148,2; BAdd² 41; BAPD 310422.

37 568; see also 678–679.

38 304–305.

39 The ancient sources are collected by W. H. Roscher, in: W. H. Roscher (ed.), Ausführliches Lexikon der griechischen und römischen Mythologie, 1,1 (1886) 148 s.v. Aigimos; 537–539 s.v. Argos 2. For the epithet *panoptes* see also W. Burkert, GrRomByzSt 7, 1966, 101 n. 74.

40 BAPD 201519; Iozzo 2006 116 n. 55 no. 1. The information about the provenance surely is taken from J. D. Beazley, Attic Red-Figured Vases in American Museums (1918) 14, where the accession number of the Boston plate is wrongly recorded (03.385 instead of 03.785), but the names Xenophon and Dorotheos are unequivocal.

41 Iozzo 2006 116 n. 55 no. 5, pl. XII,1, with bibliography. In 2006, at the suggestion of this author, the Passerini Collection was purchased by the Italian State for the National Archaeological Museum in Chiusi. Published in part by G. Paolucci, Sinalunga e Bettolle. Due centri etruschi della Valdichiana (1996) 14–18. 100–121 figs. 5–8. 10; 80–85. 87–109, this collection is in the process of being studied and republished by the author. For the Passerini jewelry, which already had been acquired in 1890 by the National Archaeological Museum in Florence, and is at present housed in temporary storage in the Civic Archaeological Museum in Cortona, see now M. Giuman, in: S. Fortunelli (ed.), Il Museo della Città Etrusca e Romana di Cortona. Catalogo delle collezioni (2005) 249–252 nos. VI, 119–137 (which also probably joins the diadem no. VI, 113: Paolucci (supra) 101 n. 185.

42 Height 2.2 cm; diameter of the rim 18.9 cm; diameter of the foot 11.3 cm; diameter of the inside tondo 12.5 cm.

43 ABV 294,21; ARV² 11,30; Para 128; BAdd² 77; BAPD 320367; B. Cohen, The Colors of Clay. Special Techniques in Athenian Vases, exh. cat., Malibu 2006 (2006) 199–200 no. 52; A. Shapiro, Re-Fashioning Anakreon in Classical Athens (2012) 17 n. 18 (with bibliographical references to recent works by S. Price, A. Lear, and I. Kantzios).

44 D. C. Kurtz – J. Boardman, in: Greek Vases in The J. P. Getty Museum 3 (1986) 50–56.

45 For the instrument and the position of her fingers, see J. G. Landels, Music in Ancient Greece and Rome (1999) 24–26; S. D. Bundrick, Music and Image in Classical Athens (2005) 34–42; on the mythical context of the aulos, see P. A. Leven, JHS 130, 2010, 35–48. Like the floral crown of the dancer, our aulos very likely was white (with short incisions to indicate the *holmos* and the edge of the shortest pipe); Paseas often uses red as an added-color in his red-figured vases, such as, for instance, for the small leaves of vine-branches, floral crowns, and ribbons. The instrument played on the plate in the Metropolitan Museum of Art must have been white, while the reference to the one at Yale (1913.170) given by T. Mannack, in Vollkommer (supra n. 23) s.v. Paseas 626, must be an error, since the satyr does not have an aulos.

46 J. Neils, in: B. Cohen (ed.), Not the Classical Ideal. Athens and the Construction of the Other in Greek Art (2000) 215–216.

47 F. M. Snowden, Jr., Blacks in Antiquity. Ethiopians in the Greco-Roman Experience (1970) 164–165. 187; N. R. E. Fisher, Slavery in Classical Greece (1993) 55; B. Cohen (supra n. 46) 9. The bibliography on the subject is extensive (see the one recently put together by K. Vlassopoulos, JHS 131, 2011, 115–130), yet the phenomenon of pairs or groups of servile performers such as ours also should be studied.

48 H. Herter, JbAC 3, 1960, 70–111, Italian transl. Il mondo delle cortigiane e delle prostitute, in: G. Arrigoni (ed.), Le donne in Grecia (2008) 367–369. 375–378; J. Davidson, Courtesans & Fishcakes. The Consuming Passions of Classical Athens (1999) 80–82. 104–108 (*megalomisthos*). 124–126, and for the price of flute-girls, 190. 196–198. 204; and see, more recently, L. K. McClure, Courtesans at Table: Gender and Greek Literary Culture in Athenaeus (2003) 21–22; A. Glazebrook, Dike 8, 2005, 45; A. Glazebrook, in A. Glazebrook – M. M. Henry (eds.), Greek Prostitutes in the Ancient Mediterranean 800 B.C.E.–200 C.E. (2011) 47; H. A. Coccagna, in: ibid., 106–122 (119 n. 3, with additional bibliography); N. Sorkin Rabinowitz, in: ibid, 138–139. The word auletris, not "officially" linked to prostitution, is not listed by K. Kapparis, in: ibid. 222–255. Exceptionally, respectable women are depicted playing the aulos, but, obviously, not associated with a sympotic context; see A. Kaufman-Samara, in: APP 285–296; Bundrick (supra n. 45) 92–99.

49 Pl. *Symp.* 2.1, 9.2ff.; Davidson (supra n. 48) 96.

50 ARV^2 1530,2; Para 501; BAdd^2 385; BAPD 231211; H. A. Shapiro, Hesperia 52, 1983, 305; Cohen (supra n. 43) 268–269 no. 79.

51 ARV^2 1630,12bis; CVA Berlin 8 Germany 62 55 pl. 38,1–3; 6–7 Beil. 19,1; BAPD 1006348.

52 Although this writer never received credit for his attribution to Paseas, which was proposed by A. Rastrelli in 1993, he was shown images of the plate at the time when studies were being prepared by Paolucci (supra n. 41) and A. Rastrelli, in: G. Capecchi et al. (eds.), In memoria di E. Paribeni (1998) 339–358 (especially 350). On the painter, see: ARV^2 163–164. 1630; Para 160. 174. 334; BAdd^2 95. 104. 182; Mannack (supra n. 45) 626–627 with bibliography; C. Wagner, in: S. Deacy – A. Villing (eds.), Athena in the Classical World (2001) 99.

101–102; Karoglou (supra n. 22) 46. 84–85 no. 69 fig. 35; ibid. 46 n. 143; 118–119 no. 207 fig. 96 (the *pinax* 1984.131/2 in Oxford, the attribution of which to Paseas has not been accepted by everyone). A bilingual eye-cup signed by Pamphaios, once on the market (in London in 1994 and now whose whereabouts are unknown to me: Sotheby's, New York Parke Burnett, 8 December 1995, no. 65; Mannack [supra n. 45] 627), has been tentatively attributed to Paseas by R. Guy, when the cup belonged to the dealer Bruce McAlpine (information kindly due to Michael Padgett and Robert Guy), but Dietrich von Bothmer did not agree with this attribution; I see the hand of someone close to Paseas (and not far from Oltos), but the letters are very different from his type. I agree with Robert Guy's attribution to Oltos of an unpublished fragmentary plate that once belonged to Robin Symes (now still in London *sub iudice*, among those fragments that the liquidators of Symes' assets are considering giving back to Italy); it represents a female musician holding a *phorminx*; Dietrich von Bothmer attributed it to Paseas (I thank Michael Padgett and Robert Guy for this information).

53 ARV^2 163,12. I thank G. Kavvadias for providing the photos.

54 B. Cohen (supra n. 43) 106–108; see also 122–124 nos. 29–30.

55 Cohen (supra n. 43) 116 n. 7; E. A. Mackay, in: A. J. Clark – J. Gaunt – B. Gilman (eds.), Essays in Honor of D. von Bothmer (2002) 206–207; E. A. Mackay, Tradition and Originality: A Study of Exekias (2010) 6–7 n. 48 pl. 51.

56 Florence, inv. no. 153086 (formerly PD 147): ARV^2 163,11. From the San Cerbone necropolis, close to the Tomba dei Carri.

57 ARV^2 163,4; BAdd^2 182; BAPD 201522; on the spelling of the name Katadra with the omitted nasal, see L. Threatte, The Grammar of Attic Inscriptions, I: Phonology (1980) 488. 450. For the plate see now CVA Yale 1 USA 38 42–44 pls. 45. 47,1 no. 37, with full bibliography.

58 J. B. Connelly, in: J. Holliday (ed.), Narrative and Event in Ancient Art (1993) 88–129.

59 Theseus's wreath is identical to that worn by our small black dancer, a type that Paseas fully shares with Epiktetos.

60 ARV^2 163,7; Cohen (supra n. 23) 63 n. 73 fig. 21; BAPD 201533.

61 LIMC VI (1992) 580–581 s.v. Minotauros (S. Woodford); S. Muth, MüJB 55, 2004, 7–31; see also F. Díez Platas, Despalabro 5, 2011, B 55.

62 Callipolitis-Feytmans 215 n. 16.

63 Besides the types distinguished by Callipolitis-Feytmans, also see Agora XII 144–150.

64 Callipolitis-Feytmans 214 n. 9; 217. The Villa Giulia cup (without inv. no.) + Heidelberg B 25 (Kr. 20): ARV^2 163,10, where the references to inv. no. 20 lists W. Kreiker, Katalog der Sammlung antiker Kleinkunst der Universität Heidelberg, I. Die rotfigurigen attischen Vasen (1931) pl. 4 no. 20; BAPD 201528; H. Bloesch, Formen attischer Schalen von Exekias bis zum Ende des strengen Stils (1940) 28–29 no. 11; J. Keck, Studien zur Rezeption fremder Einflüsse in der chalkidischen Keramik. Ein Beitrag zur Lokalisierungsfrage (1988) 287 no. 25. The cup shows in the tondo a hetaira with a phallus-bird and

the right-handed letters EI painted between her left arm and thigh. On A, Herakles and Geryon, with Ge arriving quickly from right. On B a puzzling scene, with Artemis to right, a man seated on a *thakos*, in front of another figure seated (feet on a *hypopodion*). To this side Robert Guy added, in 1981, a small rim fragment with part of the right-handed inscription (APO)LLON. While I was preparing this paper, he also suggested to me that a small fragment in Amsterdam (Allard Pierson Museum, inv. no. 2892) can possibly belong to the same cup; following this brilliant idea, I made the purely hypothetical photomontage in Fig. 15, where the leg of the Amsterdam *diphros* could be placed above the small fragment in the Villa Giulia with part of a simple foot (even though *diphroi* usually have animal paws). The fragment in Amsterdam: CVA Amsterdam 1 The Netherlands 6 29 pl. 19,4.

65 See n. 12.

66 ARV^1 44; in ARV^2 the plate is listed in the index on p. 1756, but then it does not appear on p. 69 as expected); Callipolitis-Feytmans 214. 372 no. 9 fig. 54: Class of Berkeley '815' (unfortunately, the number is wrong; it should be 8/5); BAPD 1012156; R. F. Sutton, Jr, in: APP II 271–272 fig. 6; Idem, in: C. Kosso – A. Scott (eds.), The Nature and Function of Water, Baths, Bathing, and Hygiene from Antiquity through the Renaissance (2009) 73 n. 35.

67 ARV^2 1630; Callipolitis-Feytmans 373 no. 23 fig. 55; CVA Tübingen 5 Germany 54 13 pl. 1,8–9 fig. 2.

68 Paolucci (supra n. 41) 111–112 fig. 94; Iozzo 2006 116 no. 5; n. 55 fig. XII,1.

69 With the help of Luca Cappuccini (Università di Firenze), who executed the drawings of the plate.

70 Immerwahr (supra n. 34) 58 figs. 78–79 (the Boston plate with Chsenophon and Dorotheos).

71 The obvious connection is the substantive *hippotes*, the most famous use of which is for Nestor, called "the horseman" twenty-one times in the *Iliad* and ten times in the *Odyssey* (the full Homeric title is *Gerenios hippota Nestor*, but the meaning of the epithet is still obscure; simply *hippota Nestor* once in the *Iliad*): D. Frame, Hippota Nestor (2009), Introduction, n. 1.

72 Kapparis cit. (n. 48) 230–231. 235.

73 For an aetiological discussion of the names, see: E. Crisci, in: G. Cavallo – E. Crisci – G. Messeri – R. Pintaudi (eds.), Scrivere libri e documenti nel mondo antico, exh. cat., Firenze 1998 (1998) 103–104 no. 22 (PSI XI 1220) pl. XIX; T. Corsten (ed.), A Lexicon of Greek Personal Names, V.A. Coastal Asia Minor: Pontos to Ionia (2010) 231. Hippotima: P. M. Fraser – E. Matthews (eds.), A Lexicon of Greek Personal Names, III.B. Central Greece: From the Megarid to Thessaly (2000) 210. The masculine names Hippotas and Hippotion: P. M. Fraser – E. Matthews (eds.), ibid. I. The Aegean Islands, Cyprus, Cyrenaica (1987) 237; P. M. Fraser – E. Matthews (eds.), ibid. III.A. The Peloponnese, Western Greece, Sicily, and Magna Graecia (1997) 223; Fraser – Matthews ibid., III.B, 210; P. M. Fraser – E. Matthews (eds.), A Lexicon of Greek Personal Names IV. Macedonia, Thrace, Northern Regions of the Black Sea (2005) 177. On Hippotion as a horseman or stable-boy in Corinthian ceramics, see LIMC V (1990) s.v. Hippotion I 475 (P. Müller); LIMC VI (1992) s.v. Laodamas II (P. Müller) 191 no. 1.

74 M. J. Osborne – S. G. Byrne (eds.), A Lexicon of Greek Personal Names, II. Attica (1994) 24; Fraser – Matthews (supra n. 73) III.A 32.

75 J. Boardman, JHS 78, 1958, 1–3; D. von Bothmer, GettyMusJ 9, 1981, 1–4; idem, in: H. de Meulenaere – L. Limme (eds.), Artibus Aegypti. Studia in Honorem B. von Bothmer (1983) 15–23; J. Boardman, in: Papers on the Amasis Painter and his World. Colloquium J. Paul Getty Museum 1986 (1987) 148–150.

76 1.30 and 2.177–179; 3.39–43 and 122–125.

77 ARV^2 144,8; 686 and 145,14; Para 60; BAdd^2 39–40; Mackay 2010 (supra n. 55) 201–213 no. 18 pls. 49–51; 291–303 no. 27 pls. 69–71.

78 The signature Kleophrades eposiesen Amasidos on the Douris cup in Malibu: BAdd^2 395. 403. 405; BAPD 13342. The inscription from Megara: Fraser – Matthews (supra n. 73) III.B, 26.

79 From the collection of Dr. Volker Gross, in Bad Nauheim, the lekythos was acquired at Christie's, London, 3 July1996, 54–55 no. 65, by Brian Aitken (Akanthus Gallery, New York), on behalf of a Boston private collector. I warmly thank Michael Padgett and Robert Guy for generously sending me information about this and other vases.

80 G. Hedreen, in: Yatromanolakis (supra n. 34) 200–239; Shapiro (supra n. 43) p. 32; and Hedreen in this volume.

81 W. Helbig, BullInst 11, 1879, 241.

82 New York 2010.64 (diameter of the rim 19.1 cm); passed to William Hoek, in Brussels, and later sold to Robert Haber, in New York: Iozzo 2006 116 no. 6 and n. 55, and add: A. Greifenhagen, JbBerlMus 3, 1961, 130 n. 30; R. Lullies, Griechische Plastik, Vasen und Kleinkunst: Leihgabe aus Privatbesitz, exh. cat., Kassel 1964 (1964) front cover and no. 56; C.A. Picón, BMetrMus 68,2, Fall 2010, 8.

83 Herter (supra n. 48) 375 n. 140; Davidson (supra n. 48) 92–93; Landles (supra n. 44) 7; Bundrick (supra n. 45) 115 (in contrast to the "respectable" *auletrides*: 92–99).

84 S. Corner, in: Glazebrook – Henry (supra n. 48) especially 78–79.

85 For the phenomenon of paired vases see recently C. Isler-Kerényi, Pallas 61, 2003, 46–47 (with previous bibliography).

86 S. A. Hemingway, in: J. M. Padgett (ed.), The Centaur's Smile. The Human Animal in Early Greek Art, exh. cat. Princeton, NJ – Houston 2003–2004 (2003) 280–281 no. 71; Cohen (supra n. 43) 254–257 nos. 72–73.

87 Iozzo 2006 132 pl. XII,4–6; A. Villa, in: D. Barbagli – M. Iozzo (eds.), Etruschi; Chiusi, Siena, Palermo: La Collezione Bonci Casuccini, exh. cat., Siena and Chiusi 2007–2008 (2007) 146–151 nos. 55. 55a. 55b.

88 M. Iozzo, in: N. Chr. Stampolidis – Y. Tassoulas (eds.), Eros. From Hesiod's Theogony to Late Antiquity, exh. cat., Athens 2009–2010 (2009) 164–167 n. 133 (with bibliographical references for both).

89 B. A. Sparkes, The Red and the Black. Studies in Greek Pottery (1996) 69–70 fig. III, 3 with bibliography.

90 M. Iozzo, AttiMemMagnaGr S. III, vol. II, 1993 (1994) 67. 198, nos. ME 2–3, pls. LXXIII–LXXIV. LXXVI, 2.

91 Ast 132–133; M. Iozzo, in: Rocco – Gaunt – Iozzo – Paul (supra n. 28), in press, where I also have gathered some examples of pairs of vases, along with some bibliography on the phenomenon of "repetition".

92 For the two pelikai, Ast 731–732, and some other twin vases connected with them see G. Rocco, in: Rocco – Gaunt – Iozzo – Paul (supra n. 28) in press.
93 M. Iozzo, in: E. M. Moorman – V. Stissi (eds.), Shapes and Images. Studies on Attic Black Figure and Related Topics in Honour of H. A. G. Brijder (2009) 63–85; LIMC Suppl (2009) 413–414 add. 1 s.v. Peleus (M. Iozzo).
94 M. P. Baglione, in: M. Bentz – C. Reusser (eds.) Attische Vasen in etruskischem Kontext: Funde aus Häusern und Heiligtümern, Beihefte zum CVA Deutschland II (2004) 89–90 fig. 8.
95 Callipolitis-Feytmans 215–215. 216 n. 19.
96 British Museum E 138: ARV^2 163,2; Beazley (supra n. 40) 14 fig. 6; for the join see D. Ridgway, ARepLond, 1967–68, 48 fig. 25; Para 337,2.
97 For recent proposals concerning the revision of the chronology of the Pioneers (and others), see R. T. Neer, Style and Politics in Athenian Vase-painting. The Craft of Democracy, ca. 530–460 B.C.E. (2002) 186–205; S. Rotroff, in: Oakley – Coulson – Palagia (supra n. 48), who lowers the introduction of red-figures to 520–515 BC, a date which I would move even slightly later, to around 515 BC, following R. Tölle-Kastenbein, Bemerkungen zur absolute Chronologie spätarchaischer und frühklassischer Denkmäler Athens, AA 1983, 573–584.
98 E. Csapo, The Dionysian Parade and the Poetics of Plenitude (2013) 1–2.

10 Some Greek Vases in the Museum of Mediterranean Archaeology at Nir David (Gan Hashlosha), Israel

Sonia Klinger

The Museum of Mediterranean Archaeology at Nir David (Gan Hashlosha) in the Beit She'an Valley was founded in the early 1960s. It was established to house the archaeological collection belonging to the Swiss collector, archaeologist and artist Dan Lifschitz who arrived at the Kibbutz Nir David in the summer of 1958.[1] The main and most important part of this collection consists of about 135 vases, Attic and non-Attic, ranging in date from the Geometric to the Hellenistic periods. Many of the pieces are fragmentary, and like most vases in private collections, they have no archaeological context. With a few exceptions, many of these vases remain unknown and unpublished.[2] Although a fascicule in the Corpus Vasorum Antiquorum series is in the offing, the project will take a while to complete, and so I was delighted to have been given the opportunity to write a brief account of the collection and present some of its vases here. They are worth a second look, as they touch on some of the core issues of style and iconography in vase-painting scholarship.

Standing out among the non-Attic vases is a Middle Corinthian round aryballos (Figs. 1–3).[3] It has a heavy mouthpiece and broad handle-plate and belongs to Payne's shape A.[4] The vase is complete except for missing parts around the lip, and there are surface abrasions in many places. The clay is buff, and the decoration is executed in black gloss, but some of it has fired light brown and much is quite faint now. Abundant traces of incision can still be seen on the figured scene on the vase's body.

At the top of the lip are radiating tongues between three lines around the mouth and one around its outer edge. Crosshatching covers the handle's top. On the edge of the lip and handle is a zigzag pattern between lines. On the back of the handle, within framing parallel lines, is a finely drawn head, neck and shoulder of a female rendered in outline technique. She looks to the right and has long, brown, wavy hair with a reserved hair-fillet encircling her head. On the field around her are three crosses. Radiating tongues fill the shoulder followed below by a band of zigzag pattern between lines that connect with one on the handle's edges.

Close examination of the vase's body allows us to identify the faint, poorly preserved but richly decorated figured scene framed below by a Z-pattern between parallel lines. The scene comprises seven hoplites in battle and two horsemen, with some of the figures overlapping the upper band and the handle's end; all are surrounded by incised rosettes and other filling ornaments. At the center, opposite the handle, a battle scene shows four fighting helmeted hoplites armed with spears and holding circular shields. Two young, long-haired, beardless riders frame and move toward them (Fig. 3). To their right and left three additional fighting hoplites complete the scene; the central one kneels exactly beneath the handle. The figures are rendered in a variety of postures with plentiful incised decoration marking the anatomy, drapery, and ornament, such as the details that identify the helmets as Corinthian, the circles on the borders of the hoplites' shields and the fillets encircling the riders' heads. Underneath is a whirligig of alternating dark brown, purple and reserved crescents around a depression at the centre.

The vase belongs to a type of aryballos decorated with women's heads on their handles which was described by Humfry Payne,[5] most of which have been attributed to the Boar-Hunt Painter and the Liebieghaus Group, both active during the Middle Corinthian period (595/590–570 BC).[6] Normally the body of these aryballoi is decorated with florals, stars or wheel motives,[7] but some do have interesting figured scenes such as duellists and horsemen, a dancing contest or komasts.[8]

The vase's shape and dimensions, syntax and painting style are closest to an aryballos from Isthmia whose decoration has been attributed by Oscar Broneer to Payne's Early Corinthian Warrior Group, though he identified the shape as Middle Corinthian.[9] Another parallel is the aryballos in Athens from Perachora, decorated on the handle with a woman of similar look and framed within similar parallel lines, though its body is decorated with a gorgoneion and a helmeted head. This aryballos was dated by Payne to the Early Corinthian period, but Neeft has now rightly placed it near the Liebieghaus Group.[10]

The poor condition of the Nir David aryballos detracts from our ability to appreciate its quality, but it was probably as fine as the Isthmia aryballos and may have been painted by the same hand, probably within the Liebieghaus Group in the Middle Corinthian period. The very few differences – the patterns on the handle frame and shoulder, and the different numbers of warriors and their postures – are outweighed by the numerous and obvious affinities: note the very similar sharp profile of the woman and the filling decoration around her, the type of battle scene combining horsemen and armed hoplites around the vase's belly (with some figures also overlapping the upper band), the identical decoration on the hoplites' shields and the similar whirligig and zigzag bands on the vase's rims and handles.

The combination of a woman's head with riders and fighting males on the Isthmia and Nir David aryballoi, or the Perachoran woman and warrior head composition, bring to mind other Middle Corinthian vase paintings with combinations of women's heads and male scenes studied elsewhere.[11] In that study I argued that female heads and protomai, with or without identifying names, are not hetairai but young, respectable Corinthian women approaching marriageable age; the male figures probably represent the male (heroic or communal) role and the padded dancers relate to *Frauenfest* scenes. A look at the iconography of the painted decoration on the aryballoi attributed to the Boar-Hunt Painter, the Liebieghaus Group and those from Isthmia and Perachora with female heads on the handles or underneath the vase, and males in hunting, duels, a competition scene, a padded dancers' scene and warrior friezes or warrior heads, suggest a similar allusion to female and male roles in Corinth. But is there also a link between the scenes, the vase's shape and its use in Corinth?

Aryballoi, oil or perfume containers, are traditionally linked to male athletic activities and were obviously considered suitable gifts for both male and female deities, as exemplified by the Isthmia aryballos offered to Poseidon, the Perachora aryballos, offered to Hera Limeneia, and additional aryballoi also found there.[12] Not many aryballoi were found in the sanctuary of Demeter and Kore at Corinth,[13] but we see them held by male youths in a number of terracotta sculptures and terracotta figurines.[14]

What about the women? Our very limited knowledge on their possible use of aryballoi in Corinth does not allow us to draw definite conclusions. However, there is clear evidence that aryballoi were also linked to women's work and activities. One example is the early Corinthian aryballos in Corinth decorated with a weaving scene illustrating the contest between Athena and Arachne.[15] Not

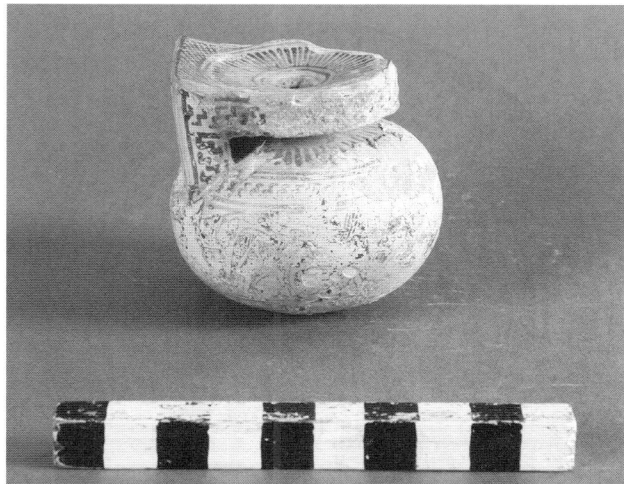

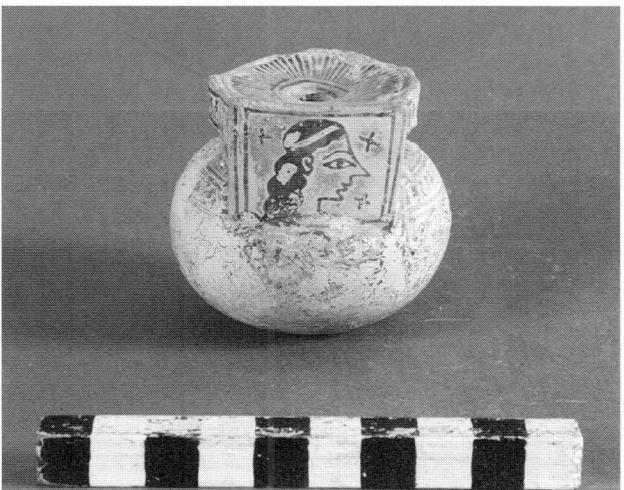

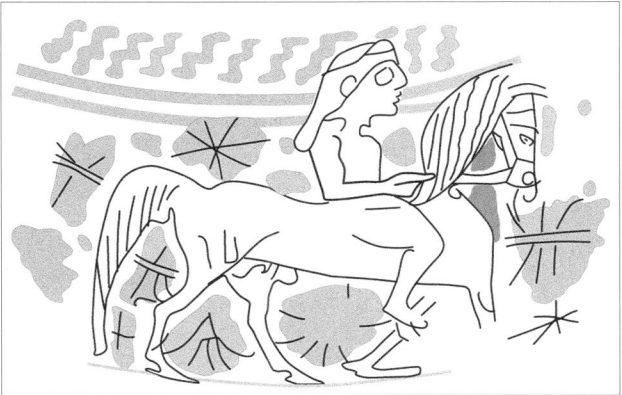

Figs. 1–3 Middle Corinthian aryballos, Probably the Liebieghaus Group, IAA, Inv. 72.5476.

only is the scene obviously linked to the women's world, but two aryballoi are actually illustrated, next to other tools (reels of thread, loom weights?), on the second shelf of the cupboard beneath the handle. These may allude to the concrete use of oil in wool-working.[16] A similar role is suggested by the aryballos represented in another wool-working scene on an Attic red-figure lekythos.[17]

Evidence for a more significant use of aryballoi by women is provided by additional Attic vase paintings: aryballoi turn up in grave offering scenes,[18] and in many athletic/bathing scenes.[19] Although we have no Corinthian vase paintings depicting women making offerings at the grave or athletic/bathing scenes, we do have evidence for female athletic activities in Corinth. As Gloria Merker and Nancy Bookidis argued, there is evidence regarding boys' and girls' athletic competitions held in the sanctuary of Demeter and Kore, including a Corinthian early fifth-century BC kotyle dedicated to Demeter with a crowned female on one side and a foot race on the other.[20] This later vase and the evidence on female athletic activities may help explain the presence of the woman's head on the Nir David aryballos and on the numerous aryballoi produced by the Boar-Hunt Painter and the Liebieghaus Group. They may allude to their presence in athletic competitions and/or be related to the female deities to whom these aryballoi may have been dedicated.

Turning now to the Attic black-figure vases in the Nir David collection,[21] one fine example is a fragmentary one-piece panel amphora of type A (Fig. 4).[22] Its inside is reserved and shows wheel marks. Outside is preserved part of the neck and panel bordered by a lotus-palmette chain between two glossed lines with a red line on top. Details of the panel border are incised and decorated with added red (central sepals and cuffs of lotuses, cores of palmettes). On the panel, and slightly overlapping its border, is a chariot scene with a female figure, Dionysos and the heads of three horses. The branch between the female and Dionysos may have been held by either of them. Some of the gloss is thinly applied (Dionysos' face, second horse's forelock) but most is shiny black. Added white is applied over the black silhouette for the female flesh, and added red is used on the figures and horses.

The female stands on the left in profile view to the right. Her white-painted face and a bit of her black eye, forehead curls and red wreath are preserved. Facing her, Dionysos is standing in profile view to the left. His well-preserved head displays very careful incision that marks his profile's outline, large frontal eye with round pupil and tear duct, long, curved eyebrow, round nostril, slightly open mouth with prominent, fleshy lips, hairy moustache, the separate locks for his long beard and hair, the curly spirals on the forehead, and the elaborate wreath with alternating red and black ivy leaves sprouting out of a knotty branch encircling his head. Note also the meticulous incision used in rendering the horses' profiles, their large eyes with round pupils and long tear duct lines, eyebrows marked with three parallel lines, upright ear, round jawbone, parallel wrinkles at the throttle, and short unconnected lines on the hanging red mane and forelock. Incision defines also the bridle's parts (cheek strap, bit cheekpieces and browband) and the chariot's pole and its vertical end.

The painting style is close to some of the best black-figure work by Psiax. Note especially the similarity to the old man's nose, long eye and hairy moustache on side B of the one-piece amphora in Brescia[23] and Triton's identical pointed nose rendered with incision on the neck amphora in Palermo;[24] also compare Adrastos' similar protuberant lips and moustache and the almost identical markings of the horses' heads on a hydria in Würzburg;[25] the similar profile, protuberant lips and the moustache of Herakles on side B of the bilingual one-piece amphora in Munich;[26] and Dionysos' moustache also on side B of the bilingual one-piece amphora in Madrid, as well as the latter's elaborate wreath with alternating red and black ivy leaves sprouting out of a similar branch.[27] The drawing's meticulous quality and interest in decorative surfaces recalls Mertens' recent description of Psiax' figure work, especially that of his later period (520–510 BC).[28] Scenes with Dionysos and/or members of his entourage abound in Psiax's work,[29] and although the fragment is too small to allow a closer identification of the scene, it would fit well, for example, in a wedding scene or in a mounting chariot scene.[30]

The Nir David collection also includes some unpublished Attic red-figure vases that deserve further study.[31] One fragment stands out for its fine quality and remarkable iconography (Fig. 5).[32] It belongs to a closed shape, possibly the shoulder of a kalpis. The inside is reserved and shows wheel marks. The wall is fairly flat, slightly concave and thicker at the top, but convex and thinner at the bottom.

The scene takes place in the *gynaikonitis*, the women's quarters. The fragment preserves the upper parts of three women. The leftmost one stands in profile view to the

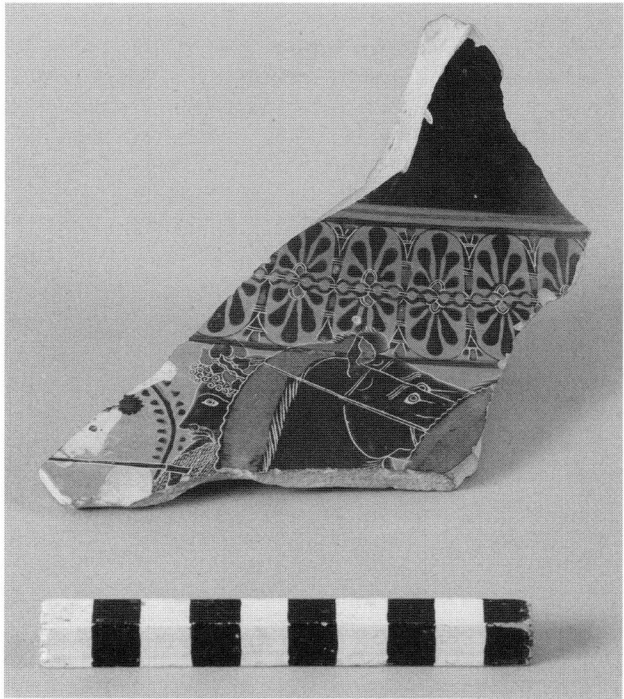

Fig. 4 Attic black-figure fragment, Psiax, IAA, Inv. 72.5454.

right, spinning while facing toward the central woman. She holds a distaff up in her left hand around which threads are wound while her right hand (only its upper part is preserved) draws the white, vertically hanging thread that was probably wound around a spindle but is now mostly faded. Her head is slightly bent as she carefully eyes the thread. The preserved part of her head and arm suggests that she wears a chiton and a hair covering of some sort. The central woman stands in frontal view and looks left toward the spinner while displaying a necklace in white with both hands. She is dressed in chiton and himation, her hair, gathered in a bun, is uncovered, and she wears a small rounded pendant earring. The rightmost female sits on a klismos to the right and faces right suggesting that she is looking toward another figure or figures in the scene. She wears a chiton and himation, her hair is enclosed in a sakkos decorated with two bands of dots and white upright leaves, and, like the central woman, she wears a small rounded pendant earring.

The contour lines are sometimes sloppy, overlapping the edges, for example, of the leftmost and central figures' hands. Dilute gloss is used for the distaff's thread and some anatomical details of her arm, while traces of added white paint are preserved on the hanging yarn, the necklace and the leaves on the leftmost female's head cover.

The painting style is Polygnotan, and details of anatomy and drapery are especially close to Polygnotos' neck-amphora in London belonging to the vase painter's mature phase (440–430 BC).[33] Note particularly the figures' idiosyncratic profile, their eyes crowned by long, round brows, the typical ear composed of a well-defined helix that breaks into a sharp angle at the top, and a round lobe. Note also the middle figure's himation folds, still thick and stiff at the top and combined with straight vertical hooks below. These stiff himation folds are also apparent on the leftmost symposiast on a stamnos from the same phase of the painter's career also in London,[34] while the more unusual thumbnail drawn on the left figure's hand also occurs occasionally during the painter's mature phase.[35]

At first glance, since the scene preserves only women, with one engaged in wool-working, it could be described as domestic. However, modern scholarship has convincingly shown that scenes of women engaged in textile production often stand for much more than mere literary descriptions of female work, frequently juxtaposing textile production with other women-related images in combinations that are often metaphorical constructs.[36] A unique combination among these constructs is the display of jewelry with wool-working present on the Nir David scene.[37] The prominent, white necklace held by the woman standing in frontal view, either preparing to wear it or, more probably, displaying it for all to see, underscores its importance and refers not just to women's adornment but also to nuptial imagery.[38] Necklaces were the typical husband's gift that sealed the imminent wedding, and necklaces are depicted in scenes of mortal and mythical wedding preparations.[39] The allusion to nuptial imagery evoked by the necklace fits well with the image of the spinning woman. It refers to one of the bride's main skills – a prerequisite to marriage – and proclaims her as "industrious",[40] a suitable quality for the bride and the married woman. The well-dressed woman seated on the klismos, a piece of furniture often found in such scenes, may have depicted another vignette in this metaphorical construct, perhaps including the mistress of the oikos herself. This type of scene, filled with figures on the kalpis' shoulder, is typical of Polygnotos' work, reflecting his interest in multi-figural compositions, especially on kalpides, and in *gynaikeion* scenes associated with weddings.[41]

We conclude this study with a look at one of the Attic white-ground lekythoi belonging to the collection.[42] It is of the full-sized cylindrical variety (Figs. 6–8; Color Pl. 12A),[43] and has a calyx mouth, notch at the neck-mouth join, offset at the neck-shoulder join, and disc foot attached to the body by a fillet marked above and below with an incised line. The lip, neck and handle are black-glossed, as is the lower part of the body and upper surface of the foot. The vertical edge of the foot is covered in a red wash.

Very little is left of the decoration on the shoulder, but it appears to be all in black matt, including the parallel lines that mark the top. The decoration consists of three palmettes, their hearts arc-shaped with a dot on top, and tendrils that do not join. At the top of the scene on the body of the vase between parallel lines drawn in gloss is a band of sloppy, running, broken meanders facing right that alternate with dotted saltire squares.

The picture on the body shows a conflation of two scenes: the ferryman Charon preparing to row the deceased youth across the river Styx to Hades and a visit to the grave. Only the outlines of the youth's hair and Charon's boat are still preserved; the red matt used for this ranges from pink to light red. On the left the youth stands in profile to the right, extending his right arm toward the

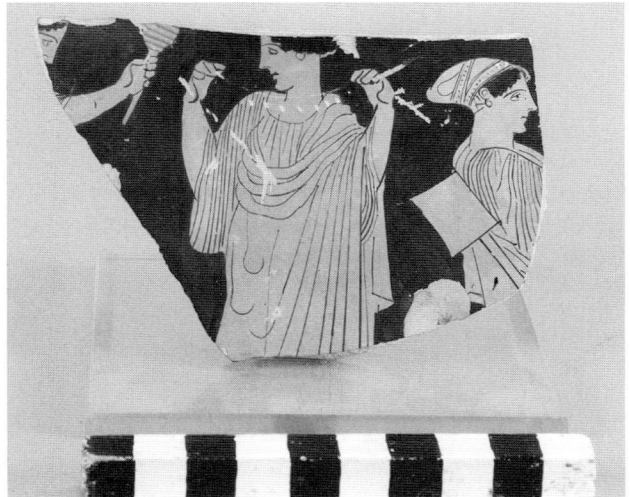

Fig. 5 Attic red-figure fragment, Polygnotos, IAA, Inv. 72.5553/4.

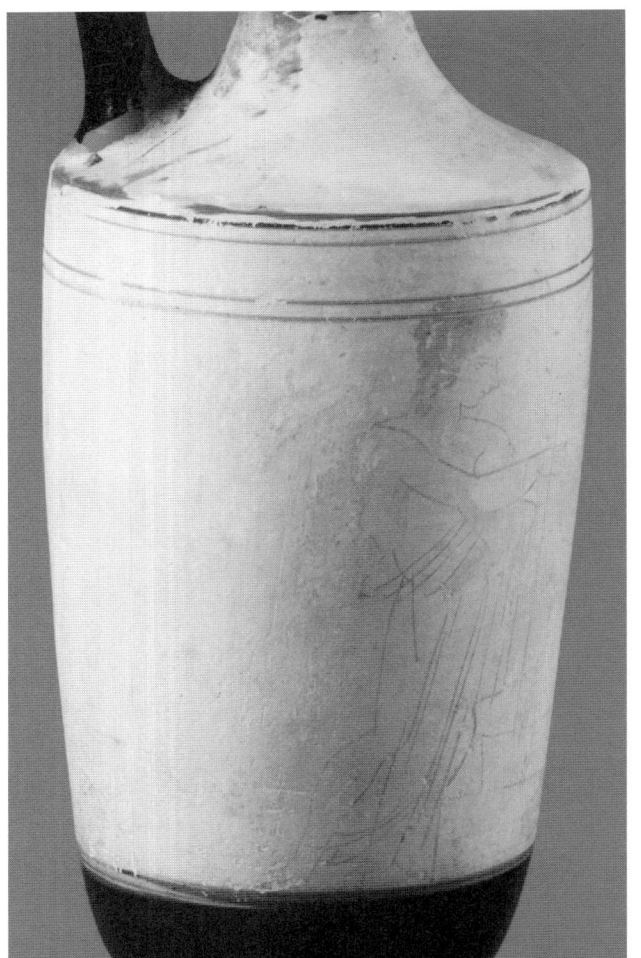
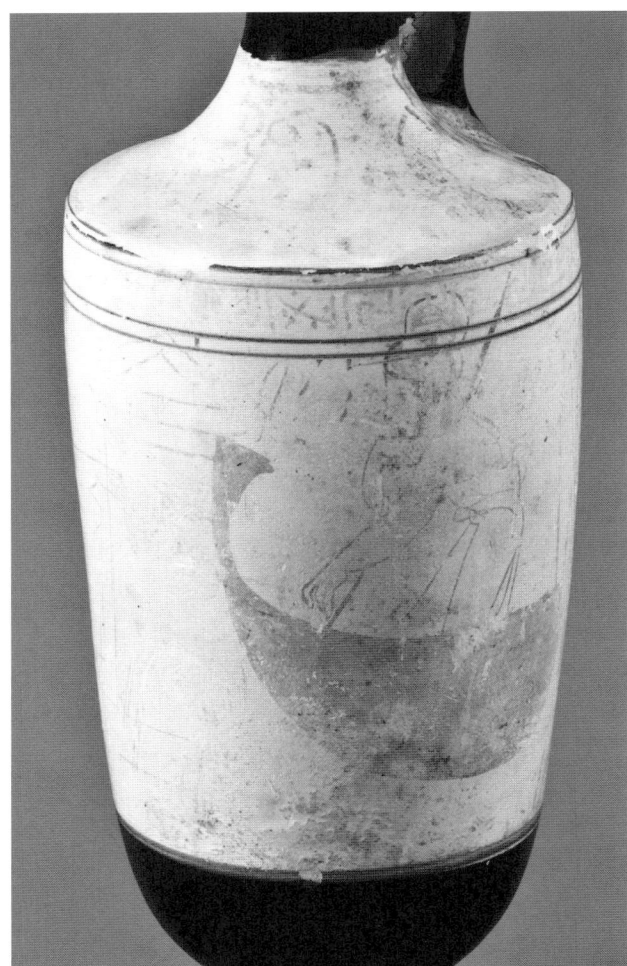
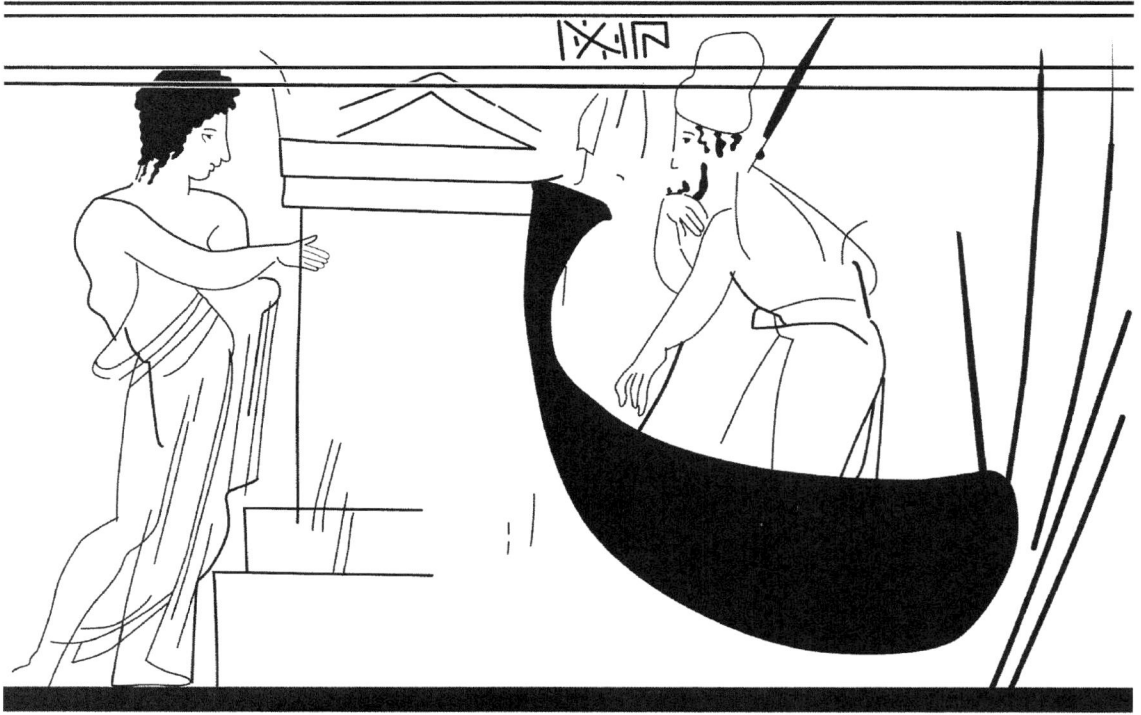

Figs. 6–8 Attic White-ground Lekythos, Reed Painter, IAA, Inv. 72.5550.

center. He is barefoot and wears a himation. In the center is a broad grave stele crowned with a pediment and decorated with *tainiai* (now mostly faded) that were tied around it. Another tainia hangs in the background to the right of the stele. On the stele's right Charon stands in profile to the left, leaning on his oar in his boat. His beard is sparse, he wears his traditional workman's *exomis,* and his head is covered with a conical rustic *pilos*. A clump of reeds behind the boat decorates the area beneath the lekythos' handle.

The vase can be attributed to the Reed Painter (420's–410 BC).[44] As described in detail elsewhere,[45] his work offers good parallels for the vase's shape, pattern work, painting style and iconography.[46] Note, for example, his typical use of black matt paint for the patterns, the red matt for the figures, the shoulder palmettes of type IIA type, and the meander band beneath it.[47] Note also the distinctive figure work: the similar shape of the youth's eye and eyebrow, his short, pointed chin, his luxuriantly curling red hair, and the sketchy lines used on both figures' anatomy.[48] Also typical of the painter's work are Charon's sparse facial hair, his body and drapery, the vase's composition with Charon standing on one of the scene's sides leaning on his pole opposite a figure, the grave stele between them and the vegetation that gives him his name.[49] The grave stele is of Norio Nakayama's type B-V,[50] and there are good parallels for similar grave stelai with pediment and acroteria on lekythoi by the Reed Painter.[51]

The polychromy still preserved on some of these lekythoi[52] allows us also to visualize our lekythos' now vanished rich palette. The latter would have emphasized not only the figures' drapery, the stele's architecture and decoration, and the vegetation behind the boat, but would have also underscored the vase painter's interest in extending the scene beyond the upper border into the ornamental band framing the scene, another typical peculiarity of his style.[53]

Charon is often portrayed in the Reed Painter's works.[54] On twenty of his lekythoi the boat protrudes from the reeds that allude to the shore where it is moored; Charon either stands or sits in the boat on the vase's right or left, and the other figure is either a youth or a woman. The addition of a grave stele to the scene adds a twist to its meaning. The Reed Painter produced at least two other white lekythoi with a similar conflation: one is in Copenhagen, the other in Hamburg.[55] Our scene is especially close to the Copenhagen version, except there the scene is flipped, Charon is less pensive and gestures more actively, and the youth gestures less actively and is more pensive. Nevertheless, these small differences do not seem to change the scene's basic message. As Francisco Díez de Velasco and John Oakley have suggested, this conflation was probably meant to create a symbolic fusion of the imaginary and the factual reality of the youth's death. Thus, the stele becomes a symbolic gate to the underworld and to the youth's crossing as well as the location of his physical remains on earth where he would be remembered.[56] Such a vase would have been a fitting funerary offering that refers to death but also comforts the living.

The study of the four vases housed in the Museum of Mediterranean Archaeology at Nir David (Figs. 1–8) has provided us here the opportunity to attribute them to known workshops – the Middle Corinthian Liebieghaus Group (595/590-570 BC), and the Attic vase painters Psiax (520–510 BC), Polygnotos (440–430 BC) and the Reed Painter (420's–410 BC) – and to speculate on their iconographies. Though we are missing the vases' ancient contexts and settings, we have gained some knowledge about the workshops that produced them and on some of the iconographical nuances developed during their times. This brief glimpse invites us to look further into a collection that includes numerous other objects, such as Greek and South Italian terracotta figurines and lamps, small bronzes, a fine collection of Etruscan objects and archaeological finds from local sites, most of which have received very little scholarly attention. It is my hope that, by presenting this material, I have helped remind scholars and visitors of the museum's existence and its treasures.

Acknowledgements

I am very grateful to John Oakley for his suggestion to write a paper on the Nir David vase collection. I am particularly indebted to Dror Segal, Director of the Nir David Museum, for allowing me access to the vase collection, and to him and Yael Barschak of the Israel Antiquities Authority for making available the images published here. Special thanks are due to Susan Matheson, who commented on my attribution of the red-figure fragment to Polygnotos. The drawings are by S. Haad.

Abbreviations

Amyx	D. A. Amyx, Corinthian Vase-Painting of the Archaic Period (1988)
APP II	J. H. Oakley – O. Palagia (eds.), Athenian Potters and Painters, The Conference Proceedings II (2009)
Kahane	P. P. Kahane, Museum of Mediterranean Archaeology, Nir David, Israel (1966)
Kurtz	D. C. Kurtz, Athenian White Lekythoi: Patterns and Painters (1975)
Matheson	S. B. Matheson, Polygnotos and Vase Painting in Classical Athens (1995)
Oakley 2004	J. H. Oakley, Picturing Death in Classical Athens: The Evidence of the White Lekythoi (2004)
Payne	H. Payne, Necrorinthia, a Study of Corinthian Art in the Archaic Period (1931)

Notes

1. For a fuller account of the museum's history, see G.Bar Or, The Journal of Israeli History 31.1, 2012, 167–186.
2. For the single catalogue of the collection, that includes black and white photos of some of the vases and other objects but no further information, see Kahane.
3. IAA, Inv. 72.5476 : H. 5.56 cm; D. of rim 4.48 cm; Max. D. of body 6.08 cm; W. of handle (above) 3.65 cm. The aryballos is described in the list of plates of the museum's catalogue as follows: "Arybalos (scent bottle). On the handle head of a girl. Protocorinthia," Kahane 29 pl. II.7.
4. Payne 287. 303; R. H. Hopper, BSA 44, 1949, 198.
5. Payne 101. 287.
6. See D. A. Amyx – P. Lawrence, The Archaic Corinthian Pottery and the Anaploga Well, Corinth VII, ii (1975) 32 no. 85 pl. 14; Amyx 163–165; C. W. Neeft, Addenda et Corrigenda to D. A. Amyx, Corinthian Vase-Painting of the Archaic Period (1991) 49–50. For a more recent addition, see CVA St. Petersburg 7 Russia 14 pl. 29,5–7.
7. On the wheel motif in Attic vase painting, see A. Lezzi-Hafter, in: APP II 147–158. One wonders, for example, if its appearance on Corinthian vase painting is merely decorative or whether it is connected with other motives appearing on aryballoi, an inquiry that is obviously beyond the scope of this study.
8. Respectively: Nîmes attributed to the Boar-Hunt Painter, Amyx 164,7; Corinth C-54-1, related to the Liebighaus Group, Amyx 165, C-1; and London, BM A 1042, Payne 303 no. 805 pl. 31,7–8.
9. Isthmia, IP 88, O. Broneer, Hesperia 24, 1955, 131–132 pl. 51, 1, a, b, c.
10. Athens, NM 16426, T. J. Dunbabin et al., Perachora. The Sanctuaries of Hera Akraia and Limenia II (1962) 147–148 no. 1558 fig. 12a pl. 61; Neeft (supra n. 6) 50, B-1.
11. For a summary of various, often divergent, early interpretations of this iconography, see S. Klinger, in: APP II 100–107.
12. Dunbabin (supra n. 10) 146–148 nos. 1555.1568; in addition, there were also bronze aryballoi from the seventh and early sixth century BC, H. Payne et al., Perachora, the Sanctuaries of Hera Akraia and Limenia I (1940) 158 pl. 61,1–2.
13. E. G. Pemberton, The Sanctuary of Demeter and Kore. The Greek Pottery, Corinth XVIII,i (1989) 53.
14. G. S. Merker, The Sanctuary of Demeter and Kore. Terracotta Figurines of the Classical, Hellenistic, and Roman Periods, Corinth XVIII,iv (2000) 104. 240 nos. C 195 (MF-14058), H320 (MF-11908), pls. 17. 51; N. Bookidis, The Sanctuary of Demeter and Kore. The Terracotta Sculpture, Corinth XVIII,v (2010) 124. 135. 34B pl. 27f.
15. Corinth, Archaeological Museum, CP 2038, E. J. W. Barber, in: J. Neils (ed.), Goddess and Polis. The Panathenaic Festival in Ancient Athens (1992) 106 fig. 65.
16. For example, acid mordants used on the dyes can be derived from vegetable oils, see E. J. W. Barber, Prehistoric Textiles. The Development of Cloth in the Neolithic and Bronze Ages (1991) 236.
17. See the suspended aryballos on a red-figure lekythos by the Bowdoin Painter with a woman with wool at a table, A. Crispino – A. Musumeci (eds.), Musei Nascosti, Collezioni e raccolte archeologiche a Siracusa dal XVIII al XX secolo (2008) 153 no. 11.
18. On the aryballos as a grave offering, see Oakley 2004 4. 9. 62. 119. 120. For examples, see the name-vase of Paris, Musée du Louvre, CA 613, ARV^2 1197,1; BAdd^2 343; and the following white ground lekythoi: Athens, National Museum, A 15041, by the Painter of Munich 2335, L. Parlama – N. Chr. Stampolidis (eds.), Athens: the City beneath the City (2000) 252–253 no. 233; Providence, Rhode Island School of Design, 25.082, and Arlesheim, S. Schweizer, 217668, both by the Reed Painter, ARV^2 1376,5; 1376,8; BAdd^2 371.
19. See, for example: the amphora in Six's technique by the Andokides Painter, Paris, Musée du Louvre, F203, ABV 253 middle.3; ARV^2 4–5,13; BAdd^2 150; the red-figure cups: Berlin, F3218 (lost), in the manner of the Brygos Painter, ARV^2 390,44; Jerusalem, Bible Lands Museum 4647, by the Triptolemos Painter, APP II 150 fig. 6B; and Warsaw, National Museum, 142313, by the Boot Painter, ARV^2 821,4; BAdd^2 293; the column-kraters: once Küsnacht, Hirschmann Coll. G57, by Myson, Para 349,29bis; BAdd^2 201; Dresden, Staatliche Kunstsammlungen, Albertinum 321, by the Painter of the Louvre Centauromachy, ARV^2 1089,29; BAdd^2 329; and Vienna, Kunsthistorisches Museum 2166, by the Painter of Tarquinia 707, ARV^2 1111,1; Para 452; BAdd^2 330; and the pyxis in Berlin, Antikensammlung, 3403, by the Painter of Athens 1243, ARV^2 1319,1.
20. On an extensive discussion of the competitions held there and their link to Demeter and Kore, see Merker (supra n. 14) 334–335; and Bookidis (supra n. 14) 269–272, both with extensive bibliography. Further evidence for these competitions are the bronze strigils, including a miniature one, that have been found in the Demeter and Kore sanctuary and are to be published in a separate fascicle of Corinth XVIII, together with all the miscellaneous finds. On the kotyle, see Pemberton (supra n. 13) 133–134 no. 292 fig. 34 pl. 32.
21. For some of these, see Kahane 29 pls. IV–VI; BAPD 4847–4853. The latter, oinochoe Inv. 72-5460, was traced by N. Levin to the Luzern Market, see Para 144,6. 192; N. Levin, A Black-figure Oinochoe from Gan Hashlosha: Identification and Meaning, unpublished MA thesis (University of Haifa, 2007) and a forthcoming publication.
22. IAA, Inv. 72-5454: P.H. 12.5 cm; P.W. 13 cm. The fragment is described in the list of plates of the museum's catalogue as follows: "Fragment of amphora. Attic black-figure, about 530 B.C.E. with representation of Dionysos," see Kahane 29 pl. IV.6 .
23. Brescia, Museo Civico, ABV 292,1; BAdd^2 76.
24. Palermo, Museo Archeologico Regionale 1110, ABV 292,4; BAdd^2 76.
25. Würzburg, Universität, Martin-von-Wagner Mus. L319, ABV 293,10; BAdd^2 76.
26. Munich, Antikensammlungen und Glyptothek 2302, ABV 294,23; BAdd^2 77.
27. Madrid, Museo Arqueológico Nacional 11008, ABV 294, 24; BAdd^2 77.
28. J. R. Mertens, in: K. Lapatin (ed.), Papers on Special Techniques in Athenian Vases. Proceedings of a Symposium held in Connection with the Exhibition 'The Colors of Clay: Special Techniques in Athenian Vases', at the Getty Villa, June 15–17, 2006 (2008) 141–142. On some of his latest black-figure work, see: B. Cohen, Attic Bilingual

Vases and Their Painters (1978) 235 n. 119; B. Cohen, in: B. Cohen et al., The Colors of Clay: Special Techniques in Athenian Vases (2006) 28.

29 On Psiax' special interest in Dionysiac scenes, see J.R. Mertens, AntK 1979, 1, 26; and P. Pelletier-Hornby, Revue du Louvre 50.4, 2000, 32–34.

30 A representative example is the panel scene on a black-figure hydria of unknown whereabouts attributed to the Priam Painter with Hermes mounting a chariot that includes a white skinned female to the right who faces Dionysos looking left; see W. G. Moon, in: W. G. Moon (ed.), Ancient Greek Art and Iconography (1983) 114 n. 1 fig. 7.20a.

31 The Attic red-figure vases in the collection include kylikes, skyphoi, a kantharos and small red-figure lekythoi.

32 IAA, Inv. 72-5553/4: Preserved H. 7.1cm; Max. W. 11cm. Th. top .719 cm, bottom .525 cm. Unpublished.

33 London, British Museum E 281, Matheson 40–43 P 41 pl. 31. On the painter's mature style, see 39–64.

34 London, British Museum E 454, Matheson 56 P 14 pl. 42.

35 New York, Metropolitan Museum of Art 45.11.1, Matheson 58–59 P 60 pl. 44.

36 For a clear summary of early interpretations of this iconography, their diverse and often divergent readings, and the view that these scenes represent women's contributions to the household and the city of Athens during the classical period, see most recently S. D. Bundrick, Hesperia 77, 2008, 283–334. For some of the more important studies of this iconography, see D. Williams, in: A. Cameron – A. Kuhrt (eds.), Images of Women in Antiquity (1983) 94–97; E. C. Keuls, in: W. G. Moon (ed.), Ancient Greek Art and Iconography (1983) 209–230; K. Carr, in: D. Cardon (ed.) Archéologie des textiles des origines au Ve siècle: Actes du Colloque de Lattes, octobre 1999 (2000)163–166; K. Stears, in: G. Hoffmann – A. Lezzi-Hafter (eds.), Les pierres de l'offrande: Autour de l'oeuvre de Christoph W. Clairmont (2001) 107–114; and G. Ferrari, Figures of Speech (2002) 35–60; on standing spinners see her list on 215 and Matheson's description of the lekythos by the Two-Row Painter, CVA Yale 1 USA 38 29–30 no. 24 pl. 33,1–4.

37 Wool-working and jewellery display are more typically conflated by adding a kalathos, the wool basket, rather than actual spinning. See, for example, the scene of a youth offering a necklace to his bride, who stands next to a kalathos while tying her girdle: black-figure alabastron, London, BM GR 1892.7-18.10 (E 719): V. Sabetai, in: J. Oakley – W. D. E. Coulson – O. Palagia (eds.), Athenian Potters and Painters (1997) 321–322 fig. 4. For the problematic interpretation that the woman is a prostitute rather than a bride, see P. Badinou, La laine et le parfum (2003) 95 A 256 pl. 99. For one example of a seated spinner in a scene conflating different components of the wedding rite but without the display of a necklace, see the red-figure hydria attributed to the Orpheus Painter in New York, The Metropolitan Museum of Art, ARV² 1104,16; BAdd² 329.

38 On the adornment of the parthenos, see Ferrari (supra n. 36) 52–53; on necklaces in nuptial iconography, see J. H. Oakley – R. H. Sinos, The Wedding in Ancient Athens (1993) 16–20.

39 On the connotations of necklaces as gifts typically offered by husbands, on the famous necklace wrought by Hephaistos that Kadmos offered to Harmonia on their wedding day, and additional mythological references linking necklaces to nuptial iconography, see A. Kauffmann-Samaras, Revue du Louvre 51, 2001.2, 37–38; V. Sabetai's description of the lebes gamikos in Athens, the Benaki Museum 31117, CVA Benaki 1 Greece 9 38–39 pls. 31–32; and V. Sabetai, in N. Kaltsas – A. Shapiro (eds.), Worshiping Women. Ritual and Reality in Classical Athens (2008) 294–295. For an illustrative example linking necklaces to Harmonia, wedding iconography and allusions to wool-working, see the preparation of Harmonia on the epinetron (the most symbolic of tools linking women with wool-working) by the Eretria Painter, Athens, National Archaeological Museum 1629, ARV² 1250–51,34; 1688; Para 469; BAdd² 354; Oakley – Sinos (supra n. 38) 41 fig. 128.

40 On the adjective ΦΙΛΕΡΓΟΣ, "industrious" added to a scene of a spinning woman, see the red-figure lekythos by the Villa Giulia Painter in Paris, Cabinet des Médailles, ARV² 624,81.

41 On his multi-figural compositions on kalpides and on the type of scenes, see Matheson 74–78. 287–292 respectively. More generally, note the escalating popularity of textile production scenes depicted on hydriai during the High Classical period, Bundrick (supra n. 36) 288 Table 1, 290.

42 These comprise a number of white-ground lekythoi, among them two decorated with patterns and florals and four with figured scenes. They are published elsewhere and attributed to the Bowdoin Painter, the Painter of Taranto 2602, the Two-Row Painter and the Reed Painter: see S. Klinger, Israel Museum Studies in Archaeology 5, 2006, 5–22 figs. 1–13. 20–23.

43 IAA, Inv. 72.5550: H. 24 cm; D. of mouth 4.8 cm; D. of foot 4.9 cm; W. of handle (above) 3.65.

44 On the Reed Painter, see ARV² 1376–1382; Kurtz 58–68 (including Group R); Parlama and Stampolidis (supra n. 18) 238–239 no. 220; 351–352 no. 384; Oakley 2004, 18. 29–30. 110 list 11 nos. 32–50. 119–120; and J. H. Oakley, in: R. Panvini – F. Giudice (eds.), Ta Attika. Veder Greco a Gela. Ceramiche attiche figurate dall'antica colonia (2004) 212. 214, with a short discussion of the painter's revised chronology and further bibliography.

45 Klinger (supra n. 42) 15–17 figs. 20–23.

46 For a close parallel in shape and size, though slimmer, see the lekythos in the Basel market by the Reed Painter, Kurtz pl. 47,2; for the type of shoulder palmettes, see Kurtz 61 fig. 24c.

47 For the type of band with meander and saltire squares, see Kurtz fig. 5h pl. 47,2; for a close parallel for the shoulder and figural decoration, see the lekythos from Athens also by him: Parlama and Stampolidis (supra n. 18) 351. 353 no. 384.

48 So, for example, the figure's style on the lekythos in Arlesheim ARV² 1376,8, (supra n. 18). For reproductions of some of the usual types of youths used by the painter, see S. Papaspyridi, ADelt 8, 1923, 123γ. 124α-β. 126α. 127α-γ.

49 For a Charon of similar anatomy and posture, though with a thicker beard, see the lekythos in Arlesheim (supra n. 18). For reproductions of some of the usual types of Charon depicted by the painter, see Papaspyridi (supra n. 48) 120–121; and F. Díez de Velasco, AEspA 64, 1991, figs. 1–6.

50 For the grave stele of this type by the Reed Painter, see N. Nakayama, Untersuchung der auf weissgrundigen Lekythen dargestellten Grabmaeler Ph.D. diss. (Albert-Ludwigs-Universität zu Freiburg im Breisgau, 1982) 20. 221–223 B-V-6 to B-V-25 pls. 14–15.

51 For example, see the following: Copenhagen, National Museum, Dept. of Classical and Near Eastern Antiquities 729, ARV² 1377,13; Nakayama (supra n. 50) B-V-10; Oakley 2004 110 list 11 no. 45; 121 figs. 80–81; Paris, Musée du Louvre, MNB 616, ARV² 1378,44; Kurtz pl. 46,2; Nakayama (supra n. 50) B-V-6; Hamburg, Museum für Kunst und Gewerbe, 1917.817, ARV² 1381,111; BAdd² 371; Kurtz pl. 47,1; Oakley 2004 110 list 11 no. 49; and Gt. Neck, Long Island, Pomerance coll. 115, now in Brooklyn Museum 98, no. 115, Nakayama (supra n. 50) B-V-22.

52 For lekythoi with well-preserved colors, see for example, the lekythos in Freud's collection, P. Gay, Sigmund Freud and Art. His Personal Collection of Antiquities (1989) 90–91.

53 Oakley 2004 120.

54 On scenes with Charon on white-ground lekythoi, and on those specifically by the Reed Painter, see respectively Oakley 2004 113–125 and 110 list 11 nos. 32–50.

55 For the Copenhagen and Hamburg lekythoi, see supra n. 51. On scenes mingling grave stelai with Charon which started to materialize in Attic vase paintings ca. 430 BC and on their use by the Quadrate Painter, the Reed Painter and others, see Oakley 2004 118–125.

56 Díez de Velasco (supra n. 49) 239; Oakley 2004 118.

11 Trade of Athenian Figured Pottery and the Effects of Connectivity

Kathleen Lynch and Stephen Matter

Connectivity is a term borrowed from population ecology, and in archaeology it is a way to describe how interconnected and inter-related sites and their populations are both physically and conceptually related. In the influential book, *The Corrupting Sea*, Peregrine Horden and Nicholas Purcell describe connectivity as: "The various ways in which microregions cohere, both internally and also one with another – in aggregates that may range in size from small clusters to something approaching the entire Mediterranean." They emphasize that the perception of space rather than actual physical features is most critical to connections among sites.[1] Theirs is a useful way of understanding why certain sites form networks of exchange and communication. The original ecological meaning, however, provides other dimensions of the theory that can also be applied to the trade in Athenian pottery. In population ecology, connectivity is a descriptor of how individuals move between populations.[2] Populations in ecology are groups of individuals living in particular places. Ecological connectivity is particularly interested in how migrants move from population to population and what factors affect this movement including distance, terrain, and how attractive the new and old populations are.

The study of the trade in Athenian pottery has many parallels to the study of population ecology. There are local populations of pots, that is, a site assemblage, and the study of pottery trade is essentially an interest in what motivated the pots to "migrate" from their home, production population, to a new, consumer population. The trade in Attic pottery raises important ecological issues: how difficult is it to move the pottery? Is there terrain that effectively limits trade? Does the demand for imported pottery at the consumer site provide strong enough motivation to overcome distance and terrain?

In ecological studies movement of individuals from one population to another can be observed, and then predictive models can be created. For example, the models can predict how a reduction in a population's resources would affect the amount of movement to and from that population. In theory the movement of pottery from its production population to its consumer population could be similarly modeled. Just as models can predict how a population of, say, butterflies will adjust as its food source changes, in theory similar models should be able to predict how a reduction in demand for Attic pottery at a particular site affects the entire network of exchange. Connectivity models are based upon quantifiable, observed data: counts of butterflies and its food source. Unfortunately, the data for the movement of pots is far less robust for several reasons. First, not all archaeological sites are published, so our picture of networks is incomplete. Second, even when published, sites are rarely fully excavated, and published pottery is usually representative, not exhaustive. The portions of a site excavated are also not random or representative but more often opportunistic or pragmatic. Therefore, any model would contain a large number of assumptions and speculations making it no more useful than direct observation of patterns. Short of a predictive model, however, the principles of ecological connectivity can enlighten interpretations of patterns by providing insights on likely trade routes and highlighting sites unusually "attractive" to Attic pottery.

The site of Gordion, in central Anatolia, provides a test case to demonstrate how the principles of connectivity can help explain observed patterns of pottery imported from Athens.[3] Gordion is far inland, about 500 kilometers from the Ionian coast, 200 kilometers from the Black Sea, and 400 from the southern coast of Asia Minor (Fig. 1). The site lies at the junction of two rivers, the Sangarios, with an outlet on the Black Sea, and a tributary of the Sangarios, the Tembris. There are several possible routes for Attic pottery to travel to Gordion, and this paper examines how likely each was. Unfortunately, because of uneven data sets – some sites are not excavated, others unpublished – it is not possible to use rigorous

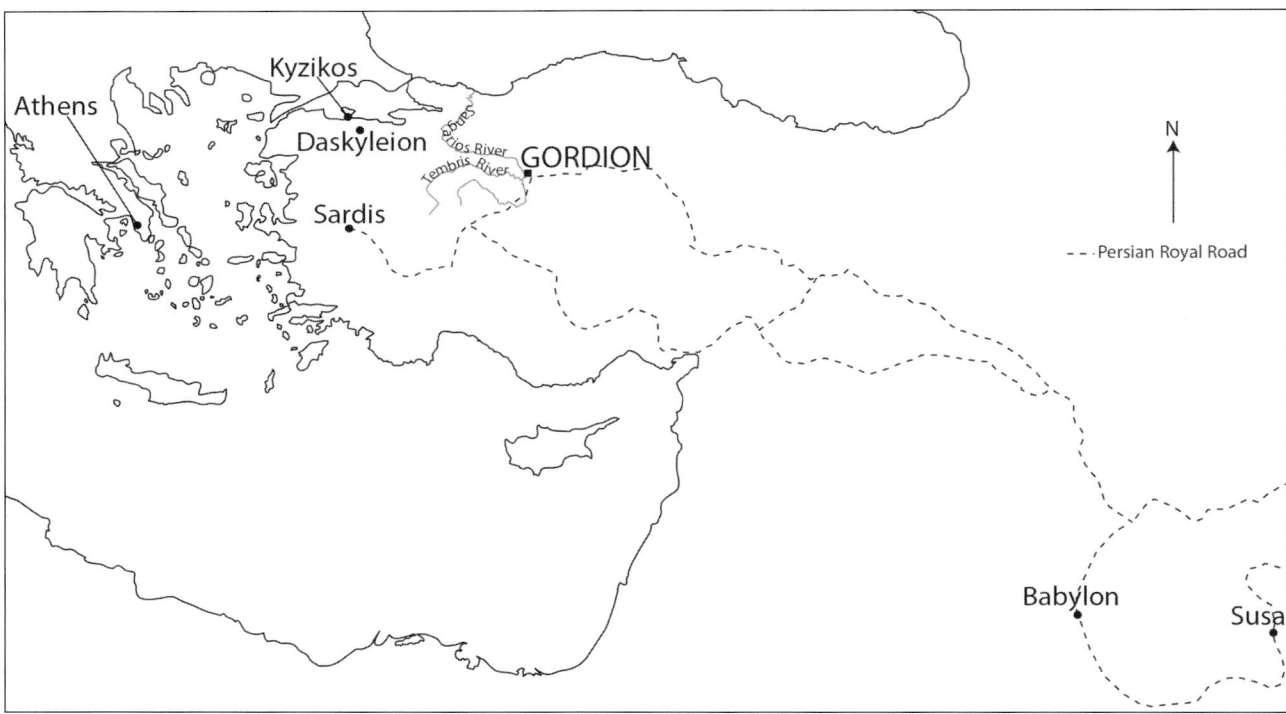

Fig. 1 Detail of Eastern Aegean basin and Anatolia, redrawn by Lynch, after Brill's Historical Atlas of the Ancient World, New Pauly, Supplements (2010) 87.

statistical modeling to identify the most reasonable route. Nevertheless, the principle of connectivity describing an "immigrant" population provides a new approach to the data we do have.

In the Anatolian Iron Age Gordion was a thriving capital of the Phrygian empire.[4] The site featured a citadel with a palace sector and a production quarter in its support. Even a fiery destruction, recently redated to ca. 800 BC, could not quash the power of the Gordion Phrygians.[5] The Phrygians rebuilt the citadel on the same conceptual lines.

The fortune of the Phrygians changed in the sixth century BC. First Lydians took control of the site, and then around 540 BC the Persians seized the site after a difficult battle with the Lydians. Remnants of a Persian siege ramp attest to the campaign.[6] The site remained in Persian control until Alexander the Great arrived to cut the Gordian knot in 333 BC.[7]

The import of Greek pottery began in the late eighth century BC with a handful of Corinthian skyphoi of the Late Geometric and Early Protocorinthian periods.[8] Imports from Greek production sites on the Ionian coast followed in the seventh century. At the 1994 "Athenian Potters and Painters [I]" conference in Athens, Greece, Keith DeVries gave a snapshot of the variety of Athenian pottery found at Gordion.[9] Athenian pottery began to arrive in the first quarter of the sixth century BC and continued to increase in quantity during the period of Lydian control. The peak quantity of Attic imports, however, came under the period of Persian rule.[10]

The "immigrant population" of imported Athenian pottery at Gordion is a small percentage of the overall ceramic assemblage. By one estimate, imports represent less than two percent of the site assemblage, which had a thriving local tradition of pottery production.[11] Nevertheless, these imports have been critical to understanding the chronology of the more ubiquitous but less chronologically distinctive local pottery. Most of the imported pottery comes from residual or reuse contexts, but patterns of deposition may provide clues to loci of original use. The function of many of the Phrygian buildings reused in Lydian and Persian times remains unclear, although we know that some of the former Phrygian palatial structures were re-purposed as workshops with a residential component.[12] With the exception of one unusual structure, the Painted House, constructed at the beginning of the fifth century BC (thus under the Persians), there are no other clear candidates for religious buildings.[13] Unfortunately, no imported pottery was found in a context of use associated with the Painted House.

Nevertheless, even though original context is often missing, the very presence of Attic pots documents trade from Athens to Gordion. In fact, comparison to other contemporary Anatolian sites makes it clear that the trade with Gordion and the quality of pottery that arrived from Athens, especially in the fifth century BC, was exceptional. Gordion is the farthest site inland in Anatolia to receive a steady and reasonably large flow of Athenian pottery in the sixth and fifth centuries BC.[14] Especially notable is that Athenian pottery is scarce, although not absent, in the Persian heartland of modern Iraq and Iran.[15]

The principle of ecological connectivity underscores the importance of Gordion. The null hypothesis or the condition that would exist if there were no pressure on the system – in our case, no focused trade to Gordion by Athens or demand for trade by Gordion – is diffusion. The amount of Attic pottery should simply decrease with increasing distance from Athens. Since Gordion is farther from Athens than coastal Ionian sites, the null hypothesis predicts that the Ionian sites should contain more Attic pottery. This prediction is false, and the absence of diffusion puts the spotlight on sites that violate the null hypothesis.[16] Gordion is one of these sites, far from Athens, and yet is an active consumer of Attic pottery. What path did the pottery take to Gordion, and can we explain why Athenian pottery was more popular here than elsewhere in Anatolia?

Several potential trade routes exist. The Persian Royal road system served to connect the Achaemenid satrapal capitals of Sardis to Susa with an extension to the port of Ephesos (Fig. 1).[17] The Persian Royal Road, created by Darius I in the late sixth century BC, followed many pre-existing Assyrian and Phrygian roads, but there is some disagreement about its main route through central Anatolia, since there was a northern and a southern trunk.[18] Whether it was on the main route or a secondary branch, Gordion was well-connected, and a road passed through Gordion at least by the mid-sixth century BC and probably even earlier.[19] Gordion researchers have assumed that the Royal Road was the main trade route for ceramics and other commodities.[20] Unfortunately, Athenian pottery data do not exist for many of the sites along the route of the Royal Road with the exception of the satrapal capital at Sardis, which has been well published.[21]

A comparison of Attic pottery from Sardis and Gordion shows, in fact, that these sites had very different trade relationships to Athens, and the null hypothesis – that Sardis should receive more Athenian pottery by virtue of its shorter distance to Athens – does not hold. Sardis and Gordion receive similar amounts of black-figure; however, the pattern differs dramatically with red-figure and black-gloss (Fig. 2). Gordion receives about ten times as much fifth- and fourth-century BC Athenian pottery. The publisher of the Sardis Attic pottery, Nancy Ramage, speculated that the reduction in Attic pottery at Sardis may be related to the tastes of the Persians living at Sardis, that they may not have appreciated the more complex iconography of red-figure.[22] If that were so, then Attic imports to other sites under Persian control including Gordion and Daskyleion, the satrapal capital of Hellespontine Phrygia, should also have decreased, but they did not. The population at Sardis during the Achaemenid period was probably larger than Gordion's, although population estimates are notoriously difficult.[23] If we modify our null hypothesis to assume demand increased with population size, Attic pottery would be even more over-represented at Gordion in comparison to Sardis. More likely is that preferred trade routes changed.

A second hypothesis assumes that Roman roads reflect pre-Roman "best routes."[24] The Orbis website from Stanford has been particularly helpful in understanding the various possible routes.[25] One Orbis route from Athens to

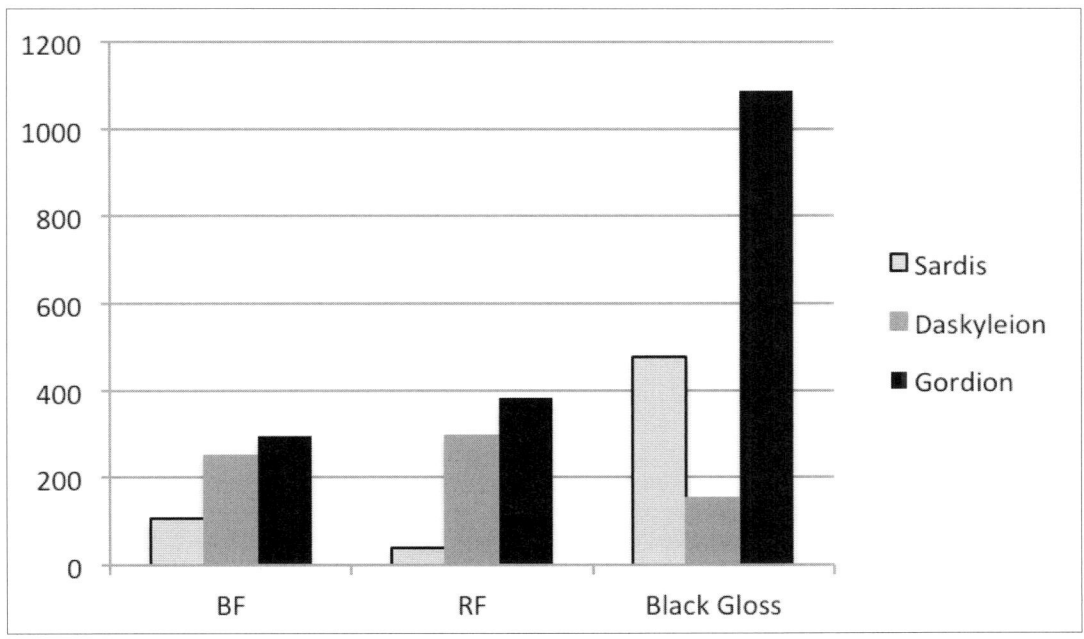

Fig. 2 Comparison of number of Attic black-figure, red-figure, and black-gloss vessels from Sardis, Daskyleion, and Gordion. Data for Sardis from Ramage (infra n. 21); for Daskyleion from Görkay and Tuna-Nörling (infra n. 33).

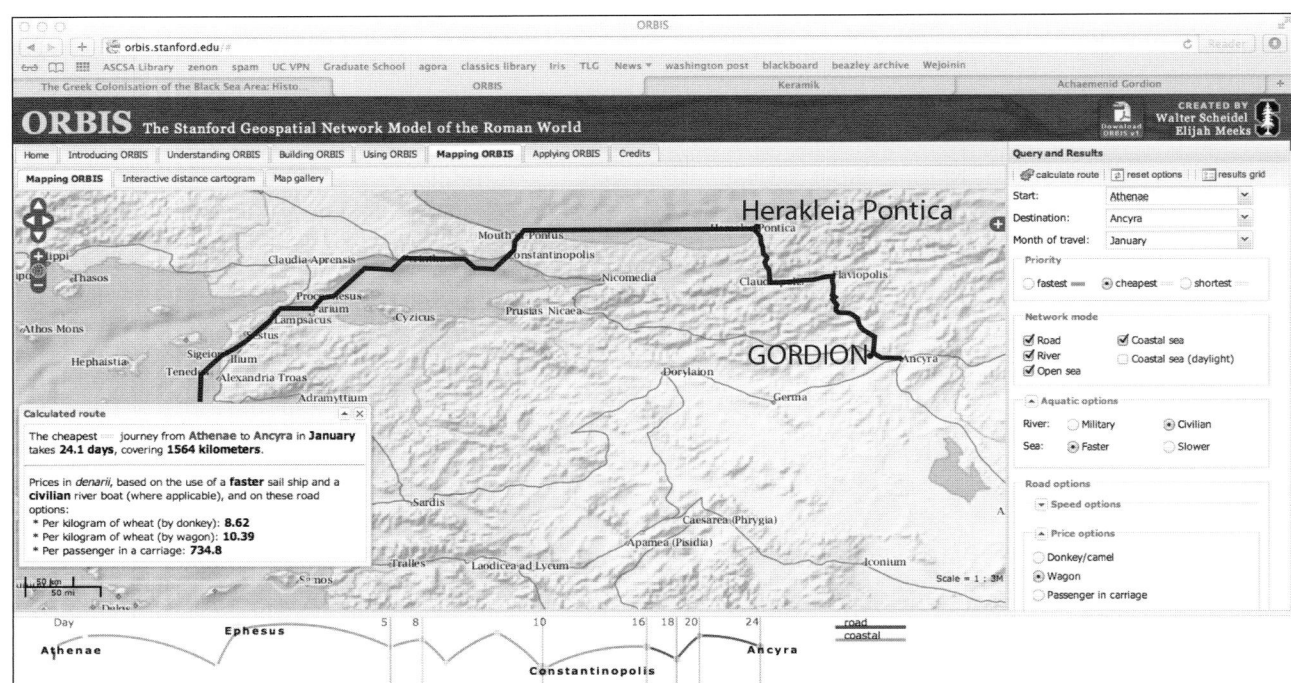

Fig. 3 Best route, optimized for using the Orbis Geospatial Network Model of the Roman World (www.orbis.stanford.edu). Originating in Athens and terminating in Ancyra (Ankara) because Gordion is not a site option.

Ancyra (Ankrara), optimized for cost but not speed, goes up the Ionian coast, through the Hellespont, into the Black Sea, and turns inland at Herakleia Pontica (Fig. 3).[26] In Mark Lawall's largely unpublished study of the transport amphoras from Gordion, he notes an unusual presence at Gordion of Herakleian jars in the late fifth to fourth centuries BC in comparison to coastal Asia Minor sites.[27] Herakleia Pontica lies due north of Gordion, and modern transhumance routes attest to the possibility of an ancient overland route, although a difficult one due to mountain ranges and valleys oriented east-west, not north-south.[28] During the fifth century BC Athenian trade expanded into the Black Sea, and it is possible that Gordion's connectivity switched from being based on Ionian ports to Pontic or Hellespontine ports. However, little evidence of Athenian pottery has been found at Herakleia Pontica itself, and the colony was founded in 554 BC,[29] after Attic pottery had already started to arrive at Gordion, so, in our opinion, this reduces its pottery connectivity to Gordion. Sheep, occasional amphoras, and other goods may have made the journey, but not Athenian pottery, and not throughout the Late Archaic and Classical periods.

A third, more likely route crossed through the Persian satrapy of Hellespontine Phrygia, and reached Gordion using the valley of the Tembris River (Fig. 4). This route dates back to the Hittite kingdom.[30] Gordion belonged to the Achaemenid satrapy of Hellespontine Phrygia, which had Daskyleion as its capital from the middle of the sixth century BC.[31] Daskyleion had a similar character to Gordion with an old Phrygian population and Persian newcomers. Unlike Gordion, there are at Daskyleion clear signs of Persian bureaucracy including a large archive of bullae sealings.[32] Of all the sites with Athenian pottery in Ionia and northern Asia Minor, the volume and character of Attic pottery from Daskyleion most closely matches that from Gordion (Fig. 2).[33] In a 2011 article on the trade in transport amphoras to Daskyleion, Aylin Koçak Yaldır saw a similar pattern for the end of the sixth to beginning of fifth centuries BC.[34]

Athenian pottery probably made the journey by sea until it landed at the Greek colony of Kyzikos, then crossed the flat plain to Daskyleion.[35] After Daskyleion, the route probably proceeded through the inland coastal plain through to one of the river valleys leading into the Anatolian heartland. Consensus is that the Sangarios was not navigable, and its river bed too gorge-like to be a conduit for foot traffic.[36] Alternatively, the route could have run along the valley but crossed south to Dorylaion and used the more reliably navigable Tembris River to reach Gordion.[37] Yaldır, in her amphora study, independently considered the same three routes, and she came to the same conclusion that we did: that the northern, Hellespontine Phrygia route accounts for more of the import trade than the Persian Royal Road.[38]

The Persian Royal Road and its pre-Achaemenid predecessor may have accommodated trade until the end of the sixth century BC. The shift to a northerly route for the fifth and fourth centuries may have been related to Athens' interest in the Propontis area. The old Athenian colony of Sigeion in the Troad flourished in the fifth

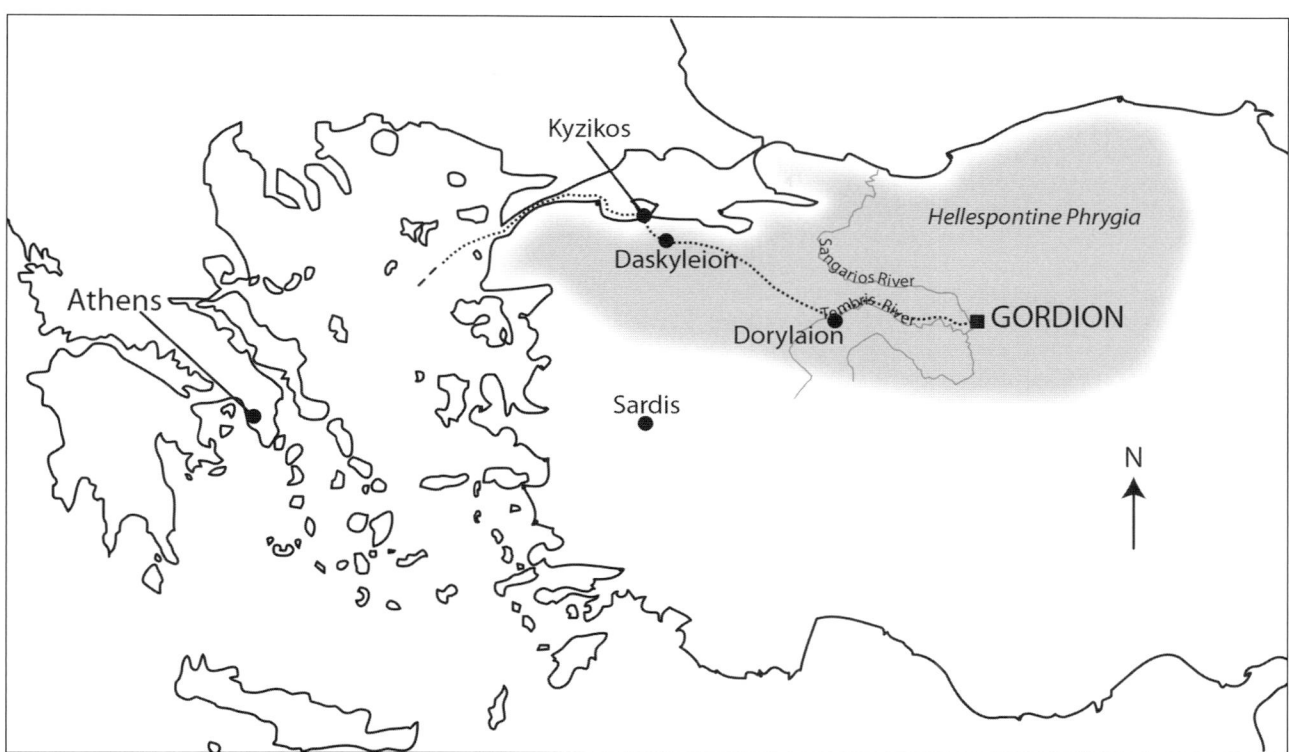

Fig. 4 Detail of Eastern Aegean basin and rough limits of Persian satrapy of Hellespontine Phrygia, redrawn by Lynch, after Brill's Historical Atlas of the Ancient World, New Pauly, Supplements (2010) 87.

century BC and played a part in Athenian foreign affairs in the fourth century, although it was contested by others during that period.[39] Similarly, opposite Sigeion, Elaious on the Thracian Chersonnesos, was an important Athenian stronghold in the fifth and again in the fourth century BC.[40] Even if, as is likely, Athenian pottery was not being traded by Athenian merchants, the protection of the Athenians from both sides of the Hellespont may have favored trade to the Propontis and Black Sea. In the fifth and fourth centuries BC Athens' interest in the area followed its need for grain from the Black Sea region, although the extent to which it depended on this trade is debatable.[41]

Now that we have identified a probable trade route, what accounts for the consumer demand motivating the trade of Attic pottery? Gordion is the terminus for the trade. There are no sites farther east in Anatolia with substantial or even notable amounts of Athenian pottery.[42] Three examples of the kinds of Athenian pottery that reached Gordion underscore the specificity of the trade. DeVries argued that a rhyton with Amazonomachy reflected Athenian marketing of "eastern" subjects to "eastern" customers (Fig. 5; Color Pl. 14A).[43] A second distinctive piece is a fragment of a white ground cup, which is one of only two white ground cups in all of modern Turkey.[44] The other example is from the Artemesion at Ephesos and features Apollo before an omphalos.[45] The Gordion white ground cup is by the Penthesilea Painter and depicts a winged youth with a female figure whose arm rests on his shoulder (Fig. 6). The figures may be Aphrodite and Eros, on analogy with the painter's white ground pyxis in the Metropolitan Museum of Art, where a youthful, tousled-hair Eros looks up to Aphrodite.[46] The owner of the cup from Gordion, however, may have seen Kybele, the Phrygian mother goddess and main Phrygian cult figure, and her consort, Attis. Attis is sometimes winged, but Kybele is not assimilated with Aphrodite as she is, for example, with Demeter and Artemis.[47] Thus, the cup may be an instance of local interpretation being at variance with the painter's intended meaning. The find spot of the fragment is not helpful, although in the Greek world, non-funerary white ground cups are usually votive offerings at sanctuaries.[48] A third, less dramatic example is a black-figure, white ground lekythos by the Athena Painter with a centaur defeating a Greek (Fig. 7).[49] Although this particular scene and composition are very common in the Athena Painter's oeuvre, this is the only example of it from Anatolia. The image is usually taken to be the defeat of the Greek transgendered hero Kaineus during the Centauromachy, which the Greeks, of course, ultimately win.[50] Hybrid creatures, including centaurs, have a long history in Phrygian iconography, which may have been the appeal;[51] on the other hand, the unusual instance of a Greek in defeat may have instead appealed to a Persian living at Gordion ca. 500 BC. This lekythos was found tucked away under a cellar wall, as if it were deposited whole as an offering.[52] Stratigraphy and other datable pottery indicate that it was new when deposited. Other pieces of Attic pottery from Gordion are more ordinary – Beldam

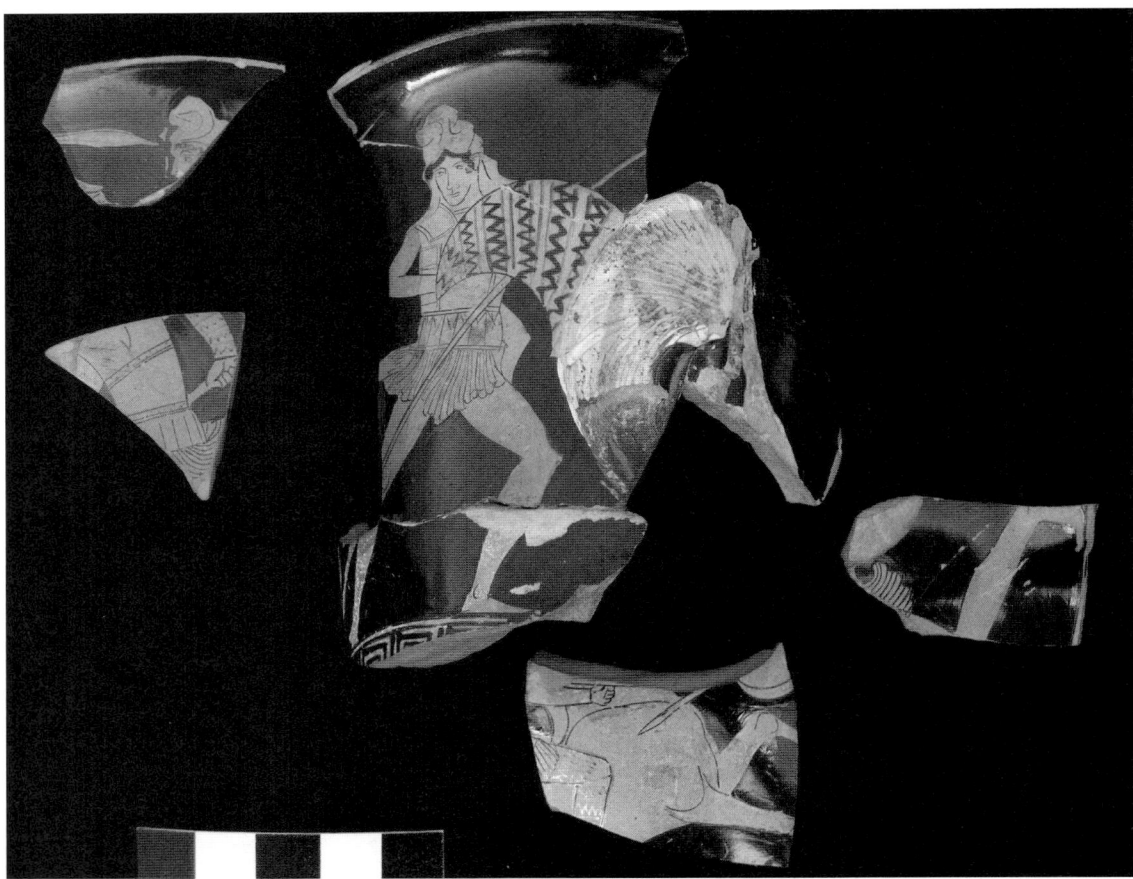

Fig. 5 Gordion P 380 a, b + P 3356 + P 4688. Sotadaean rhyton in form of an Amazon on horseback (plastic figure largely missing); Amazonomachy on neck. Photo: Lynch with permission of the Gordion Excavations, University of Pennsylvania.

Painter lekythoi, Haimon Painter cup-skyphoi, and red-figured kraters. Thus, the more unusual pieces speak to a keen understanding of the market at Gordion, either on the part of the painters or the traders who served the site.

This study started out as an ambitious attempt to use quantitative methods to address patterns of trade in Athenian pottery. Regrettably our field lacks data robust enough to use statistical modeling, but the principles underlying the modeling emphasize that the sketchy patterns we see are not accidental. In ecological terms, the null hypothesis of diffusion predicts that Gordion should receive very few immigrant Athenian pots. However, connectivity can be affected by factors such as accessibility of the site, the size of the population, or the attractiveness of the market. By all measures, Gordion is not very accessible. Its population size is hard to determine, but it is likely smaller than Sardis or Daskyleion. It was certainly not a metropolis with a large population whose demand could alter trade (for example, more sneakers will be sold in New York City than Kansas City simply because more people live in New York, but Kansas City may be a bigger consumer of sneakers per capita.) So that leaves attractive consumer demand as the most likely factor influencing the trade.

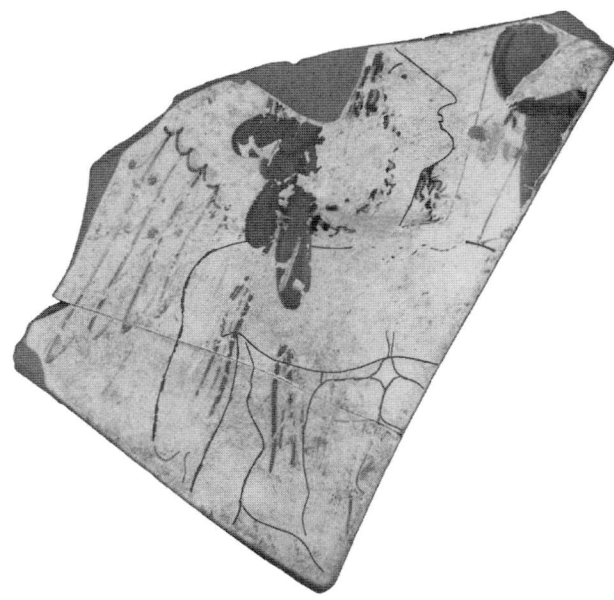

Fig. 6 Gordion P 475. White ground cup interior with a winged youth and female. Figure outline enhanced bu Lynch for clarity. Photo: Lynch with permission of the Gordion Excavations, University of Pennsylvania.

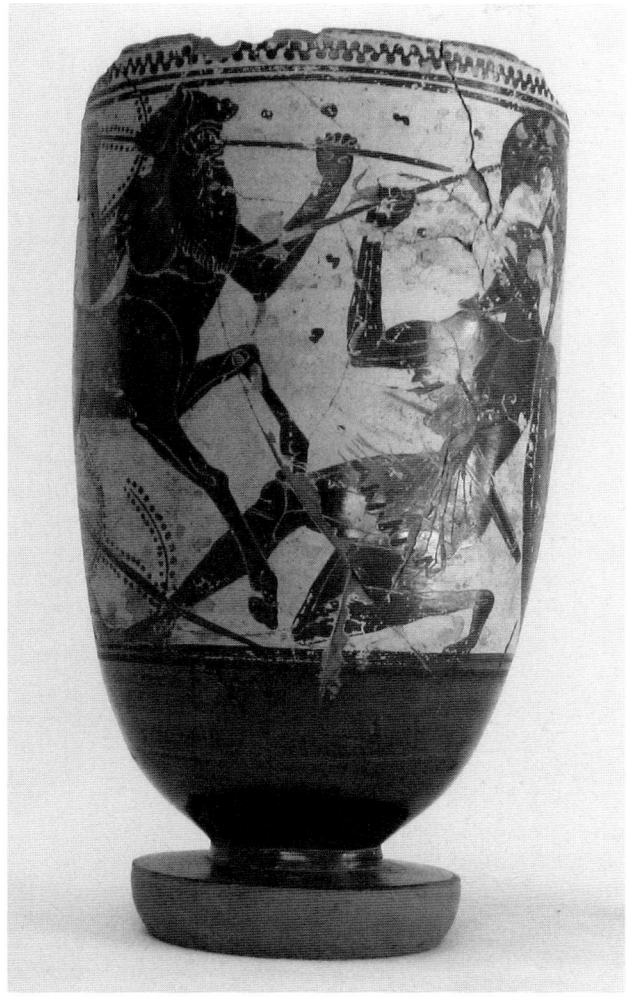

Fig. 7 Gordion SF 89–130. White ground, black-figure lekythos attributed to the Athena Painter. Centaur defeats Kaineus. Photo: author with permission of the Gordion Excavations, University of Pennsylvania.

Why, then, was Gordion, a provincial city in the Persian period, such an active consumer of Athenian pottery? There is no clear answer, and we can only speculate at this point. Unlike Daskyleion, there is little evidence for a large, Persian elite presence at Gordion. The number of Achaemenid seals and sealings is small – twenty-nine.[53] There is one possible Persian period administrative building, the Mosaic Building, but no Attic pottery was found in it or around it.[54] Instead of the ruling Persians driving demand, it is possible that the old Phrygian families were the active consumers of Athenian pottery. A reference in Herodotos indicates that the Phrygian royal line was still in existence at the time of Persian conquest, although no longer in power since the Lydian takeover.[55] Athenian pottery began to be imported before the Persians arrived. Perhaps the Phrygians had adopted Athenian pottery for social or religious customs that they then maintained under both the Lydians and the Persians.

Phrygian graffiti occur occasionally on Attic black-gloss pots, although never on figured wares.[56] Archaeological data from other Phrygian sites such as Midas City and Pessinous confirm that their inhabitants did not buy as much Attic pottery as the residents of Gordion.[57] At Persian sites along coasts, such as Daskyleion (discussed above), Pitane on the Ionian coast, or even Tel Dor in Israel, among many others, Attic pottery arrived reliably and was happily purchased even during the peak of animosity between Athens and Persia.[58] Even a small Persian presence at Gordion may have amplified the pre-existing Phrygian market for imported pottery; and the probable trade route through Hellespontine Phrygia, where Daskyleion was another good customer with a large Phrygian population mixed with Persians, ensured a steady flow of pottery.[59]

Although unable to use the robust quantitative techniques we originally intended, this paper demonstrated that the pottery trade to Gordion was substantial and that Gordion was most likely in the trade orbit of Daskyleion near the Hellespont, not cities along the Black Sea Coast or the Ionian coast.

Notes

1. P. Horden – N. Purcell, The Corrupting Sea: A Study of Mediterranean History (2000) 123. 124.
2. A. Moilanen – N. Nieminen, Ecology 83, 2002, 1131–1135; S. F Matter – J. Roland – A. Moilanen – I. Hanski, Ecological Applications 14, 2004, 1526–1534.
3. For a history of excavations, see G. K. Sams, in: L. Kealhofer (ed.), The Archaeology of Midas and the Phrygians: Recent Work at Gordion (2005) 10–21 and M. Voigt, in: L. Kealhofer (ed.), The Archaeology of Midas and the Phrygians: Recent Work at Gordion (2005) 22–35. Annual preliminary reports are published in the *Kazı Sonuçları Toplantısı*, a summary of archaeological work presented to the Turkish Ministry of Culture.
4. For an overview of the Phrygian period of the site, see C. B. Rose (ed.), The Archaeology of Phrygian Gordion, Royal City of Midas, Gordion Special Studies 7 (2013).
5. For a summary of the evidence for redating the conflagration, which is no longer associated with the Kimmerian invasion, see C. B. Rose – G. Darbyshire (eds.), The New Chronology of Iron Age Gordion, Gordion Special Studies 6 (2012).
6. M. J. Mellink, Chapter 3e. Anatolia, in CAH, 2nd edition, Vol. 4 (1988) 228; K. DeVries, in: L. Kealhofer (ed.), The Archaeology of Midas and the Phrygians (2005) 51.
7. For the Hellenistic period of the site see S. M. Stewart, Gordion after the Knot: Hellenistic Pottery and Culture, Ph.D. diss. (University of Cincinnati, 2010) and M. G. Wells, A Cosmopolitan Village: The Hellenistic Settlement at Gordion, Ph.D. diss. (University of Minnesota, 2012).
8. DeVries (supra n. 6) 37 fig. 4–3; K. DeVries, AncNearEastSt 45, 2008, 38–40.
9. K. DeVries, in APP 447–455.
10. Lynch is preparing the publication of Archaic and Classical pottery imported to Gordion.

11 DeVries (supra n. 9) 453.
12 M. M. Voigt – T. C. Young, Jr., IrAnt 34, 1999, 220–224.
13 M. J. Mellink, in: K. DeVries (ed.), From Athens to Gordion: The Papers of a Memorial Symposium for Rodney S. Young, University Museum Papers 1 (1980) 91–98.
14 DeVries (supra n. 9) 453–454.
15 K. DeVries, AJA 81, 1977, 546, n. 14; C. Clairmont, Berytus 11, 1954–1955, 85–141; C. Clairmont, Berytus 12, 1956–1957, 1–34, with Appendix A, Attic Black Vases from Susa, Persia; J. Y. Perreault, in: H. A. G. Brijder (ed.), Ancient Greek and Related Pottery (1984) 224–228; J. Y. Perreault, BCH 110, 145–175.
16 Y. Tuna-Nörling, Die Ausgrabungen von Alt-Smyrna und Pitane: Die attisch-schwarzfigurige Keramik und der attische Keramikexport nach Kleinasien, Istanbuler Forschungen 41, 1995, 101–149 present an overview of Attic pottery in Asia Minor.
17 D. F. Graf, in: H. Sancisi-Weerdenburg – A. Kuhrt – M. Cool Root (eds.), Achaemenid History VIII. Continuity and Change, Proceedings of the last Achaemenid History Workshop, April 6–8, 1990 – Ann Arbor, MI (1994) 167–189.
18 Hdt. 5.52–54; 7.26–44; Graf (supra n. 17) 177–180; D. French, Iran 36, 1998, 22. French sees the Persian Royal road on a more southerly route, through Ikonion to Tarsos, although other scholars including Rodney S. Young, the first director of excavations at Gordion, argue for a northern route, or at least a northern trunk of the Royal Road, R. S. Young, Proceedings of the American Philosophical Society, 107, 1963, 348, n. 6; J. D. Winfield, AnSt 27, 1977, 151–166; E. Dusinberre, Aspects of Empire in Achaemenid Sardis (2003) 16.
19 Young (supra n. 18) 350; J. M. Birmingham, AnSt 11, 1961, 186–190.
20 G. K. Sams, Expedition 21, 1979, 9–10; G. K. Sams, ANews 2/3, 1979, 49–50; K. DeVries, AJA 94, 1990, 399; M. C. Miller, Athens and Persia in the Fifth Century B.C.: A Study in Cultural Receptivity (1997) 70–72.
21 N. H. Ramage, in: J. S. Schaeffer – N. H. Ramage – C. H. Greenewalt, Jr., The Corinthian, Attic, and Lakonian Pottery from Sardis, Sardis Monograph 10 (1997) 63–130.
22 Ramage, (supra n. 21) 68.
23 J. M. Marston, AJA 116, 2012, 382–385. 393–396 uses both archaeological settlement data and archaeobotanic data to identify changes in population size, but he does not estimate population at Gordion.
24 French (supra n. 18) 15.
25 W. Scheidel – E. Meeks, Orbis. The Stanford Geospatial Network Model of the Roman World, <http://orbis.stanford.edu> (25.01.2013). Note that Gordion is not listed as a possible site, so Ancyra (Ankara) was selected as the destination.
26 Another Roman Road ran east to west from Nicaea over mountain terrain, but there is no evidence that this difficult route was a viable trade option before the Romans. See D. French, Roman Roads and Milestones of Asia Minor, Part 2, BIAA Monograph no. 9, BAR International Series 392 (1988) 544 map 10. 560 map 18.
27 Preliminary publications of amphoras from Gordion have appeared as: M. Lawall, in: M. Voigt – K. DeVries – R. C. Henrickson – M. Lawall – B. Marsh – A. Gürsan-Salzman – T. C. Young, Anatolica 23, 1997, 21–23; M. Lawall, in: D. Kassab Tezgör – N. Inaishvili (eds.), PATABS I. Production and Trade of Amphorae in the Black Sea, Actes de la Table Ronde internationale de Batoumi et Trabzon, 27–29 Avril 2006, Varia Anatolica 21 (2010) 159–165; but Lawall has revised some interpretations for the final publication, M. Lawall, Transport Amphoras at Gordion: Rhythms of Trade in the Seventh through Second Centuries B.C., forthcoming.
28 A. Gürsan-Salzmann, Expedition 43:3, 2001, 24–25; topography discussed by C. A. Burney, AnSt 6, 1956, 179–180; A. K. Yaldır, World Archaeology 43, 2011, 374.
29 S. Saprykin, Heracleia Pontica and Tauric Chersonesus before Roman Domination (1997) 21.
30 Burney (supra n. 28) 179 and passim.
31 T. Bakır, Anadolou/Anatolia 25, 2003, 2.
32 Bakır (supra n. 31), 4; D. Kaptan, The Daskyleion Bullae: Seal Images from the Western Achaemenid Empire I–II (2002).
33 Lynch thanks MaryBeth Wagner, a student in her 2012 archaeology seminar at the University of Cincinnati, for permission to use data she collected for a seminar paper using K. Görkay, Attic Black-Figure Pottery from Daskyleion, Studien zum antiken Kleinasien IV, Asia Minor Studien 34 (1999) 1–100 and Y. Tuna-Nörling, Die attische Keramik, Daskyleion I (1999). Note that black-gloss from Daskyleion is under-published, so this figure is not accurate.
34 Yaldır (supra n. 28) 364–379; K. İren, in: R. S. Bagnall – K. Broderson – C. B. Champion – A. Erskine – S. R. Heubner (eds.), The Encycopedia of Ancient History, Vol. 4 (2013) 1930–1931.
35 Yaldır (supra n. 28) 372–373. Miller (supra n. 20) 71 also suggests this route to Gordion.
36 Burney (supra n. 28) 179.
37 This valley had a higher density of settlement in the Iron Age, Burney (supra n. 28) 192.
38 Yaldır (supra n. 28) 375–376.
39 M. H. Hansen – T. H. Nielsen (eds.), An Inventory of Archaic and Classical Poleis (2004) 1014 no. 791, s.v. Sigeion (S. Mitchell).
40 Hansen – Nielsen (supra n. 39) 906 no. 663, s.v. Elaious (L. Loukopoulou); the area of the Hellespont is well represented on the Athenian Tribute Lists, see B. Merritt – H. T. Wade-Gery – M. F. McGregor, The Athenian Tribute Lists, 4 vols. (1939–1953); J. Cargill, The Athenian Settlements of the Fourth Century B.C., Mnemosyne Supplement 145 (1995) 9–12, with fifth-century BC background to Athenian involvement in the area, although there was a gap in Athenian presence after the Battle of Aigospotami in 405 BC.
41 Grain trade argument summarized with references: J. K. Davies, Society and Economy, CAH, 2nd ed., vol. V, The Fifth Century (1992) 300–301.
42 For example, there is no significant Attic pottery from Hattuşa, even though it is farther along the Persian Royal Road, S. M. Stewart, pers. comm., September 2012.
43 P 380 a, b + P 3356 + P 4688: DeVries (supra n. 9) 450 fig. 6. K. DeVries (supra n. 15) 544–548 presents evidence for eastern iconographic preferences.
44 P 475: DeVries (supra n. 9) 450 fig. 5.
45 Ephesos cup, BM 1907.12-1.798, I. Wehgartner, Attisch weissgrundige Keramik, Keramikforschungen 5 (Mainz

46 1983) 69. 97 no. 74 pl. 23,3. Lynch thanks Jenifer Neils for mentioning the Ephesos fragment.
46 MMA. 07.286.36, ARV² 890,173; 1673; Para 428; BAdd² 302; D. von Bothmer, Greek Vase Painting (1987) 54–55 no. 27.
47 Although the myth of Aphrodite and Adonis shares some folk elements with the myth of Kybele and Attis, L. Roller, In Search of the God Mother (1999) 255.
48 J. R. Mertens, MetrMusJ 9, 1974, 108.
49 SF 89–130, DeVries (supra n. 9) 448–449 fig. 3.
50 LIMC V (1990) 884–891 s.v. Kaineus (E. Laufer).
51 For example, the revetment plaques from Pazarlı, see H. Z. Koşay, Les Fouilles de Pazarlı, Türk Tarih Kurumu Yayınlarından V. Seri 4 (1941) pl. 29.
52 Mentioned in Voigt – Young (supra n. 12) 223–224, but not illustrated; preliminary publication G. K. Sams – M. M. Voigt, Kazı Sonuçları Toplantısı 12.1, 1991, 460, fig. 16; 470, but note that Voigt now thinks the lekythos was under the cellar wall, pers. comm. June 2012.
53 E. Dusinberre, Gordion Seals and Sealings: Individuals and Society (2005) 24.
54 R. S. Young, Bulletin: University Museum, 17:4, 1953, 11–14; R. S. Young, Expedition 7:3, 1965, 5–7; Voigt – Young (supra n. 12) 220–223. A single fragment of Attic pottery was found outside the building.
55 Hdt. 1.35–1.45.
56 L. Roller, AnSt 37, 1987, 106–107.
57 Midas City: C. H. E. Haspels, La cité de Midas, céramique et trouvailles diverses, Phrygie, Explorations Archéologique, vol. 3 (1951); Pessinous, unpublished, but personal observation and pers. comm. Roland Docter, June 2006.
58 DeVries (supra n. 15); Clairmont (supra n. 15); Perreault (supra n. 15), Miller (supra n. 20) 65–72; Pitane and Old Smyrna: Tuna-Nörling (supra n. 16); Tel Dor: A. Stewart – R. Martin, BASOR 337, 2005, 79–94; R. Martin, Near Eastern Archaeology, 68, 2006, 24–25; R. Martin, "Hellenization" and Southern Phoenicia: Reconsidering the Impact of Greece before Alexander, Ph.D. diss. (University of California, Berkeley, 2007).
59 Bakır (supra n. 31) 13.

12 Beautiful Men on Vases for the Dead

Thomas Mannack

The Ashmolean Museum houses a large number of Athenian black- and red-figure lekythoi. 184 complete specimens and three fragments are displayed in a large showcase at the foot of the stairs to the Ancient Greece rooms. Among the complete vases, not always provided with a precise provenance, but because of their excellent state of preservation most probably found in tombs, are a number of lekythoi bearing inscriptions. One of them, a red-figure lekythos from Gela[1] attributed to an artist working near the Pan Painter (Fig. 1; Color Pl. 12B), is decorated with a man leaning on a staff wearing a himation and elegant shoes. He holds an object in his right hand. Behind him hangs a cage with a plump bird painted in silhouette-technique. In front of the man's head, the painter inscribed HIPPON KALON, Hippon is beautiful. Klein and Beazley recognized two *beaus* of that name; the Oxford vase praises Hippon II.[2] This Hippon is otherwise unknown; he does not feature among the aristocratic families in Attica[3] and merits only a brief mention in the *Lexicon of Greek Personal Names*. Equally little is known about the process of exporting Athenian vases. The lekythos was made in Athens and was sold to a customer in Sicily who placed the vase in a grave and had probably never heard of the Athenian Hippon. The painter may have decorated the vase with no specific use in mind, since caged birds could be presented to the dead and the living.[4] However, the use of a *kalos* inscription in a grave overseas may suggest that the inscription was perceived as decoration.

Kalos-names are still rather enigmatic, although they have been studied for about two centuries. In 1828 and 1848, Theodor Panofka suggested on the basis of the relatively few vases known then that these inscriptions were commissioned in the workshop and named their owners. This was clearly incorrect, but he also noted regional clusters of names.[5] Two monographs cataloguing these names were published in 1890 by Wilhelm Klein[6] and a much better one by Konrad Wernicke.[7] Klein produced a second edition in 1898, and his opinion that kalos-names are homoerotic praise of aristocratic youths has become the accepted view.[8]

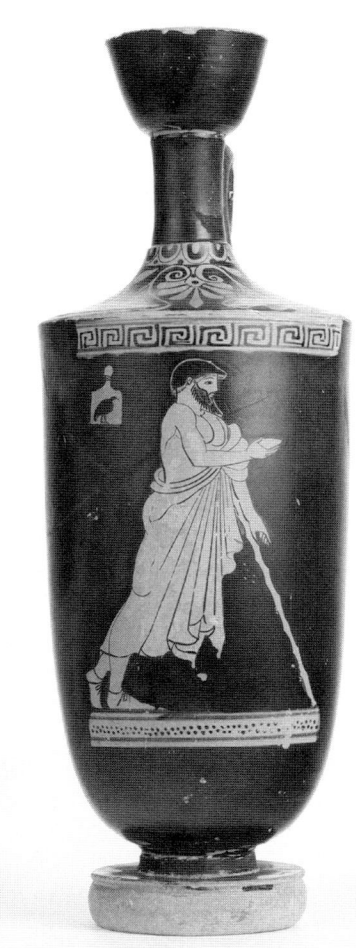

Fig. 1 Oxford, Ashmolean 1888.1402, red-figure lekythos attributed to Near the Pan Painter.

Hippon I and II

The first to praise Hippon was the painter of a black-figure neck-amphora made around 530/520 BC.[9] Around 500 BC, the Epeleios Painter wrote 'Hippon kalos' on the shield of a fighting warrior on the obverse of a cup found in Vulci,[10] and inscribed 'ho pais kal[os]' in added red in the field. He placed nonsense inscriptions on the reverse. Myson named Hippon on a calyx-krater in Berlin,[11] found in Falerii and dated round 490 BC. This krater is decorated with a battle scene. Between the fighting warriors, Myson inscribed the name 'Nikon', wrote 'kalos' on a shield below and placed the name 'Hippon' on another shield. The Oxford lekythos is attributed to a painter working in the manner of the Pan Painter, a pupil of Myson. This could indicate that names were passed on within a workshop or connected with a workshop, rather than inspired by aristocratic youths. The Providence Painter named Hippon on four lekythoi decorated between 480 and 460 BC, three of which were found in Thebes in Boeotia.[12] Hippon also links Nolan amphorae made between 480 and 470 BC in the workshops of the Charmides, Providence and Dresden Painters.[13] Pictures of mortal symposia show only pointed amphorae, suggesting that Nolan amphorae were not used at aristocratic feasts.

It seems that the name Hippon was used continuously for about sixty years and the distinction of two men of that name, Hippon I and II appears necessary, but somewhat arbitrary. The Oxford container illustrates some of the problems connected with the reading of kalos-names as homoerotic praise in symposia: vases inscribed with Hippon's name were exported to Sicily and Italy, where they were placed in graves, which implies that the name itself was not important to the buyers. Hippon would not have been known overseas, and does not appear in any Athenian context outside the vase-painters' realm. The occurrence of Hippon on three lekythoi attributed to the Providence Painter exported to Boeotia may suggest a workshop or trade connection. The use of the kalos-name 'Charmides' may also hint at workshop or trade connections. Charmides is named 'kalos' on four lekythoi, four cups and twenty Nolan amphorae from various workshops, including those of the Providence, Charmides, Dresden, and Nikon Painters, and the Painter of the Yale Lekythos.[14]

Vases for the Dead

While one cannot determine whether the Oxford lekythos praising Hippon was made with its funerary use in mind or not, one can be more certain about other inscribed lekythoi in Oxford. A lekythos (Fig. 2; Colour Pl. 13A) made around 460 BC and also found in Gela in Sicily[15] is decorated with the departure of a beardless male dressed in a short chlamys and holding two spears. A young woman draped in a chiton and black ependytes extends both her hands towards his chin. The scene is painted on a buff slip, the woman's skin in secondary white. The painter wrote 'kalos' between their faces, and added the name 'Timokrates' vertically between the figures. The white-ground technique used at this time, and the height of almost 35 cm suggest that the container was not made for use in daily life.

'Timokrates kalos' is also inscribed on a stele on a red-figure neck-amphora in Mykonos[16] which was once placed in a tomb in Delos, and later carried to Rheneia and deposited in a purification pit. The scene appears to pertain to the funeral: a youth whose mantle is drawn up over the back of his head and mouth leans on a staff and gazes at a stele. Ancient texts attest to graffiti calling lovers 'kalos' on almost any object, but it is more likely that the painter intended the inscription to be seen more clearly than it would have been, if done in added red on black, so he placed it on the red ground of the stele, where it would also remind viewers of the inscription naming the deceased.

The inhabitants of ancient Gela appear to have been unusually fond of placing Athenian lekythoi with kalos inscriptions in their graves. A white-ground lekythos in

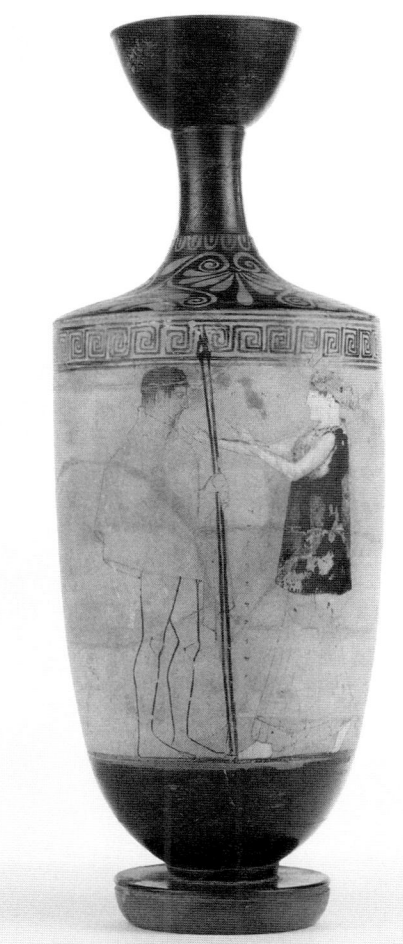

Fig. 2 Oxford, Ashmolean 1891.686, white-ground lekythos by the Timokrates Painter.

Oxford[17] (Fig. 3; Color Pl. 13B) attributed to the Achilles Painter was also found there and bears the carefully arranged stoichedon inscription:

ΑΛΚΙΜ[Η]ΔΗΣ
ΚΑΛΟΣ
ΑΙΣΧΙΛΙΔΟ

Alkimedes, the son of Aischylides, is beautiful. Its white-ground technique and size of 36 cm suggest that it was intended for a burial. At any rate, the domestic scene on the body showing a seated and a standing woman holding musical instruments is not suitable for use in an aristocratic symposium. Like many other beautiful men, Alkimedes is not mentioned elsewhere and does not appear to have been a member of the landed gentry.

The Achilles Painter also favoured a Hygiainon, and seems to have used this name mainly on white-ground lekythoi with domestic scenes. Among these is a fairly badly preserved white-ground lekythos in the Ashmolean Museum (Fig. 4), said to have been found in Greece,[18] and decorated with a woman holding an alabastron on the left and another woman on the right holding a sash. The Achilles Painter placed the carefully arranged inscription

HYGIAINON
KALOS

between their heads. Several of the Achilles Painter's white-ground lekythoi[19] praising Hygiainon (Fig. 5) are decorated with so-called 'mistress and maid' scenes, which would not normally have been thought to be suitable for a symposium or aristocratic males. Moreover, on lekythoi in Copenhagen[20] and Worcester,[21] the "maids" are carrying a flat basket with grave-offerings.

The Usual Suspects

The use of kalos-names on lekythoi, especially on grave-lekythoi, is not necessarily typical of their use. On such vases, the kalos-inscription may have replaced the epitaphs of carved marble grave-monuments.[22] It is, therefore, useful to examine some of the most famous kalos-names.

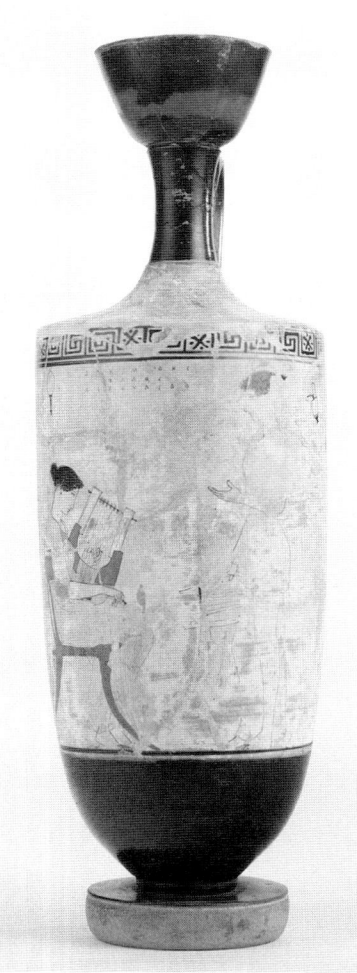

Fig. 3 Oxford, Ashmolean 1889.1016, white-ground lekythos by the Achilles Painter.

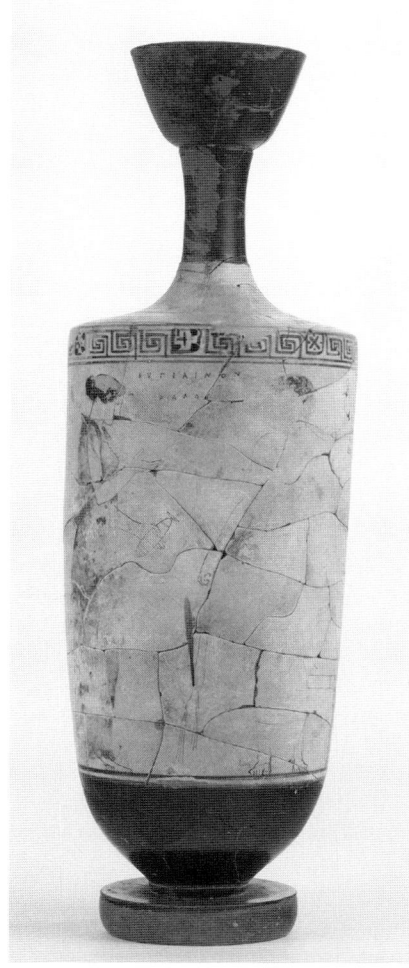

Fig. 4 Oxford, Ashmolean 1934.341 white-ground lekythos by the Achilles Painter.

Leagros

The most famous *beau* praised on Athenian pots is Leagros, whose name is inscribed on around seventy vases spanning a period of over twenty years[23] and who was once turned into a woman, Leagre, by Euphronios on a psykter in St. Petersburg.[24] Thus, Euphronios treated Leagros with the same levity as his colleague, Smikros, whom he made into the naked beauty Smikra on the same vase.

Occasionally, kalos-names have been connected with the figures next to which they have been written. These present the same baffling variety as the simple 'kalos' tags: 'Leagros kalos' occurs next to a beautiful reclining youth playing kottabos on the neck of an amphora with twisted handles (Fig. 6) attributed to Euphronios.[25] His youth is emphasized by an additional 'pais' written vertically below his cup. Another symposiast combined with 'Leagros kalos' on a cup by the Eleusis Painter (Fig. 7)[26] is entirely different: he is an aged roué preparing to have intercourse with a young, naked hetaira. His debauched lifestyle has left its mark: his brow is wrinkled and his beard wispy. Onesimos and the Colmar Painter made the point more forcefully and combined the beautiful Leagros with satyrs.[27]

Leagros, son of Glaukon, is known from other sources; around 480 BC he dedicated a statue to the Twelve Gods in the Athenian Agora,[28] and in the 460's he served as *strategos*. Apparently, the status as a favourite of vase-painters or aristocrats could be inherited. It is not unlikely that Glaukon, a brother of Leagros, was praised on a white-ground cup in Berlin signed by Euphronios as potter and attributed to the Pistoxenos Painter,[29] as well as on a white-ground cup in London assigned to the same artist.[30]

The vast majority of vases embellished with the name of Leagros were found in Italy; among the find-spots are Vulci, Cervetri, Capua, Viterbo, and Chiusi; one cup was excavated in Olbia. Only six of the around seventy examples were found in Greece: Three fragmentary cups were dedicated on the Acropolis of Athens,[31] and two cups were dedicated in the sanctuary of Demeter at Eleusis.[32]

Glaukon, the son of Leagros, was also acclaimed on vases,[33] among them a number of funerary lekythoi.[34] The long period of popularity of Leagros, and the use of his son's name for around another fifteen years, and on vases not connected with Athenian feasts, could mean that the family of Leagros had a long-standing relationship with Athenian potteries, perhaps as their landlord, banker or trade agent.

Onesimos named a range of males on his vases, all of which were found in Italy. Moreover, the painter inscribed a kyathos 'PANAITIOSKALO[S]. The shape is an Etruscan one, and the vast majority of Attic kyathoi were exported to the west. This vase was excavated in Vulci.[35]

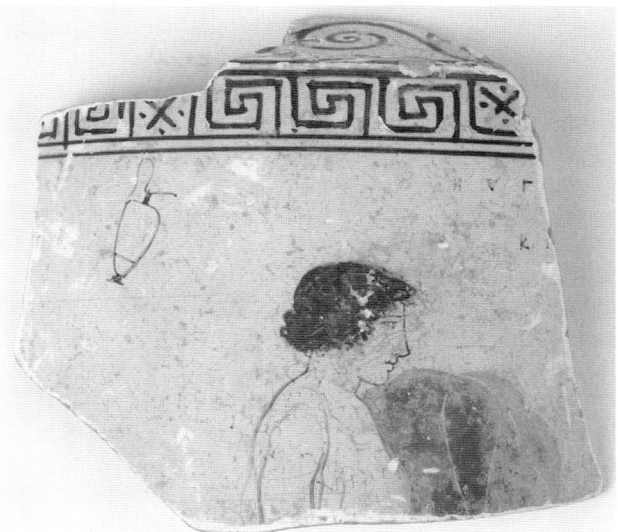

Fig. 5 Oxford, Ashmolean 1928.507, white-ground lekythos by the Achilles Painter.

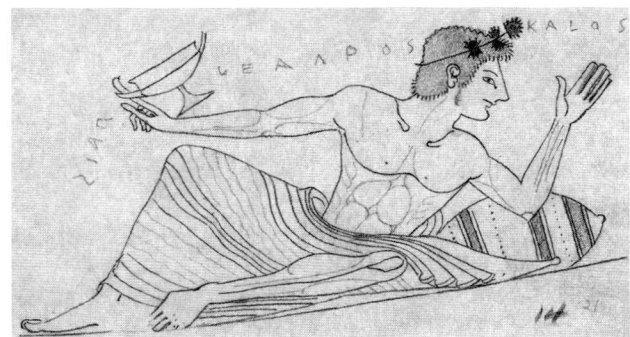

Fig. 6 Paris, Louvre G 30, red-figure neck-amphora with twisted handles by Euphronios.

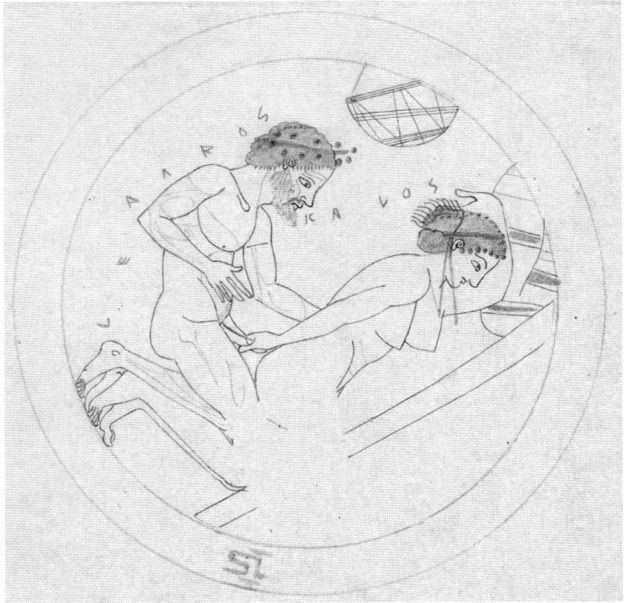

Fig. 7 London, BM 1865.11-18.46, red-figure cup by the Eleusis Painter.

Onetorides

Exekias' favourite was Onetorides, whom he called *kalos* on four vases.[36] Onetorides poses some problems if kalos-names are to be read as homoerotic praise of young aristocrats on vases used at the symposium: the three amphorae were found at Vulci in Etruria, where Onetorides would have been unknown. The calyx-krater was found in a sanctuary at Athens and does not show any traces of sympotic use. On all four vases, the kalos-names are combined with other inscriptions such as names, signatures and – on the Vatican amphora – speech-bubbles. Moreover, Exekias praised Onetorides throughout his long career,[37] far longer than he would have excited jaded aristocrats in the palaistra; while Exekias may have remained faithful to Onetorides, the artist's customers would not. The name may not have been a personal favourite, since it was not only used by a painter working near Exekias,[38] but was also handed on to the next generation, a painter whose work is akin to that of the Lysippides Painter.[39] Moreover, when the Edinburgh Painter decorated one of his few belly-amphorae,[40] he did not only use the master's theme of Kastor and Polydeukes, but also added an abbreviated form of Exekias' favourite, 'Onetor kalos'.

Other names follow workshop-lines too and are sometimes used as names for figures. Alkimachos was a favourite of the Achilles Painter,[41] a painter working in his manner,[42] the Group of Polygnotos,[43] the Chicago Painter,[44] and the Alkimachos Painter.[45] The Lykaon Painter inscribed 'Alkimachos kalos' on a bell-krater in Warsaw[46] and named a symposiast Alkimachos on a bell-krater in the British Museum.[47] He may have been the son of Axiopeithes, another *beau* inscribed on vases assigned to the Achilles Painter.[48] Kallias was another beautiful man who was praised on vases,[49] and whose name was used for labelling figures.[50] The Polygnotan painters and the Kleophon Painter's follower may have associated Kallias with music, since he appears once as a spectator at a Pyrrhic display[51] and twice as a flute player.[52]

Megakles

Megakles I, son of Alkmaion, Megakles II, father of Kleisthenes and Hippokratos, and Megakles III, ostracised in 471 BC, were members of one of the noblest families of Athens. Two hydriai,[53] made around 500 BC, praise Megakles as kalos; the painter of a black-figure lekythos made around the same time, wrote 'Megakles' next to a jumper with halters.[54] More than twenty years later, two fragments of a cup already inscribed with 'Megakles kalos' were used in an attempt to ostracise another Megakles,[55] and an even younger Megakles was called kalos by the Orestes and Kleophon Painters.[56]

Of particular interest is a polychrome white-ground plaque (Fig. 8) from the Athenian Acropolis decorated with a warrior advancing to the left; his shield is emblazoned with a black-figure satyr.[57] It is roughly contemporary with the Pioneer hydriai. The painter inscribed 'Megakles' to

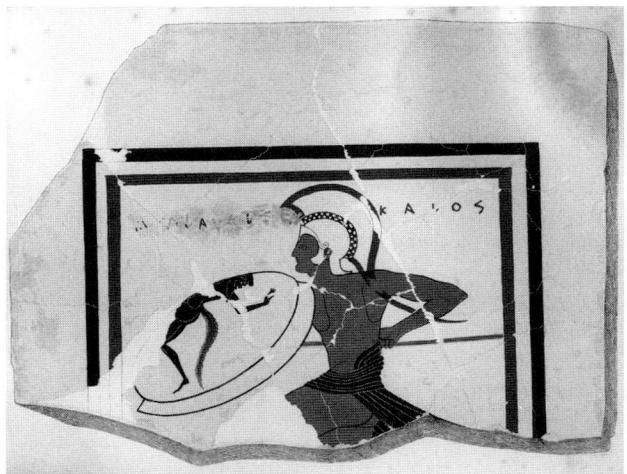

Fig. 8 Athens, Acropolis 2.1037, polychrome plaque from the Acropolis.

the left of the warrior's head, and 'kalos' to its right. At a later time, perhaps still in the workshop, 'Megakles' was partially erased and replaced with the name 'Glaukytes'. This name has no aristocratic pedigree and occurs only on Athenian pots. Glaukytes signed three black-figure Little Master cups as potter[58] and is perhaps called kalos on the reverse of a red-figure neck-amphora with twisted handles, which preserves the inscription ...]YTES K[....[59] The obverse of the vase shows a pipes-player named Smindyrides. Athenaeus and Herodotus[60] relate that a Smindyrides of Sybaris wooed the daughter of the Sikyonian tyrant Kleisthenes. This could link the name Glaukytes with the house of Megakles, who had named one of his sons after the tyrant of Sikyon, and thus explain the change of names on the Acropolis plaque. However, there could also have been a pottery connection. The potter Glaukytes is known from three signatures. About sixty to seventy years later, a potter signed a pyxis decorated by the Pistoxenos Painter with Megakles epoiesen.[61] It is not inconceivable that Athenian potters adopted and used the aristocratic names which pleased them, since there was no copyright on names; after all, at least three vase-painters took the liberty to sign with the name of the famous painter Polygnotos of Thasos.[62]

Kalos

'Kalos' is normally translated as 'beautiful' and is thought to have been applied not only to desirable young males, but also to parts of the body, one's character, and objects, and it was also frequently used ironically[63] and could also mean 'good' or 'bravo'.[64] Of special interest is the use of the epithet on vases. Here it can be written in its masculine and feminine forms next to figures, probably implying that the figure is beautifully or skilfully drawn. Vase-painters applied the soubriquet to a wide variety of figures. The Sabouroff Painter wrote 'kalos' next to a rather unassuming draped youth seated on an altar on a lekythos in a private collection,[65] while the unnamed painter of a white-ground lekythos excavated in Thebes in Boeotia, used the word to describe a bearded male holding a helmet,[66] and the Oionokles Painter (Fig. 9) applied the epithet to an older man without any apparent aristocratic traits.[67] Even a grotesquely ugly dancing satyr on an oinochoe in Boston (Fig. 10)[68] could be labelled 'kalos', as could a conventionally ugly satyr on a lekythos assigned to the Flying Angel Painter.[69] The god Dionysos[70] leaning on a staff in the manner of an Athenian citizen, bearded and nonathletic in appearance, and therefore not displaying the aristocratic ideal, is also called beautiful, as are a bearded rapist and his victim,[71] who may be Hermes and an unknown woman, or Menelaos and Helen (Fig. 11).

Beautiful banausoi

Among the around 900 kalos inscriptions are a considerable number naming *banausoi*.[72] Best known is Smikros, who portrayed himself in a symposium on a stamnos in Brussels[73] and was also shown at a feast by his colleague Euphronios.[74] A fellow Pioneer inscribed 'Smikros kalos' next to two naked women washing at a laver on a hydria in Berlin.[75] All three vases bear numerous further inscriptions. As a Pioneer, Smikros has long been deemed worthy of appearing in an aristocratic context, but Scheibler has drawn attention to the many kalos inscriptions naming potters and painters.[76] The Taleides Painter wrote 'Andokides ka[l]os dokei' on a black-figure hydria in the Louvre;[77] the painter of a black-figure Nikosthenic pyxis added the inscription 'Nikosthenes kalos'[78] to a picture of musicians, and an unknown painter wrote 'ho Mys kalos dokei' and nonsense inscriptions in the spaces between blacksmiths working at a forge.[79]

Conclusion

Vase-painters of Beazley's Group E were the first to inscribe kalos-names on vases around 550 BC. These inscriptions were most popular in the Late Archaic period, and continued to be added to scenes until the late fifth century. From the beginning, they were frequently

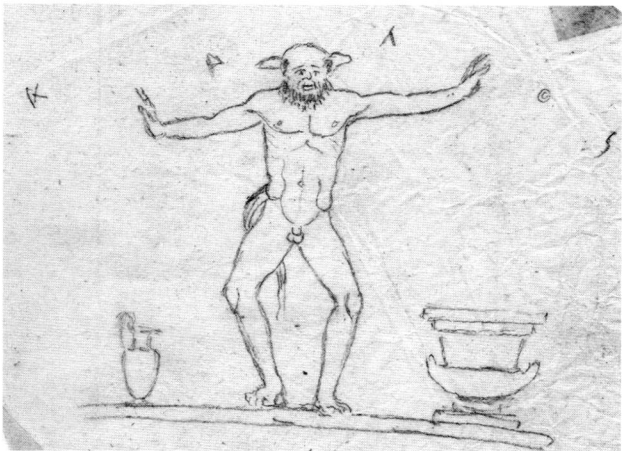

Fig. 10 Museum of Fine Arts, Boston 95.56, red-figure oinochoe by the Painter of Louvre CA 1694.

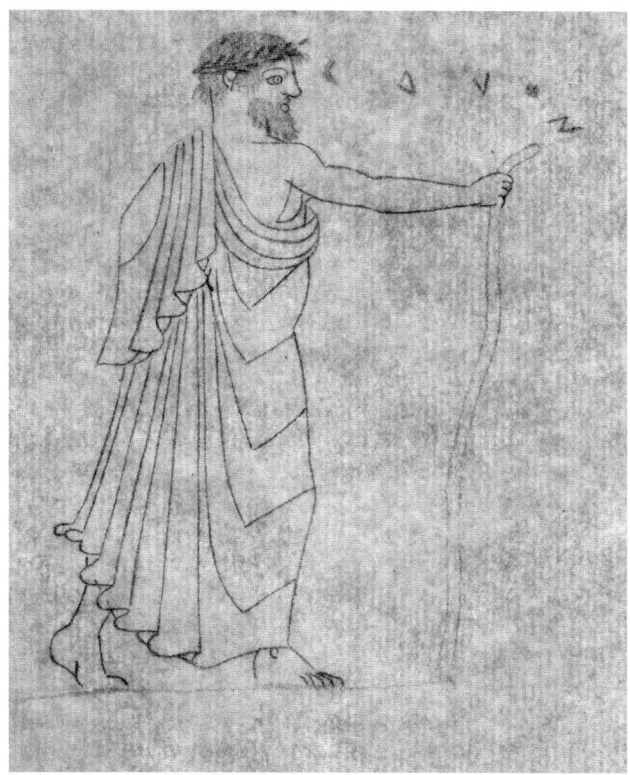

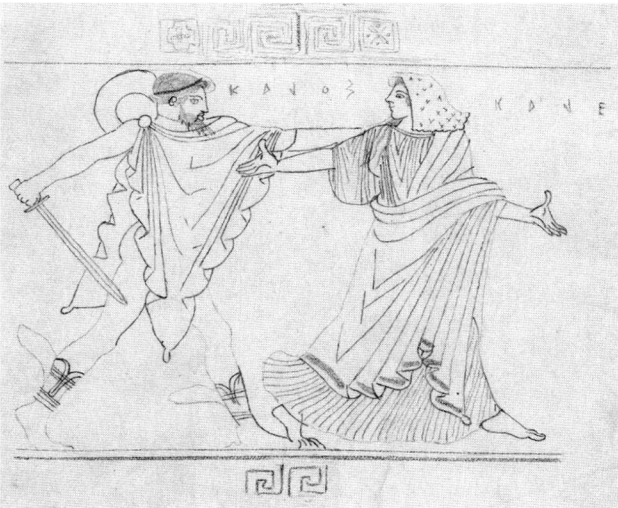

Fig. 9 Vienna, Kunsthistorisches Museum 846, red-figure Nolan amphora by the Oionokles Painter.

Fig. 11 Los Angeles, County Museum A5933.50.16, red-figure lekythos by the Oionokles Painter.

combined with other inscriptions such as signatures, names and nonsense. More than three-quarters of the around 900 vases inscribed with kalos-names with a known provenance were exported to Italy and Sicily, and many were dedicated in sanctuaries in Greece or placed in graves and not used in symposia. Abroad, the beautiful individuals would have been unknown. Many males were kalos for more than fifteen years. The names themselves are baffling: well-known aristocrats, potters and painters, and entirely unknown persons occur. Moreover, the status of favourite of a vase-painter could be inherited.

Shapes bearing these inscriptions imply an aristocratic connotation: more than fifty percent are cups. The subjects to which kalos-names have been added are decidedly aristocratic: around 140 inscribed vases show warriors, one hundred athletes, and seventy symposia.

The use of the same name in different burials and of potters' names suggests that customers bought inscriptions, which enhanced the cultural status of vases, not names. Vase-painters would, therefore, have been free to choose any name coming to mind. That they were not too imaginative in their selection is demonstrated by the occurrence of female versions of the names of their male favourites. Equally baffling is the meaning of kalos, and it is unlikely that there was only one, which vase-painters used with abandon for a very wide range of figures. So who were these beautiful men? Some were aristocrats, in the case of Leagros and Glaukon, perhaps the landlords of potteries, others, such as Kallias, popular musicians. Some names may have been borrowed from fellow potters and painters whose signatures have not yet been discovered, or they were inspired by their agents in trade or merchants; this would explain the use on shapes from different workshops and clusters of kalos-names overseas.

Acknowledgements

I am most grateful to John Oakley for the invitation to Athenian Potters and Painters III, and to Elke Böhr, Adrienne Lezzi-Hafter, and Heide Mommsen for valuable discussions and advice. I would also like to thank Tom Carpenter and Robert Cromey for valuable information.

Abbreviations

Oakley, Death	J. H. Oakley, Picturing Death in Classical Athens, The Evidence of the White Lekythoi (2004)
Shapiro, Leagros	A. Shapiro, in: C. Marconi (ed.), Greek Vases: Images, Contexts and Controversies (2004) 1–11
Ta Attika	R. Panvini – F. Giudice (eds.), Ta Attika, Attic Figured Vases from Gela (2003)
Wernicke	K. Wernicke, Die griechischen Vasen mit Lieblings-namen (1890)

Notes

1. Lekythos, Ashmolean Museum 1888.1402, ARV^2 561,9; Para 388; CVA Oxford 1 Great Britain 3 29 pl. 38,5; Ta Attika 336.I40; CAVI 5903; BAPD 206412.
2. ARV^2 1586.
3. J. K. Davies, Athenian Propertied Families, 600–300 B.C. (1971); Lexicon of Greek Personal Names.
4. Love token, cup, Havana, Museo Nacional 210, ARV^2 1259,8. White-ground funerary lekythos, Athens, National Museum 1769, Oakley, Death 209 fig. 171; BAPD 216406.
5. E. Gerhard – T. Panofka, Neapels antike Bildwerke (1828) 385–386 no. 1925. T. Panofka, 'Die griechischen Eigennamen mit ΚΑΛΟΣ im Zusammenhang mit dem Bilderschmuck auf bemalten Gefäßen,' Abhandlungen der Königlichen Akademie der Wissenschaften zu Berlin (1849) 37–126.
6. W. Klein, Die griechischen Vasen mit Lieblingsinschriften (1890).
7. Wernicke.
8. W. Klein, Die griechischen Vasen mit Lieblingsinschriften, 2nd ed. (1898). The bibliography is too extensive to be listed here; cf. D. M. Robinson – E. J. Fluck, A Study of Greek Love Names, Including a Discussion of Paederasty and a Prosopographia (1937); N. W. Slater, in: E. A. Mackay (ed.), Signs of Orality: The Oral Tradition and its Influence in the Greek and Roman World (1999) 143–161; K. J. Dover, Greek Homosexuality, 2nd ed. (1989); F. Lissarrague, in: S. Goldhill – R. Osborne (eds.), Performance Culture and Athenian Democracy (1999) 359–373; H. A. Shapiro, Hesperia 52, 1983, 305–310; idem., ZPE 68, 1987, 107–118.
9. Boston, MFA 01.8059, ABV 667; CVA Boston 1 USA 14 26–27 fig. 29 pls. 36,1–2; 38,1–2; BAPD 306438.
10. London, BM E 7, ARV^2 149,16; 1585; CAVI 4421; BAPD 201341.
11. Berlin Antikensammlung 3257, ARV^2 239,17; 1586; 1602; CAVI 2462; BAPD 202366.
12. Boston, MFA 95.45, ARV^2 640,74; 1586; CAVI 2644. 95.43, ARV^2 640,75; 1586; CAVI 2642. 95.44, ARV^2 640,76; CAVI 2643; New York, Metropolitan Museum of Art 07.286.67, ARV^2 641,90; CAVI 5572.
13. Providence Painter, Boston, MFA 03.789, ARV^2 636,14; 1586; CAVI 2727; Dresden Painter, from Ruvo, Naples, Museo Archeologico Nazionale 81538, ARV^2 655,9; 1586; CAVI 5429; Charmides Painter, Dresden, Albertinum 291, ARV^2 654,8; 1586; CAVI 3366.
14. Providence Painter, Paris, Cab. Med. 362, ARV^2 636,18; 1571; CAVI 6116. Nikon Painter, Oxford, Ashmolean Museum 1885.671, ARV^2 651,12; 1571; CAVI 5887. Charmides Painter, London, BM E 290, ARV^2 653,1; 1571; CAVI 4553. Dresden Painter, Mariemont, Musée Royal G 129, ARV^2 655,13; 1572; CAVI 5070. Painter of the Yale Lekythos, London, BM E 291, ARV^2 662,1572; CAVI 4554.
15. Oxford, Ashmolean Museum 1891.686, ARV^2 743,3; 1610; CAVI 5885; Oakley, Death 62 fig. 34; Ta Attika 209 fig. 4 376.I210; BAPD 209184.
16. Mykonos, Archaeological Museum, ARV^2 534,7; 1610; CAVI 5406; BAPD 207289.
17. Oxford, Ashmolean Museum 1889.1016, ARV^2 1001,195; 1563; J. H. Oakley, The Achilles Painter (1997) pl. 137c–d; BAPD 214017.

18 Oxford, Ashmolean Museum 1934.341, ARV² 997,147; 1586; Oakley, Death pl. 106b–c; BAPD 213969.
19 E.g. London, BM D 48, ARV² 997,148; 1586; CAVI 4411. Oxford, Ashmolean Museum 1928.507, ARV² 997,147; 1586; CAVI 5979.
20 Copenhagen, National Museum 5624, ARV² 997,150; 1586; CAVI 3249; BAPD 213972.
21 Worcester, Art Museum 1900.65, ARV² 997,151; 1586; CAVI 8036; BAPD 213973.
22 Shapiro (supra n. 8) 107–118.
23 Shapiro, Leagros 1–11.
24 St. Petersburg, Hermitage ST 1670, ARV² 16,15; 1619; CAVI 7353; BAPD 200078. See Hedreen in this volume for Smikra.
25 Paris, Louvre G 30, ARV² 15,9; 1619; CVA Louvre 5 France 8 pls. 27,8–9; 28,1. 4; Shapiro, Leagros 1–11; BAPD 200071.
26 London, BM 1865.11-18.46, ARV² 315,2; 1592; CVA British Museum 9 Great Britain 17 22 fig. 5a pl. 11,a–b; BAPD 203238.
27 Shapiro, Leagros 1–11. Colmar Painter, Colmar University, University Museums 1977.3.103, ARV² 1593; CVA Baltimore, Robinson Collection 2 USA 6 12 pls. 2,2; 3,1; BAPD 9004973. Onesimos, Boston, MFA 10.179, ARV² 327-318,110; 1567; CB II pl. 38; BAPD 203364.
28 H. G. G. Payne, JHS 54, 1934, 185–186; G. Karo, AA 49, 1934, 128; T. L. Shear Jr., AJA 39, 1935, 177.
29 Berlin, Antikensammlung F 2282, ARV² 859,1; 1589,1; 1703; CVA Berlin 3 Germany 22 8–9 figs.1–3 pls. 102,1–5; 103,1–6; BAPD 211324.
30 London, BM D 2, ARV² 859. 862,22; 1580,3; 1672; J. Boardman, Athenian Red Figure Vases, The Classical Period (1989) 38 no. 3 fig. 67; BAPD 211350.
31 Athens, National Museum 15214, ARV² 17,18; BAPD 200081. Athens, Acropolis Museum 211, ARV² 29,20; BAPD 200125. Athens, Acropolis Museum 862, ARV² 1612; BAPD 9017232.
32 Eleusis, Archaeological Museum, ARV² 1592,31; BAPD 9017610. Eleusis, Archaeological Museum, 619, ARV² 1592; BAPD 203232.
33 Lekythos, Oxford, Ashmolean Museum G 298, ARV² 864,13; 1581,6; CVA Oxford 1 Great Britain 3 29 pl. 38,10; BAPD 211374.
34 Lekythos, Paris, market, ARV² 1582,27; CAVI 6777; BAPD 9017847. Bonn, Akademisches Kunstmuseum 64, CVA Bonn 1 Germany 1 49 pls. 41,1–3; 42,1; BAPD 9005530. Madison, Elvehjem Museum 70.2, CAVI 4875; BAPD 1433.
35 Berlin, Antikensammlung F 2322, CAVI 2358; ARV² 329,134; 1604, 1645; BAPD 203389.
36 Neck-amphora, Berlin, Antikensammlung F 1720, ABV 143,1; 686; neck-amphora, London, BM 1836.2-24.127, ABV 144,7; 672. 686; amphora type A, Vatican City, Museo Gregoriano Etrusco 16757, ABV 145,13; 686; calyx-krater, Athens, Agora Museum AP 1044, ABV 145,19.
37 W. Technau, Exekias (1936) 8–11.
38 From Spain, Barcelona, Museo Arqueologico 4485, ABV 148; BAPD 310420.
39 Hydria, St. Petersburg, Hermitage ST 142, ABV 264,2; 672; BAPD 302300.
40 Amphora type B, London, BM B 170, ABV 671,1; BAPD 306453.
41 Geneva, Musée d'Art et d'Histoire, Oakley (supra n. 17) pl. 74a–d; BAPD 19764.
42 Boston, Museum of Fine Arts 13.202, ARV² 1561; BAPD 214046.
43 Plovdiv, Regional Museum of Archaeology 1812, ARV² 1562; BAPD 213559.
44 Boston, Museum of Fine Arts 13.191, ARV² 1562; BAPD 207322.
45 London, British Museum E318, ARV² 1561; BAPD 205996.
46 Warsaw, National Museum 142355, ARV² 1562; 1568; BAPD 213561.
47 London, British Museum 1772.3-20.1, ARV² 1045; BAPD 213563.
48 Munich, Antikensammlungen S 80, ARV² 1568; BAPD 213977; Wernicke 117.
49 Neck-amphora, Athens, Agora Museum P 1690, ARV² 1587; BAPD 207625.
50 Pronomos-Vase, Naples, Museo Archeologico Nazionale 81673; ARV² 1336,1; CAVI 5435; BAPD 217500.
51 Hydria, Florence, Museo Archeologico Etrusco 4014, ARV² 1588,1 s.v. Kallias II.
52 Pelike, Naples, Museo Nazionale 3211 and bell-krater, Boston, Museum of Fine Arts 95.25 ARV² 1588,3. 4 s.v. Kallias II.
53 Phintias, London, BM E 159 ARV² 24,9; 1620; CVA British Museum 5 Great Britain 7 pls. 70,1; 72,1; BAPD 200130. Euthymides, Bonn, Akademisches Kunstmuseum 70, ARV² 28,12; BAPD 200141.
54 Toronto, Royal Ontario Museum 963.59, ARV² 1699; CVA Toronto 1 Canada 1 22 pl. 27,15–18.
55 Athens, Ceramicus, 7715, CAVI 1763; AM 106, 1991, pls. 26,1; 27–28; C. Mann, et al. (eds.), Rollenbilder in der athenischen Demokratie, Medien, Gruppen, Räume im politischen und sozialen System, Beitrage zu einim interdisziplinaren Kolloquium in Freiburg i. Br., 24.–25. November 2006 (2009) 153–155 figs. 1–4; BAPD 28994.
56 Bell-krater from Cyprus, Paris, Louvre A 258, ARV² 1113,10; 1599; CVA Louvre 4 France 5 pl. 23,9. 12; BAPD 214718. Stamnos, St. Petersburg, Hermitage 2353, ARV² 1144,7; 1590, 1599; S. B. Matheson, Polygnotos and Vase Painting in Classical Athens (1995) 144 pl. 127; BAPD 215147.
57 Athens, Acropolis 2.1037, Epiktetos or related to Euthymides, ARV² 1598,5; CAVI 1463; Euphronios der Maler (1991) 142; BAPD 46837.
58 London, BM 1857.8-5.1, ABV 160,2; 163,1; Munich, Antikensammlungen 2243, ABV 160,2; 163,2. Berlin, Antikensammlung, F 1761 ABV 164,3.
59 Paris, Louvre CP 11187, ARV² 18; CAVI 6612; Euphronios der Maler (supra n. 57) 142–143 no. 16; BAPD 200094.
60 Ath. 12.58; Hdt. 6.126; Euphronios der Maler (supra n. 57) 142–143; CAVI 6612.
61 Brussels, Bibliothèque Royale 9, ARV² 862,31; 1555; BAPD 211359.
62 The Lewis Painter, Nausicaa Painter and Polygnotus.
63 H. G. Liddell – R. Scott, A Greek-English Dictionary (1983) 737–738 s.v. καλός.
64 Wernicke 118.
65 Once Northwick, Spencer-Churchill, ARV² 846,191; HASB 1, 1975, pl. 4,2.
66 Thebes, Archaeological Museum 46.84, V. Aravantinos, The Archaeological Museum of Thebes (2010) 234.

67 Vienna, Kunsthistorisches Museum 846, ARV² 648,27; CVA Vienna 2 Austria 2 12–13 pl. 60,1–3; BAPD 207539.
68 Boston, MFA 95.56, ARV² 787,5; BAPD 209689.
69 London, BM E 583, ARV² 282,40; CAVI 4631; BAPD 202549.
70 Pelike, Geras Painter, New York, Metropolitan Museum of Art 01.8.8, ARV² 286,19; RH pls. 22. 173; BAPD 202590.
71 Red-figure lekythos, Oionokles Painter, Los Angeles, County Museum A5933.50.16, ARV² 649,44; LIMC V (1990) pl. 269, Hermes 873; BAPD 207556.
72 Wernicke 118.
73 Brussels, Musées Royaux A 717, ARV² 20,1; 1619; CVA Brussels 2 Belgium 2 pls. 12,1a–d; 13,1a. 1b. 1c; BAPD 200102.
74 Calyx-krater, Munich, Antikensammlungen 9300+; ARV² 1619,3bis; 1705. 1699; CAVI 5363; BAPD 275007.
75 Berlin, Antikensammlung 1966.20, Para 503; CVA Berlin 9 Germany 74 18–20 figs. 2. 3 Beilage 1,3 pls.4,1–5; 56,3; BAPD 340207.
76 Der Neue Pauly VII (1999) 181–183 s.v. Lieblingsinschriften (I. Scheibler).
77 Paris, Louvre F 38, ABV 174,7; 664; CVA Louvre 6 France 9 pl. 62,1–4; BAPD 301126.
78 Vienna, Kunsthistorisches Museum IV 1870, ABV 671; CAVI 7899; BAPD 306451.
79 London, BM 1846.6-29.45, CAVI 4338; A. Chatzidimitriou, Parastaseis Ergasterion kai Emporiou stin Eikonographia ton Archaikon kai Klasikon Chronon (2005) pl. 22,X2; BAPD 303253. Mys signed a lekythos from Tanagra as painter, Athens, National Museum, 1626, ARV² 663; N. Kaltsas (ed.), Athens-Sparta (2006) 235 no. 122; BAPD 207770.

13 The View from Behind the Kline: Symposial Space and Beyond

Timothy McNiven

In several groups of images of the Athenian symposion, attempts were made to render the space in which the symposion was set. An examination of these images provides an opportunity to accomplish several things. First, to examine the methods that were developed to depict space in images of the symposion. Second, to examine how the understanding of these images affects our conceptions of the space of actual symposia. Third, I would like to propose an explanation for why these images were added to the developing iconography of the Athenian symposion.

The rendering of space is not usually associated with Greek vase painting, at least not before the middle of the fifth century when the experiments of the wall painter Polygnotos appear on the Niobid Krater in Paris. Later in the fifth century, as Gisela Richter demonstrated in her classic study, there were attempts at true linear perspective and the development of perspective seems to have continued in the fourth century.[1] Earlier, in the Late Archaic period, however, space was not something that was on a vase painter's mind, or at least that has been the common view. However, as with so many innovations, the Pioneer Group began experimenting with space, and some of their ideas continued to be used by later artists.[2]

One such experiment shows up in symposion scenes, usually in connection with the typical arrangement with a row of couches against the blank background, with servers and entertainers and male figures on each couch, when at the right of the scene the painter depicts a couch end-on, creating as it were a corner of the symposion space. The most sophisticated example of this is a cup attributed to Douris in the British Museum (Fig. 1; Color Pl. 14B).[3] Three couches are shown. The one on the right is turned at a right angle to the others, so that it projects into the viewer's space. The man on the end-view couch is shown from the back, leaning on his left elbow and facing the other two men and two serving boys to the left. To indicate space, Douris overlapped the furniture to demonstrate that the front-view couch in the middle is behind the end-view serving table, which is overlapped in turn by the end-view couch. Kylikes and oinochoai hang from the wall in the background.

This kind of image goes back to the beginning of the fifth century. The earliest example of this, in my opinion, is by Epiktetos (Fig. 2).[4] He shows us a very stripped down version, where the space is ambiguous since none of the furniture overlaps (although the scene makes sense enough). Another, more complex version is preserved on a fragment attributed to the Hegesiboulos Painter. There is little left, but it does show us this composition with the end-view couch with the back of the symposiast, the serving table that goes with the couch to its left, and the right side of the frontal couch and symposiast to the left of that.[5] Late Archaic artists such as the Kleophrades Painter, the Foundry Painter and the Brygos Painter also experimented with this composition.[6] Douris seems to have particularly liked this image, using it on both sides of the London cup, discussed above, as well as on both sides of a cup in Florence.[7] Later artists, such as the Painter of the Louvre Symposion, continued the series into the Classical period, but these images need not occupy us further.[8]

Depictions like those on the cup in London, combined with excavated dining rooms in various places, such as the Athenian Agora, Eretria and Olynthos, formed the basis for Piet de Jong's reconstruction of the space of the symposion as a cozy room lined with couches, where men recline and interact across the open space in the center (Fig. 3).[9] It is a testimony to the power of such well-informed and carefully rendered depictions that they are popular, and have become a part of the way we all think about the Greek symposion. But there is a problem. In a few ancient images, there is a space behind the kline seen end-on, a space which our standard reconstruction does not account for. Douris, for instance, created a tondo composition on another cup in London that focuses only on the end couch and its table, surely an excerpt from

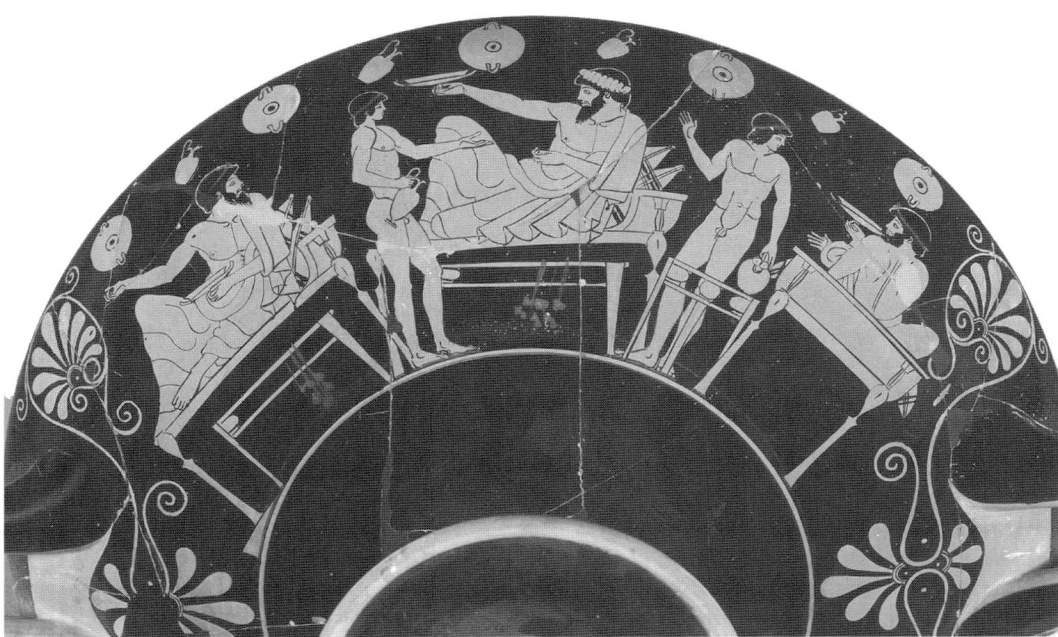

Fig. 1 Athenian Red-figured Cup, attributed to Douris, 485–480 BC. London, British Museum 1843.11-3.15. ©The Trustees of the British Museum. Photo: Museum.

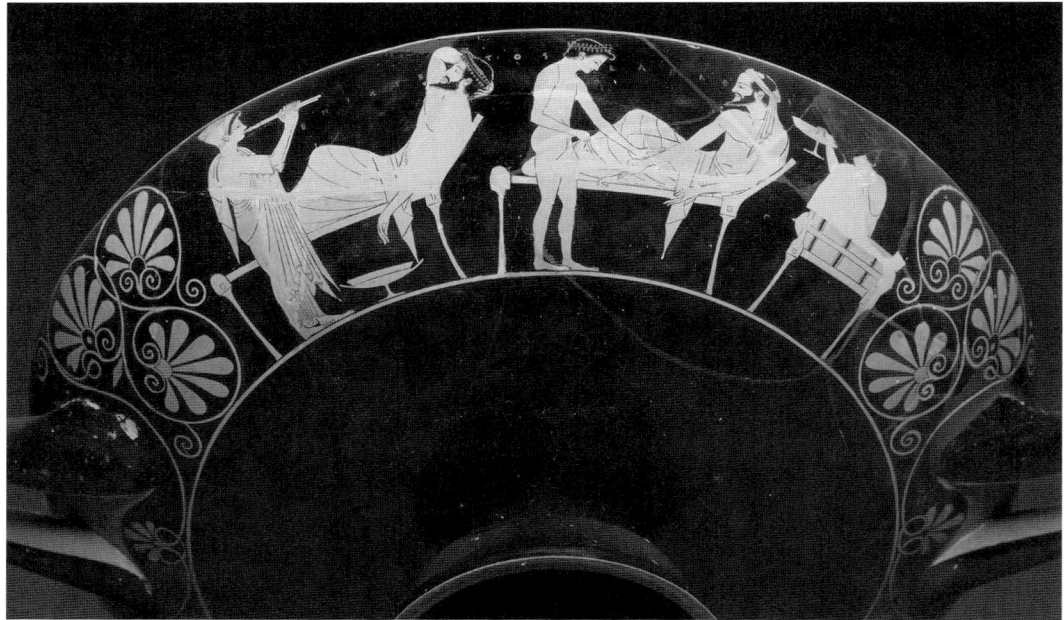

Fig. 2 Athenian Red-figured Cup, attributed to Epiktetos, 500 BC. London, British Museum E38. ©The Trustees of the British Museum. Photo: Museum.

his larger compositions.[10] The youthful symposiast faces right and reaches back with his kylix. It is not clear what he is doing: it does not look like playing kottabos, so he may be displaying his empty cup to call for a refill. In any case, Douris does not seem to imagine him against the wall. On another cup there is a lampstand behind the kline, although this could be imagined as standing against the wall.[11] However, on a third cup, a krater stands at the right behind the kline seen end-on (Fig. 4).[12] Regular access to the krater was important during the drinking, so it does not seem likely that it was set up between a couch and the wall.[13]

During the last ten years, scholars of domestic architecture, such as Lisa Nevett, have pointed out that

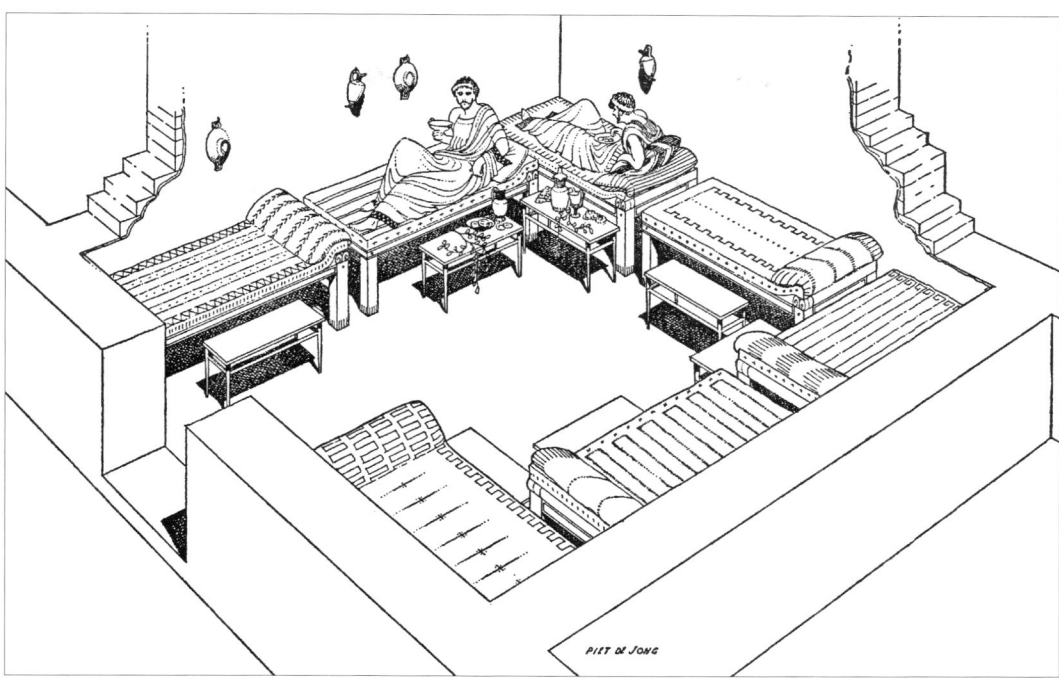

Fig. 3 Reconstruction of a dining Room in the South Stoa, Athenian Agora, by Piet De Jong. Image: Agora Excavations, American School of Classical Studies at Athens

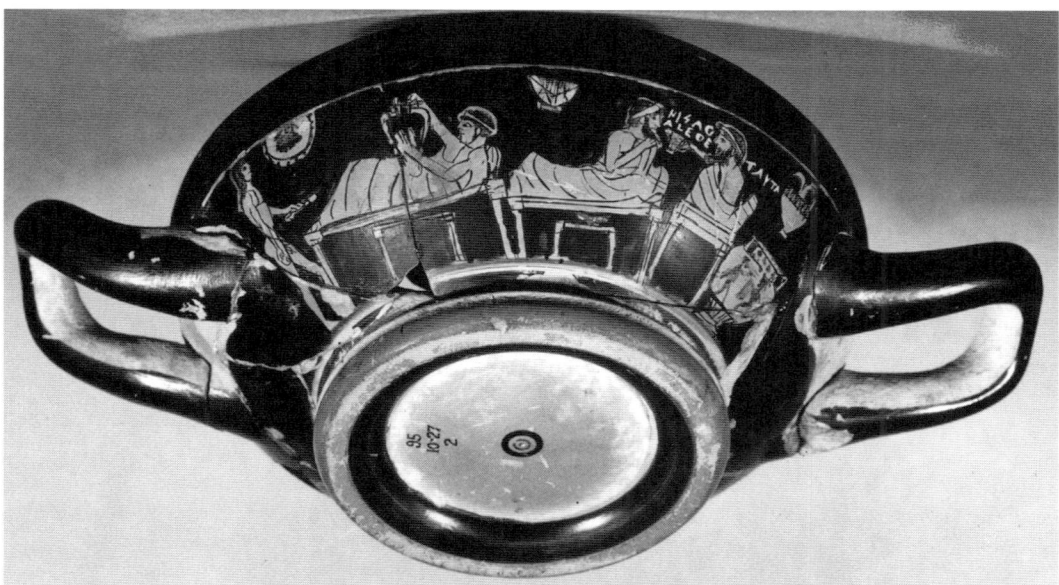

Fig. 4 Athenian Red-figured Cup, unattributed, 480 BC. London, British Museum 1895.10-27.2. © The Trustees of the British Museum. Photo: Museum.

the excavated dining rooms on which Piet De Jong's reconstruction is based are dated to the late fifth or early fourth century or even later, and that the admittedly scanty remains of houses from earlier periods, even ones contemporary with these images, do not possess a specially designed *andron*, as the room designated for dining and drinking was called.[14] It is therefore anachronistic to put these vase paintings with those excavated spaces. In fact, there is no reason why anyone would have been limited to the andron for a symposion, if the symposion was larger than the andron could hold. An example of such a situation (admittedly mythical) is found in the depiction of the battle between the Lapiths and Centaurs on the neck of a volute krater in New York, where a Lapith fights a centaur from behind the kline.[15] Clearly a royal wedding feast, especially one that includes Centaurs, would demand an unusual amount of space! It is therefore a logical suggestion that a symposion could be held in the courtyard of a house. I suspect that not only was this often the case, but that it was especially true during the summer in Athens, when a closed room would have been stuffy, and dining and drinking under the sky would have made more sense. But normal symposion scenes, even if they do not show objects hanging on the wall, almost never show a person behind the couches. A rare exception is the Hegesiboulos Painter's name piece, where one of the serving boys runs behind his master's kline with an oinochoe.[16] It can be argued that this is not a symposion, since there is only one man, and not a cup in sight, and because seemingly modest women are present. The image is unusual in so many ways, but we certainly are made aware of the space behind the kline here.[17]

This is mapping known territory, but things become less familiar in some symposion images that turn the view around, as it were. Epiktetos seems to have been the innovator here as well. Even before the earliest example of a kline shown from the end, he experimented with a different viewpoint, one that has greater implications about the placement of the kline. This is a composition where the symposiast reclines to the left, with his feet to the right. The oldest example seems to be Epiktetos' symposiast in a tondo at Oberlin College (Fig. 5).[18] A youth reclines on a kline, as indicated by the board that forms the platform beneath the pillows and his hips. This is not a ground line, since his cloak drops down over the far side of the board. Later versions of the image will include objects on the other side of the kline, as on a cup attributed to the Painter of the Louvre Komos, where a storage amphora decorated with a wreath stands on the floor beyond the kline, creating a more substantial presence in the symposial space.[19] By the middle of the fifth century, some artists, especially ones in the Penthesilea Workshop, depict another person, a serving boy or girl standing on the other side of the couch.[20] Space is visible in front; space is indicated in back. The kline must stand in the open, and not against a wall. We are behind the kline looking over the reclining figure and out into the space in the middle of the symposion.[21] The food basket hanging from the porthole frame in Epiktetos' Oberlin College tondo complicates this open space a little, as does the case for auloi hanging on the right on a slightly later cup by Epiktetos.[22] Such hanging objects show the painter toying with the frame, much as he did in showing each symposiast pushing his left foot up again the reserved circle of the tondo.

In these and comparable examples, the reclining figure is shown in profile, with his back usually against a pillow. Each figure has both hands full, or is busy in such a way that it is impossible for him to recline normally on his left elbow, because he plays a barbitos, holds several cups or even a storage amphora. Like the symposion with end-on kline, this composition also continued to be used by later generations.[23] In every case these compositions show only a single symposiast.

The Oberlin cup looks a little odd, since the youth sits in profile but leans on his left elbow while holding a cup in his left hand and playing kottabos with his right. The space is also a little awkward here, since the pillow seems to be beyond the youth rather than beneath him. The awkward placement of the pillow is repeated on another early tondo, but with an important difference (Fig. 6).[24] Here the youth turns his back towards the viewer in a three-quarter view and faces back to the left as he spins the cup on his finger. Such images are repeated throughout the fifth century with increasing grace and spatial sophistication.[25]

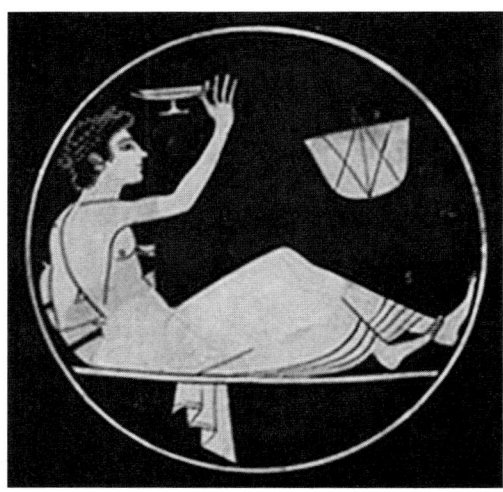

Fig. 5 Athenian Red-figured Cup, attributed to Epiktetos, 520–510 BC. Oberlin, OH, Oberlin College, Allen Memorial Art Museum 1967.61, General Acquisition Fund, 1967. Photo: Museum.

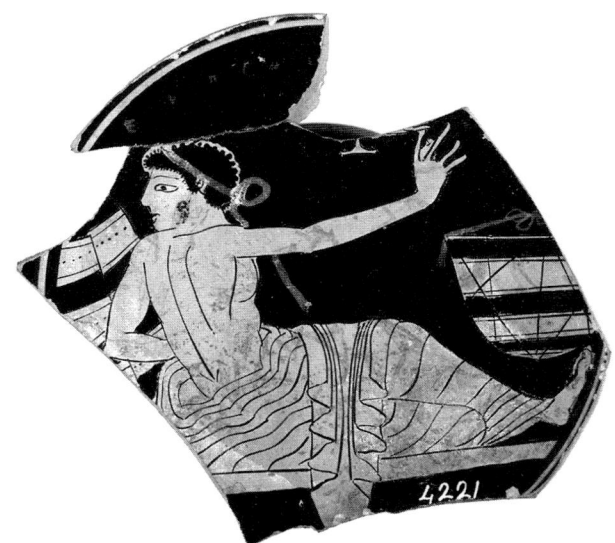

Fig. 6 Athenian Red-figured Cup, by an artist akin to the Elpinikos Painter, 500 BC. Florence, Museo Archeologico 4221. Photo: by permission of the Soprintendenza per i Beni Archeologici della Toscana-Firenze.

These figures recline on a kline shown from behind, often reduced to a single board, although sometimes the legs and end pieces of the couch are depicted.[26] Often, the youth's cloak drops over the other side of the couch, and there may be a walking stick propped there as well. The three dimensional quality of the space is particularly clear on a sadly fragmentary cup in Adria, where the reclining figure wraps his arms around his chest and pulls his knees up on the couch, treating us to a view of the soles of his feet.[27] Pulling in the extremities like this may indicate that the figure feels cold, or that he is insecure. Beyond the couch, the serving table is visible, as well as the figure's staff. While they indicate the space on the far side, the view of the feet makes us all the more conscious of the space on this side of the kline. Members of the Penthesilea Workshop particularly favored the dorsal symposiast in the middle of the century, but clarified the space by depicting a figure on the other side of the kline, a serving boy or a girl musician (Fig. 7).[28] (This composition was repeated *ad nauseam* and degraded into a formula.) There is no doubt in these cases that the viewer is behind the kline, looking past the figures and out into the central space of the symposion.

Perhaps the most curious image of a symposiast shown from the back is on a column krater attributed to the Nausicaa Painter.[29] The musician in the center is framed by two symposiasts. The youth on the left reclines with his feet to the left, his chest in a normal frontal view, while the man on the right has his feet to the right and is depicted from behind. Each has a serving table in front of him, which means that the table on the right is on the other side of the kline from us. The youth on the left holds a fruit that overlaps the aulist's shoulder, while her pipes overlap the headboard of the couch on the right. This would seem to indicate that there is a simple spatial progression from left to right. The youth on the left is in front, the woman is behind or next to him, and the man is farthest back of all. But if that is so, it is hard to imagine how the furniture could be arranged in space. It seems that the youth closest to the picture plane faces us; the man farthest away faces away from us. Neither could see the other, or the musician. There is no central space to this symposion, where the woman is standing.

It is never a strong argument to suggest that the artist has made a mistake, but if the painter had not overlapped the attributes, it is possible to see the three people relating to each other in three distinct layers in space. The man on the right, shown from behind, would be in the foreground seen from behind, facing the aulos player in the middle ground in the center of the space, and the youth on the left in the background beyond her. Without perspective, however, and with the overlapping hands, this is a flattened mess.

What I have proposed that the Nausicaa Painter was attempting to draw is actually accomplished on a fourth-century calyx-krater in the Hermitage.[30] Here, the use of stacked ("Polygnotan") space makes everything clear. Across the top of the field, four symposiasts recline

in normal fashion, feet to the left, in front of a row of columns. In front of these symposiasts, lower down in the middle ground, a female aulist performs. In front of her, at the bottom of the field, is a couch with two symposiasts, feet to the right, shown from behind. The space of the symposion is then well-defined: the viewer

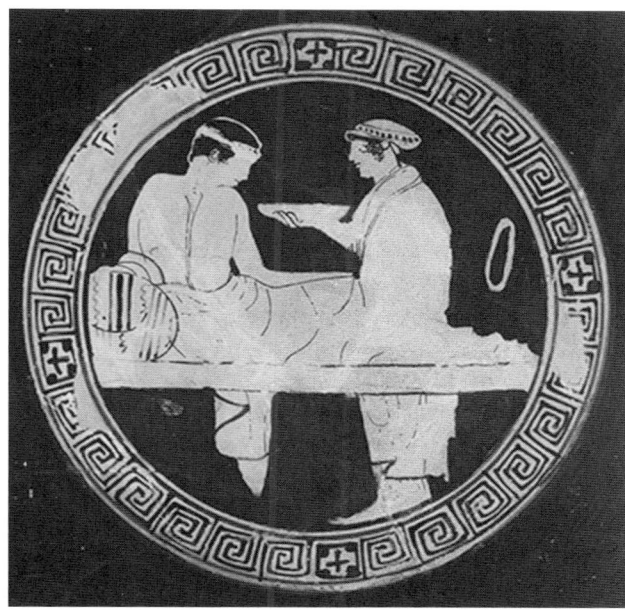

Fig. 7 Athenian Red-figured Cup, attributed to the Painter of Brussels R330, 450 BC. New York, Metropolitan Museum of Art 19.192.67. © The Metropolitan Museum of Art. Photo: Art Resource, NY.

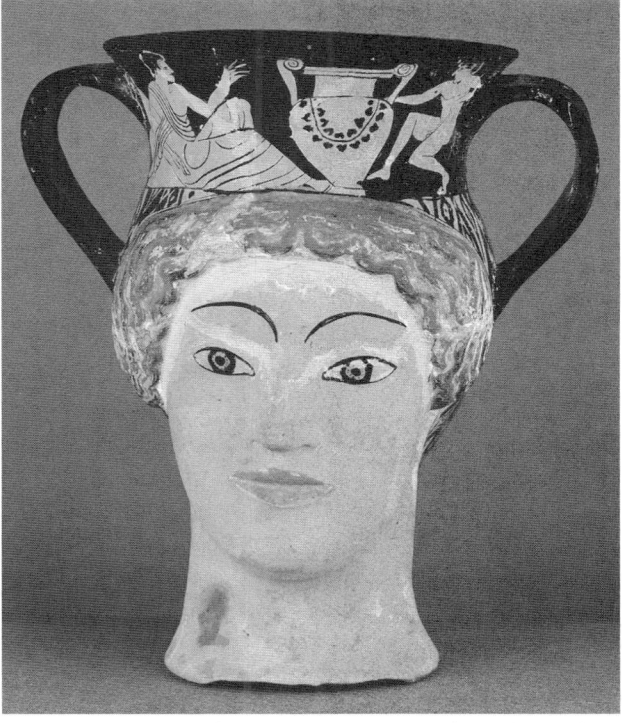

Fig. 8 Athenian Red-figured Kantharos, Recalling the Epeleios Painter, 510–500 BC. Paris, Louvre Museum H 46. Photo: Lessing.

looks over the dorsal-view of the symposiasts as they face their companions across the open space, very possibly a courtyard as indicated by the columns at the rear. There are awkward elements, such as the need to shorten the legs on the foreground couch, and the way the aulist seems to step on the youth below, but actually in front of, her. There are also subtle spatial touches, such as the hand that the serving boy (lower left) lays on the back of the youth in the foreground, and the foot of the serving man (lower right) that appears below and beyond the foreground couch. After a century of experimentation, we are finally shown a symposion in space, but also made conscious of the limitations of the flat black of the background, and how altered our view of the world is after the invention of linear perspective.

Spatial cues are crucial in all these images. Without the simple elements such as sticks or servants that indicate the space beyond the couch, and without the later convention of stacked "Polygnotan" space, it could be argued that dorsal symposiasts are simply reclining the opposite way, on pillows placed at the left end of the couch rather than the right. A practical reason that argues against this is that the typical kline had a headboard but no footboard, so pillows would slide off in real life. Figures do occasionally lay the wrong way, as on another tondo signed by Epiktetos.[31] A satyr, in this case, reclines in profile with his feet to the right and drinks directly out of a storage amphora. His tail hangs over this side of the board, and neither end of the couch is indicated. Satyrs often turn the world upside down, something already indicated by the way this one drinks unmixed wine right out of the amphora.[32] Clearly satyrs can recline backwards too. But this in itself is an odd image, because satyrs are only rarely depicted reclining on couches.[33] When satyrs do recline, they usually recline on the ground, which raises another issue about symposia.[34]

Sometimes, a symposiast is reclining not on a kline but on a mattress or the ground line, that is, out of doors, as on a the rim of a head kantharos (Fig. 8; Color Pl. 15).[35] These images of a symposion on the ground have been much discussed.[36] Frauke Heinrich connects them with the Dionysiac realm;[37] Kathryn Topper believes that these are images of ancestral custom, citing mythological examples.[38] However, neither of these specific interpretations seems possible in the light of Euphronios' psykter, where a hetaira named Smikra reclining with her companions on a mattress dedicates her kottabos throw to Leagros. This must be a contemporary scene, even if it is imaginary.[39] I believe that images of symposia without klinai simply show us a less formal version of the summer symposion, which could be held completely out of the house, in a garden or in the countryside.[40] The images may depict the age of heroes, a ritual situation or the Dionysiac realm, but the position on the ground only indicates that the setting is rustic.

In reference to symposiasts seen from behind, the space of the symposion is altered when it is outdoors and on the ground. Unlike couches, mattresses can be placed in any orientation. This is indicated by images in which a figure stands behind a symposiast in this setting, as when an aulist plays between the two drinkers.[41] In the later fifth century, when Polygnotan space had become common, figures seen from behind while reclining on the ground render the symposial space quite elegantly. These are often satyrs, as on a famous volute krater from Spina by Polion, who appear at an outdoor symposion given by Dionysos for Hephaistos.[42] The satyrs in the foreground project into the space, thereby creating it, like the mourners in the foreground of Giotto's *Lamentation*.

Symposia on the ground allow a great deal of flexibility of posing and positioning, and therefore, from early on, artists were able to show figures from different sides, which can challenge the viewer to understand the space. For instance, Euthymides, depicted young men back to back playing music on mattresses on the ground.[43] The one on the right is shown in profile with his feet to the right, but there is no unusual depiction of space. The view is from the front; only the seating has been re-arranged. In other examples a symposiast on the ground with his feet to the right is sometimes shown from the front, not supporting himself on his elbow, so that he seems to be rolling around.[44] Sometimes, however, an equivalent figure is shown in back view, with his head turned over his shoulder to his normally positioned comrades to the left.[45] In such cases, this flexible arrangement allows for symmetry, and certainly for variety from the serried ranks of normal symposiasts; it does not have much to tell us spatially.[46]

It is a threadbare truism, but one that needs to be kept in mind, that images in Greek art are not documentary photographs. They present us with what French scholars have named "the imaginary," a representation of what the world ought to be like.[47] Athenian vase paintings are as constructed as Egyptian wall paintings, and it is only their convincing realism that lures us into thinking, or wanting to think, that they show us the real world. We know this when we are looking at an image of a satyr, but forget it too easily when we are looking at a human. At the same time, this imaginary world is still tied to the real world.[48] Some things are the same: gravity still works (mostly), and human anatomy is consistent. Symposiasts always recline on their left elbows and play kottabos with their right hands, whichever way they are lying, and whichever way we view them. (There are no left-handed people in Greek art.) It is an edited world, ruled by convention and expressing commonly held views.This has important implications for the images examined so far. If the symposion was always held in an andron, a Greek artist would not have thought of showing us a view from beyond the kline. He did not need to be able to see something to draw it, as images of monsters demonstrate, but a composition from such a point of view would make no sense if it were impossible in actuality. It is easy to believe, as many scholars have proposed, that some symposia took place outdoors, in the courtyard of a private house or in open spaces in the city or in the countryside. Images of the symposiast from behind the kline strengthen those arguments with ancient evidence. But a question remains: What did these images add to the developing iconography of the Athenian symposium?

In order to create these images, the artist had to think about the view from behind the kline. But who would have viewed the kline from behind? As previously discussed, in ordinary symposion scenes, servers or entertainers are almost never shown behind the klinai. So the dorsal view is not a servant's viewpoint; and a vase painter probably would never show his customers a servant's viewpoint anyway. If we imagine it from the point of view of another guest at the symposion, this puts us, literally, in an interesting position. At a symposion in a courtyard or in the open, we are approaching the kline from behind. We are looking at a symposiast in profile or from the back. In the earlier images this was often an adult man, but soon all the images showed youths. Care was spent on the depiction of the musculature of the back and the torsion of the torso. To some extent we are being given an implicit invitation to join the person on the kline, to become a symposiast ourselves. Maybe we are just arriving and choosing a companion. Maybe we are returning to our places after answering a call of nature. On the Adria fragment the lone symposiast curls up on his couch and folds his arms from the cold.[49] Maybe his pose suggests that he would welcome a companion.

An important parallel exists in the Tomb of the Diver from Paestum.[50] The walls of the tomb are encircled by a symposion, with the krater at the head end, three couches down each side, and a trio arriving on the foot end.[51] Lying in the tomb means being in the symposion, even in the andron. On the left end of each side wall, a man occupies a kline alone. The one near the feet of the dead youth extends a cup to the three figures painted on the end panel: an aulos girl, a youth and a young man. The nude youth strides forward and extends his left hand, returning the greeting of the man on the couch around the corner.[52] The youth clearly has his choice of drinking companions: the young man he is arriving with or either of the two men reclining alone. He seems most interested in the man with the cup of wine. Thinking about this, the viewer is suddenly conscious of the dilemma of the man walking behind him. When the youth makes his choice, where will his older companion end up?

The artist of the Tomb of the Diver has focused on the opportunities of the youth, presumably the youth buried in this tomb. In a similar way, the artists who depicted lone symposiasts from behind also focused on the late arrival, the viewer, but he can be assumed to be an adult male, the presumed typical buyer for drinking equipment in ancient Athens. The male viewer gazing at an image of a lone symposiast is always presented with an opportunity, perhaps an invitation, to join him (occasionally her) on the couch. When the view is from the front, there can be eye contact, and possible rejection. When the view is from behind, the possibility of rejection is less, and perhaps one can assume that the reclining symposiast will welcome the companion who is joining him.

Notes

1   G. Richter, Perspective in Greek and Roman Art (1970) 32–47.
2   D. Williams, in: D. Buitron-Oliver (ed.), New Perspectives in Early Greek Art (1991) 292–293 discusses the rare use of foreshortening in the early fifth century.
3   London, British Museum 1843.11-3.15 (E49): ARV² 432,52; BAPD 205096; CVA British Museum 9 Great Britain 17 pls. 28–29.
4   London, British Museum E38: ARV² 72,16; 1623; BAPD 200460; I. Peschel, Die Hetäre bei Symposion und Komos in der attischen-rotfigurigen Vasenmalerei des 6.-4. Jahrh. v. Chr. (1987) fig. 55. The end-view kline does allow the painter to explore drawing in a back view, something Epiktetos seems to have enjoyed judging from his well-known penchant for rendering shoulder-blades. The discussion about the relative dating is summarized in D. Paleothodoros, Épictétos (2004) 42–44.
5   Basel, H. A. Cahn 680, attributed by D. von Bothmer to the Hegesiboulos Painter: BAPD 41449; Williams (supra n. 2) 291 fig. 8. Not discussed in M. Moore, MetrMusJ 43, 2008, 11–37.
6   Copenhagen, National Museum 13365: ARV² 185,32 (Kleophrades Painter); BAPD 201684; CVA Copenhagen 8 Denmark 8 259. Cambridge, Corpus Christi College: ARV² 402,12; 1651 (Foundry Pt.); BAPD 204353; Peschel (supra n. 4) fig. 64. Paris, Bibliothèque Nationale 717 etc.: ARV² 372,28 (Brygos Painter); BAPD 203926; G. Mylonas (ed.), Studies Presented to David Moore Robinson on his Seventieth Birthday II (1953) pl. 26.
7   See n. 3, and Florence, Museo Archeologico 3922: ARV² 432,55; BAPD 205099; CVA Florence 3 Italy 30 pl. 90,1–3.
8   Paris, Louvre G 415: ARV² 1070,2 (Painter of the Louvre Symposion), BAPD 214408; CVA Louvre 4 France 5 pl. 20,3–4. Other later images include Florence, Museo Archeologico 3999: ARV² 275,47 (Harrow Painter); BAPD 202883; CVA Florence 2 Italy 13 pls. 39,2; 42. Mainz, University 3239: ARV² 525,38 (Orchard Painter); BAPD 205922; CVA Mainz 2 Germany 43 pl. 10,2–3. Basel, Antikenmuseum und Sammlung Ludwig BS 486 (neck): ARV² 612,2 (Painter of Bologna 279); BAPD 207096; CVA Basel 3 Switzerland 7 pl. 4,6. Tarquinia RC 1996: ARV² 1058,110 (Group of Polygnotos); BAPD 213740; unpublished.
9   J. Papadopoulos, The Art of Antiquity. Piet de Jong and the Athenian Agora (2007) 26. 29 fig. 41. Compare the color version in P. Connolly – H. Dodge, The Ancient City. Life in Classical Athens and Rome (1998) 52.
10 London, British Museum 1892.5-18.1: ARV² 443,227; 1653; BAPD 205273; CVA British Museum 9 Great Britain 17 pl. 34.
11 Karlsruhe, Badisches Landesmuseum 70.395: not in Beazley; BAPD 4704; CVA Karlsruhe 3 Germany 60 pls. 31–32.
12 London, British Museum 1895.10-27.2: unattributed; BAPD 11911; Hesperia 60, 1991, pl. 97. Thoroughly

discussed in E. Csapo – M. Miller, Hesperia 60, 1991, 367–382. This looks to be a poor copy of Douris. On copies, see S. Hoyt, in: C. Mattusch – A. Donohue – A. Brauer (eds.), Common Ground: Archaeology, Art, Science and Humanities (Proceedings of the XVIth International Congress of Classical Archaeology, Boston, August 13–16, 2003) (2006) 352–354.

13   F. Lissarrague, The Space of the Krater, in: The Aesthetics of the Greek Banquet, trans. A. Szegedy-Maszak (1990) 29–46.

14   L. Nevett, Domestic Space in Classical Antiquity (2010) 43–62. L. Nevett, in: R. Westgate – N. Fisher – J. Whitley (eds.), Building Communities. House, Settlement and Society in the Aegean and Beyond (2007) 5–10. K. Lynch, in: Westgate – Fisher – Whitley supra 242–249. A. Rabinowitz, in: S. Hodkinson (ed.) Sparta. Comparative Approaches (2009) 138–142. K. Lynch, The Symposium in Context, Hesperia Suppl. 46 (2011) 76–77.

15   New York, Metropolitan Museum of Art 07.286.84: ARV² 613,1; BAPD 207099; J. Mertens, How To Read Greek Vases (2010) 128.

16   New York, Metropolitan Museum of Art 07.286.47 (A): ARV² 175; BAPD 201603; B. Cohen, The Colors of Clay, Special Techniques in Athenian Vases (2006) 50 fig. 8; 296 fig. 3. Thoroughly studied by Moore (supra n. 5).

17   This is not true when the kline is used as a bed rather than as a symposion couch, such as when women stand behind the kline in prothesis scenes. Note also the figures behind the bed on which the baby Herakles strangles the snakes on an amphora in the Louvre, G192: ARV² 208,160 (Berlin Painter); BAPD 201979; CVA Louvre 6 France 9 pl. 55,2.

18   Oberlin, OH, Oberlin College 67.61: Para 329,14bis; BAPD 352425; W. Moon, Greek Vase-Painting in Midwestern Collections (1979) 133.

19   Orvieto, Museo Faina MC 589: ARV² 359,19; BAPD 203780; CVA Umbria 1 Italy 16 pl. 7,2.

20   New York, Metropolitan Museum of Art 19.192.67: ARV² 925,5; BAPD 211258; photo Beazley Archive.

21   Symposiasts shown from behind have occasionally been noted, e.g., M. Napoli, La Tomba del Tuffatore (1970) 112 figs. 39–40, but I am not aware of any scholarly discussion of the space beyond.

22   London, British Museum E37: ARV² 72,17; 1623; BAPD 200461; E. Pfuhl, Malerei und Zeichnung der Griechen (1923) pl. 324. Compare Malibu, Getty Museum 86.AE.279: Para 329,83ter (Epiktetos); BAPD 352426; CVA Malibu 8 USA 33 pl. 398,1; and Adria, Museo Archeologico 22171: ARV² 110,11 (Hermaios Painter); 1626; BAPD 200946; CVA Adria 1 Italy 28 pl. 3,3. The figure's feet are cut off by the frame on Würzburg, Martin von Wagner Museum L472: ARV² 137 (not far from the Aktorione Painter); BAPD 201146; P. Jacobsthal, Göttinger Vasen. Nebst einer Abhandlung Symposiaka (1912) 43 fig. 67.

23   Bryn Mawr, University P-206: ARV² 476,273; BAPD 204952; CVA Bryn Mawr 1 USA 13 pl. 19. London, British Museum E 27: ARV² 98,14 (manner of the Euergides Painter); BAPD 200852; JdI 6, 1891, 253. Paris, Louvre MNB 2040: ARV² 1796,1 (Chairias Painter); BAPD 201605; P. Devambez, Greek Painting (1962) pl. 101. Orvieto, Museo Civico 589: ARV² 359,19 (Painter of the Louvre Komos); BAPD 203718; CVA Umbria 1 Italy 16 pl. 7,2. Later compositions have another figure, standing or walking on the other side of the kline, e.g., Heidelberg, University 147: ARV² 916,178 (Painter of Bologna 417); BAPD 211115; Peschel (supra n. 4) pl. 175.

24   Florence, Museo Archeologico 4221: ARV² 119. 1576 (akin to the Elpinikos Painter); BAPD 201002; CVA Florence 3 Italy 30 pl. 86,4.

25   Mannheim, Reiss-Museum 62: ARV² 866,4 (Cat-and-Dog Painter); BAPD 211393; CVA Mannheim 1 Germany 13 pl. 21,3 (a walking stick beyond the kline). Palermo, Museo Nazionale NI 2093: ARV² 812,57 (follower of Makron); BAPD 210038; CVA Palermo 1 Italy 14 pl. 13. Perugia 0.3651: ARV² 349,3 (Cage Painter or near him); BAPD 203651; StEtr 26, 1958, 260. Christie's, Antiquities, New York, 10 June 2010, lot 92 is a late example.

26   E.g., Palermo, Museo Nazionale NI 2093 (n. 25) and Adria, Museo Archeologico 22148: attributed to the Brygos Painter by Riccioni; BAPD 9009458; CVA Adria 1 Italy 28 pl. 18,4.

27   Adria, Museo Archeologico 22148 (supra n. 26).

28   New York, Metropolitan Museum of Art 19.192.67: ARV² 925,5 (Painter of Brussels R330); BAPD 211258; unpublished. Other Penthesilean examples: New York, Metropolitan Museum of Art 96.18.131: ARV² 911,70 (Painter of Bologna 417); BAPD 211007; Peschel (supra n. 4) pl. 176. Oxford, Ashmolean Museum 1929.466: ARV² 911,73 (Painter of Bologna 417); BAPD 211010; CVA Oxford 2 Great Britain 9 pl. 52,5. Florence, Museo Archeologico 77922: ARV² 911,75 (Painter of Bologna 417); BAPD 211012; CVA Florence 4 Italy 38 pl. 136. Florence, Museo Archeologico 20B4: ARV² 911,77 (Painter of Bologna 417); BAPD 211014; CVA Florence 1 Italy 8 pl. 20,4. Leipzig, University T3635, etc.: ARV² 911,78 (Painter of Bologna 417); BAPD 211015; CVA Leipzig 3 Germany 80 pl. 67,2. Florence, Museo Archeologico PD 470: ARV² 911,79 (Painter of Bologna 417); BAPD 211016; CVA Florence 4 Italy 38 pl. 138,4. Milan, Collection H.A.: attributed to the manner of the Painter of Bologna 417 by Paribeni; BAPD 10354; CVA Milan, Collection H.A. 2 Italy 51 pl. 6,1. St. Petersburg, Hermitage B 1612a: ARV² 895,82 (Splanchnopt Painter); BAPD 211838; unpublished. Champaign-Urbana, World History Museum W22.1.38: attributed to the Splanchnopt Painter by D. von Bothmer; BAPD 18469; CVA Champaign-Urbana 1 USA 24 pl. 27.

29   Rome, Villa Giulia 3583: ARV² 1109,27; BAPD 214666; CVA Villa Giulia 1 Italy 1 pl. 10,1–3.

30   St. Petersburg, Hermitage B 2338: unattributed; BAPD 41005; T. Sini, in: O. Palagia (ed.), Greek Offerings. Essays on Greek Art in Honour of John Boardman (1997) 159–60 figs. 1–2.

31   Baltimore, Johns Hopkins University 83: ARV² 75,56; BAPD 200500; CVA Robinson 2 USA 6 pls. 1–2. Compare the drawing of lost tondo formerly in the Petersen Collection in Rome: ARV² 1624,15; BAPD 275037; D. Paleothodoros (supra n. 4) pl. 32 fig. 2.

32   F. Lissarrague, in: M.-L, Desclos (ed.), Le rire des Grecs (2000) 112–116.

33   Satyrs reclining on couches: Boston, Museum of Fine Arts RES08.31H: ARV² 142,4; BAPD 201238 (Painter of Adria B300); AntK 12, 1969, pl. 12,2. Paris, Louvre Museum G24: ARV² 354,20 (Colmar Painter); BAPD 203702. Rome, American Academy 322: ARV² 781,5 (Akestorides

34 Painter); BAPD 209615; JdI 88, 1973, 11 fig. 10. Oxford, Ashmolean Museum 1954.230: ARV² 1422,1 (Nostell Painter); BAPD 260038; JdI 88, 1973, 3 fig. 2.

34 Satyrs reclining on the ground: Northampton, MA, Smith College 1955.45: ARV² 153 (manner of the Epeleios Painter); BAPD 201399; D. Buitron, Attic Vase Painting in New England Collections (1972) 77 no. 35. Basle, Wilhelm Collection: ARV² 189,73 (Kleophrades Painter); BAPD 201721; AntK 7, 1976, 2 fig. 12. Bremen, private collection: attributed to Onesimos; BAPD 13466; Greek Vases in the J. Paul Getty Museum 4, 1989, 89 fig. 2. Paris, Louvre Museum G201: ARV² 201,63 (Berlin Painter); BAPD 201871; O. Murray, Sympotica. A Symposium on the Symposion (1990) pl. 22A. New York, Metropolitan Museum of Art 12.234.5: ARV² 382,183 (Brygos Painter); BAPD 204082; Richter (supra n. 1) fig. 86. Ex Arlesheim, Schweitzer Coll.: ARV² 266,84 (Syriskos Painter); BAPD 202765. Florence, Museo Archeologico 73749: ARV² 355,39 (Colmar Painter); BAPD 203722; F. Lissarrague, Greek Vases. The Athenians and their Images (2001) 209–210. Brunswick, ME, Bowdoin College 30.2: ARV² 779,9 (Group of Philadelphia PH 2272); BAPD 209607; photo Beazley Archive. Leipzig, University T532: ARV² 861,18 (Pistoxenos Painter); BAPD 211342; CVA Leipzig 3 Germany 80 pl. 62,1–2.

35 Paris, Louvre Museum H46: ARV² 1534,13 (London Class); BAPD 218370; MonPiot 9, 1902, pl. 13. Compare Dresden, Staatl. Kunstsammlungen, Albertinum 305, etc.: ARV² 354,26 (Colmar Painter); 1647; BAPD 203708; VerAmstMeded 34, 1985, 2–3; CVA Tübingen 5 Germany 54 Beil. 1,2.

36 B. Kaeser, in: K. Vierneisel – B. Kaeser (eds.), Kunst der Schale. Kultur des Trinkens (1990) 306–309. E. Baughan, AJA 115, 2011, 37–41.

37 F. Heinrich, in: M. Meyer (ed.), Besorgte Mütter und sorglose Zecher: mythische Exempel in der Bilderwelt Athens (2007) 101–153.

38 K. Topper, The Imagery of the Athenian Symposium (2012) 5–52.

39 St. Petersburg, Hermitage B 1650: ARV² 16,15; BAPD 200078; Peschel (supra n. 4) 70–71 pl. 42. Csapo – Miller (supra n. 12) 377 pl. 98. Topper (supra n. 38) 120. G. Hedreen, in: D. Yatromanolakis (ed.), An Archaeology of Representations. Ancient Greek Vase-Painting and Contemporary Methodologies (2009) 222–225, argues for the imaginary quality of the scene.

40 Probably connected with the Greek words stibas-stibadeion, as shown by K. Dunbabin, in: W. Slater (ed.), Dining in a Classical Context (1991) 121–148. See also Heinrich (supra n. 37) 115. Topper (supra n. 38) 32. 50–52. D. Yatromanolakis, in: Yatromanolakis (supra n. 39) 432–444. A. Shapiro, Re-Fashioning Anakreon in Classical Athens (2012) 33.

41 Vatican, Museo Gregoriano 16561: ARV² 427,2; BAPD 205046; C. Bérard et al., A City of Images. Iconography and Society in Ancient Greece, trans. D. Lyons (1989) 20 fig. 20.

42 Ferrara, Museo Nazionale di Spina 3033: ARV² 1171,1; BAPD 215539; CVA Ferrara 1 Italy 37 pl. 12.

43 Bonn, Akademisches Kunstmuseum 70: ARV² 28,12; BAPD 200141; CVA Bonn 1 Germany 1 pl. 16.

44 Cambridge, Fitzwilliam Museum GR19.1937: ARV² 135,13 (Circle of the Nikosthenes Painter); BAPD 210128; CVA Cambridge 2 Great Britain 11 pl. 7.2b.

45 Hannover, Kestner Museum 1966.99: BAdd² 397 (attributed to the Colmar Painter by Follmann); BAPD 1926; CVA Hannover 1 Germany 34 pl. 34,2. New York, Metropolitan Museum of Art 16.174.41: ARV² 355,35; BAPD 203718; Lissarrague (supra n. 13) 12 fig. 1. Paris, Louvre Cp11229: ARV² 865; BAPD 211384; photo Beazley Archive.

46 E.g., maenads on an askos in Providence, Rhode Island School of Design 25.074: ARV² 480,338; BAPD 205021; CVA Providence 1 USA 2 pl. 17,4. Satyrs on a lid attributed to Onesimos, Malibu, Getty Museum 81.AE.214B.1: BAPD 23879; photo Beazley Archive.

47 C. Bérard (supra n. 41); Lissarrague (supra n. 32).

48 R. Osborne, in: J. Sofaer (ed.), Material Identities (2007) 34.

49 Adria Museo Archeologico 22148 (supra n. 26).

50 Napoli (supra n. 21); R. Holloway, AJA 110, 2006, 365–388.

51 Napoli (supra n. 21) 147 demonstrates that this trio can be interpreted as late arrivals or early departures; both he and Holloway (supra n. 50) 376, prefer to see them as leaving. For other opinions, see Holloway's n. 44.

52 Since gestures of greeting and farewell are generally parallel, the youth's gesture can only be interpreted on the basis of the meaning of the whole scene. Since Napoli (supra n. 21) interprets the proffered cup of the reclining symposiast as the target for the kottabos-player to the right, he does not see these figures as interacting. The use of another symposiast as the target for a kottabos throw is unlikely, and the target is rarely shown in fifth century (Athenian) scenes: P. Jacquet-Rimassa, ΚΟΤΤΑΒΟΣ. Recherches iconographiques. Céramiques italiote, 440–300 av. J. C., Pallas 42, 1995, 138–139.

14 Chariots in Black-figure Attic Vase-painting: Antecedents and Ramifications

Joan R. Mertens

The chariot – particularly the war chariot – was one of the most long-lived subjects in Greek art and one of the most conspicuous in Attic vase-painting. It was a real, tangible, functional, complex object that appears in all kinds of representations on Attic vases, identifiably mythological or not. It became important as a vehicle in the Late Bronze Age, reappeared prominently in Geometric iconography, and grew increasingly popular through the sixth century BC. Surviving chariots and depictions have received serious scholarly attention as to their construction – particularly the Bronze Age, Egyptian, Near Eastern and Etruscan examples – and, in Greece, as to their iconographic typology.[1] By the Archaic period, the motif had already had a long history and the vehicles themselves had gone out of use in warfare.[2] In the sixth century BC, it became essentially a mythological subject readily combined with others, mythological or not. My interest is to sketch a broader context in which black-figure war chariots can usefully be seen. Our considerations will begin with war chariots during the Greek Bronze Age and briefly note that this military technology was still significant in Assyria and the Levant during the Greek Geometric period. Such a wider framework raises questions as to the meaning or meanings that the chariots bring with them and, by extension, as to the functions of the vases on which they are represented. The topic leads to a number of major issues, such as the degree of continuity between the Bronze Age and the first millennium in Greece. In *Horse, Bird, and Man*, Jack Benson offered one of the first wide-ranging investigations of iconographical motifs common to both the late second and early first millennium BC and possible modalities of transmission.[3] I wholeheartedly subscribe to his viewpoint, though not to all particulars. Among more recent books, *Pictorial Pursuits: Figurative Painting on Mycenaean and Geometric Pottery*, that appeared in 2006 as the proceedings of two conferences, is a goldmine of information and thought-provoking ideas.[4]

An impetus for the present inquiry comes from my sense that studies of chariot scenes in black-figure vase-paintings tend to focus on the accompanying figures who might include a god (often Apollo, Athena or Dionysos), a hero (notably Herakles) or a mortal warrior. Especially challenging are the scenes without clear indications for the identity of the figures in the chariot. A hydria of the Leagros Group[5] in The Metropolitan Museum of Art (Fig. 1; Color Pl. 16) shows the iconographical and historical context with which we today most readily associate Greek war chariots. The vase depicts Ajax and Achilles gaming before Troy[6] in the panel on the body and a chariot departing on the shoulder. The detail on the shoulder makes quite clear that the departure is for war. A fully armed hoplite stands at the far left, and the charioteer's Boeotian shield is slung over his back. The male figures seated holding staves and the dog at the right indicate the domestic setting that the warriors are leaving. The representation combines features of the sixth century BC – like the hoplite, the folding stools, the garments and hairstyles of the men – with a military technology that had not been used for war in Greece since about the eleventh century BC.

The source of the chariot's use and meaning takes us back to the Greek Bronze Age. It figures prominently in the *Iliad* and *Odyssey* of Homer, one of our firmest and most complex links between Greek prehistory and the first millennium BC.[7] As a piece of equipment, the chariot in the first millennium has not only a remembered existence, as considered by John Boardman in *The Archaeology of Nostalgia*,[8] but also a specific functional one. With the development of pan-Hellenic and local festivals beginning in the eighth century BC, chariots served most conspicuously in competitions, notably the races so familiar from both visual and literary sources as well as the apobates contests.[9] The representations depict ceremonialized, institutionalized transformations of an originally military technology. In looking at war chariots, it is important to note their continued use in Egypt and the Near East during the centuries contemporary with Geometric and Early Archaic art in Greece. The ever-growing tangible evidence for Greek exposure to Near Eastern objects attests to this contact before the long and intense confrontation between West and East during the Persian Wars.

The second half of the second millennium BC in the Near East, Egypt, and the eastern Mediterranean has been called the cultural period of the war chariot.[10] As an indication, in the most famous battle, that at Kadesh in 1275 BC between the Egyptians under Rameses II and the Hittites under Muwatalli, the number of Hittite chariots has been estimated at about 4000. Although the size of the Egyptian force cannot be as precisely quantified, it was considerable, if not comparable.[11] The images of the encounter that Rameses had sculpted at Abu Simbel, the Ramesseum, and other sites give an impressive picture of the fray, from the Egyptian point of view, of course.[12] In Greece, chariots seem to have been introduced at the end of the Middle Bronze Age,[13] possibly via Crete,[14] with the earliest direct evidence provided by the eleven decorated stone stelai found in Grave Circle A at Mycenae dated to the Late Helladic I period in the sixteenth century BC. The representations carved into the soft limestone are now difficult to read.[15]

Although there is evidence for their use in both hunting and competitions,[16] chariots were most important in warfare during the Late Bronze Age, the Mycenaean period (ca. 1600–1100 BC). A major scholarly debate concerns how they were employed. One constituency, represented most especially by the late Mary Littauer and the fortunately active Joost Crouwel, views the chariot primarily as transportation, as a "battle taxi", conveying combatants to the field but not participating in the actual conflict.[17] This is how they are usually described in the *Iliad*.[18] To cite but one example (Hom. *Il*.11.15–16. 47–50, trans. R. Lattimore):

And Atreus' son cried out aloud and drove the Achaians to gird them, while he himself put the shining bronze upon him. ...
Thereupon each man gave orders to his charioteer
to rein in the horses once again by the ditch, in good order,
while they themselves, dismounted and armed in their war gear, swept onward...

Besides such evidence from Homer, other arguments have been advanced for the chariot's absence from combat, notably the Greek terrain with its relatively scarce flat, open expanses; the difficulties of fighting from a chariot at close range with spears and bows; as well as the lack of representations in Mycenaean iconography.[19]

A dissenting view, presenting particularly thought-provoking arguments, is that of Klaus Tausend, at the university in Graz.[20] He notes that the major Mycenaean centers of power – Mycenae and Tiryns, Orchomenos,

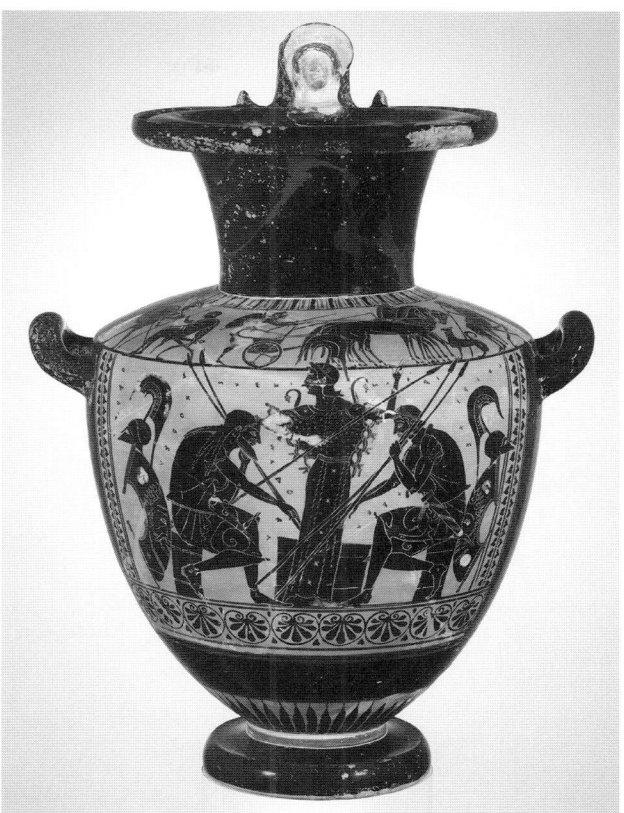

Fig. 1 Hydria attributed to the Leagros Group. Attic, ca. 510 BC. New York, The Metropolitan Museum of Art, 56.171.29. Fletcher Fund, 1956. Image © The Metropolitan Museum of Art.

Thebes, and Gla, Knossos and Phaistos – dominated extensive plains and were also the repositories of the actual chariots. Linear B tablets enumerate about 600 at Knossos and about 120 at Pylos, for example. The presence of such a considerable number, with the attendant costs for both the vehicles and the horses, indicate that they served as more than status symbols for the upper classes to ride around in.[21] The tablets further show that the chariots and horses did not belong to those who used them but to the palace centers that produced and housed them, making them available when needed. Moreover, the same tablets document that, in addition to a chariot and horses, a warrior could also receive a corselet – one or two. Two corselets suggest that not only he, but also the driver faced danger in combat.

Among other arguments that Tausend discusses, I should like to mention his interpretation of several fresco fragments on the north wall of the megaron at Mycenae. The decoration of this room has provoked controversy since the first publication by Gerhardt Rodenwaldt in 1921,[22] partly because the evidence is so incomplete. Its importance lies in the inclusion of an unusually large number of war chariots. The upshot of Tausend's close analysis is that the detail from the center of the north wall depicts a galloping horse from a chariot above a fallen warrior, and he juxtaposes a similar representation from the wall reliefs of the battle of Kadesh at Abu Simbel (Fig. 2).[23] From the aggregate of available evidence, including that of Homer, Tausend concludes that the Mycenaeans used chariots in massed formations like the Hittites; unlike the Hittites, however, the Mycenaeans also fought individually, armed with a heavy spear rather than several light spears or a bow.[24] Furthermore, the variant of driving to battle and jumping off to fight – the original action of the apobates – is well attested. Finally, according to Tausend, war chariots and light-armed – therefore easily maneuverable – foot soldiers may have been deployed together.[25]

The major points that I should like to derive from the foregoing discussion concern the connections that can be made among the dominant Mycenaean palace centers, the use of chariots, as well as certain shared features with the chariotry of Egypt and the Near East, such as how they were deployed. Particularly notable, in my view, is that the connections were forged in the Bronze Age and are acquiring an ever stronger factual basis, thanks particularly to on-going studies of contemporary evidence. What has always been interpreted as myth is proving, in fact, to be anchored in increasingly tangible reference points.

The very end of the Bronze Age – the Late Helladic III period (ca. 1425–1125 BC) – brings a further cluster of objects pertinent to our considerations, the Mycenaean chariot kraters. They were one manifestation of the Pictorial Style that, roughly speaking, extended through Late Helladic III.[26] The sources of their iconography probably included wall paintings of the kind from Mycenae briefly considered above.[27] However incomplete, a krater from Tiryns[28] corresponds very much to what we think of as a "Homeric" chariot scene. The two warriors wear tunics and greaves and they carry shields. The one in the front drives; the one behind carries two spears. A later example in Amsterdam (Fig. 3)[29] displays the standard composition with the chariot rolling along the uppermost groundline and the horses' legs partly obscured by the lines below. Three figures occupy the car, a warrior with sword walks behind, and a rider of sorts leads. Such a representation is all about status. The longevity and tenacity of such iconography, moreover, is exemplified by the Metropolitan Museum's famous Cypriot sarcophagus from Amathus,[30] dated to the second quarter of the fifth century BC. It perpetuates the same line-up: cavalry escort, the chariot with eminences, and foot soldiers in the rear.

A large quantity of chariot kraters was made in the Argolid for export and came to light on Cyprus and in the eastern Mediterranean.[31] Indeed, in her contribution to the Festschrift for Malcolm Wiener, Louise Steel has written,

> The quintessential Mycenaean pictorial vase in the Levant is...the chariot krater...The iconography of the chariot procession might originate from Syria. Certainly, the messages inherent in such a representation would be an appropriate expression of status in a Near Eastern context. Chariots and horses were explicitly linked to the members of a warrior elite or ruling class throughout the Aegean and Near East and the formulaic diplomatic greetings preserved in the Amarna archives refer frequently to the maintenance of chariots and their horse-teams, indicating their symbolic importance. The close association of this highly symbolic iconography with an exotic and novel vase form, presumably the central element of the drinking ceremonies performed by the *marzeah*, is very suggestive of the value that was placed on the Mycenaean pictorial style by the receptor societies in the east.[32]

The *marzeah* mentioned here was an institution attested in the Levant from the fourteenth century BC to the sixth century AD. It refers to a group of significant men who owned or leased a building to which additional property was attached. Participation was hereditary, and the group was under the protection of a deity. The building housed their meetings that included a good deal of drinking. Jane Carter has argued that such a tradition existed also in Mycenaean times and progressively evolved into the

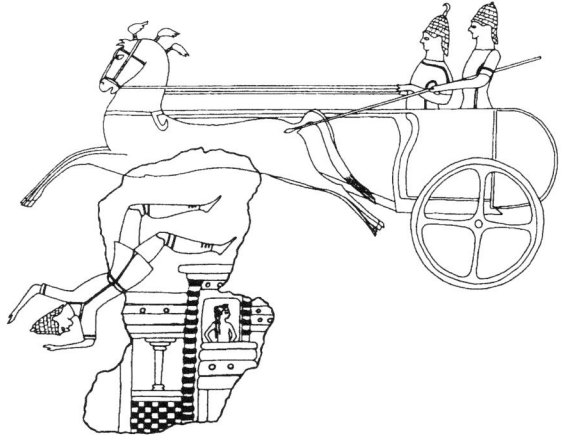

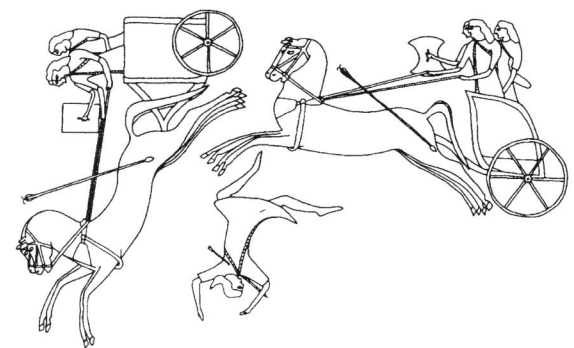

Fig. 2 Reconstruction of a detail from the north wall of the megaron at Mycenae (Late Bronze Age, second half of the thirteenth century BC) by Klaus Tausend and detail of the Battle of Kadesh at Abu Simbel (second quarter of the thirteenth century BC). After Tausend 2007 393 figs. 1–2. Drawings by Margit Linder.

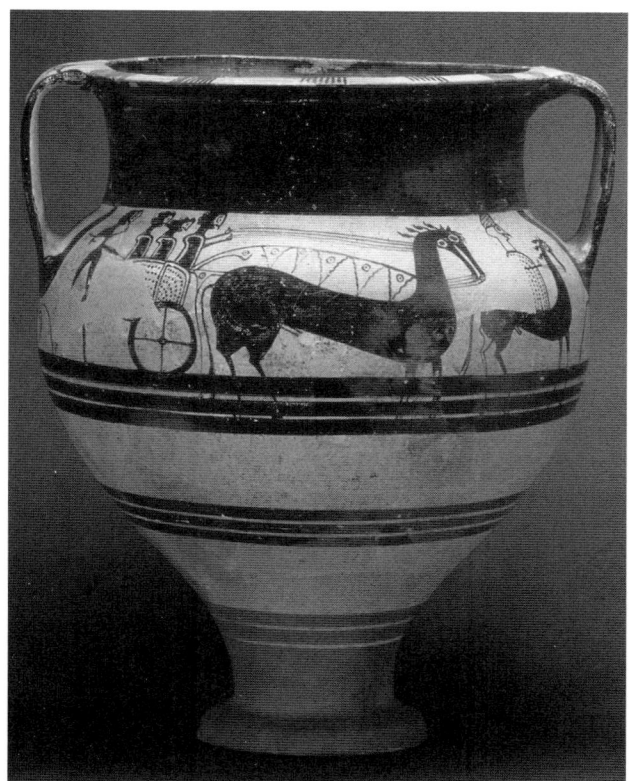

Fig. 3 Chariot krater. Late Bronze Age, Mycenaean, ca. 1300–1250 BC. Amsterdam, Allard Pierson Museum inv. APM 1856. Image © Allard Pierson Museum.

Greek symposium. Moreover, drawing on work of Oswyn Murray and John Boardman, Carter associates the elite character of warfare in the Late Bronze Age with the rituals for the aristocratic dead, as for Patroklos. In later centuries, she proposes, "the *symposium* replaced warfare as the characteristic activity of the elite classes".[33]

Our discussion has gotten a little ahead of itself but, once again, the points of interest are the popularity of the chariot kraters and their considerable diffusion eastward, to Cyprus and the Levant, before the ultimate end of Mycenaean Palace society. The other really important ingredient in Jane Carter's work is the interrelation of cultural practices and traditions as well as the associated realia, be it in types of warfare, civic conventions like the symposium or the evolution of the kline from a funerary bier to a symposiast's couch.

In addition to the martial contexts and processions that have constituted our focus, there is strong evidence for the use of chariots during the Greek Bronze Age for hunting and racing.[34] Thus, iconographical precedents exist for many kinds of chariot representations in Greek art of the first millennium. The connection is, of course, the big question. One of the most compelling elements of continuity is the structure of the vehicle that underwent remarkably little change over a period of about 400 years. Our knowledge of the development depends particularly on the meticulous, exhaustive research of Joost Crouwel. There are three major chronologically successive types: the Box Chariot, the Dual Chariot, and the Rail Chariot, differing predominantly in the construction of the car. What they shared are a pair of four-spoked wheels on a fixed axle, a draught pole with a horse on either side, harnessed under a yoke and controlled with a bridle.[35] The earliest type attested in the Greek world is the Box Chariot. Crouwel dates it about 1550 to 1450 BC and locates its origins in the east, very possibly Syria.[36] Most prevalent and most frequently depicted is the Dual Chariot, datable about 1450 to 1200 BC. Developed in the Aegean world, it has the distinct wing-like extensions that Crouwel suggests might have served as mud-guards, protecting against dust and flying debris.[37] Though less well documented, the Rail Chariot is the descendant of the Dual Chariot and is datable between about 1250–1150 BC. The car, or box, is now open, with only a rail; it is, therefore, considerably lighter and more maneuverable, especially on the battlefield. The earliest surviving representations of chariots in the first millennium BC – during the eighth century – are structurally related to the Mycenaean Rail Chariot.[38] The best evidence comes from bronze and terracotta models of the eighth century BC.[39] Finally, the type of vehicle that comes to prevail from the seventh century BC until Hellenistic times is known as the High-front Chariot and, like its immediate predecessors, was of Greek origin. The shape of the car is rectangular, with a higher rail at the front and a lower one on each side. The wheels normally have four spokes. By about 600 BC the High-front Chariot, which would have accommodated two people, was drawn by four horses. The pole horses, on the inside, provided the draught, while the trace horses may have helped in turning; Crouwel suggests that their principal contribution may have been display.[40] These are the typical chariots in black-figure representations of the sixth century BC.

Good evidence documents the continuity of the chariot as a vehicle.[41] However, from the mid-eighth century on there is a thoroughgoing divergence between the function of the war chariot, in particular, and how it is depicted on vases and other works of art. A number of factors underlie this divergence. One major development was the decline of chariotry in favor of cavalry which took place not only in the greater Greek world but gradually and progressively in Egypt and the Near East as well.[42] In Mesopotamia and the Levant, war chariots continued to be used as they had been during the second millennium BC, both in number and manner of deployment, until the second half of the eighth century BC when the Assyrians developed effective cavalry forces. Thereafter, as Robin Archer observes, "even stripped of its military functions, the chariot was still the most visually impressive mode of transport available. As it happens, the very fact of their uselessness might well have served to make them even more desirable as status symbols".[43] The situation in Egypt is unclear due to a lack of records, although there may have been some use of chariots and horses during the Twenty-Fifth Dynasty centered in Nubia during the ninth and eighth centuries BC.⁴⁴ The war chariot seems to have remained operational in Cyprus, and in North Africa until the fourth century BC.⁴⁵ In Greece and the Aegean, the disappearance of the palaces withdrew the essential, centralized economic foundation, leading instead to the development, first, of cavalry and, by the seventh century BC, hoplite forces in warfare. This change in military technology is reflected in Herodotos. Among the many polities that the historian enumerates, only the Salaminians of Cyprus and the Libyans are singled out for their use of the chariot in battle.⁴⁶ The combat forces were overwhelmingly infantry and cavalry.

As ceramic production revived in Athens during the ninth century BC, the first reappearance of chariot-related iconography assumes the form of pyxides with lids surmounted by modelled terracotta horses, singly or in groups of two, three or four. The earliest example is dated about 900 BC.⁴⁷ The subsequent development is towards a lower box, denser ornament, and a larger number of animals. The articulation of the horses' bodies, with glaze and/or incision, in many cases renders their harness, indicating that they were thought of in relation to a chariot.⁴⁸ The horse pyxides are a specifically Attic phenomenon.⁴⁹

Depictions of chariots, often in procession, become frequent on vases of the eighth century BC (Fig. 4). Manakidou comments on the variety of accompanying figures and, usefully, cautions against interpreting the meaning of scenes too narrowly.⁵⁰ However, through other components of the decoration, such as prothesis and mourning scenes, or the addition of plastic snakes, the function of many vases can with certainty be identified as funerary.

An especially significant study of Geometric military iconography is Gudrun Ahlberg's *Fighting on Land and Sea in Greek Geometric Art* (1971). Her lists and discussion concern us in two respects. The first is the decided rarity of combats with chariots.⁵¹ Two examples are cited most frequently. The fragmentary krater, Louvre A 519 (Fig. 5; Color Pl. 17A) ⁵² is described by Villard and Ahlberg as depicting a warrior with a Dipylon shield falling from a chariot, thus in the midst of battle.⁵³ The oinochoe Agora P 4885⁵⁴ has occasioned much discussion as to the identity of the warrior twosome behind the chequered square: one mounting the car, the other – with a sword – battling the warrior towards whom he turns. Ahlberg opts for the twins Akterione-Molione.⁵⁵ The scene seems to show a "battle-taxi" situation.

A second, most important, aspect of Ahlberg's study is that of Near Eastern features in Geometric military iconography, which she pursues in considerable detail. She observes that battle scenes in Assyria and the Levant of the ninth and eighth centuries BC mainly glorify the ruler, while in Geometric art the context is primarily funerary.⁵⁶ Louvre A 519 incorporates a number of motifs that she derives, compellingly, from Assyrian models. She associates the large chariot wheels with the recurrent Near Eastern motif of a chariot driven over the fallen enemy.⁵⁷ She draws parallels between the corpses piled to the right of the wheels and the many instances in Egyptian and Assyrian scenes of conflict.⁵⁸ While we cannot be certain

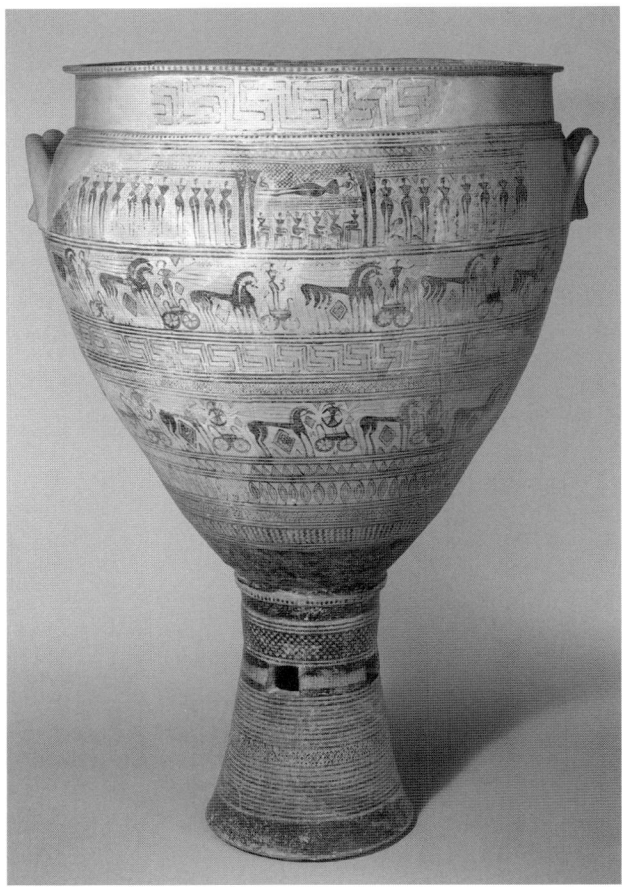

Fig. 4 Krater. Attic, ca. 725 BC. New York, The Metropolitan Museum of Art, 14.130.15. Rogers Fund, 1914. Image © The Metropolitan Museum of Art.

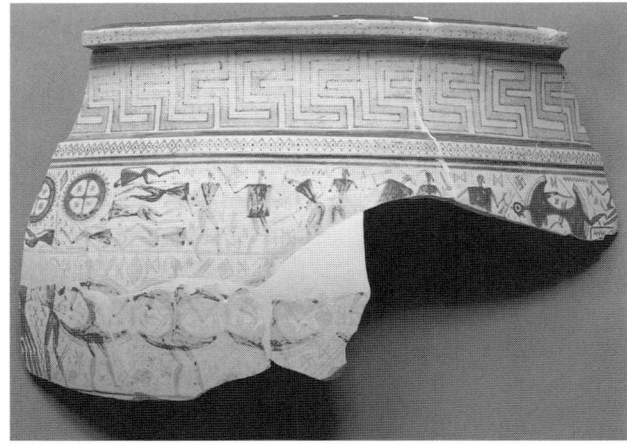

Fig. 5 Krater, fragment. Attic, ca. 750 BC. Paris, Musée du Louvre A 519. Image © Musée du Louvre.

that the "Dipylon warrior" is falling from a chariot, the motif of the falling combatant is, once again, an Eastern conceit.[59]

Ahlberg's work was based on that of others, such as Lorimer and Dunbabin,[60] and has been followed by others, notably Joost Crouwel. It is noteworthy, however, that, within the larger field of Near Eastern-Greek connections in the first half of the first millennium BC, the iconography of chariots and warfare has not attracted much attention. On the other hand, the available scholarship takes its place with that of Klaus Kilian, Imma Kilian-Dirlmeier, Walter Burkert, Hans-Volkmar Herrmann among many, many others in demonstrating the pervasiveness of Near Eastern tangible and intangible imports into the Greek world. The greatest concentrations of material evidence have been found in major Greek sanctuaries, preeminently Samos and Olympia, but also in others such as Athens, Delphi, the Argive Heraion, Perachora, Philai, and Delos, all with dates in the latter part of the eighth century BC.[61] Imma Kilian-Dirlmeier's study in 1985 of foreign dedications in Greek sanctuaries of the eighth to early seventh centuries BC includes a series of maps that are no longer up-to-date, but make the point succinctly.[62] The Heraion in Samos proved particularly rich in horse trappings.[63] Mention here will be limited to the famous frontlet of Syrian style with an Aramaean inscription naming King Hazael of Damascus, whose reign ended ca. 820–800 BC. It was found in a deposit in Samos of the late seventh or early sixth century BC and was therefore above ground and in transit for about two centuries.[64] Of extraordinary note is that two horse blinkers, one of which naming the same ruler – King Hazael – with an identical text came to light at Eretria. According to the archaeological context, it was deposited in the last quarter of the eighth century BC and is considered to have been part of the same ensemble as the frontlet from Samos.[65]

This period of the eighth century into the seventh century BC is so important because it provides evidence in some quantity for the convergence of the strands that I have been trying to distinguish. By then, there was an established and evolving Geometric pictorial language into which earlier Bronze Age elements had been assimilated. Here lies the significance of the chariot: its extraordinary longevity was due, first, to the evolution of its function over time – basically from war to competition – and to the associations with aristocratic status and heroic glory that remained pertinent, meaningful, and therefore artistically viable. The turn of the eighth to the seventh century BC was the time when the Orientalizing influx began to become potent and recognizable, then increasingly so during the seventh century which saw the breakthrough to new iconography and pictorial expression. During the Geometric period, the influences that Ahlberg distinguished are rendered in Geometric fashion. During the seventh century, the pictorial world underwent thoroughgoing change – and, incidentally, it is interesting that the scale in Proto-Attic tends to be large while in Protocorinthian it is decidedly small. The most far-reaching import from the Levant into the Greek world, probably sometime before 800 BC, was the alphabet and its most influential application was the epic poetry of Homer. It manifests much of the same cultural convergence that we are considering in the visual arts, but time does not permit discussion of this subject.

Casting our glance forward as far as the end of the sixth century BC, we see a complicated pattern of iconographical continuity and innovation. Most notably, after a dearth of "military chariots" in both Geometric and Proto-Attic, they become one of the most popular subjects in Attic black-figure.

Attic vase-painting of the seventh century BC reveals the concurrent emergence of narrative subject matter and – for want of a better formulation – increasingly full-blooded representation. Compared with Geometric decoration, mature Proto-Attic scenes provide the modern observer considerably more information to work with. A good example is the Metropolitan Museum of Art's expansive neck-amphora attributed to the New York Nessos Painter,[66] datable in the second quarter of the century. The subject is Herakles, Deianeira, and the centaur Nessos. A vase such as this features the chariot in a readily recognizable mythological context. The scale and the fact that figural decoration is confined to the obverse have led to the identification of the vase's function as a funerary marker.

In her consideration of chariot iconography during the seventh century BC, Manakidou notes the absence from Athenian iconography of military engagements with warriors either on a chariot or on horseback.[67] Chariots in procession[68] and in races[69] are frequent, and other subjects that are familiar from the beginning of our considerations appear as well. For instance, though rare, the chariot advancing over a fallen enemy and the "battle taxi" still survive. Some of the motifs are attested on vases, others at this time on bronzes. Manakidou also emphasizes that most of the vases with such scenes are funerary.[70]

Proof of the vitality and potential inherent in the chariot motif at this time lies in the introduction of new subjects that become prominent in black-figure. The first to emerge is the departure scene. The evidence is extremely poorly preserved. The more legible of two very early examples is the so-called Schliemann pithos or krater, datable about 675 BC.[71] On the left is a warrior standing in a chariot. He has a helmet, possibly a sword, and a shield, its device a wheel. At the far right, facing him is a woman wearing an elaborate over-garment and holding a small child that is barely visible. Semni Karouzou suggests that the scene might depict the departure of Amphiaraos. An even more fragmentary scene, reconstructed with the help of the previous example, shows a comparable composition, mirror reversed. The woman is at left; the warrior stands in the chariot box.[72]

Noteworthy in these representations is the centrality of the chariot as well as its scale. These features are manifest also in the earliest chariot procession on a vase that can be considered black-figure not only in execution but also in the interrelation of shape, ornament, and subject matter – the large neck-amphora attributed to the Piraeus Painter.[73] The two bigas move at a stately pace towards the right, driven by a man in front and a youth. The solemnity and grandeur of the representation are striking. The chariot procession, which typically appears among many other motifs on Geometric vases, once again takes center stage. An interest in emphasizing the narrative may have been a factor behind the scale of the New York Nessos neck-amphora but does not apply to the Piraeus Painter's vase. Both works, moreover, served a funerary function. The suddenness and amplitude that mark the return of chariot iconography as the centerpiece of vase decoration suggest a powerful motivating force about which I offer some thoughts in my conclusion.

In the succeeding generation of black-figure artists, the Gorgon Painter warrants special attention (Fig. 6; Color Pl. 17B). On his great dinos, Louvre E 874,[74] the shoulder frieze depicts Perseus and the Gorgons; the actions of the three protagonists are rendered with evident energy. Further along is a balanced, rather frozen duel between two warriors with their "battle taxis" waiting. Each of the charioteers looks round, almost as though the Gorgon episode was occurring around or above them. The juxtaposition of the two subjects and the difference in their energy levels is striking.

The Gorgon Painter interests us also because one of his standed kraters – as Beazley calls them – from the Akropolis, introduces the earliest preserved representation of a frontal chariot in black-figure.[75] Though it has Geometric antecedents,[76] the subject's greatest popularity occurs in Athens during the third quarter of the sixth century, and in other sixth-century fabrics (Fig. 7; Color Pl. 18A). The attributes of the figures in and around the car differentiate the racing chariots from the war chariots. The invention of a new type of chariot representation testifies to the unwavering popularity and significance of the subject. Whether the frontal view is primarily an artistic conceit displaying the painter's virtuosity or whether it originated for other reasons is unclear. As Mary Moore has documented, it remained popular in Athens through the end of the sixth century BC.[77]

After the frontal chariot, a second major iconographic innovation in Attic black-figure is the chariot wheeling round, introduced by a painter of Group E[78] (Fig. 8; Color Pl. 18B). Frontal chariots are stationary, those wheeling round are dynamic.

A third, quite different, category of subject enters at the beginning of the sixth century BC. Although attested previously in Egyptian and Assyrian examples,[79] the harnessing of chariots is new, and quite rare in Attica. The earliest preserved harnessing scene occurs on the famous fragmentary kantharos by Nearchos from the Akropolis.[80]

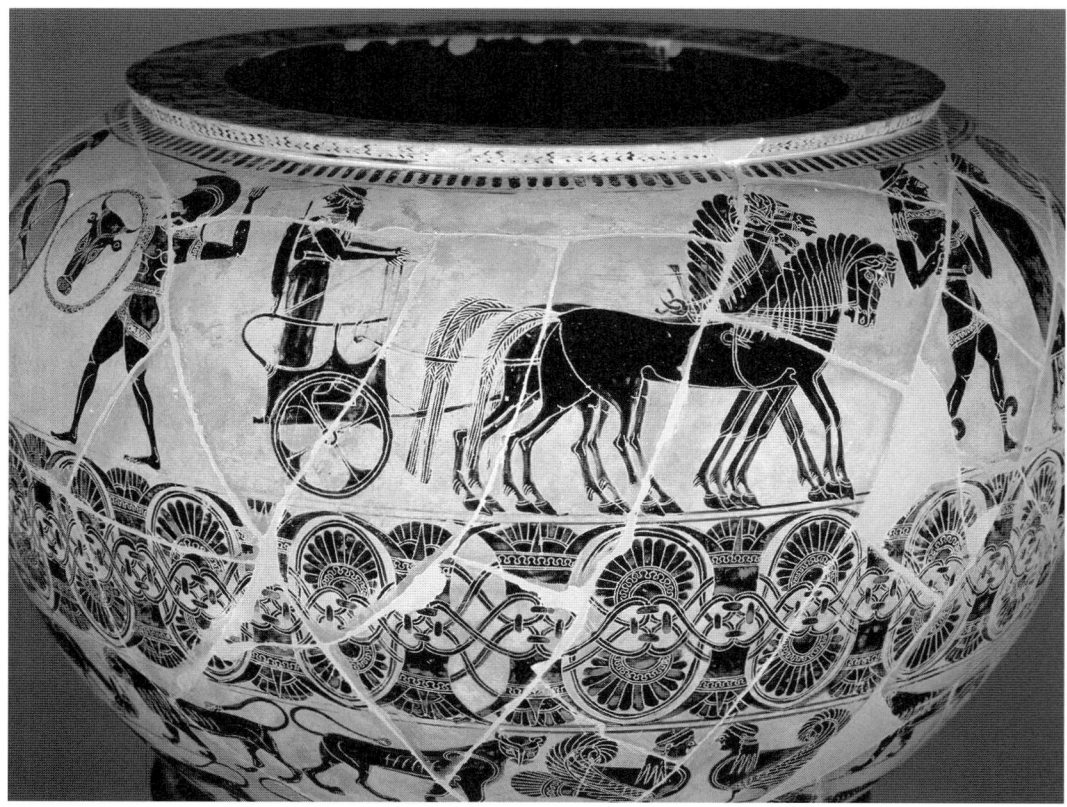

Fig. 6 Dinos attributed to the Gorgon Painter. Attic, ca. 580 BC. Paris, Musée du Louvre E 874. Image © Musée du Louvre.

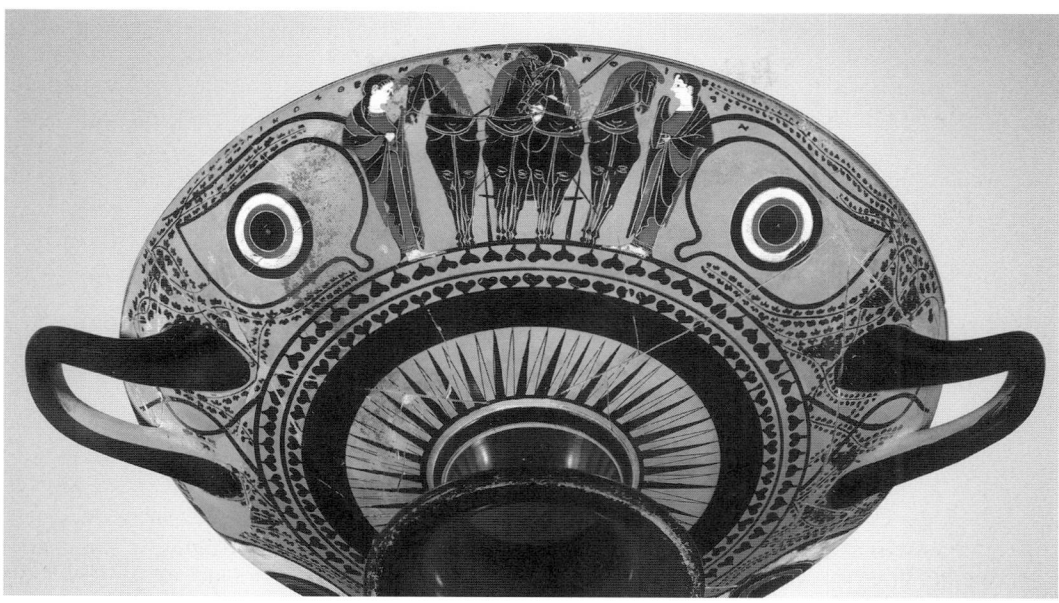

Fig. 7 Kylix signed by Nikosthenes as potter. Attic, ca. 530 BC. New York, The Metropolitan Museum of Art, 14.136. Rogers Fund, 1914. Image © The Metropolitan Museum of Art.

The other known examples are datable to the second half of the sixth century.[81] The process of harnessing widens the narrative scope of the representation. In a "standard" chariot scene, the viewer sees the warrior in his designated role. In a depiction of harnessing, the viewer becomes privy to more of the warrior's world, very particularly in the intimate moment rendered by Nearchos.

These iconographical inventions revitalized a by then traditional, venerable, on occasion conventional subject with bold artistic effects, such as the vehicle wheeling around, or with episodic detail, such as the preparation of the chariot. This was my interest in the scene on the dinos by the Gorgon Painter; compared with the vigorous Perseus and the Gorgons, the battle scene is bloodless. If we look for a motivation behind the new types of chariot depictions, the canonization of the Homeric epics under the Peisistratids is likely to have been significant. In addition to the innovations just mentioned, mythological combats with chariots also grew increasingly popular on black-figure vases.[82]

The close of the sixth century BC and the transition from black-figure to red-figure mark the end of our inquiry. Having reviewed depictions of chariots, particularly war chariots, over roughly a millennium, what conclusions may one draw? What questions does one pose?

We have repeatedly encountered scenes with war chariots on vases to which a funerary function can quite confidently be ascribed. How "funerary" is an Attic black-figure vase with a chariot? What do we make of the many hydriai with a war chariot or a warrior's departure on the shoulder (Fig. 1; Color Pl. 16)? In this

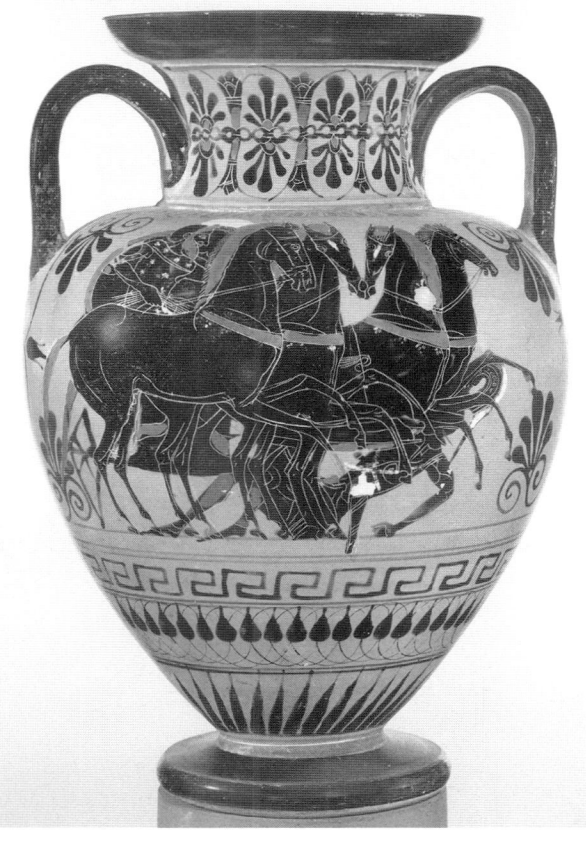

Fig. 8 Neck-amphora attributed to the Manner of the Lysippides Painter. Attic, ca. 520 BC. New York, The Metropolitan Museum of Art, 23.160.60. Rogers Fund, 1923. Image © The Metropolitan Museum of Art.

secondary decorative field, are chariots comparable to their counterparts in the friezes on Geometric works? Do they have a different significance in the primary panel? Black-figure hydriai pose an especially knotty and compelling problem given their considerable number and the variety of uses attested for the shape (Fig. 9). Is this a situation when "sometimes it is funerary and sometimes it isn't" – depending on the intentions of the user/owner? Could the motif make a vase "appropriate" for funerary use regardless of the other functions that it served during an owner's lifetime, principally as a water jar? The connection with water adds to the interpretive difficulties of the shape. The same questions apply especially to amphorae and neck-amphorae whose uses are even more difficult to pinpoint.

This matter of how much significance to attribute to vases with chariots is also bound up with their prevalence. Even a cursory look through *Attic Black-figure Vase-painters* indicates that during the second half of the sixth century BC hydriai, neck-amphorae, and amphorae with chariots are numerous. They were also exported in quantity to Etruria, especially Vulci.[83] This is a fascinating subject for which time allows only a few words. As the work of many scholars has demonstrated – notably that of Adriana Emiliozzi – chariots were an important feature in Etruscan life and iconography from the eighth century BC on. In contrast to Greece, considerable physical evidence for these vehicles exists, in fragments or – exceptionally – in fairly well preserved examples. In her book, *Carri da guerra, principi etruschi*, Emiliozzi lists over 250 pieces, mainly from Central Italy.[84] Was the production of pots with chariots in Athens also driven by the Western market? And a concomitant question is: are we wrong to think that all pots with chariots had special meaning to Athenians when in fact they were made for export? Going a step further: should we be considering the iconography of a vase that was exported differently from that of a vase found in Athens?

A related topic: how Homeric are the scenes with war chariots? To this immense question, Gregory Nagy's studies of the transmission and progressive codification of Homeric poetry provide one viewpoint. In *Homeric Questions*, Nagy proposes "at least five distinct consecutive periods of Homeric transmission – "Five Ages of Homer," as it were, with each period showing progressively less fluidity and more rigidity".[85] Those that apply here are the first period, from the early second millennium to the mid-eighth century BC without written texts; the second, what Nagy calls "pan-Hellenic" period from the mid-eighth to mid-sixth century, still without texts; and third, "A definitive period, centralized in Athens, with potential texts in the sense of transcripts, at any or several points from the middle of the sixth century to the later part of the fourth".[86] He continues "A context for the definitive period in my evolutionary model is a pan-Hellenic festival like the Panathenaia at Athens, which served as the formal setting, established by law, of seasonally recurring performances of the Homeric *Iliad* and *Odyssey*".[87] At the present time, we cannot securely identify "Homeric" chariot scenes without inscriptions, but it seems likely that through the existence of oral and, later, some form of written texts, the narrative would have been in circulation. The important consideration is that the stories would have been available not only to the elite who bought and commissioned the vases, perhaps also read written versions, but also to the potters and painters who produced the vases.

Before leaving Nagy's work on Homer, one additional thought-provoking assertion deserves mention. In his *Poetry as Performance: Homer and Beyond*, discussing the epic cycle, Nagy says, "I propose that the metaphor of *kúklos* as the sum total of Homeric poetry goes back to the meaning of *kúklos* as 'chariot-wheel'.... The metaphor of comparing a well-composed song to a well-crafted chariot-wheel is explicitly articulated in the poetic traditions of Indo-European languages".[88]

This paper has touched lightly and selectively on only a few features that lurk in the many chariot depictions on Attic – and, of course, other – vases. The chariot-borne warrior was one of the fundamental Greek contributions to Western iconography (Fig. 10), and I wonder whether the warrior with chariot did not represent a body of traditions, standards, and ideals that was progressively replaced by the kouros and his classical progeny.

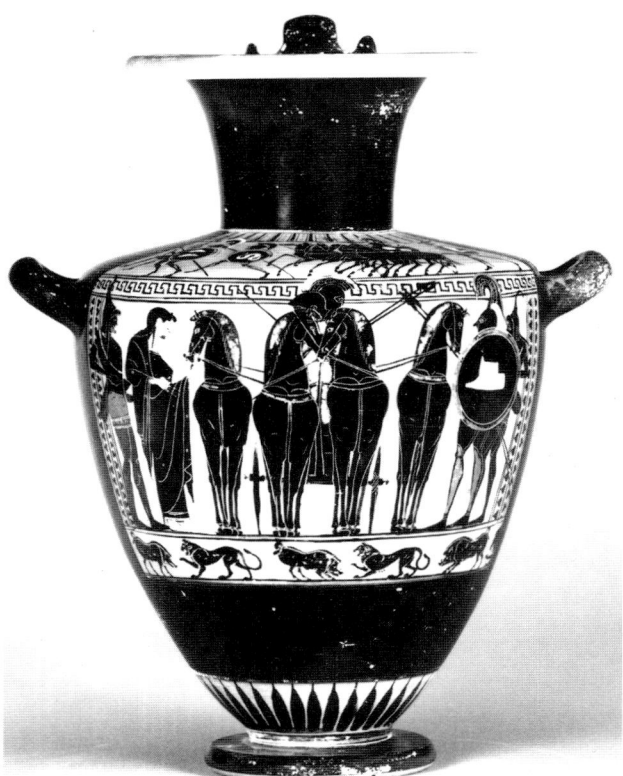

Fig. 9 Hydria attributed to the Painter of London B 343. Attic, ca. 510–500 BC. London, The British Museum, B 343. Image © The British Museum.

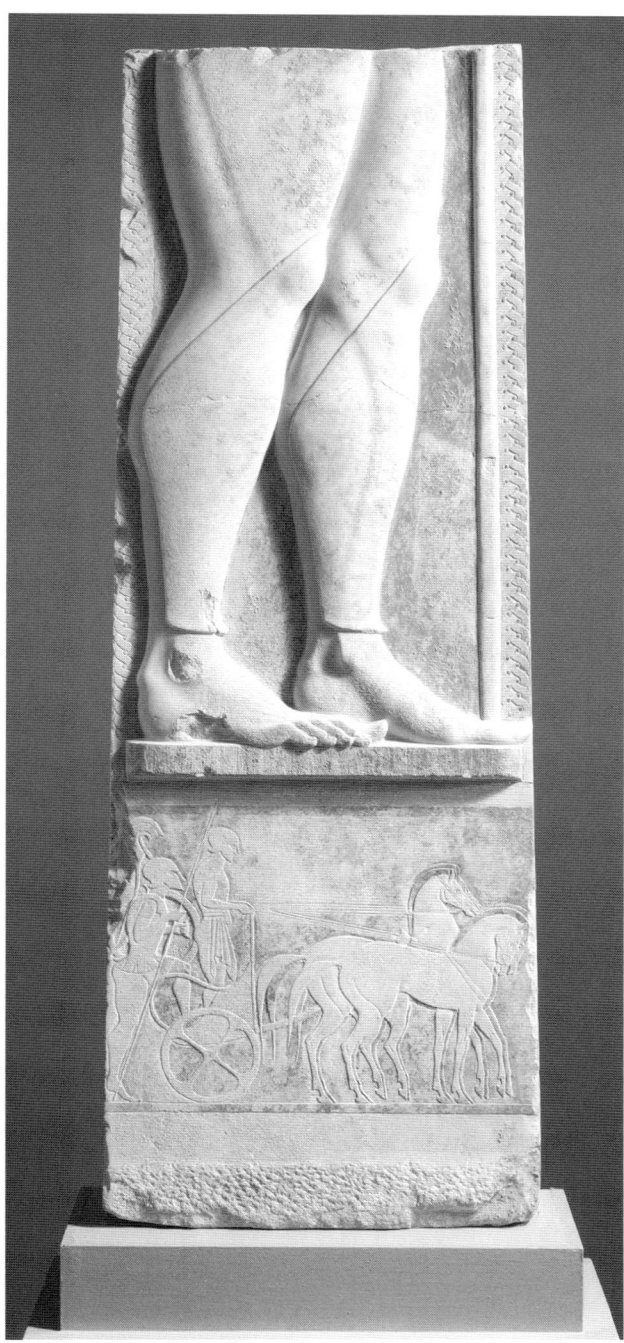

Fig. 10 Marble grave stele. Attic, ca. 525–515 BC. New York, The Metropolitan Museum of Art, 38.11.3. Fletcher Fund, 1938. Image © The Metropolitan Museum of Art.

Acknowledgements

My first thanks are due to John Oakley and to the College of William and Mary for the invitation to speak at the Athenian Potters and Painters III conference and their generous hospitality. Mary B. Moore has given me the benefit of her exceptional expertise on ancient Greek horses and Attic black-figure vase-painting. Matthew Noiseux helped unstintingly with all computer issues. I thank Klaus Tausend for permitting me to use his drawings of the fresco fragments from the megaron at Mycenae and of the detail of the Battle of Kadesh at Abu Simbel. Anne Coulié at the Musée du Louvre, Geralda Juriaans-Helle at the Allard Pierson Museum, Lesley Fitton and Alexandra Villing at the British Museum enabled me to use images in their collections. Eileen Sullivan facilitated use of images from the Metropolitan Museum of Art.

Abbreviations

Ahlberg 1971	G. Ahlberg, Fighting on Land and Sea in Greek Geometric Art, Skrifter Utgivna av Svenska Institutet I Athen 16 (1971)
Archer 2010	R. Archer, in: G. G. Fagan – M. Trundle (eds.), New Perspectives on Ancient Warfare, History of Warfare 59 (2010) 57–79
Crouwel 1981	J. H. Crouwel, Chariots and Other Means of Land Transport in Bronze Age Greece, Allard Pierson Series 3 (1981)
Crouwel 1992	J. H. Crouwel, Chariots and Other Wheeled Vehicles in Iron Age Greece, Allard Pierson Series 9 (1992)
Manakidou 1994	E. P. Manakidou, Parastaseis me armata (8os-5os ai. p. Ch.) (1994)
Moore 1971	M. B. Moore, Horses on Black-figured Greek Vases of the Archaic Period: ca. 620–480 BC, Ph.D. diss (New York University, 1971)
Tausend 2007	K. Tausend, in: E. Christof – G. Koiner – M. Lehner – E. Pochmarski (eds.), Potnia Theron. Festschrift für Gerda Schwarz zum 65. Geburtstag (2007) 383–394

Notes

1 See, for instance, Manakidou 1994.
2 A. Snodgrass, Early Greek Armor and Weapons (1964)162–163.
3 J. Benson, Horse, Bird, and Man (1970). See, for example, 20–26. 50–56. 109–114. 114–123.
4 E. Rystedt – B. Wells (eds.), Pictorial Pursuits. Figurative Painting on Mycenaean and Geometric Pottery. Papers from Two Seminars at the Swedish Institute at Athens in 1999 and 2001 (2006).
5 Accession number 56.171.29. ABV 362,30.
6 See H. Mommsen, in: H. A. Cahn – E. Simon (eds.), Tainia. Roland Hampe zum 70. Geburtstag dargebracht (1980) 139–152.
7 Still a basic point of departure is J. Wiesner, Fahren und Reiten, Archaeologia Homerica, I, F (1968).

8 (2002).
9 See, for instance, J. Neils, Goddess and Polis. The Panathenaic Festival in Ancient Athens (1992) 89–91; P. Schultz, in O. Palagia – A. Choremi-Spetsieri (eds.), The Panathenaic Games. Proceedings of an International Conference held at the University of Athens, May 11–12, 2004 (2007) 59–72.
10 Tausend 2007 383.
11 Archer 2010 76. Tausend 2007 383.
12 Discussed with particularly good drawings in T. G. H. James, Ramesses II (2002) 98–123.
13 M. A. Littauer – J. H. Crouwel, in: P. Raulwing (ed.), Selected Writings on Chariots and Other Early Vehicles, Riding and Harness (2002) 66–74.
14 Crouwel 1981, 149.
15 W. A. Heurtly, BSA 25, 1921–3, 126–146. G. Karo, Die Schachtgräber von Mykenai (1930/33) 29–35. E. Vermeule, Greece in the Bronze Age (1964) 90–94. Crouwel 1981 119–144.
16 Crouwel 1981 145.
17 Archer 2010 58–60; M. A. Littauer – J. H. Crouwel, in: Raulwing (supra n.13) 61.
18 Wiesner (supra n. 7) F27–29.
19 Archer 2010 58–63.
20 Tausend 2007.
21 See also Archer 2010 59.
22 Der Fries des Megarons von Mykenai (1921).
23 For a contrary view, see Crouwel 1981 130–132.
24 Tausend 2007 386. Archer 2010 66 proposes that small clusters of chariots could effectively attack the flanks and rear of a larger force, causing it to break up.
25 Tausend 2007 390–391.
26 The point of departure is E. Vermeule – V. Karageorghis, Mycenaean Pictorial Vase Painting (1982); for a discussion of the chariots specifically, see Littauer – Crouwel (supra n. 13) 181–187. Of particular interest within the very extensive bibliography are the contributions in E. Rystedt – B. Wells (supra n. 4), notably that by S. Hiller 63–71.
27 L. Steel, Wine Kraters and Chariots: The Mycenaean Pictorial Style Reconsidered in P. P. Betancourt – V. Karageorghis – R. Laffineur – W.-D. Niemeier (eds.), Meletemata, Studies in Aegean Archaeology Presented to Malcolm H. Wiener as He Enters His 65th Year 3 (1999) = Aegaeum 20, 806. E. Vermeule – V. Karageorghis (supra n. 26) 15. Crouwel 1981 139.
28 K. Kilian, AA 1982, 412. W. Güntner, Figürlich bemalte mykenische Keramik aus Tiryns, Tiryns Forschungen und Berichte 12 (2000) 23–24. W. Güntner, in: Rystedt – Wells (supra n. 4) 56–61.
29 Allard Pierson Museum, inv. 01856. E. Vermeule – V. Karageorghis (supra n. 26) 201, V.17, 39–40.
30 Accession number 74.51.2453. V. Karageorghis – J. R. Mertens – M. E. Rose, Ancient Art from Cyprus (2000) 201–204. A. Hermary – J. R. Mertens, The Cesnola Collection of Cypriot Art: Stone Sculpture (2014) cat. 490.
31 Steel (supra n. 27) 806–809. Among the many studies of the diffusion of Mycenaean vases, note particularly J. Balensi – J.-Y. Monchambert – S. Müller Celka (eds.), La céramique Mycénienne de l'Égée au Levant: Hommage à V. Hankey, Travaux de la Maison de l'Orient et de la Mediterranée 41 (2004).
32 Steel (supra n. 27) 808–809.
33 J. B. Carter, in: J. B. Carter – S. P. Morris (eds.), The Ages of Homer. A Tribute to Emily Townsend Vermeule (1995) 300. 304–305.
34 Crouwel 1981 119–145.
35 Crouwel 1981 112–115.
36 Crouwel 1981 59–62.
37 Crouwel 1981 63–70.
38 Crouwel 1981 70–74.
39 Crouwel 1992 52.
40 Crouwel 1992 52–53.
41 Crouwel 1992 53–54; J. Crouwel, in: Rystedt – Wells (supra n. 4) 165–168.
42 Archer 2010 especially 66–73; M. A. Littauer – J. H. Crouwel, Wheeled Vehicles and Ridden Animals in the Ancient Near East (1979) especially 99–160 on the first millennium B.C.
43 Archer 2010 78.
44 Archer 2010 74–75.
45 A. M. Snodgrass, Arms and Armor of the Greeks (1967) 45–47. 87–88. See also G. R. Bugh, The Horsemen of Athens (1988) 26. Crouwel 1992 59.
46 R. B. Strassler (ed.), The Landmark Herodotus (2007) V.113.1, VII.86.2, VII.184.4.
47 B. Bohen, Die geometrischen Pyxiden, Kerameikos Ergebnisse der Ausgrabungen 13 (1988) 45.
48 Bohen (supra n. 47) 10–12.
49 Bohen (supra n. 47) 10.
50 Manakidou (1994) 8–11.
51 Ahlberg 1971 42–43. 55–57.
52 Ahlberg 1971 42. 55.
53 Ahlberg 1971 15–17.
54 Ahlberg 1971 12–15. 56.
55 For early bibliography, Ahlberg 1971 12 n. 12. LIMC I (1981) 472–476 s.v. Aktorione (R. Hampe).
56 Ahlberg 1971 72.
57 Ahlberg 1971 84–88. Cf. A. Lezzi-Hafter, in: APP II 147–157.
58 Ahlberg 1971 88–102.
59 Ahlberg 1971 103.
60 Ahlberg 1971 105.
61 An invaluable point of departure is I. Kilian-Dirlmeier, JRGZM 32, 1985, 215–254. For a useful summary, I. Strøm in: G. Kopcke – I. Tokumaru (eds.), Greece Between East and West: Papers of the Meeting at the Institute of Fine Arts, New York University, March 15–16, 1990 (1992) 46–60.
62 Kilian-Dirlmeier (supra n. 61) 223. 227. 233. 239.
63 U. Jantzen, Ägyptische und orientalische Bronzen aus dem Heraion von Samos, Samos 8 (1972) 58–62.
64 H. Kyrieleis – W. Röllig, AM 103, 1988, 37–75.
65 Kyrieleis – Röllig (supra n. 64) 69–75. A. Charbonnet, Annali: Archeologia e Storia Antica 8, 1986, 117–156. See also Strøm (supra n. 61) 48 and W. Röllig, in: Kopcke – Tokumaru (supra n. 61) 97.
66 Accession number 11.210.1. CVA Metropolitan Museum of Art 5 USA 37 pls. 42–44.
67 Manakidou 1994 23.
68 Manakidou 1994 20.
69 Crouwel 1992 56–65. Manakidou 1994 28.
70 Manikidou 1994 21. 23.
71 Athens NM 17762; CVA Athens 2 Greece 2 pl. 1; E. Brann, Hesperia 30, 1961, 358–359.

72	Athens, Agora P 17403; Brann (supra n. 71) 358–359.	81	Moore 1971 407. Note also J. H. Crouwel, in: Moormann – Stissi (supra n. 80) 145–151.
73	Athens 353. ABV 2, bottom.	82	Manakidou 1994 268–271.
74	ABV 8,1.	83	See indices of ABV and the BAPD; also, C. Reusser, Vasen für Etrurien I (2002) 49–55.
75	Athens, Akropolis 474. ABV 8,2. See Moore 1971 411–416.		
76	Wiesner (supra n. 7) 66.	84	A. Emiliozzi (ed.), Carri da Guerra e Principi Etruschi. Exhibition catalogue Viterbo and Rome (1997) 305–336.
77	Moore 1971 421 ill.17.		
78	Moore 1971 416.	85	G. Nagy, Homeric Questions (1996) 41.
79	Moore 1971 405–406.	86	Nagy (supra n. 85) 42.
80	Athens, Akropolis 611. ABV 82,1 below. See H. Mommsen, in: E. M. Moorman – V. V. Stissi (eds.), Shapes and Images. Studies on Attic Black Figure and Related Topics in Honour of Herman A. G. Brijder (2009) 51–62.	87	Nagy (supra n. 85) 42.
		88	G. Nagy, Poetry as Performance: Homer and Beyond (1996) 74.

15 "Whom are You Calling a Barbarian?" A Column Krater by the Suessula Painter

J. Michael Padgett

In matters of style, Attic vase-painters tended to be relatively conservative and to work within the parameters of tradition. In every period, however, individual painters experimented with new techniques, or strayed outside the strictures of convention, to create novelties that either were still-born or that were admired and copied by contemporaries and followers, giving rise to new conventions. New subjects, too, were continually introduced, but if they are not defined by recognizable narrative action, and the portrayal of protagonists borrows too closely from established visual vocabularies, we may, at a distance of millennia, be left uncertain or unable to correctly interpret particular paintings. The will to do so persists, of course, and there is a temptation to escape confusion even at the risk of error. This is not necessarily a bad thing, if in the process we are compelled to re-examine our premises and to ask from what errors they, too, may have been born.

In 2007, the Princeton University Art Museum acquired an Attic red-figure column-krater that had been for many years in a private collection in Dijon (Figs. 1–5; Color Pl. 19).[1] Although it has some minor repairs, the vase is complete and in excellent condition. Its size is impressive: 42 cm. tall and 45 cm. wide at the handles. The Museum lacked an example of the Ornate Style of Attic vase-painting from the end of the fifth century, and the scene on the obverse of this krater is particularly ornate, showing a pair of figures in a quadriga drawn in three-quarter view. The legs of the horses, as usual, are all raised in unison, as though flying over the landscape, the latter indicated by a few weeds. The horses are vividly portrayed, their teeth gnashing at the bits. The artists made use of nearly every technique at his disposal: relief lines, dilute brown lines, added color, and even applied clay pellets to add texture to the cheek pieces of the horses.

The passenger in the chariot is a bearded man carrying a pair of spears and wearing a so-called Phrygian cap (Fig. 2; Color Pl. 19), a Greek artistic invention combining elements of a Persian tiara with Scythian and even Thracian elements to create a chapeaux that tells the viewer that the owner is not a Greek, but a barbarian. This particular example is of a type often encountered, with the curling peak lined with spiky protrusions, like the fins on the back of a sea-monster, a *ketos*. Reinforcing the message of barbarian otherness is the man's long-sleeved tunic, woven with zigzag patterns. Over this he wears a long robe, a fuller version of the Persian kandys, decorated with long rays, zigzags, and bands of undulating *ketea*, a popular textile design of the period, by no means

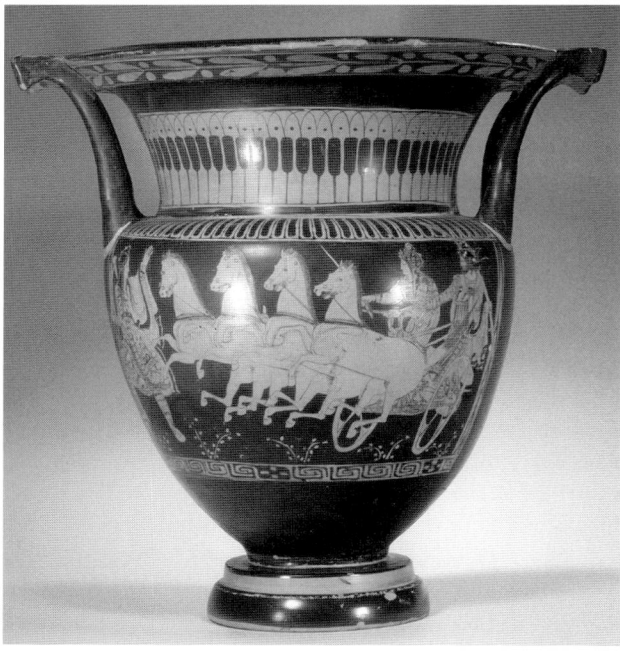

Fig. 1 Attic red-figure column-krater, attributed to the Suessula Painter. Princeton University Art Museum. Museum purchase, Fowler McCormick, Class of 1921 Fund, Carl Otto von Kienbusch, Jr. Memorial Collection Fund, and Classical Purchase Fund, 2007–98.

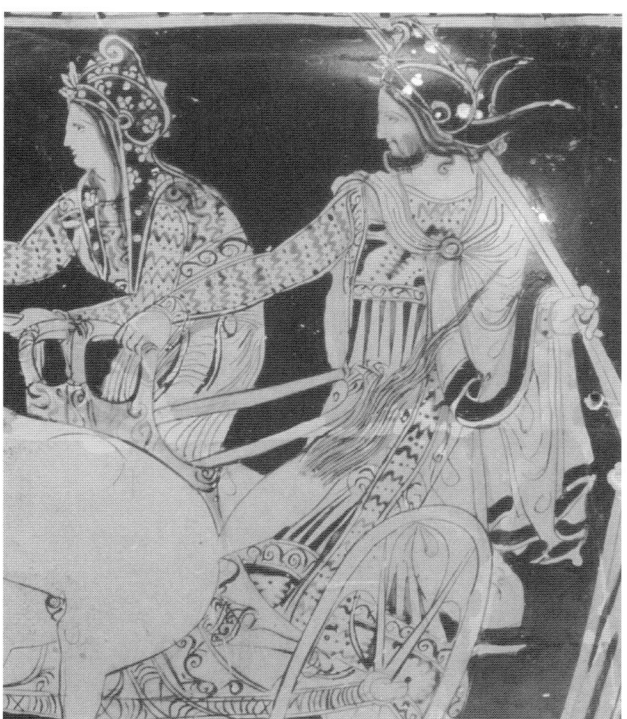

Fig. 2 Detail of the vase in Fig. 1. *Fig. 3 Detail of the vase in Fig. 1.*

exclusive to garments of barbarian origin. As a final accessory the man wears a chlamys, a short cloak, pinned at the shoulder, a garment impeccably Greek but suitable for heroes of all stripes. With his right hand he holds the rail of the chariot, the front of which the painter wishes us to know is itself decorated; to the left of the wheel and disappearing behind the horse, one can make out the leg and swirling, patterned chitoniskos of a human figure in action, possibly in a fight (Fig. 2; Color Pl. 19). This figural decoration, however abbreviated, may be unique among Attic depictions of chariots.

The man, whoever he is, leaves the driving to a charioteer, who stands beside him, holding the reins and wielding a goad (Fig. 2; Color Pl. 19). The driver also wears a sleeved under-garment and a spiky Phrygian cap, the latter now decorated with flowers. Instead of a *kandys*, there is what appears to be a short vest, perhaps a chest protector, below which emerge the folds of a long, belted chiton, appropriate garb for a charioteer, at least a Greek one. The driver's beardless face, delicate features, and long hair, falling well past the shoulders, suggest that she might be a woman. As though wishing to drive home this impression, the artist provides us with a third figure, at the left (Fig. 3; Color Pl. 19), whose hair and features are essentially identical to the driver's. This is a classic Amazon, armed with a war hatchet and wearing full barbarian regalia: Phrygian cap, patterned trousers, sleeved tunic, and a billowing, belted *kandys*, richly woven with waves, palmettes, and bands of sea monsters. Like the man, she too sports a chlamys. Placed beyond the hooves of the farthest trace horse, she is not being trampled; her reeling posture is a convention of the genre that occurs in many formats.[2] Instead, the Amazon on our vase runs ahead or alongside the chariot, as part of the retinue. *Whose* retinue is a question to which we shall return.

The decoration of the Princeton krater may be confidently attributed to the Suessula Painter, an artist active in the last decade of the fifth century.[3] He was a contemporary of the Talos and Semele Painters and, like them, in the larger ambit of the Pronomos Painter. Beazley named the painter after Suessula, the town in Campania, between Capua and Nola, where four neck-amphorae by him had been discovered. The chariot and horses recall those on the painter's masterpiece in the Louvre, a neck-amphora with twisted handles, both sides of which are devoted to a splendid depiction of the Gigantomachy, which Arnold von Salis convincingly associated with the painting of this subject on the interior of the shield of Pheidias' colossal statue of Athena Parthenos.[4] This is a fascinating subject, but not relevant to the interpretation of the painting on this krater.

On the obverse of the Princeton vase, numerous details in the drawing of the figures and their ornate attire support an attribution to the Suessula Painter, as do the three draped youths on the reverse (Fig. 4). The latter are crudely drawn, as is common among the "back-men" of even the most talented vase-painters of the period, but they have close correspondents among the acknowledged works of the Suessula Painter, particularly the youth holding a stick.[5] The capstones of the attribution are the vessel's shape and subsidiary ornament, the former rare

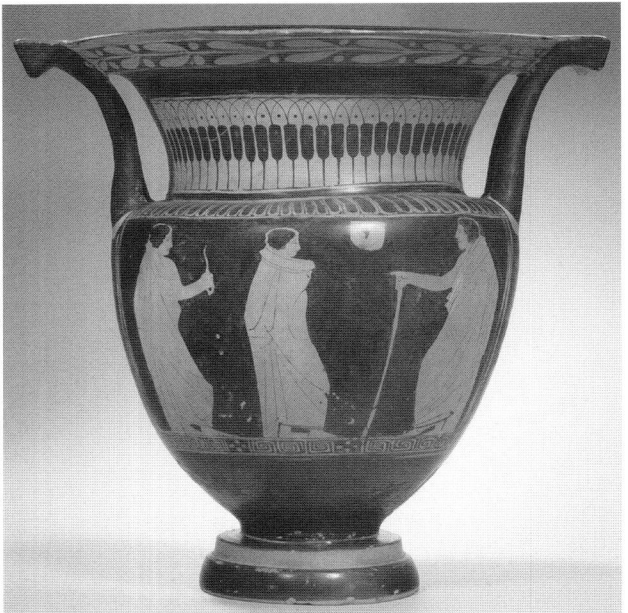

Fig. 4 Reverse of the vase in Fig. 1.

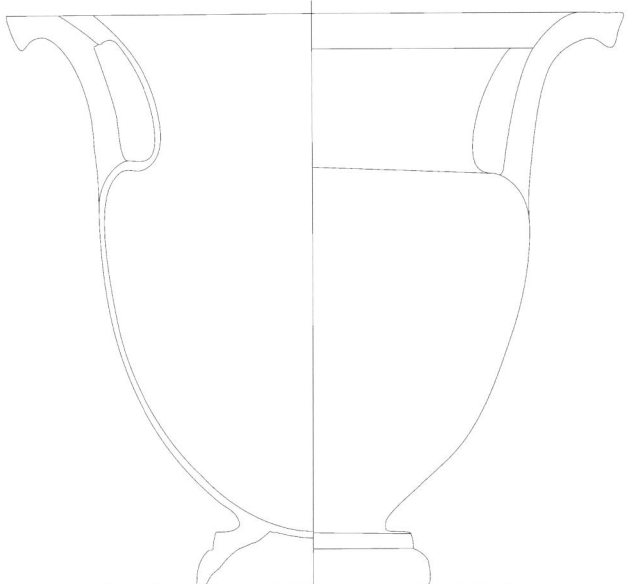

Fig. 5 Profile drawing of the vase in Fig. 1. Drawing by Elliot Lopez-Finn.

in this period and the latter, in most particulars, unique to the Suessula Painter.

By the end of the fifth century the column-krater had nearly run its course as a field for decoration by Athenian vase-painters, a decline that began well beforehand. After the Pan Painter, the best artists increasingly turned away from the column-krater, leaving it to the Late Mannerist workshop to extend its life into the last quarter of the century, though there were others, such as the Marlay Painter, the Painter of Munich 2335, and the Kadmos Painter, who still turned to it regularly. By the end of the fifth century, however, the only painter of note who decorated column-kraters in any numbers was the Suessula Painter. Beazley attributed, with degrees of certainty, fifteen vases to his hand: six neck-amphorae with twisted handles, five bell-kraters, one calyx-krater, and three column-kraters. Of the five vases that have or should be added to this list, four are column-kraters, which for the time being makes it the painter's most favored shape.[6] It is notable that after the Suessula Painter, neck-amphorae with twisted handles disappear almost immediately; indeed, the six that Beazley attributed to him may be the last.

The column-krater did not last much longer. After the Meleager Painter, the shape fades rapidly away and is gone by the second quarter of the fourth century, though it retained its popularity in southern Italy, particularly Apulia, throughout much of the century. Kleopatra Kathariou has identified the reverse of a column-krater in the Conradty collection – contemporary with the Princeton krater – as an early work by the Meleager Painter, while instead assigning the splendid Amazonomachy on the obverse to the Painter of the New York Centauromachy, an artist otherwise not known to have decorated this shape.[7]

When the contemporaries of the Suessula Painter ventured to paint a large and ambitious subject in high style, they normally resorted to the more fashionable bell-krater, calyx-krater, or volute-krater. In the case of the Princeton vase, however, the Suessula Painter turned to the krater shape with which he was most familiar, the column-krater, perhaps asking the potter for an extra-large one to accommodate his ambitious composition.[8] Although, as a shape, the column-krater lacks the elegance of the calyx-krater or the majesty of the volute-krater, the potting of the Princeton vase does exhibit a certain refinement, its "columns" arcing gracefully into the line of the overhanging rim (Fig. 5). Emphasizing the vase's special character, the artist placed a laurel wreath around the outer rim and red-figure palmettes on top of the handle plates. Instead of the usual ivy vines framing the panels, there are vertical columns of black and reserved chevrons, a motif that otherwise seems to occur only on the Amazonomachy krater in the Conradty collection, mentioned above. The lotus buds on either side of the neck of the Princeton vase – standard ornament in this position since the late sixth century – are curiously pinched and attenuated in their lower extremities, something unimportant in itself but of interest for occurring nowhere else but on column-kraters by the Suessula Painter (Figs. 1. 4; Color Pl. 19). They occur again on another, smaller column-krater by the artist in Naples (Fig. 6), with Eros driving the chariot of Aphrodite.[9] On the Naples krater one notices another distinctive element: the framing ornament is the usual ivy, but the leaves are curiously flattened and stylized, ranging in shape from a Y to a T. This tendency is even more pronounced on the painter's column-kraters in London and Madrid.[10]

These distinctive motifs – attenuated buds and T-shaped ivy – recur on a large column-krater in Salerno, and were no doubt among the clues, along with the distinctive back-men, that enabled Giada Giudice to attribute it to the Suessula Painter.[11] The principal scene on the Salerno krater has been called a Persian symposium, and the garb of the beardless banqueters does look more Persian than Scythian. Just before Giudice's attribution of the Salerno krater, Konrad Schauenburg drew a connection between it and another column-krater in an Italian private collection, with Herakles riding the chariot of Nike.[12] Both kraters have the same large lotus-and-palmette frieze on the obverse neck, above a band of astragals, and the attenuated buds on the reverse neck that occur on all of the column-kraters by the Suessula Painter. Schauenburg rightly assigned both kraters to the same, unnamed workshop, and there can be no doubt that the privately-owned krater with Nike and Herakles, which was unknown to Giudice, is also the work of the Suessula Painter. To these we may now add a third, unpublished column-krater, currently in the Barcelona art market, with identical ornament – lotus-and-palmette, astragals, attenuated buds, T-shaped ivy – and a variation of the painter's usual trio of back-men on the reverse. The picture on the obverse is in some ways a standard departure scene, with a woman libating before a youth, who stands facing her and holding a pair of spears. A second spearman is seated on the left, while a third, at right, holds the reins of a white horse. What sets this departure apart is that each of the males wears the trousers, sleeved tunic, patterned cloak (*zeira*), and animal-skin cap (*alopekis*) of the Thracian warrior. This casting of a familiar Greek tableau "against type," with barbarian protagonists, relates the Barcelona krater most strongly to the Suessula Painter's "Persian symposium" in Salerno.

The splendid horses drawing Nike's chariot on the column-krater in the Italian private collection find their closest parallels in the steeds pulling the chariot on the Princeton krater. What remain unsettled are the identities of the occupants of the Princeton chariot.

Why is a bearded, male barbarian riding a chariot being driven by what appears to be a woman in barbarian dress? As stated earlier, the similarity to the Amazon in the scene might suggest that the driver, too, is of the sisterhood. Amazons are great riders, of course, and one sees them mounted in many situations, notably the west metopes of the Parthenon. Amazons, however, are only rarely represented as charioteers. A century before, a few Attic vases show Amazons harnessing or driving chariots into battle,[13] and as late as the 460s the Niobid Painter included an Amazon charioteer on a magnificent volute-krater in Naples.[14] No Amazon charioteers occur in Attic vase-painting after mid-century, however, and one searches in vain for an Amazon of any period who chauffeurs a male of any kind, let alone a bearded barbarian.

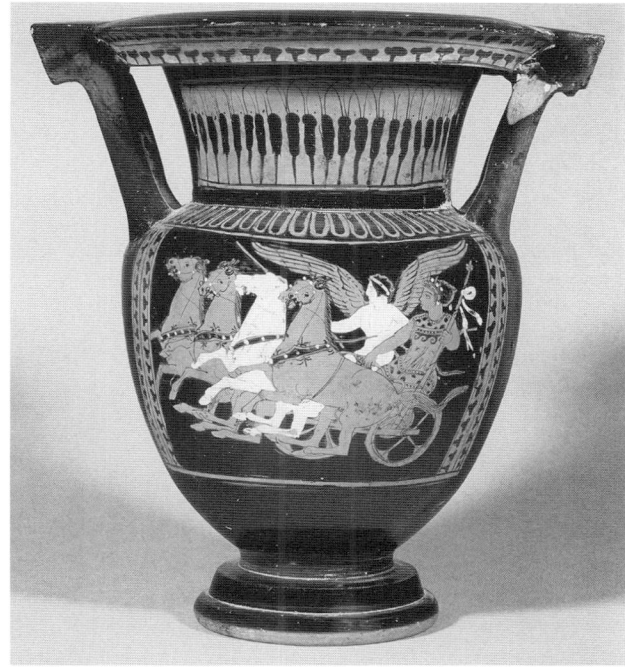

Fig. 6 Attic red-figure column-krater, attributed to the Suessula Painter. Naples, Museo Archeologico Nazionale, 146740.

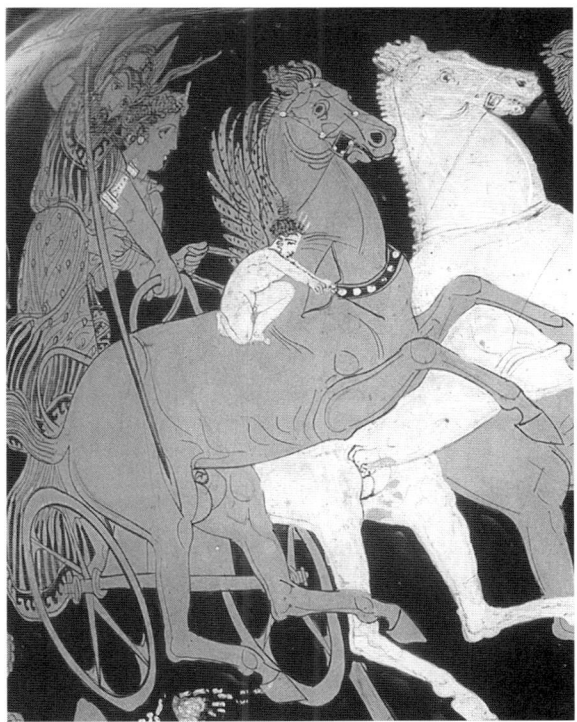

Fig. 7 Attic red-figure neck-amphora with twisted handles, attributed to the Suessula Painter. Paris, Musée du Louvre S 1677.

If she is not an Amazon, what other female drivers are possible? There are many female charioteers, of course, and we need look no farther than the Suessula Painter's Gigantomachy on the neck-amphora in the

Louvre to find Nike driving the chariot from which Zeus has disembarked, just as she also conducts Herakles to Olympus on the artist's privately owned column-krater in Italy, discussed above, a task often assumed instead by the hero's patroness, Athena. On the reverse of the Louvre neck-amphora, Aphrodite holds the reins of a quadriga while her lover, Ares, does the fighting, with little Eros riding shotgun and shooting his arrows (Fig. 7; Color Pl. 20). Perhaps the Giants thus pierced fell in love with their opponents, making them easy prey. On a volute-krater in Paris, by the Painter of the Woolly Satyrs, Artemis drives a chariot drawn by deer,[15] and does so elsewhere on many occasions. In this period Artemis is often depicted in rich and vaguely oriental garments, as on a bell-krater near the Painter of the Athens Wedding, where she is dressed in a sleeved tunic and a vest decorated with Ketos-bands.[16] She wears no trousers or Phrygian cap, however, and of course deer are not horses.

In this period the Colchian witch Medea was frequently represented in barbarian garments – sleeved tunic, *kandys*, and Phrygian cap, with or without a spiky crest.[17] But although Medea is famously associated with the dragon-borne chariot from which she escaped the wrath of Jason – a subject depicted several times in South-Italian red-figure, though never on Athenian vases – she is never represented as a driver of horses. She and Jason fled from Colchis in a chariot, but she presumably let Jason do the driving while she chopped up her brother Apsyrtos, dropping his pieces behind to slow down their father's pursuit. There is no golden fleece in our chariot, and we would not expect to see Jason depicted in barbarian attire.[18] A few other exotic mythical females appear occasionally in barbarian garb – Andromeda, for instance – but not driving a man around in a chariot.[19]

What, then, of the male passenger? Many male deities and heroes take to a chariot, though only a select few were of foreign birth, and so liable to be represented in barbarian costume. On a fourth-century lekythos in St. Petersburg, for example, Paris prepares to drive off with his bride Helen, but it is he who holds the reins, while she stands at his side, nude and white-skinned.[20] The fact is that there are few mythical couples that we *would* expect to see in barbarian garb, the both of them, and no instance in which the woman would be driving the man in a chariot.

Having said that, it is time to ask whether there is not something wrong with our premises, in particular the assumption that the vase-painter, having given similar features and garments to both the charioteer and the Amazon in the same scene, is inviting us to identify the driver as an Amazon, too. On one of his neck-amphorae in the Metropolitan Museum of Art, the Suessula Painter depicts a young Greek warrior with features no less delicate and tresses no less lengthy than those of the adjacent Amazon (Fig. 8).[21] The beardless and presumably young Persians gathered at supper on the artist's bell-krater in Salerno are even more to the point.[22] On the famous squat lekythos signed by Xenophantos the Athenian, in St. Petersburg, a

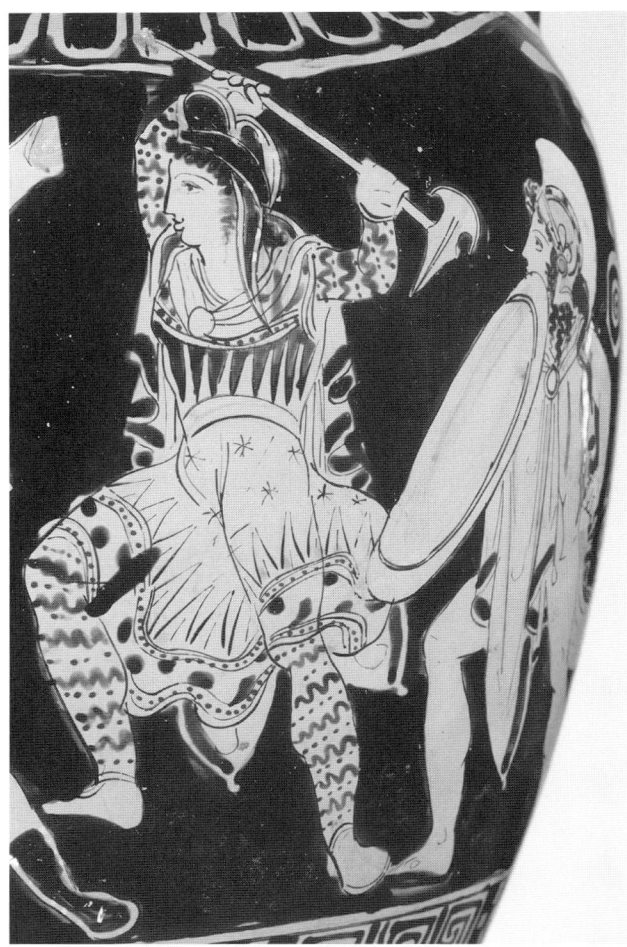

Fig. 8 Attic red-figure neck-amphora with twisted handles, attributed to the Suessula Painter. Metropolitan Museum of Art, New York, 44.11.12. Fletcher Fund, 1944.

bearded Persian, alone in a chariot, hunts creatures both earthly and fantastic, accompanied by beardless young countrymen on foot and on horseback.[23] Similar scenes appear on both sides of an earlier volute-krater in Naples, with the Persian grandee now on horseback and his beardless young huntsmen on foot (Fig. 9).[24] Is the bearded man in the chariot on the Princeton krater a Persian noble out hunting in his paradise? If so, we are denied a glimpse of his prey, which would have made the subject explicit, and an Amazon makes an odd huntsman.[25] For the same reasons it seems unlikely that our passenger is the Great King. Such a depiction would be unprecedented, and His Majesty presumably would have been served by an older, more seasoned driver, like the bearded charioteer in the Alexander Mosaic, or the one driving a king or noble in the gold chariot from the Oxus Treasure.[26]

Rather than explain the subject of the Princeton krater as a meaningless depiction of generic Persians charging through the rye, there may be other possibilities for interpreting a scene that seems to cry out to be identified with a specific narrative or particular characters. When we consider what famous mythical figure was both a foreigner and strongly associated with chariots, the name of Pelops inevitably arises. Pindar said Pelops was from Lydia, but most other ancient authors placed his home in Phrygia.[27] For a century after his first appearance in Attic vase-painting, Pelops was represented no differently from other Greek heroes, but on a kalpis from Spina, attributed to Polygnotos, he is shown dressed in a patterned gown and Phrygian cap, and driving the chariot drawn by the winged steeds that Poseidon had given him.[28] To ensure that he

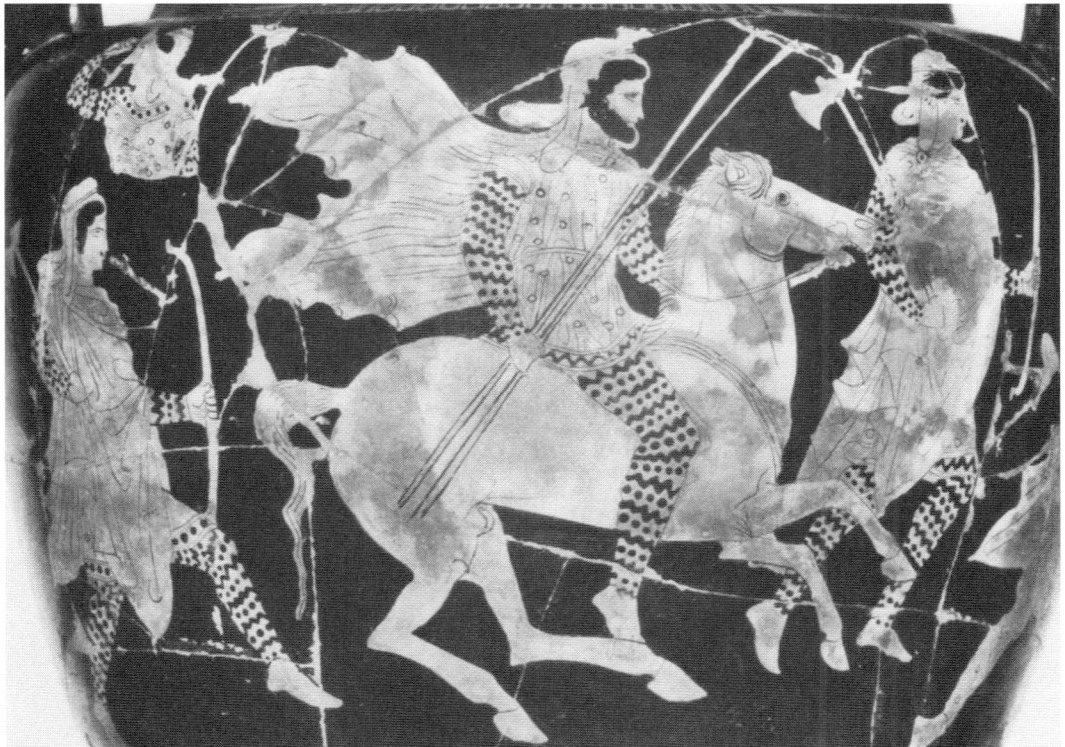

Fig. 9 Attic red-figure volute-krater. Naples, Museo Archeologico Nazionale, 81671.

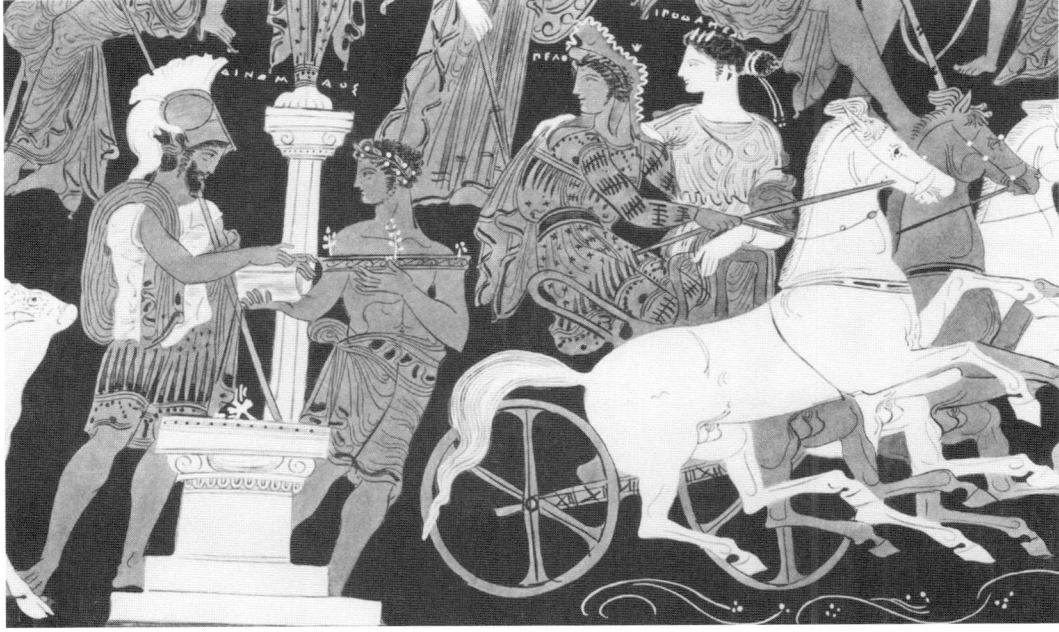

Fig. 10 Attic red-figure bell-krater, attributed to the Oinomaos Painter. Naples, Museo Archeologico Nazionale, M2731. After A. Furtwängler – K. Reichhold, Griechische Vasenmalerei, Vol. III (1932) pl. 146.

won the race against King Oinomaos of Pisa and, thereby, the hand of his daughter, Hippodameia, Pelops bribed Oinomaos's charioteer, Myrtilos, to put wax linchpins on his master's chariot so that, when they melted, the haughty ruler fell to his death. On the name-vase of the Oinomaos Painter, in Naples, a bell-krater painted a decade or so after the krater by the Suessula Painter, Oinomaos sacrifices before the race while Myrtilos, wearing a sleeveless Greek chiton, brings up the king's chariot.[29] To the right of Oinomaos, Pelops and Hippodameia stand beside one another in his chariot, as though already victorious (Fig. 10). Pelops is represented wearing rich oriental garments, complete with sleeved tunic and spiky Phrygian cap. We may wonder whether Pelops appeared on stage in similarly exotic garb in Euripides' play, *Oinomaos*, produced in 409 BC.[30]

What is sometimes forgotten is that, like Oinomaos, Pelops, too, had a charioteer, who did not live to accompany his master to Pisa. His name was Killas, also known as Sphaeros.[31] I know of no depiction of Killas in vase-painting, though Pausanias was told that he appeared on the East Pediment of the Temple of Zeus at Olympia.[32] The kneeling figure from the pediment that is sometimes identified as Killas is in Greek dress,[33] as is Pelops, but in a vase-painting from the end of the century we would expect that, as Easterners, both he and his master would be depicted in barbarian costume. Another celebrated driver, Baton, the charioteer of Amphiaraos, is shown in oriental garb on some Apulian vases.[34] One reason that we would not expect to find Killas on the Olympia pediment is that, according to the fourth-century historian Theopompos, Pelops set off for Olympia with Killas at the reins, but as the winged steeds flew over the straits toward Lesbos, Killas was thrown and killed.[35] Prompted by a dream in which Killas appeared to him, Pelops made a splendid tumulus for his ashes on Lesbos, beside which grew up the city of Killa and the sanctuary of Killaian Apollo. Might the Princeton krater show Pelops and Killas departing for Greece, with a dashing Amazon as appropriate local color? If so, would a Greek viewer, whether in Athens or Italy, have recognized them? Perhaps, if we imagine Pelops and his faithful driver being pressed into a symbolic role, advancing the interests of parties friendly to another noble barbarian king.

Martin Robertson, in a subtle analysis of the paths of descent and influence among the vase-painters of the later fifth century, noted that the painters of the better known Ornate Style works, such as the Talos Painter and the Pronomos Painter, and lesser artists like the Suessula Painter, could not always have painted such large and extraordinary works.[36] The bell-kraters attributed to the Pronomos Painter, for example, are much more everyday works, as are, in comparison to his splendid neck-amphora in the Louvre, the other neck-amphorae by the Suessula Painter, which Beazley dismissed as "tawdry work".[37] These ordinary productions belong to a continuous tradition descended from the Dinos Painter and weaker artists like the Pothos and Nikias Painters. While the more elaborate vases of the end of the century also clearly descend from the Dinos Painter and the Meidias Painter, they are different in character, and nothing really follows on from them; unless, that is, the better works of such ostensibly later artists as the Painter of the New York Centauromachy were actually produced just *before* the end of the century, like that painter's wonderful Amazonomachy in the Conradty collection.[38] Behind this brief fashion for ceramic extravaganzas Robertson recognized the patronage of the Thirty Tyrants, the pro-Spartan regime that took power in Athens in 403 BC.[39] Robertson pointed to a trio of complete and fragmentary bell-kraters that Beazley felt were connected both with the Semele Painter and (less closely) the Suessula Painter. Among them is a bell-krater in S. Agata de'Goti, with Leda and the Egg;[40] and a fragment from the Kerameikos that likely shows one of the Dioskouroi from a scene with the same Laconian subject. The fragment was found in, or near the Grave of the Lacedaemonians who fell in 403,[41] and a clear argument can be made for a distinctly Laconian–Theban strain in many of the finer vases from the end of the century; for instance, the name-vase of the Semele Painter, with the Theban birth of Dionysos;[42] and the appearance of the Theban musician Pronomos on the name-vase of the Pronomos Painter.[43]

Robertson's identification of this Peloponnesian strain in the iconography of some of the finest vases of the end of the fifth century, his suggestion that this may reflect the patronage of the Thirty Tyrants and their party, whether in office or not, and his recognition that the early works of some of the best artists of the first decade of the fourth century may actually have been made before 400, allow us to look with fresh eyes at the Suessula Painter's enigmatic column-krater in Princeton. In the final years of the Peloponnesian War, Persia was in close alliance with Sparta and its allies, and Cyrus the Younger and the satrap Tissaphernes were active in the fighting. It was immediately after the war that Xenophon and the Ten Thousand went to Mesopotamia to fight for Cyrus in the war of succession following the death of Darius II. In this brief but revolutionary period, when the world was upside down, is it possible that a partisan of the Thirty Tyrants and of the pro-Spartan/pro-Persian party at Athens may have commissioned a work expressing admiration for the valuable assistance and martial prowess of the Persians, if not overtly – something difficult to imagine, even for a Medizing oligarch – then through an evocation of their mythological ancestors? The Suessula Painter worked briefly in Corinth, decorating a locally-made bell-krater, suggesting that he might himself be Corinthian by birth or politics.[44] We have already noted his occasional casting of barbarians in traditionally Greek tableaus. What better artist from whom to commission a grand and functional symposium vessel depicting Pelops – whom Herodotus has Xerxes himself evoke as a forbearer[45] – with his loyal charioteer, Killas, setting out to establish a new order in Greece?

Acknowledgements

I am grateful to John Oakley for inviting me to participate in the Athenian Potters and Painters III conference, to helpful comments from colleagues present in Williamsburg, and to Ian McPhee, Adrienne Mayor and Margaret Miller for discussing this vase with me.

Notes

1. Princeton University Art Museum. Museum purchase, Fowler McCormick, Class of 1921 Fund, Carl Otto von Kienbusch, Jr. Memorial Collection Fund, and Classical Purchase Fund (2007-98). Record of the Princeton University Art Museum 67, 2008, 116–117 (illus); Royal-Athena Galleries, Art of the Ancient World, vol. XIX (2008) no. 128 (detail on cover). The vase was sold in April 1970 to Jean Michel Robert, of Dijon, by Paris dealer Michelle Cohen ("La Reine Margot"), along with a second column-krater. In 2007, M. Robert sold both vases back to La Reine Margot, which in turn sold them to Royal-Athena Galleries, New York.

2. The same position and posture are adopted by Hermes on a slightly later vase by the Painter of London F 64, where Herakles rides the chariot of Nike: S. Agata de'Goti, Mustilli coll.; ARV² 1420,5. There are many other examples.

3. Suessula Painter: ARV² 1344-1346. 1691; Para 482; BAdd² 367. 368; I. D. McPhee, Attic Vase Painters of the Late 5th Century B.C., Ph.D. diss. (Univ. Cincinnati, 1973) 161–207. Beazley firmly attributed fourteen vases to the artist, and said another was "probably also" from his hand. Tiverios has added a pelike from a grave near Pydna, but I do not believe it is by the Suessula Painter: M. Tiverios, in: J.-P. Descoeudres (ed.), Eumousia. Ceramic and Iconographic Studies in Honour of Alexander Cambitoglou (1990) 119–124 pls. 28. 29.

4. Louvre S 1677; ARV² 1344,1; 1691; Para 482; BAdd² 367; A. von Salis, JdI 55, 1940, 90–169. See also P. Devambez, in: Charistérion eis Anastasion K. Orlandon, I (1964) 102–109; M. Denoyelle, Chefs d'oeuvre de la céramique grecque dans les collections du Louvre (1994) 154 cat. 72.

5. In particular, cf. the back-figures on the column-kraters London E 490 and Madrid 11045 (ARV² 1345,7. 8).

6. Beazley felt that the bell-krater fragment Cambridge N 146 was "probably" by the Suessula Painter: ARV² 1345.(a). I agree and would make it no. 15 in his list. In addition to the four new column-kraters discussed in this paper, a fifth addition should be a calyx-krater fragment, Leipzig 4729 (T 656), that Beazley said "is not far from the Suessula Painter" (ARV² 1346 top).

7. E. Simon (ed.) Mythen und Menschen. Griechische Vasenkunst aus einer deutschen Sammlung (1997) 140–144 cat. 39; K. Kathariou, To ergasterio tou zographou tou Meleagrou kai e epoche tou (2002) 191. 213. 389 fig. 9 cat. MEL 14.

8. The Conradty krater – supra n. 7 – is even larger: h. 52 cm, w. with handles 52 cm.

9. Naples 146740; ARV² 1345,9; M. Denoyelle, in: Vasi antichi, Museo Archeologico Nazionale di Napoli (2009) 86. Denoyelle is surely correct in identifying the chariot's occupants as Eros and Aphrodite.

10. Supra n. 5.

11. Salerno, Museo Nazionale T228; K. Schauenburg, AM 90, 1975, 114. 115 pl. 38.2; K. Schauenburg, Studien zur Unteritalischen Vasenmalerei, Band IX/X. Studien zur attischen Vasenmalerei (2006) 65. 66. 182 fig. 169; G. Giudice, Il Tornio, la nave e le terre lontane. Ceramografici attici in Magna Grecia nella seconda metà del V sec. a.C. Rotte e vie di distribuzione (2007) 208 fig. 203 cat. 430.

12. Schauenburg 2006 (supra n. 11) 64–66. 181 figs. 167a.b; 222 color pl. XLIV.

13. E.g. Würzburg 310; ABV 667. 666,2; Para 317; BAdd² 148 – Frankfürt, Städel STV1; ABV 409. 1696; Para 165,81bis; BAdd² 106 – London B 322; ABV 363,32; Para 161; BAdd² 96.

14. Naples 81672 (2421); ARV² 600,13; Para 395; BAdd² 266; Denoyelle supra (n. 9) 68. 69.

15. Louvre CA 3482; ARV² 613,3; Para 397; BAdd² 269.

16. Vienna KM 1771; ARV² 1318; BAdd² 363. On the same vase, the garments of Apollo are equally sumptuous, but the most Greek of the gods does not – could not – wear sleeves.

17. The most striking Medea of this period is on the name-vase of the Talos Painter: Ruvo, Jatta 1501; ARV² 1338,1; Para 481; BAdd² 366. On a calyx-krater by the Kekrops Painter, her Phrygian cap has a spiky crest: Adolphseck 78; ARV² 1346–1347,2; Para 482; BAdd² 368.

18. One is intrigued, however, by a passage in Pindar's description of Jason: "A tunic of Magnesian fashion fitted close his magnificent limbs" (*Pyth.* 4, 80).

19. For example, the Andromeda on an unattributed calyx-krater in Berlin, who wears a tiara and sleeved tunic: Berlin 3237; ARV² 1336. 1690; Para 480; CVA Berlin 11 Germany 86 pl. 31.

20. St. Petersburg ST 1929; K. Schefold – F. Jung, Die Sagen von der Argonauten von Theben und Troja in der klassischen und hellenistischen Kunst (1989) 123 fig. 101. Schefold earlier had attributed this vase to his "Helena Painter," an artist not recognized by Beazley: K. Schefold, Untersuchungen zu den kertscher Vasen (1934) 86.

21. NewYork 44.11.12; ARV² 1344,3; BAdd² 368.

22. Supra n. 11.

23. St. Petersburg P 1837.2; ARV² 1407,1; Para 488; B. Cohen (ed.), The Colors of Clay: Special Techniques in Athenian Vases (2006) 140–142 cat. 37.

24. Naples 81671 (H 3251); K. Schauenburg, Jagddarstellungen in der griechischen Vasenmalerei (1969) 13 pl. 6; Schauenburg 1975 (supra n. 11) pl. 42; A. C. Montanaro, Ruvo di Puglia e il suo territorio. Le necropoli. I corredi funerari tra la documentazione del XIX secolo e gli scavi moderni (2007) 548. 549 figs. 461–463 cat. 116.1.

25. Some of the beardless young Persians on the Naples hunt krater – which is unattributed but vaguely Polygnotan in style, ca. 440 BC – carry war hatchets like that of the Amazon on the Princeton krater. The latter's rich garments, however, and her similarity to the more broadly drawn Amazons on one of the Suessula Painter's neck-amphorae in New York – (supra n. 21) – incline me to keep her on the distaff side.

26. A. Cohen, The Alexander Mosaic: Stories of Victory and Defeat (1997) 89 fig. 54; O. M. Dalton, The Treasure of the Oxus (1964) 3. 4 pl. IV.

27 Pind. *Ol.* 1, 24. Pelops: LIMC VII (1994) 282–287 pls. 219–223 s.v. Pelops (I. Triantis); M. C. Miller, in: E. S. Gruen (ed.), Cultural Borrowings and Ethnic Appropriations in Antiquity (2005) 70–75.

28 Ferrara 3058 (T.271); ARV² 1032,58; 1679; Para 442; BAdd² 318; Miller (supra n. 27) fig. 4; Triantis (supra n. 27) 283 pl. 219 no. 3.

29 Naples M2731 (H 2200); ARV² 1440,1; Para 492; BAdd² 377; Triantis (supra n. 27) 284 no. 13; LIMC V (1990) 436 pl. 310 no. 10 s.v. Hippodameia I (M. Pipili).

30 I agree with Miller that developments in Attic iconography should not be attributed too casually to the influence of the theater, but rather as "parallels in manner of presentation… independently motivated by the same ideological cause"; Miller (supra n. 27) 70.

31 Killas: LIMC VI (1992) 47 pl. 66 s.v. Killas (P. Müller).

32 Paus. 5.10.7.

33 B. Ashmole – N. Yalouris, Olympia: The Sculptures of the Temple of Zeus (1967) 16 pls. 55–57; Müller (supra n. 31) 47 no. 1.

34 The Darius Painter represented Baton in oriental garb on at least two volute-kraters: formerly Cleveland 88.41; RVAp 496 cat. 18/41 pl. 177 – Boston 61.113; J. M. Padgett et al., Vase-Painting in Italy: Red-figure and Related Works in The Museum of Fine Arts, Boston (1993) 122 cat. 44. On a third, Baton is in Greek attire but wears a Phrygian helmet: St. Petersburg B 1710; LIMC I (1981) 703 pl. 568 no. 74 s.v. Amphiaraos (I. Krauskopf)

35 Theopomp. FGrHist 115 F 350.

36 M. Robertson, The Art of Vase Painting in Classical Athens (1992) 258–259. What follows in this paragraph leans heavily on Robertson's arguments.

37 CB III 89.

38 Supra n. 7.

39 Robertson (supra n. 36) 259. Tiverios earlier had suggested that the iconography of the Gigantomachy on the pelike Athens 1333 (ARV² 1337,8), with its focus on Poseidon and the Dioskouroi, may have been influenced by the Spartan domination of Athens after Aegospotami: Tiverios (supra n. 3) 123 n. 37. He has since expanded on the notion of Laconian influence on vase iconography of the period: M. Tiverios, in: G. Giudice – E. Giudice (eds.), "Ἀττικὸν… κέραμον": Veder Greco a Camarina, dal principe di Biscari ai nostri giorni vol. II (2011) 171f.

40 S. Agata de'Goti, Mustilli coll.; ARV² 1344,1 (top).

41 Kerameikos; ARV² 1344,3 (top). It is not certain whether this fragment was in the actual 'Grave of the Lacedamonians' or in the earth nearby. Fragments of Laconian red-figure now have been found in the grave: J. Stroszeck, AA 2006, 101–120.

42 Berkeley 8.3316; ARV² 1343,1; 1691; BAdd² 367.

43 Naples 3240; ARV² 1336,1; 1704; Para 480; BAdd² 365–366.

44 Corinth 37–447; ARV² 1345,13; S. Herbert, The Red-figure Pottery, Corinth VII Part IV (1977) 47. 48 no. 76 pl. 13. E.G. Pemberton, in: APP 415 fig. 26. 416–417; I. D. McPhee – E. Kartsonaki, Hesperia 79, 2010, 124 fig. 10; 125. 136. Chemical analysis has confirmed that the krater was made in Corinth. Pemberton (supra) 417 n. 5 notes the use of Doric letter forms on the Madrid krater (supra n. 5) and suggests that the Suessula Painter may have been Corinthian. McPhee rejects Herbert's attribution of a second locally-made bell-krater fragment to the Suessula Painter: Corinth 37–445; Herbert (supra) 48 no. 77 pl. 14; McPhee (supra n. 3) 207. From what remains, it is certainly hard to distinguish from the other example.

45 Hdt. 7.11.

16 Good Dog, Bad Dog: A Cup by the Triptolemos Painter and Aspects of Canine Behavior on Athenian Vases

For Domino, a good dog

Seth D. Pevnick

Two extremes of canine behavior play out on an Athenian red-figure cup painted by the Triptolemos Painter early in his career (ca. 490–480 BC): a good dog and a bad dog, perhaps; or a single dog in two quite different states.[1] Whereas the male hound on the cup's exterior (Fig. 1) stands nicely, head and tail erect, left forepaw gently lifted and held in the right hand of a nude youth, the dog within the bowl of the cup (Fig. 2; Color Pl. 21C) viciously bites an infibulated youth on the upper thigh, with the resulting blood or bruising indicated by dilute glaze. Simultaneously – and quite literally adding insult to injury – this bad dog squats and defecates along the frame of the tondo. The bite occurs in the center of the tondo, the defecation at the bottom, making it the final thing that a drinker would see upon draining the cup.[2] On the basis of initial glimpses of the head and upper body of the youth, in other words, one would never guess that such a shock was in store below. Clearly the tondo scene is related to the exterior, for in addition to the dog and youth, they share a sponge and aryballos hanging in the background, and a staff in the hand of the youth. Side A also includes another nude youth with staff, looking on from the left, and a strigil and pair of sandals suspended above the dog. Side B (Fig. 3) lacks a dog, but retains the nudity and accoutrements of the palaistra, here with three youths. Each wears the same apicate fillet seen in the tondo and on the other side, and they hold the following (from left to right): a folded himation; a staff and aryballos, strapped to his arm; and a strigil. In the field above is another aryballos (this one fragmentary), plus a pair of sandals and pair of shoes.

Formerly in the Hunt Collection, this cup has been explicitly discussed and illustrated in just three publications – once in an exhibition catalogue and twice in auction catalogues.[3] In each case, it has been presented as a fairly straightforward depiction of dog training, beginning in

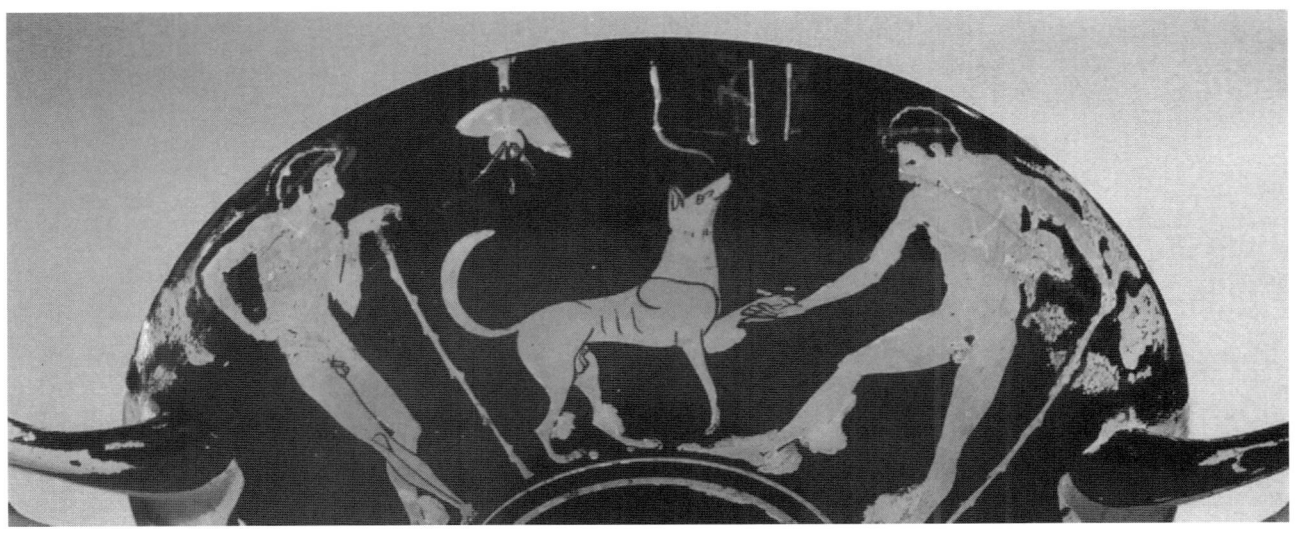

Fig. 1 Attic red-figure kylix by the Triptolemos Painter. Side A (after Sotheby's [n. 3]).

the tondo and completed on side A. It has even been suggested that the narrative may progress onto Side B, with the successful trainer, his work now complete, preparing to don his himation and move along.[4] At least one other work by the Triptolemos Painter – a Type B skyphos in Princeton, with a long jumper first preparing, then leaping – might also be read as a temporal narrative, but even here there is room for doubt, as Michael Padgett has shown; we might see one jumper preparing, another leaping.[5] Some would argue for an analogous reading of a cup by the same painter in Tampa – with an athlete first preparing the *skamma* and then stretching (or vice versa).[6] But even if we read them as narratives, these skyphoi have only two fields of decoration and were probably done a bit later in the painter's career, making them imperfect analogies for the former Hunt cup, which I believe need not be read in this way.[7]

Small differences between the decorative fields of the kylix suggest that the settings are related but not necessarily identical. For example, the items hung in the field differ slightly in each case, and the youth in the tondo is infibulated while those on the exterior are not. This last difference is perhaps especially significant, since Phrynichos tells us that *kynodesmai* (dog leashes) are "the things with which the Athenians tied up their private parts when they stripped, because they called the penis a dog".[8] In other words, the painter has created a visual pun in which the unleashed dog attacks the 'leashed' youth.[9]

But to return to the idea of narrative, it is important that on this cup, unlike the Princeton *glaux* with jumping (and unlike so many mythological vases showing episodes already well known to the viewer), we cannot be certain in which order to read the various scenes. Indeed, far more than any questions of narrative that it raises, this cup presents an opportunity to look more closely at a wide range of canine behavior on Greek vases, from bad to good and in between. For although dogs appear with great frequency on painted pottery, they often escape mention, even in basic descriptions of vases; canine iconography still awaits a comprehensive study.[10] This is not the place for that type of study, but rather an occasion to explore some of the more interesting dogs in Attic black- and red-figure, helping to place the former Hunt cup in a broader iconographical context.

To begin with the bad, the particularly offensive combination of dog attack and simultaneous defecation shown in the tondo is, as far as I can tell, unparalleled. In fact, my list of Greek vases with defecating dogs is quite short, comprising just this cup and three others. Moreover, it is not clear that all – or even any – of these dogs should be deemed 'bad' on account of their defecation. First on the list, chronologically speaking (ca. 540–530 BC), is a dog below the handle of an unattributed Droop cup in Athens (Fig. 4).[11] Decorated on both sides with banquet

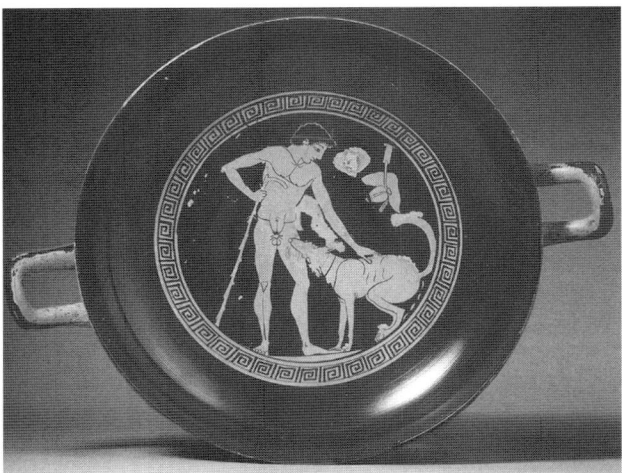

Fig. 2 Attic red-figure kylix by the Triptolemos Painter. Tondo (after Sotheby's [n. 3]).

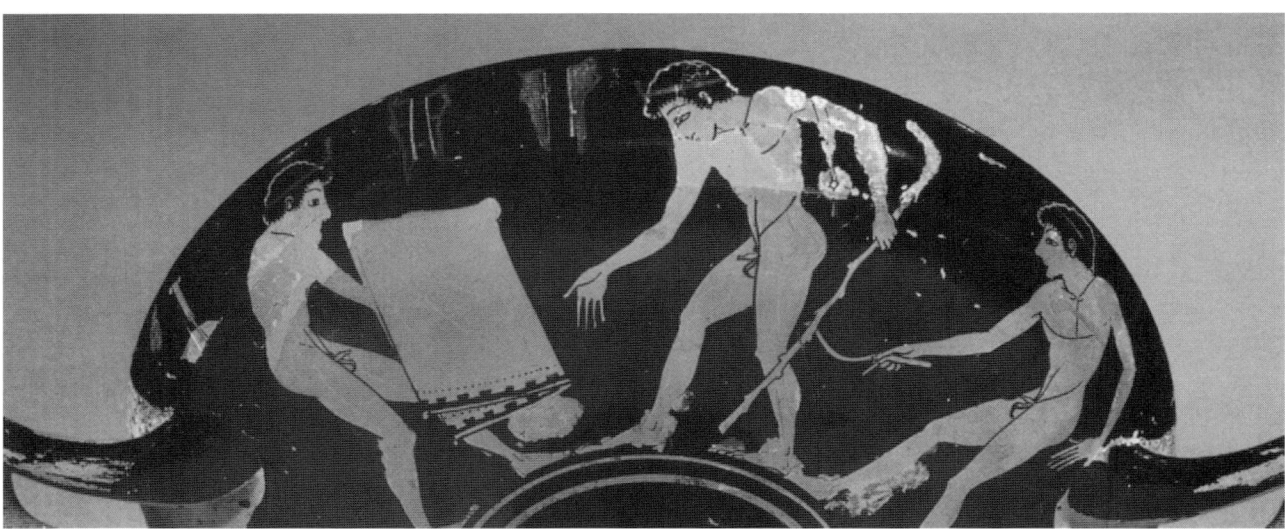

Fig. 3 Attic red-figure kylix by the Triptolemos Painter. Side B (after Sotheby's [n. 3]).

scenes, the cup actually includes three dogs: one beneath each handle, and another under the couch or banquet table on side B. This dog seems to be sniffing for food, like so many of the dogs on Greek vases – and these we shall turn to shortly.[12] But first the dogs beneath the handles – one wheeling around to look above and behind, the other squatting in profile with left forepaw raised, five black dots in a neat line beneath the rear end. Kallipolitis-Feytmans, author of the *CVA* entry for this cup, does not specifically mention these dots, perhaps because they so closely resemble those found around and between other figures on the cup; these she refers to, in general, and rightly, I think, as mock inscriptions. Martin Kilmer and Robert Develin follow Alan Boegehold in reading the five dots beneath the dog as feces, however, and this seems the logical interpretation.[13] In fact, with these dots placed so much more suggestively than the many others scattered about the cup, one wonders whether we ought to read something more, perhaps a special message beyond a randomly defecating dog. If the painter truly could not write letters, or viewed his literate colleagues and/or clients with disdain, he may have used these five carefully placed dots to draw an implicit parallel between vase inscriptions and the excrement of dogs.[14] Or, on a cup already full of revelers, perhaps the painter thought a defecating dog not so far out of place. It is also worth noting, however, that the dog attends to such needs beneath the handle, away from the main action of the party; in this sense, it is perhaps a good dog, as many people now refer to pets that void in appropriate places.[15]

To move now to the most famous – or infamous – defecating dogs of Attic painted pottery, we turn to an eye cup of Type A in Boston, attributed to the Amasis Painter (ca. 520 BC; Fig. 5).[16] Discussed more for its large and unusual male eye-siren on one side, and for the two reclining men masturbating on the other, the cup features a dog crouching beneath each handle. Just behind the pillow of a reveler on one side, and beyond the outstretched hand of the siren on the other, squats a dog, adding to an already outsized pile of excrement below. As Alexandre Mitchell has recently noted, these dogs act somewhat like ancient marginalia, adding to "the mixture of incongruous elements and visual puns" on the cup.[17] For Sir John Beazley, this cup was a response by Amasis to Exekias,[18] a sort of parody of the Type A eye cup recently invented by his colleague and rival.[19] Beazley does not mention the dogs themselves, but I think that he, like the Amasis Painter, must certainly have thought of these defecating dogs as integral components of the overall satire.[20] The effect, it seems, is an amplification of that just observed on the Athens Droop cup. In the world of Athenian black-figure, in other words, defecating dogs could be funny.

Chronologically speaking, the ex-Hunt cup comes next, a generation or so later. But we turn first to an unattributed red-figure skyphos in Tampa (Fig. 6). On this vessel, dating to about 470 BC (just later than the Triptolemos Painter's cup), the defecating dog is not nearly so explicit

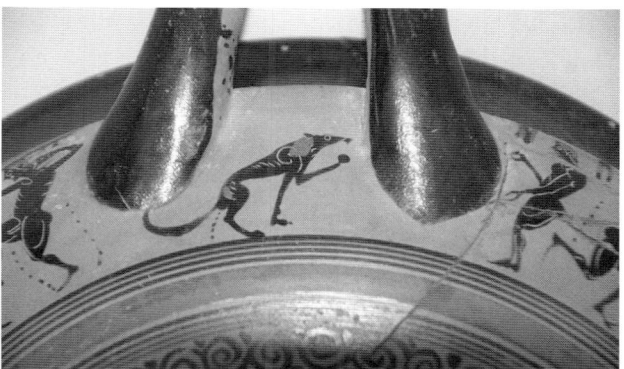

Fig. 4 Unattributed Attic black-figure Droop cup, National Archaeological Museum, Athens 359. Under Handle (Detail). © Hellenic Ministry of Education and Religious Affairs, Culture and Sports /Archaeological Receipts Fund.

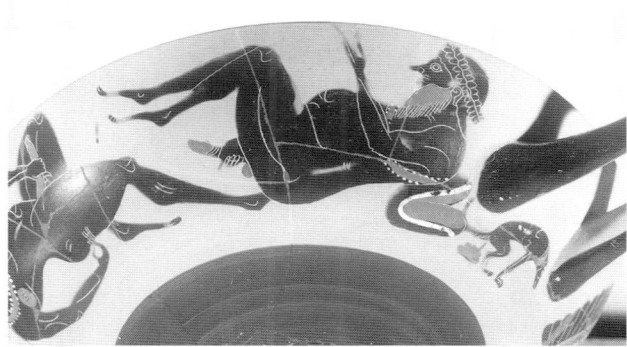

Fig. 5 Attic black-figure Eye-Siren cup by the Amasis Painter. Museum of Fine Arts, Boston 10.651, Gift of Edward Perry Warren, 1910. Under Handle (Detail). Photograph © 2013 Museum of Fine Arts, Boston.

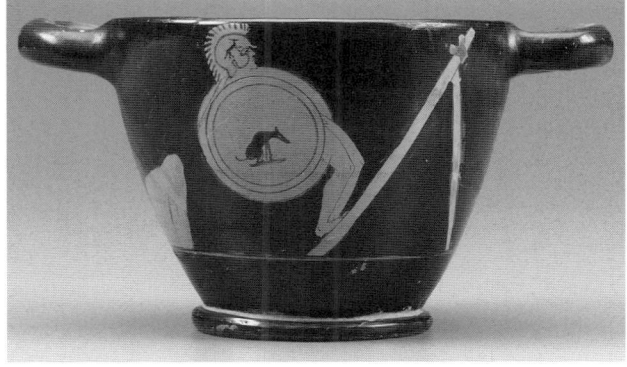

Fig. 6 Unattributed Attic red-figure skyphos. Tampa Museum of Art, Joseph Veach Noble Collection 1986.093. Side A. Photography by Eagle Photographics & Digital Imaging, Inc.

– not an actual figure in the scene, or even on the margins, but rather the silhouetted device on the facing shield of a helmeted acrobat.[21] The dog squats with nose down and tail raised, adopting the unambiguous position of canine defecation, even if no feces are actually shown.[22] The surprise of seeing this type of shield device is heightened by the contrast between the dog on the shield and the deer on the acrobat's helmet above. As with the leashed youth and unleashed dog of the Triptolemos Painter, here the images suggest a momentary role reversal, with the predator caught in a moment of vulnerability, the potential prey casually striding by. Indeed, the cup would be far less remarkable if the dog adorning the shield were not defecating, for canine shield devices are not especially uncommon on Athenian red-figure vases. Unlike the Tampa dog, however, most appear in the form of hunting or guard dogs, either standing in profile or crouching, as if about to pounce.[23] Dog heads alone can allow for more ferocious detail, as one might expect in the martial context of a shield, though here it is sometimes difficult to distinguish a dog from its wild cousin, the wolf.[24]

Perhaps more curious are several examples on which a canine *episema* takes the decidedly un-terrifying form of a little Maltese, the type of lapdog so favored in Athens in this period.[25] At times, this would seem to be ironic, as on a fragmentary cup in Paris by Skythes, who gives his leading *hoplitodromos* an appropriately athletic shield device, the laggard a cuddly lapdog (Fig. 7). Scholars differ as to whether Skythes actually was, as Boardman once termed him, "a comic by intention," but I think this shield device and at least two others by his hand are unambiguously ironic.[26] On a cup in Malibu recently published by David Saunders, for example, Skythes has given a fleeing warrior a shield paradoxically emblazoned with a charging peltast, itself an echo of a figure in Thracian garb on the opposite side of the cup.[27] Similarly, he adorned the shield of a *hoplitodromos* in Cambridge with a fox gorging on grapes, quite contrary to the famous fable attributed to Aesop.[28]

Going back to the cup in Paris (Fig. 7), Skythes' unexpected juxtaposition of cuddly companion borne by allegedly strapping athlete may be seen as a sort of parallel for the unusual dog on the shield of the Tampa acrobat-warrior (Fig. 6). For this figure, perched on an inclined board, we cannot be sure of the precise context, but he seems to be preparing for some sort of acrobatic feat, perhaps a back-flip. The figure seems connected with the aulete approaching a potter's wheel on the other side of the cup, and this would seem to belong to a number of vases showing some sort of performance possibly connected with the Panathenaia, whether officially or otherwise.[29] A somewhat analogous performer on a pseudo-Panathenaic amphora in Paris holds two shields unusually adorned with concentric crescents, a motif which Francois Lissarrague has suggested "accentuates the twirling effect of the exercise".[30] On the vase in Tampa, there is no twirling effect, but the unusual pose of the dog emblazoned on his shield might accentuate – in a very different way – the equally odd pose of the acrobat. If not an official event but rather a diversion from serious competition, perhaps the unusual shield device added to the levity of the occasion.[31]

If a defecating dog was somehow seen as humorous, as seems likely on the basis of these cups in Athens, Boston, and Tampa, what about one that bites (or that does both, as on the Triptolemos Painter's cup)? Every dog owner knows well that a dog must void, but no dog need bite a human, and this may not at first glance seem either funny or ironic. Certainly dog attacks must have happened in ancient Athens, as they still sometimes do wherever man and dog share space, but as Louise Calder points out in an important recent monograph surveying Greek attitudes to animals, neither literary accounts nor material culture provide much evidence of ancient dog aggression.[32] Calder goes on to cite the story of Aktaion as the most famous ancient instance of a dog attack, and the tondo of our cup certainly brings that tale to mind, as we can see by comparison to numerous Greek vases showing Aktaion.[33] But there is no sign of incipient antlers on the youth in the tondo of the Triptolemos Painter's cup, nor of the goddess Artemis, nor of the other hunting dogs one would expect in such a scene. The athletic kit and other indications of a *palaistra* setting also seem to place the bad dog outside the realm of myth; so too the good dog on the exterior.[34] As an example of non-mythological bad dogs, both Mitchell and Calder have recently cited the pair of fighting dogs in an oil shop on a black-figure pelike in Florence.[35] One lekythos is already broken, another knocked over, as a result of the dogfight. This is certainly bad behavior, but the only visible aggression is between the two dogs, not toward a human being as in the Aktaion tale and on the ex-Hunt cup.

Both authors cite other examples of badly behaved dogs as well, but not of such an aggressive sort. Dogs are often characterized as thieves, for example, stealing food from banqueters and even from butchers or other men preparing meat – perhaps for sacrifice, as Mitchell has suggested for a black-figure olpe in Heidelberg.[36] Mitchell also cites a black-figure amphora with dogs apparently stealing from an altar, and the only question here is whether the vase – and with it perhaps the dogs – is Attic or Etruscan.[37] As Calder points out, this type of thieving seen on vases corresponds in a general way to a number of incidents in the comedies of Aristophanes.[38] If these chronologies do

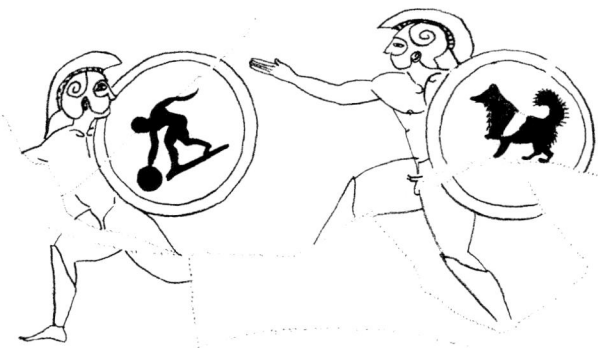

Fig. 7 Attic red-figure kylix by Skythes. Musée du Louvre, Paris G76. Side A (Detail drawing, by author).

not precisely align, there are also thieving dogs in Aesopic fables that may well date earlier (though dates for these fables are notoriously difficult to fix).[39] In one such tale we hear of an unwanted dog thrown out of a dinner party by the chef,[40] and since dogs appear so frequently beneath banquet couches and tables on vases, it is worth looking at a few of them in a bit more detail.

On a pointed amphora attributed to the Acheloos Painter and now in Basel, for example, we see three dogs beneath three different couches: the first lying in wait, raising a paw and eying a strip of meat; the second gnawing on a bone, whether stolen, dropped, or gifted; and the third also gnawing on a bone, perhaps with an eye to the meat above.[41] Given the raucous nature of the party taking place above, with one reveler vomiting and others absorbed in their music and drinking, the dogs would seem to have little to fear in the way of reprisal. Some three additional thieving dogs by the same painter take similar advantage of distracted banqueters: one on either side of an amphora in Havana; and another on an amphora in Würzburg, although here the gesture of the woman at right suggests that she may be about to intervene.[42]

In red-figure, although dogs beneath couches occur frequently enough, few are so brazen as to steal. Perhaps the best unequivocal example occurs on a fragmentary bell krater once on the Swiss market, where a single dog grabs a strip of meat from a table before a couch.[43] On a slightly earlier column krater, now in Milan, the Leningrad Painter included two dogs, one already eating, the other inching its nose closer to the scraps above. Here the dog need not steal, but only nose up to a playful young symposiast wearing the ass ears of King Midas; looking away from the game of *kottabos*, this boy seems to offer tidbits from above.[44] The interaction also brings to mind the sort of 'handshake' between dog and master with which we began on the former Hunt cup – an action that people take today as a sign of the best of dogs, so well trained that they can shake on command. On Athenian vases this canine-human 'handshake' is, as far as I can tell, unparalleled, although Timothy McNiven pointed out to me two examples of apparently very good dogs raising one paw, perhaps preparing to "shake".[45]

Much more common is the image of a person – most often a man or youth – holding one hand aloft, presumably with a morsel of food, while the dog below rears up to grab it. A good example occurs in a fragmentary cup tondo in Brussels by the Brygos Painter, where a himation-clad youth stands to right above a leaping Maltese (Fig. 8; Color Pl. 21A).[46] We see such dogs similarly poised before women and children as well, as on a lekythos by the Providence Painter in Rome and a chous decorated in Six's Technique in Cambridge, Massachusetts.[47] Whether these postures represent moments of teasing or training we cannot be sure, but even with small dogs the former would not likely have been a safe possibility had the dogs not previously been trained. Dogs posed dutifully alongside warriors or hunters also hint at training, as do collars and leashes on numerous vases (including the ex-Hunt cup),[48] but unambiguous scenes of dog training remain elusive.

The name vase of the Cat and Dog Painter, a red-figure cup dated before the middle of the fifth century, has been cited in this regard,[49] but here, too, the issue of training is more implicit than explicit. The decoration of the cup, which also bears two *kalos* names, seems much more concerned with beautiful young men and their love gifts than with the training of animals. Like the hare in the tondo and the cock on side B, the cat on side A would seem to be a present, held on a leash atop a stool by the nude youth to whom it was given. José Dörig, author of the most complete publication of the cup, rightly notes this theme, although – as Louise Calder has recently noted – he perhaps overstates the rarity of the cat, suggesting that the dog is staring at it in wonder.[50] Rather than signifying astonishment at such an unusual creature, we might read the good posture of the unleashed dog as an indication of its fine training and self-control. This is perhaps reinforced by the gestures of the man and youth, lest the situation escalate to something like that seen on the famous "Cat and Dog" statue base in Athens. If the dog on this base is "eager yet hesitant" in its attack – as G. M. A. Richter once described it – the cat is clearly fearful, arching its back and inching away.[51] To judge from the human spectators, all leaning in with great interest, both cat and dog are behaving as expected. Douris has given us a similar pairing on a cup once in the Hirschmann collection, but with a decidedly fiercer dog and a curiously canine-looking cheetah. Although the figures are partially lacking, they seem somewhat less pleased than their carved counterparts on the statue base

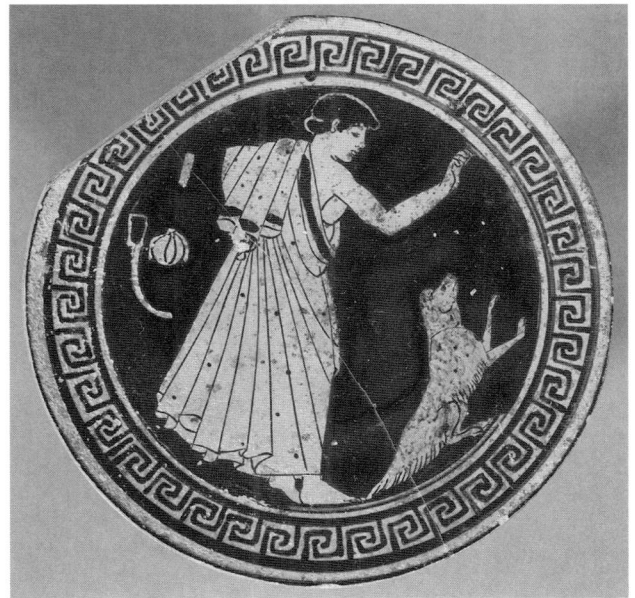

Fig. 8 Tondo of an Attic red-figure kylix by the Brygos Painter. Musées Royaux d'Art et d'Histoire, Bruxelles R350. Photograph: Museum.

– the man at left appearing flustered, the figure at right perhaps about to flee.[52] On another related vase, a red-figure pelike attributed to the Tyszkiewicz Painter, a large cat, again probably a cheetah, rears up towards a seated dog. For Calder, this dog is "exceedingly disconcerted," but to me he seems quite well behaved, particularly under the circumstances: nicely seated, tail raised.[53] The Tyszkiewicz Painter drew another interesting dog on his amphora in The Hague, genuinely interested either in the herm or in the supplicating gesture that the man makes toward it.[54] Perhaps we can understand this dog as doubly faithful, both to his master and to the god.

Among the most common scenes including dogs on Greek vases are those of homosexual courting, and here they are often quite well behaved. A pelike from very late in the career of the Triptolemos Painter (Fig. 9), perhaps about 470 BC, provides a good example. The dog stands calmly and looks up at a youth receiving a hare.[55] On another late pelike, the Triptolemos Painter shows a courtship advanced well beyond gift-giving, the hare held high by the *eromenos* and a dog sitting quietly by, its good behavior apparently enforced by a tightly held leash.[56] On each of these vases, from the same hand as the cup with which we started (but painted a decade or two later), both hare and hound have been interpreted as gifts associated with the courtship. Indeed, as Richard Neer has pointed out in his *CVA* entry for the former vase, now in Malibu, "the grouping of lovers, a hare, and a hound is a conceit that, in red-figure, goes back at least as far as the Gotha cup".[57] On that cup, of course, the hound leaps up along the tondo, apparently toward the caged hare. A Maltese on a courting cup in Munich by Douris also leaps up along the tondo, though looking back at the copulating couple.[58] Despite these small differences, both dogs recall the leaping Maltese on the aforementioned cup in Brussels (Fig. 8; Color Pl. 21A). There, as on the lekythos and chous also mentioned above, the dog seems to leap at a tasty morsel, but the athletic kit hanging in the background reminds us that dogs, whether as companions or courting gifts, spent time in the *palaistra*. There they could be enticed not only by food, but also by *gloios*, the accumulation of oil, sweat, and dirt that athletes scraped off their bodies by means of a strigil following exercise. We see this quite explicitly on another kylix by the Brygos Painter, this one in Boston, as Caskey and Beazley noted many years ago (Fig. 10).[59] Similarly, on a kalpis in Berlin by the Triptolemos Painter (probably painted after the ex-Hunt cup, but before the pelikai just discussed), a Maltese bares its teeth and appears to sniff the ground, probably intrigued by the mixture cleaned off the strigil by the youth at left (Fig. 11).[60]

A youth on a cup in Florence in the manner of the Tarquinia Painter performs the same task, and while the dog beside him does little, standing rather idly, its petite size and lack of ferocity make possible a sort of pun linking the *kalos*-inscription of the tondo to the imagery. Thus, as noted by Esposito and De Tommaso, *Lykos kalos* may refer perhaps not so much to a youth named Lykos as to the Maltese, a sort of "piccolo volpino".[61] Dogs on other cups also show special interest in strigils, and before we scorn the dogs for fascination with what might strike

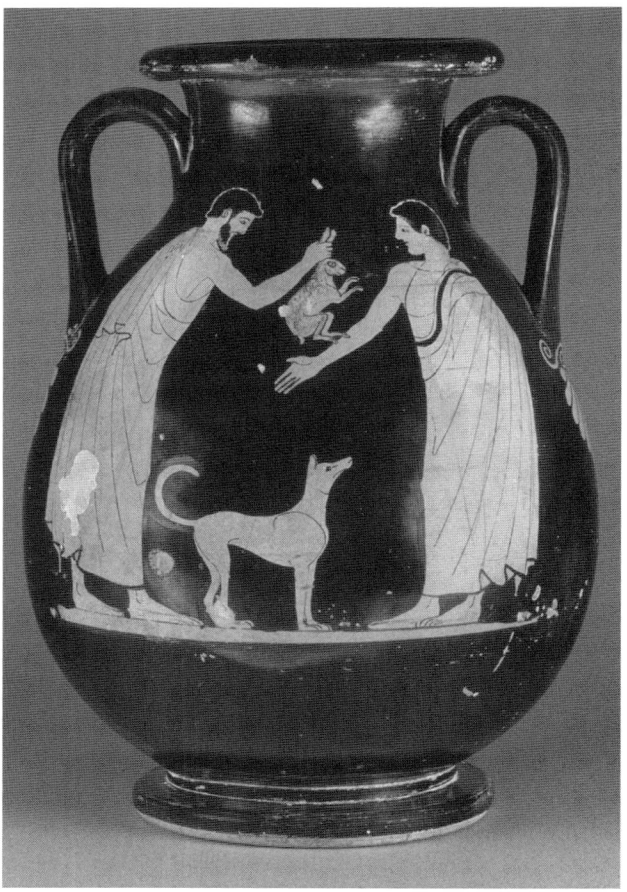

Fig. 9 Attic red-figure pelike by the Triptolemos Painter, J. Paul Getty Museum 86.AE.195. Photograph: Museum.

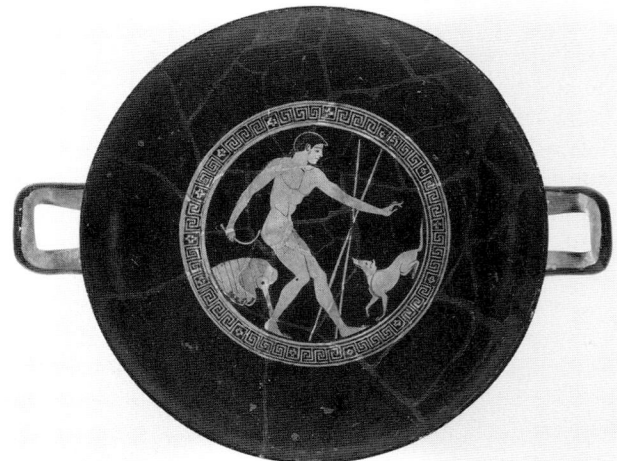

Fig. 10 Kylix by the Brygos Painter. Museum of Fine Arts, Boston 01.8038, Henry Lillie Pierce Fund. Photograph © 2013 Museum of Fine Arts, Boston.

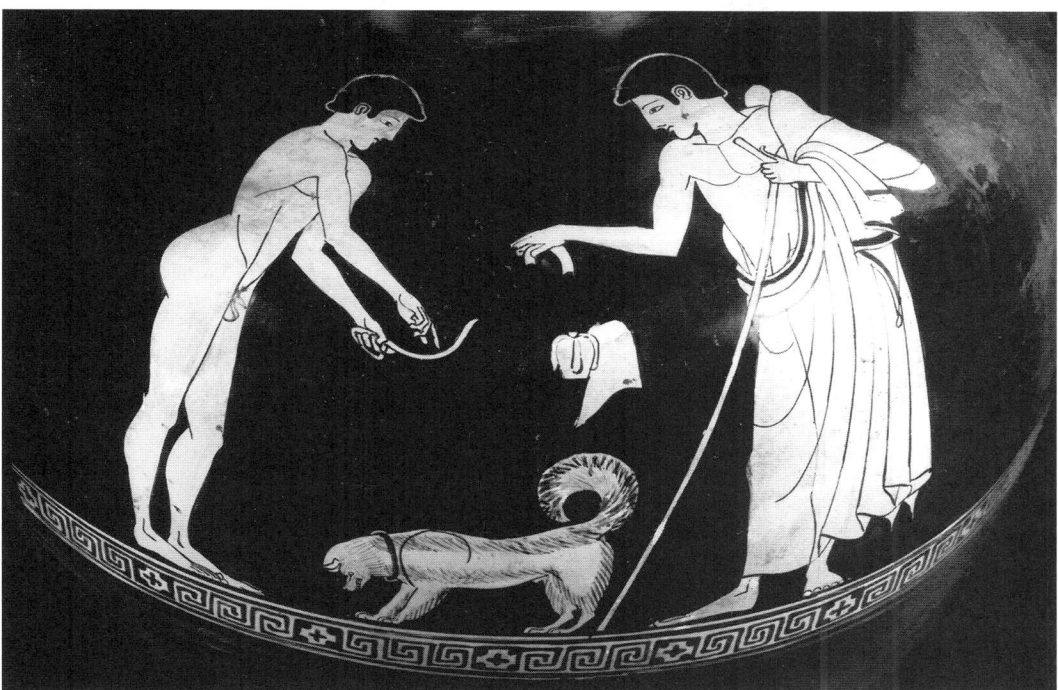

Fig. 11 Attic red-figure kalpis by the Triptolemos Painter. Shoulder (Detail). Antikensammlung. Staatliche Museen zu Berlin, F 2178; Photography by Johannes Laurentius.

us as an unappealing blend, it is worth recalling that many humans also held *gloios* in high esteem, selling it for great sums and touting its medicinal powers.[62] Moreover, for dogs, whose sense of smell is many times more sensitive than that of humans, this material must have held a great deal of information, especially because much of the unique smell of a given individual derives from his or her sweat.[63] For the dog on a Proto-Panaitian cup apparently much intrigued by his master's vomit, a similar explanation can probably be sought, even if we find the behavior still more repugnant (and perhaps the lowered tail of the dog shows his own displeasure).[64]

As pointed out by Caskey and Beazley in their discussion of the Boston Brygan cup, a similar motif with dog and strigil appears on a roughly contemporaneous grave relief from Delphi.[65] In fact, the appearance on such monuments of a dog alongside man or youth is quite common, beginning with the so-called "Man-and-Dog stelai" in the Late Archaic period. Whatever their origin (whether Attic, Ionic, East Greek, or otherwise), these stelai remain a common type well into the Classical period, especially in Attica, with the lap dog eventually joining the hunting dog as worthy companion to the deceased.[66] Dogs on stelai often look or even leap up for food in the hand of a master, or nose around for it on the ground, but never – so far as I have found – do they blatantly misbehave in the manner seen on certain vases. This should not be surprising, of course, given the much higher relative expense of a stele, and its intended use as lasting marker for the deceased.

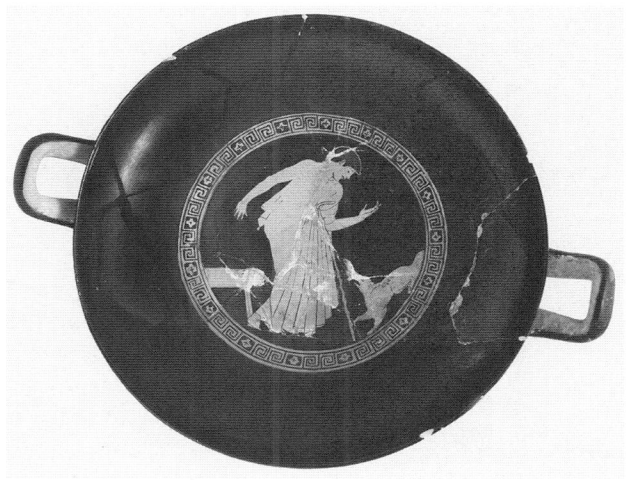

Fig. 12 Attic red-figure kylix by the Brygos Painter. Copyright © Phoebe A. Hearst Museum of Anthropology and the Regents of the University of California, Photography by Alicja Egbert, Catalogue No. 8-921.

On a painted ceramic vase, on the other hand, humor was a viable objective, as Alexandre Mitchell has recently shown so well.[67] Thus, with many well-behaved dogs in mind, whether from real life or from their appearance in a variety of artistic media, a vase painter could use the occasional badly behaved dog as a surprising and humorous contrast. This may explain why the Maltese grabbing the staff of a youth on a cup in Berkeley (Fig.

12; Color Pl. 21B) – and pulling quite hard, as Mary Moore has recently pointed out – strikes us as funny, particularly given that the same artist – the Brygos Painter – has given us other, more agreeable dogs (e.g., Figs. 8. 12; Color Pl. 21A–B).[68] Likewise, the comical image on a cup in Vienna, with the god Hermes approaching an altar accompanied by a dog disguised as a pig (or vice versa?), gains more traction in light of a pair of cups from the same hand showing a hound as noble companion to a debonair man.[69] Just so, I suggest, the Triptolemos Painter, an artist who shows a soft spot for dogs throughout his career, has shown effectively on the former Hunt cup how these animals can both disgust (Fig. 1) and delight us (Fig. 2; Color Pl. 21C) – a message that rings as true for dog owners today as for our forebears so many centuries ago.

Acknowledgements

I thank my family for their support, and John Oakley for the invitation to participate in this conference and volume. In addition, I am grateful to the conference attendees in Williamsburg and to audiences in Tampa and Gainesville, Florida, for many helpful questions and insights.

Notes

1 BAPD 8843, unknown to Beazley; additional references listed below (n. 3).
2 I thank Mark Stansbury-O'Donnell for this insight.
3 Summa Galleries. Auction Catalogue 1. 18, September 1981, lot 10. D. von Bothmer et al. (eds.), Wealth of the Ancient World: The Nelson Bunker Hunt and William Herbert Hunt Collections (1983) cat. 11. Sotheby's, Antiquities. New York, 19 June 1990, lot 11. More recently published images of the cup suggest that it may be housed today in the Villa Giulia in Rome, following its seizure together with thousands of other antiquities from the Geneva warehouse of Giacomo Medici, but I have been unable to confirm this with the Villa Giulia. I thank Timothy McNiven for the following references to photographs of the cup in this context: E. Bensard, Archéologia 430, February 2006, 18–22; A. Slayman, Geneva Seizure, Archaeology Magazine online feature, last update 14.09.1998, story <http://archive.archaeology.org/online/features/geneva/index.html>; photograph <http://archive.archaeology.org/online/features/geneva/captions/63.html> (16.01.2013).
4 von Bothmer et al. (supra n. 3) 71: "SIDE B. BATHING SCENE. The central figure in this side also wears the red fillet and carries a staff like the trainer in the other two scenes. He may be the same man at his bath".
5 J. Michael Padgett, Record of the Art Museum, Princeton University 61, 2002, 37–48 (40–42 for this cup).
6 Tampa Museum of Art, Joseph Veach Noble Collection 1986.092. ARV² 367,102. BAPD 203894. Padgett (supra n. 5) 42 fig. 6.
7 It is worth noting a remark penned by J. R. Guy (The Triptolemos Painter, M.A. thesis [University of Cincinnati, 1974] 62) with regard to the Tampa cup (then still with Noble) and one in Berlin with satyr on either side (ARV² 367,105): "their decorative schemes are minor violations of a rule formulated in chapter 3: that the Triptolemos Painter never allows one scene to be read continuously round the vase, that he respects the natural division of the surface by the handle zone".
8 For more on *kynodesmai*, see S. Miller, Ancient Greek Athletics (2004) 12–13 and Phrynichos 85 (Miller [supra] 13). For a youth by the Triptolemos Painter actually in the act of infibulating, see New York MMA 14.105.7; BAPD 203873, ARV² 366,81.
9 I thank Timothy McNiven for this insight.
10 For the most recent work on dogs on Greek vases, with extensive bibliography, see L. Calder. Cruelty and Sentimentality: Greek Attitudes to Animals 600–300 BC (2011); M. B. Moore, MetrMusJ 43, 2008, 11–37 and M. Iozzo, RdA 36, 2012 (2013), 5–22.
11 Athens, National Museum 359 (CC821). CVA Athens 3 Greece 3 50 pls. 40. 41; BAPD 43016 (not in ABV). I thank G. Kavvadias for photographs.
12 D. Callipolitis-Feytmans notes on side A (CVA [supra n. 11]), "table servie, d'où pend une branche de vigne". On side B, no mention of the table is made, but both couch and table resemble those on the other side, perhaps again with bunches of grapes hanging down.
13 M. Kilmer – R. Develin, The Amasis Painter: Erotica, Scatologica and Inscriptions, Electronic Antiquity 2.1, 1994, last update 24.02.2012 <http://scholar.lib.vt.edu/ejournals/ElAnt/V2N1/kilmer.html> (17.01.2013) n. 20, citing personal communication with Boegehold. Kilmer and Develin describe the position of the dog, but not the dots of feces, while Boegehold (CAVI entry 0704) lists simply "A, B, each: nonsense: a large number of rows of dots". I am grateful to William Knight Zewadski for alerting me to Kilmer and Develin's article, and thereby to this cup. That the dog raises its forepaw to adopt an unlikely sort of posture for the act of defecation should not be surprising on a cup full of exuberant komasts in unusual postures, often with one or both feet positioned well above the ground-line.
14 Even on other vases with dogs and copious mock inscriptions, I have yet to find a precise parallel for this one. Perhaps closest are the dogs attacking a boar on either side of a black-figure cup from a private collection, but the artist here has not positioned either dogs or dots as suggestively as on the Droop cup in Athens: W. Hornbostel (ed.), Aus der Glanzzeit Athens. Meisterwerke griechischer Vasenkunst in Privatbesitz (1986) 40–41 cat. 4; BAPD 16051.
15 Numerous conference attendees and audience members made this point to me, too many to acknowledge individually.
16 Boston, Museum of Fine Arts, 10.651, Gift of Edward Perry Warren, 1910. ABV 157,86; BAPD 310515. I thank P. Segal for photographs of this cup and Fig. 10 below.
17 A. Mitchell. Greek Vase-painting and the Origins of Visual Humour (2009) 43–44 figs. 8a. b.
18 As cited by D. von Bothmer. The Amasis Painter and his World. Vase-Painting in Sixth-Century B.C. Athens (1985) 221–222 cat. 61. Unlike Mitchell [supra n. 17], von Bothmer sees the eye-siren as male.
19 J. D. Beazley. The Development of Attic Black-Figure (1986) 56–57. The cup of Exekias is Munich 2044 (ABV

20 If sheer numbers necessitated brevity for Beazley's descriptions in ABV, ARV², etc., the same cannot be said for The Development of Attic Black-Figure (supra n. 19). Rather, it seems that Beazley omitted reference to defecating dogs as a nod to modesty, just as he made no explicit mention of masturbation, referring instead simply to "the effrontery of the picture on the other half" (56); in ABV, he resorted to the Greek *dephomenoi* (though no *chezontes* for the dogs, which receive no remark at all). For the act of *chezein* in Attic black-figure, see M. Iozzo. Ceramica attica a figure nere, Monumenti, musei e gallerie pontificie vasi antichi dipinti del Vaticano, La collezione Astarita nel Museo gregoriano etrusco 2, 1 (2002) 203–204 n. 4 (with cat. 288). I thank Mario Iozzo for this reference. See also B. Cohen – H. A. Shapiro, in: A. J. Clark – J. Gaunt (eds.), Essays in Honor of Dietrich von Bothmer (2002) 83–90.

21 Tampa Museum of Art, Joseph Veach Noble Collection 1986.093. BAPD 9054. A third concentric circle passing behind the figure makes clear that he holds another shield on his left arm.

22 It is not clear to me why Kilmer and Develin (supra n. 14) suggest that this dog has diarrhea.

23 Many additional instances of dog blazons on Athenian red-figure vases can now be added to the three listed over a century ago by G. H. Chase, HarvStClPhil 13, 1902, 103 (XCIII.2–4), including one recently discovered in the Athenian Kerameikos (inv. 4845) which will be published by Heide Freilinghaus. One of those listed by Chase, a kantharos by Douris in Brussels, actually depicts the dog somewhat awkwardly: BAPD 205305 (Douris, Brussels A718, ARV² 445,256 = Chase [supra] 103 XCIII.3). A few examples of the more usual type on roughly contemporaneous cups: BAPD 200731 (Euergides Painter: Toledo 1961.25, ARV² 90,36); BAPD 201440 (Painter of Berlin 2268: Cambridge 37.16, ARV² 155,37); BAPD 203902 (Brygos Painter, Louvre G154, ARV² 369,3); BAPD 204538 (Painter of Louvre G265: Leiden PC75, ARV² 416,7); BAPD 206929 (Niobid Painter, Bologna 18108, ARV² 598,1). For additional bibliography on shield blazons, see D. Saunders, Getty Research Journal 4, 2012, 9 n. 6.

24 Dog/Wolf head blazons: BAPD 205229 (Douris, Florence 3960, ARV² 441,184); BAPD 215777 (Painter of Munich 2332, Florence 4020, ARV² 1192,3); BAPD 275130 (with inscription; Goettingen Painter; Brindisi, ARV² 1638,10bis). For examples and distinguishing characteristics of dogs and wolves, see Calder (supra n. 10) 67–74, with associated catalogue entries.

25 Maltese blazons: BAPD 200676 (Skythes, Louvre G76, ARV² 84,16); BAPD 203841 (Triptolemos Painter, Vatican 629/16537, ARV² 364,49; Guy (supra n. 7) Period 3 [Middle]); BAPD 204502 (Dokimasia Painter, Hermitage B657, ARV² 413,19); perhaps BAPD 214641 (Nausicaa Painter, Marseilles 3198/7198, ARV² 1107,3).

26 J. Boardman, Athenian Red Figure Vases, The Archaic Period (1975) 59, with additional quotation from J. D. Beazley, Attic Red-Figured Vases in American Museums (1918) 21: Skythes "purposely paints men worse than they are". *Pace* M. Robertson, The Art of Vase-painting in Classical Athens (1992) 39: "[Skythes'] little figures have sometimes a comic look to us, but it is doubtful if that was intended".

27 Saunders (supra n. 23) 1–12. The cup is Getty 83.AE.247.

28 Fitzwilliam Museum 48.1864 (ARV² 85,23; BAPD 200685). I am grateful to David Saunders for this reference. The fable is "The Fox and the Grapes" (Babrius 19).

29 J. Neils (ed.), Goddess and Polis. The Panathenaic Festival in Ancient Athens (1992) 96. 176 cat. 47. See also P. Russell, Ceramics and Society. Making and Marketing Ancient Greek Pottery (1994) 15 cat. 2 with further bibliography.

30 F. Lissarrague, Greek Vases. The Athenians and their Images, trans. K. Allen (2001) 77 fig. 63. The vase is Paris, Cabinet des Médailles 243 (BAPD 1047). For other "whirligig" shield devices, cf. mounted warriors on a late Middle Corinthian column krater in Providence (inv. 62.059; A. Ashmead – K. Phillips, Jr., Classical Vases. Excluding Attic Black-Figure, Attic Red-Figure and Attic White Ground. Museum of Art, Rhode Island School of Design (1976) 20–21 cat. 16).

31 That entertainment was the primary goal of the two men on the Tampa skyphos would perhaps be further supported if we could confirm that the pipe-player on the opposite side intends to use the potter's wheel as a stage, thereby increasing the degree of difficulty of his performance. For other performers on potter's wheels, see Neils and Russell (supra n. 29). For another canine *episema* with possible humorous intent, see Palermo 2104/1517/V652 (Oltos, ARV² 47,151; 57,38; BAPD 200630), where Oltos has painted a dog with unusually prominent penis.

32 Calder (supra n. 10) 70.

33 Cf., e.g., the name vase of the Pan Painter, slightly later in date (Boston 10.185; ARV² 550,1; BAPD 206276).

34 As an aside, it is worth noting that the dogs of Aktaion can be understood as behaving precisely as trained – i.e., by attacking their prey, since Aktaion had, by the moment of the attack, been transformed by Artemis. Cf. L. Lacy, JHS 110, 1990, 39: "The outraged Artemis gives Aktaion the outward appearance of his erstwhile quarry and offering and thereby instigates the hounds' aggression". Lacy also provides a useful discussion of the transgression of Aktaion, based on various accounts in ancient sources.

35 Florence 72732; BAPD 9458, 15585; Calder (supra n. 10) 70 cat. 181; Mitchell (supra n. 17) 56–57 fig. 17.

36 Heidelberg, Ruprecht-Karls-Universitat 253; BAPD 10598. Mitchell (supra n. 17) 50. 54–58.

37 Mitchell (n. 17) 58 n. 81 (as Attic, 530–520 BC, but citing Das Tier in der Antike [1974] 54 pl. 56 cat. 325, which lists the vase as Etruscan, ca. 500 BC).

38 Calder (supra n. 10) 69–70.

39 Mitchell (supra n. 17) 58 cites "The dog and the butcher" (Chambry 1958: Fab. 254), and there is also "The dog and his shadow" (Babrius Fab. 79; cf. also Phaedrus Fab. 4). On Aesop and Aesopic portraiture and iconography, including in Athenian vase-painting, see F. Lissarrague, in: B. Cohen (ed.), Not the Classical Ideal. Athens and the Construction of the Other in Greek Art (2000) 132–149.

40 Babrius, Fab. 42: "The Departure of a Well-Sated Guest".

41 Basel BS 2405. I am grateful to J. Michael Padgett for reminding me of this vase.

42 Havana 219, ABV 383,15; 483,2; BAPD 302860. Würzburg HA175/L207; ABV 383,14; BAPD 302859.
43 As J. Robert Guy discovered, a joining fragment in the Louvre gives the rest of the scene — Herakles at the house of Dexamenos, with the centaur Eurytion presumably asking for the hand of the king's daughter, Mnesimache. I am grateful to Francois Lissarrague and J. Michael Padgett for alerting me to Guy's join of the fragmentary krater (formerly with Cahn) and the Louvre fragment (G345, attributed to the Nausicaa Painter: ARV² 1108,16; BAPD 214655); see also T. Gantz, Early Greek Myth. A Guide to Literary and Artistic Sources I (1993) 423–424.
44 Milano, Banca Intesa 13/354 (ex Torno), ARV² 567,4; BAPD 206491.
45 Eucharides Painter, stamnos, Copenhagen, National Museum 124: ARV² 229,35; BAPD 202230. Harrow Painter, pelike, Louvre Cp 10789: ARV² 274,32; BAPD 202868. Although each shows a dog with raised paw, neither of these vases shows a human quite ready to reciprocate.
46 Brussels, Musées Royaux d'Art et d'Histoire R350: ARV² 377,99; BAPD 3997. I thank N. Massar for the photograph. For *felines* tempted by meat on Greek vases, see the short listing by A. Ashmead, in: R. D. De Puma – J. P. Small (eds.), Murlo and the Etruscans. Art and Society in Ancient Etruria (1993) 146.
47 The lekythos is Accademia di Lincei 2478, ARV² 642,107; BAPD 207462, labeled "a novelty" for its playfulness (K. Bulas, JHS 72, 1952, 119). The chous is Harvard Art Museums/Arthur M. Sackler Museum, Loan from Estate of Donald Upham and Mrs R. U. Hunter, 24.1908; BAPD 13419. Cf. also the choes in Karlsruhe (Badisches Landesmuseum 271; BAPD 12474) and Basel (Antikenmuseum und Sammlung Ludwig BS 1941.122; BAPD 16283), each with youth and Maltese similarly poised: teasing/training in Karlsruhe; imminent crowning with wreath in Basel (CVA Basel 3 Switzerland 7 68). On Maltese dogs more generally, see most recently Moore (supra n. 10) 16–18 and Calder (supra n. 10) 83–84; et passim, both with bibliography.
48 For a very fine example of a well-behaved hunting dog with collar, see the red-figure lekythos by the Pan Painter in Boston (13.198; ARV² 557,113; BAPD 206356). For the question of whether this is "just a hunter, or … a particular hunter," namely Kephalos, see CB II 54 cat. 97.
49 E.g. Sotheby's (supra n. 3). The cup is said to be in a Zurich private collection (ARV² 866,1; BAPD 211392).
50 J. Dörig, Art Antique. Collections privées de Suisse romande (1975) cat. 215; Calder (supra n. 10) 85 cat. 227 with bibliography.
51 G. M. A. Richter, Animals in Greek Sculpture. A Survey (1930) 31. 77. fig. 175. See also Calder (supra n. 10) 85 cat. 226. The statue base is Athens NM 3477, ca. 510 BC.
52 BAPD 7242. Calder (supra n. 10) 86 cat. 201, with bibliography.
53 Boulogne, Musée Communale 134, ARV² 293,47; BAPD 203021. Calder (supra n. 10) 82 cat. 209
54 The Hague, Gemeente Museum 2026, ARV² 292,32; BAPD 203006. On vases showing supplication of herms, see T. McNiven, in: D. Yatromanolakis (ed.), An Archaeology of Representations. Ancient Greek Vase-Painting and Contemporary Methodologies (2009) 298–324 (esp. 316–19). I thank Timothy McNiven for this reference.
55 Para 364,21bis; BAPD 275939, J. Paul Getty Museum 86.AE.195.
56 Mykonos 7, from Rheneia, ARV² 362,21; BAPD 203813; also ARV² 280,18 for the other side (attributed to the Flying-Angel Painter).
57 CVA Malibu 7 USA 32 21; the "Gotha cup" is Gotha, Schlossmuseum 48 (ARV² 20, top; BAPD 200100).
58 Munich, Antikensammlungen 2631, ARV² 443,224; BAPD 205269.
59 Boston 01.8038, ARV² 376,93; BAPD 203991; CB I 24–25 cat. 28.
60 Berlin Antikensammlung F2178, from Vulci; ARV² 362,24; BAPD 203815. I thank U. Kästner for the photograph.
61 Florence, Museo Archeological Nazionale 4220, ARV² 872,23; BAPD 211513; A. M. Esposito – G. de Tommaso (eds.), Vasi Attici (1993) 69. On Lykos as a *kalos*-name, see further ARV² 1595–1596.
62 S. Miller, Arete. Greek Sports from Ancient Sources (2004) 18. 218 with references to Plin. HN 15.4.19; 28.50–52, and SEG 27.261.
63 S. Coren. How Dogs Think. What the World Looks Like to Them and Why They Act the Way They Do (2004) 66–67. 83. It is worth noting that dogs generally lack the human sensitivity to (and craving for) salty tastes, suggesting that their interest in *gloios* would have been one of scent rather than taste. See also A. Horowitz, Inside of a Dog. What Dogs See, Smell, and Know (2009) 67–78 with additional references at 309–310.
64 Paris, Musée du Louvre G25, ARV² 316,5; 1592; BAPD 203243. For a list of other scenes of vomiting on Attic vases compiled by Mary Moore, updating that in CB I 23, see CVA Malibu 8 USA 33 28–29.
65 CB I 25. Delphi 330.
66 D. Woysch-Méautis, La representation des animaux et des êtres fabuleux sur les monuments funéraires grecs de l'époque Archaïque à la fin du IVe siècle av. J.-C., Cahiers d'archeologie romande 21 (1982) 53–60. 124–130 with bibliography.
67 Mitchell (supra n. 17).
68 Berkeley, Phoebe A. Hearst Museum of Anthropology 8–921; ARV² 377,96; BAPD 203994. Moore (supra n. 10) 17–18 fig. 15. I thank A. Egbert for the photograph.
69 Dog/Pig: Vienna 321/3691, ARV² 118,8; BAPD 200986. Noble Companions: St. Petersburg (Russia), Hermitage 664, ARV² 117,4; BAPD 200982; ex Canino Coll., ARV² 117,5; BAPD 200983.

17 A Scorpion and a Smile: Two Vases in the Kemper Museum of Art in St. Louis

Susan I. Rotroff

In 1904, St. Louis hosted the World's Fair, celebrating the centennial of the Louisiana Purchase and the Lewis and Clark Expedition and touting the city's position as a thriving modern center of arts and industry. Among the objects on view were 11,000 works of art, brought together for the occasion by Halsey C. Ives, director of the Fair's Department of Art. Ives taught art at Washington University, where an endowed chair now bears his name, and founded the St. Louis School and Museum of Fine Arts, an institution that was to evolve into the St. Louis Art Museum and the School of Art of Washington University. Thanks to his inclusive definition of the arts, a small collection of ancient Greek vases counted among the works displayed at the Fair. Adolf Furtwängler, who visited St. Louis in the autumn of 1904, provided a brief description of "eine hübsche kleine Vasensammlung" of nineteen pieces in his report to the Bavarian Academy of Sciences the following year.[1] While most of the art displayed at the fair was dispersed after its closing, the vases stayed. Through the generosity of Robert Brookings, then president of the university's Board of Trustees, and local collector Charles Parsons, the University was able to purchase them, and fifteen of the nineteen vases described by Furtwängler are now in the Kemper Museum.[2] They form the core of a small collection, to which only a few pieces have been added in the past century. In its current configuration, however, the Museum is steadfastly devoted to the art of the twentieth and twenty-first centuries; the vases remain in storage and, despite a modest history of publication, are less well known that they might be.[3]

The vases appear to have been chosen to represent the range of Greek ceramic art as it was known and appreciated in the early twentieth century: mostly figured ware, including representatives of Corinthian, Attic, and Apulian pottery. In this paper, however, I will examine two black-gloss vessels, at first sight perhaps among the least prepossessing items in the collection. Both, nevertheless, have features that have been overlooked or misrepresented in publication, and I take this occasion both to set the record straight and to look more closely into the cultural background that these details reflect.

A Piping Scorpion

A black-gloss stamnos (WU 3268, Fig. 1) standing thirty-nine centimeters high impresses by its size and the brilliance of its gloss. Barbarba Philippaki included it in her book, *The Attic Stamnos*, as a plain black example of the shape, dating it in the late 480s on the basis of comparison with figured stamnoi.[4] What she apparently did not notice was the tiny image of a scorpion on its shoulder, originally painted over the gloss but now almost invisible, surviving only in the discoloration of the underlying surface (Fig. 2). Although the animal has six legs instead of the anatomically correct eight and its two forward-reaching appendages lack pincers, the curved, jointed tail leaves no doubt as to its identity. John Oakley drew attention to the scorpion in his monograph on the Achilles Painter, moving the vase into Philippaki's Spotlight Group,[5] stamnoi with a small figured vignette in just this position. These images are regularly executed in red figure, but despite the different technique, it is clear that this is where the St. Louis stamnos belongs. In technique the scorpion finds good parallels in scorpions painted as white devices on black shields,[6] and indeed it is as a shield device that the animal most commonly appears in vase painting.[7]

In a previous paper, I considered why the painter chose this particular vignette to decorate the shoulder of the St. Louis stamnos, speculating that it may have been intended as a joke, an apotropaic device, or an allusion to a drinking song.[8] The only explicit connection between scorpion and symposium that I was able to find was a scrap of sympotic poetry attributed to Praxilla of Sikyon, who wrote about a generation after the St. Louis scorpion was painted.

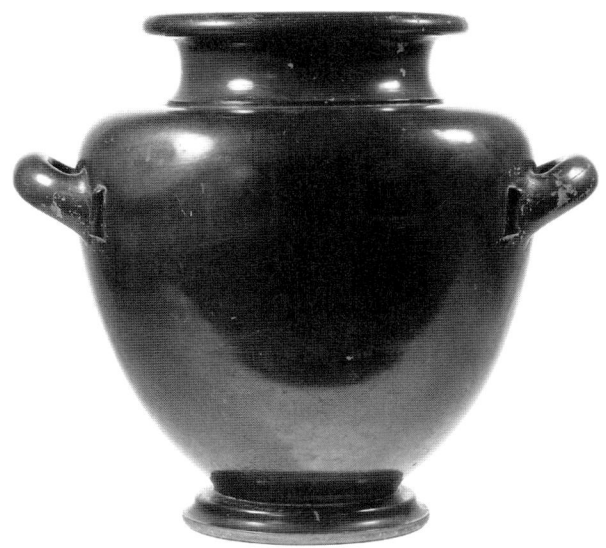

Fig. 1 Black-gloss stamnos in the Kemper Museum of Art, St. Louis (WU 3268). Photograph: Douglas Gaubatz.

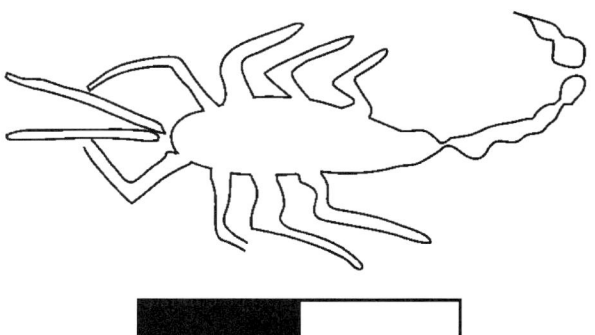

Fig. 2 Scorpion on the shoulder of the stamnos. Drawing: Susan Rotroff.

ὑπὸ παντὶ λίθῳ σκορπίος, ὦ ἑταῖρ', ὑποδύεται.
φράζευ μή σε βάλῃ· τῷ δ' ἀφανεῖ πᾶς ἕπεται δόλος.

A scorpion creeps about under every stone, friend. Watch out he doesn't sting you; tricks go hand-in-hand with the unseen.[9]

An unmistakable link to the symposium, however, is provided by a detail that I had misread: what I took for anatomically incorrect antennae projecting from the scorpion's mouth are in fact auloi, which the scorpion holds with his pincerless appendages.[10] This scorpion is a musician and thus rightly takes his place in the andron.

The St. Louis scorpion is not the only invertebrate with an unexpected ability to play the pipes. A particularly fine instance occurs on a black-figured white-ground phiale in the British Museum.[11] That scorpion has the correct eight legs, but its frontal appendages are human arms. Vigorously coiling snakes flank the scorpion, giving the composition an apotropaic air, although the rest of the imagery shows birds, foxes, and a rabbit hunt. A second piping scorpion combines musicianship with protection, as a device on the shield of a young warrior on a cup in Basel; the inscription ΗΟ ΠΑΙΣ encircling the animal maintains the symposiac atmosphere.[12] Like the scorpion on the stamnos, this one has only six legs, and its frontal appendages, though summarily drawn, are not arms but end in proper scorpion pincers. Crabs, which, like scorpions, are eight-legged animals with claws, may also turn musical. Euphronios painted a piping crab as a shield device for the warrior at the center of the arming scene on the famous krater formerly in the Metropolitan Museum of Art.[13] There the painter makes a visual pun, as François Lissarrague realized,[14] pointing to a comic fragment where a practiced kottobos player instructs a beginner that he must "crab" (καρκινοῦν) his fingers in the manner of a flute player before making his throw.[15] Perhaps the artistic idea began with the crab and migrated to the similarly eight-legged scorpion;[16] whatever the chronological sequence, all of these images cluster in the late 6th and early 5th century BC.

A final question is why the painter chose the overpainted technique in place of the red-figure normally employed on spotlight stamnoi. His intentions are not recoverable, but it is tempting to surmise that the faintness of the image is intentional. If painted in red instead of white paint, the image would have been muted even when fresh, and a nearly ἀφανής scorpion would accompany – and illustrate – Praxilla's song.

A Deceptive Smile

The only other non-figured piece among the World's Fair vases is a close contemporary of the stamnos: a moldmade kantharos presenting the smiling face of an African woman (WU 3284; Figs. 3–4; Color Pl. 22A–B). The vessel is only seventeen cm tall and the head thus less than half life size. When fresh from the shop, it was enlivened by details in incision and in paint that has now largely disappeared. The eyebrows were orange, the whites of the eyes white; an incised circle still distinguishes the pupil from the black iris. The lips are orange, open in a smile displaying prominent white teeth. Earlier accounts described the pink tip of a tongue between those teeth,[17] but close examination reveals this to be simply the protrusion of the teeth themselves, from which both gloss and white paint have worn away. Traces of bright red paint are preserved in the nostrils and on the teeth. The crinkly texture of the hair is effectively rendered with zigzag incision. Over it the woman wears a *sakkos*, arranged in the usual double points at the back. The vessel rests on the low column of the woman's neck. Above the head, the high rim of the kantharos flares out, and a painted myrtle garland hangs between the two upper handle attachments.

In his foundational 1929 study of head vases, Beazley included the St. Louis vase in his Group G, a large collection of head vases depicting women (eighteen European and three African) and Dionysos (three).[18] He dated them between ca. 510 and 480, with the St. Louis vase not among the earliest; others have concurred, placing it in the early fifth century.[19]

Athenian head vases representing Africans have become increasingly familiar with growing interest in the Greeks' reaction to peoples other than themselves, and increased attention to issues of race and class generally. These vases occur in some numbers from perhaps as early as 515 down to the Early Classical period. Thereafter they are rarer, although they never disappear. The shape repertoire is limited, with about equal numbers of aryballoi, kantharoi, and oinochoai, a few mugs, and a single wine thief among those I reviewed for this study. About half are janiform, with the two sides chosen for contrast; a common pairing links an African man with a European woman.

Various notions have been advanced to explain the adoption of Africans as subjects for Athenian head vases, but there is no agreement on the social identity of those subjects and therefore none on the reason they were considered appropriate in vases for the gymnasium and the symposium. The Africans have most often been thought to represent slaves or servants,[20] suitable in almost any ancient Athenian setting. Some observers have pointed out, however, that there is nothing inherently servile in the representations,[21] and Alain Bourgeois argued that the heads represent Homer's blameless and beautiful Ethiopians.[22] Beazley dismissed any deeper meaning in this choice of subject, concluding that the similarity between African skin and Attic black gloss was enough to suggest the idea to Athenian potters.[23] He and others have explained the appeal of these vessels in all settings as simple "curiosities" or "novelties".[24] Some have posited an apotropaic function for African portraits,[25] which others have summarily dismissed.[26] Scholars writing before the middle of the twentieth century sometimes saw the recurrent contrast between African and European as a juxtaposition of an ugly or grotesque African physiognomy and a beautiful European one.[27] More recently it has been diagnosed rather as a symptom of the ancient interest in the differences between races attested slightly later by the text of Herodotus,[28] or as an invitation to the alternative world that the drinker will enter by consuming the wine in the cup.[29] Beth Cohen, however, sees an affinity between the often paired African man and European women, casting them as slave and hetaira, representatives of two exploited groups serving to boost the assurance of the elite Greek male athletes and drinkers who used the vessels.[30]

Women are significantly outnumbered by men among the Africans represented on Late Archaic and Early Classical Athenian head vases. I know of only seven examples (listed at the end of this paper), in contrast to about thirty men. All are kantharoi, and we can be

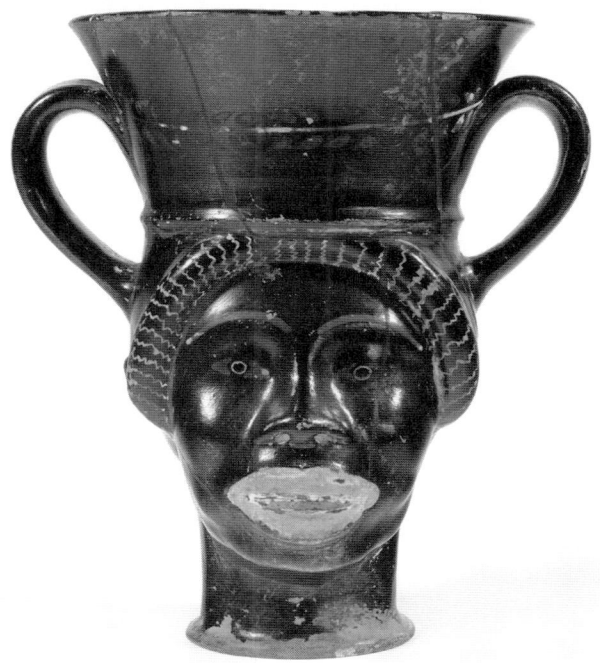

Fig. 3 Head vase in the Kemper Museum of Art, St. Louis (WU 3284). Photograph: Douglas Gaubatz.

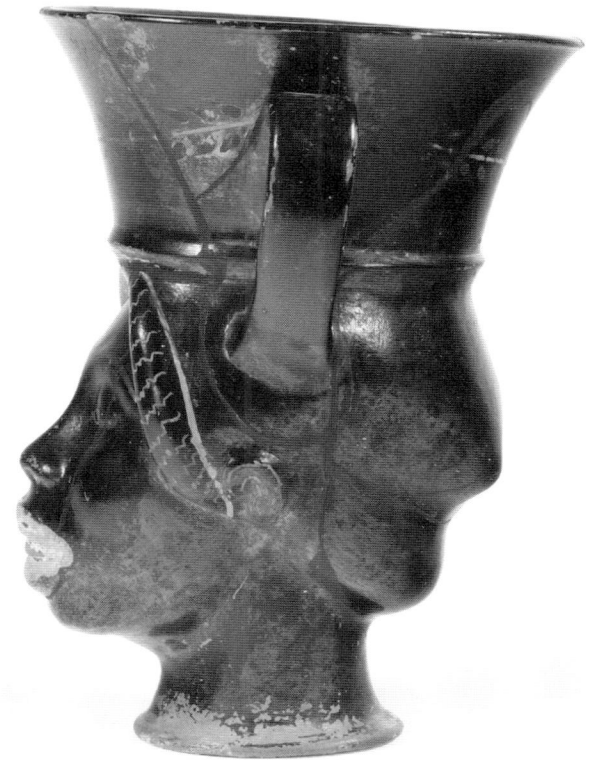

Fig. 4 Profile view of the head vase in the Kemper Museum. Photograph: Douglas Gaubatz.

confident that they functioned in the context of the symposium. There are only two single-headed examples: the kantharos in St. Louis and one in the Kunsthistorisches Museum in Vienna, both provided with a low stand (nos. 1, 2; Figs. 3–5; Color Pl. 22A–C). The other five are janiform, all pairing an African woman with a European one and standing on a high pedestal (nos. 3–7; Figs. 6–12; Color Pls. 22D. 23). These seven cups are spread among as many museums, and without direct comparison it is difficult to gauge the technical relationships among them. At least two of the janiform vessels (nos. 3 and 4, in Rome and Boston) may have been made using the same molds.[31] The African head in Cambridge (no. 5) seems, from photographs, to resemble that in Rome closely (no. 3); but the European heads of the two vessels were clearly made in different molds. Three heads share the same distinctive dot-rosette earring (nos. 2–4; Figs. 5. 6; Color Pl. 22C–D), and three or four bear inscriptions praising a *pais kalos* (nos. 2–4 and probably 7; Figs. 5. 6. 11. 12; Color Pls. 22C–D. 23C–D). The St. Louis and Vienna single kantharoi share features like the pyramidal form of the nose and the modeling of chin and cheeks (compare Figs. 3 and 5; Color Pl. 22A. 22C). The Vienna face looks broader, but measurement of the photographic images suggests the proportions of the two are about the same, and it is possible, though not verifiable at present, that the two were made in the same mold. In any event, the seven head vases depicting African women are a close-knit group. Furthermore, they all share a highly unusual feature, one that sets them markedly apart from the male faces: a wide, toothy smile.

The smile *per se* is not surprising, for almost all of the head vases show smiling faces. The Athenian head vase was created in the Archaic period, when the smile was a regular feature of the representation of the human face. The old molds continued to be used in the Classical period, when that smile had faded, so even head vases dated considerably later retain the smile.[32] None of the

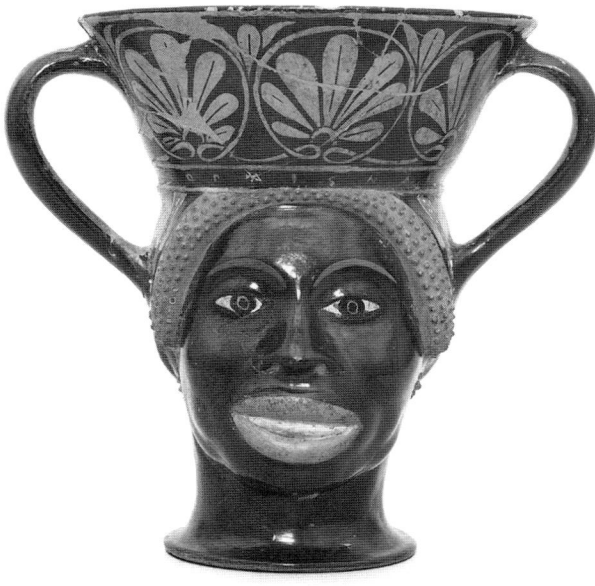

Fig. 5 Head vase in Vienna, Kunsthistorisches Museum 3714. Photograph: Kunsthistorisches Museum, Vienna.

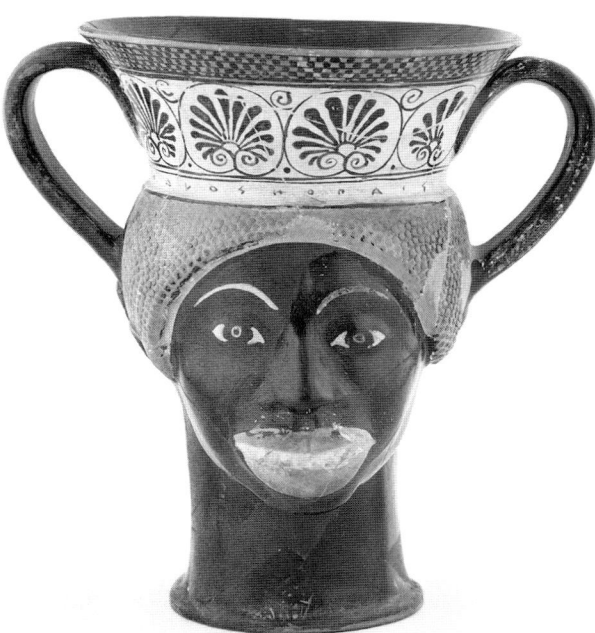

Fig. 6 Janiform kantharos in the Museum of Fine Arts, Boston, 98.926. Photograph: Museum of Fine Arts, Boston.

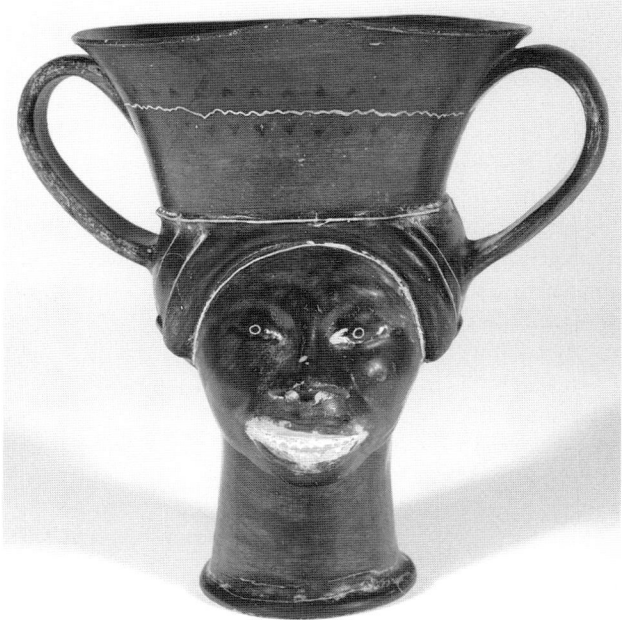

Fig. 7 Janiform kantharos in Cambridge, Fitzwilliam Museum GR.2.1999. African woman. Photograph: © Fitzwilliam Museum, Cambridge.

European women and few of the African men, however, expose their teeth, while all of the African women do so. The gleaming white teeth made a nice contrast to the rich black skin; but if that were the reason for these smiles, they would be spread among all of the Africans, not concentrated among the women.

Only a handful of African men expose their teeth, and most of them do so without smiling at all. Teeth are suggested by a painted white line between the smiling lips of the male African of an early janiform aryballos in the Louvre,[33] but the teeth themselves do not appear. The teeth of a bearded African paired with a European woman on a mid-fifth-century janiform kantharos in the Hearst Collection[34] are visible between his lips, but barely, and those lips do not turn up in a smile. A contemporary bearded African on a janiform kantharos in Cleveland bares his teeth in a sort of grimace, an expression he shares with the satyr with which he is paired.[35] Both look threatening and their exposed teeth perhaps signal their wildness. Equally disquieting are a pair of African men on an aryballos formerly in the Brummer Collection,[36] where the teeth, heavily outlined in black, and large, bloodshot eyes again present a threatening visage. Moving from the horrible to the apparently ridiculous, a janiform kantharos found in the grave of a woman at Akanthos, in the Chalkidiki, and associated with the Syriskos Painter pairs a man with a European woman.[37] The man's protruding teeth are like those of the African women, but his mouth does not turn up in a smile, and other features of the portrait set it apart from the African head vases. The skin is reddish-brown rather than black, the hair is black and straight, not the universal barbotine red of African men, and the man wears sideburns, a thin moustache and a goatee, facial hair that is not paralleled on other images of Africans that I am aware of. An accompanying graffito reads: "Timyllos is beautiful, like this face" – a joke, it seems, but the whole presents an unsolved puzzle.

A final group of African men who expose their teeth may be found in a series of Sotadean rhyta depicting a black youth caught in the jaws of a crocodile.[38] The painted details of the faces are the same as those of the head vases and so provide an apt comparison, despite the smaller scale. The teeth are clearly visible between the parted lips, painted white and sometimes outlined in black, but there is no smile, and the furrowed brow emphasizes the youth's distress. His face most obviously expresses pain and terror, although I am aware of the suggestion that what is depicted here is an ethnic dance, not a tragedy.[39] In sum, the few African men who expose their teeth glare, grimace, or present a baleful stare; none display the wide and seemingly open-hearted smile of the African women.

Toothy smiles are all around us in the twenty-first century, thanks to advertising, where they project unqualified satisfaction with whatever product is on offer. A smile was not such a common thing in times past, however, and cultural conditions mediate its significance.[40] To anyone who grew up on pancakes in the 1950s, a widely grinning African woman cannot help but evoke the nurturing but now embarrassing figure of Aunt Jemima. Today we recognize this as a caricature, created by marketers against the background of the unique history of Africans in the United States. The smiling African woman of the Athenian head vases is surely no less a caricature, but one that we are less well equipped to decipher.

While a history of bared teeth in Greek antiquity is beyond the scope of this paper, even a superficial survey suggests a complex series of meanings. Teeth in the poetry of Homer are a barrier that keeps the breath inside the body. Hastily uttered words escape the fence of the teeth (ἕρκος ὀδόντων), and the soul escapes the same way with the dying breath. Gritted teeth denote grim determination or berserker rage.[41] In art, the monstrous smile of the Gorgon is well known, and predators, like the Nemean lion, bare their teeth, as do braying donkeys[42] and spirited horses.[43] On humans and other anthropomorphic figures teeth are associated with effort, pain, and death. The villains Antaios and Kyknos clench their teeth as they "bite the dust" (also a Homeric metaphor for death, e.g. Hom. *Il.* 2.418; *Od.* 22.269), and the clenched teeth of the huge Sarpedon bespeak the rictus of death.[44] Patroclus grits his teeth in agony as Achilles binds his wound on the well-known cup of the Sosias Painter in Berlin.[45] Similarly, in sculpture, the dying warrior of the east pediment of the Temple of Aphaia on Aigina pulls

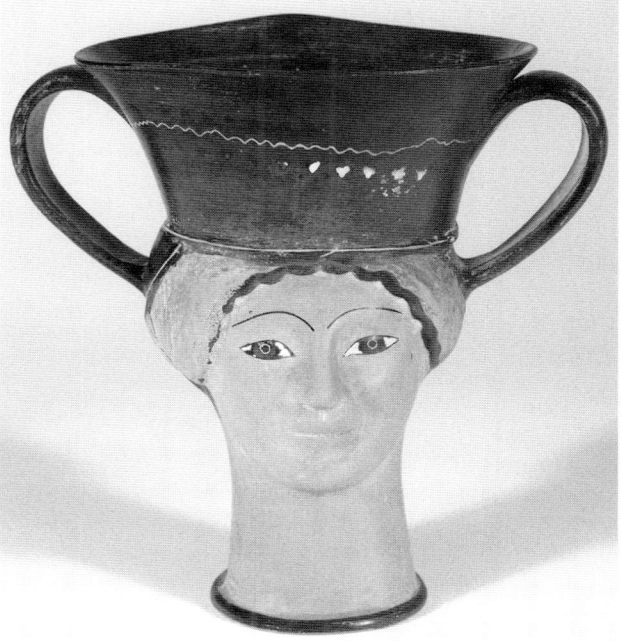

Fig. 8 Janiform kantharos in Cambridge, Fitzwilliam Museum GR.2.1999. European woman. Photograph: © Fitzwilliam Museum, Cambridge.

back his lips to reveal teeth, though they would have been barely visible to the viewer standing below. More prominent are the silver teeth of Riace Warrior A. The Homeric association of teeth and speech suggests he may be speaking,[46] but Paolo Moreno has read them as a sinister attribute of the cannibalistic Tydeus.[47]

Given these cultural conventions of bared teeth, the smile of the St Louis kantharos is unlikely to have had positive associations in antiquity. It does not, however, fit easily into any of the models described above. The woman is not speaking, for her teeth effectively close her mouth. She clearly is not dead or dying, nor is there reason to think she is in pain. Possibly, then, the teeth represent a threat or a predisposition to violence, as in the case of the Gorgon and of predatory animals, or, in Moreno's interpretation, Riace Warrior A.

Nearly a century ago, Charles Seltman expressed the opinion that the smiling African women of the Athenian head vases represent the African bogeywoman, Lamia.[48] The idea probably originated in a vase in his own collection, a small janiform oinochoe pairing a leering female face with a bearded male, whom Seltman identified as Dionysos.[49] The female figure wears a kerchief, appropriate to feminine gender, and bares oversized teeth in a wide grin. In form and overall appearance the vessel differs significantly from Athenian head vases and is probably not Attic;[50] but Seltman also applied the Lamia identification to the African woman of the kantharos in Rome (no. 3 below), the only example of our group that he knew.

Lamia was a familiar figure of the fifth-century imagination.[51] She was the title character of a play by the comic poet Krates[52] and provided one-liners for Aristophanes, who characterized her as an unwashed and farting hermaphroditic monster (Ar. *Pax* 758, *V* 1035, 1178). Surviving accounts of her fuller story are much later and paint a rather different picture.[53] Lamia started life as an African princess outstanding for her beauty; an affair with Zeus aroused the anger of Hera, who caused her children to die. Lamia subsequently developed into an ugly monster that snatched and killed other women's babies, and a specter with which Greek mothers regularly threatened naughty children.

We have no clear idea of what the ancient Greeks thought Lamia looked like, and it is unlikely that there was unanimity on the topic.[54] The puzzlement of modern scholars on the same point is illustrated by a black-figure oinochoe once in Berlin,[55] on which each of two confronted monstrous figures has been proposed as her portrait: a hairy woman with pendulous breasts, outstretched arms, and clawed fingers spread to grasp her prey,[56] and a fire-breathing, four-footed monster similar to the sphinx, equipped with both animal teats and huge human breasts, and the head of a woman, incongruously wreathed.[57] In a single other example, she has been captured by Herakles, who leads her away on a leash.[58]

A slightly different monster, also captured by Herakles, lacks the human breasts and has an enormous head, open mouth, teeth and protruding tongue; she, too, wears a wreath or fillet, as well as earrings.[59] These tableaux, if they have anything to do with Lamia at all, illustrate a different story, in which Lamia is a man- and livestock-eating monster who lived in a cave on Mount Parnassos and was slain by a virtuous youth (Antoninus Liberalis, *Metamorphoses* 8). The final and best known candidate for Lamia is the victim of torture on the name vase of the Beldam Painter;[60] an ungainly hermaphroditic figure with sagging breasts and belly and an ugly face with projecting lips and prominent teeth, bound to a tree and tormented by satyrs.

No one now wants to add the African head vases to this list. Scholars who have quoted Seltman's identification have done so only to reject it. Grace Beardsley considered even the grotesque head in Seltman's collection "not sufficiently hideous for the conception of Lamia," and she expressed the opinion that the faces on the Attic head vases "are not grotesques or caricatures – they are simply naturalistic".[61] George Mylonas, too, rejected Seltman's interpretation. For him, the African faces represent "an earnest attempt to represent the racial features of the negro face," and the smile is simply a pleasant facial expression.[62]

But if, as other ancient grins suggest, exposed teeth are not friendly but threatening, then Seltman's suggestion deserves consideration. While it has been argued that any image of Lamia must be ugly,[63] the attractive qualities of the African faces on the head vases may allude to the beauty that the texts insist Lamia once possessed.[64] In addition, Diodoros Siculus (20.41.5) provides a reason why Lamia would be appropriate to the symposia at which these cups were used. He describes the unfortunate princess as a great drinker, claiming that "when she was drunk, she gave everyone licence to do what they wanted unobserved" (ὅτε δὲ μεθύσκοιτο, τὴν ἄδειαν διδόναι πᾶσιν ἃ βούλοιντο ποιεῖν ἀπαρατηρήτως). Lamia would then join Herakles, the satyrs, and Dionysos in a gallery of famous drunks on these ancient Toby mugs.

One of the African heads, that on the janiform kantharos in Athens (no. 6; Fig. 9), preserves a final detail that may be related to Lamia's story. Although paint has been applied to the lips and hair and to a garland on the high rim of the kantharos, the woman's eyes are blank, lacking both painted and incised detail. The quality of the piece is not high, and the omission may have been a simple oversight, but it recalls another part of Lamia's story. Diodoros Siculus (20.41.6), Herakleitos (34), and Plutarch (*de curiositate* 516A) agree that Lamia was in the habit of removing her eyes and tossing them into a cup or a basket, behavior that both ancient authors and modern commentators have associated with her drunkenness,[65] and it is just possible that the kantharos in Athens depicts Lamia in her blind drunken state.

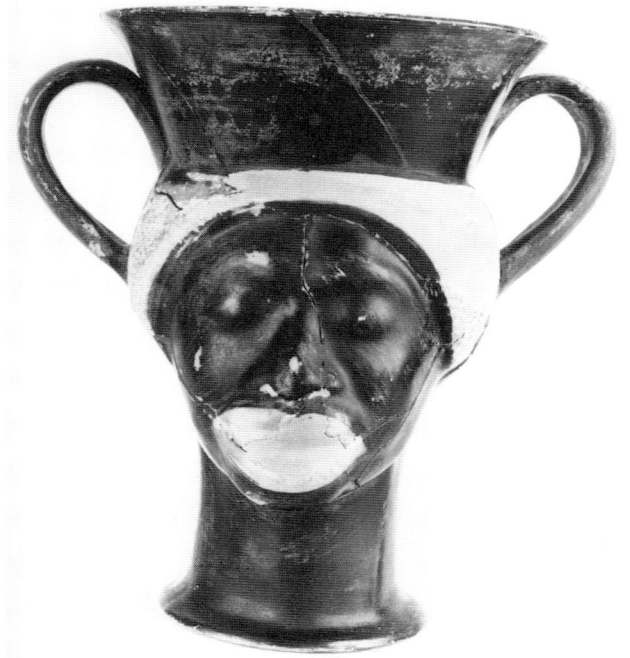

Fig. 9 Janiform kantharos in the National Archaeological Museum, Athens (inv. 2056). African woman. Photograph: National Archaeological Museum, Athens.

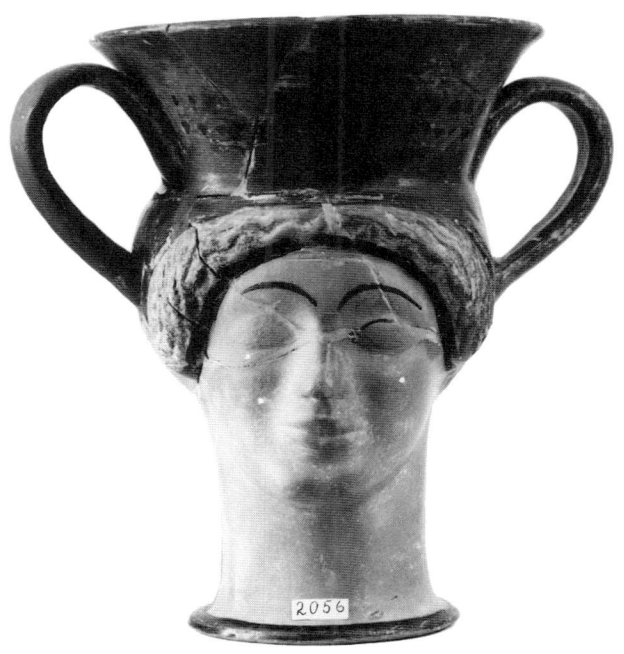

Fig. 10 Janiform kantharos in the National Archaeological Museum, Athens (inv. 2056). European woman. Photograph: National Archaeological Museum, Athens.

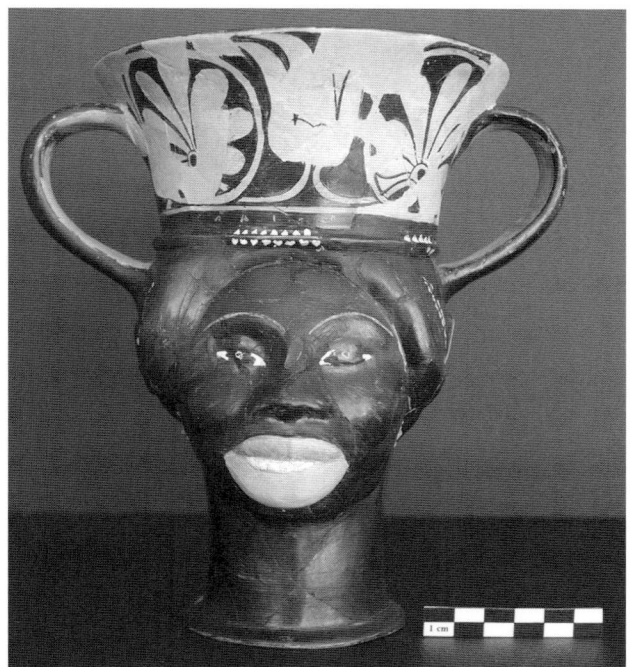

Fig. 11 Janiform kantharos in the Archaeological Museum of Aiani. African woman. Photograph: Archaeological Museum of Aiani, reproduced by courtesy of Georgia Karamitrou-Mentessidi.

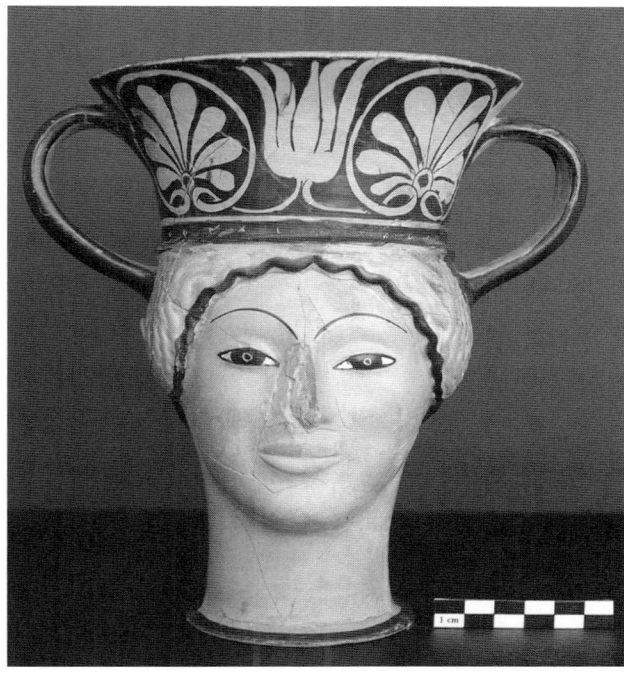

Fig. 12 Janiform kantharos in the Archaeological Museum of Aiani. European woman. Photograph: Archaeological Museum of Aiani, reproduced by courtesy of Georgia Karamitrou-Mentessidi.

Attic head vases representing African women:

1. St. Louis, Kemper Museum of Art WU 3284. Figs. 3. 4; Color Pl. 22A–B. ARV² 1534,19; Beazley 1929 49, Group G, no. 11; Beardsley 1929 28 no. 48; Furtwängler 1905 cols. 243–244 no. 8; Mylonas 1940 205–207 fig. 18; Herbert – Symeonoglou 1973 24 fig. 31; Moon – Berge 1979 149.
2. Vienna, Kunsthistorisches Museum 3714. Fig. 5; Color Pl. 22C. ARV² 1534,18; Beazley 1929 49, Group G, no 10; Beardsley 1929 28 no. 49; CVA Vienna 1 Austria 1 36–37 pl. 45, 1–2.
3. Rome, Villa Giulia 50571. From Tarquinia. Janiform, African and European women. ARV² 1534,10; 1697; Beazley 1929 47, Group F, no. 2; Beardsley 1929 29 no. 50.
4. Museum of Fine Arts, Boston 98.926. Fig. 6; Color Pl, 22D. Janiform, African and European women. ARV² 1534,9; Beazley 1929 47, Group F, no. 1 fig. 3; Beardsley 1929 26 no. 40.
5. Cambridge, Fitzwilliam Museum GR.2.1999. Figs. 7. 8; Color Pl. 23A–B. Janiform, African and European women. ARV² 1697,10bis.
6. Athens, National Archaeological Museum 2056. Figs. 9. 10. From Thebes (Kabirion). Janiform, African and European women. ARV² 1534,11; G. Nicole, Catalogue des vases peints du Musée National d'Athènes, Supplément (1911) 283 no. 1232; Beazley 1929 47–48, Group G, no. 5; Beardsley 1929 23 no. 30.
7. Aiani, Archaeological Museum. Figs. 11. 12; Color Pl. 23C–D. Janiform, African and European women. G. Karamitrou-Mentesidi, Aiani: A Guide to the Archaeological Sites and the Museum (2008) 116 fig. 186.

Acknowledgements

I would like to thank the following colleagues for their assistance in the preparation of this paper: Maria Chidiroglou, Christina Giannakos-Avronidaki, Elizabeth Langridge-Noti, Georgia Karamitrou-Mentessidi, Michael Padgett, Robert Lamberton, Phoebe Segal, and Christina Ziota.

Abbreviations

Beazley 1929	J. D. Beazley, JHS 49, 1929, 38–78
Beardsley 1929	G. M. Beardsley, The Negro in Greek and Roman Civilization: A Study of the Ethiopian Type (1929)
Cohen 2006	B. Cohen, The Colors of Clay: Special Techniques in Athenian Vases (2006)
Furtwängler 1905	A. Furtwängler, Sitzungsberichte der Philos.-Philol. Klasse der Kgl. Bayer. Akademie der Wissenschaften 1905, cols. 241–280
Herbert – Symeonoglou 1973	K. Herbert – S. Symeonoglou, Ancient Collections in Washington University (1973)
Moon – Berge 1979	W. G. Moon – L. Berge, Greek Vase-Painting in Midwestern Collections (1979)
Mylonas 1940	G. E. Mylonas, AJA 44, 1940, 187–211

Notes

1 Furtwängler 1905 col. 241.
2 A sixteenth is in the Saint Louis Art Museum (39:1921) (Furtwängler 1905 col. 243 no. 5), another apparently in private hands (ARV² 1117,6; Furtwängler 1905 col. 244 no. 11 BAPD 214782). I have not been able to discover the whereabouts of the other two.
3 The principal publications are Furtwängler 1905, Mylonas 1940, Herbert – Symeonoglou 1973, and scattered entries in Moon – Berge 1979.
4 B. Philippaki, The Attic Stamnos (1967) 88. 92 pl. 15,1. See also Herbert – Symeonoglou 1973 22 fig. 28. P. P. Betancourt included a brief discussion of the stamnos in his unpublished master's thesis for Washington University (Greek Vases at Washington University [no date] 36). Furtwängler did not list the stamnos in his 1905 article, but the Museum's records indicate that it entered the collection with the other vases from the Fair.
5 J. H. Oakley, The Achilles Painter (1997) 81. For the group, see Philippaki (supra n. 4) 89–93 pls. 15–18.
6 E.g., Munich Antikensammlungen 1411 (CVA Munich 1 Germany 3 28–29 pl. 43,1); Paris, Cabinet de Médailles 232 (CVA Paris, Bibliothèque Nationale1 France 7 32 pl. 43,3).
7 The BAPD lists over 50 instances of scorpions as shield devices.
8 S. I. Rotroff, in: S. Aybek – A. K. Öz (eds.), The Land of the Crossroads: Essays in Honour of Recep Meriç (2010) 223–225.
9 Ath. 15.695d; Page, PMG 388 no. 750.
10 I am grateful to the conference participants, many of whom pointed out my mistake to me, in the most tactful of ways.
11 London, British Museum GR 1873.8-20.388, ca. 520; Cohen 2006 194–195 no. 50.
12 Basel Antikenmuseum und Sammlung Ludwig LU36 by the Bonn Painter, ca. 500 BC (E. Berger – R. Lullies [eds.], Antike Kunstwerke aus der Sammlung Ludwig I [1979] 97–100 no. 36 [A]).
13 Rome, Museo Nazionale Etrusco di Villa Giulia L.2006.10 (Euphronios: Peintre à Athènes au VIe siècle avant J.-C. [1990] 85). A second instance may be found on a volute krater in the Metropolitan Museum of Art (59.11.20; ARV² 224,1; Cohen 2006 195) by the Karkinos Painter, so named from this detail.
14 F. Lissarrague, in S. Schmidt – J. H. Oakley (eds.), Hermeneutik der Bilder: Beiträge zur Ikonographie und Interpretation griechischer Vasenmalerei, CVA Beifhefte Band IV (2009) 17.

15 αὐλητικῶς δεῖ καρκινοῦν τοὺς δακτύλους / οἶνόν τε μικρὸν ἐγχέαι καὶ μὴ πολύν· / ἔπειτ' ἀφήσεις (Antiph., Birth of Aphrodite, apud Ath. 15.667a; R. Kassel – C. Austin, Poetae Comici Graeci II (1991) Antiph. fr. 57.
16 For ancient recognition of the similarity between the two, see Nic., Ther. 786–796; Ael., NA 6.20.
17 Mylonas 1940 206; Moon – Berge 1979 149.
18 Beazley 1929 47–52; the St. Louis vase is his no. 11. By the time of the publication of ARV² the list had grown to 42, still dominated by European women and now known as Class G (ARV² 1533–1536).
19 Mylonas 1940 207, no later than 500–490; Moon – Berge 1979 149, early fifth century.
20 E.g., P. Hartwig, AEphem 1894 col. 126; H. Schrader, BWPr 60 (1900) 11; Beardsley 1929 36; F. Lissarrague, Source 15, 1995, 4–7; Cohen 2006 268. 273.
21 C. Bérard, in: Sciences et Racisme (1986) 22; K. L. Wrenhaven, in: R. Alston – E. Hall – L. Proffitt (eds.), Reading Ancient Slavery (2011) 109.
22 A. Bourgeois, La Grèce antique devant la négritude (1971), 90.
23 Beazley 1929 39.
24 Beardsley 1929 36; Moon – Berge 1979 149; K. Rhomiopoulou, in: Ἄμητος. Τιμητικός τόμος για τον καθηγητή Μανόλη Ανδρόνικο (1987) 726.
25 C. T. Seltman, AJA 24, 1920, 14; Mylonas 1940 206–207, both citing J. B. Wace, BSA 10, 1903/1904, 103–114, who includes Graeco-Roman bronze images of Africans among charms against the evil eye. See more recently R. Nenova-Merdjanova, KölnJb 33, 2000, 303–312, though also in reference to much later times.
26 Beazley 1929 39.
27 E. Pottier, MonPiot 9, 1901, 144.
28 E.g., J. Ober – C. W. Hedrick (eds.), The Birth of Democracy: An Exhibition Celebrating the 2,500th Anniversary of Democracy at the National Archives, Washington, DC, June 15, 1993–January 2, 1994 (1993) 137; Wrenhaven (supra n. 21) 109.
29 R. Osborne, The History Written on the Classical Greek Body (2011) 140.
30 Cohen 2006 268.
31 Beazley 1929 47.
32 Beazley 1929 52 discusses the case of Naples 2952, which combines an Archaic head with Apulian red-figure decoration of the second half of the fourth century.
33 Paris, Louvre CA 987; Epilykos Group, ca. 515–500 BC. See Cohen 2006 268–269 no. 79 for excellent color photographs of all views.
34 San Simeon, Hearst 9904. Wrenhaven (supra n. 21) 109 fig. 5,3.
35 Cleveland, Museum of Art 1979.69 (CVA Cleveland 2 USA 35 40 pl. 78,1–4; A. P. Kosloff, BClevMus 67, 1980, 206–211).
36 The Ernest Brummer Collection II: Ancient Art (1979) 324 no. 691 where it is said that there is another by the same hand in the Metropolitan Museum of Art in New York (27.122.21).
37 Rhomiopoulou (supra n. 24) 723–732.
38 H. Hoffman, Sotades: Symbols of Immortality on Greek Vases (1997) 155–156 nos. F1–F9, figs. 1. 5. 7. 11.
39 D. Williams, in: S. Keay – S. Moser (eds.). Greek Art in View: Essays in Honour of Brian Sparkes (2004) 103.
40 For discussion of the smile in life and art, see A. Trumble, A Brief History of the Smile (2004).
41 D. Lateiner, Liverpool Classical Monthly 14, 1989, 18–23.
42 E.g. Florence, Museo Archeologico Etrusco 4235 (CVA Florence 2 Italy 13 63–64 pl. 72,2).
43 E.g., Munich, Antikensammlungen 2620; J. Boardman, Athenian Red Figure Vases: The Archaic Period (1975) fig. 26.
44 Paris Louvre G 103 (Antaios); New York, Shelby White & Leon Levy Collection (Kyknos); Rome, Mus. Naz. Etrusco di Villa Giulia L.2006.10 (Sarpedon). Euphronios: Peintre à Athènes au VIᵉ siècle avant J.-C. (1990) 73. 85. 96–97.
45 Berlin Antikensammlung F 2278. CVA Berlin 2 Germany 21 pl. 49,1.
46 F. Maiullari, QuadUrbin n.s. 82, 2006, 113–156.
47 P. Moreno, I bronzi di Riace: il Maestro di Olimpia e i Sette a Tebe (1998).
48 Seltman (supra n. 25) 14–18.
49 The object later formed part of the collection of David M. Robinson (Beardsley 1929 29 no. 54 fig. 8).
50 Among other differences, gloss is restricted to the stand and the neck, rim, and handle of the vessel, and the lip of the trefoil rim is split. Nonetheless, both Seltman and Beardsley identified it as Attic.
51 For recent discussions of Lamia, see M. Halm-Tisserant, Kernos 2, 1989, 67–82; S. I. Johnston, in: M. Meyer – P. Mirecki (eds.), Ancient Magic and Ritual Power (1995) 361–387; E. Difabio de Raimondo, Circe 5, 2000, 105–108; M. Rybakova, The Child-Snatching Demons of Antiquity: Narrative Traditions, Psychology and Nachleben, Ph.D. diss. (Yale University, 2004) 66–113; F. L. Gattinoni, Aristonothos 2, 2008, 161–175.
52 R. Kassel – C. Austin, Poetae Comici Graeci IV (1983) Crates, frr. 20–25.
53 The most significant accounts for my purposes are Duris FGrH 76 F17; Diod. Sic. 20.41.2–6; Herakleitos the Paradoxographer, περὶ ἀπίστων 34, Plut., de curiositate 515F–516A. Additional sources are collected by J. Fontenrose, Python: A Study of Delphic Myth and its Origins (1959) 100 n. 17 and Johnston (supra n. 51) 367.
54 LIMC VI (1992) 189 s.v. Lamia (J. Boardman). Johnston (supra n. 51) 371–372 comments on the wide range of forms and traits attributed to Greek demons, a phenomenon that is paralleled in ethnographic accounts of their modern Greek counterparts.
55 Berlin F 1934. Details of the picture are clearest on a drawing from the original publication (M. Mayer, AZ 43, 1885, 119 pl. 7,2), reproduced by S. Fritzilas, in APP II 42 fig. 8.
56 Boardman (supra n. 54) identifies her as Lamia. Cf. a similar figure on a fourth-century Kabiric skyphos: P. Levi, JHS 84, 1964, 155–156 pl. V.
57 Identified as Lamia by Meyer (supra n. 55) and others (e.g. E. T. Vermeule, in: U. Höckmann – A. Krug [eds.], Festschrift für Frank Brommer [1977] 296).
58 Boston MFA 98.924 (Vermeule [supra n. 57] 295–296 pl. 80,1–2).
59 Athens National Museum, Acropolis Collection 1306 (Vermeule [supra n. 57] pl. 81,1) and a skyphos in a private collection (M. Reho-Bumbalova, BABesch 58, 1983, 53–60). Cf. also Copenhagen 834 (Vermeule [supra n. 57] pl. 80,4) and perhaps Cyrene, Museum 417.9 (M. B.

Moore, in D. W. White [ed.], The Extramural Sanctuary of Demeter and Persephone at Cyrene, Libya: Final Reports III [1987] 40–41 no. 275 pl. 44).
60 Athens National Archaeological Museum 1129; Halm-Tisserant (supra n. 51) pl. I fig. 1.
61 Beardsley 1929 35.
62 Mylonas 1940 206.
63 Johnston (supra n. 51) 372.
64 ταύτην... γυναῖκα καλὴν γένεσθαι... (Duris FGrH, 76, F17); ...Λάμιαν τῷ κάλλει διαφέρουσαν (Diod. Sic. 20.41.3); καλῇ αὐτῇ οὔσῃ ὁ Ζεὺς ἐπλησίασε... (Heraklitos, 34).
65 For discussion of Lamia's eyes, see J. Stern, TAPA 133, 2003, 89; Difabio de Raimondo (supra n. 51) 107–108: Rybakova (supra n. 51) 71.

18 Demographics and Productivity in the Ancient Athenian Pottery Industry

Philip Sapirstein

Athenian figured vases are of unique value for understanding ancient pottery production. Over a century of research has identified the work of individual vase-painters from the enormous corpus of pots. Signatures inscribed on some vases give us direct evidence of authorship and are supplemented by the detection of individual styles in the rich figural decoration, the border patterns, and the shapes of the vases. The foundational work on painting styles was by J. D. Beazley, who studied and classified tens of thousands of Athenian figured vases.[1] He dedicated his career to compiling comprehensive catalogues of Athenian pots structured primarily by the painters. He designated a painterly "hand" when he felt confident that a group of vases represented the work of an individual, and he had other categories to deal with uncertainty – such as pots that resembled the work of a particular painter but might have been by an imitator.[2] Although Beazley wrote relatively little about how he discerned one hand from another, he did articulate the characteristics of several prominent hands.[3] The review of his attributions by later scholars has largely confirmed the validity of his work.

The present chapter summarizes the results of my ongoing research on Athenian pottery production at the level of the individual artisan, the workshop, and the industry as a whole.[4] This work is founded on a new statistical analysis of Beazley's attributions informed by analogy to the ethnographic record for pre-modern, Mediterranean pottery production. This chapter presents the project methods, defines a model for artisanal activity, and defends a new estimate of the total population of painters active in Athens during the sixth and fifth centuries BC.

The Population of Athenian Painters

It is usually assumed that by the mid-fifth century BC about 500 to 1000 people were making pottery with figural decoration in ancient Athens. This figure can be traced to an innovative paper by R. M. Cook, who pioneered a quantitative approach to Beazley's corpus of vase-painters to estimate, among other things, the size of the Athenian industry.[5] He employed two methods. First, Cook began with the roughly 500 red-figure painters designated by Beazley at the time. Assuming each painter had an average career length of twenty-five years, he estimated roughly 125 painters were active simultaneously during the main century of red-figure production. Second, Cook approached the problem from the total number of vases in modern collections. If he could estimate how many vases one of Beazley's painters made in a typical year, then he could determine the total population of individuals required to produce the 40,000 known vases. Cook suggested that a typical painter had about three to four extant vases for each year of activity, and he worked out that on average about seventy-five painters must have been active over the main 150 years of black- and red-figure production. Combining the two methods to arrive at about 100 painters in total, Cook added three more artisans (potters and workshop assistants) to come up with the estimate of about 400 people in all engaged in pottery production, and presumably many more during the industry's Early Classical heyday.

While his approach is compelling, Cook's results are problematic. The first method relies on an assumption that Beazley's 500 Athenian vase painters were active for twenty-five years on average. It also assumes that even the hundreds of Beazley hands with just a handful of attributions were real, unique artisans. Fig. 1 shows the underlying problem by plotting each of Beazley's hands – more than 630 by the time of his death – against their total number of attributed vases. More than half of Beazley's "hands" have fewer than ten extant works, whereas only the fifty-four most prolific hands have more than 100 attributed works. This great disparity in the lists shows that vase painters did not have equal career lengths, meaning that the twenty-five year average career assumed by Cook

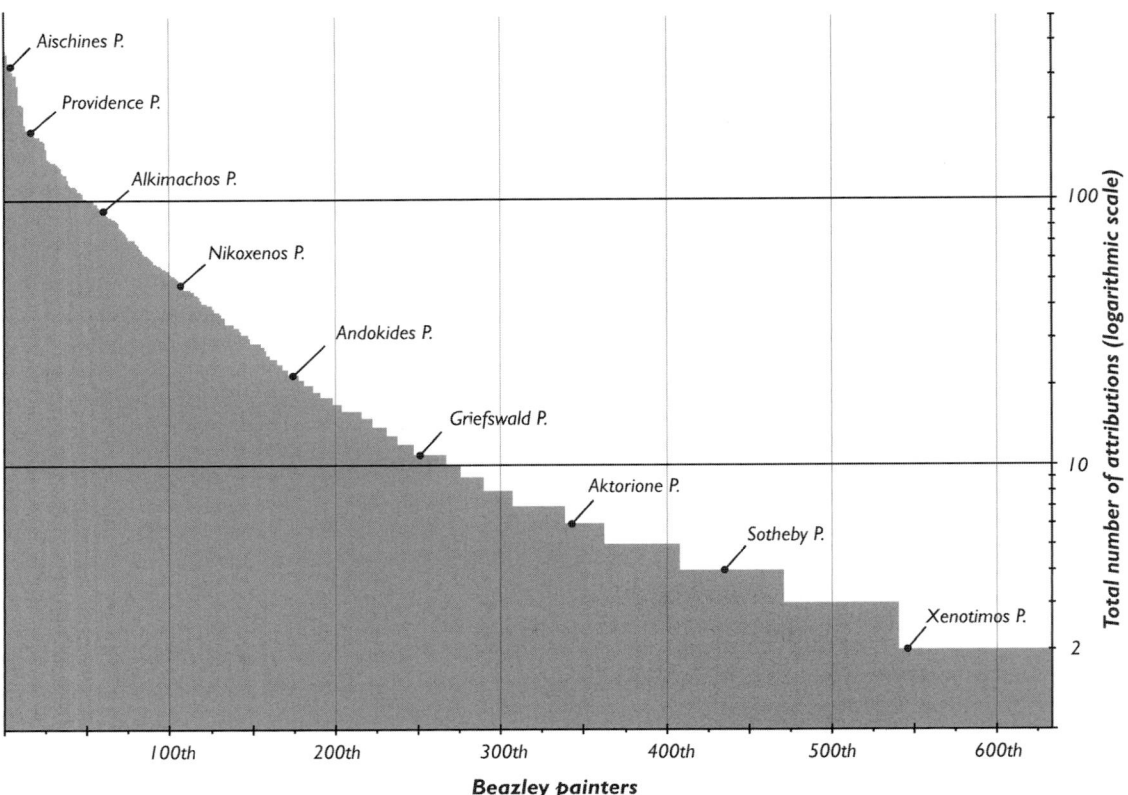

Fig. 1 Beazley's painters in the ABV, ARV², and Para in descending order by total attributions.

is arbitrary. It also indicates a great deal of uncertainty in the designations at the right half of Fig. 1, many of which are probably not real individuals, but rather works which have yet to be linked into a complete artisanal persona.[6] In other words, we cannot assume that every minor hand is equivalent to a unique artisan.

Cook's second method is more promising. However, he did not explain how he determined that a typical painter would have left three to four extant works per year. This figure, the annual *attribution rate*, can in fact be estimated by examining a number of well-defined, prolific individual painters. A good starting point is Douris, whose painting style and attributions are confirmed by his many *egrapsen*-signatures, and who has been the subject of a detailed monograph in the *Kerameus* series.[7] With a corpus of more than 250 extant vases produced over thirty to thirty-five years, roughly eight vases have survived from each year Douris was active. Epiktetos, who also signed an unusually high percentage of his vases, has a similar annual attribution rate.[8]

Annual Productivity of Vase-painters

My examination of many other hands revealed a surprising consistency in the attribution rate of about 8 vases per year of activity. It demonstrates that an individual painter left us about twice as many works per year as assumed by Cook. Moreover, the accidental discovery that vase-painters worked at consistent rates inspired my formal examination of annual productivity as a potential tool for examining the careers of individual painters.

I designed a formal methodology to test the consistency in attribution rate among black- and red-figure painters. First, it is necessary to select only the painters who worked a long time, because the majority of Attic vases cannot be dated more precisely than to timespans of about five to ten years. Any painter that worked fewer than fifteen years should be excluded from the study, because his chronology will be too coarse to estimate his annual productivity reliably. A solution is to include only painters with at least 150 attributions, which eliminates the hands which might be poorly defined, selects all the painters who were active long enough for us to have a relatively accurate idea of their career lengths, and favors the most-studied and best-defined hands.[9]

Several other rules are necessary for internal consistency. First, every published attribution through 2011 has been included.[10] Most painters have a number of attributions which are uncertain, such as vases "near" the hand. Half of the vases which might be by the painter himself have been tallied. The chronological precision is a quarter of a decade (2.5 years) to accommodate cases where a painter seems to have worked "a few years" before or after a particular five-year interval.[11] Finally, there are a few unusually rich deposits in Athens and Thasos that produced vast numbers of figured sherds, and which have clearly introduced a bias favoring the painters represented in these deposits. Only one-third of the attributions from these deposits has been tallied.[12]

The results of the comprehensive study are presented in Fig. 2. Including recently published vases, there are thirty-six painters with at least 150 attributed works. The group has left on average about 8.2 vases for each year of activity.[13] Considering the approximations involved, there is an astonishing consistency in the annual attribution rate, seven to nine vases per year, across this diverse group of painters active from the mid-sixth century to the later fifth century BC. Evidently, this metric is a valid proxy for the actual productivity of Athenian vase painters in antiquity.

Makron, the Late Archaic cup-painter, is a notable exception. His painting of over twenty extant pots per year is more than twice the norm for the other thirty-five artisans. His large corpus exists in spite of the relative high

	Works	Career dates (B.C.)	Span (yr)	Works / year
Polos Painter	204	< 580 – 555 >	30	6.8*
Taras Painter	156	565 – 550 >	< 20	8.9
Heidelberg Painter	158	< 560 – 545 >	20	7.9
Centaur Painter	161	545 – 525 >	< 25	7.2*
Swing Painter	173	540 – 520	20	8.7
Oltos	173	520 – 500	20	8.7
Epiktetos	171	515 – 490	25	6.8*
Edinburgh Painter	167	< 510 – 490	< 25	7.4
Gela Painter	322	< 510 – 480 >	35	9.2*
Theseus Painter	269	510 – 480 >	< 35	8.3
Onesimos	178	505 – 485 >	< 25	7.9
Diosphos Painter	253	505 – 475	30	8.4
Douris	259	< 500 – 470 >	35	7.4
Berlin Painter	325	< 500 – 460	< 45	7.6
Athena Painter	213	500 – 475 >	< 30	7.7
Makron	599	500 – 470	30	20.7**
Eucharides Painter	187	< 495 – 475	< 25	8.3
Brygos Painter	262	< 495 – 470	< 30	9.5*
Haimon Painter	182	495 – 475 >	< 25	8.1
Syriskos	174	< 485 – 465	< 25	7.7
Bowdoin Painter	339	< 480 – 440	< 45	8.0
Pan Painter	163	480 – 460	20	8.2
Providence Painter	170	480 – 460 >	< 25	7.6
Hermonax	215	475 – 450 >	< 30	7.8
Aischines Painter	289	475 – 445 >	< 35	8.9
Penthesilea Painter	212	470 – 445	25	8.5
Carlsruhe Painter	186	< 465 – 445	< 25	8.3
Sabouroff Painter	322	< 465 – 435 >	35	9.2*
Splanchnopt Painter	177	465 – 445	20	8.9
Achilles Painter	340	465 – 430 >	< 40	9.1
Euaion Painter	174	< 460 – 440	< 25	7.7
Painter of Bologna 417	246	< 460 – 435	< 30	8.9
Phiale Painter	218	450 – 425	25	8.7
Painter of Munich 2335	179	440 – 420 >	< 25	8.0
Washing Painter	217	< 435 – 410	< 30	7.9
Reed Painter	174	430 – 410	20	8.7
TOTAL: 35 (excl. Makron)	7608	< 930 years		8.20

Fig. 2 Prolific Athenian vase-painters. High and low annual rates are starred.

quality and detail of his painting, mostly cups potted by Hieron (Fig. 3). Here, the nature of the collections may have introduced a positive bias into his corpus. Although Beazley gave Makron fewer than 350 vases, the recent *Kerameus* monograph raises the total to over 600 works.[14] This unusually large expansion from the lists in ARV[2] can be traced to private collections of small fragments that surfaced after Beazley's death. It is rare for even the largest museums to have more than a dozen works by any one vase painter, yet almost 180 of Makron's works come from a single private collection.[15] Because of this peculiarity, Makron must be eliminated as an outlier (a standard practice in statistical analysis).

Makron aside, the number of vases painted by an artisan appears to be directly proportional to how long he was active.[16] An annual attribution rate of 8.2 is the norm for the most prolific hands defined within the Athenian vase-painting industry. However, the picture presented in Fig. 2 is incomplete, because it includes only prolific artisans. It is necessary also to test whether any other well-defined hands had a *lower* annual production than seven extant works, because any such painters will have been excluded from the study by the 150-vase-minimum rule.

In fact, there are also quite a few painters with a low attribution rate (Fig. 4). Some well-known, intensively studied artisans appear in this list, such as Exekias, Euphronios, or the Amasis Painter. These painters also worked for a long enough period that their very low productivity cannot be explained merely by imprecisions in the chronology. If an imprecisely dated, short career were to blame, then we would expect there to be as many painters with high attribution rates as low. With only about two to six extant vases per year, this under-performing group is a significant exception to the pattern established for their prolific colleagues.

One explanation might be that these are unusually fastidious painters who took extra time adding minute detail to their work. For example, vases by Exekias and Euphronios include exceptionally detailed scenes that obviously would have taken longer to paint than the normal Athenian fare. However, this explanation is not particularly persuasive. Not all the works by Exekias and Euphronios are more greatly complicated than the vases typical of other Athenian painters (e.g., Fig. 5), and many of the prolific artisans also produced very detailed showpieces from time to time (e.g., Fig. 6). The lower-production group also includes artisans like Nikosthenes, who is a relatively sloppy painter.[17]

A more convincing explanation for low productivity begins with the inscriptions left by Euphronios and Exekias. Both signed their names to many of their vases, often with the verb *epoiesen*. Although the meaning of *poietes*-signatures is debated, on the most basic level it indicates the person who fashioned the vase with his own hands.[18] The signatures of Exekias reveal that he was a potter who also painted on occasion.[19] Euphronios, in contrast, appears to have signed only as a painter early in his career, and after he had ceased painting altogether his signature as *poietes* appears on several vases decorated by other hands, such as Onesimos.[20] He is believed to have

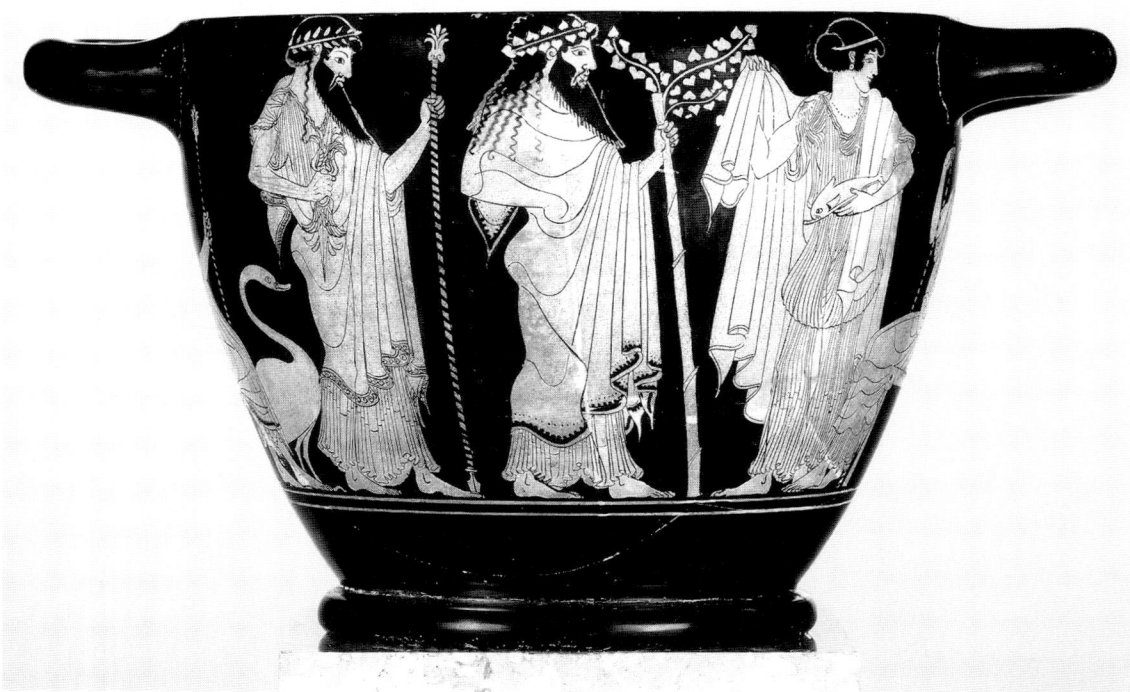

Fig. 3 London E140, attributed to Makron, signed by Hieron as poietes (ARV² 459). Photo: © Trustees of the British Museum.

	Works	Career dates (B.C.)	Span (yr)	Works / year
Gorgon Painter	55	595 – 580 >	< 20	3.1
Sophilos	67	585 – 570	15	4.5
KY Painter	75	< 575 – 565	< 15	6.0
Malibu Painter	59	565 – 550	15	3.9
Red-black Painter	55	< 560 – 550 >	15	3.7
Griffin-bird Painter	131	555 – 535 >	< 25	5.8
Tleson Painter	124	555 – 535 >	< 25	5.5
Amasis Painter	142	555 – 520	35	4.1
Hermogenes Painter	39	< 550 – 535	< 20	2.2
Painter N (Nikosthenes)	129	545 – 510	35	3.7
Elbows Out	61	545 – 530 >	< 20	3.5
The Affecter	132	< 540 – 520	< 25	5.9
Exekias	35	< 540 – 525	< 20	2.0
Euphronios	51	515 – 500	15	3.4
Red-Line Painter	129	510 – 490	20	6.5
Sappho Painter	114	510 – 485 >	< 30	4.1
Niobid Painter	139	470 – 450 >	< 25	6.2
Calliope Painter	107	440 – 420	20	5.4
Codrus Painter	71	< 435 – 420 >	20	3.6
Shuvalov Painter	100	435 – 420 >	< 20	5.7
TOTAL	1815	< 415 years		4.4

Fig. 4 Athenian vase-painters with few attributions annually.

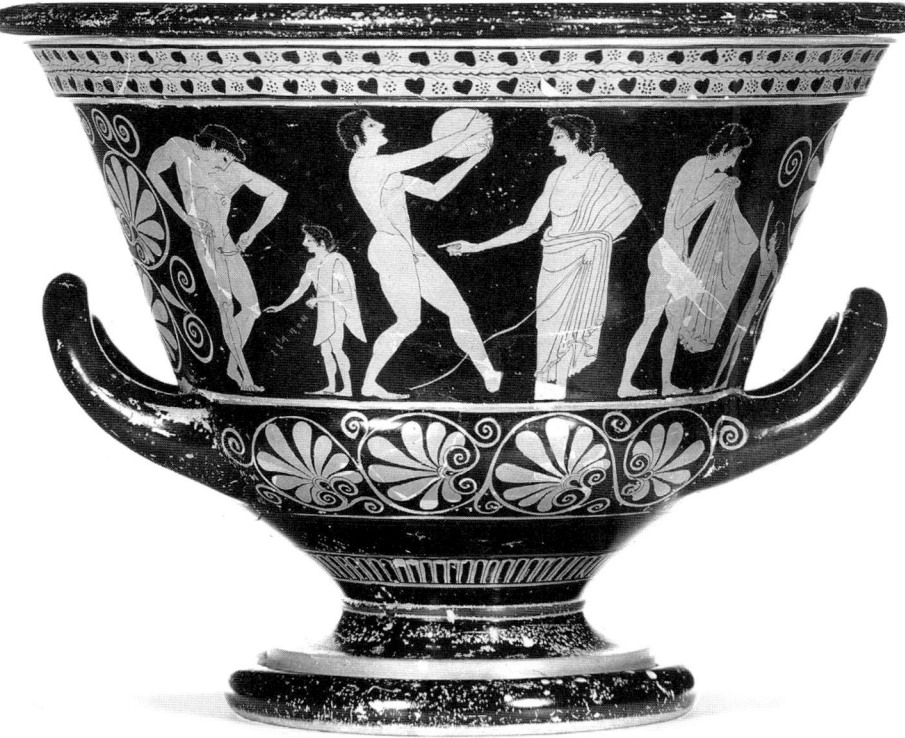

Fig. 5 Berlin F2180, attributed to Euphronios (ARV² 13–14). Photo: © bpk/Antikensammlung, SMB/Johannes Laurentius.

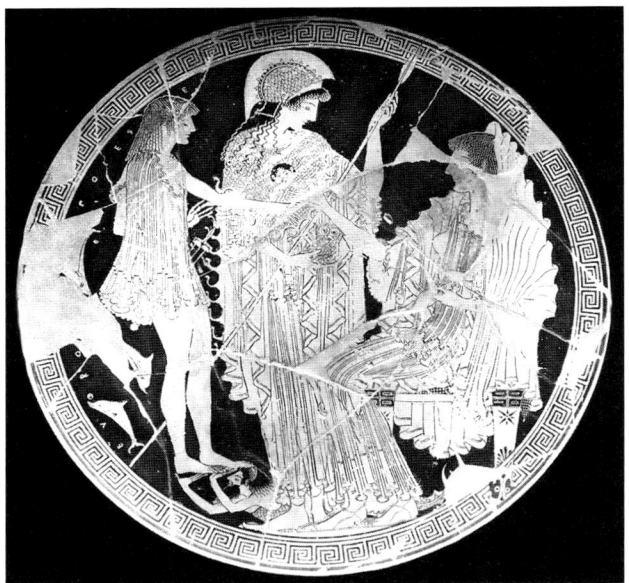

Fig. 6 Louvre G104, attributed to Onesimos, signed by Euphronios as poietes (ARV² 318). Photograph: Wikimedia Commons, public domain image, user Bibi Saint-Pol, last update 22.01.2013, <http://commons.wikimedia.org/wiki/File:Theseus_Athena_Amphitrite_Louvre_G104.jpg>.

risen to the position of the master potter in his workshop, where he threw vases full-time and employed others to decorate his wares. The cases of Exekias and Euphronios suggest a more diverse mode of production, in contrast to the prolific vase-painters, who presumably spent the majority of their time painting vases and thus had the highest annual attribution rates.

Specialist Painters vs. Potter-painters

The existing *egrapsen* and *epoiesen* signatures are consistent with this binary model of activity. The signatures of several of the prolific painters, including Douris, Epiktetos, and Makron, provide clear indications that they spent most of their time painting vases thrown by other potters. The *poietes*-inscriptions on their works include the majority of the potters known from the later Archaic Period (Fig. 7). Douris is clearly distinguished from his lead potter, Python,[21] as was Epiktetos from Hischylos,[22] and Makron from Hieron,[23] meaning that Douris, Epiktetos, and Makron almost certainly worked as specialist painters for these three different potters. Although they each have many signatures as *poietes*,

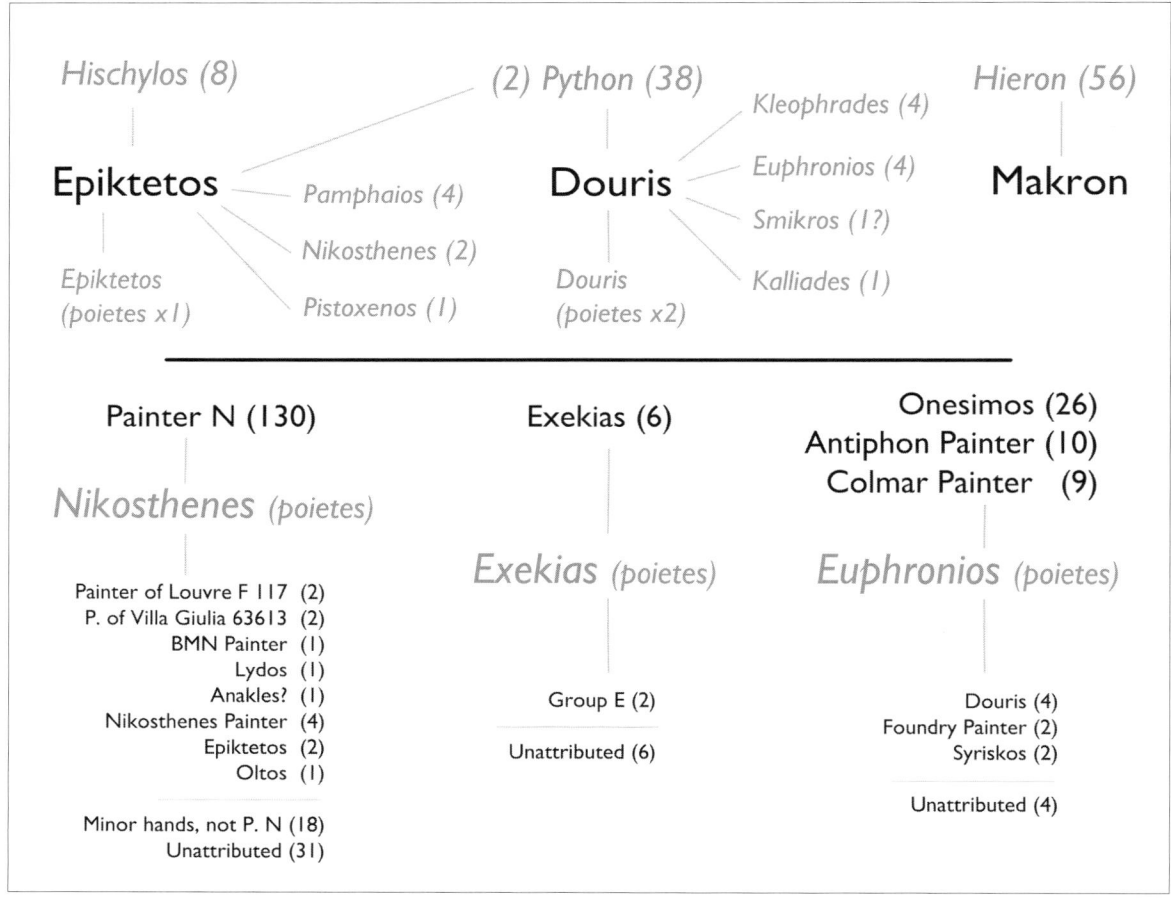

Fig. 7 Major artisans and their associations (painters in black text, poietes in gray; with number of probable links).

Hischylos, Python, and Hieron never seem to have painted themselves (or at least are named only as *poietes*). Even if one disputes that these three names belonged not to the respective potter but rather to the workshop or owner, it is clear from the many other *poietes* named on their attributed vases that Epiktetos and Douris painted for many different potters and/or workshops. This "itinerancy" is usually assumed in the literature to mark a specialist painter.

In contrast to this specialist painter is the painter who also potted (Fig. 7). For example, Exekias has few apparent associates. Signatures on his vases make clear that he was both the potter and the painter, and his painterly hand appears on other vases which he must have potted.[24] Group E is not clearly the work of an individual, but rather comprises painting of lesser quality that is slightly earlier than the secure attributions to Exekias himself.[25] More than 80% of the vases with the *poietes*-inscription of Nikosthenes are decorated by the anonymous Painter N, almost certainly the hand of Nikosthenes himself.[26] The potter-painter Nikosthenes also seems to have recruited other artisans to paint a small number of vases, the majority for special techniques like red-figure which Nikosthenes, who painted in black-figure, may have felt unable to execute himself.[27]

In contrast to Exekias and Nikosthenes, who had comparatively few interactions with outside painters, Euphronios as a full-time potter worked with several different painters, including relatively large numbers of pots decorated by Onesimos, the Antiphon Painter, and the Colmar Painter.[28] Other full-time potters such as Brygos,[29] Kleophrades,[30] and Hischylos[31] exhibit a similar pattern, where one potter maintained stable alliances with multiple painters. These examples support a model where potter-painters neither work regularly with other painters – except for special pieces – nor paint for other potters. The latter habit is important because it sharply contrasts with specialist painters like Douris and Epiktetos, who roved about various workshops in the Kerameikos and decorated vases by a variety of potters.

The binary model can be justified by reference to the ethnographic record. Typically in pre-modern production at the workshop level, the lead potter also manages the shop, from the digging of clay through the firing and bulk sales of finished pots.[32] In ethnographies of pre-modern commercial production, a master potter could turn out 10,000 or more vases per year. In order to maximize his efficiency at the difficult job of throwing vases, the master tends to hire assistants for labor-intensive, low-skill jobs like treading clay or gathering fuel for kilns. The significant investment in facilities and labor mean that he is tied to a single workshop, where he usually stays throughout his career.[33] In the case of ancient Athens, a master-potter who also painted would be decorating his own vases, and would have little time or motivation to paint for other workshops – his competitors.

In contrast, vase painters have much simpler needs. Besides a steady supply of new pots, the painter would need brushes and a place to sit.[34] A specialist vase-painter would have no physical obstacle to moving among workshops fluidly, as is evident for Epiktetos, Douris, and others. There is at least one ethnographic parallel among the faience-painting specialists in Morocco who roved among local workshops on short-term contracts with different potters.[35]

Of course, we have only indirect evidence to determine which mode of activity was typical of an artisan in ancient Athens. Scholars have relied on two major proxies for mobility. Inscriptions identify who potted a vase, or at least the workshop, but are rare after the Archaic Period. The other is based on the analysis of vase profiles.[36] While it is hard to be sure that a group of vases of highly consistent profiles are necessarily the work of a single potter, we can at least conclude that vases with *inconsistent* profiles are unlikely to have been thrown by the same person. When examining the corpus of one painter, we can conclude that he was probably working with multiple potters – and thus a specialist – if there are significant variations in the potting of vases of one type.

However, a painter who decorated a highly consistent set of shapes is not necessarily the potter himself. For example, Makron worked almost exclusively for the potter Hieron, whose cups are very standardized. Without a "Makron *egrapsen*" inscription to distinguish him from his *poietes* Hieron, the evidence of the vase-profiles alone might lead us to misidentify Hieron as both potter and painter of all of his cups. One possibility, which is suggested both by ethnographic comparisons and by father-son and sibling relationships attested in various Archaic *poietes*-inscriptions, is that Makron and Hieron were brothers in a family workshop who developed complementary specializations. In any case, vase shapes are a useful proxy for distinguishing non-mobile potter-painters from roving specialist painters, but a specialist painter who has a stable alliance may be falsely identified as a potter-painter.

With this caveat in mind, the combined results for the model are presented in Fig. 8. In fact, the binary model is strongly correlated to the attribution rates of these painters. Those who roved about various workshops are almost all highly productive.[37] Those who decorated consistent vase shapes include almost all of the artisans with low attribution rates, but, as predicted by the model, the "potter-painter" group includes a number of false positives who have relatively high attribution rates. The Swing Painter, for example, may have been a full-time specialist allied with a single potter over most of his career.[38]

This comparison confirms that the number of extant vases per year by a painter is not just a coincidence: it is a meaningful proxy for his actual productivity in antiquity. The annual attribution rate has a strong statistical relationship to the variability in vase shapes. Such a correlation of a painter's annual productivity to the profiles of his vases and his inscriptions is extremely unlikely to be due to chance.[39]

Worked with multiple potters				Consistent potter-work			
Oltos	8.7	8.0	P. Munich 2335	Exekias	2.0	4.1	Amasis P.
Epiktetos	6.8	8.0	Antimenes P.	C P.	7.4*	3.7	Nikosthenes (P. N)
Douris	7.4	8.3	Theseus P.	KY P.	6.0	5.9	The Affecter
Hermonax	7.8	8.3	Eucharides P.	Heidelberg P.	7.9*	6.5	Red-Line P.
Sabouroff P.	9.2	8.0	Bowdoin P.	Red-black P.	3.7	4.1	Sappho P.
Euergides P.	9.1	8.3	Carlsruhe P.	Griffin-bird P.	5.8	6.2	Niobid P.
Triptolemos P.	7.4	5.4*	Calliope P.	Tleson P.	5.5	5.7	Shuvalov P.
Achilles P.	9.1	7.7	Eretria P.	Centaur P.	7.2*	–	(Makron)
Phiale P.	8.7	7.9	Washing P.				
Providence P.	7.6						
	8.02 works / yr				5.05 works / yr		

incomplete evidence							
Gela P.	9.2	9.5	Brygos P.	Euphronios	3.4	8.7*	Swing P.
Onesimos	7.9	7.6	P. Paris Gigantomachy	Syriskos	7.7*	8.4*	Diosphos P.
Berlin P.	7.6	8.5	Penthesilea P.	Polos P.	6.8	7.4*	Edinburgh P.
Athena P.	7.7	8.9	Splanchnopt P.	Taras P.	8.9*	7.1	Beldam P.
Haimon P.	8.1	8.9	P. Bologna 417	Malibu P.	3.9	8.0*	Altamura P.
Pan P.	8.2	6.0*	P. London D 12	Hermogenes P.	2.2	3.6	Codrus P.
Villa Giulia P.	8.0	6.9	Veii P.				
	8.13 works / yr				6.55 works / yr		

Fig. 8 Attribution rates of painters with evidence for specialization or potting.

Consequently, we can use the attribution rates for each painter to determine whether he was more a specialist painter or a potter-painter. Those with more than 7.5 extant vases per year are likely to have been specialists, whereas those with fewer than 6.5 vases per year were probably painting part-time. The results for the seventy-five painters in the study are plotted chronologically in Fig. 9 (Color Pl. 24).

This visualization reveals a stark transition in the Athenian vase-painting industry. We begin in the early sixth century with a small number of potter-painters, like Sophilos, active when Athens was vying with Corinth as the major producer of figural vases. One of the earliest identifiable specialists is Lydos, a skillful black-figure painter who worked for different potters by his later career. The Swing and Antimenes Painters in the latter half of the sixth century are the first specialists with a high attribution rate, even while most of their contemporaries appear to have both painted and potted.

The situation changes in the following generation. By about 530 BC, Athenian potters were experimenting with a host of new painting techniques. White-ground, the Six's technique, and coral red were new techniques becoming popular at this time, but it was the development of red-figure in the 520's which led to a major revolution in the structure of the pottery industry.[40] Many of the painters employing these special techniques appear to have worked as specialists, such as the itinerant Psiax.[41] Red-figure obviously was difficult to learn to paint well, and the Athenian industry had grown sufficiently during the previous generation to support full-time specialists. We see large numbers of red-figure specialists appearing just before 500 BC when this technique was in high demand for elite dining wares. Funerary vases continued to be painted in the black-figure technique, but increasingly the decoration was done by specialists like the Theseus Painter.

By the time of the Persian invasions, there were very few prominent potter-painters that I have been able to detect. Because this study has filtered out less productive hands, however, we should not assume that there were no more potter-painters, but this trend does indicate that a majority of Classical potters preferred to hire red-figure specialists rather than doing the painting themselves. In other words, Fig. 9 charts the rise of the specialist painter in the Late Archaic Period, which went hand-in-hand with a booming export business and the new red-figure technique.

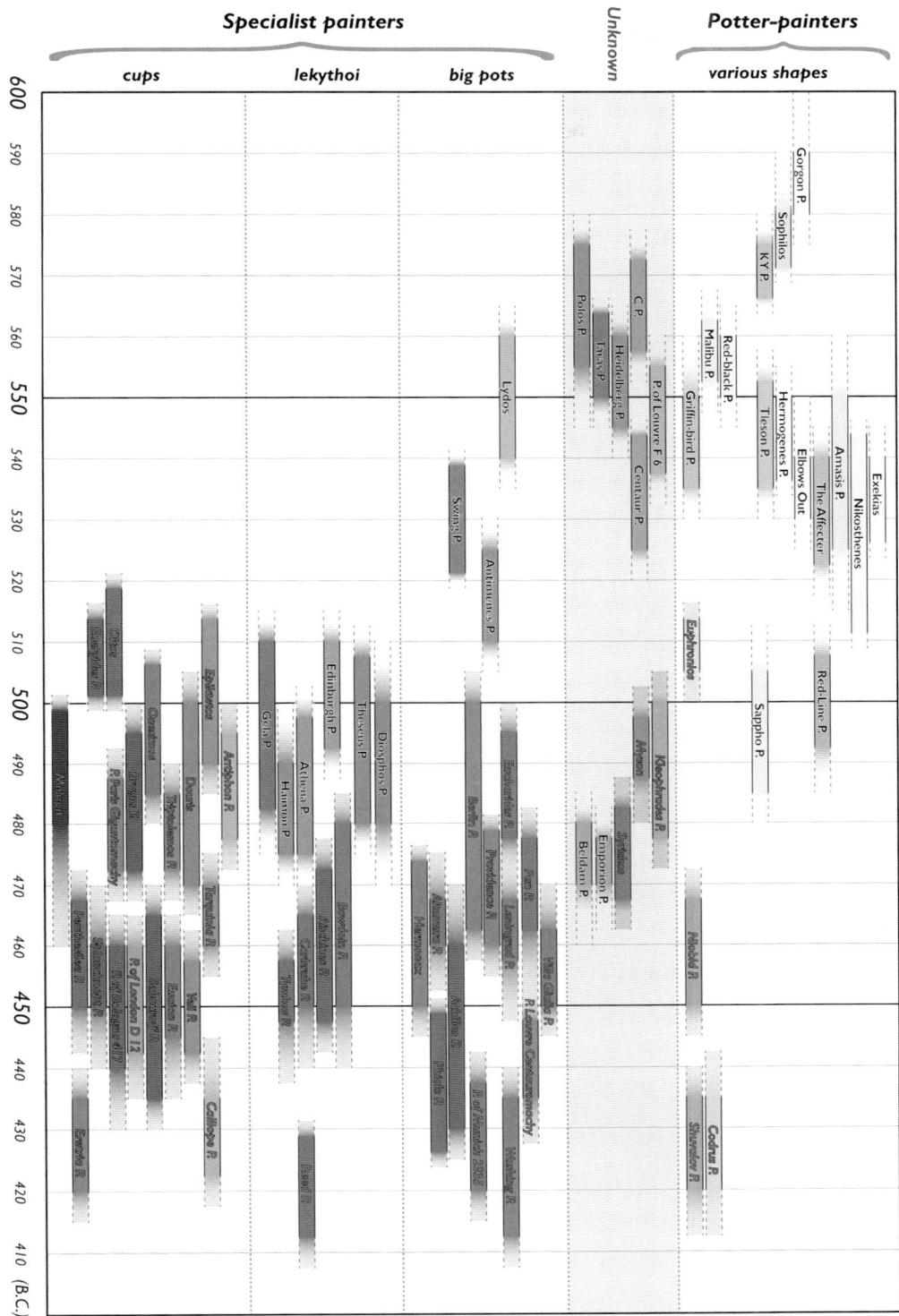

Fig. 9 Specialists and potter-painters in Archaic and Classical Athens.

The Population of the Athenian Pottery Industry

At this point we may return to the question that initially sparked this investigation, the population of the whole industry. If we estimate the total number of attributed vases over a given period, then we can deduce the minimum number of full-time painters working simultaneously from the individual productivity of ca. 8.2 vases. Cook's estimate of 40,000 figure-decorated vases which have been attributed was close to the mark. Of course there are vast numbers of other Attic sherds which have been excavated, but the 38,830 vases in Fig. 10 include the published pieces, which is a large, representative sample of the whole.

The estimation of the total population of painters is not quite as simple as dividing the total number of attributed vases by the specialist attribution rate. For example, it would take about forty-five specialist painters active at once to decorate all of the ca. 9300 vases from the first quarter of the fifth century BC. However, this must be seen as a minimum population, because in reality a sizeable number of artisans probably were potter-painters, and thus would have painted fewer vases per year.

I have also estimated the ratio of painting specialists to part-time painters in Fig. 10 for each quarter-century in light of several considerations. We can assume there were no specialists in the early sixth century BC, and the ratio probably did not change rapidly except during the Late-Archaic shift toward specialization. Furthermore, we should expect the number of relatively prolific hands designated by Beazley in each period to correlate to the actual population. The number of Beazley's painters with at least thirty attributions each happens to correspond relatively well with the estimate of the population in each period.

In the following twenty-five year segments, the number of attributed vases reflects the growth of the Athenian pottery industry. The total population of potter-painters and specialists rose quickly during the Archaic period, leveled out in the Early Classical, and declined after ca. 450 BC. At its maximum, the total population should never have exceeded seventy artisans engaged directly in painting vases. We can see a dramatic decline at the end of the fifth century, which has been convincingly connected to the hardships of the Peloponnesian War.[42]

Up until this point the study has focused only on attributed works. However, we can also estimate roughly the total ancient production of figural vases. Assuming the 0.5–1.0% preservation rate derived for Panathenaic amphorae can be generalized to the overall preservation rate, the 8.2 extant vases from one specialist painter would be equivalent to perhaps 800–1600 vases per year.[43] If this actual production estimate is near the mark, a painter working full time would have completed several pots per day. By the Early Classical period, the total annual production in Athens might have peaked at around 50,000 figured pots, and the gross from sales would have been in the neighborhood of ten talents.[44]

Upon review, the total population of potters was probably much smaller than Cook had estimated. Since painting vases would have been the most time-consuming step of the production, a comparatively small number of potters could have supplied the cohort of ca. thirty or fewer specialized painters. Ethnographic parallels show that the seventy-five painters and potter-painters would have required about one assistant each for their workshops to operate efficiently.[45] The whole population could easily have been as small as 120–200 workers including painters, potters, and low-skill assistants.[46] This workforce would have included enough potters to produce several times more than just the 50,000 figure-decorated vases. These same workshops probably were also supplying plain black-gloss pottery and smaller unpainted wares.

There are compelling patterns revealed by Beazley's corpus of painter attributions. Regardless of how they are interpreted, such strong correlations of ostensibly unrelated factors – like a painter's career length, total number of vases, and the consistency of the profiles of his vases – demand explanation. If the interpretive framework presented here is accepted, then there are several repercussions. First, we can use annual productivity to determine whether a painter was more of a specialist or a potter. Second, we can establish a higher annual production for vase-painters than guessed by Cook, and

Period	Beazley attributions	Potter-painters		Specialist painters	Beazley hands with at least 30 works
600 – 575	760	11	+	0	10
575 – 550	1,600	16	+	2	19
550 – 525	3,170	29	+	5	35
525 – 500	5,180	36	+	12	32
500 – 475	9,260	41	+	30	63
475 – 450	9,390	43	+	30	74
450 – 425	7,510	45	+	20	56
425 – 400	1,960	10	+	6	12
Total	38,830	30	+	22	(av. 550 – 400 B.C.)

Fig. 10 Estimated population of painters in Archaic and Classical Athens.

that the Athenian pottery industry is much smaller than once believed – perhaps a half or a third of previous estimates.

Finally, this analysis casts doubt on the many hands designated by Beazley with fewer than twenty or thirty attributions. Beazley's methods, as a result of his safeguards against making false stylistic links among vases, have inadvertently over-divided the material. The recent trend in scholarship is to refine Beazley's system even further by designating more painters within the same material. Accordingly to my study, this has given us many more painterly hands than there were actual ancient painters.

There is a simple solution which permits sub-dividing the material to reflect our uncertainties about linkages without inflating the apparent size of the Athenian industry. I advocate a revised classification scheme where a "Painter" is reserved only for a well-defined and widely recognizable style that is likely to represent the whole corpus of an individual painter. The hundreds of "Painters" in the ABV and ARV² with small and uncertain corpora (Fig. 1) should be given a new label that does not imply a fully fledged artisanal persona, but merely a tight stylistic linkage among several vases. A new, unambiguous term is in order, such as a "Hand".[47] Eventually we might promote a combination of these small stylistically bound "Hands" into "Painters", but this is a matter for future study.

Notes

1 ABV; ARV²; Para.
2 BAdd² xviii–xix.
3 J. D. Beazley, JHS 42, 1922, 70–98; idem, JHS 47, 1927, 63–92.
4 P. Sapirstein, Painters, Potters, and the Scale of the Attic Vase-Painting Industry, AJA 117.4, 2013, 493–510.
5 R. M. Cook, JdI 74, 1959, 119–121.
6 This was a natural result of Beazley's method, which began with a grouping of vases by style. When he was uncertain whether similar groups of vessels belonged together, Beazley often designated separate painters, which he felt free to combine into a single identity, if he identified stronger links. For example, only in the second edition of Beazley's red-figure catalogue (ARV² 318–332) does Onesimos absorb the works of the Panaitios Painter: M. Robertson, The Art of Vase-Painting in Classical Athens (1992) 43–51. While the corpus for a major painter can be assumed to be relatively complete, dozens of the minor hands might be recombined. Recently, Pevnick has asserted that three of Beazley's hands should be combined as one artisan, Syriskos: S. D. Pevnick, Foreign Creations of the Athenian Kerameikos: Images and Identities in the Work of Pistoxenos-Syriskos, Ph.D. diss. (University of California, Los Angeles 2011) 87–166.
7 D. Buitron-Oliver, Douris: A Master-Painter of Athenian Red-Figure Vases, Kerameus 9 (1995) 1–3. 72–88.
8 D. Paléothodoros, Épictétos, Collection d'Études Classiques 18 (2004) 7–56. 139–170. Epiktetos has about 8.5 attributions per year during the first two decades of his career, although his productivity apparently declines after ca. 500 BC; see Robertson (supra n. 6) 137–138; D. Williams, in: A. Verbanck-Piérard – D. Viviers (eds.), Culture et cité: l'avènement d'Athènes à l'époque archaïque. Actes du colloque international organisé à l'Université Libre de Bruxelles du 25 au 27 avril 1991 (1995) 154–155.
9 Assuming eight extant works per year, the 150-vase cutoff eliminates vase-painters who were active fewer than 18.75 years (150 vases ÷ 8 vases/year).
10 In order to deal with new attributions made after Beazley's time, I have included all attributions that I could find through 2011 in fascicules of the CVA, monographs, and other publications referenced in the BAPD.
11 While a particular vase is seldom dated to less than a five or ten year interval, a painter's *career* can be established more precisely from dozens of individually dated vases.
12 The adjustments for preservation bias are generally minor and have no significant effect on the overall results. Of the thirty-six painters in the study, only the Washing and Theseus Painters have a significant number of works from the unusually rich contexts at the Sanctuary of Nymphe.
13 Makron, an outlier, has been excluded from the calculations.
14 ARV² 458–481. 1654–1655. 1706; Para 378–379; N. Kunisch, Makron, Kerameus 10 (1997)160–223.
15 These works from "Centre Island, N.Y." belonged to D. von Bothmer; another nineteen vases attributed to Makron are in large private holdings: D. von Bothmer, in: D. C. Kurtz – B. Sparkes (eds.), The Eye of Greece: Studies in the Art of Athens (1982) 33–39; Kunisch (supra n. 14) 233–235. 244–246.
16 For the thirty-five remaining hands, the correlation coefficient between career length and total number of attributions is very strong (0.947). The consistency of this metric across many painters suggests that the number of vases preserved represents a stable fraction of an artisan's total production.
17 Beazley (Para 106) describes the "extraordinarily worthlessness" of the painting; also see V. Tosto, The Black-figure Pottery Signed ΝΙΚΟΣΘΕΝΕΣΕΠΟΙΕΣΕΝ, Allard Pierson Series 11 (1999) 8. 53–58. 96.
18 J. D. Beazley, Potter and Painter in Ancient Athens, Proceedings of the British Academy 30, 1944, 25–26; R. M. Cook, JHS 91, 1971, 137–138; M. M. Eisman, JHS 94, 1974, 172; Robertson (supra n. 6) 3–4. 31–32. 45–46; Tosto (supra n. 17) 182–187.
19 H. R. Immerwahr, Attic Script: A Survey (1990) 31–36. 171; E. A. Mackay, Tradition and Originality: A Study of Exekias, BARIntSer 2092 (2010) 4–5.
20 Immerwahr (supra n. 19) 63–65; Robertson (supra n. 6) 46; D. Williams, in: Greek Vases in the J. Paul Getty Museum 5, 1991, 41–64.
21 Buitron-Oliver (supra n. 7) 56–61; Immerwahr (supra n. 19) 85–88.
22 Immerwahr (supra n. 19) 61–63; Paléothodoros (supra n. 8) 9. 38–39. 55–56.
23 Kunisch (supra n. 14) 6–7; Immerwahr (supra n. 19) 89–90.
24 Supra n. 19.
25 On Group E, Beazley (BSA 32, 1931–1932, 3) wrote that "one day we may be able … to establish … group E or part of it, as early work of Exekias himself" but ultimately kept it separate: ABV 133; Beazley (supra) 1–22.

26 Tosto (supra n. 17) 1–8. 87–88. 173–192. 229–232.
27 Tosto (supra n. 17) 1. 252.
28 Supra n. 20.
29 ARV² 368. 398–399; H. Bloesch, Formen attischer Schalen von Exekias bis zum Ende des strengen Stils (1940) 81–90.
30 ARV² 191. 429. 1555; Bloesch (supra n. 29) 58. 161.
31 ABV 166–167. 172. 688; ARV² 41. 45. 70–71. 78–79. 161–162. 165–166; Bloesch (supra n. 29) 31–35. 64. 161.
32 D. E. Arnold, Ceramic Theory and Cultural Process (1985) 225–231; D. P. S. Peacock, Pottery in the Roman World: An Ethnoarchaeological Approach (1982) 9–10. 25–46.
33 This stability even carries over to some itinerant potters. The *pitharia*-makers from Thrapsano maintained a stable staff, with the whole workshop team traveling together to work in different regions each summer: R. Hampe – A. Winter, Bei Töpfern und Töpferinnen in Kreta, Messenien und Zypern (1962) 1–46.
34 B. Cohen (ed.), The Colors of Clay: Special Techniques in Athenian Vases (2006); J. V. Noble, The Techniques of Painted Attic Pottery, rev. ed. (1988) 99–121.
35 A. Bel, Les industries de la céramique à Fés (1918) 188. 200–201.
36 Bloesch (supra n. 29).
37 Only the Calliope Painter has an unusually low annual production, although his mode of activity is also compatible with having been a potter for a significant part of his career: A. Lezzi-Hafter, Der Eretria-Maler: Werke und Weggefährten, Kerameus 6 (1988) 48–57.
38 However, the documentation of his potter-work is incomplete: E. Böhr, Der Schaukelmaler, Kerameus 4 (1982) 16. 57; D. von Bothmer, Review of Der Schaukelmaler by E. Böhr, AJA 88, 1984, 82.

39 To be more precise, the Mann-Whitney test gives a P-value of less than 0.0001 (less than 1 / 10,000) that the two original populations originally had equal medians.
40 Cohen (supra n. 34) 18–23. 45–46. 52. 73–74.
41 Excluded from the chart due to his small corpus; see ABV 292–295. 692; ARV² 6–9.
42 B. R. Macdonald, AJA 85, 1981, 165–168.
43 M. Bentz, Panathenäische Preisamphoren: eine athenische Vasengattung und ihre Funktion vom 6.-4. Jahrhundert v. Chr., AntK Beiheft 18 (1998) 17–18; I. Morris, in: J. G. Manning – I. Morris (eds.), The Ancient Economy: Evidence and Models (2005) 95–99; V. V. Stissi, Pottery to the People: the Production, Distribution and Consumption of Decorated Pottery in the Greek World in the Archaic Period (650–480 BC), Ph.D. diss. (University of Amsterdam, 2002) 26–29.
44 The revenue estimate is derived from the prices inscribed on individual vases; see A.W. Johnston, Trademarks on Greek Vases (1979) 33–35; Stissi (supra n. 43) 190–195.
45 P. Sapirstein, On the Scale and Organization of the Attic Red-Figure Pottery Industry, AIA 111th Annual Meeting Abstracts 33, 2010, forthcoming. A publication examining workshop structures in more detail is in preparation.
46 Assuming two to three painters (2.5) per full-time potter, and one to two assistants (1.5) per potter, the seventy painters/potter-painters active ca. 475 BC would imply a minimum industry population of 120 at maximal efficiency, although the actual figure including part-time laborers was probably around 150–200 artisans.
47 For example, we denote the "Painter of Athens 1237" – comprising three to five vases "related to the Pistoxenos Painter" (ARV² 865–866) – as the "Hand of Athens 1237" within in the "Manner of the Pistoxenos Painter".

19 An Amazonomachy Attributed to the Syleus Painter

In memory of Eleni Hatzivassiliou

David Saunders

Introduction

This paper is devoted to an Athenian red-figure calyx-krater, datable to around 480–470 BC and attributed to the Syleus Painter (Figs. 1–4; Color Pls. 25–26).[1] Following its reconstruction from fragments, the vase was displayed in 2008–09 in an exhibition at the Getty Villa titled *Fragment to Vase: Approaches to Ceramic Restoration* but to date has not been fully published. For its size alone, it demands study, but a number of iconographic curiosities also warrant attention. After having addressed these matters, I will situate the vase in the broader context of Athenian Amazonomachies, calyx-kraters and the oeuvre of the Syleus Painter, and conclude with some observations regarding its context.

Reconstruction

The vessel was acquired by the museum in fragments during the 1980s. For its reconstruction, the positioning of the fragments was based on several factors, including the thickness of the wall, turning marks, poses of the figures, costume and orientation of attributes. An interactive feature in the website for the exhibition *Fragment to Vase* presented two approaches to the reconstruction of the figures and the in-painting of the reassembled vase.[2] The first leaves all modern additions black, so that the only figurative features are ancient, while the second fills in much of the missing areas, albeit without details. It was the latter method that was employed in restoring the vase.

Shape

As reconstructed, the Syleus Painter's krater has a certain squatness of form, visually reinforced by the dense decoration on the cul. It is not quite so boxy as earlier, Pioneer examples, but likewise not as elongated as those attributed to the Niobid Painter; in general, its proportions are typical of kraters of the first quarter of the fifth century.[3] Its dimensions were initially estimated from existing fragments which, although non-joining, provided evidence for the reconstruction of most of the profile. The calculation of the diameter of the rim was based on the arc of one rim fragment and, using an approximate 1:1 height-diameter ratio, this gave the height as well. The vase stands 64.5 cm tall (25 3/8"), with a maximum diameter of 68.9 cm (27 1/8"). This is, in other words, a very large vessel indeed. Contemporary or earlier calyx kraters rarely reach dimensions beyond 50 cm, and the closest comparison of similar date of which I am aware is a calyx-krater formerly at the Getty, which measures 58.2 cm in height, with a diameter of 61.6 cm.[4]

Decoration

The ambitious scale of the Syleus Painter's vase is matched by its decoration. The krater is topped by a chain of lotus and addorsed palmettes, with a break in the pattern just above the collapsing Amazon near one of the handles – presumably where the painter started or finished the frieze.[5] On the cul, beneath a continuous ovolo pattern, is a rich palmette complex. The two rows of encircled palmettes are largely preserved on one side (A), and the missing sections have been reconstructed. The decoration is scanty on the other side, and it has not been possible to restore two fragments that clearly belong (Figs. 5–6). One shows a bristly form below the ovolo band, the other a rounded shape with two protrusions at the lower right beside a palmette. The rounded shape is decorated with rows of small black dots, and its edge framed by dashes similar to those on the smaller fragment. Comparable are the foreparts of the lion on the neck fragments of a volute-krater found at Al Mina, also attributed to the Syleus Painter,[6] and we probably have a similar creature here.

The expansive palmette complex on the cul of the Getty krater would be notable for its extent – generally red-figure painters prefer a single line of ornament at this point – but the inclusion of figural decoration is very unusual, and all the more so given its apparent incorporation into the floral pattern.[7]

The body of the vase is decorated with a battle scene, which by the presence of Herakles and a number of (partially preserved) names is immediately identifiable as an Amazonomachy. The fight takes place among four overlapping but self-contained groups: a trio consisting of Herakles about to inflict the fatal blow against the fallen Andromache as her comrade comes to protect her (Fig. 1; Color Pl. 25A]; a collapsing Amazon, fleeing from two Greeks (Fig. 2; Color Pl. 25B); an Amazon prevailing over a fallen Greek as his comrade comes to defend him (Fig. 3; Color Pl. 26A); and a similar group to the preceding, with an Amazon archer on the left (Fig. 4; Color Pl. 26B).

Herakles (Fig. 1; Color Pl. 25A)] is identifiable by his lion skin, and the pelt is indicated by rows of neatly arranged black dots running across its surface, the edges marked with a darker wash. The lion skin is bound by a waistband, from which hangs the partially-preserved gorytus (no bow is visible). Herakles wears a chitoniskos beneath the lion skin, visible at his left thigh. He strides forward, wielding his sword in his right hand and reaches out with his left to grasp the throat of his opponent below.[8] She is Andromache (the letters ...]NΔP[... are painted retrograde near her head), one of Herakles' regular foes,[9] and she wears a scale-patterned cuirass over a light chitoniskos, with a scabbard hanging across it. The left shoulder flap bears a star, but the force of Herakles' attack has caused the flap on her right to come loose so that it stands upright, exposing the chitoniskos beneath. Upright shoulder flaps are depicted in arming scenes, and there is a superb example on a red-figure cup that shows Achilles tending to Patroklos' injured arm,[10] but I do not know of an example from the mêlée of battle. Our painter evidently relished the detail, since it recurs for the collapsing Amazon to the right.

Andromache's posture – supporting herself on her shield – is typical for a defeated figure, and her combative character is reinforced by the open-mouthed Centaur emblazoned on her shield. She holds her sword in her right hand, but as her strength fails, two of her fingers have lost their grip. The use of such a detail to convey weakness has a long history. From the second quarter of the sixth century a number of black-figure vases show a defeated warrior losing grip of his shield,[11] but the unfurling of individual fingers from the handle of a sword is a feature introduced by red-figure painters.[12] As Herakles grips Andromache's throat, her mouth is open as if struggling for breath and – another detail that is widely used to convey weakness – her eye begins to roll upwards. Her vulnerability is further emphasized by the fact that her head is exposed, for her helmet lies on the ground. Fallen helmets can be found in other contemporary battle-scenes,[13] but its presentation here is exceptional, for it serves effectively as a second face for Andromache, its frontal aspect a typical motif for dead and dying figures.[14] With empty 'eyes' and a limp crest, it provides a silent commentary on her impending fate.

To the right of Andromache's head are preserved the thighs and chiton of her defender, whose name may be partially preserved on an adjacent fragment: ...]ΟΠΙΣ – perhaps Lykopis.[15] To her right, above the handle, is a collapsing Amazon (Fig. 2; Color Pl. 25B), the occasion for whose fall is the spear that has penetrated the right side of her chest. No blood is preserved but the emergent spear-head is visible beside her right arm. As noted, the painter repeats the detail of the upright shoulder flap, loosened by the force of the spear blow.

A leg of this collapsing Amazon crosses that of her attacker, which, as restored, overlaps what would be the front of another figure's foot. The attacker is otherwise unpreserved, save for a fragment depicting his bearded head and part of the arm that holds the spear. As restored, his stabbing gesture is unusual, but not unparalleled.[16] The head is bearded and a partial inscription to the left preserves part of a name, ...]ΠΑΛΚΟΣ (retrograde), for which I have not been able to find any parallels.[17] A second Greek strides beside him, with much of the shield and the central portion of his torso preserved. Initially, it was thought that only one figure attacks the fleeing Amazon, but given the reconstructed shape of the vase, it became evident that there is room for a second, and one of the fragments preserves a tiny amount of drapery that belongs to the figure in front. If correctly restored, the pairing is noteworthy. Numerous contemporary Amazonomachies show Amazons acting as pairs, and partially overlapping, too,[18] but I know of no other Amazonomachy of this period where a comparable composition is used for Greeks.

The next three figures form a triangular composition (Fig. 3; Color Pl. 26A), similar to that on the front. The attacker on the left has her name preserved, ΑΝΤΙΟΠΕ. Amongst the extant Amazon-scenes that carry inscriptions, she is first encountered not in battles *per se*, but in depictions of her abduction by Theseus.[19] There are various versions of this story – Theseus either goes with Herakles to attack the Amazons at Themiskyra or acts separately. In the former case, he either abducts Antiope or receives her as a reward. There is no sign of Theseus on this vase, and it is unusual to find Antiope named as being in action amongst Herakles' opponents.[20] She thrusts her spear against a fallen enemy – presumably a Greek – who is almost entirely missing. To the right is his defender, who extends his shield and brandishes a spear.

Red-figure Amazonomachies regularly include an archer, usually as a companion to an Amazon warrior. On this vase (Fig. 4; Color Pl. 26B) she is distinguished from the other figures by her sleeved and patterned clothing, over which she wears a cuirass, and soft head-gear of oriental type. A fragment to the right preserves the final alpha of her name. She supports one of the more fully

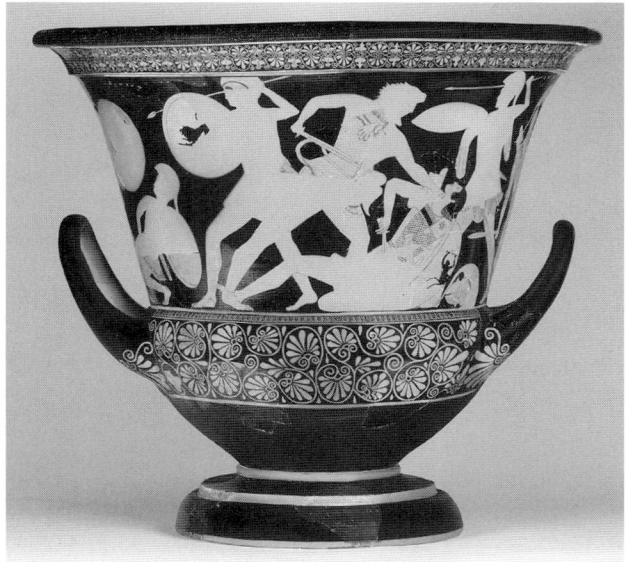
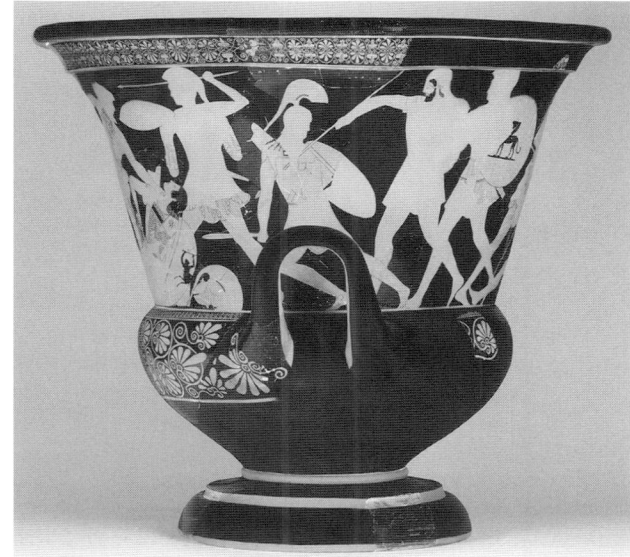
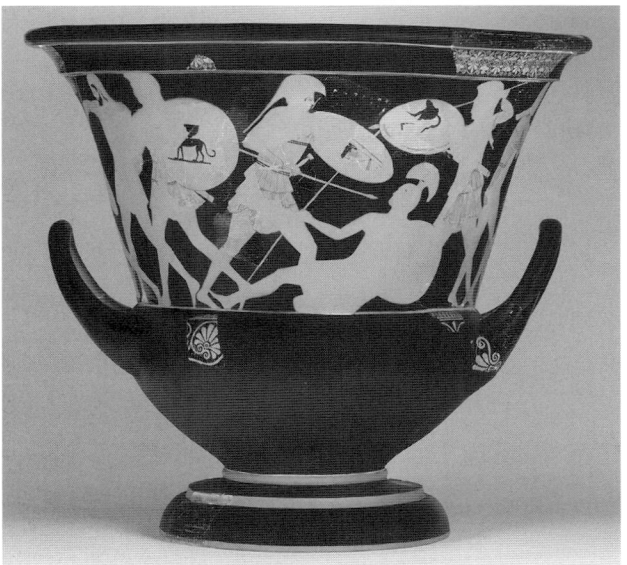
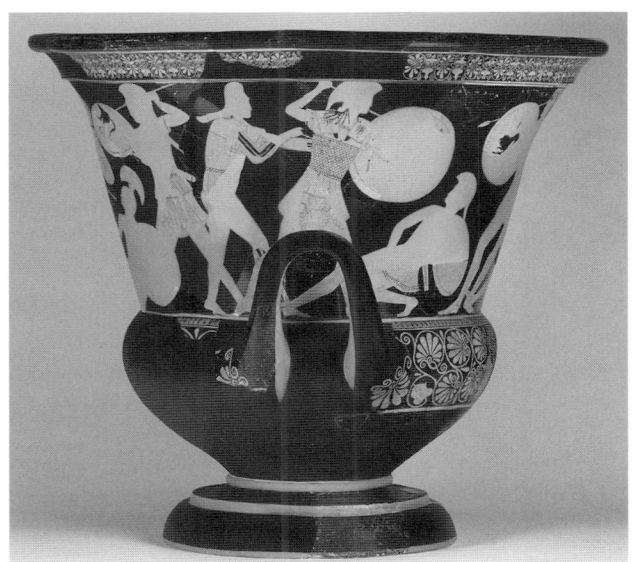

Figs. 1–4 The J. Paul Getty Museum, Villa Collection, Malibu, California (81.AE.219.2) Calyx krater attributed to the Syleus Painter. 480–470 BC. H. 64.5 × 68.9 cm (25 3/8 × 27 1/8 in).

preserved Amazons. Standing above the handle, this figure advances to the right with her spear poised for a downward thrust. She wears a scale-patterned cuirass with stars on the epaulettes, over a short chitoniskos. The partial inscription near the upper border reads …]ΟΔΑΜΕΙΑ, perhaps Androdameia.[21] Her fallen opponent is only partially preserved. The warrior who defends him is likewise only minimally extant (Fig. 1; Color Pl. 25A), with a tiny portion of his back and scabbard beside Herakles, the upper part of his helmet and crest, and his spear and shield (the curl of the lion's tail on the shield offering a neat echo of that of Herakles' lion-skin). On Euphronios' volute-krater in Arezzo,[22] the equivalent Greek (with a similar lion-blazon shield) is named as Telamon, and comparable figures who make up this V-shaped composition with Herakles in other red-figure Amazonomachies are often identified as such.[23] But here, the inscription identifies the figure not as Telamon, but ΤΥ[ΔΕ]ΥΣ (written retrograde).[24] The name has no parallels, to my knowledge, in other Amazonomachies. Rather, Tydeus is, most famously, one of the Seven who fought against Thebes. He is notorious for disgusting Athena – who would have given him the reward of immortality – by eating the brains of the dead Melanippos.[25] Perhaps this was a simple slip on the painter's part – Tydeus and Telamon were approximately of the same generation; their offspring (Diomedes, Ajax and Teucer) fight together at Troy. Taking into account Martin Robertson's suggestion that the Syleus Painter's

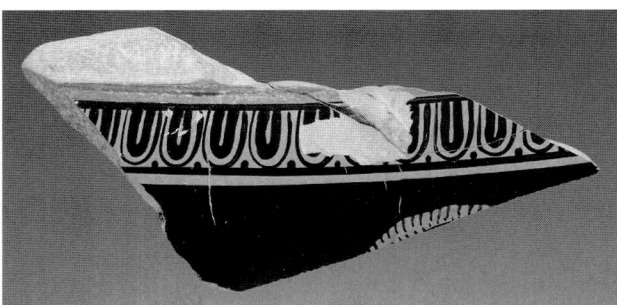

Fig. 5 The J. Paul Getty Museum, Villa Collection, Malibu, California (81.AE. 219.11) Fragment of a calyx krater attributed to the Syleus Painter. 480–470 BC. H. 4.5 × W. 10 cm (1 3/4 × 3 15/16 in).

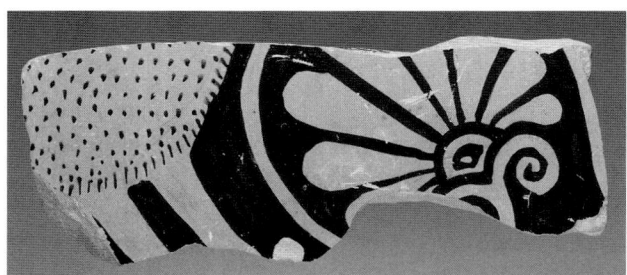

Fig. 6 The J. Paul Getty Museum, Villa Collection, Malibu, California (81.AE. 219.9) Fragment of a calyx krater attributed to the Syleus Painter. 480–470 BC. H. 4 × W. 10 cm (1 9/16 × 3 15/16 in).

name was Sikelos,[26] we might even consider whether the painter's ethnicity might have been a factor. In terms of the representation and identification of figures, however, there is nothing else in his oeuvre that would suggest a non-Athenian's misunderstanding of Greek mythology. We have already encountered one unusual name for another of the Greek warriors on this krater (…]ΠΑΛΚΟΣ), which reminds us of the variability of the painter's sources or inspiration, and perhaps Tydeus' presence refers to a variant of the myth unknown to us today. It is possible, for example, that his juxtaposition with Herakles could have been meaningful: Tydeus was son of Oineus, and thus half-brother to Deianeira, who was married to Herakles.[27]

The Syleus Painter

The vase for many years after its acquisition had been attributed to the Altamura Painter. However, a note in the museum's object file states that it was attributed by Robert Guy to the Syleus Painter, and the completion of the vase's restoration provided the opportunity to reassess this attribution. The identification of the hand as that of the Syleus Painter was confirmed by Michael Padgett. The painter's name vase itself provides valuable points of comparison with our krater:[28] the fat, linked, encircled palmettes; the closed lotus flower; and the double-lined heart-shaped form of the knot that ties Herakles' lion-skin. Likewise, the shading around Antiope's eye finds parallels on a footed dinos attributed to the Syleus Painter.[29] Other points of connection include Antiope's cuirass and the rear-end of a horse as a shield blazon: both find parallels on a kalpis formerly in the Bastis collection.[30] Further comparanda will be noted below, but one detail to note here is that the inscriptions appear to have been painted with white. I am not aware of any parallels on other vases attributed to the Syleus Painter. Indeed, it is a feature that only seems to come into frequent use later in the fifth century.[31]

The "Syleus Sequence" – the Syleus Painter and the other hands that might be earlier phases in the painter's development – is notoriously problematic,[32] but it is nonetheless worthwhile to examine how the Getty's calyx-krater fits into the range of vases presently attributed to the Syleus Painter, both in terms of shape and iconography, and how it compares to other contemporary Amazonomachies.[33]

Named after the stamnos now in Copenhagen,[34] the vases attributed to the Syleus Painter are mainly large closed shapes – pelikai, stamnoi, hydriai and amphorae of various forms. There are, nevertheless, fragments from another calyx-krater and two volute-kraters. The calyx-krater fragments were found at Locri Epizyphrii, as were those of one of the volute-kraters.[35] The other volute-krater fragments were found at Al Mina, and these remain the only examples among the attributed vases that have been found outside of mainland Greece or Italy.[36]

The painter's scenes range from the down-to-earth to the Olympian. Many, particularly on the pelikai, involve pairings of men and youths or men and women, while the stamnoi carry the lion's share of recognizably mythical narratives. These scenes are usually depicted in what was the conventional manner for the time, but occasionally there is something more elaborate, such as a kalpis that shows Theseus leaving Ariadne, and Dionysos and Athena interceding.[37] An amphora in Kansas City has received particular scrutiny, and if correctly interpreted as the vote for Achilles' arms, presents an alternative version of this scene, with the heroes using leaves rather than pebbles.[38] Battles – and indeed, warriors – are few and far between. Unfortunately fragmentary is what must have been an impressive vase in Paris with two rows of figures and at least one Homeric duel.[39]

I know only of one other Amazonomachy attributed to the Syleus Painter; it is on a stamnos now in a private collection.[40] It uses the same trio-composition as the Getty krater, and one can compare the shield blazon and the depiction of the defeated Amazon's limp hand. She, like the archer on the krater, wears Oriental sleeves and trousers beneath a cuirass. Here, however, she should be identified as Penthesilea, for her attacker is named as Achilles.

The four Gigantomachies attributed to the Syleus Painter provide further parallels for posture types, armor and shield blazons. On the Brussels pointed amphora,[41] the Gigantomachy is juxtaposed with a Centauromachy, which provides the fullest comparanda for the scene on the Getty's krater. Not only does it show the painter to be capable of ambitious work, but here again we encounter a balanced conflict made up of a series of individual, but related, combats. Of special note is the use of a continuous frieze for the Centauromachy, which is a format well-suited to this vase, and to battle-scenes in general. It is deployed effectively on the Getty krater, and its occurrence is worth stressing, for, in the late sixth and early fifth centuries, most calyx-kraters were decorated with separate scenes on either side.[42]

Introduced around 530 BC, calyx-kraters were invariably treated like amphorae and other 'two-sided' vases: despite the continuous picture field that was available, painters deemed the handle zone a natural separation, and in black and earlier red-figure examples, florals or other subsidiary ornament (or even empty space) are often found at these points. Of course, as on other shapes, there was scope for pairings and juxtapositions, but a continuous frieze that wraps around the entire surface of the vase is surprisingly rare on early fifth-century calyx-kraters. The only contemporary examples of which I am aware are a fragmentary vase attributed to the Berlin Painter, the previously-mentioned krater with the death of Aegisthus, and two examples by the Kleophrades Painter.[43] As an aside, there are further aspects that encourage the investigation of links between the Kleophrades and Syleus Painters.[44] Herakles' use of a sword, for example, is unusual in red-figure Amazonomachies, but occurs on the Getty krater and on two Amazonomachies attributed to the Kleophrades Painter, as do centaurs as shield blazons.[45] Palmettes appear, unusually, under the handles of the Getty krater, and a similar feature is found on the Kleophrades Painter's calyx-krater in Paris.[46] Further clues to the proximity of these two painters are that both decorated pointed amphorae, and that the Panathenaics bearing the name Sikelos – perhaps the Syleus Painter, following Martin Robertson – show Athena with Pegasos on her shield, which was the distinctive logo of the Kleophrades Painter's panathenaics.[47]

Amazonomachies

Returning to the continuous frieze on the Getty krater, the Syleus Painter's decision to use this format can also be seen as part of a contemporary trend of what might be termed encircling Amazonomachies – most famously Euphronios' Arezzo krater and the Berlin Painter's very similar neck-amphora in Basel.[48] These combine Herakles' battle on one side with Amazons running up to join in on the other, producing a unified frieze devoted to the conflict. The Getty's collection includes the most elaborate example, on a volute-krater attributed to the Kleophrades Painter.[49] Such scenes betray a curious fascination with the Amazons as paradoxically different, yet similar. They arm themselves in the same way as Greek hoplites – and even, on the Kleophrades Painter's krater, transport their dead as Ajax did Achilles – yet remain incontrovertibly other. This view behind enemy lines reveals much about the Greek conceptualization of this mythical race of warrior women, but most immediately, makes clear that the Amazons were truly worthy opponents for Herakles and his men.

However, despite using an encircling frieze, and incorporating typical motifs of an Amazonomachy, such as the V-shaped back-to-back composition with Herakles and his counterpart or the Amazon archer, the Syleus Painter does not show us the Amazons' preparations. Rather, the entire surface of the vase is devoted to the action on the battlefield. Comparable is Douris' kantharos in Brussels,[50] which pairs Herakles' attack with that of his comrade on the other side. This pair of scenes leave no doubt that the Greeks are dominant, which is typical for contemporary red-figure Amazonomachies; as Susanne Muth has shown, Herakles and his men are virtually always shown to be winning in Amazon battles of the late sixth and early fifth centuries.[51] By contrast, on the Getty krater, Greeks are winning two battles, and Amazons the other two. Although we need not doubt the final outcome, at this stage the fight is presented as evenly-balanced. In doing so, the krater preserves the idea that the Amazons were serious opponents, and that the victory of Herakles and the Greeks is indeed heroic.

Ostensibly formulaic in terms of its composition and subject, the Syleus Painter's calyx-krater bears a number of curious details of iconography and identification, and testifies that even for Herakles' battle with the Amazons, a scene that can be traced back almost a century to early black-figure, there remained scope for variation. Yet this still-vibrant pictorial tradition seems to have come to an abrupt halt, and the krater must be among the latest extant vases to depict this mythical battle. For in the aftermath of the Persian Wars, and the wall-paintings that commemorated or alluded to it in the Stoa Poikile and elsewhere,[52] the Heraklean Amazonomachy swiftly disappeared from the Athenian vase-painter's repertoire. In its stead came a new version of the encounter, in which the invading Amazons – analogues for the Persians – are repelled from Athens. And in this context, Athenian vase-painters regularly depict defeated Greeks,[53] as if, following the successful dispersal of the Persian threat, there was now room for an even-handed presentation of the conflict.

Context

Thus far, I have concentrated on the Athenian context of the vase, and the krater's decoration with themes that were pertinent to a male audience: martial values and the heroic prowess of Herakles would no doubt have been apposite in a sympotic setting. Regrettably, the findspot of the vase has not been documented, but there is a very evident clue on the interior. Incised just below the rim is a graffito (Fig. 7). Its prominent location and the comparanda cited below suggest that it should be read retrograde (and upside-down) as SU[..., i.e., the beginning of śuthina, an Etruscan term meaning "for the tomb".[54]

The Etruscan practice of "śuthinizing" appears to have been a localized one.[55] Around 130 examples are known to date, and the great majority is found on metal vessels and mirrors dating to the late fourth and early third centuries BC. Where the provenance of these objects is known, they occur mainly in north-central Etruria, in the area of Volsinii. In some cases, multiple examples come from a single tomb, such as a group now in the Metropolitan Museum of Art in New York.[56] Śuthina inscriptions have been found on terracotta vases of the sixth and fifth centuries, but to date, only around a dozen have been published.[57] On some, the word is written across the surface of the vase, defacing the figural scene.[58] On others it is inscribed on the interior of the lip.[59] Just one of these Athenian vases is decorated with figures that has a śuthina-inscription has a secure context: a bell-krater from the Banditaccia necropolis at Cerveteri, which depicts Herakles and Busiris.[60] Paul Fontaine notes, however, that the presence of a four-bar sigma on other examples suggests a central Etruscan provenance,[61] and this letter-form occurs on the Syleus Painter's krater. At the very least, then, it can be concluded that this magnificent Athenian mixing bowl was a valuable possession in Etruria, and was ultimately deposited in a grave.[62] The krater's decoration with one of Herakles' famous deeds would certainly have been appreciated in this setting, for Herakles (as Hercle) was worshipped in Etruria, and there was a sanctuary dedicated to him at Cerveteri.[63]

It is unlikely that the krater would have been buried in isolation, and although evidence is lacking to reconstruct a tomb group of any sort, I take this opportunity to illustrate seven vase fragments in the Getty's collection which preserve similar inscriptions that mark them for an Etruscan burial. Two have been published previously: a fragmentary black-figure Panathenaic amphora attributed to the Euphiletos Painter (Fig. 8) and a red-figure kalpis attributed to the Berlin Painter (Fig. 9).[64] The others are presented here for the first time: a black-figure neck-amphora (Fig. 10),[65] a red-figure plate (Fig. 11),[66] a red-figure astragalos fragment (Fig. 12),[67] part of an unusual red-figure *keras* (Fig. 13)[68] and the base of a red-figure figure-vase (Fig. 14).[69]

These seven examples substantially increase the corpus of śuthina inscriptions on Athenian vases, and further sifting through museum storerooms and excavation deposits will likely bring more to light. The first point to note with this group, of course, is that they are not inscribed with śuthina, but rather śutil or śuthil. Conveying the same meaning,[70] this variant spelling links the group together, and given that only the first two letters survive complete on the Syleus Painter's krater, it remains plausible that it, too, had been inscribed with

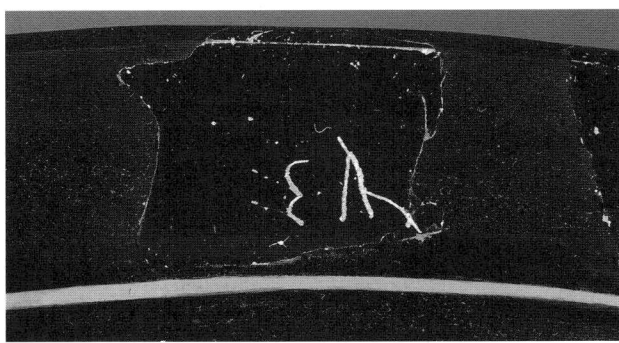

Fig. 7 The J. Paul Getty Museum, Villa Collection, Malibu, California (81.AE. 219.2) Detail (interior) of calyx krater attributed to the Syleus Painter. 480–470 BC.

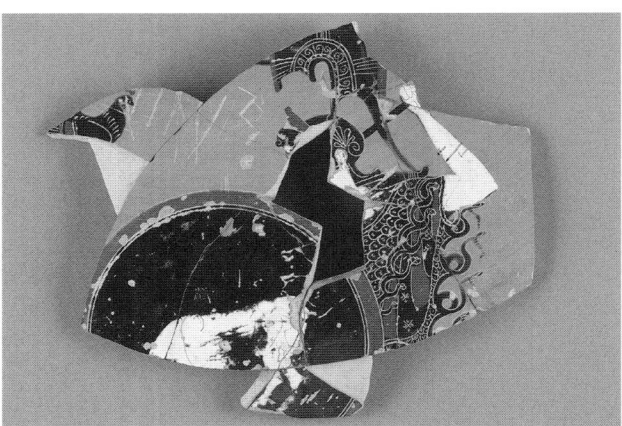

Fig. 8 The J. Paul Getty Museum, Villa Collection, Malibu, California (81.AE.203.6.2.1) Fragment of a Panathenaic amphora attributed to the Euphiletos Painter. 530–500 BC. H. 16 × W 23 cm (6 5/16 × 9 1/16 in).

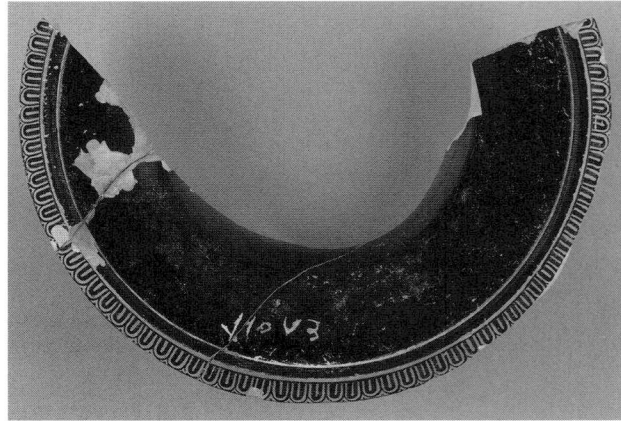

Fig. 9 The J. Paul Getty Museum, Villa Collection, Malibu, California (81.AE.206.D.2005) Fragment of a red-figure hydria attributed to the Berlin Painter. About 480 BC. Diam. 21 cm (8 1/4 in).

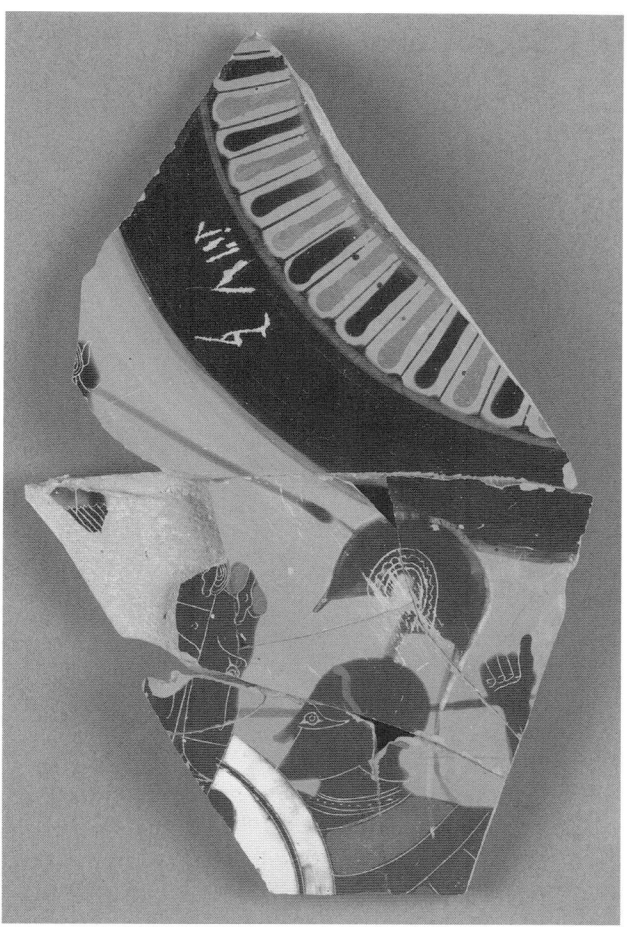

Fig. 10 The J. Paul Getty Museum, Villa Collection, Malibu, California (81.AE.200.35.3) Fragment of a black-figure neck-amphora. 530–500 BC. H. 11.5 × W. 11.7 cm (4 1/2 × 4 5/8 in).

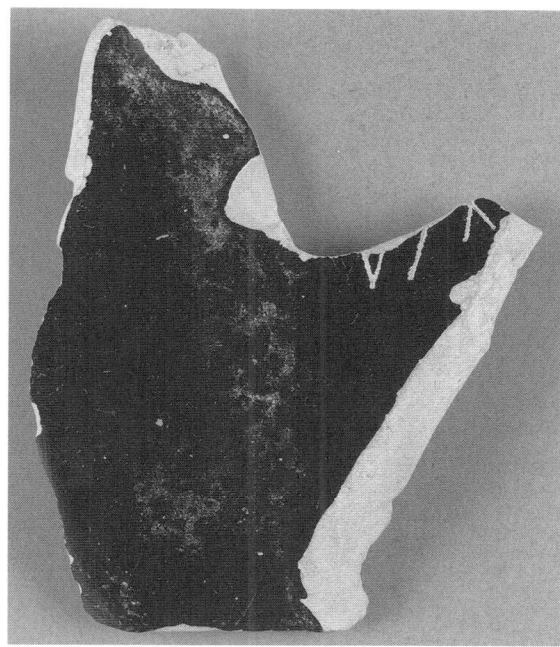

Fig. 12 The J. Paul Getty Museum, Villa Collection, Malibu, California (81.AE.216.E.12) Fragment of a red-figure astragalos attributed to Syriskos. About 470 BC. Greatest extent: 8.4 cm (3 5/16 in).

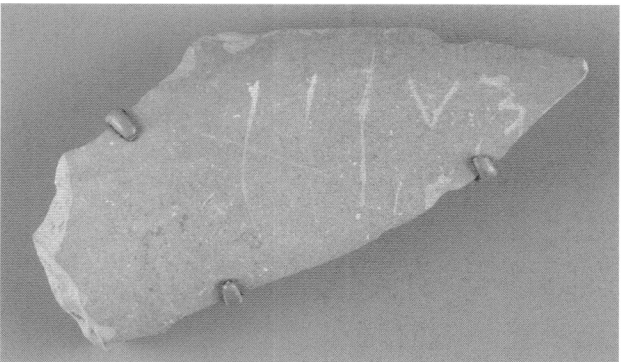

Fig. 13 The J. Paul Getty Museum, Villa Collection, Malibu, California (81.AE.216.H.10) Fragment of a red-figure keras. About 470 BC. Greatest extent 9.3 cm (3 5/8 in).

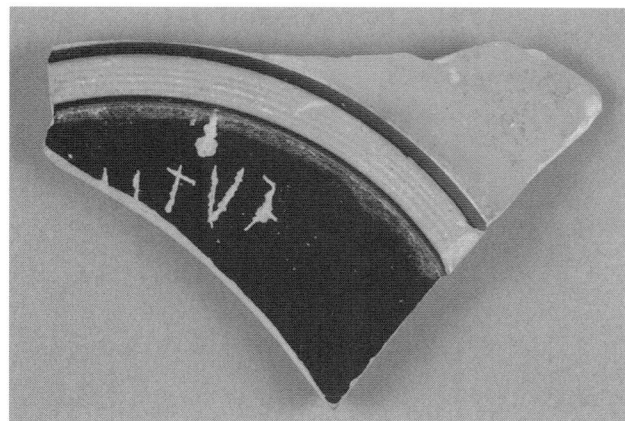

Fig. 11 The J. Paul Getty Museum, Villa Collection, Malibu, California (81.AE.206.A.7) Fragment of a red-figure plate attributed to Phintias. About 500 BC. Greatest extent 8.6 cm (3 3/8 in).

Fig. 14 (right) The J. Paul Getty Museum, Villa Collection, Malibu, California (81.AE.216.J.1.3) Fragment of a red-figure figure vase. 500–490 BC. H: 11.8 × W. 14 cm (4 5/8 × 5 1/2 in).

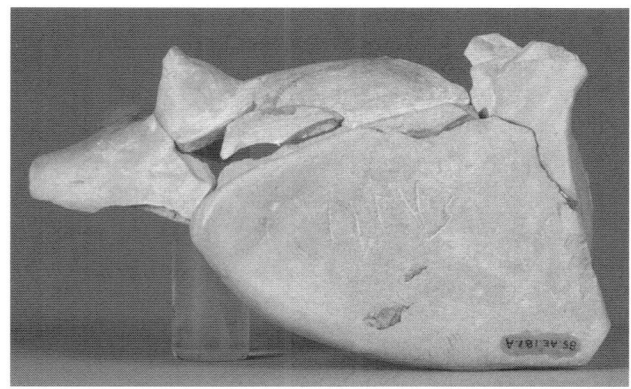

śutil rather than śuthina. The 'śutil group' also shows, where preserved, the four-bar sigma, which points to a possible origin in Central Etruria; it appears that at least the Panathenaic amphora and the figure-vase were inscribed by a common hand. Furthermore, whereas the previously published Athenian vases with śuthina inscriptions tend to date to the second quarter of the fifth century, the Getty vases seem to be a little earlier, spanning the last quarter of the sixth and the first of the fifth. Additional evidence would be required to allow us to conclude that they all came from the same grave or even the same necropolis, but it bears stressing that this 'śutil group' comprises some quite remarkable products from the Athenian Kerameikos – notably the astragalos, the keras and the figure-vase, as well as the huge Syleus Painter's krater. They demonstrate that the Etruscan market received some of the most innovative and unusual products of the Athenian Kerameikos, and it is to be hoped that further research will allow us to learn more about the role of these Athenian vases in Etruscan funerary assemblages.

Acknowledgements

I am indebted to Jeffrey Maish and Michael Padgett for their manifold contributions and readiness to answer questions. Numerous colleagues read or heard earlier versions of this paper or provided valuable points of information, and it is a pleasure to acknowledge them: Karol Wight, Claire Lyons, Kenneth Lapatin, Mary Louise Hart, Alexandra Sofroniew, Niki Stellings-Hertzberg, Seth Pevnick, Dyfri Williams, Andrew Clark, Jasper Gaunt, Athena Tsingarida, Natacha Massar, Giorgos Kavvadias, Alexandra Alexandridou and Sophie Padel-Imbaud. For photographs, I am grateful to Rebecca Truszkowski and Tahnee Cracchiola. Finally, I am indebted to John Oakley for the generous opportunity to present this paper at Athenian Potters and Painters III.

Notes

1 Malibu, J. Paul Getty Museum 81.AE.219.2; BAPD 23214; H. Immerwahr, Attic Script: a Survey (1990) 136 no. 921; C. Rozeik – J. Dawson – L. Wrapson, in: C. Rozeik et al. (eds.), Conservation and the Eastern Mediterranean: Contributions to the Istanbul Congress 20–24 September 2010 (2010) 27 fig. 6. The majority of fragments were acquired in 1981 from Werner Nussberger. Further fragments were purchased from Galerie Nefer (Zurich) between 1985 and 1988. Two fragments are on loan from Robin Symes. The vase was reconstructed by Jeffrey Maish, Associate Conservator, Department of Antiquities, at the behest of Dr. Marion True with the guidance of Jerry Podany, Senior Conservator of Antiquities and Andrew Clark.

2 http://www.getty.edu/art/exhibitions/fragment_to_vase/

3 On calyx-kraters, see K. Huber, in: M. Seifert (ed.), Komplexe Bilder (2008) 61–83; A. Tsingarida, in: P. Rouillard – A. Verbanck-Piérard (eds.), Le vase grec et ses destins (2003) 99–109; K. Hüber, in: I. Wehgartner (ed.), Euphronios und seine Zeit (1992) 57–72; S. Franck, Attische Kelchkratere (1987). The profile of the Getty krater's rim, with an instep above and below the lotus-palmette band occurs on Paris, Musée du Louvre G162 (Kleophrades Painter; ARV^2 186,47; BAPD 201699) and also formerly Malibu, J. Paul Getty Museum 77.AE.5 (Berlin Painter; BAPD 8859). A comparable echinus foot occurs on Tarquinia, Museo Nazionale RC 4196 (Kleophrades Painter; ARV^2 185,35, BAPD 201687). Not enough of the krater's handles survive to tell how high they extended.

4 Formerly Malibu, J. Paul Getty Museum 88.AE.66 (Aegisthus Painter; BAPD 12959).

5 This pattern appears to be relatively unusual on red-figure calyx-kraters; see Agora XXX 29 n. 22, to which add formerly Malibu, J. Paul Getty Museum 88.AE.66 (supra n. 4) and Paris, Musée du Louvre G164 (Aesigthus Painter; BAPD 205657). Another unusual feature are the individual palmettes at the handle bases; see Agora XXX 30 n. 30, to which add formerly Malibu, J. Paul Getty Museum 92.AE.6 (signed by Syriskos; BAPD 28083).

6 Antioch, Museum; ARV^2 251,28; BAPD 202505.

7 For figures on the cul of red-figure calyx-kraters, see Agora XXX 28 n. 10 (add the fragments attributed to the Andokides Painter; Emory University, Michael C. Carlos Museum 2002.43.18–22).

8 Compare the kalpis, London, British Museum E167 (Leningrad Painter; ARV^2 571,77; BAPD 206568).

9 See D. von Bothmer, Amazons in Greek Art (1957); LIMC I (1981) 774 s.v. Andromache II.

10 Berlin, Antikensammlung F2278 (Sosias Painter; ARV^2 21,1, BAPD 200108).

11 E.g., Athens, National Archaeological Museum, Akropolis Collection 1.2211 (BAPD 3363).

12 E.g., pelike, Paris, Musée du Louvre G65/CP709 (Pioneer Group; ARV^2 21,5; BAPD 200106); calyx-krater, Boston, Museum of Fine Arts 97.368 (Tyszkiewicz Painter; ARV^2 290,1; 1591; BAPD 202631).

13 E.g., the kalpis mentioned above (supra n. 8).

14 See F. Frontisi-Ducroix, Metis 1, 1986, 197–213; Y. Korshak, Frontal Faces in Attic Vase Painting of the Archaic Period (1987) 58–63.

15 See von Bothmer (supra n. 9) 234. LIMC VI (1992) 302 s.v. Lykopis.

16 See e.g., red-figure kyathos, Berlin, Antikensammlung F2321 (Oinophile Painter; ARV^2 333,3; 1605; BAPD 203429).

17 Henry Immerwahr (Corpus of Attic Vase Inscriptions, no. 4956) suggests Epalkos.

18 E.g. red-figure volute-krater, Arezzo, Museo Archeologico di Arezzo 1465 (Euphronios; ARV^2 15,6; 1619; BAPD 200068).

19 See von Bothmer (supra n. 9) 124–130.

20 A red-figure hydria signed by Hypsis (Munich, Antikensammlungen 2423; ARV^2 30,1; BAPD 200170) names Antiope arming alongside Andromache. Antiope and Andromache are named together in a battle – but not involving Herakles – on the later calyx-krater, Ferrara,

Museo Nazionale di Spina T1052/ 2890 (Achilles Painter; ARV² 991,53; 1568. 1677. BAPD 213874).
21 Androdameia occurs on a fragmentary psykter that depicts the abduction of Antiope: Vatican City, Museo Gregoriano Etrusco Vaticano AST428 (Myson; ARV² 238. 242,77; BAPD 202178).
22 Supra n. 18.
23 See also the neck-amphora, Basel, Antikenmuseum und Sammlung Ludwig BS453 (Berlin Painter; ARV² 1634,30bis; BAPD 275091). Neils identifies the leftmost warrior on the volute-krater, Museo Archeologico di Morgantina 58.2382 (Euthymides; ARV² 28,10; 1620; BAPD 200145) as Telamon on account of his pose (and shield blazon), even though he is separate from Herakles (J. Neils, AJA 99, 1995, 432).
24 The apex of the third letter (Δ) and the top bar of the fourth (E) survive.
25 See LIMC VIII (1997) 142–145 s.v. Tydeus (E. Simon – S. Lorenz); J. D. Beazley, JHS 67, 1947, 1–9.
26 C. M. R. Robertson, AntK 13, 1970, 13–16.
27 Another approach might posit Herakles as representative of Athens and seek a 'political' allusion in this mutually supportive juxtaposition. Tydeus had been born in Aetolia, but later fled to Argos. Argos was allied with Athens in 462 BC, but this seems too late for this vase, and during the Persian invasions of 480–479, Argos was famously neutral. An Attic tradition that the Seven against Thebes, including Tydeus, were buried at Eleusis (see Aesch. Eleusinians; Paus. 1.39.2) offers another field for speculation; see further, J. Boardman, JHS 95, 1975, 1–12, with references to Herakles' initiation at Eleusis.
28 Copenhagen, National Museum 3293; ARV² 251,36; BAPD 202489.
29 J. Paul Getty Museum 89.AE.73; BAPD 43376.
30 ARV² 252,43; BAPD 202496.
31 Immerwahr (supra n. 1) 115. Examples occur on the calyx-krater Athens, National Archaeological Museum, Akropolis Coll. 2.735 (Syriskos Painter; ARV² 259,1; BAPD 202955). I am grateful to Seth Pevnick for this reference.
32 ARV² 245–255. On the development of Beazley's attributions, see C. M. R. Robertson, The Art of Vase-Painting in Classical Athens (1992) 121–123. On the Syleus Painter, see L. Berge, in: W. G. Moon, Greek Vase-painting in Midwestern Collections (1979) 157; J. M. Padgett, in: APP 213–230; M. Tiverios, Μια "κρίσις των όπλων" του Ζωγράφου του Συλέα (1985); R. von Kaenel, HASB 17, 2000, 41–47; Y. Tuna-Norling, AA, 2001, 27–44; M. Tiverios, in: Epitumvion Gerhard Neumann (2003) 113–121.
33 The BAPD (checked November 28th, 2012) records seventy-two vases attributed to the Syleus Painter and another fourteen are listed as 'near to', 'perhaps', 'compare' or 'recalls'.
34 Supra n. 28.
35 Calyx-krater: Reggio Calabria, Museo Nazionale (ARV² 1639,2bis; BAPD 275141); volute-krater: Reggio Calabria, Museo Nazionale 4379 (ARV² 251,27; BAPD 202504). Michael Padgett (pers. comm.) has brought to my attention another fragmentary calyx-krater attributed to the painter by Robert Guy, once on the market and unpublished.
36 Antioch Museum (supra n. 6). Tuna-Norling (supra n. 32) attributes the column-krater from Tekirdağ to the Syleus Sequence, but argues that the vase supports the idea that all the works of this group are by a common hand (i.e., the Syleus Painter).
37 Berlin, Antikensammlung F2179; ARV² 252,52; 1639; BAPD 202898.
38 Nelson Atkins Museum of Art 30.13; ARV² 249,1; BAPD 202480 on which, in addition to Berge and Tiverios (supra n. 32), see H. A. Shapiro, BABesch 56, 1981, 149–150; G. F. Pinney – R. Hamilton, AJA 86, 1982, 581–584.
39 Paris, Musée du Louvre CP10823; ARV² 253,54; BAPD 202900.
40 ARV² 251,35; BAPD 202488.
41 Brussels, Musée du Cinquantenaire R303; ARV² 249,6; 1639. BAPD 202485.
42 Continuous friezes occur most commonly on later calyx-kraters, especially when the double register format is employed (see J. H. Oakley, in: H. A. G Brijder (ed.), Ancient Greek and Related Pottery – Proceedings of the International Vase Symposium 12–15th April, 1984 (1984) 119–127).
43 Berlin Painter: supra n. 3; Aegisthus Painter: supra n. 4; Kleophrades Painter: Louvre G162 (supra n. 3) and Cambridge, Arthur M. Sackler Museum, 1960.236 (ARV² 185,31; BAPD 201683).
44 See Padgett (supra n. 32) 224; Berge (supra n. 32), who sees "reflections of the Kleophrades Painter's work in the Syleus Painter's predilection for the running key border", and compares the Dionysiac scene on the reverse of the Syleus Painter's name vase with that on Munich, Antikensammlungen 2344 (ARV² 182,6; BAPD 201659).
45 Volute-krater, Malibu, J. Paul Getty Museum 77.AE.11 (ARV² 187,52; BAPD 201704) and cup, Paris, Cabinet des Médailles 535 (ARV² 191,103; BAPD 201751).
46 Supra n. 3.
47 On Sikelos, see supra n. 26. For the Pegasos blazons, see M. Bentz, Panathenäische Preisamphoren. Eine athenische Vasengattung und ihre Funktion vom 6.-4. Jahrhundert v. Chr. (1998) 49. 207.
48 Arezzo krater and Basel amphora (supra ns. 18. 23). See M. Schmidt, in: H. A. Cahn – E. Simon (eds.), Tainia. Festschrift für Roland Hampe (1980) 153–169. Schmidt rejected the possibility that the Arezzo krater might be close in date to the Basel neck-amphora, but recent arguments for down-dating early red-figure by Richard Neer (Style and Politics in Athenian Vase Painting: The Craft of Democracy, ca. 530–460 BCE [2002] 186–205) and Susan Rotroff, in APP II 250–260 suggest that this possibility be kept open.
49 Supra n. 45.
50 Brussels, Musée du Cinquantenaire A718 (ARV² 445,256; 1569. 1653; BAPD 20530).
51 S. Muth, Gewalt im Bild (2008) 357–367.
52 See D. Castriota, Myth, Ethos and Actuality (1992).
53 E.g. volute-krater, New York, Metropolitan Museum 07.286.84 (Painter of the Woolly Satyrs; ARV² 613,1; BAPD 207099).
54 The tip of a third letter is just visible. By itself, *su* can be a trademark; see A. W. Johnston, Trademarks on Greek Vases (1979) 164. 230 noting that some examples are likely to be abbreviations for śuthina. However, in Trademarks on Greek Vases – Addenda (2006) 158–159, Johnston moves away from this suggestion.

55 This term was coined by Richard De Puma, AJA 112, 2008, 429–440, and I am grateful to him for discussion on this subject. On śuthina inscriptions, see also N.T. de Grummond, in: M. Gleba – H. Becker (eds.), Votives, Places and Rituals in Etruscan Religion. Studies in Honor of Jean Macintosh Turfa (2009) 171–182; P. Fontaine, in: J-R. Jannot (ed.), Vaisselle Métallique, Vaisselle Céramique: Productions, Usages et Valeurs en Étrurie – REA 97 (1995) 201–226.
56 Discussed by De Puma, supra n. 55.
57 Fontaine (supra n. 55) 204–205 records eleven examples – seven Attic and four Etruscan. Add to these the Syleus Painter fragments in the Louvre mentioned above (supra n. 39) and noted by Beazley (ARV² 253,54) and the fragmentary phiale, formerly Malibu, J. Paul Getty Museum 81.AE.213 (BAPD 15527).
58 E.g., the red-figure pelike, Hamburg, Museum für Kunst und Gewerbe 1980.174 (Painter of the Birth of Athena; BAPD 5647). See also the discussion by E. Rystedt, in: E. Herring – I. Lemos – et al. (eds.), Across Frontiers. Etruscans, Greeks, Phoenicians and Cypriots. Studies in Honour of David Ridgway and Francesca Romana Serra Ridgway (2006) 504.
59 E.g., the red-figure stamnoi, Paris, Musée du Louvre G188bis (Deepdene Painter; ARV² 498,6; BAPD 205592) and G415 (Painter of the Louvre Symposium; ARV² 1070,2; BAPD 214408).
60 Cerveteri, Museo Nazionale Cerite (BAPD 8910).
61 Fontaine (supra n. 55) 205. See also D. Briquel (supra n. 55) 217–223, suggesting that a provenance from Cerveteri or Vulci is more plausible than Nola for Louvre G188bis and G535.
62 On Athenian vases in Etruscan contexts, see C. Reusser, Vasen für Etrurien (2002). See also N. Spivey, in: D. Yatromanolakis (ed.), An Archaeology of Representations (2009) 50–75. Given the large scale of the Syleus Painter's krater, note M. Guggisberg, in: B. Hildebrandt – C. Veit (eds.), Der Wert der Dinge – Güter im Prestigediskurs (2009) 103–141; A. Tsingarida, in: T. Mannack et al. (eds.), Greek Pots Abroad (Oxford forthcoming).
63 See N. T. de Grummond, Etruscan Myth, Sacred History, and Legend (2006) 180–188. On the sanctuary of Hercle at Cerveteri, see M. A. Rizzo, Mediterranea V, 2008, 91–120; eadem, in: S. Fortunelli – C. Masseria (eds.), Ceramica attica da santuari della Grecia, della Ionia e dell'Italia. Atti convegno internazionale Perugia 14–17, Marzo 2007 (2009) 369–386. In addition to the large red-figure cup with an incised dedication to Hercle from this site, Guggisberg (supra n. 62) 124–125 fig. 6 draws attention to fragments of a large black-figure cup with Herakles battling (perhaps) the Amazons from the same sanctuary.
64 81.AE.203.6.2 (J. Frel, in: J. Frel, Studia Varia (1994) 25 fig. 8; BAPD 9016244); 81.AE.206.D.2005 (M. Kotansky – K. Manchester – J. Frel, in: Greek Vases in the J. Paul Getty Museum 2, 1985, 76 fig. 1).
65 81.AE.200.35.3
66 81.AE.206.A.7
67 81.AE.216.E.12
68 81.AE.216.H.10.
69 81.AE.216.J.1.3.
70 On the association of śuthina and śutil (perfect genitive, meaning 'of the tomb'), see M. True, Pre-Sotadean Attic Red-Figure Statuette Vases and Related Vases with Relief Decoration, PhD diss. (Harvard University, 1986) 48 n 26.

20 Democratic Vessels? The Changing Shapes of Athenian Vases in Late Archaic and Early Classical Times

Stefan Schmidt

"Form ever follows function:" This famous phrase by the Chicago architect Louis Sullivan[1] could apply especially to the shapes of Athenian pottery. Even vases with sophisticated decoration were never art for art's sake, but vessels determined by a – at least imagined – practical function. I only call to mind, for instance, the Greek hydria as an impressive functional shape with its two horizontal handles for fetching water and lifting the vessel and with the vertical handle for pouring (Fig. 1). We find the handling of hydriai depicted on a good number of vase paintings. Although almost all researchers agree that the delicate painted specimens of this shape might never have been used this way at Athenian fountains,[2] their form follows the fundamental functions of an everyday tool. Or, to cite another example, the shape of an oinochoe with trefoil mouth and high curved handle is best suited to ladle wine from a krater without getting the fingers wet, and then to serve the wine to symposiasts.[3]

Nevertheless, despite the fundamental role of function, the Athenian potters had a certain degree of freedom to decide how to form the actual vase. For the Attic oinochoai Sir John Beazley defined ten types with distinct features, adopted and sometimes modified by other authors (Fig. 2).[4] But, in spite of the differences in shape, most of these vessels seem to have served the same purposes: the holding and pouring of wine. Additionally, we find for every one of these types of oinochoai a wide range of proportions. This may show how broad the variation within a single functional field could have been. But what was the motive for the potter to choose one or the other type for his work, or to employ the one set or another set of proportions? Was it the wish to design a shape all the better for a specific use, or was it a question of fashionable aesthetics?

To anticipate an answer, there seems to have been a couple of reasons for changing types and forms in Attic pottery. Most important were certainly the wishes of the customers. Good examples for the interdependencies between a purchaser's preferences and a producer's ideas are to be found with the amphora, one of the most common shapes in Attic fine ware pottery.

Well known is the use of the so called Nikosthenic amphora and some other Etruscan shapes in the repertoire of Attic pottery, as a reaction to the demands of Italian or

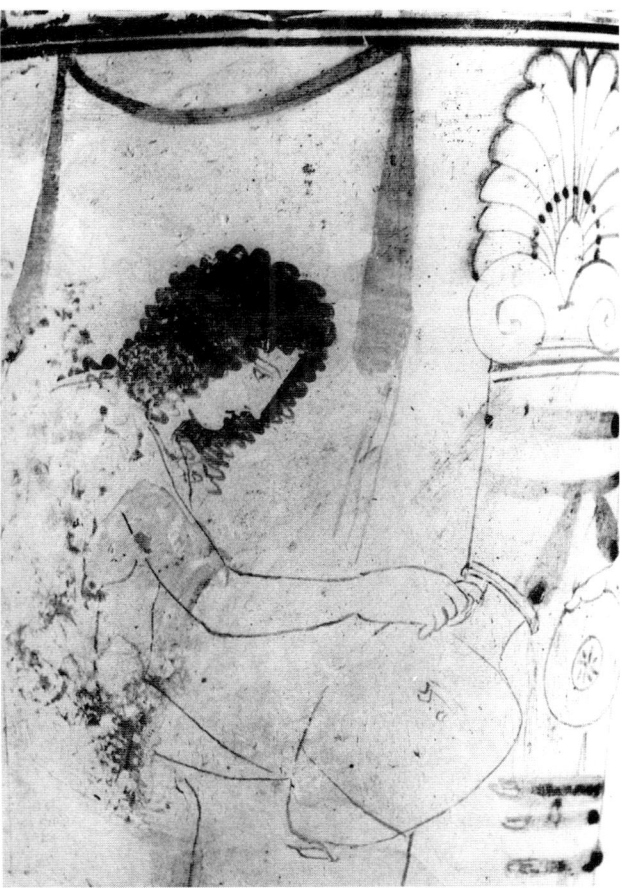

Fig. 1 Pouring from a hydria (after Karlsruhe, Badisches Landesmuseum B 1528: M. Maaß, Wege zur Klassik [1985] color pl. 18).

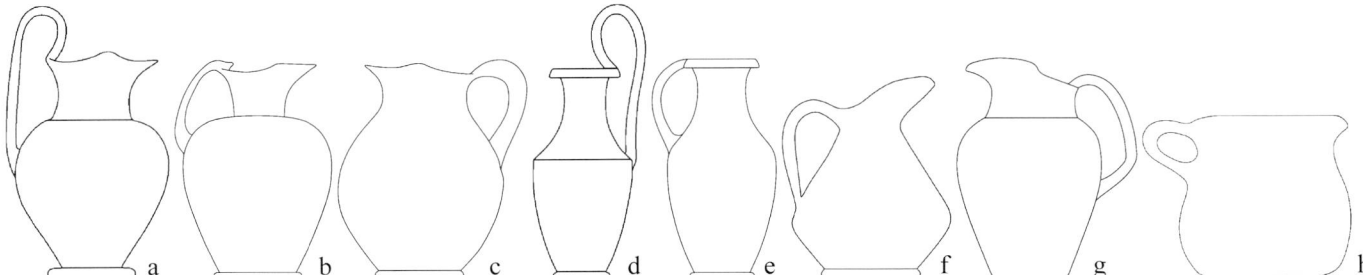

Fig. 2 Oinochoai of eight shapes (after J. Boardman, Athenian Red Figure Vases. The Archaic Period. A Handbook [1975] 209).

to be more precise Caeretan purchasers (Fig. 3).[5] Vases of these shapes were developed and produced in the Athenian workshop of Nikosthenes and almost exclusively shipped to the region of Caere, modern Cerveteri. The rather straight conical form of the Nikosthenic amphora with articulated edges and broad flat handles follows exactly Etruscan Bucchero types, which themselves were clearly inspired by metal-ware. Although there are no extant Etruscan bronze amphorae of exactly this shape, one could imagine the construction of the vessel from several sheets of metal which are connected by folding and hammering. Such a construction is used for a bronze amphora from a warrior's grave in Tarquinia (Fig. 4).[6]

Whereas the products of the Nikosthenic workshop match very closely with Etruscan shapes, other influences of Etruscan customers on Attic vase shapes are less obvious, although it seems that a certain 'metallic' appearance of the vases was well received by the Etruscans. Indeed, the development of the Attic neck amphorae in the second half of the sixth century BC shows a gradual 'metallization' of the shape that goes together with an almost exclusively export oriented production of this shape. Although the shape itself with its two vertical handles has nothing that reminds strongly of metal vessels, the articulation of details follows the appearance of high quality metal vases (Fig. 5a). The profiled foot is inspired by cast bronze feet. As part of a clay vessel such a protruding edge could be easily damaged. The wide body and high shoulder used by Group E and Botkin neck amphorae in the middle of the sixth century may also have been prompted by metal-ware models.[7]

Similarly, there is a parallel development of the Attic shouldered hydriai in the second half of the sixth century BC. Their vertical handles have attachments and rounded knobs at the rim like contemporary bronze examples (Fig. 5b).[8] Additionally, the profile of the Archaic hydria with its sharp angle between body and shoulder looks like an imitation of bronze models. The potters may have exaggerated the sharp but mostly rounded curve for the bronze hydriai, as they tried to make their products more 'metallic' than the metal-ware itself.

The potters' efforts to give their products an elegant shape that could compete with the prestigious metal vases was certainly pushed forward by the wishes of their customers. One should assume that in these cases

the most influential customers were the Etruscans, since the great majority of the black-figured vases with emphasized 'metallic' characteristics have been found in Italy. Especially the shoulder hydria and the so-called standard amphorae are relatively rare in Athenian and Greek contexts, although they compose a high number of the total number of vases known.[9] Most come from Etruscan graves, especially from Vulci.

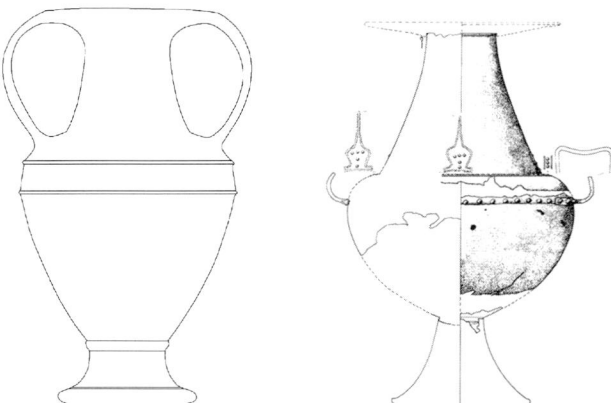

Fig. 3 (left) Nikosthenic Amphora (after P. E. Arias – M. Hirmer, Tausend Jahre Griechische Vasenkunst [1960] pl. xiii).

Fig. 4 (right) An early seventh century Etruscan bronze amphora from Tarquinia (after K. Kilian, JdI 92, 1977, fig. 11).

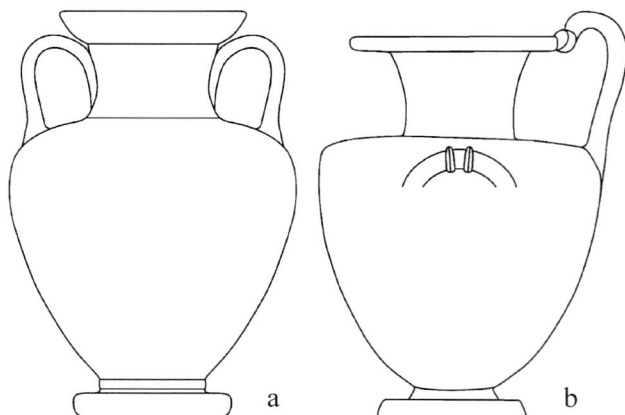

Fig. 5 Standard neck amphora and shouldered hydria (after T. Mannack, Griechische Vasenmalerei [2002] endpaper and Berlin, Staatliche Antikensammlungen F 2174).

On the other hand, belly or one-piece amphorae are as frequent in Athens as in Etruria. Apparently this shape matched Athenian needs (Fig. 6a). The best evidence of how they were used by the Athenians is supplied by the depictions on the vases themselves. In contrast to neck amphorae of the standard shape which never appear in the pictures,[10] one-piece amphorae are sometimes shown together with men in mantles or filled with grain.[11] Ingeborg Scheibler has convincingly argued that the decorated one-piece amphora was inspired by the everyday kados and seems to be somehow connected with typical Athenian rituals or feasts. Nevertheless, although the development of the shape was obviously influenced by Athenian needs, the vases were likewise attractive to Etruscan customers. And maybe, therefore, the amphora – especially the type A amphora – also underwent a slight 'metallization' (Fig. 6b).

These few examples may show the variety of influences on the development of a certain vase shape in Athenian potteries. In not every case can the reasons for having chosen the one variety or the other may be traced back with the same certainty. But a hermeneutical network of information about the use, the distribution, and the origin of certain shapes could lead to a better understanding of the intentions of both the producers and the purchasers of Attic pottery.

This study will evaluate the intentions behind the development of vase shapes during an exiting period of Athenian history. In the Late Archaic and Early Classical periods not only the polis as a whole saw far-reaching changes, but also the potters' workshops in the Kerameikos. The most obvious was the invention of the red-figure technique in vase-painting around 530 BC. Not only did the aesthetics of decoration change, but in the following years several new shapes found their way into the Attic repertoire. The characteristics of these newly invented shapes and their semantics will be the focus of the following paragraphs.

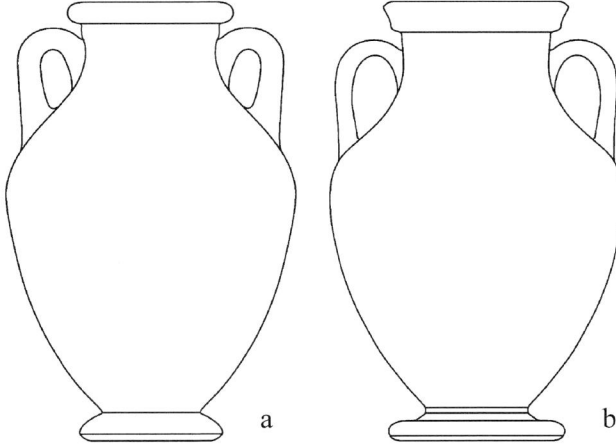

Fig. 6 One-piece amphorai of shape C and A (after T. Mannack, Griechische Vasenmalerei [2002] endpaper).

In 1951 Dietrich von Bothmer gave a list of Attic vase shapes invented in the early red-figure period. Beside the so called pelike, which was the focus of his article, he mentioned the psykter, the stamnos, the kalpis, and the bell krater.[12] This list was repeated by numerous scholars with slight modifications,[13] and it serves as an appropriate starting point for this investigation. Two of the new shapes mentioned are easily explained. The psykter was a new type of vessel developed for new functional needs. The refinement of symposium culture led to a wish to cool the wine not only by adding fresh water directly to the wine, but to cool the whole wine container. For this purpose the psykter was developed. Containing unmixed wine, it was put into a krater where it was surrounded by water or ice.[14]

The psykter was a rather short-lived shape. By the middle of the fifth century it went out of fashion. It seems that the complicated procedure of cooling was no longer of interest. If one assumes – as some scholars do[15] – that this equipment was necessary for serving unmixed but cool wine, the history of the shape could mirror changing habits of the Late Archaic and Early Classical symposium.

The second shape that von Bothmer lists, the stamnos, was one of the shapes that seems to have been invented to meet the wishes of Etruscan customers. Older hypotheses saw the shape in the tradition of either the Attic Geometric belly-handle amphora or common Greek household jars.[16] Cornelia Isler-Kerényi first, and then Juliette de La Genière convincingly argued for the Etruscan connection of the shape.[17] Like the Nikosthenic amphora or the kyathos, the stamnos is based on Italian models and was almost exclusively exported to the west.

More difficult to explain are the last three shapes mentioned by von Bothmer. Of these, only the pelike has been discussed in some depth by other scholars.[18] All agree that the name is a purely modern convention, going back to Eduard Gerhard.[19] The shape is often seen as a variation of the amphora, particularly of the type C one-piece amphora (Fig. 6a).[20] But, although the two vertical handles and the torus-like rim show that the shape had a similar function, it also has been pointed out that the pelike was somewhat odd in the Athenian repertoire of the late sixth century BC. Compared to the other vases with high shoulders and articulated details – for example, the above mentioned contemporary neck amphorae – the pelike is an ugly duckling. With its sagging belly on a broad simple foot, it seems to contradict all aesthetic principles of the time (Fig. 7).[21]

These characteristics have been explained by shape's function. The low center of gravity is appropriate for vessels which filled with valuable liquids needs to stand stable. The evidence for how the Athenians used these vessels is again given by the depictions on the vases themselves. The pelike is shown several times in lively market scenes, where it serves as container for scented oil (Fig. 8).[22] The salesmen had to be sure that their valuable liquid goods did not get lost. The ancient name of the shape could have been "stamnos", as Ingeborg

Scheibler suggested with good reasons,[23] a name which would likewise suit its use. As a derivation from ἵστημι it emphasizes the standing up of the vessels in contrast to commercial amphorae which had no or only small feet, so that they needed an additional piece of equipment to be stood in an upright position.[24]

On one black figured vase in Berlin we find the depiction of pelikai used for fetching water (Fig. 9).[25] With a rope between the handles they were treated like a bucket. This picture may hint at one of the inspirations for the new shape. Normally the buckets used in this way in other depictions can be identified with the kados which was a very common vessel in Attic and Greek domestic pottery (Fig. 10).[26] These common household pots resemble the pelikai with their two vertical handles, the continuous profile, and the wide mouth. That both pelikai and kadoi could serve the same purposes, and that they had functional similarities makes it very likely that the Late Archaic potters had in mind to create the pelike as a fine ware version of the kados. Indeed, the simple and less articulate form of the pelike seems to have been inspired by the widely disseminated domestic vessels.

As mentioned above, the kados was even considered as a model for the one-piece amphora by Ingeborg Scheibler.[27] Indeed, the kados and one-piece amphora have a lot in common, especially the continuous curved profile. The close resemblances between the one-piece amphora, especially of Type C, and the pelike suggest that the kados was the inspiration for both. The only difference is that the creation of the one-piece amphora took place in the late seventh century, whereas the pelike was the result of changes in the last decades of the sixth century BC.

The pelike was the most successful of the potters' inventions during these years. The shape remained in production till the end of the fourth century BC. Other experiments with new amphora shapes in the Late Archaic red-figure workshops were not as well received. Either they were not nearly produced as frequently as pelikai, or they had a rather short lifespan. It is important, nevertheless, to emphasize that the other new amphorae also took their inspiration from pottery and not from metalwork. The most obvious ones are the pointed amphora which quotes the form of the common transport amphora,[28] and the so-called amphora of Panathenaic shape that was reminiscent of the famous prize vases.[29]

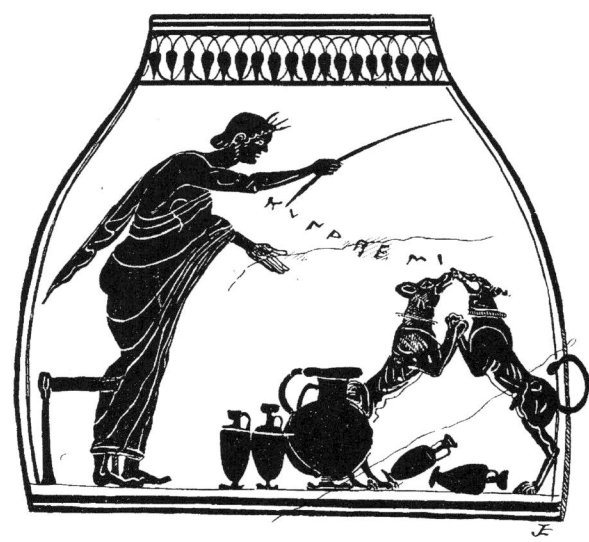

Fig. 8 Pelike, Firenze, Museo Archeologico 72 732 (after RA 1926, 290 fig. 5).

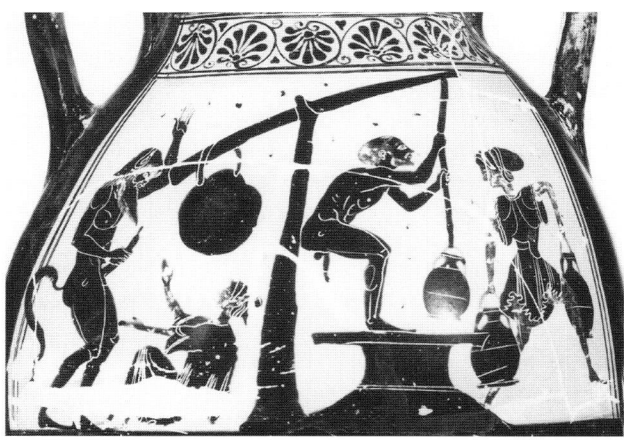

Fig. 9 Attic black-figure pelike Berlin, Staatliche Antikensammlungen V.I. 3228 (after CVA Berlin 7 Germany 61 pl. 29,1).

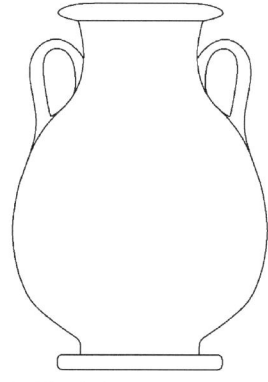

Fig. 7 Pelike (after Paris, Louvre G 65).

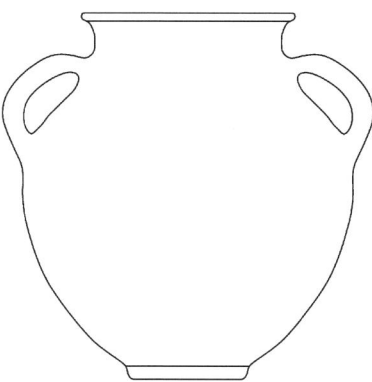

Fig. 10 Cooking ware kados (after Athens, Agora P 18347).

If we now broaden the view to other contemporary new shapes, it will be clear that the dependence of the pelike on everyday pottery is not accidental, but mirrors an overall tendency for Attic fine ware in the last decades of the sixth century BC. Going back to von Bothmer's list, we find the so called kalpis (Fig. 11a) as another new shape fitting perfectly within this tendency. With its bulging body, its continuous curved profile and the vertical handle attached not on the rim but on the neck, this newly invented form of the hydria was clearly a derivation from the conventional household hydria (Fig. 11b).[30] This marks a striking change in the potters' interests. Up to this time the shaping of the Attic hydria followed primarily metal-ware models, as mentioned above (Fig. 5b). The invention of the common household shape in the repertoire of fine ware seems to have taken place again in the same workshops that specialized in the new red figure technique.[31] And coincidently, the shape was attractive also to the metal workers, for at the same period of time even the bronze hydriai followed this everyday model.[32]

One vessel not included in von Bothmer's list should be mentioned here: the chous (Fig. 2c). As I have shown elsewhere, this shape was inspired by the plain household jug which was used in Athens as early as the seventh century BC (Fig. 12).[33] Painted and plain jugs have in common not only the simple curved profile, the broad foot ring and the low handle, but also the more or less standardized capacity that is known in Athens nomenclature as a chous. It is true that the earliest examples of choes in fine ware can be found in the work of the Amasis and Taleides Painters who are claimed to be the inventors of this shape.[34] This would be a little earlier then 530 BC. But their black-figured choes were mere singletons. Only in red figure did the chous become the standard oinochoe in Athens. With the choes it was the same as with the hydriai and the pelikai: Shapes that recalled clearly the vessels every Athenian used in his kitchen were taken up by the most ambitious potters' workshops.

Another shape must be mentioned here. Conventionally considered an oinochoe, although its use as wine pitcher is not certain, Beazley's oinochoe shape VIII is a rather simple mug with a flat bottom, convex body and short offset rim (Fig. 2h).[35] It has been suggested that such simple mugs originally were carried by soldiers or travelers in their pack, perhaps inspired by Laconian predecessors.[36] Interesting for us is that this shape appears in some early red figure workshops alongside other everyday models. Although there were only a few early workshops producing it – namely that of the Epeleios Painter and the Painter of Berlin 2268[37] – this experimental shape also reflects the tendency we have seen.

The last novelty listed by von Bothmer was the bell krater. Named because its shape resembles an inverted bell, this rather simple krater was an invention of the late sixth century BC too (Fig. 13). Although the earliest extant examples are by the Berlin Painter from the early fifth century BC,[38] the shape may well have been in the repertoire of Athenian potters and painters even before that, for there are two fragments by late sixth-century painters which may come from bell kraters.[39] In addition, a tub-like krater with rounded lugs instead of handles is frequently depicted on cups of the Euergides Painter and some other Late Archaic painters,[40] and these cups are certainly earlier than the Berlin Painter's bell kraters (Fig. 15). However, it is not entirely clear if the images refer to early bell kraters or to vats used for preparing grapes to make vine.[41] But even this uncertainty makes the source of inspiration clearer. Also for the bell krater the potters looked at these everyday wine vessels.[42] A tub with lug handles from an Archaic house south of the Athenian Agora illustrates what models they may have had in mind (Fig. 14).[43]

To complete the picture, I have to mention here the second krater shape invented in the Attic repertoire during the last decades of the sixth century BC, the calyx krater. It first appeared in the workshop of Exekias slightly earlier than the shapes we have considered so far in this paper.[44] The creation of this krater shape seems to be first of all caused by functional needs. A new wide-mouthed vessel was necessary for using the almost simultaneously invented psykter.[45] This functional pairing off can be proved by the depictions of psykters in use. They were exclusively shown in calyx kraters, but never with other shapes, the only exception being a cup in Compiègne

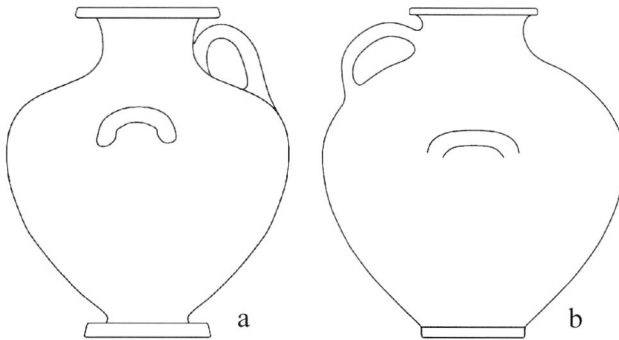

Fig. 11 Kalpis and cooking ware hydria (after Berlin, Staatliche Antikensammlungen 1966.20 and Athens, Agora P 20558).

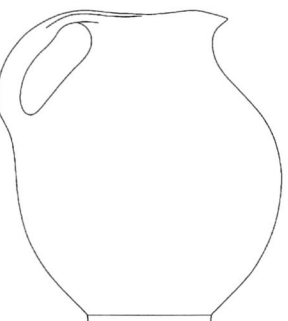

Fig. 12 Cooking ware jug (after Athens, Agora P 12528).

where the psykter sits in a big skyphos or bell krater.⁴⁶ So, the invention of the calyx krater and the psykter was directly connected. Nevertheless, the calyx krater developed independently even after the psykter ceased. It was still in production in Athens and South Italy during the fifth and fourth centuries BC.

To sum up, this short overview has shown a conspicuously increasing number of new shapes in the last decades of the sixth century that were inspired not by elegant metal-ware but rather by clumsy, everyday pottery. We should ask, why was there a return to everyday pottery models in a time that saw increasing competition between metal and clay? As I pointed out, one of the driving forces for the orientation towards metal vessels was the demand of Etruscan customers. Were they no longer interested in Attic vases? Definitely not! The new shapes found their way to the West as well. Not just the traditional black-figured standard neck amphorae or the shoulder hydriai were bought by the Etruscans, but almost all the experiments of the Athenian potters and painters – were the red figure technique as well as the new shapes – were highly welcome in Etruria, judging from the enormous corpus of such vases unearthed in Italy.

Also improbable is that all these new shapes were invented to meet new functional needs. This may have been the reason for the creation of the psykter and the calyx krater, but this does not explain the change from the shoulder hydria to the kalpis or the success of the pelike and the chous. These were indeed created due to new aesthetic values. But why did these values change so significantly?

If we look for similar changes in other fields of art, one phenomenon comes to mind. At the beginning of the fifth century BC a radical change in Athenian clothing styles took place, especially in women's dress when the patterned and delicate chiton and himation were replaced by the woolen and austere peplos.⁴⁷ Like the name, the significance of this early fifth-century garment and the connotations of its use are not perfectly clear to us,⁴⁸ but it is obvious that instead of using imported luxury fabrics, even rich Athenians gave preference to homemade Attic woolen cloth. This preference seems to acquire a political significance, if we see it together with other evidence of latent criticism of luxury of the same time, as for instance the end of lavishly decorated aristocratic family burials, a change which is often connected with a sumptuary law,⁴⁹ or the mocking of luxurious lifestyles in written sources like Aeschylus or Xenophanes.⁵⁰ All these phenomena have been seen by historians as part of the great processes of democratization, a turning to the values of the majority. To a certain degree, the peplos seems to have served as a statement that emphasized the community of isonomic and autochthonic Athenians.

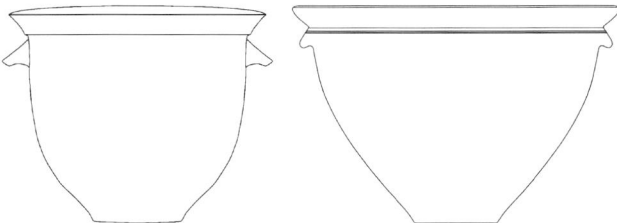

Fig. 13 (left) Lugged bell krater (after Tarquinia, Museo Nazionale RC 7456).

Fig. 14 (right) Household ware tub (after Athens, Agora P 26237).

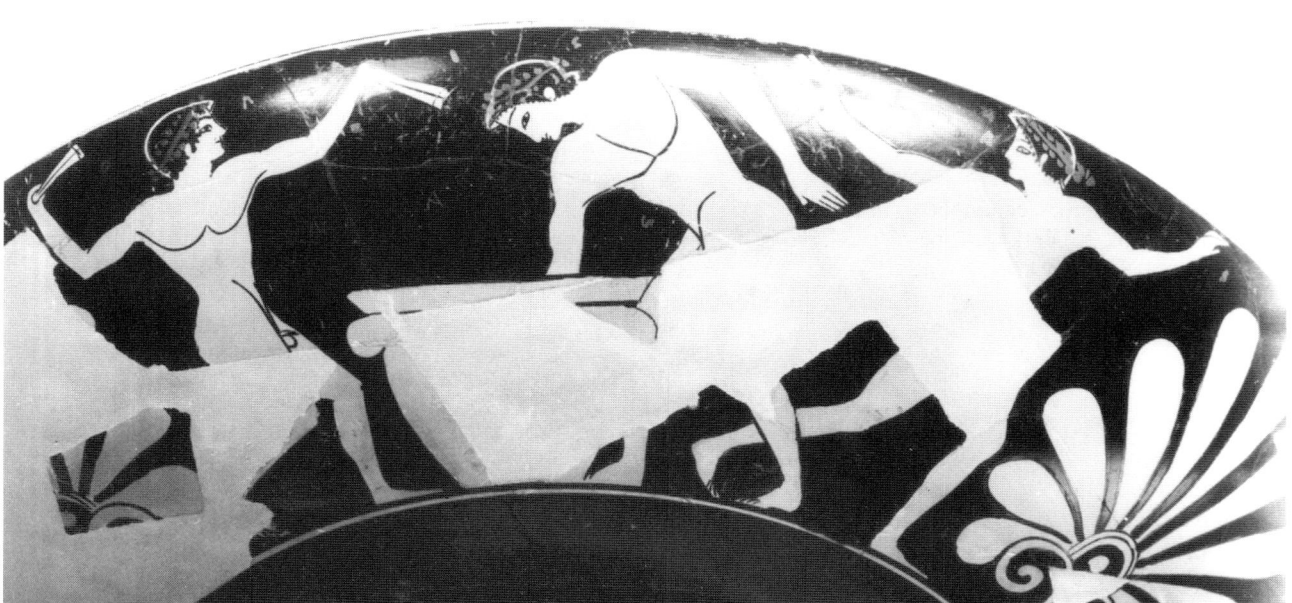

Fig. 15 Attic red-figure kylix, Leipzig, Antikenmuseum T 3373 (after CVA Leipzig 3 Germany 80 pl. 12,3).

However, did the new style of pottery we have observed belong to these phenomena? Were the pelike, the kalpis or the chous "democratic" vessels? Did their shapes emphasize the simple lifestyle of ordinary Athenians? As Alan Shapiro outlined at the first Athenian Potters and Painters conference, there is a remarkable accumulation of pictures on black figure pelikai depicting scenes of craftsmen or working people. Far more detailed and more frequent as on all other shapes, these pictures gave special praise to the world of Athenian banausoi.[51] One wonders if the depictions aimed to underline the significance of a banausic shape. Should the shape of the pelikai likewise highlight the habits of the average Athenian versus the sophisticated lifestyle of the aristocracy?

Although I insinuated this to be the case with the title of this paper, there are good reasons to argue against this hypothesis. First of all, there are chronological discrepancies. The changes of pottery shapes we have observed started as early as around 530 BC, a time when no one in Athens thought about democracy and when sophistication of aristocratic lifestyles reached a peak. The later success of these simple shapes in Athenian workshops might have been fostered by the same attitudes that caused the appearance of the peplos. But for the invention of the pottery shapes some fifty years earlier, this cannot be the case.

Secondly, we would misunderstand these revolutionary changes in Athenian society during Kleisthenic and even later times, if we were to assume that aristocratic values were totally replaced by new democratic values. Isonomia, the slogan of the Kleisthenic reforms, did not mean the deprivation of power for Athenian aristocrats, but only the political and juridical equality of all *politai*. Even in the first half of the fifth century BC aristocratic lifestyles did not meet with disapproval. Moreover, participating in former aristocratic occupations like the symposium, sports or horse races was the ideal of most Athenian democrats.[52] To a certain degree, democratization in fifth-century Athens means the aristocratization of the life of the many.

Since there are no clear hints of a special appreciation of austerity in Late Archaic or Early Classical Athenian society, we have to look for other reasons for the obvious change of fashion in Athenian pottery. Most promising for understanding the invention of the new shapes is the fact that this was contemporary with the invention of the red figure technique; especially, since most of the shapes were developed in the same workshops in Athens that gave favor to this new, revolutionary manner of decoration. We have to assume a direct link between these two developments.

As Richard Neer has convincingly pointed out in his study of the political attitudes of the Pioneers, the invention of the red figure technique was part of a broad, innovative climate in the Late Archaic Kerameikos. Potters and painters experimented a lot with new techniques in order to give their products a more striking appearance[53] – especially in respect to some of the efforts undertaken to compete with metal-ware. The red figure technique, too, may have been caused first by a wish to imitate the glossy surface of metal vessels. But the painting of bright red figures surrounded by a black background turned out to surpass the possibilities of metal-ware decoration. The potters and painters had by chance developed a new aesthetic based on purely ceramic means. The great success of this experiment, confirmed by the almost complete change of techniques within the next decades, may have been one of the reasons for the increasing wealth and above all the pride of the artisans. There is some evidence for the social advancement and newly found self-confidence of the former banausoi. Often discussed are the self-portraits on vases of some Pioneers in sympotic or other aristocratic contexts.[54] Likewise well known are the remains of costly votives of potters and painters in Athenian sanctuaries.[55]

The great aesthetic and economic success of red figure seems to have, on the other hand, encouraged potters to look more closely at clay traditions than to metal-ware to develop new shapes. Since red figure's painterly lines outdid the old black figure incisions, so similar to toreutics, why should not a shape that brought the potter's craft to perfection be more attractive than one that was inspired by metal-ware? So, in a period of artisans' growing self-confidence, referring to Athenian common pottery makes sense.

The vase shapes examined in this paper are, therefore, not evidence for the special wishes of the customer. They hint neither at new functional needs nor at a new aesthetic of the sober and simple. The shapes are first of all evidence for the intentions of their producers. They hint at the changing self-awareness of the potters and painters in the Athenian Kerameikos. In doing this, the new pottery shapes add a tiny aspect to our view of the development of an Athenian middle class, so to speak. Beside other evidence, the trends in shaping fine ware pottery shed additional light on the growing importance of salesmen, artisans and industrialists in Late Archaic Athenian society. The increasing wealth and self-confidence of these groups allowed them to participate in the political process. Balancing out these needs with the power of the landowning aristocrats was one of the aims of the Kleisthenic reforms. Athenian democracy was later built on this foundation of the participation of the many in decisions for the polis. So indeed, the pottery shapes let us grasp a little bit of the atmosphere in which democratic ideas began to grow. And only in this respect may one speak of "democratic" vessels.

Abbreviations

Agora VIII	E. T. H. Brann, Late Geometric and Protoattic Pottery, The Athenian Agora VIII (1962)
Kerameikos IX	U. Knigge, Der Südhügel, Kerameikos. Ergebnisse der Ausgrabungen IX (1976)

Notes

1. L. H. Sullivan, Kindergarten Chats and Other Writings (1947) 208 (reprinted from L. H. Sullivan, The Tall Office Building Artistically Considered, Lippincott's Magazine, March 1896).
2. Cf. I. Scheibler, Griechische Töpferkunst. Herstellung, Handel und Gebrauch der antiken Tongefäße, 2nd ed. (1995) 29; V. Liventhal, AnalRom 14, 1985, 44; B. Sparkes, The Red and The Black. Studies in Greek Pottery (1996) 80; S. Schmidt, Rhetorische Bilder auf attischen Vasen. Visuelle Kommunikation im 5. Jahrhundert v. Chr. (2005) 226; – for the use of hydriae see E. Trinkl, in: Tsingarida, Shapes 155–158.
3. Cf. B. Kaeser, in: K. Vierneisel – B. Kaeser, Kunst der Schale – Kultur des Trinkens (1990) 187; A. J. Clark, in: Tsingarida, Shapes 90–92.
4. ARV² xlix–l; J. R. Green, BICS 19, 1972, 6–9; J. Boardman, Athenian Red Figure Vases. The Archaic Period. A Handbook (1975) 208–209; M. G. Kanowski, Containers of Classical Greece. A Handbook of Shapes (1984) 108.
5. Scheibler (supra n. 2) 172–173; T. Rasmussen, AntK 28, 1985, 33–39; V. Tosto, The Black-figured Pottery Signed ΝΙΚΟΣΘΕΝΕΣΕΠΟΙΕΣΕΝ (1999) 17–43.
6. K. Kilian, JdI 92, 1977, 33 fig. 11. For critics on the relationship between metal and clay: D. K. Hill, AJA 51, 1947, 248–256; see remarks in Agora XII 15.
7. See H. Mommsen, in: Tsingarida, Shapes 31–46 rejecting the older assumption of an Origin from East Greek Fikellura models: D. A. Jackson, East Greek Influence on Attic Vases (1976) 13–37.
8. E. Diehl, Die Hydria. Formgeschichte und Verwendung im Kult des Altertums (1964) 58; J. Boardman, Athenian Black Figure Vases. A Handbook (1974) 186.
9. A. W. Johnston, in: H. A. G. Brijder (ed.), Ancient Greek and Related Pottery (1984) 208–211. On the distribution of standard neck amphorae: M. Bentz, in: Tsingarida, Shapes 83.
10. Bentz (supra n. 9) 82–83.
11. I. Scheibler, JdI 102, 1987, 63–75.
12. D. von Bothmer, JHS 71, 1951, 42; going back to J. D. Beazley, Attic Black-figure, A Sketch (1928) 24.
13. H. Bloesch, JHS 71, 1951, 29; Agora XII 49; W. Schiering, Die griechischen Tongefässe. Gestalt, Bestimmung und Formenwandel, 2nd ed. (1983) 52; Agora XXX 12.
14. On the use of the psykter, see the erroneous conclusions of S. Drougou, Der attische Psykter (1975) 31–35. – Cf. Agora XXIII 20–21; K. Vierneisel, in: Vierneisel – Kaeser (supra n. 3) 259–264; C. Tombretti, La breve vita dello psykter. Parabola dell'Harosyne sulla scorcio dell'archaismo, Frankfurter elektronische Rundschau zur Altertumskunde 16, 2011, 11–41 (http://s145739614.online.de/fera/ausgabe16/Trombetti.pdf).
15. G. M. A. Richter – M. J. Milne, Shapes and Names of Athenian Vases (1935) 12, referring to Poll. 6.99; K. Vierneisel, in: Vierneisel – Kaeser (supra n. 3) 261.
16. B. Philippaki, The Attic Stamnos (1967) xxi; Schiering (supra n. 13) 51–52; Kanowski (supra n. 4) 141.
17. C. Isler-Kerényi, NumAntCl 5, 1976, 33–52; J. de La Genière, MEFRA 99,1, 1987, 43–61; C. Isler-Kerényi, Gnomon 66, 1994, 48; J. de La Genière, in: M. C. Villanueva Puig (ed.), Céramique et peinture grecques. Modes d'emploi (1999) 418.
18. Von Bothmer (supra n. 12); R.-M. Becker, Formen attischer Peliken von der Pionier Gruppe bis zum Beginn der Frühklassik (1977) (D. von Bothmer, Review of Becker 1977, AJA 83, 1979, 361–362); H. A. Shapiro, in: APP 63–70; Γ. Καββαδίας, Τό Μουσεῖον 2, 2001, 29–31.
19. Richter – Milne (supra n. 15) 5; Shapiro (supra n. 18) 63; Καββαδίας (supra n. 18) 29.
20. von Bothmer (supra n. 12) 44; Agora XII 49; Schiering (supra n. 13) 38; Agora XXIII 20; Shapiro (supra n. 18) 63.
21. Schiering (supra n. 13) 38; von Bothmer (supra n. 18) 362; Shapiro (supra n. 18) 68. For the overall tendency see Bloesch (supra n. 13) 29.
22. Scheibler (supra n. 2) 17 fig. 7; Shapiro (supra n. 18) 64; Schmidt (supra n. 2) 29 fig. 1.
23. Scheibler (supra n. 2) 147; cf. A. W. Johnston, ZPE 12, 1973, 265–266.
24. Cf. D. A. Amyx, Hesperia 27, 1958, 193; Kanowski (supra n. 4) 141.
25. Berlin, Staatliche Museen Antikensammlung V.I.3228: CVA Berlin 7 Germany 61 pls. 28. 29,1–2; Shapiro (supra n. 18) 64 fig. 1. – Cf. for pelikai actually used as buckets: K. M. Lynch, Hesperia 70, 2001, 171–173.
26. Agora VIII 54–55; Agora XII 201–203; Kerameikos IX 192 pl. 95,1. For depictions in vase-paintings see Scheibler (supra n. 2) 61 n. 19; Trinkl (supra n. 2) 157.
27. Scheibler (supra n. 11) 60–63.
28. Boardman (supra n. 4) 208; Schiering (supra n. 13) 36.
29. J. D. Beazley, BSA 19, 1912/13, 239–240; Boardman (supra n. 4) 208; M. Bentz, Panathenäische Preisamphoren. Eine athenische Vasengattung und ihre Funktion vom 6.–4. Jahrhundert v. Chr. (1998) 21.
30. Agora VIII 56 pl. 12. Agora XII 200–201 pl. 71 – Cf. R. M. Cook, Greek Painted Pottery (1960) 226; Diehl (supra n. 8) 58–59.
31. ARV² 34; F. W. Hamdorf, Pantheon 32, 1974, 220; Agora XXIII 38; Agora XXX 38; CVA Berlin 9 Germany 74 19. Add New York, Market: BAPD 19827; Würzburg K 2025: E. Simon (ed.), Die Sammlung Kiseleff im Martin-von-Wagner-Museum der Universität Würzburg 2. Minoische und griechische Antiken (1989) 109 no. 180 pl. 77; BAPD 46203.
32. Diehl (supra n. 8) 58.
33. Schmidt (supra n. 2) 157–158.
34. Cf. Agora XII 63; Agora XXIII 42. – Amasis Painter: A. J. Clark, in: Tsingarida, Shapes 35–51; D. von Bothmer, The Amasis Painter and his World (1985) 154–162. Taleides: ABV 174,3. 4; BAPD 301122. 301123.
35. Green (supra n. 4) 8; Agora XXX 43; F. Lissarrague, L'autre guerrier (1990) 165.
36. Agora XII 70–71; Lissarrague (supra n. 35) 165–166.
37. ARV² 152. 156–158. 1676; Agora XXX 43 nos. 30–31; Lissarrague (supra n. 35) 166; D. Paleothodoros, Epictetos (2004) 50–52.
38. Paris, Louvre G 174: CVA Louvre 2 France 2 pl. 12,2; ARV² 205,123; BAPD 201932; Paris, Louvre G 175: CVA Louvre 2 France 2 pl. 12,5. 7; 14,3. 4; ARV² 205,124; BAPD 201933; Rome Market: ARV² 205,125; BAPD 201934; Tarquinia, Museo Nazionale RC 7456: ARV² 205,126; BAPD 201935. – Cf. Agora XXX 31; CVA Berlin 11 Germany 86 43.
39. Rome, Villa Giulia 50590: ARV² 162,5; BAPD 201518; Agora XXX 31 n. 5 (Hischylos Painter). – Paris, Cab.

Méd. 387: ARV² 31,5; BAPD 200190; Agora XXX 31 n. 6 (Dikaios Painter).

40 Euergides Painter etc.: ARV² 89,14. 20; 90,29; 91,50. 54; 92,61. 65; 95,126. 127; 97,10; BAPD 200710. 200716. 200724. 200745. 200749. 200758. 200762. 200822. 200823. 200848; add: Frankfurt, Museum für Vor- und Frühgeschichte β402: CVA Frankfurt 2 Germany 30 pl. 59,2; BAPD 10535; Taranto, Museo Nazionale Vinc 108/2: CVA Taranto 4 Italy 70 pl. 21,3; 22,2; BAPD 23633. Others: ARV² 133,4; BAPD 201096 (Circle of Nikosthenes Painter); ARV² 151,51; CVA Baltimore 1 USA 28 pl. 45,3; BAPD 201375 (Manner of Epeleios Painter); ARV² 152,5; BAPD 201392 (akin to Epeleios Painter); Para 336; BAPD 352457 (Manner of Epeleios Painter). – Cf. J. H. Oakley, CVA Baltimore 1 USA 28 45; F. G. Lo Porto, CVA Taranto 4 Italy 70 17. – See a depiction of a similar vessel on a neck amphora by the Berlin Painter, Paris Louvre G 201: ARV² 201,63 BAPD 201871.

41 Agora XII 55.

42 J. D. Beazley, Der Berliner Maler (1930) 12; H. R. W. Smith, CVA San Francisco 1 USA 10 45; ARV² 1632.

43 Agora XII 217. 366 no. 1847 pl. 88.

44 Cf. Agora XXIII 26–27; K. Huber, Werkstattgesellen. Zur Produktion früher Kelchkratere, in: Euphronios und seine Zeit (1992) 57–72; Agora XXX 26–28; A. Tsingarida, in: P. Rouillard – A. Verbanck-Piérard (eds.), Le vase grec et ses destins (2003) 99–109; A. Schöne-Denkinger, CVA Berlin 11 Germany 89 26.

45 Agora XXIII 21; Agora XXX 36; Tsingarida (supra n. 44) 100.

46 Compiègne, Musee Vivenel 1102: ARV² 341,1; BAPD 203525 (Manner of Antiphon Painter).

47 W. Martini, in: K. Zimmermann, Der Stilbegriff in den Altertumswissenschaften (1993) 75 80; E. B Harrison, in: S. J. Barnes – W. S. Melion (eds.), Cultural Differentiation and Cultural Identity on the Visual Arts (1989) 41–44; J. M. Hall, in: S. E. Alcock – R. Osborne (eds.), Classical Archaeology (2007) 343–347.

48 There is no evidence for peplos as a name for the classical garment: see M. M. Lee, The Myth of the Classical Peplos (1999) 5–8. 351–355, who argues that the depicted garment was not in everyday use, but an iconographical construct of Hellenic identity: 359–361.

49 J. Engels, Funerum sepulcrorumque magnificentia. Begräbnis- und Grabluxusgesetze in der griechisch-römischen Welt mit einigen Ausblicken auf Einschränkungen des funeralen und sepulkralen Luxus im Mittelalter und in der Neuzeit (1998) 97–106.

50 Aesch. Pers. 181–187; Xenophan. Fr. 3 (Heitsch; DK 21 B 3); Cf. Martini (supra n. 47) 78. – For modest dressing see Thuc. I, 6.3–5.

51 Shapiro (supra n. 18) 63–70.

52 Cf. C. Mann, Klio 80, 1998, 20; Hall (supra n. 47) 347.

53 R. Neer, Style and Politics in Athenian Vase-painting. The Craft of Democracy, ca. 530–470 B.C.E. (2002) 32–37.

54 L. Giuliani, in: Euphronios (supra n. 44) 16–18; Scheibler (supra n. 2) 130–132; E. C. Keuls, Painter and Poet in Ancient Greece. Iconography and the Literary Arts (1997) 288–290; J. Boardman, The History of Greek Vases (2001) 146–149 fig. 179; Neer (supra n. 53) 87–134; G. Hedreen, in: D. Yatromanolakis (ed.), An Archaeology of Representations. Ancient Greek Vase-painting and Contemporary Methodologies (2009) 200–239.

55 Scheibler (supra n. 2) 124–127.

21 A Kantharos in the Museum of Fine Arts, Boston and the Reception of Athenian Red-figure in Boeotia

In Memoriam, Natalie Boymel Kampen

Phoebe C. Segal

The reception of Athenian vases by non-Athenians, Greek and non-Greek alike, has attracted significant attention in the past two decades. Yet, despite its proximity to Athens, the status of Boeotia as an importer of Attic vases has only recently been given serious consideration, principally by Victoria Sabetai.[1] The subject of this paper is an Athenian red-figure kantharos attributed to the Brygos Painter (Figs. 1–3; Color Pl. 27) which features on each side Zeus pursuing one of his erotic interests.[2] The noted antiquities collector Edward Perry Warren, who must have been attracted to the kantharos' elegance and erotic subject matter, purchased it in 1895 for the Museum of Fine Arts, Boston and recorded in his notes that it was "said to have been found at Thebes".[3] The kantharos remains one of the most widely discussed vases in the MFA's esteemed collection, but its Theban audience has not yet been given critical consideration.

Sabetai has suggested that in Boeotia, where the black-figure technique was dominant through the Classical period, all red-figure pottery, whether of Boeotian, Attic or Corinthian manufacture, carried a "more elevated tone" than black-figure, and that red-figure vases were prized items, even if they were not intrinsically valuable.[4] Deposited in limited numbers even in very rich graves, it would seem that red-figure vases were selected carefully, especially in the Late Archaic period.[5] Thus, it is important to pursue the question of why the images these esteemed vases carried might have appealed to a Boeotian, in this case Theban, audience. To that end, this paper seeks to contextualize the kantharos within the historical setting of its manufacture in Athens and export to Thebes and offers some suggestions on why it might have appealed to a Theban.

The absence of a scientifically excavated find-spot in Thebes demands that one proceed with caution, yet the alleged provenience of the kantharos should not be ignored. While it is the only published example of an Athenian red-figure kantharos to have been found, or "said to have been found," in Thebes, it is difficult to ascertain how much of an outlier it was in the Late Archaic period when it was most likely buried. Thebes has been the site of continuous human occupation since the Early Bronze Age (circa 2,500 BC) and this has presented a logistical challenge with regard to carrying out systematic excavations on a grand scale. Recent excavations in the Archaic, Classical and Hellenistic cemeteries have yielded significant quantities of terracotta figurines, marble sculpture, and vases, but most of these unfortunately remain unpublished.[6]

The Vase

Side A of the kantharos (Figs. 1. 3; Color Pl. 27A) features Zeus, partially draped in a himation, scepter in hand, chasing after a female figure usually identified as the nymph Aegina, but on occasion as Semele.[7] The speed of the pair is palpable in every detail of the iconography. The woman energetically lunges, desperately attempting to evade Zeus' grasp, the gentle arc of her body echoing that of the vase. Her advancing right leg bends forward so powerfully, and flexibly, that her knee emerges from behind her chiton, which swells around her legs, billowing out behind her. With both feet on tiptoes, she barely even touches the ground. Up top, she slows herself, turning her head towards Zeus, her left arm raised, palm outstretched, begging to be spared. But Zeus charges after her nonetheless, his right arm reaching out and past what may be read as a supplicating gesture. Behind him stands an altar accompanied by a palm tree.[8]

Side B (Figs. 2–3; Color Pl. 27B) of the vase depicts another pursuit scene, and this time Zeus hunts Ganymede, shown with his identifying hoop and stick.[9] The magnitude of Ganymede's effort to escape Zeus is apparent in the composition of the scene, chiefly in the dramatic forty-five degree lurch forward of his entire body. In addition to his himation, Zeus is shod in elaborately laced sandals

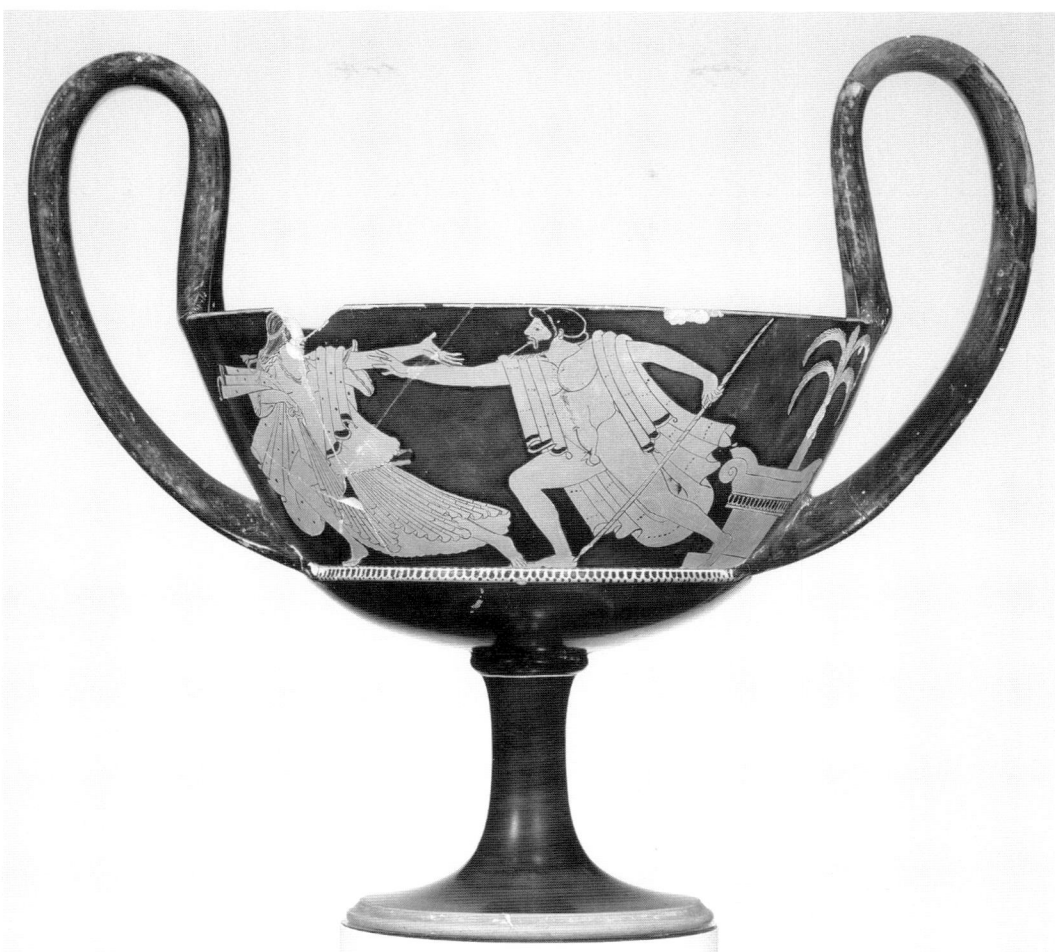

Fig. 1 High-Handled cup (kantharos) with Zeus pursuing Aegina, attributed to the Brygos Painter, ceramic, red-figure, Greek Late Archaic period, about 490–480 BC, *Catharine Page Perkins Fund. (95.36) Photo: © 2013 Museum of Fine Arts, Boston.

and gaiters, both painted in red.[10] As on the other side, he extends both arms forward, and carries a scepter. Ganymede, too, turns backward to face the god, but there is no gesture of appeal.

Attention to this remarkable vase has focused on the very aspects that mark it as exemplary. The elegance of its shape – Caskey and Beazley's kantharos sub-type form A – in particular, its near-perfect symmetry and the beautifully curved handles, has secured its place among the most attractive ceramic kantharoi.[11] Next is its style – perfectly emblematic of that of the Brygos Painter, with its dynamic composition and swift, animated figures.[12] But much of the discussion about the kantharos has centered on its subject, the sexual pursuits of Zeus, which was an enormously popular theme in Athenian vase painting between 490 and 440 BC.[13] The taste for pursuit scenes in these years has been attributed to aesthetic, religious and even political reasons, however no single argument has explained the phenomenon completely.[14]

The myth of Zeus' pursuit of Ganymede has often been characterized as the paradigm of the *erastes – eromenos* relationship.[15] Alan Shapiro observed that the myth became especially popular in Athenian vase painting at the time when the courtship scenes that had celebrated homosexual relationships in the second half of the sixth century under Peisistratid rule increasingly fell out of favor. He argued that in the early years of the Athenian Democracy, the followers of Kleisthenes chose to play down the *erastes – eromenos* relationship in the visual arts for political reasons, because the institution of pederasty had come to be so closely associated with the aristocracy under Peisistratos and his sons, particularly Hipparchos.[16] Instead, artists in the fifth century elevated homoerotic love and removed it from everyday life by casting it into mythological terms.[17]

While the image of Zeus hunting Ganymede has tended to dominate discussions about the kantharos, the identification of the female figure on the other side of the kantharos has proved challenging. Caskey and Beazley admit freely that they identify her as Aegina by ruling out Europa, Danae, and Semele in the absence of any specific iconographical clues to suggest them.[18] Martin Robertson

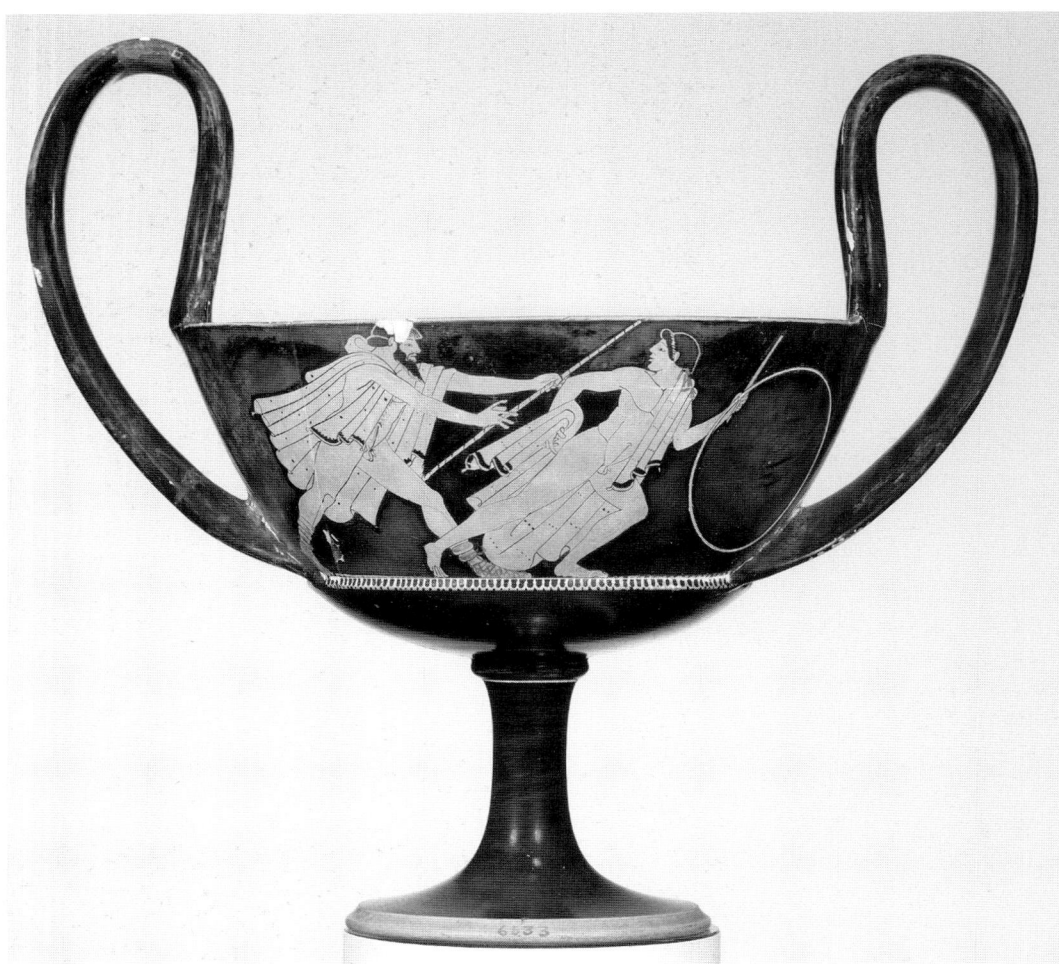

*Fig. 2 High-Handled cup (kantharos) with Zeus pursuing Ganymede, attributed to the Brygos Painter, ceramic, red-figure, Greek Late Archaic period, about 490–480 BC, *Catharine Page Perkins Fund. (95.36) Photo: © 2013 Museum of Fine Arts, Boston.*

inclines to Semele because of the kantharos' association with Dionysos and the fact that this particular vase was found in Dionysos' birthplace. Indeed, Dionysos and Semele are seen flanking a black-figure kantharos on the name vase of the Kallis Painter, a clear demonstration that the association between the god and the kantharos extended to his mother. Kaempf-Dimitriadou warns of the dangers of reading mere attributes, such as Zeus' thunderbolt, as narrative devices in pursuit scenes. A column-krater in the Metropolitan Museum of Art depicting Zeus about to hurl a thunderbolt at a woman, whom one would be tempted to read as Semele, but is, in fact, inscribed Aegina, is a case in point. In short, while Semele cannot be ruled out, I will argue that there is equally good reason to interpret the female figure as Aegina.

What remains puzzling is that the iconography of Zeus' pursuits – so very much in vogue in Athens at the moment the kantharos was created, between 490 and 480 – was drawn on a shape which the Athenians used seldomly and made in very few numbers. In fact, of the nearly 400 vases catalogued by Kaempf-Dimitriadou, the Boston kantharos is one of only two kantharoi that carry pursuit scenes. The other, also depicting Zeus and Ganymede, is a kantharos of the stemless type (Caskey and Beazley's Form D) attributed by Beazley to the Schifanoia Group and dated about a decade after the Museum of Fine Arts' kantharos.[19] The Brygos Painter's decision, and subsequently that of his follower, to place this popular motif on a relatively unpopular vase shape is curious, and all the more so when one considers that it was likely found in Thebes.[20]

Kantharoi in Athens and Boeotia

Writing about the Boston kantharos in 1931, L. D. Caskey and J. D. Beazley remarked, "the history of the kantharos in Greek pottery remains to be written".[21] The situation has been remedied to a large extent since then. The origins of the kantharos, defined broadly as a drinking cup with a deep bowl and high handles, can be traced back to the Middle Bronze Age.[22] However, its evolution from the time of its reemergence in the Middle Geometric period

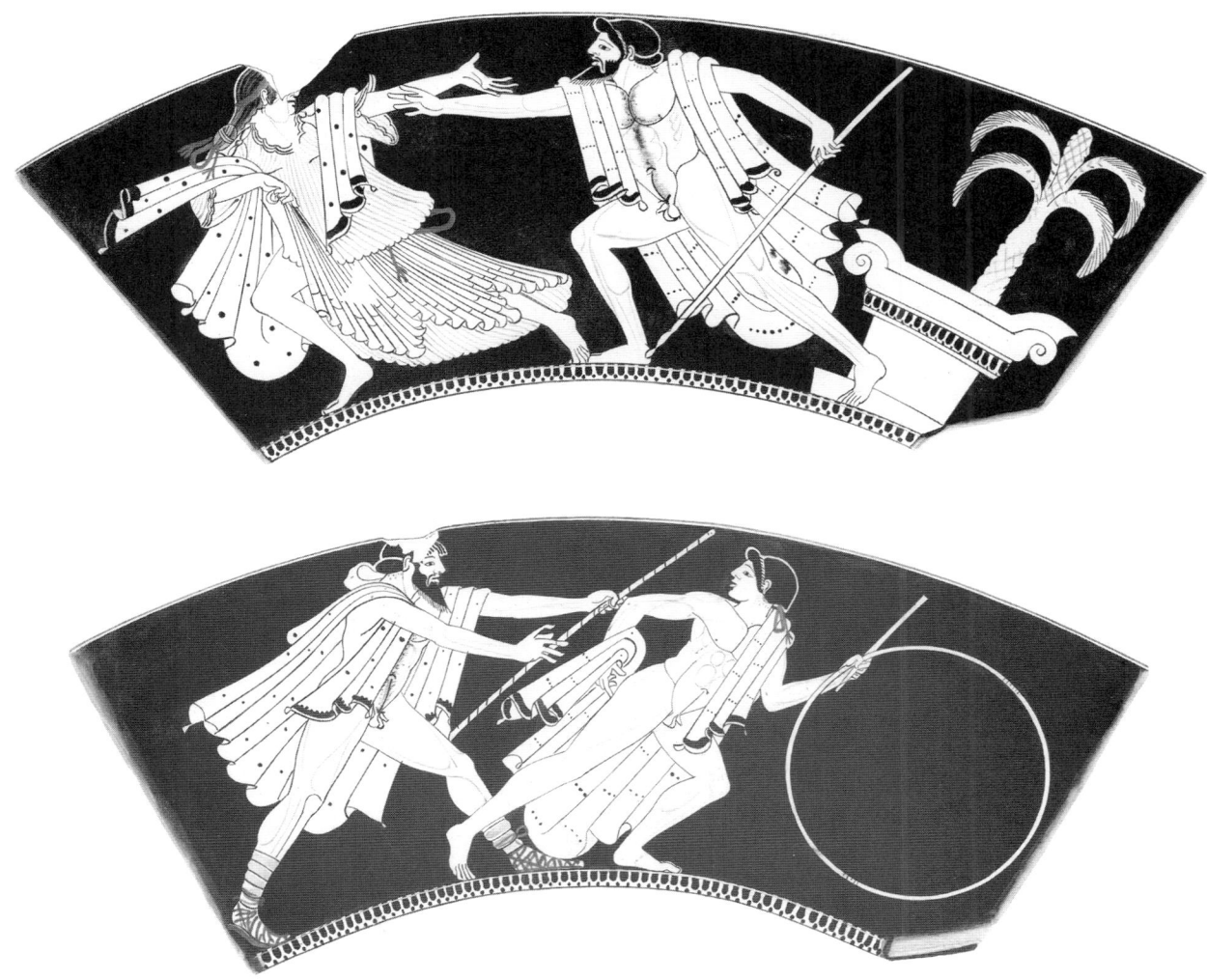

*Fig. 3 Drawing of High-Handled cup (kantharos) with Zeus in pursuit, attributed to the Brygos Painter, ceramic, red-figure, Greek Late Archaic period, about 490–480 BC, *Catharine Page Perkins Fund. (95.36) Photo: © 2013 Museum of Fine Arts, Boston.*

through the Archaic period in Attica and Boeotia and the extent to which the sub-types of both regions developed interdependently is still questionable. In 1953, Paul Courbin posited that the Archaic kantharos in Boeotia developed in response to Attic models, which were themselves influenced by Etruscan bucchero kantharoi. Karl Kilinski argued against this hypothesis, first by demonstrating that the Archaic kantharos appeared in Boeotia and in Attica at about the same time, circa 585–580 BC, and second, by pointing out that the Attic and Boeotian shapes are quite different from one another.[23] The foundational typologies of the kantharoi from the two regions set forth by P. N. Ure for Boeotia in 1913 and Caskey and Beazley for Attica in 1931 support Kilinksi's argument.[24]

Caskey and Beazley made two very important observations that still largely hold true today. The first is that the quantity of kantharoi found in Boeotian contexts vastly outnumbers those found at Athens.[25] Sparkes and Talcott include only twenty-four examples of Archaic and Classical black-gloss kantharoi in Agora XII and among the thousands of vases from the Athenian Akropolis catalogued by Graef and Langlotz, many of them kylikes, just fourteen fragments belong to kantharoi (seven black-figure and seven red-figure).[26] By contrast, excavations and survey in Boeotia have revealed denser concentrations of kantharoi in cemeteries (Rhitsona, Thespiae) and sanctuaries (Kabeirion, Ptoios, Hyettos) than anywhere else in Greece, including Athens.[27] While the Attic kantharoi of the Geometric period may very well have influenced the Archaic shape of the Boeotian kantharos, in Athens the ceramic kantharos seems to have fallen out of favor in the Protoattic period, possibly for religious or aesthetic reasons (or both).[28]

	Black-figure	Red-figure	Total
Number of Attic ceramic kantharoi	69	263	387
Number of representations of kantharoi on other Attic vase shapes	754	765	1519

Caskey's second observation is that Attic kantharoi are few in number when compared with how many representations of them one finds in Athenian vase painting.[29] In the decade following 580 BC, about the time that Attic workshops began to turn out kantharoi, representations of them on Athenian vases began to appear.[30] The earliest example is found on the famed dinos by Sophilos in London on which Peleus holds up a kantharos of the Boeotian, deep-bottomed shape, as he faces his oncoming wedding procession.[31] As the table above (based on figures from the BAPD) shows, kantharoi were represented in Attic black-figure vase painting more than ten times more often than the number of actual black-figure kantharoi. For red-figure, representations of kantharoi in vase painting appear about three times more often than actual kantharoi. Indeed the number of actual red-figure kantharoi is about four times greater than the number of black-figure kantharoi.

Overwhelmingly, the kantharos is associated in Attic vase painting with Dionysos and Herakles, both of whom were famously of Theban origin and had numerous cults in Boeotia.[32] As many others have noted, kantharoi depicted in the hands of Dionysos and Herakles undoubtedly represent vessels made of precious metals, not terracotta. While Dionysos was first seen in possession of a kantharos on vases by the KX Painter and Sophilos, dated to 580–570 BC, the shape only comes to be linked to Herakles at the time of the bilingual vases (approximately 525 BC), as the hero gained prominence in Athens under Peisistratos. Thomas Carpenter has speculated that the enhanced status of the kantharos in Athenian art in the middle of the sixth century may have signaled the tyrant's thanks to his Theban allies for their support in his return to Athens in 546, of which Herodotus writes in Book I.60.[33] To this point we shall return.

The abundance of kantharoi discovered in Boeotian cemeteries and sanctuaries together with the elevated status of the kantharoi in the Boeotian visual arts, principally its frequent appearance on the coinage of a number of Boeotian city-states beginning in the mid-fifth century, supports the view held by Kilinksi that the kantharos had a special ritual function in Boeotia beginning in the Archaic period.[34] François Lissarrague has characterized the kantharos as a *sema* of the Boeotians in his recent study on the use of vases as emblems, and in particular, as shield devices.[35] A prime example is a mid-fifth-century red-figure amphora in St. Petersburg attributed to the Nikon Painter[36] on which a warrior's shield is emblazoned with a kantharos and beside it the adjectival ethnic "Boiotios".[37]

This juxtaposition demonstrates conclusively that by the middle of the fifth century the vase shape had come to be inextricably linked with the Boeotians.

To sum up the situation before moving forward, the vase in question is an exquisite work of art by one of the best talents of his generation and depicts a subject that was very fashionable in Athens at the moment it was created. The shape of the vase was demonstrably unpopular in Athens, but evidently so highly prized by the Boeotians that it came to function as their national symbol. At some point, the vase was deposited in a tomb in Thebes. From this seeming paradox (i.e. popular theme on a distinctly unpopular shape), a number of pressing questions emerge. When did it travel to Thebes and under what circumstances? What kind of person bought it and was buried with it? Why did the imagery appeal to him or her? And finally, is it possible that a Theban patron may have commissioned it?

The Historical Context

To approach these questions, the historical and political events that shaped the tense relationship between Athens and Thebes at the end of the Archaic period must be considered. Herodotus reports that in 546 BC, a group of Theban noble families had provided support to Peisistratos in his successful bid to regain Athens.[38] Dedications made by elite Athenians, Alkmaeonid Alkmaeonides and Peisistratid Hipparchos, in the third quarter of the sixth century at the Boeotian Sanctuary of Apollo Ptoios indicate that at that time relations between the leaders of the neighboring regions were still cordial.[39] However, after the Plataeans refused to join the nascent Boeotian League in 519 BC and instead chose, on Spartan advice, to ally themselves with the Athenians, the Thebans's attitude towards the Athenians soured considerably.[40] In 507/6 BC, in cooperation with Kleomenes of Sparta, the Boeotians and Chalkidians marched on the Parasopia and northern Attica. The Boeotians took the Attic demes of Oinoe and Hysiai, but were soon confronted by the Athenians. The encounter resulted in a fiasco for the Boeotians, many of whom were killed and 700 were taken as prisoners.[41] The Athenians commemorated their decisive victory with a tithe in the form of a bronze four-horse chariot, which was reportedly erected near the statue of Athena Promachos on the Acropolis. The remains of this victory monument survive in a base with the inscription: "With iron bonds they vanquished their pride, the sons of the Athenians, by deeds in battle, when they defeated the Boeotians and Chalkidians, from whom these horses, as a tithe, they dedicated to Pallas Athena".[42] Recent excavations in Thebes revealed the Boeotian side of the story: A fluted *kioniskos* with a partially preserved inscription that proudly names the Attic demes the Boeotians captured – Oinoe, Phylai, Hysiai, and Eleusis – and refers to the Chalkidians who were held for ransom by the Athenians.[43]

In the wake of their defeat, the Thebans sought the counsel of the Delphic Oracle, who instructed them that they would only be able to take their revenge on the Athenians if they enlisted the help of those closest to them. Herodotus reports that after much debate in the assembly, the Thebans ruled out the possibility that the oracle was referring to their fellow Boeotians (the Tanagrians, Coronaeans, and Thespiai) and instead had referred to those who were closely related genealogically, the Aeginetans, since after all the nymphs Aegina and Thebe, the daughters of Asopos, had been sisters (Hdt. 5.79–80). With the support of the Aeginetans, the Thebans advanced on Athens, but the Athenians defeated them once again (Hdt. 5.81).

The greatest and most lasting source of strain between Athens and Thebes was the Thebans' betrayal of the Greek cause in the fight against the Persians, as reported by Herodotus. The Boeotian League remained neutral in Darius' campaign, but did send 400 men to Thermopylae, eventually surrendering to the Persians there.[44] A Theban pro-Persian faction led by Attaginus and Timagenidas welcomed Macedonian officers loyal to Xerxes into the city, invited them to a lavish banquet, and allowed Thebes to become an important base of operations for his invasion of Attica.[45] At the conclusion of the Battle of Plataea, in which tens of thousands of Boeotians fought on the Persian side against their fellow Greeks, (a few hundred with extraordinary valor and commitment to the Persian cause, Hdt. 9.67), the Greek allies resolved to ravage Thebes unless the Thebans gave up Attaginus and Timagenidas. The Thebans were unwilling and on the eleventh day after the battle, the Greeks vanquished Thebes completely (Hdt. 9. 86). The MFA kantharos is traditionally dated between 490 and 480, and it is difficult to imagine that it was carried to Thebes after the events of 480/479 BC.[46] Indeed, the finds from Thebes, Thespiae and Halai – indicate that the Boeotians did not resume buying Athenian red-figure until a couple of decades later, around 460 BC.[47]

A Theban Perspective

The rape of Aegina by Zeus was a recurrent narrative in Boeotian poetry beginning with the Hesiodic *Catalogue of Women*.[48] In a passage devoted to the daughters of Asopos, the river god of Thebes, the poem recounts how Zeus abducted the nymph from her fatherland and brought her to Aegina where she gave birth to a son, Aiakos (Hes. *Cat.* fr. 205). Pindar related the myth in *Isthmian* 8 (dated to 478 BC), which he composed for an Aeginetan patron, adding that Aegina had a twin sister, Thebe, who went on to become the queen of Thebes. The Theban poet sang of the rape once again in *Paean* 6. Greg Nagy has argued that the *Catalogue of Women* was performed at the Panathenaia at some point between 540 and 520, during the years that Peisistratos was tyrant.[49] The myth of Zeus abducting Aegina first appeared in the visual arts some years later, at the end of the sixth century in Aegina. Dieter Ohly identified a number of late sixth-century sculptural fragments found in the temenos of Aphaia (now in the Munich Glyptothek) as belonging to a group that was perhaps originally intended for a pediment but was displayed in an "open-fronted", specially built structure beside the altar instead.[50]

If, as I believe, the Boston kantharos indeed depicts the rape of Aegina by Zeus, it would be the earliest of some thirty (or more) representations on Athenian vases dating from 490 to 440 BC to do so.[51] It would seem plausible that the display of a monumental sculptural group on the nearby island could have inspired vase painters working in the Kerameikos in Athens. The reasons why the imagery became so popular remain elusive, but I do not believe, as Karim Arafat has argued, that the pursuit of Aegina by Zeus needs to be read as an allegory for the Athens' literal pursuit of Aegina from 491 to its submission in 458 BC.[52] The existence of an Aeginetan model for the subject renders an exclusively Athenian reading highly problematical.

Turning to the question of why the imagery of Zeus pursuing Aegina would have appealed to a Theban audience, we recall the fact that the eponymous nymphs of the two cities were sisters was the basis, according to Herodotus, for the Thebans seeking Aeginetan help in taking revenge on Athens in 506, after the debacle with Chalkis. The strong genealogical bond between Aegina and Thebes was not only celebrated in the poetry of Hesiod and Pindar (as well as Baccyhlides and Korinna, whose dates remain unresolved) and referenced by Herodotus, but was also the basis, according to Stephanie Larson, for the use of the "cut-out" (often known as Boeotian) shield on their coinage beginning at the end of the Archaic period.[53] The shield type, she maintains, had stronger iconographic associations with Ajax and Achilles than any other epic heroes, and through this "heroicizing symbol" the Boeotians asserted their noble Aiakid lineage.[54] The myth of Asopos and his daughters acted as a cornerstone of Theban and Aeginetan identities and bound the two cities together.[55] For this reason, the image of Zeus pursuing Aegina would have appealed to a Theban patron eager to celebrate his or her exalted lineage.

The Boeotian fascination with Zeus' pursuit of Thebe's sister is demonstrated by the fact that fifth-century vase painters adopted this story into their repertoire of images. A Boeotian red-figure lekythos dating around 430 BC which was discovered in the Polyandrion at Thespiae (Thebes Museum 697) depicts the scene. D. Schilardi identified the female figure as Semele and hypothesized that the lekythos was a "copy" of an Athenian lekythos attributed to the Achilles Painter, now in the MFA, Boston (01.8077).[56] This interpretation is difficult to accept because the Boston vase is said to have come from Selinus, but Schilardi's premise – that an Athenian vase with this subject circulating in Boeotia inspired Boeotian vase painters to adopt the scene – is surely the case.

The scarcity of Late Archaic and Early Classical red-figure found in Boeotia, even in wealthy burials, very tentatively suggests that the eventual owner of the Boston kantharos may have been a member of the clique of elite ruling families described by Thucydides (3.62). It would seem plausible that the original owner of the kantharos could have been part of this small elite group of Thebans. Further, the fact that it is the only Athenian red-figure vase of this shape found in Boeotia, that it is the best example of its shape to carry a pursuit scene, and that its subject and findspot are so closely related both mythologically and historically, may even suggest that the vase may have been made with a Theban patron in mind. Despite the fact that these very tentative suggestions can never be proven, it seems unlikely that our kantharos ended up in Thebes completely by chance.

Acknowledgements

I'd like to extend warm thanks to John Oakley for the opportunity to present this paper in Williamsburg and publish it here. Seth Pevnick, Lydia Herring-Harrington, Christine Kondoleon and Mary Comstock read drafts and offered valuable feedback, for which I am very grateful. Special gratitude is due to Joan Mertens, whose extensive and penetrating comments encouraged me to be more careful and precise in my writing and conclusions. I dedicate this paper to the memory of Natalie Boymel Kampen (February 1, 1944 – August 12, 2012), a treasured advisor, teacher and friend.

Notes

1 See V. Sabetai, in: S. Schmidt – A. Staehli (eds.), Vasenbilder im Kulturtransfer: Zirkulation und Rezeption griechischer Keramik im Mittelmeerraum, CVA Germany Beiheft 5 (2012) 121–138 and in: S. Scherup – B. B. Rasmussen (eds.), Red-figure Pottery in its Ancient Setting (2012) 81–98.

2 E. Robinson, Trustees of the Museum of Fine Arts, Boston Twentieth Annual Report, 1895, 20 no. 24, "kantharos, unsigned, but undoubtedly by Brygos". F. B. Tarbell, A Cantharus from the Factory of Brygos in the Boston Museum of Fine Arts, Decennial Publications 6, 1902, 7–9. The first lengthy discussion of it appeared in CB 1 13–18 no. 17. ARV² 381,182 ascribes the attribution to John Marshall.

3 Warren's taste for erotic art is demonstrated in his private collection as well as the antiquities he bought for the Museum of Fine Arts, Boston and has been the subject of numerous publications in recent years. See C. Kondoleon, in: C. Kondoleon – P. C. Segal, Aphrodite and the Gods of Love (2011) 11–15; D. Sox, Bachelors of Arts: Edward Perry Warren and the Lewes House Brotherhood (1991).

4 Sabetai, in: Schmidt – Staehli (supra n. 1) 122 notes that red-figure vases were given as gifts to the gods, as we learn from a red-figure vase signed by Epilykos and inscribed as agalma discovered at the Helikonian Cave of the Leibethrian Nymphs.

5 The graves at Rhitsona yielded only two examples from the Late Archaic period. Grave 18, in which 270 objects were found, contained only one red-figure kylix, depicting a nude woman carrying a wash-basin and dated between 510 and 500. A second example, from Grave 22, a skyphos of hybrid shape, depicts an ithyphallic satyr, draped in a panther skin, wielding a phallic staff, paired with, on the other side, a young Thracian peltast; it is the only vase by the Brygos Painter with an archaeological find-spot in Boeotia. See CVA Thebes 1 Greece 6 80–82 pls. 73–74; R. M. Burrows – P. N. Ure, BSA 14, 1907–1908, 294–295 pl. 13a; 301–304 fig. 23 pl. 14.

6 V. Aravantinos, in: A. G. Vlachopoulos (ed.), Archaeology: Euboea and Central Greece (2009) 243.

7 Aegina: CB I 14 admits that the identification is based on "process of elimination". S. Kaempf-Dimitraidou, Die Liebe der Götter in der attischen Kunst des 5. Jahrhunderts v. Chr., AntK Beiheft 11 (1979) 23 provisionally, as "Aigina" but with more certainty in LIMC Vol. I (1981) 368 no. 1 pl. 281 s.v. Aigina (S. Kaempf-Dimitriadou); K. W. Arafat, Classical Zeus. A Study in Art and Literature (1990) 80 follows CB I noting that "Semele and certainly Thetis are usually distinctive". Semele: M. Robertson, The Art of Vase-Painting in Classical Athens (1992) 99, "and if the woman were Semele, on whom he begot Dionsysos in Thebes (where this vase was found), a Dionysiac association would be established for the whole…Given the association of the shape [to Dionysos] I incline to Semele".

8 The use of an altar in vase painting typically signifies sacred space, and O. Jahn suggests that here it may indicate that the abduction takes place at a religious festival, where girls enjoyed greater liberty: Archäologische Aufsätze (1845) 149–150. C. Sourvinou-Inwood interprets the altar in combination with a palm tree as a reference to the sanctuary of Artemis Brauronia in BICS 32, 1985, 126 n. 31.

9 J. Barringer addresses the metaphorical hunt of Ganymede by Zeus in The Hunt in Ancient Greece (2001) 119–123.

10 Arafat (supra n. 7) 69 identifies Zeus' footwear as boots though Caskey and Beazley rightly observes that he wears sandals covered by gaiters. Zeus is not often seen wearing boots or gaiters in Late Archaic and Early Classical vase-painting, however, a pair of fragments also depicting Zeus pursuing Ganymede and also attributed to the Brygos Painter (Athens, National Museum 2.545; ARV² 383,196) depicts Zeus wearing black boots with horizontal stripes.

11 R. Carpenter praises its "beautifully running contours", in AJA 25, 1921, 23; G. M. A. Richter, The Craft of Athenian Pottery. An Investigation of the Technique of Black-figured and Red-figured Athenian Vases (1923) 23

cites the kantharos as an example of how Athenian vase handles sprung from the body of the vase as "organic, living things".

12 To my knowledge, the attribution, first made by John Marshall, to the Brygos Painter has never been publically challenged. Tarbell (supra n. 2) 8 attributes the dots on all four himations, the obliquely striped scepter, the use of shades of brown in the female figure's hair, the liberal treatment of Zeus' body hair and the peculiar arrangement of Zeus' hair on the back of his neck definitively to the Brygos Painter. A. Cambitoglou puts forth similar observations in The Brygos Painter (1968) 13–14. For the Brygos Painter's style, see also M. Wegner, Brygosmaler (1973).

13 Kaempf-Dimitriadou deems this vase so emblematic of the genre of the loves of the gods that her book (supra n. 7) opens with a discussion of it.

14 Arafat (supra n. 7) 64 cites the format of pursuit scenes as particularly well suited to shapes on which single figures were typically featured on each side, e.g. the Nolan amphora. J. Boardman, Review of Kaempf-Dimitriadou, ClR 30.2, 1980, 306 notes that the scenes are "no doubt to be explained in terms of new equations of mortal and divine".

15 H. A. Shapiro, in: A. Richlin (ed.), Pornography and Representation in Greece and Rome (1992) 58–64.

16 H. A. Shapiro, AJA 85, 1981, 133–143.

17 It is interesting to note that this practice has continued to the present day. A photograph of the vase graced the cover of The Journal of the American Medical Association in 1972, as an illustration for the article, "Youthful Male Homosexuality. Homosexual Experience and the Process of Developing Homosexual Identity in Males Aged 16 to 22 Years".

18 CB I 14.

19 Paris, Louvre G248: ARV^2 387,2; Kaempf-Dimitriadou (supra n. 7) 77 no. 12. The find-spot of the kantharos is unknown.

20 The connection between the shape of the vase and its find-spot was noted by B. A. Sparkes, JHS 87, 1967, 124.

21 CB I 14.

22 K. Kilinski II, Ancient World, 2005, 182.

23 Ibid. 182.

24 P. N. Ure's classification of Boeotian kantharoi, based on the finds from the graves at Rhitsona, deems that the shallow-bottomed type, in vogue initially, was superseded in popularity by the deep-bottomed variety after 575 BC. See P. N. Ure, Black Glaze Pottery from Rhitsona in Boeotia (1913) 4–13. CB I 14–18 arranged the Athenian kantharoi into four principle types (A–D), of which the Brygos Painter's kantharos is type A.

25 Agora XII 113 records only twenty-four sixth and fifth century black-glaze kantharoi out of a total of 2040 black-gloss specimens: just over 1%.

26 B. Graef – E. Langlotz, Die antiken Vasen von der Akropolis zu Athen (1925–1933) Vol. I 214–216 cat. nos. 2133–2139; Vol. II 49–50 cat. nos. 551–557.

27 Kilinski (supra n. 22) 182: "The question of derivation is important since Boeotian canthari of the Archaic and Classical periods are legion, far surpassing in numbers all those from other contemporary Greek pottery schools combined". D. Schilardi, The Thespian Polyandrion (424 B.C.). The Excavations and Finds from a Thespian State Burial, PhD. diss. (Princeton University, 1977) 301 states that "the most predominant type of vase from the Thespian Polyandrion is undoubtedly the black-glazed kantharos". The graves at Rhitsona yielded more than four hundred black-glaze kantharoi, Ure (supra n. 24) 8. The findings of the Boeotian Survey Project compared with those of surveys conducted in Lakonia, Asea, Methana and Keos demonstrated the overwhelming presence of kantharoi in Boeotia, particularly in cemeteries and sanctuaries, as opposed to settlements. See E. Mulder, Boeotia, Land of the Kantharos. Explanations, BA Thesis (University of Leiden, 2012) 44–48 for the high number of kantharoi present in the Archaic and Classical periods in Boeotia.

28 Sparkes (supra n. 20) 121: "Of all the shapes which the Boeotians cultivated, the kantharos with its many different forms was the favourite". Kilinski (supra n. 22) 183. 185 notes the relatively high importance of the Archaic kantharos in Boeotia compared with that of Athens.

29 Agora XII 113 n. 1: "Dionysos' kantharos, one of the most familiar shapes seen in Attic vase-painting, is rare in Attic pottery at the time when Dionysos and Herakles are often seen holding it. Presumably the kantharoi they hold are of metal; see D. K. Hill, AJA 51 (1947) p. 254 (Hill)."

30 Kilinksi (supra n. 22) 184.

31 London, British Museum 1971.11: Para 19,16bis; BAdd^2 10–11; Greek Vases in the J. Paul Getty Museum 1, 1983, 23 fig. 25.

32 T. H. Carpenter, Dionysian Imagery in Archaic Greek Art (1986) 122–123. See A. Schachter, Cults of Boeotia, Vol. I, BICS Suppl. 38.1 (1981) 172–195 for Dionysos' cults in Boeotia (virtually every important city-state in Boeotia – Akraiphia, Chaironeia, Eleutherae, Haliartos, Orchomenos, Tanagra, Thebes and Thespiai – is represented) and Vol. II, BICS Suppl. 38.2, 1–37 for Herakles. See Aravantinos (supra n. 6) 238–239 for an account of the 2004 excavations in Thebes that revealed the existence of a temenos dedicated to Herakles, his ancestors and his descendants.

33 Carpenter (supra n. 32) 122–123.

34 Kilinski (supra n. 22) 185.

35 F. Lissarrague, in: Tsingarida, Shapes 241–243.

36 St. Petersburg, Hermitage 4305: ARV^2 652,1; 1663.

37 The earliest use of the ethnic "Boiotios" to describe the people who inhabited the territory of Boeotia and were commonly descended from the hero Boiotos is found in Homer's Catalogue of Ships (Il. 2.494–759). S. L. Larson, Tales of Epic Ancestry. Boeotian Collective Identity in the Late Archaic and Early Classical Period (2007) 10.

38 Hdt. 1.61.

39 A. Schacter, in: S. Hornblower – R. Osborne (eds.), Ritual, Finance, Politics. Athenian Democratic Accounts Presented to David Lewis (1994) 291–306. Schachter proposes that the Ptoion may have served as a pan-hellenic substitute for the Sanctuary of Apollo at Delphi in the wake of the fire that destroyed the second temple in 546.

40 Hdt. 6.108.

41 Hdt. 5.77.

42 Larson (supra n. 37) 150 n. 100 (translation after C. Fornara, Translated Documents of Greece and Rome: Archaic Times to the End of the Peloponnesian War [1977] no. 42). Hdt. 5.74–78, who quotes the epigram verbatim

and locates the monument, which was probably destroyed by the Persians in 480, whereas Paus. 1.28.2 places it near Pheidias' Athena. C. Keesling, in: M. Baumbach – A. Petrovic – I. Petrovic (eds.), Archaic and Classical Greek Epigram (2010) 123–125 proposes that the original dedication took the form of an athletic chariot.

43 V. Aravantinos, BSA 101, 2006, 369-377. The Boeotian inscription is dated based on its letter forms to the end of the sixth century, and the column (H. 0.57 m; Diam. [top] 0.193 m; Diam. [base] 0.198 m), which was found in a rectangular cist, in which it was probably buried in the late fifth century, must have supported a votive tripod or statue. Aravantinos reasons that it was originally set up in an "athletic/military complex" dedicated to a martial and/or athletic deity. The inscription is difficult to reconstruct in its entirety but would seem to have been set up by a collective of men, likely the survivors of the attack on Athens.

44 Hdt. 7.205.3 notes that "Leonidas had made a special effort to bring the Thebans from among all of the Hellenes, because they had been strongly accused of medizing," adding that "though their hearts were not in it, they did send men". Hdt. 7.233: The Thebans surrendered to the Persians, claiming that they had been forced to fight against their will.

45 Hdt. 9.5.1; N. G. L. Hammond, "The Expedition of Xerxes," CAH Vol. 4, 2nd ed. (1988) 565.

46 Personal discussion with Vassilis Aravantinos, Ephor Emeritus of Boeotia.

47 These finds were catalogued by P. N. Ure and presented more recently by Victoria Sabetai in CVA Thebes 1 Greece 6.

48 M. L. West, The Hesiodic Catalogue of Women. Its Nature, Structure and Origins (1985) 127 maintains that although the poem was undoubtedly not composed by Hesiod himself, it was consistently attributed to him in antiquity. West (136) suggests that the poem was composed between 580 and 520 BC.

49 G. Nagy, in: D. Fearn (ed.), Aegina: Contexts for Choral Lyric Poetry. Myth, History and Identity in the Fifth Century BC (2011) 41–44.

50 D. Ohly, The Munich Glyptothek. Greek and Roman Sculpture (1974) 64–66. For the most recent mention of these, see D. Watson, in: Fearn (supra n. 49) 83.

51 On some of the vases, Aegina is depicted alone with Zeus and on others with her father Asopos and/or her sisters. See LIMC I (1981) 367–371 s.v. Aegina (S. Kaempf-Dimitriadou).

52 Arafat (supra n. 7) 78.

53 Larson (supra n. 37) 80–83.

54 Larson (supra n. 37) 87.

55 Larson (supra n. 37) 82 discusses the close ties between the two cities: "It is not just that Pindar needs to redeem himself for being Theban – the poem [*Isthm.* 8], after all, was performed in 478, in the aftermath of the Persian wars, unkind to Thebes and Boeotia in general – but the poet may also have included this genealogy to remind his Aiginetan relatives, grieving over so many men lost, that their family tree is shared with the whole city of Thebes; Thebes grieves with them, too, as it is also celebrates Aigina's victor".

56 Schilardi (supra n. 27) 121.

22 Oikos and Hetairoi: Black-figure Departure Scenes Reconsidered

Martina Seifert

An Attic black-figure belly amphora in Karlsruhe (Fig. 1) attributed to the Painter of Munich 1410 and conventionally dated soon after 530 BC[1] shows in the central part of side A a scene comprising fifteen figures and one quadriga. On the left, two bearded men looking to the right are depicted: the one in front, who is dressed in a long garment (*xystis*), stands in the carriage holding the reins with both hands, while the man in the back, who is clad in a warrior's armor stands with one leg on the ground, the other in the chariot box. Directly in front of and looking at both men is a woman dressed in a richly decorated garment and mantle. She balances a small naked child on her shoulders. The child raises its right hand towards the warrior's face. Looking in the same direction und partly covered by the backs of the horses are another warrior, a white haired bearded man – the opaque white has flaked off – , and a woman, each with a child on their shoulders. Next, two naked, short-haired boys are attending the horses. A third warrior with a lance turned towards a bearded man clad in a mantle and a woman with a child conclude the scene. The picture lacks inscriptions.

A very similar scene, although composed of fewer figures, is displayed on an Attic black-figured belly amphora in Rome, Vatican Museums 1770 (Fig. 2)[2] which is dated to the middle of the sixth century BC. There are 9 figures: To the left, an armed warrior stands in the chariot box accompanied by a bearded man, both of whom face a woman carrying a child. Next to her a second warrior with two lances and a white-haired man are depicted; both are half-covered by the backs of one white and three black horses constituting the quadriga. In front of the horses' forelegs there stands a small male figure with drapery over one arm. Another woman with a child completes the group on the right half of the image. On this vase, too, there are no inscriptions.

Both scenes belong to a group of images commonly denoted by scholars as a "warrior's departure, warrior's farewell" or in German "Kriegerabschied". The theme is represented in various ways: departing on horseback, arming, departing on foot, or performing a libation or hepatoscopy.[3] The various types of scenes appear at different times and have a different duration of use. The departing warrior in a chariot (see Mertens in this volume), as shown on both belly amphorai, probably emerges in the seventh century BC on Corinthian vessels, followed by the Attic ones. The Attic black-figured scenes are mainly painted on amphorai, hydriai, lekythoi, kylikes and column kraters. In red-figure vase painting the subject is rare.[4] Usually the warrior in the chariot is joined by other heavily-armed men and appears in the middle of a group of figures of different sexes and ages facing him. The latter are characterized as non-warriors.[5]

In the following discussion particular attention will be paid to the non-warriors, who to my mind play a key role for the interpretation of the images. By no means minor characters, they contribute essentially to the image's message by differentiating the formulaic rendering of the main theme and putting it in a wider context. In this paper I shall focus on the analysis of the function and meaning of the figures of women and children examining the development of the 'warrior's departure' and investigating also the relation between words and images.

The anonymous departure scenes decorating the two amphorae in Karlsruhe and the Vatican – there are several others similar to these two – must be discussed in the context of the so-called mythical warrior's departures. From the beginning of the seventh century BC, the departure of Amphiaraos is arguably the most famous subject on Corinthian and Tyrhennian vessels (Figs. 3[6] and 4[7]).[8] Induced by his wife Eriphyle, according to the myth, and at his brother-in-law Adrastos' (King of Argos) urging, Amphiaraos goes to war with Thebes, although he foresaw the unfortunate outcome of the campaign and his own death. Part of the figurative stock of the later pictorial transformations of the myth are the warrior entering or standing in the chariot, a charioteer, a woman carrying a child (Eriphyle, Eriphyle with Amphilochos/Alkmaion) and a second heavily-armed man, a hoplite. Inscriptions on the vases help to identify most of those figures in the scenes with Amphiaraos in the chariot. In addition to the persistence of the Amphiaraos episode on vases, the warrior's departure from home and taking leave of his wife and parents remained an established literary topos: for example Hector taking leave of Andromache as narrated in the sixth book of the Iliad (6.399ff.). Bearing in mind such literary traditions and the mythical figures in the image, scholars have occasionally seen on some vases a relationship between the anonymous and the mythical departure scenes regarding form and content. According to Spieß, anonymous departure scenes generally appear one or two decades after the inscribed images. At the beginning, there were the mythical scenes which are clearly recognizable by the inscribed names of the figures; in the course of time the mythical scenes then would have been replaced by the anonymous scenes.[9]

If we accept this line of argumentation, we would have to assume that the scene on the Vatican amphora (Fig. 2) is a pictorial set-piece derived from the Amphiaraos-theme and can be interpreted as showing Amphiaraos' departure, even if it lacks inscriptions: In this case, it would implicitly refer to the departure of the armed Amphiaraos standing in the chariot, joined by a charioteer as well as fellow warriors and taking leave of his wife Eriphyle, his sons Amphilochos and Alkmaion, his parents, and a slave.

However, it is the prevailing opinion in scholarship that the image does not show the myth but depicts a generally understandable episode of exemplary nature through unnamed figures: The farewell of the "heroic" warrior from his family members.[10] This main theme is connected with the basic iconographic pattern, which can generally be linked to mythical themes by the use of inscriptions, but remains comprehensible even without them.

The whole setting, that is the composition of the scene, indicates a distinctive hierarchy between the figures. The warrior with his charioteer standing in the carriage with the centrally positioned team of horses is the leading character. As indicated by the orientation of the bodies and the lines of view connecting the figures, the whole group's attention concentrates on the warrior. The woman standing to the left with child, for example, is directly correlated to him by physical closeness. Through composition, context is established, which dictates the placement of the figures.

It is clear that this basic iconographic scheme originally created for images of Amphiaraos is used for the scene on the amphora in Karlsruhe (Fig. 1), even if the scene is expanded by six figures. Once again, the composition of the image reveals a hierarchy between the figures expressed by the arrangement, proportions, *habitus*, and clothing of the figures. Interaction is indicated by gestures. Nevertheless, the composition as a whole is clearly focused on the warrior in the chariot.

In analogy with the departure scenes of mythical warriors, scholars like Wrede[11] or in recent years Oakley/ Sinos[12] and Stansbury-O'Donnell[13] have put forward an interpretation of the minor characters on the non-inscribed vases as family or clan members, accompanied by unnamed members at the warrior's farewell. Therefore, the figures should be understood as representations of standardized types with a certain meaning, for example warrior or wife.[14] As regards the composition of the image this would mean – in my words – that the multiplication of figure types (inter alia here: woman and child) would be an artistic means to visualize the extended family – in contrast to the depiction of just the nuclear family on the Vatican amphora (Fig. 2).

Is this a correct interpretation? Maybe, but maybe it is possible to devise a more differentiated approach. That's why I will now focus on an analysis of the meaning and the function of the women and children in the images. Reichardt[15] stresses that Eriphyle in the mythical scenes represents the figurative type of a woman who – by the infant – is characterized as mother and at the same time as

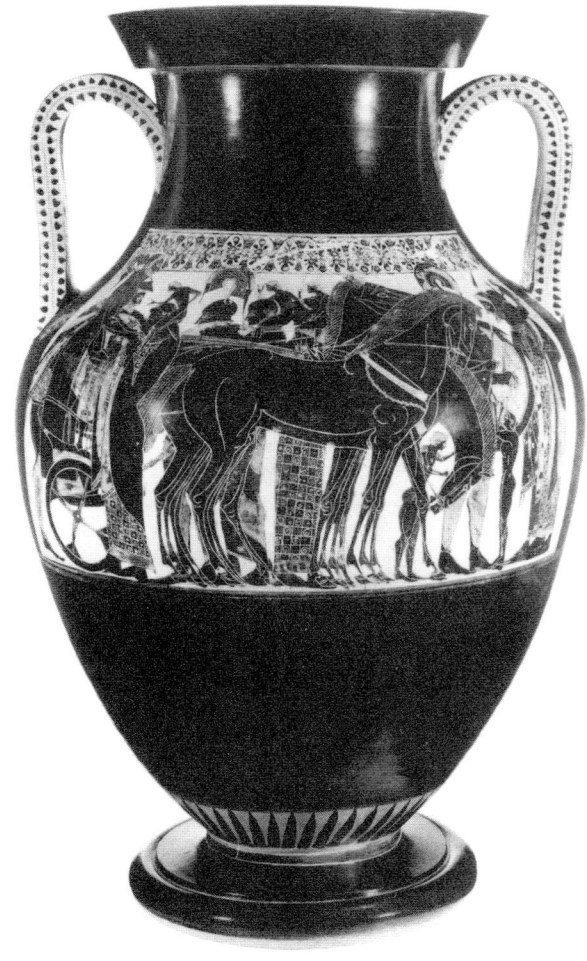

Fig. 1 Attic black-figure amphora, Painter of Munich 1410. Karlsruhe, Badisches, Landesmuseum 61.89. Photo: after CVA Karlsruhe 3 Germany 60 pl. 12,1.

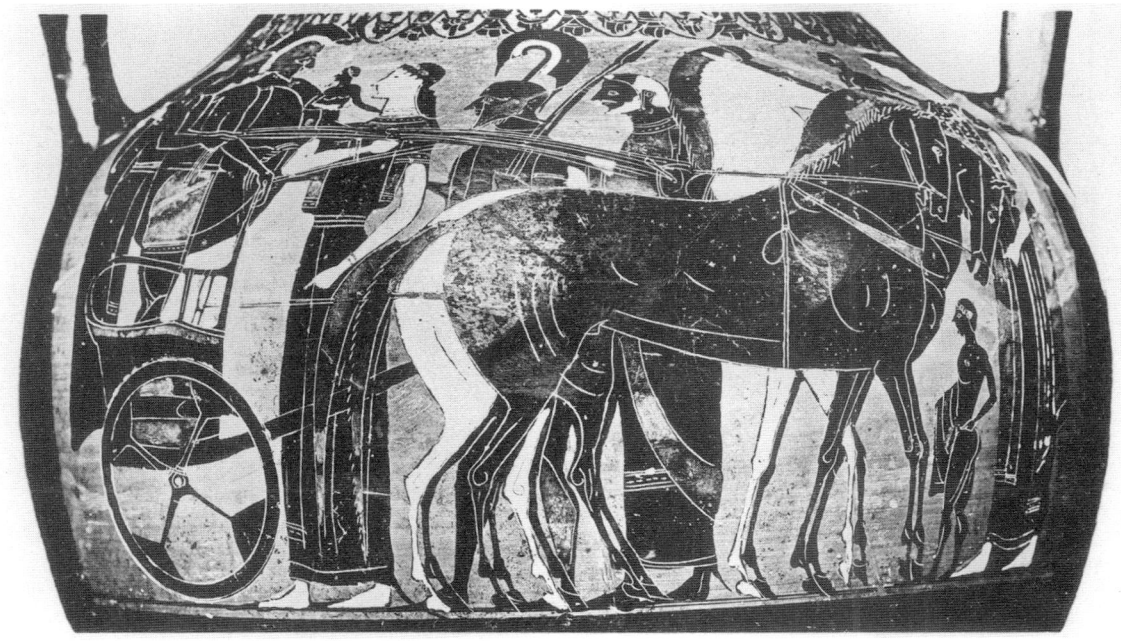

Fig. 2 Attic black-figure amphora. Attributed to Near Group E. Rome, Vatican 1770. Photo: after Wrede 1916 pl. XVII.

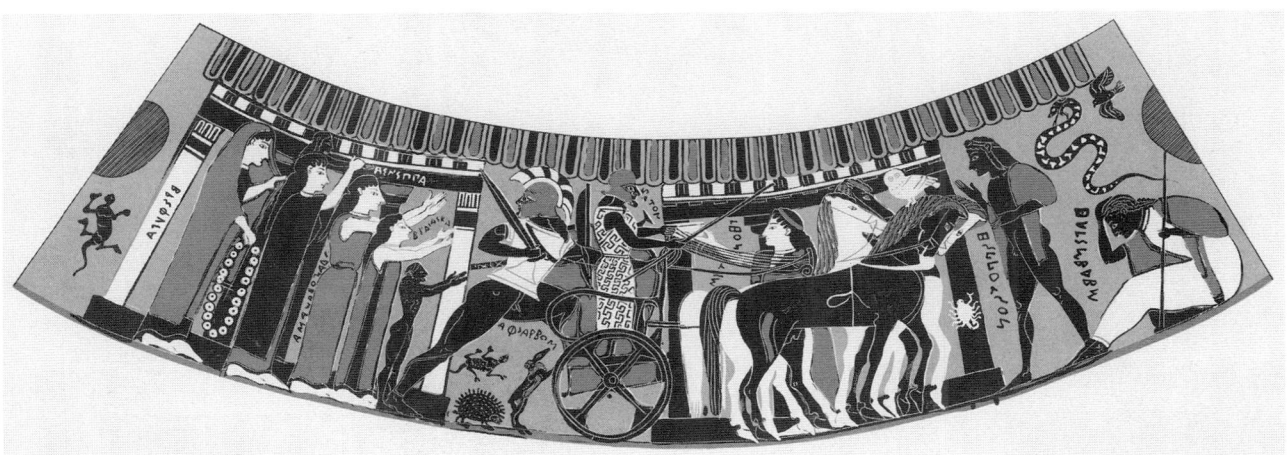

Fig. 3 Corinthian column-krater. Lost, Berlin Antikensammlung F 1655. Photo: after A. Furtwängler – K. Reichhold, Griechische Vasenmalerei III (1932) pl. 121.

wife. In the anonymous images – which she terms pictures of the world of life or *Lebenswelt*[16] – the woman generally signifies the family left behind. According to Reichert a figurative type in a mythical context produces a specific, in a non-mythical context a generalizing, message of the image. In contrast, I think that the same abstract concepts of representation constitute the basis of both pictorial groups, the mythical and the non-mythical, and that those concepts represent the form of social organization of Athenian society relating to the categories of age, sex and status.

To support this theory, we must take a closer look at the iconographical characterization of the figures. Those in the Karlsruhe departure scene (Fig. 1) are distinguished in relation to sex, status and – if necessary for the message – age. Size, *habitus* and clothing or nakedness are a further means of differentiating the figures. The female figures apparently represent upper class women without specific physiognomy of age (signifiers are again *habitus*, clothing, hair dress and the homogenous rendering of their faces). The naked children carried by the women are little boys – girls are always shown clothed in Athenian art of this time. By being carried, the boys are denoted as dependent on the women's care. In the anonymous scenes a kinship relation between the depicted women and children (like mother/child, grandmother/grandchild, sister/brother) or a

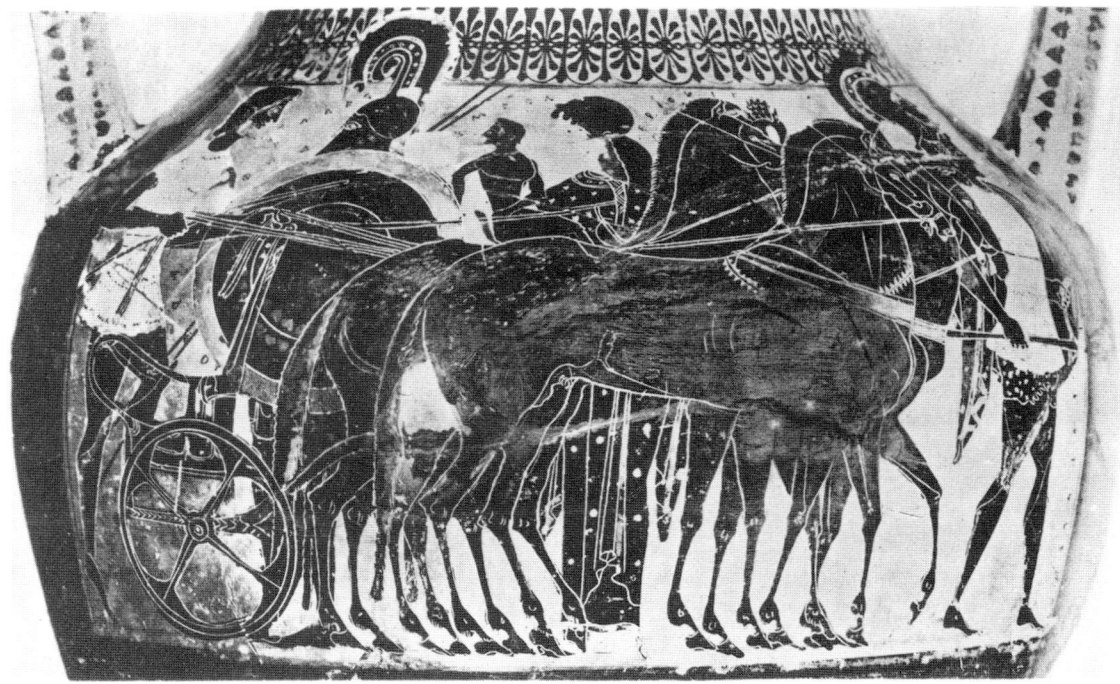

Fig. 4 Attic black-figure amphora. Chiusi, Museo Etusco 1794. Photo: after Wrede 1916 pl. XXVII.

kind of caring relationship between the two (like mother or nurse) is not indicated in how the figures are drawn. Therefore, a fixed interpretation of the group showing woman and child as denoting the female figure as wife and mother in mythological scenes and as the family in non-mythical scenes seems to be too narrow or even misleading. The Amphiaraos-scenes indicate kinship relations between warrior and woman by the identification of the figures through inscriptions. So the interpretation as mother/wife results from the inscribed names and the viewer's implicit knowledge of the myth, not from an inscribed term like 'family'.

In ancient Greek there is no word for family as we understand it nowadays, be it the nuclear family or the extended family consisting of blood relatives of different degrees. The Greek word "*oikos*" means household and designates an economic entity comprising all persons as members, regardless of age, status and assets. According to my analysis the pictorial elements "woman" and "carried infant" are a pictorial code which as *pars pro toto* stands for the social organizational form "*oikos*", both in mythical and non-mythical scenes, as well as in specific contexts. A further differentiation, for example, of the status of the woman within the *oikos* or her gender role, is subject to the pictorial context.

With this in mind, I shall now outline the preliminary conclusions that may be drawn from my analysis as regards interpretation of anonymous departure scenes in looking again at the amphora in Karlsruhe (Fig. 1). Understanding each woman in the Karlsruhe scene carrying a child as a separate element of the picture and assuming that each refers to an *oikos*, the repetition of this code serves to visualize different households and not to visualize the extended family as has been assumed by scholars. The three women wear nearly identically decorated cloths which lead to the conclusion that they represent persons of equal rank within the *oikos*, but not servants or nurses.

This interpretation corresponds with historical tradition. Cohen believes that at least during the sixth century BC Athenian society consisted of different households which stood in an indirect, communicative relationship to each other.[17] The clear division of the elite into single, largely autonomous *oikoi* independent of each other, which were not connected by nature, that is kinsman-like relationships, necessarily implies that the *oikos* as a social unit was the reference point for the actions of the individual *aristoi*. On the Vatican amphora (Fig. 2) the departing warrior's status is stressed by the demonstration of his role as head of the *oikos* and the richness of his household. Material wealth is denoted by his armor, the chariot with one white and three black horses, and the presence of fellows, maybe a *hetairos*, as well as a boy attending the horses and a slave. The continuity of his family line is denoted by the old man and the women carrying children.

The image on the amphora in Karlsruhe (Fig. 1) not only represents the dominating economic strength of the departing warrior – the horses cover the complete centre of the image and screen a good portion of the figures behind – but it also reflects that fellows from separate households go to war jointly. The warrior in the chariot is set apart from the others not the least by the formal composition of the image, for the scene represents the individual superiority of the chariot's owner within a specific hierarchy of the upper class[18] (a model *oikos* versus a clan or extended family).

The images presented in this paper illustrate the concept of a competitively structured society. It is no coincidence that the series of depictions of a warrior's departure by chariot – explicitly connected to the *aristoi* – comes to an end in the later sixth century BC. The sociopolitical changes induced by the Kleisthenic reforms also affected forms of social organization which are then reflected by the images.

Conclusion

The theory which I have suggested is transferrable to other pictorial themes of the sixth and fifth centuries BC. It also can be applied to other media, like Attic votive reliefs. However, a precondition for this would be to take these depictions as constructs in a specific historical context. The language of the images can only be understood within the narrative and the composition of the individual scene. A knowledge of the forms of social organization and the terms used to identify them, as well as literary evidence constitutes an important basis for the understanding of the images.

Abbreviations

Spieß 1992	A. B. Spieß, Der Kriegerabschied auf attischen Vasen der archaischen Zeit (1992)
Killet 1996	H. Killet, Zur Ikonographie der Frau auf attischen Vasen archaischer und klassischer Zeit, 2nd ed. (1996)
Siurla-Theodoridou 1989	V. Siurla-Theodoridou, Die Familie in der griechischen Kunst und Literatur des 8. bis 6. Jhs. v. Chr. (1989)
Wrede 1916	W. Wrede, AM 41, 1916, 221–377

Notes

1 Black-figure belly amphora, attributed to the Painter of Munich 1410, Karlsruhe, Badisches Landesmuseum 61.89; Para 135,1bis; BAdd² 84; CVA Karlsruhe 3 Germany 60 (pl. 12,1; 13,1; 14,1. 2. 3. – Cf. Spieß 1992, 239 B 295. 302 fig. 33. 303 fig. 34.

2 Black-figure belly amphora, Rome, Vatican Museums 1770, near Group E, middle of sixth century BC, ABV 138,2. – See Killet 1996 67. sf. Vasen 3, 13; Wrede 1916 no. 34 pl. XVII; Spieß 1992 247 B 347. 305 fig. 38.

3 For some images it is hard to decide whether it shows a warrior's departure or arrival; see Siurla-Theodoridou 1989 280. I am sure that an ambiguous reading can be assumed here, see M. Seifert, Dazugehören. Kinder in Kulten und Festen von Oikos und Phratrie. Bildanalysen zu attischen Sozialisationsstufen des 6. bis 4. Jahrhunderts v. Chr. (2011) 62–70.

4 In red-figure vase-painting the farewell scenes concentrate mostly on departures on foot, cf. H. Luschey, Rechts und Links. Untersuchungen über Bewegungsrichtung, Seitenanordnung und Höhenanordnung als Elemente der antiken Bildsprache (2002) 42.

5 The material has been treated in many publications, see Spieß 1992 with an overview on the scholarship. Critical of Spieß 1992 is Killet 1996 64–65; on warrior departures in general, see Killet 1996 64–90. – See also Wrede 1916 221–377; K. Dahmen, Boreas 19, 1996, 235–240. – On hepatoscopy: J. Durand – F. Lissarague, Hephaistos 1, 1979, 92–108; A. Kossatz-Deissmann, AA 96, 1981, 562–576. – So-called "Persian farewell": M. F. Vos, Scythian Archers in Archaic Attic Vase-Painting (1963) 31–33; W. Raeck, Zum Barbarenbild in der Kunst Athens im 6. und 5. Jh. v. Chr. (1981) 47–52 – Interpretation of content: H. A. Shapiro, Metis 5, 1990, 113–126; H. Hoffmann, Hephaistos 2, 1980, 142–154; I. Scheibler, JdI 102, 1987, 75–118. – Gender relations: R. F. Sutton, The Interaction between Men and Women Portrayed on Attic Red-figure Pottery, Ph.D. diss. (University of North Carolina at Chapel Hill, 1981) 226–232. For fighting warriors see C. Ellinghaus, Aristokratische Leitbilder – Demokratische Leitbilder. Kampfdarstellungen auf athenischen Vasen in archaischer und frühklassischer Zeit (1997). – Social context: R. T. Ridley, AntCl 48, 1979, 508–548; V. D. Hanson (ed), Hoplites. The Classical Greek Battle Experience (1991).

6 Lost late Corinthian Krater (Berlin, Antikensammlungen F 1655), cf. A. Furtwängler – K. Reichold, Griechische Vasenmalerei III (1932) 1–2 pl. 121; H. Luschey, Rechts und Links. Untersuchungen über Bewegungsrichtung, Seitenanordnung und Höhenanordnung als Elemente der antiken Bildsprache (2002) 42 pl. 10,2.

7 Belly amphora Chiusi, Museo Etrusco 1794; cf. Wrede 1916 42 pl. 27; Killet 1992, 3,23.

8 See P. Sineux, Amphiaraos. Guerrier, devin et guérisseur (2007); J. H. Oakley, in: Akten des 13. Internationalen Kongresses für Archäologie, Berlin 1988 (1990) 527–529; I. Krauskopf, Die Ausfahrt des Amphiaraos auf Amphoren der tyrrhenischen Gruppe, in: Tainia. Roland Hampe zum 70. Geburtstag am 2. Dezember 1978 (1980) 105–116; P. Vicaires, BAssBudé 1979, 2–49.

9 Spiess 1992 2–25. 85–89.

10 Also in early vase-painting so-called *Lebensbilder* without any mythological connotation are depicted, cf. K. Fittschen, Untersuchungen zum Beginn der Sagendarstellungen bei den Griechen (1969) 201; L. Giuliani, Bild und Mythos. Geschichte der Bilderzählung in der griechischen Kunst (2003) 63–64. 133–134.

11 Wrede 1916, 221–377.

12 J. H. Oakley – R. H. Sinos, The Wedding in Ancient Athens (1993).

13 M. Stansbury-O'Donnell, Vase Painting, Gender, and Social Identity in Archaic Athens (2006) 1–3.

14 Cf. C. Ellinghaus, Aristokratische Leitbilder – Demokratische Leitbilder. Kampfdarstellungen auf athenischen Vasen in archaischer und frühklassischer Zeit (1997) 255.

15 B. Reichardt, in: M. Meyer (ed.), Besorgte Mütter und sorglose Zecher. Mythische Exempel in der Bilderwelt Athens (2007) 13–93.

16 See B. Reichardt, in: Meyer (supra n. 15) 21 n. 55. 27 refering to A. Möller in: H. J. Gehrke – A. Möller (ed.), Vergangenheit und Lebenswelt (1996) 5–8.

17 E. E. Cohen, The Athenian Nation (2001) 9. With this assumption he argues against scholars who deduce the development of Athenian society from a "face-to-face-society", like H.-J. Hölkeskamp, in: H.-J. Gehrke (ed.), Rechtskodifizierung und soziale Normen im interkulturellen Vergleich (1994) 140. 142 who concurs with M. I. Finley, Past and Present 21, 1962, 3–24; see also J. Ober, Mass and Elite in Democratic Athens (1989) 31–33.

18 The social and economic position of the warrior as a member of the "elite" is stressed by the chariot, cf. P. Schollmeyer, Antike Gespanndenkmäler (2001) 117. See also Ellinghaus (supra n. 5) 250–251. 252.

23 The Robinson Group of Panathenaic Amphorae

H. A. Shapiro

The starting point for this paper is a well-preserved (though much restored) but little known Panathenaic prize amphora in Baltimore that is an eponym of Beazley's Robinson Group, dating from the last third of the fifth century BC (Figs. 1–3; Color Pl. 28).[1] The vase was acquired by David M. Robinson in the 1920's, allegedly as part of a tomb group from Attica that included three additional Panathenaic amphorae.[2] One of the four Panathenaics later turned out to be by the Achilles Painter,[3] and thus not officially part of the Robinson Group. At the time of Robinson's death in 1958, one Panathenaic was on loan to the Baltimore Museum of Art, and following the death of Robinson's widow in the early 'sixties', the Museum acquired it. In 2010 it was placed, along with four more vases from the BMA's collections, on long-term loan to the newly reopened Johns Hopkins University Archaeological Museum.[4]

David Moore Robinson, widely considered the dean of classical archaeologists in the United States in the first half of the twentieth century, was Professor at Johns Hopkins from 1905 until his retirement in 1947. The eventual disposition of the Robinson vases is a complicated story, beyond the scope of this paper, but three names crop up most often, an unlikely triad: Harvard University; the University of Mississippi in Oxford, where Robinson taught and lived out his final years after retirement from Johns Hopkins; and Baltimore. Perhaps emblematic of the dispersal of the collection is the fact that, of the four Panathenaics in the tomb group, two are today at Harvard (Fig. 4),[5] one at Ole Miss (Figs. 5–6),[6] and one now on loan at Johns Hopkins (cf. Figs. 1–3; Color Pl. 28).[7]

In 1943, when J. D. Beazley catalogued in an article all the prize Panathenaics then known to him, he named the workshop that produced three of these four amphorae the Robinson Group, in honor of his old friend.[8] In Bentz's monograph of 1998, there are a dozen entries for the Robinson Group, and it is dated to the years 430 to 420 BC.[9] The hallmark of the group is Athena's shield device, a flying Nike in white proffering a crown of victory, very clearly seen on the fragmentary example excavated in the Athenian Agora and first published by Eugene Vanderpool (Fig. 7).[10] The Baltimore vase has been heavily restored, and the shield device is no longer visible.[11]

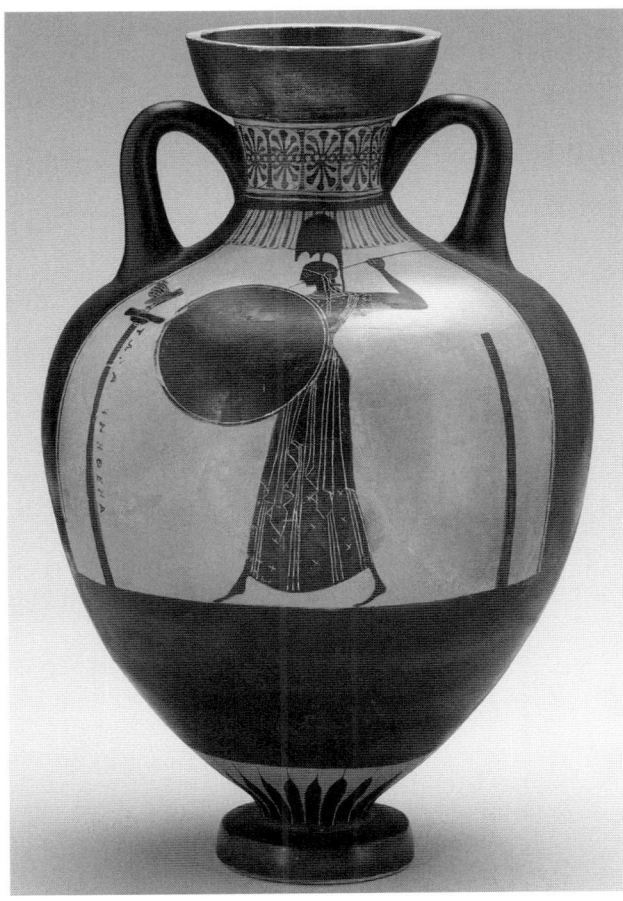

Fig. 1 Baltimore Museum of Art 1960.55.3 (on loan to the Johns Hopkins University Archaeological Museum). Panathenaic prize amphora of the Robinson Group, Side A. Photo: Courtesy Baltimore Museum of Art.

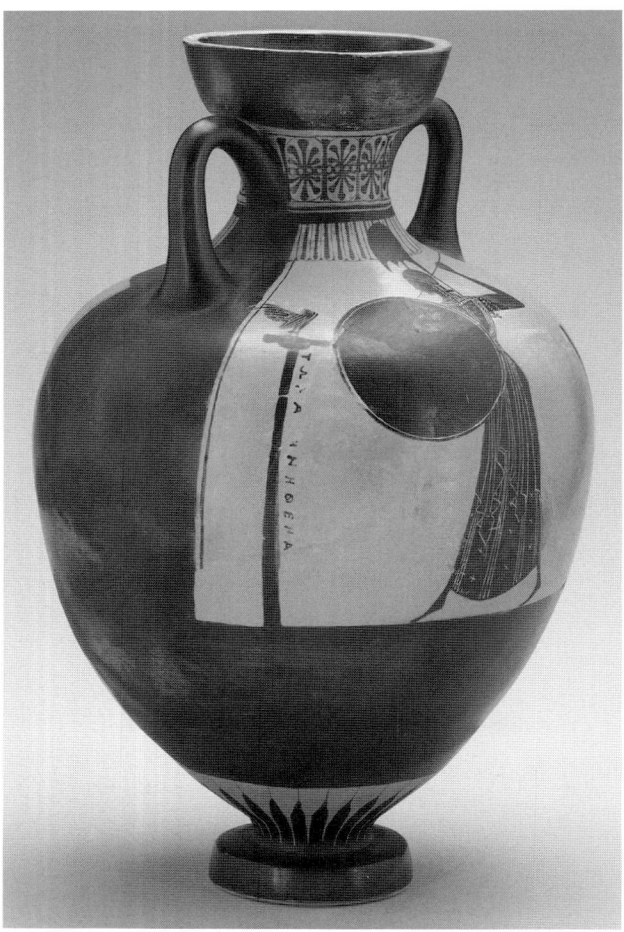

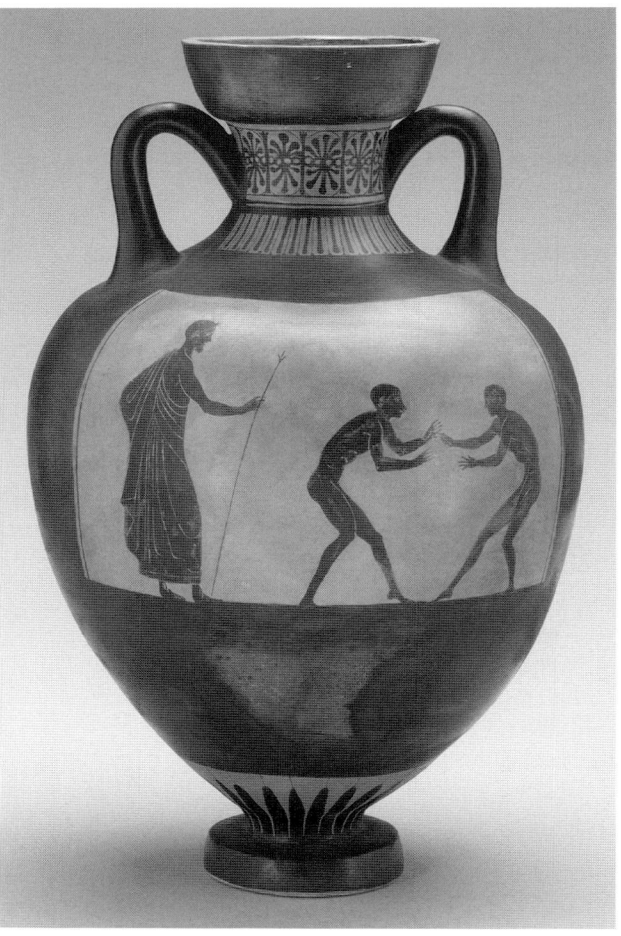

Fig. 2 Detail of the amphora in Fig. 1 showing the prize inscription. Photo: Courtesy Baltimore Museum of Art.

Fig. 3 Side B of the amphora in Fig. 1: boy wrestlers. Photo: Courtesy Baltimore Museum of Art.

The reverse of two of the three Panathenaics under discussion depicts the boys' wrestling contest (Figs. 3, 4; Color Pl. 28B), with a mature man – the umpire or judge – presiding. One of Robinson's Panathenaics now at Harvard (Fig. 4) has the same competition as the Baltimore vase, only the umpire has shifted to the other side. The vase now at Ole Miss has a wrestling match of two grown men (Fig. 6), and Robinson imagined this was the same victor, now 8 or 12 years older[12] – probably a bit of wishful thinking.[13]

The Robinson Group has always raised questions concerning the artist or artists who decorated the vases. Since prize amphorae were only awarded every four years, there would not have been enough business to keep a late fifth-century workshop going that only made these vases in the black-figure technique. This means that they must have been made as a sideline in workshops that otherwise produced red-figure vases, as well as perhaps lekythoi and other shapes in white-ground. A good example of such a multi-faceted workshop is that of the Achilles Painter.[14] As mentioned, this painter's work on Panathenaic prize amphorae includes a fragmentary vase from the Robinson Collection now at Harvard, the fourth member of the tomb group.[15]

Robinson's three other Panathenaics have usually been thought to be by the same hand, or at least from the same workshop. But which workshop? It has always been notoriously difficult to attribute vases in black-figure and in red-figure to the same hand, since the two techniques, being mirror images of each other, require different skills and produce different effects.[16] Robinson was aware of this problem and made passing comparisons between his Panatheniacs and some known red-figure painters of the same period, such as the Kalliope Painter and Aison,[17] but he did not pursue the issue. In his monograph on Panathenaic amphorae, K. Peters ventured a stylistic parallel between the Robinson Group and the Euaion Painter, which would entail raising the date of the group back toward the middle of the fifth century.[18] Independently of Peters (both writing during World War II), Beazley wrote that the Robinson Group "recalls artists on the outskirts of the Polygnotan Group, for instance the Cassel Painter."[19] This again yielded a somewhat earlier date for the group than Robinson had believed, in the 430's.[20]

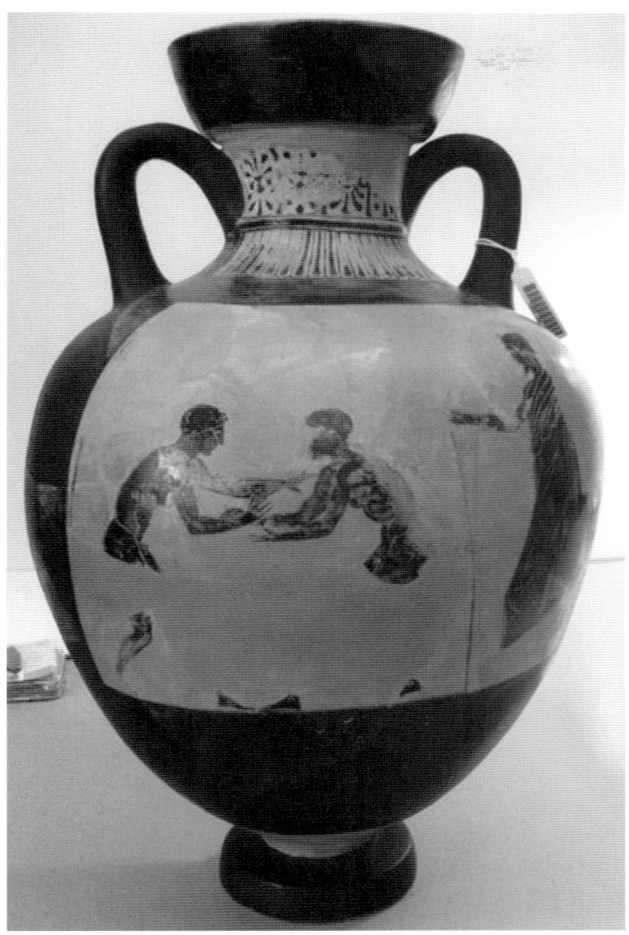

Fig. 4 Harvard University, Fogg Art Museum 1959.128. Panathenaic Prize amphora of the Robinson Group, Side B: boy wrestlers. Photo: author.

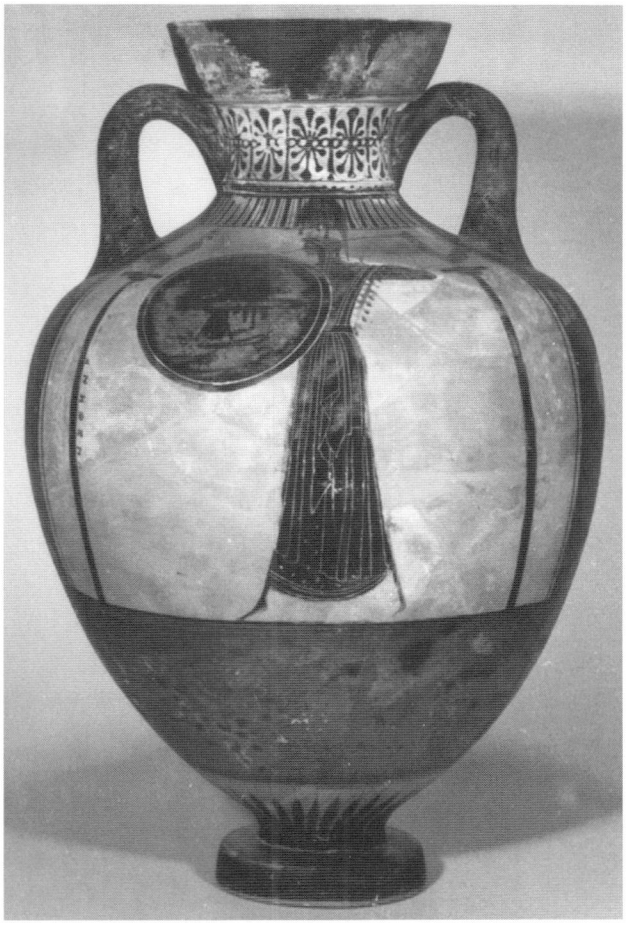

Fig. 5 Oxford, Mississippi, University of Mississippi Art Museum 1977.3.59. Panathenaic Prize amphora of the Robinson Group, Side A. Photo: Museum.

In 1980, the Ny Carlsberg Glyptotek in Copenhagen acquired a magnificent, and very well preserved, Panathenaic prize amphora (Figs. 8–9; Color Pl. 29A–B).[21] The Danish scholar who first studied it, Jette Christiansen, came to the conclusion, not only that this is the masterpiece of the Robinson Group, but also that the hand could be identified as that of one of the finest red-figure artists of the years about 430, the Kleophon Painter. Martin Bentz has accepted this identification, at least for the three largest and finest members of the Group.[22] Although I can claim no great expertise in attributions or style, I would like to suggest that a closer study of the oeuvre of this painter can help strengthen the association and shed some new light on his artistic personality.

The Kleophon Painter has long been regarded as the most 'Parthenonian' of vase-painters in the Periclean period, because some of the solemn sacrificial processions and noble Athenian citizens on his vases seem to have stepped right off the Frieze of the Parthenon.[23] A broader look at the subjects of the Kleophon Painter suggests that he shares with the Parthenon not only stylistic affinities but also a particular interest in festivals and ritual activities more generally. The great volute-krater from Spina that is always set alongside the Parthenon Frieze for its depiction of animals led to sacrifice and the prominent *kanephoros* and priest probably depicts a festival of Apollo at Delphi, with the god himself watching the procession from inside a naiskos.[24] Gualandi first suggested that it might depict the Athenian *theoria* to Delphi ("Pythais") that we hear about in the written sources.[25] A paper of mine, published some 15 years ago, collected these scenes of sacrifice in the presence of the god Apollo – a full half of them by the Kleophon Painter – and proposed that they reflect the Athenians' desire to stay in the good graces of the god who was seemingly shunted aside in favor of Athena, in the transition from Delian League to Athenian Empire.[26]

Whether this interpretation is accepted or not, it is undeniable that the Kleophon Painter has given us more scenes of sacrificial processions than any other painter in the red-figure repertoire. These include the youths leading a bull to sacrifice on a calyx-krater in the Hermitage;[27] and another sacrificial procession on a lesser calyx-krater

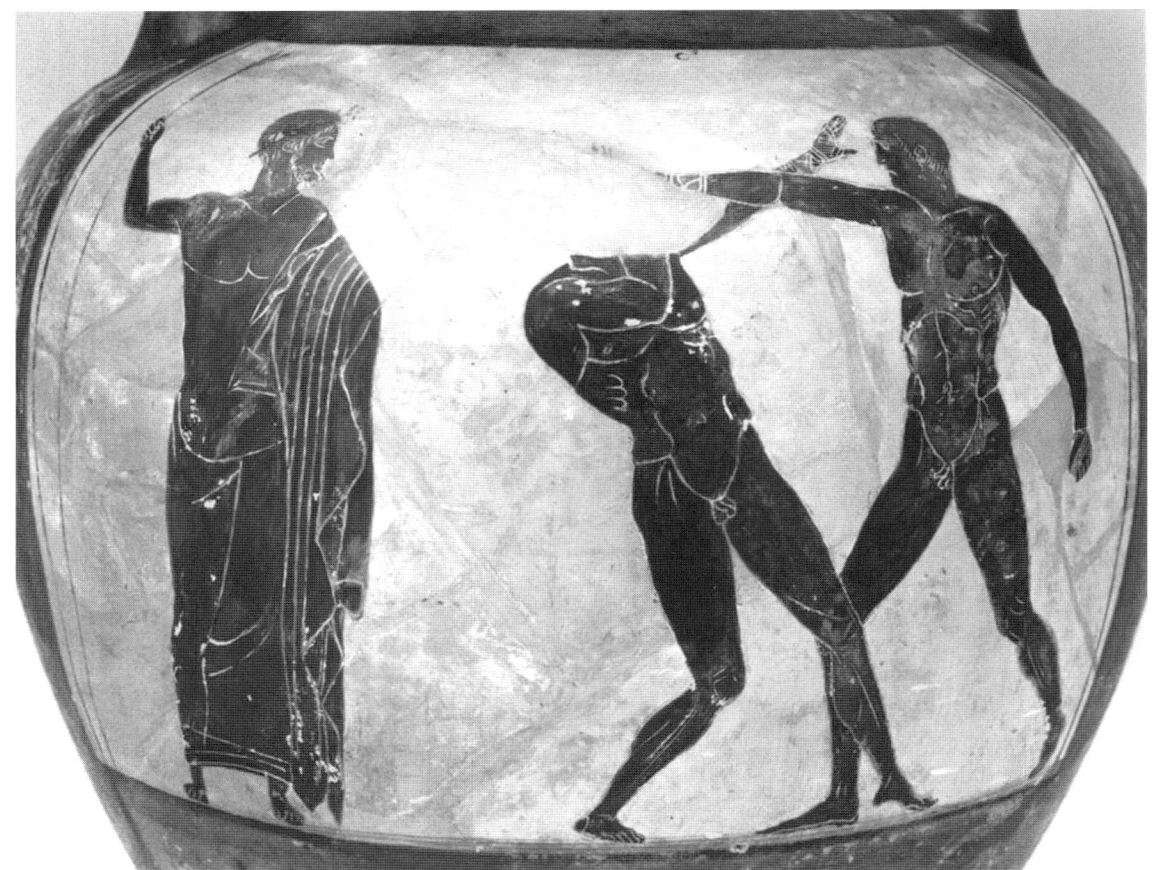

Fig. 6 Detail of Side B of the amphora in Fig. 5: boy wrestlers. Photo: Museum.

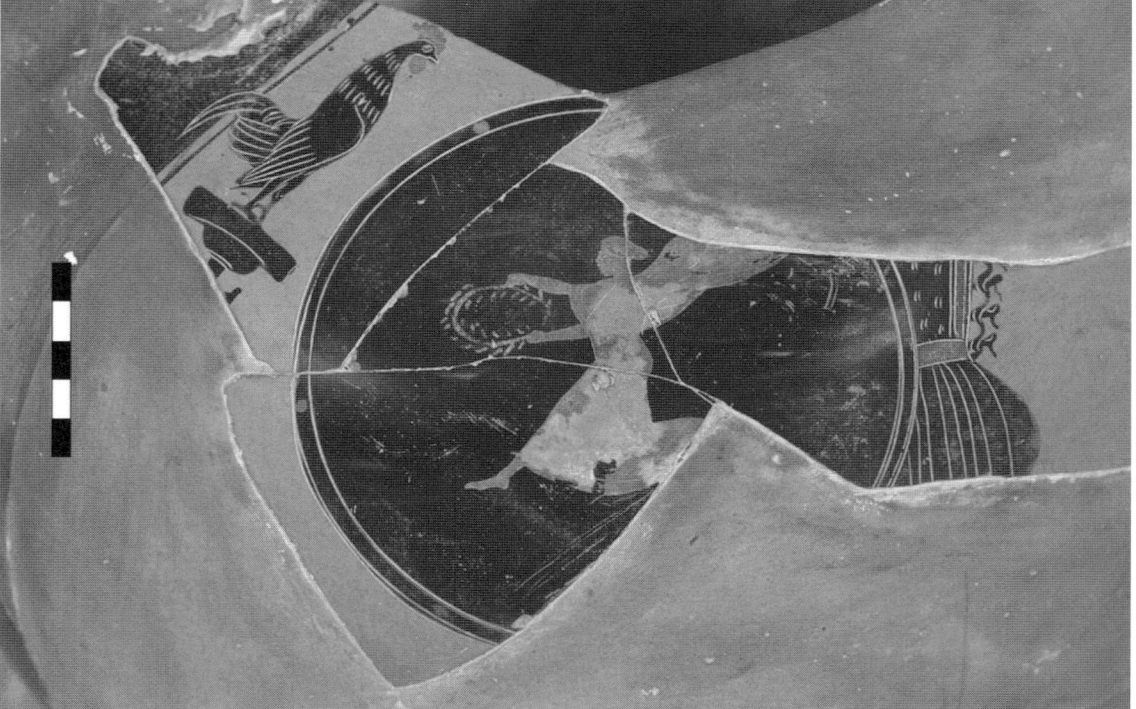

Fig. 7 Athens, Agora Excavations P 10007. Fragment of a Panathenaic prize amphora of the Robinson Group. Photo: Courtesy Agora Excavations.

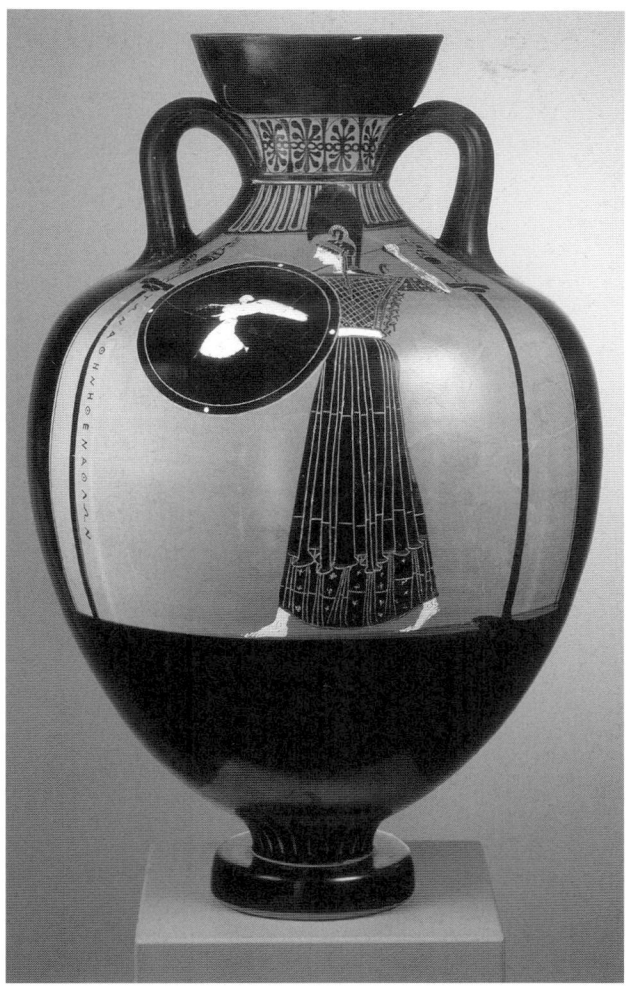

Fig. 8 Copenhagen, Ny Carlsberg Glyptotek 3606. Panathenaic Prize amphora of the Robinson Group, Side A. Photo: Courtesy Museum.

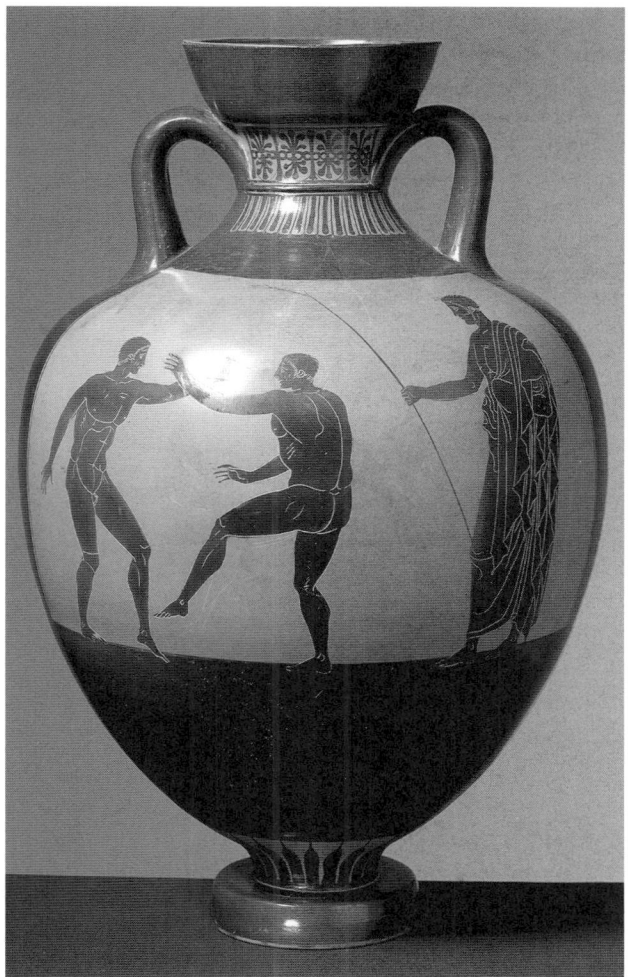

Fig. 9 Side B of the amphora in Fig. 8: youths wrestling. Photo: Courtesy Museum.

also found at Spina;[28] portions of more scenes of sacrifice on fragments now in Oxford found in far-flung locations, Al Mina and Naukratis;[29] an elaborate sacrifice of a ram by a group of named individuals on a well-known bell-krater in Boston;[30] a sacrifice to Apollo on a krater from Agrigento;[31] and a more simplified sacrifice on an amphora of Panathenaic shape now in Darmstadt.[32] I need hardly emphasize the interest in the present context of a subject plausibly identified as a ritual that formed part of the Panathenaic festival on a vase whose shape was inspired by the prizes at that festival.[33] We may also note the unique scene of a dithyrambic chorus on the painter's bell-krater in Copenhagen;[34] and a victorious kitharode with a fluttering Nike, reminiscent of the Panathenaic *mousikoi agones*, on a fragmentary calyx-krater with a most suggestive provenance, the workshop of Pheidias just outside the *altis* at Olympia.[35]

Finally, until recently, the Darmstadt vase was the Kleophon Painter's only pseudo-Panathenaic amphora. But a far more extraordinary example has now been added, thanks to John Oakley's publication of the pseudo-Panathenaic belonging to Laval University, Québec and now on loan to the Montreal Museum of Fine Arts.[36] We shall return to the vase's extraordinary funerary iconography in a moment.

Thus, the Kleophon Painter had a keen interest in festivals and ritual sacrifice and decorated two amphorae that look like special commissions for participants in the Panathenaia. Is it such a leap from pseudo-Panathenaics to making the real thing, i.e. prize amphorae? There is, of course, the key issue of the black-figure technique, but Christiansen's stylistic comparisons between the Copenhagen vase and the Kleophon Painter's work in red-figure are compelling.[37]

In 1971, Florens Felten proposed, in his Munich dissertation, that the Thanatos Painter and the Kleophon Painter are one and the same individual, the white lekythoi of the former complementing the red-figure of the latter.[38] The identification was based largely on a perception that the two painters shared a similar ethos, a sculptural quality in their drawing, and could be dated to the same years, just after the middle of the fifth century.[39] Felten's argument has not won any adherents among subsequent scholars.[40] But the realization that the Kleophon Painter decorated Panathenaic amphorae in black-figure might suggest at least a reconsideration of Felten's idea. Furthermore, the Thanatos Painter's moving scene of Hermes leading a woman to Charon's boat, on his lekythos in Munich,[41] now looks like a precursor of the related scene on the Laval Panathenaic, which depicts a youth being coaxed by Hermes into Charon's boat.[42] In effect, this would mean, as J. Christiansen first pointed out, that the Kleophon Painter, carrying on the tradition of his teacher the Achilles Painter, ran a large and diversified workshop that produced at various times all of the standard techniques of the day: black-figure for prize amphorae; white-ground for funerary lekythoi; and red-figure for a range of pot shapes, some for commemorative purposes, some for use at the symposium, such as the bell-krater, others not (especially his many pelikai).[43] In the end, I defer to the verdict of Oakley, who makes a compelling argument for the many strands of influence and appropriation between the Kleophon Painter and contemporary painters of white lekythoi while stopping short of the supposition that he was one of them.[44]

It is often said that the discovery of a single new vase can radically change our appreciation of a painter we thought we knew well. This has happened repeatedly with the Kleophon Painter over the past half-century. Such was the case with the discovery of the volute-krater at Spina in the late 1950's,[45] which immediately vaulted the painter from a good but unremarkable member of the Polygnotan workshop into an artist capable of a masterpiece on a monumental scale and worthy to be placed alongside the school of Pheidias. Ernesto De Miro's publication in the late 60's of the krater in Agrigento with a sacrifice to Apollo led to the re-attribution of the similar krater in Boston to the Kleophon Painter and established him as the pre-eminent painter of sacrificial ritual.[46] The appearance of the extraordinarily fine Prize Panathenaic in Copenhagen added a whole new dimension to his artistic personality in the early 80's,[47] as did the psuedo-Panathenaic at Laval in the late 90's.[48] On a different level, our painter was never thought of as having a particular interest in mythological narratives (outside the sphere of Dionysos)[49] or the theater until the appearance in the late 1960's of his calyx-krater with Andromeda and Perseus.[50] Nor would we have suspected that the Kleophon Painter would break new ground in the technique of mythological narrative, as on his volute-krater at Stanford,[51] published in the early 1980's, which combines a standard version of the Departure of Triptolemos with other elements of the story not depicted on any other vase. Most notable among the painter's innovations is the way in which Demeter has been moved from her usual position flanking Triptolemos and is depicted instead seated nearby on the "mirthless stone" familiar from the *Hymn to Demeter*.[52]

That two of the most recent and spectacular additions to the painter's oeuvre should both be Panathenaic in shape, when only one other modest vase of this shape had been known from the painter's hand (the Darmstadt vase[53]) seems almost too good to be true. Christiansen suggested that the Copengahen vase was most likely made for a victor at the Greater Panathenaia of 430, the date derived in part from the introduction of the Ionic alphabet, with eta for long E, in the prize inscription.[54] John Oakley independently speculated that the funerary imagery of the Laval amphora, combined with its Panathenaic shape (a unique combination in this period), could suggest that the deceased youth had won a victory in the same games of 430 or the previous ones of 434.[55] In other words, the Kleophon Painter could have decorated two vases for the same family within a year or so, the first a victory celebration, the second a tragic commemoration. Who was this talented young man cut down in his prime, whether in the Great Plague or in an early campaign of the War?

It is a striking fact that the kalos inscription from which the painter takes his name is a hapax. Kleophon is named, with or without kalos, only on a stamnos in the Hermitage that is dated to the painter's early phase in the 430's.[56] Although the name doesn't sound like an uncommon one, there are no external sources, literary or epigraphical, that can connect him securely with a known élite family (the name does not appear, for example, in J. Davies' *Athenian Propertied Families*), even though the same vase also praises Megakles, no doubt of the Alkmeonid family.[57] Perhaps that is because Kleophon never became an adult: he merely caught the eye of a young painter as a handsome youth, won his victory in wrestling in the Games a few years later, and succumbed soon after.

Unlike any other painter of his time, including Polygnotos himself, the Kleophon Painter had a penchant for sprinkling the names of contemporary Athenians across his scenes, sometimes as kalos, as on the name-vase, but more often as what Beazley called tag-kaloi, essentially labeling the real-life individuals who participate, especially in the scenes of sacrifice.[58] In one instance, the Boston bell-krater,[59] several of the names can be identified as those of known oligarchs, leading Beazley to link them to names of men who could be their ancestors, on vases nearly a century earlier, what he called *patrikoi philoi*."[60] If my suggestion about the political meaning of the sacrifice to Apollo has some merit,[61] this would imply that these oligarchs were opposed to Perikles' policy of aggressively expanding the Athenian Empire and longed for the days of Kimon's Spartan sympathies and panhellenic leadership against the Persians. These small private sacrifices to Apollo recorded on the vases contrast with the ostentatious public and 'democratic' festival of the City Goddess. The Kleophon Painter would have been these oligarchs' spokesman in the potters' quarter, yet he was not averse to making prizes for the Panathenaia as well. Decorating Panathenaic prize amphorae is certainly not tantamount to *political* conservatism, but it does at least suggest an interest in Athens' ancient religious traditions and in the now outdated technique of black-figure.

There is not space in this paper to explore all the peculiarities of the Robinson Group of Panathenaics, but two more should be noted. The amphora in Copenhagen that is the star of the Group (Figs. 8–9; Color Pl. 29A–B) conforms to the standard size for a Panathenaic prize amphora, as do the examples in the Agora (Fig. 7) and Oxford.[62] Independent of the exact proportions, a prize amphora should contain a standard measure of olive oil, a *metretes*, equivalent to about 39 litres. But most of the other members of the Robinson Group, including the three once owned by David Robinson, are at least ca. 10 cm shorter and contain about half the volume of a prize vase.[63] Nevertheless, they carry the prize inscription that marks a true prize Panathenaic and thus cannot be considered in any sense "pseudo." How to explain this anomaly?

In the most recent, careful study of the issue, Bentz has proposed the likeliest solution. He notes that, in the several-hundred-year history of Panathenaic amphorae, the undersized prize vases are few, and the majority fall into the years of the Peloponnesian War – those of the Robinson Group and a few other, contemporary examples.[64] With the Spartan army invading Attika every year and ravaging the land, it would have been extremely difficult to harvest the olives that yielded the prize oil. Thus, as a stop-gap solution, the Athenian state must have drastically reduced the amounts of oil awarded in order to continue to hold the Games at all.[65] Although the numbers are extremely small, Bentz also notes that for the years immediately following the Persian sack of Athens in 480, we have only two prize Panathenaics, and both hold only one-third the standard volume.[66]

David Robinson himself went so far as to suggest that the Panathenaic festival must have been cancelled or scaled back several times during the war years, in 430 because of the Plague and in 426 because so many young men were off on campaign.[67] But there is no independent evidence for this. One would think that, between Thucydides and all the later writers who deal with the Peloponnesian War, someone would mention the canceling of the Great Panathenaia if this had actually happened. On the contrary, when Thucydides (5.47.10) records the terms of a 100-year peace between Athens and Argos, negotiated by Alcibiades in 417, one clause states that the Argives and their allies, the Eleans and Mantineans, shall renew the oath by going to Athens ten days before the Great Panathenaia. This would seem an unlikely choice if there had been major disruptions in the festival since the outbreak of the War.

Plutarch tells the famous story of how the annual procession to Eleusis was re-routed and almost canceled owing to the danger of the Spartan occupation of Dekeleia, until Alcibiades stepped in defiantly to lead the way (Plut. Vit. *Alc.* 34.3–6). But since the entire Panathenaia took place within the walls of the city, I see no reason to think the Games were ever suspended in the fifth century –

scaled back, perhaps, in the lavishness of the prizes, but, given the festival's central importance to the Athenians' very identity, its continuity during the war years will have become more, not less, indispensible.[68] Christiansen made the interesting suggestion that the shield device of Nike holding out a victory wreath that seems to have been introduced by the Kleophon Painter for the Games of 430, the first year of the War, could have had a double meaning, not only athletic victory but military as well.[69]

Secondly, one member of the Robinson Group, found in South Russia and now in the Hermitage, has always been an anomaly among Panathenaics for a different reason.[70] It is both undersized *and* it depicts a victorious kitharode, a young man singing to the music of the kithara, with the judge at left and an audience of one. Such musical competitions are not supposed to appear on prize amphorae, since the prize in such events was not olive oil but gold and silver wreaths and cash, as we know from the famous inscription of about 380 recording the prizes in the various contests.[71] But this one *is* a prize vase – it has the inscription. Otherwise, the musical contests are mostly shown on pseudo-Panathenaics that are relatively well represented in both black-figure and red.[72] Perhaps the explanation for the Hermitage vase is related to that for the other undersized prize amphorae of the Robinson Group. That is, the Athenians were even more strapped for cash than they were for olive oil during the early years of the War, and so, exceptionally, this victor received oil as his prize. The device on Athena's shield is not the Nike typical of the Robinson Group, but only the wreath,[73] perhaps symbolizing the one in precious metal that the victor should have received.

The dating of the Robinson Group, which had long failed to find any consensus among scholars, now seems to have settled into the decade 430–20, with the masterpiece of the Group in Copenhagen at the beginning of the series and the rest falling into, and perhaps reflecting in their reduced size, the hardships of the Archidamian War years. Robinson was well aware of the strange paucity of surviving Panathenaic prize amphorae from the whole of the Peloponnesian War period. For after the Robinson Group, it is difficult to find any datable examples until Beazley's well-known Kuban Group, in which the shield device of the Tyrannicides statue group points clearly to the Panathenaia of 402, the first after the restoration of the democracy in the previous year.[74] Interestingly, Robinson himself was able to provide essential material for the chronology of Panathenaics at the turn of the fifth to fourth century by excavating at Olynthos a considerable number of them (mostly fragments but two almost complete examples) that fall into this period.[75]

David Robinson no doubt shared with the Kleophon Painter a special enthusiasm for Athenian festivals, especially the Panathenaia. One of his earliest purchases for his personal collection was a fragment of a prize Panathenaic with the Archon's name preserved that he spotted in the bazaar in Athens in 1908.[76] There is a remarkable red-figure chous of ca. 420 from his collection, now at Harvard, to which he devoted a short article and then included in the last fascicle of his three CVA's.[77] He claimed that the scene of two youths leading a bull to sacrifice copies more closely than any other vase of the period a passage from the Parthenon Frieze, a claim that has been borne out in recent attention paid to the vase by Jenifer Neils in particular.[78] Robinson's attribution of the vase to the "School of the Painter of the Berlin Dinos" (now known as the Dinos Painter) evidently did not persuade Beazley, for the vase does not appear in any of his lists, nor in Susan Matheson's recent study of the painter.[79] Nevertheless, it is interesting that Robinson's initial attribution brings us back to the latest stage of the larger Polygnotan workshop, in which the Kleophon Painter has emerged as the specialist par excellence for festival-related scenes.

Acknowledgments

I am very grateful to John Oakley for the invitation to participate in the conference in Williamsburg, as well as for the extraordinary honor that is recorded elsewhere in this volume. For help in providing photographs and other information I am indebted to the following: Amy Brauer (Harvard University Art Museums); Angela Elliott and Rachel Sanchez (Baltimore Museum of Art); Robert Saarnio and Marti Funke (University of Mississippi Art Museum); Jan Jordan (Agora Excavations); Nikoline Sauer Petersen (Ny Carlsberg Glyptotek); and Sanchita Balachandran (Johns Hopkins University Archaeological Museum).

Abbreviations:

Bentz	M. Bentz, Panathenäische Preisamphoren. AntK Beiheft 18 (1998)
Christiansen 1981	J. Christiansen, MeddelGlypt 38, 1981, 28–50
Christiansen 1984	J. Christiansen, in: H. Brijder (ed.), Ancient Greek and Related Pottery (1984) 144–48
Matheson	S. B. Matheson, Polygnotos and Vase-Painting in Classical Athens (1995)

Notes

1 Baltimore Museum of Art 1960.55.3; ABV 410,1; CVA Robinson Collection 1 USA 4 pls. 31,1; 33,1; Bentz 152 no. 5.177 pl. 80.
2 In CVA Robinson Collection 1 USA 4 46, he writes the group was "purchased in Western Europe," which I take to mean not in Greece. An inordinately large number of the vases in Robinson's collection are given the identical, somewhat vague provenance, "said to be from a cemetery in the area of Vari in Attica" (e.g. CVA Robinson Collection 1 USA 4 17 on pl. 9, the chous [infra n. 7] or 17 on pl. 10).
3 Harvard 60.309; ABV 409,5; CVA Robinson Collection 1 USA 4 pls. 31,3; 32,2; J. H. Oakley, The Achilles Painter (1997) 155 no. 304 pl. 158; Bentz 151 no. 5.167.
4 See www.*archaeologicalmuseum.jhu.edu*.
5 At Harvard, the Achilles Painter amphora (supra n. 3) and one member of the Robinson Group: 1959.128; ABV 410,3; CVA Robinson Collection 1 USA 4 pls. 31,1; 33,5; Bentz 152 no. 5.175. Cf. J. Neils, Goddess and Polis. The Panathenaic Festival in Ancient Athens, Hood Museum of Art, Dartmouth College, Hanover (1992) 86. 171 no. 40.
6 University of Mississippi Art Museum 1977.3.59; ABV 410,4; CVA Robinson Collection 1 USA 4 pls. 32,1; 33,6; Bentz 152 no. 5.176.
7 Supra n. 1.
8 J. D. Beazley, AJA 47, 1943, 450–453.
9 Bentz 151–153. A small fragment of a Panathenaic found at Aigai (Vergina) has been added to the Robinson Group by M. A. Tiverios, Μακεδόνες καί Παναθήναια (2000) 36–37 n. 135.
10 Agora P 10007; ABV 410,1; E. Vanderpool, Hesperia 16, 1946, 123; Agora XXIII 134–135 no. 256 pl. 29. For the development of similar figures of Nike with spread wings, holding either a wreath or a fillet, as a shield device on Panathenaic prize amphorae, see N. Eschbach, in: M. Bentz – N. Eschbach (eds.), Panathenaika. Symposion zu den panathenäischen Preisamphoren (2001) 87–88.
11 An examination of the Baltimore vase in ultraviolet light, conducted with S. Balanchandran, Curator of the Johns Hopkins Archaeological Museum and herself an archaeological conservator, confirmed that there are no remaining traces of the shield device. It also revealed much overpainting on the figure of Athena from the waist up, including the arm and spear, helmet and crest, with only a bit of the original spear visible between the goddess's nose and shield. The incision at the right edge of the aegis is original except for the bottom 2 cm. On Side B, more overpainting is visible, including possibly the entire staff of the umpire. The profile of the boy at left looks to be restored.
12 CVA Robinson Collection 1 USA 4 47. Robinson thought the Ionic lettering of the prize inscription could not be earlier than 426 or 422 (but see now infra 226) and dated his vases from 422 to 414.
13 Cf., however, Christiansen 1984, positing something similar, that the same victor in the boys' wrestling for 422 (Baltimore and Harvard) won again four years later (Mississippi). Yet the presence in the tomb group of the considerably earlier amphora by the Achilles Painter already makes it unlikely that all the vases should be associated with a single victor.
14 See Oakley (supra n. 3) esp. 30–31 on the relationship among the painter's styles in the three techniques.
15 Supra n. 3.
16 A notable contribution in this area is the work of P. Valavanis, Παναθηναϊκοί αμφορείς από την Ερέτρια (1991), who successfully identified the hands of fourth-century Panathenaics from Eretria with major red-figure artists of the period, the Marsyas and Pourtalès Painters, and was able to adjust their chronology accordingly.

17 Kalliope Painter: CVA Robinson Collection 1 USA 4 48 for the vase now in Baltimore; Aison: CVA Robinson Collection 1 USA 4 48 for the vase now in Mississippi.
18 K. Peters, Studien zu den Panathenäischen Preisamphoren (1942) 91–92.
19 Beazley (supra n. 8) 453.
20 Cf. M. Robertson, The Art of Vase Painting in Classical Athens (1992) 259–261, who assesses the earlier views and rightly points out that the comparisons to painters of cups and small shapes by Robinson and Peters were never plausible for a decorator of large Panathenaic amphorae, while Beazley was more on the right track looking at pot painters in the Polygnotan circle. Robertson, however, was not aware of the recent publication of a new member of the Robinson Group that may have solved the problem, discussed immediately below.
21 Ny Carlsberg Glyptotek 3606; Christiansen 1981; Christiansen 1984.
22 The Copenhagen amphora; the Agora amphora (supra n. 10; Fig. 7); and the amphora Oxford 1952.548; ABV 410,4; CVA Oxford 3 Great Britain 14 pl. 28,1–3; Bentz 152 no. 5.174. On the problem of the undersized members of the Robinson Group see below.
23 For recent overviews of the painter see Matheson 135–147 and passim; Robertson (supra n. 20) 221–223. On his 'Parthenonian quality' see, e.g., C. Isler-Kerényi, in: Zur griechischen Kunst. Hansjörg Bloesch zum 60. Geburtstage, AntK Beiheft 9 (1973) 29–30. Two fundamental studies of the painter based on the new discoveries of his work at Spina in the 1950's are those of G. Gualandi, ArtAntMod 19, 1962, 227–260; ArtAntMod 20, 1962, 341–383.
24 Ferrara T 57 CVP; ARV² 1141,1; N. Alfieri – P. E. Arias, Spina (1958) pls. 82–87; N. Kaltsas – A. Shapiro, Worshiping Women. Ritual and Reality in Classical Athens (2008) 220–221 no. 96, with selected references.
25 Gualandi (supra n. 23, AaM 19) 233–234. Cf., however, the alternative suggestion of E. Simon, Festivals of Attica (1983) 79, that the scene is set in the Pythion in Athens, on account of the tripods prominently displayed flanking the temple and associating it with the festival of the Thargelia.
26 H. A. Shapiro, in: P. Hellström – B. Alroth (eds.), Religion and Power in the Ancient Greek World (1996) 101–115.
27 St. Petersburg 774; ARV² 1144,14; A. Peredolskaya, Krasnofigurnye attischeskie vazy (1967) 184–185 no. 211 pl. 143.
28 Ferrara T416 B VP; ARV² 1144,21; BABesch 45, 1970, 64–65 fig. 27.
29 Al Mina bell-krater fragments: Oxford 1945.250; ARV² 1145,26; JHS 54, 1939, 16–17; Naukratis bell-krater fragments: Oxford G 720; ARV² 1145,27; CVA Oxford 2 Great Britain 9 pl. 66,31.
30 Boston MFA 95.25; ARV² 1149,9; Matheson 412 KL 30; 147 pl. 131.
31 Agrigento AG 4688: Veder Greco – La necropolis di Agrigento (1988) 226–227 cat. 75; Matheson 411 KL 29; 146 pl. 130.
32 Hessisches Landesmuseum 478; ARV² 1146,48; Christiansen 1981 35 fig. 6; Bentz – Eschbach (supra n. 10) pl. 32,4.
33 For this and other references to the Panathenaia on red-figure pseudo-Panathenaic amphorae see my comments in Bentz – Eschbach (supra n. 10) 119–121.

34 Copenhagen, National Museum inv. 13817; ARV² 1145,35; CVA Copenhagen 8 Denmark 8 pls. 347–349.
35 A. Mallwitz – W. Schiering, Die Werkstatt des Pheidas in Olympia. OF 5 (1964) 251–254 pls. 82–83.
36 Laval University inv. D25: J. H. Oakley, in Bentz – Eschbach (supra n. 10) 135–143 pls. 38–39.
37 Christiansen 1984 147–48. She especially notes the similarity of the priest of Apollo on the Spina krater (supra n. 24) to the umpire on the reverse of the Copenhagen Panathenaic and the fact that both embody equally the spirit of the Parthenon Frieze.
38 F. Felten, Thanatos- und Kleophon Maler (1971).
39 Felten (supra n. 38) esp. 44 on the dating; 52 on the identification of the two painters.
40 E.g. Matheson 146–147; D. C. Kurtz, Athenian White Lekythoi (1975) 36 n. 7; 220, notes that the Kleophon Painter did not decorate white lekythoi, but does not address Felten's thesis.
41 Munich 2777; ARV² 1228,11; J. H. Oakley, Picturing Death in Classical Athens (2004) color pl. IVB.
42 Oakley (supra n. 36) pl. 38.
43 Christiansen 1981, 50.
44 Oakley (supra n. 36) 142–143.
45 Supra n. 24.
46 E. De Miro, ArchCl 20, 1968, 238–248. For Beazley's re-attribution of the Boston krater (supra n. 30) from Manner of the Kleophon Painter to the painter himself, see CB 3 (1963) 76–78.
47 Supra n. 21.
48 Oakley (supra n. 36).
49 Although Dionysiac scenes, including the Return of Hephaistos, are familiar in the work of the Kleophon Painter, there was nothing to prepare us for the monumental grandeur of an enormous skyphos in Toledo attributed to him and acquired in the 1980's, with a most unusual version of this myth, including Hera chained to her throne: Toledo Museum of Art 82.88; CVA Toledo 2 USA 20 pls. 84–87. The vase has more recently been attributed to the Curti Painter: Matheson 379 no. CUR 5.
50 Basel BS 403; ARV² 1684; Para 456; LIMC I (1981) 776 no. 6 pl. 624 s.v Andromeda I (K. Schauenburg).
51 Stanford 70.12; I. K. – A. E. Raubitschek, in: Studies in Athenian Architecture, Sculpture, and Topography Presented to Homer A. Thompson, Hesperia Suppl. 20 (1982) 109–117; LIMC VIII (1997) 964 no. 127 pl. 646 s.v. Persephone (G. Günter) with further references.
52 See K. Clinton Myth and Cult. The Iconography of the Eleusinian Mysteries (1992) 12–14.
53 Supra n. 32.
54 Christiansen 1984 146. This seems to be the earliest example on a Panathenaic amphora. Cf. H. R. Immerwahr, Attic Script (1990) 184.
55 Oakley (supra n. 36) 142.
56 St. Petersburg 810; ARV² 1144,7; Matheson 407 KL 7; 144 pl. 127.
57 See ARV² 1599 for vases naming Megakles (II) as kalos. For other attestations of men named Kleophon see M. Osborne – S. Byrne, A Lexicon of Greek Personal Names II: Attica (1994) 267. The only one who falls into our period is Kleophon son of Kleippides of Acharnae, who was a candidate in the last ostrakophoria, in 417: M. L. Lang, Ostraka, The Athenian Agora XXV (1990) 90–91.

58 E.g. the stamnos by Polygnotos London E 455; ARV² 1028,9; Matheson 347 P8; 48 pl. 35, naming Archenautes, Nikodemos, and Sosibios (?); and the fragmentary companion vase, London E 456; ARV² 1051; Matheson 347 P9; 49 pl. 36, preserving only the name Diomedes.

59 Supra n. 30.

60 The names are Aresias, Manthitheos, Kallias, Hippokles, and one that Matheson 40 KL 30 (following an earlier conjecture by K. Schefold) suggests could even be restored as the later tyrant Kallias (but from only the final sigma). See Beazley, in CB III 76–78, and cf. T. B. L. Webster, Potter and Patron in Classical Athens (1972) 50, who also discusses this vase and refers to the group as "a nest of very conservative Athenians who might well have celebrated sacrifices together." Cf. especially the Kleophon Painter's fine calyx-krater (supra n. 27), where naming inscriptions are lacking, but the crowded composition, with four mature bearded men to the left of the altar and two nude boys at the right, suggests the same group of individuals as on the Boston vase. Even the two elegant satyrs flanking a maenad on Side B of the Hermitage krater (supra n. 27) have a Parthenonian flavor, recalling the Eponymous Heroes on the East Frieze.

61 Shapiro (supra n. 26) 109–110, on the named individuals in sacrifice scenes.

62 Supra n. 10. n. 22.

63 The heights are: 53.4 cm (Baltimore); 50.2 cm (Harvard); 53.4 cm (Mississippi). On normal variations in the amount held by full-size amphorae see J. L. Shear, ZPE 142, 2003, 101–102.

64 Bentz 33. 37–39. 203 Anhang 6 for a list of all undersized prize Panathenaics.

65 Bentz 38.

66 Bentz 39. 147 nos. 5.094. 5.095.

67 Robinson, in CVA Robinson Collection 1 USA 4 47.

68 See J. L. Shear, in: G. Reger – F. X. Ryan – T. F. Winters (eds.), Studies in Greek Epigraphy and History in Honor of Stephen V. Tracy (2010) 135–152 for a documented example of the cancelation of the Panathenaia in the early third century and the extremely serious ramifications of such a decision. I thank the author for this reference.

69 Christiansen 1984, 146.

70 St. Petersburg 17794; ABV 410,2; Bentz 152 no. 5.179 pl. 81.

71 IG II² 2311; Neils (supra n. 5) 15–16; fully re-studied most recently, by J. L. Shear, ZPE 142, 2003, 87–105.

72 H. Kotsidu, Die musischen Agonen der Panathenäen in archaischer und klassischer Zeit (1990) esp. 90–91 on the St. Petersburg amphora.

73 See Bentz pl. 81, right.

74 ABV 411–412; N. Eschbach, JdI 107, 1992, 33–58; Bentz 156–163 pls. 95. 97 for the Tyrannicides shield device.

75 D. M. Robinson, Excavations at Olynthos V: Vases Found in 1928 and 1931 (1934) 87–90 pl. 61; idem, Excavations at Olynthos XIII: Vases Found in 1934 and 1938 (1950) 59–66 pls. 14–19.

76 D. M. Robinson, AJA 12, 1908, 47–48; CVA Robinson Collection 1 USA 4 pl. 33,2. The Archon is Neaichmos (320/19) = Bentz 179 no. 4.118.

77 Harvard 1959.129; D. M. Robinson, AJA 38, 1934, 45–48; CVA Robinson Collection 3 USA 7 pl. 9.

78 Neils (supra n. 5) 180–181 no. 52; eadem, The Pathenon Frieze (2001) 210 fig. 45. In these publications, Robinson's attribution has been simplified to "Dinos Painter," although he was more cautious and wrote "it may be only a school piece."

79 Matheson does not contain a reference to the vase.

24 Guess Who's Coming to Dinner? Red-figure Komasts and the Performance Culture of Athens

for D. C. Kurtz and F. Lissarrague

Tyler Jo Smith

"The kōmos was essentially a processional dance through the streets, with music, song, laughter, and shouting". So claims Lillian B. Lawler in her 1964 book entitled *The Dance of the Ancient Greek Theatre* in the midst of her discussion about dance and tragedy.[1] Elsewhere in the same book, where she addresses 'the dance of comedy', Lawler explains additional types of komoi ("revel dances"), from the most raucous to the most "sedate" – i.e. those associated with informal partying as opposed to those intended to honor a god, an athletic victor, or a wedding, as well as others involving transvestism or animal mummery.[2] For the most part, Lawler's understanding of the term *komos*, and its many uses, derives from a variety of ancient literary sources. Here as elsewhere, Lawler also looks to Greek vases and their iconography to elucidate her subject, but her understanding of the evidence is often naïve or at the very least adapted to suit her needs:

> The *kōmoi* were of various sorts. In one, frequently portrayed on vase paintings, young men, feeling exuberantly happy after a drinking bout, rollicked through the town, singing uproariously, kicking up their heels in impromptu dances, scuffling, and playing practical jokes upon one another and upon luckless passersby.[3]

Like a series of scholars before her and since, Lawler was grappling with the complex relationship between dance and drama, with the unanswerable question of dramatic origins ever at the back of her mind.[4] Exactly which "vase paintings" does she refer to? And who are these exuberant young men she mentions? As there are neither illustrations in her book nor references to specific objects, we must search elsewhere for the answers. In another book published by Lawler in the same year, *The Dance in Ancient Greece*, Athenian red-figure vases are chosen to illustrate the komos, complete with captions: 'young men dancing' and an 'after-dinner dance of young men'.[5] Quite simply, Lawler's komasts are youthful, thirsty, loud, and mobile.

Many scholars of both Classical literature and art have concerned themselves with the term komos and/or the komast figures on vases, often seeking a single definition or occasion for them.[6] Lawler's more eclectic view, though flawed with regard to artistic evidence, is a good illustration of variety and type, on the one hand, and of the complicated association between image and text, on the other. Although it is not our focus here, it is important to begin any discussion of ancient Greek dance and image with a caveat: it is difficult, if not impossible, to make a direct connection between the dancers or dances chosen for decoration on the sides of Archaic and Classical vases with the figures or movements described in ancient Greek literature. Even more dubious are attempts over the past hundred years or so to recreate the choreography of named dances, which derive from many different time periods and sources, among them visual and literary.[7] That being said, it remains crucial to our modern understanding of the ancient komos that we recognize the validity of questions that have thus far dominated scholarship – the place of drama and ritual, the associations with Dionysos and dithyramb, participation in processions and symposia – while recognizing upfront that dance, regardless of its setting, occasion, participants, or level of formality, was an art-from in its own right, both intensely physical and manifestly performative.

The komast figure, defined here as a male dancer or reveler, decorates both black- and red-figure vases and is occasionally found in other artistic media. The first series of vases featuring the figures with regularity are, of course, those from late seventy-century Corinth, where male dancers are dressed up in short-red chitons that sometimes appear to be stuffed or augmented, thus earning them the title "padded dancers".[8] Their favorite gesture is undoubtedly bottom-slapping, though it is not their only one. Shown solo, in all-male groups, or in the presence of nude women, they are, on the whole, playful figures, whose dance sometimes resembles spontaneous pantomime rather more than rehearsed action. When early Athenian black-figure painters select the figure for their artistic repertoire, they are quick to alter his appearance and to incorporate him into new settings, including sympotic (i.e. Siana cups) and erotic (i.e. Tyrrhenian amphorae); though it must be said that an exact setting or location for their performance is often difficult to determine, and, where it is evident, it is often tied to an individual artisan or group.[9]

Regardless of painter, drinking and playing music regularly aid the reveler's pursuits and conjures an atmosphere of merry-making and pleasure. The short chiton and bottom-slapping gesture, both originating in Corinth, are retained by Athenian artists initially, but over time nudity becomes the norm for revelers and their range of poses and gestures is expanded to include head-tapping and kicking. Outside of Athens, the komast figure is represented widely in black-figure; from Laconia, Boeotia, East Greece, and the West, he is adapted to local tastes and fashions, as well as to native artistic needs.[10] With the advent of the red-figure technique in Athens, it is arguable that the black-figure komast changes in more ways than one. Painters working in both techniques incorporate new attributes, such as sticks, boots, and cloaks, and the body postures of the dancers and their anatomy become more ambitious artistically. This is easily illustrated with the works of the later black-figure Leagros Group and the Segment Class, or by the early red-figure 'Pioneer' painters Euthymides and Euphronios.[11] These changes, as has been suggested elsewhere, are not as abrupt as one might suspect; at least a few black-figure painters (e.g. Lydos) had begun introducing the new trends previously.[12] Taken as a whole, however, elements of a new komos become far more prevalent with the rise of red-figure but, as we shall see, they are not embraced whole-heartedly by each and every painter.

A large number of Athenian red-figure vases are decorated with komast scenes. A recent search of the BAPD for the terms 'red-figure' and 'komos' results in 1790 records.[13] If we limit the search to the date range that interests us here, 525–475, that number reduces to 380, but from 500–450 come another 840 (1220 in total). On more careful inspection of these results it becomes clear that, as in black-figure, some painters/groups active during these years specialized in komast imagery, while others merely dabbled in it. The setting, where indicated or discernible, is a symposion or, just as often, the journey to or from the andron.[14] At the same time, these painters tend to place more emphasis on aspects of performance (dancing, singing, playing music) than on sexual encounters or alcoholic overindulgence. Such iconographic choices indicate that many red-figure painters carry on the somewhat monotonous tradition of Athenian black-figure dance iconography that dominates the years leading up to the invention of the red-figure technique, or for whatever reason are throwbacks to it. From a purely stylistic perspective, many red-figure komast painters also retain their close ties to black-figure by representing dancing figures in profile with little or no foreshortening. The fact that so many of these images decorate sympotic vessels, mainly cups, but also kraters, psykters, and amphorae, hardly seems shocking.[15]

What follows here is a cursory survey of what I am labeling 'komast painters' in red-figure – namely, those who are especially interested in the subject – active in the years in and around 500 BC, and thus firmly rooted in the Archaic tradition. Komast scenes are a good indicator of a painter's or group's style, because they tended to be produced in relatively large quantities and the imagery inclines toward the repetitive. Excluded from this presentation are heavily draped komasts, among them the Anakreontic vases ("booners"), who have received a good deal of attention in their own right; these are the purview of other painters, at least some of whom seem just as interested in dress as in dance (e.g. Brygos Painter, Douris).[16]

The First Generation: Oltos, Epiktetos, Epeleios

Among the first generation of red-figure cup-painters who are particularly drawn to komast imagery we should cite Oltos and Epiktetos. Both may have been taught by the Andokides Painter, and both were active during the last quarter of the sixth century.[17] On a cup in Basle, Oltos offers up a bilingual vision of the reveler in isolation – red-figure on the exterior, and black-figure in the tondo.[18] A surprising detail here is the juxtaposition, or perhaps inversion of the old and the new: the beardless red-figure males are of the more old-fashioned nude type, involved in music and drink, while the black-figure male portrayed in the tondo is bearded and wreathed, wearing a cloak and boots. Although the figure in the tondo is probably mortal, the slightly Dionysian air about him is consistent with this painter's general love of the wine-god's entourage.[19] Like the black-figure Nikosthenes Painter, Oltos is more than willing to place satyrs and komasts on the same vessel, in this case on cups, but he consistently separates the world of myth from the world of mortals.[20]

His fellow painter, Epiktetos, shows an even greater interest in human revelry (thirty-four BAPD records as opposed to Oltos' sixteen), including group compositions, duos, or isolated studies dominating tondos or plates.[21] The tubby, bearded male decorating a plate in Paris (Fig. 1) is a much more restful version of Oltos' black-figure dancer.[22] He strides to the right, head tilted up (perhaps in song), brandishing stick, cloak, pipes-case, and a large skyphos. This painter, too, is capable of mixing the satyr revel and the mortal revel, as seen on a cup in Aberdeen and Florence, where again the two types are relegated to different decorative zones.[23] Also, in the komast scene, which is found on one exterior side (Ajax and Achilles are on the other), two youthful males holding drinking-cups face each other and dance energetically, while a bearded figure supporting an oinochoe moves off to the right, mouth open and head tilted back in song. A black-figure komast attributed to Epiktetos by Kraiker (Fig. 2) incorporates the turban, a detail more in line with Anakreontic vases, making this figure an outlier to the artist's normal repertoire of revelers.[24] In another example, this one signed 'Epiktetos egrapsen', a grotesque-looking red-figure reveler hoists up his cloak while bending over to urinate.[25] This painter's interest in movement, poses, and performance is further attested by the elegant figures on his red-figure plate in the British Museum; and such an image only further demonstrates that Epiktetos is in no way committed to a particular variety of komast imagery.[26] A much simpler version of events is seen on a cup in Munich, where the youthful reveler who carries a wine-skin and oinochoe moves right, but turns his head back to the left in a style reminiscent of a large number of black-figure examples from the mid-sixth century and earlier.[27] Indeed, Epiktetos perhaps more than any artist attempts the available range of possibilities, and his ambition in this regard is expressed in the works of lesser contemporary artists. Case in point is the Scheurleer Painter whose komastic antics range from public exhibitions of the bodily functions to impressive acrobatic displays.[28]

A more prolific painter of komast imagery (forty records in BAPD), and one certainly less well-known, is the Epeleios Painter.[29] He is highly conservative in his approach to the iconography of revelry, and in several examples his figures are so reminiscent of the Athenian black-figure dancers of the past that they almost seem to copy them. Such is the case with the crouching figures on a mug in Poland, one of whom proudly demonstrates the bottom-slapping gesture and carries an (upside down) drinking-horn.[30] A fully nude male, who decorates the exterior of a cup now in Rennes (Fig. 3), kneels to the floor while wielding a cup and slapping his bottom; on a fragmentary cup in Paris a column-krater has been added to enhance the sympotic setting.[31] Selecting among the latest choices for dress and attributes, this painter is fond of the cloak and krotala, a percussion instrument played by either men or women, and "associated with mystery, excitement, and vigorous celebration".[32] Most ambitious is this painter's cup in Basle where the setting is clearly not the andron itself, but rather a literal komos-

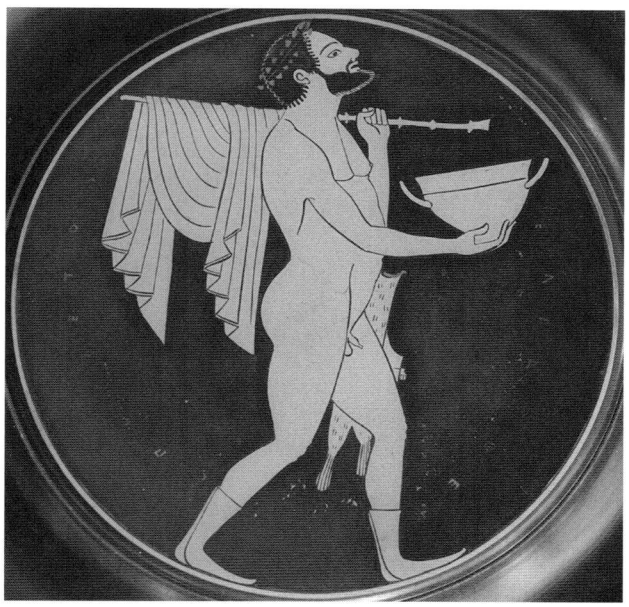

Fig. 1 Paris, Cabinet des Médailles 510. Red-figure plate. Epiktetos. Photo: ArtStor.

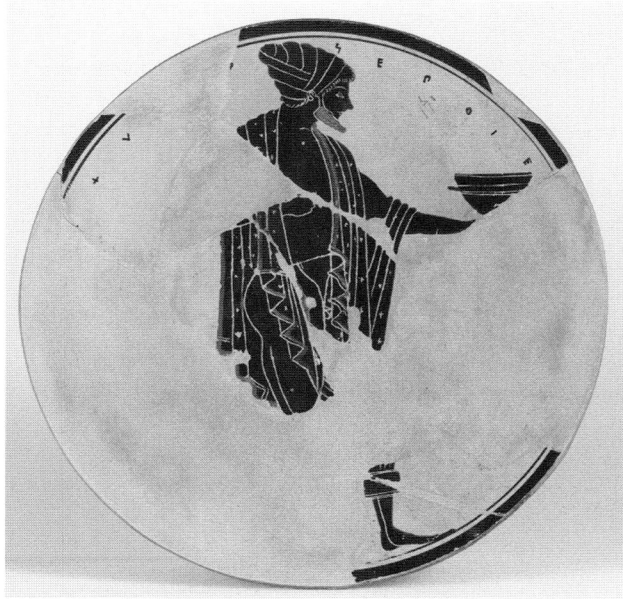

Fig. 2 Berlin, Antikensammlung F2100. Black-figure cup. Epiktetos. Photo: Art Resource.

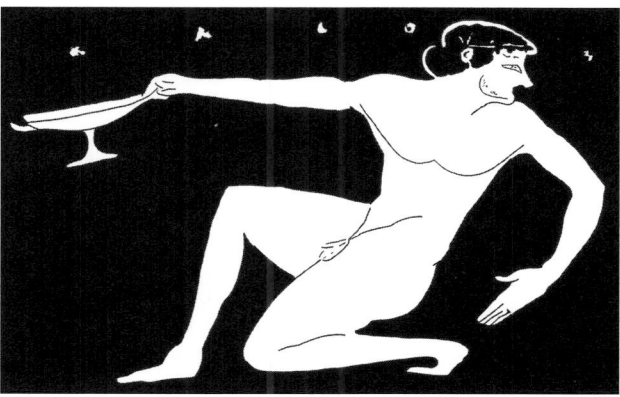

Fig. 3 Rennes, Musée des Beaux Arts 1932.725 (1909.375). Red-figure cup. Epeleios Painter. Drawing: D. Weiss after BAPD 200411.

procession headed to the drinking-party.[33] This cup is fascinating in its attention to detail. On one side (Fig. 4; Color Pl. 29C), eight fully nude youths are gathered in two groups: one group wheels a wine-skin and the others appear either to be fighting or engaged in an acrobatic routine (both are to be found in a komast's bag of tricks). On the opposite side (Fig. 5), the crowd has moved indoors. Four youthful nude males dance excitedly, while a pair of friends (one of whom is ithypallic) tends to the krater. The bearded nude male in the tondo (Fig. 6) surely attends the same party. His body posture indicates dancing, and the empty wine-skin suspended in the background places him at a more advanced stage of the evening than his beardless friends on the exterior. The lack of anatomical detailing on the mature figure, as well as his full profile body, help establish the Epeleios Painter as key to the survival of the Archaic black-figure komast type in red-figure.

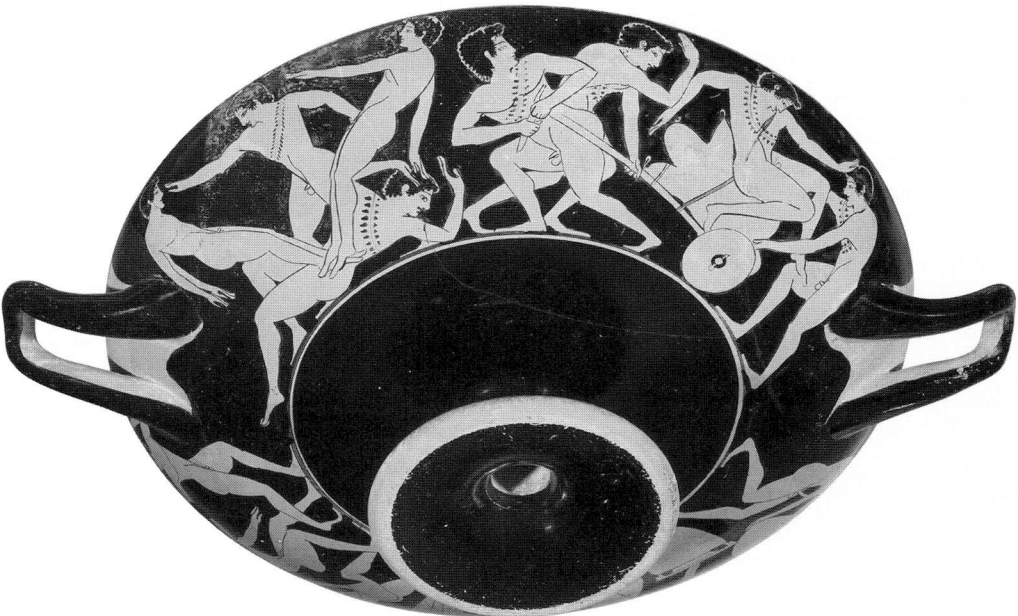

Fig. 4 Basle, Antikenmuseum und Sammlung Ludwig BS463. Red-figure cup exterior. Epeleios Painter. Photo: Antikenmuseum Basel und Sammlung/A. Voegelin.

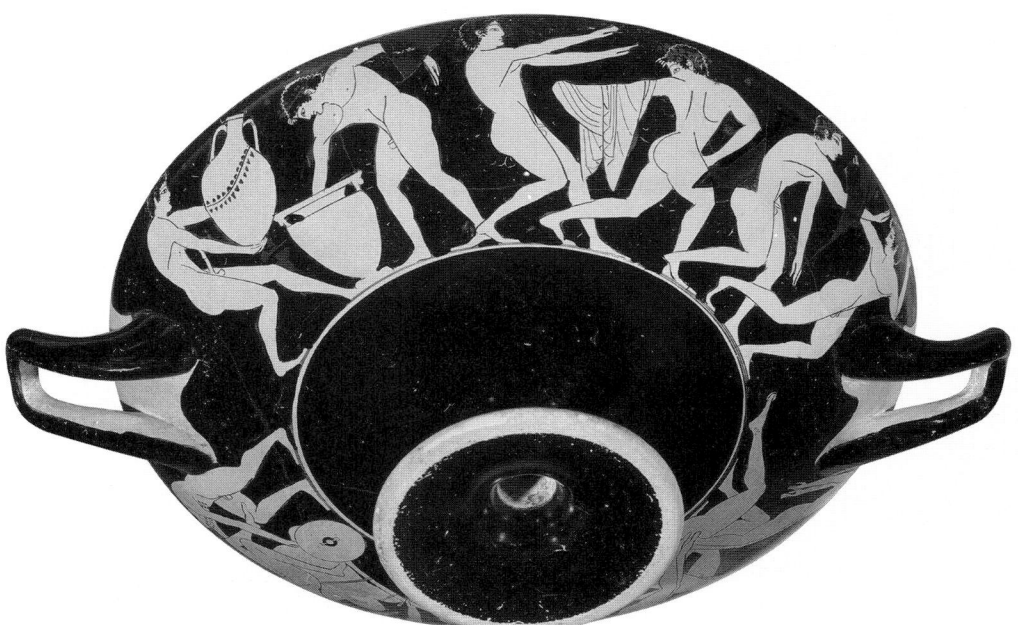

Fig. 5 Other side of vase in Fig. 4.

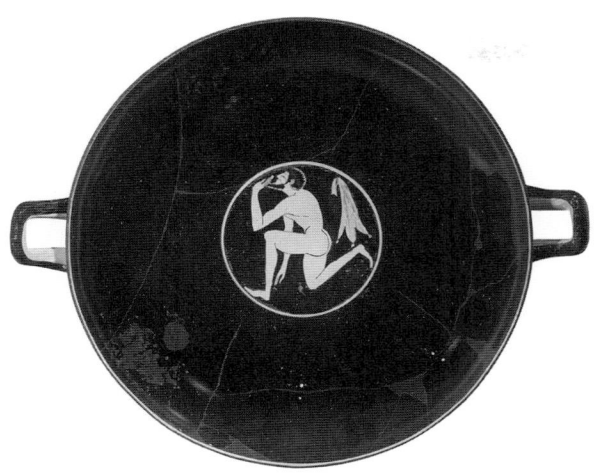

Fig. 6 Basle, Antikenmuseum und Sammlung Ludwig BS463. Red-figure cup tondo. Epeleios Painter. Photo: Antikenmuseum Basel und Sammlung/A. Voegelin.

Antiphon and Cage Painters

In the next generation of Athenian red-figure cup-painters there is one who is markedly keen on komast imagery: the Antiphon Painter. Beazley devoted his entire Chapter twenty-three in *ARV*² to the painter, finding him close in style to Onesimos, and Robertson adds that the two artists must have belonged to the same workshop.[34] No less than eighty-two komos scenes have been associated with his hand (cf. thirty-nine assigned to Onesimos, whose scenes are rather different). Where the provenance is known, it is Etruscan, with another handful coming from Athens or "Greece". Some of his cups "bear the name Euphronios as *poietes*", though his name derives from a *kalos* inscription.[35] It has been claimed by both Beazley and Robertson that it is sometimes difficult to distinguish the Antiphon Painter from his followers, yet all cups assigned or related to him reveal an interest in dance as bodily movement.[36] This painter follows three schemes for producing komast iconography on cups:

1. Single komast in tondo; exterior undecorated
2. Single komast in tondo; komos on exterior
3. Single komast in tondo; komos and/or athletes on exterior

The solo figures decorating the tondos of many cups by this painter are a diverse bunch, and no two would appear to be alike. Some hold drinking vessels (kylix, skyphos, or mug) and/or sticks, some hold or play musical instruments (the pipes, lyre, or krotala); all wear or carry their cloaks. Some of the figures are standing, while others are actively dancing. More than once a head-tapping gesture is employed, yet none of these males has time for any old-fashioned, hard-core bottom-slapping.[37] Unlike the painters discussed thus far, the Antiphon Painter experiments with frontality, foreshortening, and more complex movements of the body in three-dimensional space.[38] As seen so consistently with other red-figure painters, these male figures are nearly always youthful and beardless. Komast scenes displayed on the exterior of the Antiphon Painter's cups duplicate these individuals, placing them into dancing-reveling groups, and sometimes incorporating women, more mature males (at least some of whom recline), and sexual activities.[39] The fragmentary state of many scenes makes it impossible to determine who's doing what in every instance, but one pattern starts to emerge: youthful males carry and serve wine (even by force!) to mature symposiasts.[40] Yet, as in Athenian black-figure, there is a great deal of variety when it comes to combined komos-symposion iconography, and body posture (i.e. reclining vs. upright) or poses/gestures are often a better indicator of possible social status than any other aspect of the iconography, including age.[41] The Antiphon Painter's symposion scenes do feature beardless youths reclining on klinai, be they alone, in pairs, or sprawled alongside a bearded male. In one known example attributed to the painter by von Bothmer (Fig. 7), komast dancers decorate the exterior of the cup, while the symposion is placed inside; the figures, be they dancing or reclining, are beardless youths.[42]

A contemporary craftsman, the Cage Painter, has only a handful of komast vases assigned to his name, and even those are considered by Beazley to be related to the Antiphon Group.[43] Two fragmentary cup tondos in Paris present the familiar suspects: beardless males in motion, sporting the cloak and stick assemble.[44] Both have the

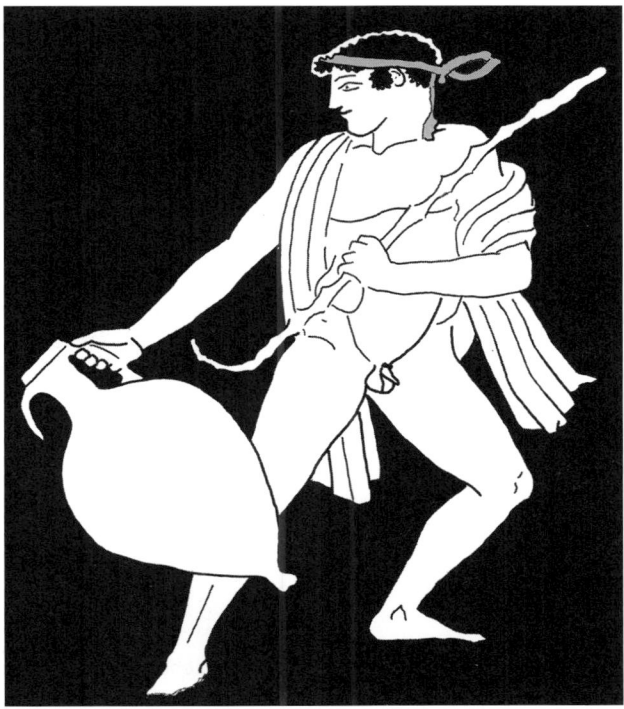

Fig. 7 New York, Bothmer Collection. Detail. Red-figure cup. Antiphon Painter. Drawing: D. Weiss after BAPD 203557.

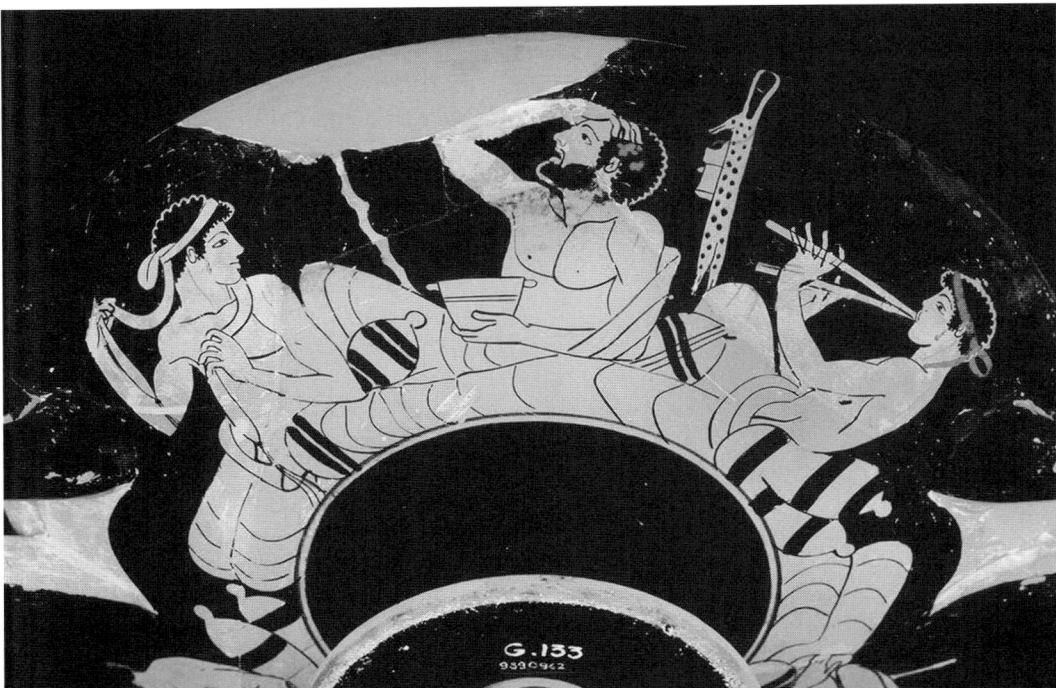

Fig. 8 Paris, Musée du Louvre G133. Red-figure cup. Cage Painter. Photo: Art Resource.

familiar short-cropped hair-do of their era, and both are shown in profile with torsos turned to the front. A bit of variety is added by the touching of the head in one case, the wearing of a fillet in the other. Another cup in Paris gives a more complete picture of what was possible, and in some respects distances this artist from the Antiphon Painter, at least with regard to komast imagery.[45] On either side of the cup's exterior, a bearded male is joined by two beardless ones, and all figures recline on cushions. On one side a frontal-faced bearded male takes a drink of wine from a skyphos. The younger males pay no attention to their more mature companion, and converse amongst themselves. Both hold drinking cups and are draped from the waist down, and one is adjusting his head-band; a basket hangs above and between them. On the other side of the cup (Fig. 8), the bearded male figure is at the center of the composition, and the youths are placed on either side. Again one of the youths is preoccupied with his hair accessory, while his friend plays the double pipes. The bearded male raises a hand to his head and with his mouth open is singing.[46] The fully nude male figure who decorates the tondo of this cup may well be a komast on break from dancing; he dips his oinochoe into a krater that has been decorated with a wreath: "The vase is treated like a guest, adorned as they are in Dionysian greenery", to quote Lissarrague.[47] Although a youthful figure, the painter has spared no detail in proving that he is well built, and the ivy wreath on his head aligns him with the more grown-up members of the party. The profile stance of this reveler is purely Archaic, but like other examples attributed to the Cage Painter – such as a kottabos-playing symposiast shown from the back[48] – his work discloses a combination of what the 'Pioneers' of the past introduced to red-figure and a newly developing Early Classical style.

Myson and Other Pot Painters

Up to this point, our attention has been given to Athenian red-figure cup-painters and their enthusiasm for the komos. Considering the assumed sympotic setting for both the shape and the dancers, this hardly comes as a surprise. But it is important to remember that the earliest red-figure komast scenes may actually have appeared on pots, such as the oft-cited amphora by Euthymides in Munich.[49] Beazley attributed a fantastic psykter in Paris to Smikros (Fig. 9), and its lively and ambitious dancing group holds much in common with black-figure dance scenes in terms of style, pose, and composition.[50] By contrast, a vase of the same shape attributed by Beazley to the Dikaios Painter, and now in the British Museum, whose long-bearded aging revelers don cloaks and boots, establishes that new dress and/or dance styles have come to town, but are either: a) not worn by everyone, or b) an indication that some painters are more conservative with the subject than others.[51] These dancers belong to a separate iconographic tradition.

The next generation of pot painting in Athens is dominated, at least in our minds, by the Kleophrades and Berlin Painters. But were these painters of "power" and "grace", with whom we associate Olympian and Trojan subject-matter, at all interested in the komos?[52]

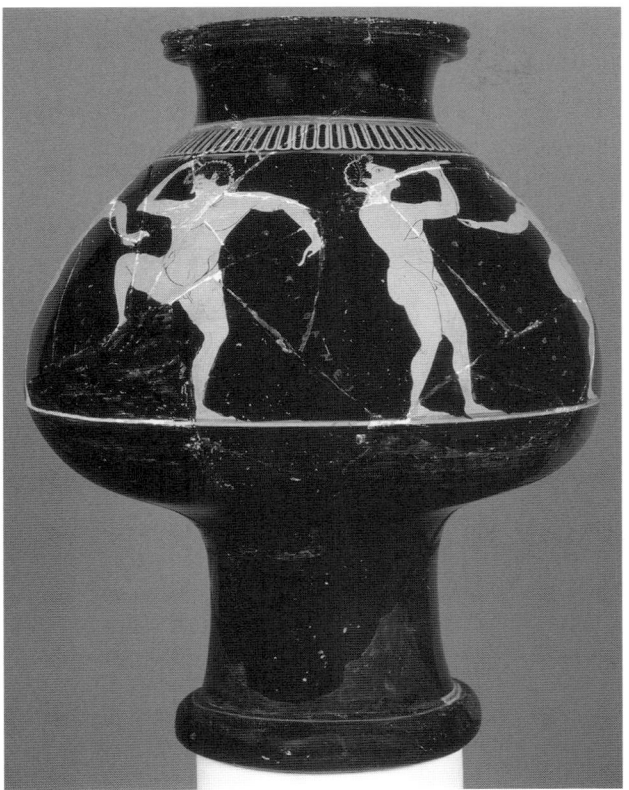

Fig. 9 Paris, Musée du Louvre G58. Red-figure psykter. Smikros. Photo: Art Resource.

The Kleophrades Painter's hand has been assigned to a neck-amphora in Würzburg, depicting a departure scene on one side and exposing a komos on the other (Fig. 10).[53] This komast scene has what may only be described as many unique features. It demonstrates an exercise in artistry rather than any direct or sustained interest in the iconography of dance and revelry. Two bearded and nude male figures are painted with abundant anatomical detail from head to toe. Steadying themselves on both legs, the slight bending of their knees is enough to suggest movement. Both men have their heads tilted down: one gazes at his own reflection in a skyphos, the other gazes at his friend's backside. Their attributes of music and drink confirm the occasion. The third figure is conspicuously female, fully nude and frontal. Rather than playing her auloi, she holds one pipe across her belly and with the other she suggestively pokes the man next to her; like her companion to the far right, her gaze is also affixed to the man in the middle.

This scene, unlike any we have viewed thus far, encourages us to think about dancing in a more complex way. Dance is entertainment, but it is also a physical, sometimes even sensual activity. Its physical aspect directs us as viewers to the body. We are directed to the body with the gaze. The gaze, like the body, can be highly erotic. The Berlin Painter, expectedly, takes a different

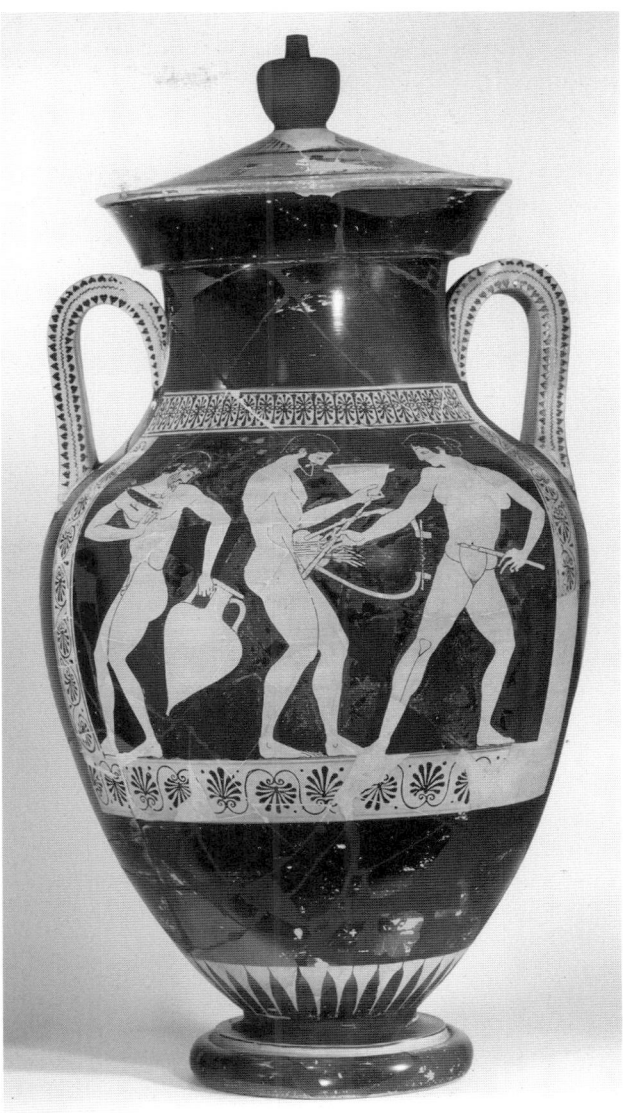

Fig. 10 Würzburg, Martin von Wagner Museum L507. Red-figure neck-amphora. Kleophrades Painter. Photo: Martin von Wagner Museum der Universität Würzburg, P. Neckermann, respectively E. Oehrlein.

approach to the topic. On several amphorae, such as one in London, he portrays a spot-lit reveler on each side.[54] As with other vases decorated by this master craftsman, we as viewers are encouraged to ponder the two sides of the object first separately and then together. By doing so here, the viewer may compare bearded and beardless, music and drink, silenic and human. With both the Kleophrades and Berlin Painters we are mere witnesses to their playful komastic tinkerings.

The Late Archaic pot painter who seems most committed to komast imagery, and indeed the last to be presented here, is Myson.[55] A specialist in column-kraters, he painted a wide range of subjects and many of them everyday (i.e. athletes, komos) or Dionysian. Although he is not the only painter of his time to explore komast imagery, he is the most prolific with at least sixty-five vases assigned to him or his manner. The findspots for these vessels are mainly in Italy and Sicily, although isolated examples come from mainland Greece and Cyprus. For the most part, Myson presents a fairly familiar variety of komast iconography, but the influence and potential of the newer technique is evident throughout. Myson prefers two different compositions for his revelers: solo dancers or groups. Solo dancers are combined on the same vessel – in a manner reminiscent of the Berlin Painter – with satyrs, athletes, or Dionysos. But as has been the case with other painters, the human revelers and the rowdy satyrs grace different sides.[56] Komos may combine with komos on opposite sides as well.

There are two dancing poses notably favored by Myson. The first and most frequent shows dancers who move in one direction but turn their heads sharply 180 degrees in the other (Fig. 11).[57] The second pose demonstrates figures who dance and face in the same direction with both feet on the ground, and very often one or both arms extended and holding objects.[58] A few of these revelers are on the verge of bottom-slapping, and the painter is also fond of using the partial back-view à la Euthymides (but with less success!). Participants are mostly short-haired, youthful males wearing little or no drapery. Several males lift pointed amphorae, skyphoi, or oinochoai, and a few even carry wine skins, or an occasional drinking-horn. Some scenes include draped lyre-players, and krotala are played by nude dancers who look to be totally engrossed in their routine.[59]

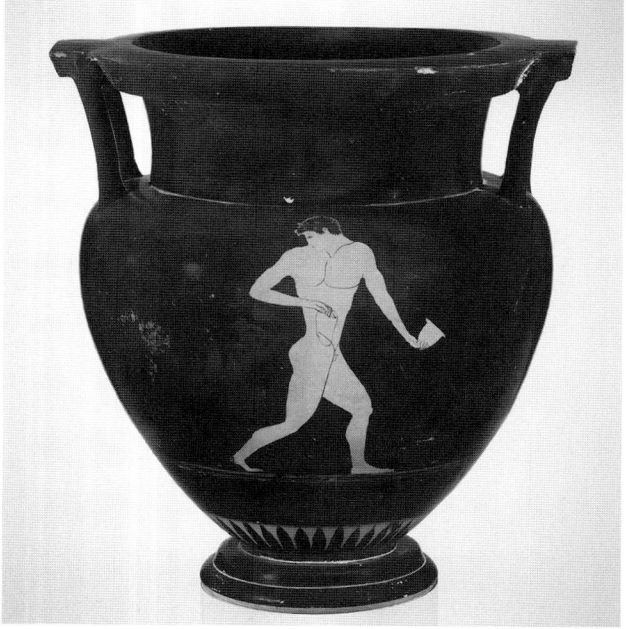

Fig. 11 New York, Metropolitan Museum of Art 21.88.82. Red-figure column krater. Myson. Photo: Art Resource.

Performing in "a man's world"

In this brief survey of red-figure komast dancers and related figures from the years in and around 500, we have highlighted painters and images that disclose the continuation of the black-figure komast iconography that dominated dance imagery through most of the sixth century. In doing so, we have demonstrated that, as in black-figure, painters and groups may not only have specialized in male dance imagery (which clearly had a huge market), but also their focus on individual groups and types.[60] By way of conclusion, let us break down this iconography into the same basic components that have been applied to the Athenian black-figure corpus: dress/attributes, poses/gestures, and context.[61] These categories may be applied to the images and objects under discussion here, because they help define the komos and the komast.

Beginning with dress, we have noticed very little amongst the cited examples. The figures are nearly always nude, and their cloaks (when included) almost serve as an element of costume that enhances the occasion rather than a necessary item of dress. Not surprisingly when dealing with informal dance and revelry, a percentage of the scenes incorporate music or drink or both in some fashion. Singing, which is not all that common in black-figure scenes, is beginning to take hold here. Their sticks, like their cloaks, signal mobility or movement between venues, and act as a sort of stage prop (affectation?). The attributes in general, which are a common addition to the scenes, serve to define the figures in their role as komasts and to distinguish them from runners and other athletes.

The poses and gestures of the figures under discussion are also reminiscent of black-figure komasts, especially after the middle of the sixth century. Dancers perform in profile, most with torsos turned to the front, and they make little or no bodily contact. An occasional painter attempts a more ambitious body position, but these examples are not representative of the overall dance aesthetic. The bottom-slapping gesture that was integral to the earliest groups of Athenian black-figure vases with dance iconography has all but disappeared, and there is no consistency of dance pose even among designated groups or painters.

The context of the dancing figures and their friends, where evident, is the symposion, but in a much abbreviated form. Unlike some other red-figure painters, such as the Brygos Painter, our craftsmen are focused more readily on bodily movement and interaction between figures than on couches or cushions for reclining.[62] The emphasis on this type of symposion entertainment as a male domain, almost to the exclusion of women performers is notable: "this"...to quote John Boardman, "is a man's world".[63] Furthermore, the male figures themselves are mostly a younger set; their bearded counterparts tend to be more heavily draped and the products of a separate and distinct iconographic tradition. Is an alternative occasion or setting the explanation, or a difference in the social status and expectations of the participants? Or, is it just as likely that different painters are adapting to different cliental, or represent a sort of conservatism among the workshops in which they have trained? We have also recognized that mortal activity and mythology do not mix, nor is there any overt indication of religious ritual. These, I would posit, are real people at a real party.[64] They dance, sing, and converse, play music and drink wine, even adjust their hair and urinate into wine jars. Using varying amounts of detail, their painters are more interested in creating a festive ambiance for the eyes of the buyers, users and viewers than in the accurate portrayal of dancing. The lack of explicit sexual activity, erect phalloi, or even courtship is notable.

Finally, because we are looking at dance imagery the question of how these images illustrate the contemporary performance culture of Athens is a valid one. Performance can be poetic, musical or theatrical display, and dancing belongs to each of these realms. The term more widely construed can also be used to mean any activity, including ritual ones, in which an individual or group behaves in a particular manner, normally before the eyes of others.[65] Such performances can be rehearsed or impromptu, they can be controlled or lewd, and they can occur indoors or outdoors. The komast dancers of these years are drawn from a repertoire of existing options. Their painters were not terribly innovative, and realistically they did not need be in order to translate their subject effectively. Taken as a whole, our youthful and sympotic red-figure revelers and the failure of the artists of these years to reinvent them, are indicative of the transition from private sympotic performances to public dramatic ones.[66] New creative challenges awaited red-figure artists with the advent of staged drama and the realization that vase surfaces were venues just as ideal to illustrate the actor and the chorus as the komast dancer – the vase-painter's performer of choice for decades.

Acknowledgments

The author wishes to thank first and foremost John Oakley for organizing the conference and for his careful editing of the papers. Thanks are also owed to Veronica Ikeshoji-Orlati for assistance with musical instruments, to Dan Weiss for preparing the drawings, and to the museums and collections that have provided photographs as well as permission to publish them. This paper is dedicated to Donna Kurtz and François Lissarrague for their help with and inspiration with things komastic and much else besides.

Notes

1 L. B. Lawler, The Dance of the Ancient Greek Theatre (1964) 48.
2 Lawler (supra n. 1) 64–65.
3 Lawler (supra n. 1) 64. On Lawler's contribution to Greek dance studies see F. G. Naerebout, Attractive Performances. Ancient Greek Dance: Three Preliminary Studies (1997) 77–85; and on her use of Greek vases as evidence see T. J. Smith, in: F. MacIntosh (ed.), The Ancient Dancer in the Modern World: Responses to Greek and Roman Dance (2010) 89–91.
4 E. Csapo – M. C. Miller (eds.), The Origins of Theater in Ancient Greece and Beyond: From Ritual to Drama (2007); T. J. Smith, Komast Dancers in Archaic Greek Art (2010) 8–11. 18–21.
5 Lawler (supra n. 1) 119 figs. 51–53. The book was criticized by J. Boardman (ClR 15, 1965, 365–366) for its inadequate understanding of representations. A useful comparison is P. Ghiron-Bistagne, Recherches sur les acteurs dans la Grèce antique (1976) 'Appendice', on komos and komoi, concerned with both text and art.
6 On this issue see T. H. Carpenter, in: Csapo – Miller (supra n. 4) 109–112; Smith (supra n. 4) 1–5; and also M. Steinhart, Die Kunst der Nachahmung: Darstellungen mimetischer Vorführungen in der griechischen Bildkunst archaischer und klassischer Zeit (2004) 32–64.
7 Outspoken against this approach is F. G. Naerebout, Pharos 3, 1996, 23–40. See further Naerebout (supra n. 3) 60–71. See, for example, F. Brommer, AA 1989, 483–494.
8 Carpenter (supra n. 6); Smith (supra n. 4) 17–23. Despite a lack of concrete evidence, the term persists; see recently A. Ziskowski, BSA 107, 2012, 211–232; M. Meyer, Talanta 34/35, 2002, 135–179 ("Dickbauchtänzer").
9 Smith (supra n. 4) ch. 3, and tables 1a. 3a.
10 Smith (supra n. 4) 5–8.
11 On later black- and red-figure komasts see: C. Bron, in: J. Christiansen – T. Melander (eds.), Proceedings of the 3rd Symposium on Ancient Greek and Related Pottery. Copenhagen August 31–September 4 1987 (1988) 71–79; K. Vierneisel – B. Kaeser (eds.), Kunst der Schale: Kultur des Trinken (1990) 293–302; T. J. Smith, in: B. Schmaltz – M. Söldner (eds.), Griechische Keramik im kulturellen Kontext. Akten des Internationalen Vasen-Symposions in Kiel vom 24.bis 28.9.2001 (2003) 387–390.
12 Smith (supra n. 4) ch. 3; Smith (supra n. 11).
13 www.beazley.ox.ac.uk. This search and all other searches conducted for this paper occurred on 15 August 2012.
14 Bron (supra n. 11); P. Schmitt-Pantel, La Cité au banquet, histoire des repas publics dans les cités grecques (1992) 24–31.
15 On sympotic vessels see now K. M. Lynch, The Symposium in Context: Pottery from a Late Archaic House near the Athenian Agora, Hesperia Suppl. 46 (2011), with bibliography. For the relationship of komos and symposion on vases see T. J. Smith, in: G. R. Tsetskhladze – A. J. N. W. Prag – A. M. Snodgrass (eds.), Periplous: Papers on Classical Art and Archaeology Presented to Sir John Boardman (2000) 309–319; T. J. Smith, Cantor Arts Center Journal, Stanford University 7, 2010–2011, 5–17; and in literature see B. Pütz, The Symposium and Komos in Aristophanes (2007).
16 Booners and Anakreon: F. Frontisi-Ducroux – F. Lissarrague, AIONArch 1983, 11–32; D. C. Kurtz – J. Boardman, in: Greek Vases in the J. Paul Getty Museum 3, 1986, 35–70, esp. 56–61 on dress; S. D. Price, GrRomByzSt 31, 1990, 146–153; M.-H. Delavaud-Roux, RA 1995, 227–263; M. C.

Miller, AJA 103, 1999, 223–253; cf. W. J. Slater, Phoenix 32, 1978, 185–194. On these painters see in general M. Robertson, The Art of Vase-Painting in Classical Athens (1992) 84–106. On varieties of komasts and their dress in the oeuvre of the Brygos Painter see M. Wegner, Brygosmaler (1973) 119–143; T. Lorenz, Perspektiven der Philosophie 17, 1991, 421–435. The less heavily draped komasts of Makron, dancing with their cloaks draped across their arms, seem to represent a separate iconography; N. Kunisch, Makron (1997) 110–115.

17 On the painters: J. Boardman, Athenian Red Figure Vases: The Archaic Period (1988) 57–58; J. Harnecker, Oltos: Untersuchungen zu Themenwahl und Stil eines früh-rotfigurigen Schalenmalers (1991); Robertson (supra n. 16) 16–18; D. Paléothodoros, Épictétos (2004), with bibliography.

18 Antikenmuseum und Sammlung Ludwig LU33; ARV² 55,20; Para 326; B. Cohen, Attic Bilingual Vases (1978) pl. 81,1–2; Harnecker (supra n. 17) 27.

19 Boardman (surpra n. 17) 57; A. Bruhn, Oltos and Early Red-Figure Vase Painting (1943) 108–110; Harnecker (supra n. 17) 160–166.

20 E.g. Vienna, Kunsthistorisches Museum 137; CVA 1 Austria 1 pls. 1,1–3; 2,1–2; Smith (supra n. 4) 88–90, on the Nikosthenes Painter.

21 Paléothodoros (supra n. 17) 95–100.

22 Cabinet des Médailles 510; ARV² 78,96; Para 329; Paléothodoros (supra n. 17) 149 no. 23 pl. 9 fig. 1; F. Lissarrague, Greek Vases: The Athenians and their Images (2001) 25 fig. 14 (color).

23 Aberdeen, University 744 and Florence, Museo Archeologico Etrusco 1B29; ARV² 73,28; BAdd² 168; Paléothodoros (supra n. 17) 158 no. 79 pl. 25 figs. 1–3.

24 Berlin, Antikensammlung F2100; ARV² 71,7; 1623; BAdd² 159; Paléothodoros (supra n. 17) 145 no. 8 pl. 2 fig. 2. On the head coverings of komasts see Kurtz – Boardman (supra n. 16) 51–57.

25 Paris, Louvre G5; ARV² 71,14; Paléothodoros (supra n. 17) 150 fig. 31 pl. 9 fig. 4.

26 London, British Museum E137; ARV² 78,95; BAdd² 169; Paléothodoros (supra n. 17) 149 no. 22 pl. 8 fig. 3. See also Boardman (supra n. 17) 58–59 on the painter's style and composition.

27 Munich, Preyess; ARV² 76,71; Paléothodoros (supra n. 17) 163 no. 115 pl. 34 fig. 4.

28 On the painter see ARV² 168–170. See the nude, erect youth who balances a skyphos on his hip (Paris, Louvre G73); ARV² 170 ("near" the painter); F. Lissarrague, The Aesthetics of the Greek Banquet: Images of Wine and Ritual (1990) fig. 62 (drawing); and the youth who squats frontally and urinates (Brussels, Musées Royaux des Beaux-Arts R 259: ARV² 169,7; Boardman [supra n. 17] fig. 84).

29 On the painter see ARV² 146–153; Boardman (supra n. 17) 61.

30 Cracow, Collections de Cracovie 1259; ARV² 52,2; CVA Carcow 1 Poland 21 pl. 10, 1a–b.

31 Rennes, Musée des Beaux Arts 1932.725 (1909.375); ARV² 50,201; 1628; CVA Rennes 1 France 29 27 pl. 22,1–4; and see further A. Schäfer, Unterhaltung beim griechischen Symposion (1997) 55. Paris, Louvre CP 12205; CVA Louvre 19 France 28 pl. 43,3.

32 T. J. Mathiesen, Apollo's Lyre: Greek Music and Music Theory in Antiquity and the Middle Ages (1999) 164. The instrument is a relative late-comer to komast iconography, although it has been said to "give visual emphasis to the dancer's movement"; J. G. Landels, Music in Ancient Greece and Rome (1999) 83.

33 Antikenmuseum und Sammlung Ludwig BS463; ARV² 147,16; BAdd² 179; CVA Basle 2 Switzerland 6 pls. 7,4; 8,1–3. On the scene, see further Schäfer (supra n. 31) 56; Lissarrague (supra n. 28) 70–72, who associates the figures with a wineskin game called *askoliasmos*.

34 ARV² 335; Robertson (supra n. 16) 106; Boardman (supra n. 17) 135.

35 Robertson (supra n. 16) 106. The inscribed vase is ARV² 335,1 (Berlin 2325).

36 ARV² 335 ("imitators"); Robertson (supra n. 16) 106.

37 The range of options can be seen by searching the BAPD for 'Antiphon Painter' and 'komos'.

38 See, for example, Chicago, University of Chicago, Smart Museum of Art; ARV² 335,5; AJA 42, 1938, 336 fig. 2, where the dancer turns his back to viewer; and New York, Metropolitan Museum of Art 16.174.42; ARV² 338,46; Para 361; RH pls. 65. 181, for a frontal dancing pose.

39 E.g, Florence, Museo Archeologico Etrusco; ARV² 339,54; M. F. Kilmer, Greek Erotica on Attic Red-Figure Vases (1993) 250 R489.

40 For wine being poured directly into the mouth: Amsterdam, Allard Pierson Museum B11001 (once Paris, Private); ARV² 338,38; CVA Amsterdam 1 Netherlands 6 pl. 26,5.

41 Smith (supra n. 4) 9, on reclining and upright.

42 New York, Bothmer; ARV² 343,33; 349 ("recalls the Cage Painter").

43 ARV² 348–349; cf. Boardman (supra n. 17) 135.

44 Paris, Louvre CP10909; ARV² 346,85 ("recalls"); BAdd² 220. Paris, Musée du Louvre G134; ARV² 348,6 ("related").

45 Paris, Louvre G133; ARV² 348,7; BAdd² 220; Lissarrague (supra n. 22) 37 fig. 26 (tondo); F. Frontisi-Ducroux, Du masque au visage; aspects de l'identité en Grèce ancienne (1995) pl. 42.

46 Vierneisel – Kaeser (supra n. 11) 238–246; Lissarrague (supra n. 22) 33–35, on song and image; and K. Lynch, in: T. J. Smith – D. Plantzos (eds.), A Companion to Greek Art (2012) 531. Interestingly, this exact same gesture, which is found elsewhere in vase-painting, is even used today in the context of Arabic folk singing at family gatherings or parties. It can represent extreme distress or emotion, as reflected in the lyrics and music, but it also signals to the larger group whose turn it is to perform.

47 Lissarrague (supra n. 22) 36.

48 Perugia, Museo Civico; ARV² 349,3.

49 Munich, Antikensammlungen 2307; ARV² 26,1; 1620; Para 323; BAdd² 156; J. Boardman, The History of Greek Vases: Potters, Painters and Pictures (2001) 83 fig. 115. A cup in Boston is signed by Euphronios as potter, but this was clearly not his shape preference; Museum of Fine Arts 95.27; ARV² 325,76; 313. 1604; BAdd² 216; AJA 71, 1967, pl. 96,3.

50 Musée du Louvre G58; ARV² 21,6; M. Denoyelle (ed.), Euphronios peintre, recontres de l'École du Louvre 10 Octobre 1990 (1992) 89 figs. 12–14; Lawler (supra n. 1) 18 fig. 1.

51 London E767; ARV² 29,6; Para 324; BAdd² 157; Boardman (supra n. 17) 47.

52 Boardman (supra n. 17) 91; Robertson (supra n. 16) 56–83.
53 Martin von Wagner Museum L507; ARV² 181,1; Para 340; BAdd² 186; Boardman (supra n. 17) fig. 129; S. D. Bundrick, Music and Image in Classical Athens (2005) 117 fig.70.
54 British Museum E266; ARV² 198,21; 1633; Para 342; BAdd² 191; CVA British Museum 3 United Kingdom 4 pls. 8,3a–b; 12,1a–b.
55 On the painter see ARV² ch. 17; Robertson (supra n. 16) 124–127, with bibliography; and also E. Reschke, Die Ringer des Euthymides (1990) 26–27.
56 E.g. on a pelike in the collection of the University of Mississippi; ARV² 238,7; Reschke (supra) pl. 4,2.
57 As on New York, Metropolitan Museum of Art 21.88.82; ARV² 242,73; BMetrMus 18, 1923, 255 fig. 7 (column krater); and on the pelike in Mississippi (supra).
58 As on Philadelphia, University of Pennsylvania Museum of Archaeology and Anthropology 5688; ARV² 241,62; I. Peschel, Die Hetare bei Symposium und Komos in der attisch rotfigurigen Malerei des 6.-4. Jhs. v. Chr. (1987) pl. 36; and on one side of the New York column krater (supra).
59 On Altenburg, Staatliches Lindenau-Museum 279, a draped dancer holds a skyphos and oinochoe on one side, while a nude male dances with krotala on the other; ARV² 241,67; CVA Altenburg 2 Germany 18 pl. 54,1–4.
60 Cf. Smith (supra n. 4) 74–77.
61 Smith (supra n. 4) passim.
62 Schäfer (supra n. 31).
63 Boardman (supra n. 17) 220.
64 Cf. Z. Archibald, in: V. Coltman, Making Sense of Greek Art (2012) 21.
65 C. Bell, in: M. C.Taylor (ed.), Critical Terms for Religious Studies (1998) 205–224; M. Verhoeven, in: T. Insoll (ed.), The Oxford Handbook of the Archaeology of Ritual and Religion (2011) 115–132.
66 Smith (supra n. 4) 246; also E. Stehle, Performance and Gender in Ancient Greece (1997) 213–227; A. Bierl, Ritual and Performativity: The Chorus of Old Comedy (2009) ch. 2.

25 Menelaos and Helen in Attic Vase Painting

Mark D. Stansbury-O'Donnell

If one were to have asked an Athenian in the sixth or fifth century BC what the most common image of Menelaos would be, the unequivocal answer would have been his reunion with Helen during the fall of Troy. Indeed, the number of images of Menelaos with Helen dwarfs all other Attic representations of the hero, and one might fairly characterize him as a one-deed hero, unlike Achilles or Herakles.[1] LIMC lists fourteen Attic black-figure and red-figure representations of Menelaos without Helen, including those regarded as uncertain. In contrast, there are 139 vases listed with Menelaos and Helen, most in the entry under Helen. Additional works cited by Hart, Recke and the Beazley Archive gives a total of 195 Menelaos/Helen scenes.[2]

Within this basic episode, though, there is a range of pictorial choices for actions and composition. Menelaos can move toward Helen, confront/stand in front of her, or lead her away, often holding her clothing or arm while turning back to look at her. Helen can stand facing Menelaos, follow him if he is moving away, or run away from him. The compositional choices have been thoroughly studied iconographically, but they can also be explored contextually, looking at the patterns of production and distribution to consider the relationship of market and narrative choice for this story.

L. Kahil has written most extensively on the iconography of the episode, first in a monograph and then in the two LIMC entries under Helene and Menelaos respectively.[3] Her lists are organized by the core action in the scene, which she links to two epic accounts of the fall of Troy. The links between literary versions and vase paintings have been critiqued and in the absence of any extensive literary sources, it is hard to associate any of the actions with a specific poem since the sequence of actions – Menelaos looking for, pursuing/charging, confronting, and leading/taking back Helen – would be included in almost any full narrative of the episode.[4]

More recent studies have focused on the scene within the context of other artistic themes. M. L. Hart looked at representations of the fall of Troy, including the rape of Kassandra, the killing of Astyanax and Priam, and the recovery of Helen.[5] These individual scenes had become established, repeated iconographic formulas as part of the set of new scenes introduced by Athenian painters after 560, as identified by Shapiro.[6] The painters, starting with Lydos, began to assemble these units into a broader Iliupersis narrative (Fig. 1; Color Pl. 30A).[7]

G. Hedreen discusses the importance of setting in the Iliupersis, noting that the Menelaos-Helen scenes showed less specificity as to location than Aias-Kassandra pictures, but suggesting the importance of a sanctuary setting for the confrontation scenes between Menelaos and Helen in red-figure painting.[8] Following Sourvinou-Inwood, he also notes the importance of the sword in these representations as a means for distinguishing it from other episodes, such as the recovery of Aithra.[9]

M. Recke explored the representation of violence and suffering in war imagery, and in particular examined the episodes involving Helen, Kassandra, Priam, and Astyanax as examples of warriors' violence against non-combatants.[10] He charts in more detail the chronology of the scenes, noting the highpoint for the confrontation scene of Menelaos and Helen in Attic black-figure of 540–520, and the revival of the Menelaos-Helen story as a love pursuit in the period 480–460, along with a de-emphasis on representing Menelaos as a fully outfitted warrior.

Most recently, A. Stelow looked at the episode within the context of Archaic representations of Menelaos, primarily poetic, but also in vase painting.[11] She rejected the association of specific actions with epic accounts of the story and noted that most visual representations of Menelaos are with Helen, and indeed that this is the only reliable way to identify him without an inscription. In recovery scenes there is an emphasis upon the mutual

Table 1 Chronological Distribution of Menelaos-Helen Scenes by Action Type.

	575–550	550–525	525–500	500–475	475–450	450–425	Total
Menelaos charges – Helen stands	1	8	5	2	0	0	16
Menelaos charges – Helen flees	0	2	1	14	33	16	66
Menelaos stands – Helen stands	2	7	5	0	1	0	15
Menelaos stands – Helen flees	0	0	0	0	1	0	1
Menelaos leads – Helen stands	5	31	36	3	0	0	75
Menelaos leads – Helen follows	1	4	5	2	1	0	13
Fragmentary scenes, undetermined nucleus	0	4	2	2	1	0	9
Total Scenes	9	56	54	23	37	16	195

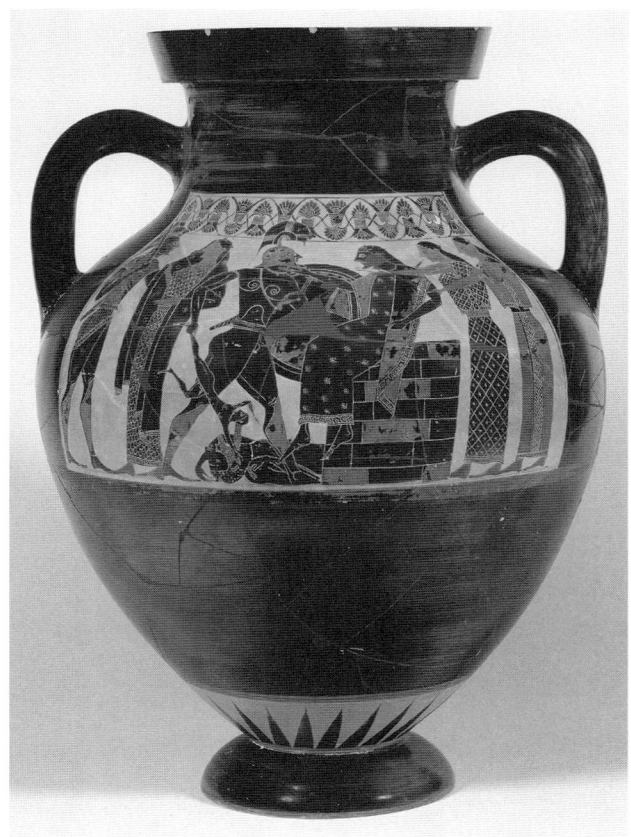

Fig. 1 Attic black-figure amphora, Berlin F1685. Photo: bpk, Berlin/Antikensammlung, Staatliche Museen, Berlin, Germany/ Ingrid Gesk /Art Resource, NY.

gaze of the two figures that distinguishes the scene from related wedding iconography, including the use of the *anakalypsis* and *cheir' epi karpo* gestures.[12]

In order to study the relationship of context and narrative choice, a database of the currently identified representations was created to track not only dates, attributions, and findspots of the pots, but also details of the action and composition. Each picture was categorized in terms of the major action of each participant and is summarized in Table 1 with their chronological distribution:

Looking first at the narrative actions favored in the sixth-century examples, the most common nucleus is Menelaos with his back to Helen, leading her away (eightly-eight examples). In most cases he either looks back at her and/or grabs her or her clothing as he moves forward, as on an amphora by the Amasis Painter in Munich (Fig. 2).[13] In thirty-four of the eighty-eight "Menelaos leads," he holds a drawn sword, while in thirty-two he holds one or two spears. Helen's action is primarily to stand facing Menelaos (seventy-five) while holding out her mantle in a position associated with the *anakalypsis* gesture of the bride (64/75). In thirteen pictures she takes a step forward to follow Menelaos, as on the Amasis Painter's amphora, but in only four of these cases does she pull her mantle forward as she does on that vase. Of the eightly-eight examples of Menelaos leading, 86% fall into the second half of the sixth century, making it the predominant formula in that period. Only six pictures are dated after 500.

Some sixth-century representations show a slightly earlier narrative moment, with Menelaos standing, facing Helen directly, as on an amphora by Lydos (Fig. 1; Color Pl. 30A). In all but one of the fifteen examples, Helen stands facing him, eleven times pulling her mantle forward. The motif of the drawn sword is less frequent in this configuration, occurring on only three vases. Like Menelaos leading, this narrative variation is developed in the second quarter of the sixth century, but 80% (12/15) are found in the last half of the sixth century and only one after 500.

A still earlier moment of the episode shows Menelaos charging or striding toward Helen. In sixteen pictures, Helen stands facing the charging Menelaos, as can be seen on an amphora near Group E in the Vatican (Fig. 3).[14] All but two of these belong to the sixth century. In

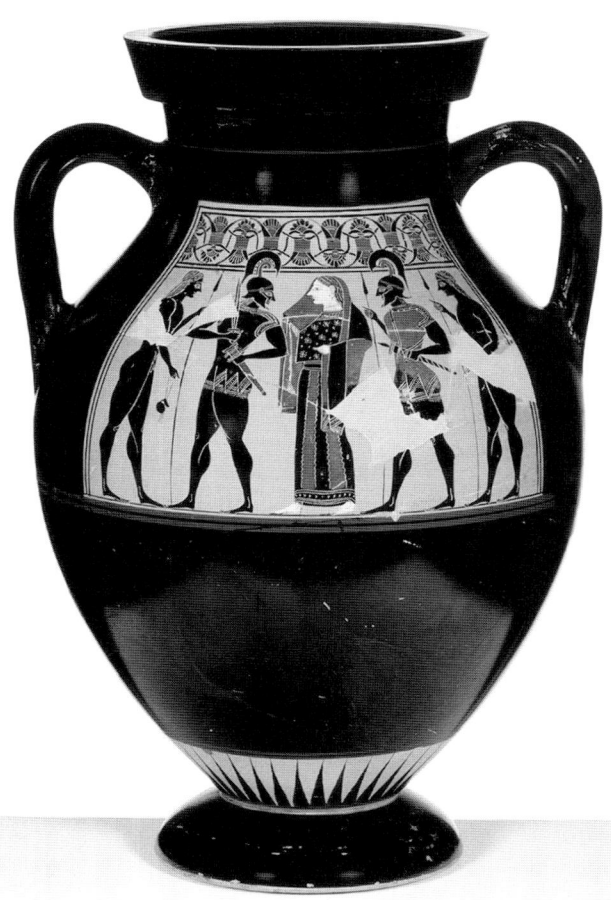

Fig. 2 Attic black-figure amphora, Munich 1383. Photo: Staatliche Antikensammlungen und Glyptothek.

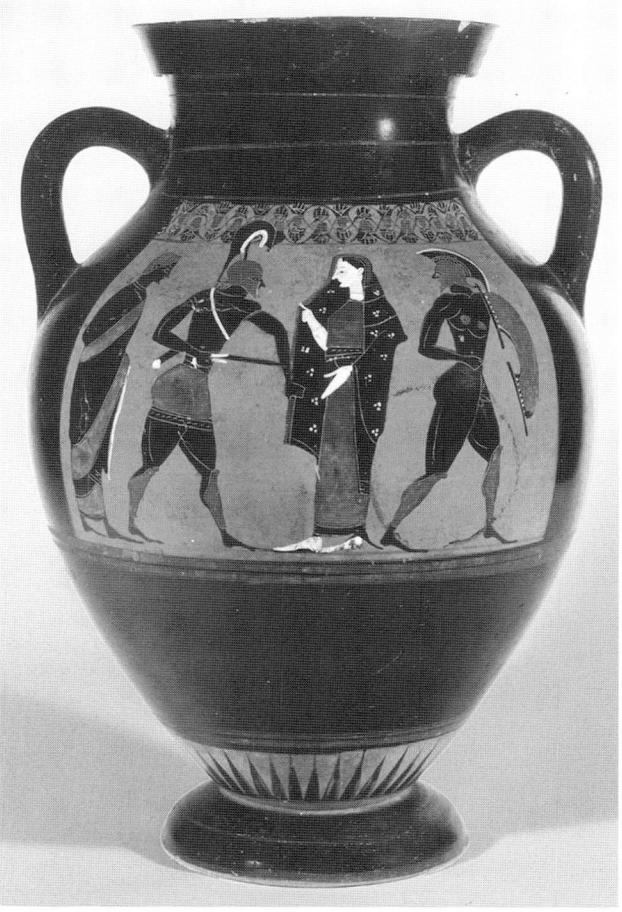

Fig. 3 Attic black-figure amphora, Vatican 16589. Photo: Scala/Art Resource, NY.

fourteen pictures Helen pulls her mantle forward, as in the Menelaos leading scenes; in eleven, Menelaos holds a drawn sword. While Menelaos charging is a more aggressive action than either standing or leading, and the level of threat that he presents is higher with a drawn sword, this formula simply picks up an early moment in the episode when he first discovers her, before confronting her and then leading her away.

Before turning to the pursuit variation of the episode (Menelaos charges – Helen flees) that dominates the fifth century, we can look at the shape and distribution of Attic vases with Menelaos-Helen scenes. Table 2 shows the distribution of scenes by shape as percentages, with the total number of vases in parentheses.

Of particular interest in this data is that following an initial period before 550 with a wide range of vase types, during 550–500 amphorae account for nearly two-thirds of all Menelaos-Helen scenes (70/110 vases, 63.6%). In contrast, during the fifth century, amphorae constitute less than a quarter of the pots, marking a clear shift in production after 500. First cups, and then kraters become the dominant shape, but in no period is there a predominance of one shape as there was in 550–500.

There is also a change from the sixth to the fifth century in the patterns of the distribution of the Menelaos-Helen vases (Table 3). Seventy-eight of the 195 vases in Table 1 have a provenance, and these are grouped into four major regions: Greece, Etruria, southern Italy/Sicily, and all others. The percentage is the proportion of vases with provenance from that period:

For those vases with a provenance from 550–500, almost two-thirds (23/36) were found in Etruria, specifically in the western areas at sites like Chiusi, Vulci, Tarquinia, and Cerveteri. Of the sixth-century vases found in Etruria, nineteen (82.6%) are amphorae. Considering this point and the sixth-century data from Table 2, one can surmise a particularly strong association between amphorae and Etruria for sixth-century Menelaos-Helen scenes. Therefore, we should consider that the Menelaos-Helen scenes were mostly for export to the western Etruscan market, and explore what structural features about the scene would favor or make it suitable for that market.

Looking at this from the painter's point of view, the composition of the episode is well adapted as a decorative choice for an amphora. The two central figures can be made large enough to fill the picture surface, and

Table 2 Distribution of Shapes by Period (percentage by period and actual number).

Shape	575–550	550–525	525–500	500–475	475–450	450–425
amphora	22.2% (2)	62.5% (35)	64.8% (35)	26.1% (6)	21.6% (8)	12.5% (2)
cup	11.1% (1)	14.3% (8)	3.7% (2)	34.8% (8)	8.1% (3)	6.7% (1)
hydria	0	1.8% (1)	0	4.3% (1)	8.1% (3)	12.5% (2)
krater	0	3.6% (2)	0	4.3% (1)	35.1% (13)	31.3% (5)
lekythos	11.1% (1)	7.1% (4)	14.8% (8)	8.7% (2)	0	6.3% (1)
olpe/oinochoe	11.1% (1)	3.6% (2)	7.4% (4)	0	8.1% (1)	6.3% (1)
pelike	0	0	0	0	0	6.3% (1)
plate	11.1% (1)	0	3.7% (2)	0	0	0
pyxis	11.1% (1)	3.6% (2)	3.7% (2)	0	5.4% (2)	0

Table 3 Distribution of Findspots (when known) by Period (percentage by period and actual number).

	575–550	550–525	525–500	500–475	475–450	450–425
Greece	33.3% (1)	21.1% (4)	11.8% (2)	20.0% (2)	9.5% (2)	12.5% (1)
Etruria	66.7% (2)	52.6% (10)	76.5% (13)	40.0% (4)	47.6% (10)	50.0% (4)
western	2	10	13	5	4	2
eastern	0	0	0	0	6	2
S. Italy & Sicily	0	21.1% (4)	0	40.0% (4)	38.1% (7)	37.5% (3)
Other	0	5.3% (1)	11.8% (2)	0	4.8% (1)	0
Total w prov.	3	19	17	10	21	8
Total Vases	9	56	54	23	37	16

additional figures like a second warrior or spectators can be placed to the sides to fill up more of the picture area as needed. The second warrior is also helpful in signaling to the viewer that this is a war scene rather than a departure. With only one picture to tell the story, the painter's narrative challenge is to enable the viewer to recognize the subject matter readily and thereby to evoke the entire story of Menelaos and Helen.[15] How, then, does a sixth-century Athenian painter get an Etruscan viewer to recognize the story of Menelaos and Helen?

There are few inscriptions on Menelaos-Helen scenes, and none on the black-figure vases, so the viewer must therefore recognize the story on the basis of the figures and actions.[16] A warrior with a spear or sword is not unusual, nor is his interaction with a woman, as numerous departure scenes attest. Menelaos's actions, whether charging, confronting, or leading, with or without drawn sword or spears, are then hardly distinctive in their own right. A forceful threat by a warrior with a drawn sword to a woman could signal Menelaos-Helen as the subject, but as can be seen in Table 4, only forty-two of the 110 pictures from 550–500 (38.2%) show a drawn sword, suggesting that this sign is not the key for identifying the story.

What is more unusual in the sixth-century pictures is that the victim would pull her mantle away from herself, the *anakalypsis* gesture of wedding scenes, or that the man, while being armed, would take her by the wrist or arm in a manner like the *cheir' epi karpo* wedding gesture.[17] As can be seen in Table 5, forty-nine out of fifty-six scenes between 550 and 525 use one or both gestures, and forty-eight out of fifty-four scenes do so between 525 and 500. Leaving out scenes where the gesture cannot be determined, 95% of the sixth-century scenes use a wedding-related gesture. The majority of scenes that do not use a wedding-related gesture show Helen walking and following Menelaos as he leads her away. In sixth-century scenes, she rarely reaches out in a pleading gesture, as might be expected in a threatening situation. That Helen stands still in the face of Menelaos's threat or use of force, rather than flees, especially when he has a drawn sword, is unexpected and incongruous.

The core of story recognition, then, comes down to an absence of commensurate actions by Menelaos and Helen, and in particular the incongruous reaction of Helen to Menelaos's actions. This is reinforced by their typically mutual gaze, which is also unusual in a scene that includes

Table 4 Menelaos with Drawn Sword.

	575–550	550–525	525–500	500–475	475–450	450–425	Total
Charges with drawn sword	1	8	4	8	13	2	36
Dropped sword	0	0	0	3	7	10	20
Stands with drawn sword	1	2	0	0	0	0	3
Leads with drawn sword	4	15	13	3	0	0	35
Total scenes with drawn sword	**6**	**25**	**17**	**14**	**20**	**12**	**94**
Total scenes	9	56	54	23	37	16	196

Table 5 Wedding-related Gestures.

	575–550	550–525	525–500	500–475	475–450	450–425	Total
Anakalypsis	8	46	39	5	4	3	105
Cheir' epi karpo	7	30	29	4	2	0	72
Both	7	27	20	0	1	0	55
Total with a wedding gesture	**8**	**49**	**48**	**9**	**5**	**3**	**122**
Undetermined/fragment	**0**	**5**	**3**	**3**	**3**	**1**	**15**
Total scenes	9	56	54	23	37	16	196

wedding gestures.[18] This incongruity, an asymmetry of actions, then, was the key for an Etruscan, or any other sixth-century viewer, to identify Menelaos and Helen as the most likely subject for the picture at hand, whichever moment the narrative nucleus showed.

This reliance on broad character type, warrior and woman, and their actions is not without problem and can create ambiguity both for the ancient viewer and the scholar today. A belly amphora in the manner of the Antimenes Painter, for example, is identified in the *CVA* and the British Museum's website as the recovery of Aithra (Fig. 4).[19] The BAPD and Recke list it as the recovery of Helen, and Kahil in LIMC as a degenerated version of that scene. The two warriors with spears could be Akamas and Demophon, but the pulling of the mantle by the woman, who is not pictured with gray hair, and the grabbing of the hem of her garment match more closely the scenes of Menelaos with drawn sword leading Helen. As Sourvinou-Inwood's semiotic study of ephebic pursuit scenes argued, a drawn sword implies a more murderous intention than a carried spear.[20] The lack of a drawn sword certainly lessens the incongruity between the gestures of the warrior and the woman and injects more potential ambiguity into the scene, but the drawn sword is not essential and there is still disparity in the actions.

While the formula may have enough ambiguity in some cases to create problems of identification, this potential for modest variation could be a factor for the success of the scene generally. Among all of the actions from the Trojan

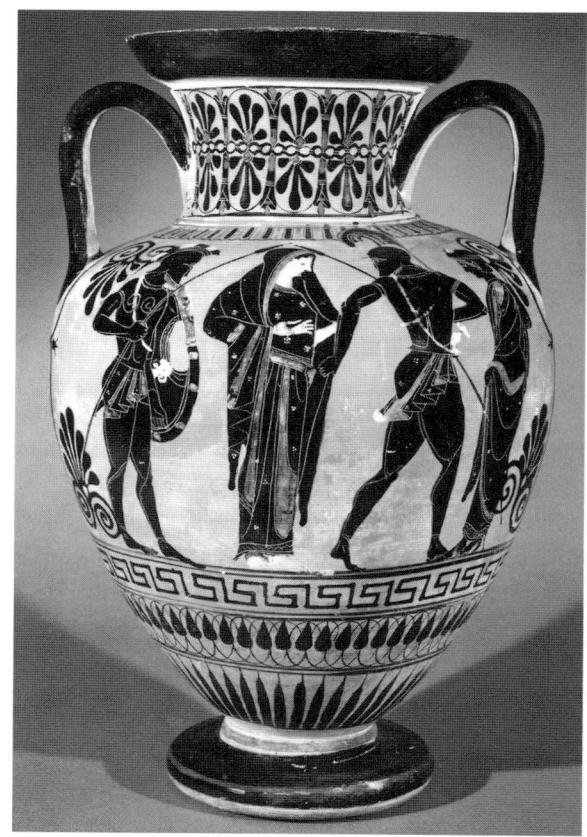

Fig. 4 Attic black-figure amphora, London B244. Photo: ©Trustees of the British Museum.

War in sixth-century vase painting, Menelaos-Helen is one of the most common, more so than other scenes from the Iliupersis such as the killing of Priam and Astyanax and the rape of Kassandra.[21] Whereas Achilles is a more popular Trojan War hero than Menelaos, even his pursuit of Troilos appears less frequently in painted pottery.[22] One reason for the popularity of both Menelaos-Helen and Achilles-Troilos in the potters' quarters that we should consider is that each scene is visually distinctive based on its character type and action. Even if both scenes were susceptible to uncertain identification in some cases, on the whole they would be successful narrative formulas for a diverse viewing audience across the Mediterranean, wherever the pots would be sold.

Indeed, we might consider A. Steiner's use of information theory in studying Greek vases to note that there is more distinctiveness in the Menelaos-Helen scenes than in a picture of two warriors fighting, and therefore a lower degree of entropy and greater clarity of the narrative message, as would also be the case for Achilles-Troilos scenes.[23] The nucleus of both scenes, beauty seducing a warrior, and a warrior who can outrun a horse, would still have distinctive compositional appeal, even if the viewer did not identify the narrative story correctly.

While popular in the sixth century, the appeal of these Menelaos-Helen scenes generally vanishes in the fifth century. As Table 1 showed, a pursuit formula, in which Menelaos charges and Helen flees, becomes the most common version of the narrative in the fifth century, particularly on red-figure works. There are some early, isolated examples of the pursuit from the third-quarter of the sixth century, including a fragmentary cup by the Centaur Painter and an unattributed amphora in Mykonos.[24] The amphora by Oltos in the Louvre is often regarded as the progenitor of the pursuit scene in red-figure vase painting (Fig. 5).[25] Menelaos advances with drawn sword as we might expect and grabs Helen by the wrist; his name is inscribed. Helen, also identified by inscription, looks back at her pursuer and raises up her free hand in a supplicating gesture. This formulation increases the sense of menace and threat in the scene. Helen's reaction is no longer incongruous, but is entirely responsive to the action of a charging warrior with drawn sword; she should fear for her life and both beg and flee. The change of the narrative nucleus changes the tone of the story considerably, from beauty overcoming arms to the consequences of defeat in war. Perhaps the inscription became necessary since the actions are not sufficient on their own to identify the story clearly and for the viewer to realize quickly that the scene does not end in death or rape as might be expected.[26]

Oltos's composition did not find any immediate successors in the sixth century. During the first quarter of the fifth century, however, there are fourteen examples of the pursuit formula, while there are only nine examples of all other formulas combined, showing a decided shift of concept and interest had taken place. Some pictures have just the two figures, but several set the pursuit either within a structure like a palace by including columns or at a sanctuary through the provision of an altar, tripod, or the presence of a god such as Aphrodite, Athena, or Apollo, as Hedreen has pointed out.[27] Additional figures, usually women, also appear as witnesses who react to Menelaos's threat. In spite of what Kahil characterized as a revitalization of the subject by abandoning the static composition favored in the sixth century, the overall number of Menelaos-Helen scenes falls in the early fifth century, from fifty-four to twenty-three scenes.[28] This occurs at a time when the overall production of Attic vases increases 75% from the last quarter of the sixth century to the first quarter of the fifth. With Attic production at its highest historical levels in the first half of the fifth century, the decrease of interest in Menelaos-Helen is even more striking.[29]

There is a rebound of interest for Menelaos-Helen scenes in the second quarter of the fifth century, but with thirty-five examples it is still less popular than it had been in the sixth century. Thirty-one of the thirty-five pictures, over 88%, are now pursuits. Most of these follow the conventions of the scenes from the early fifth century, as

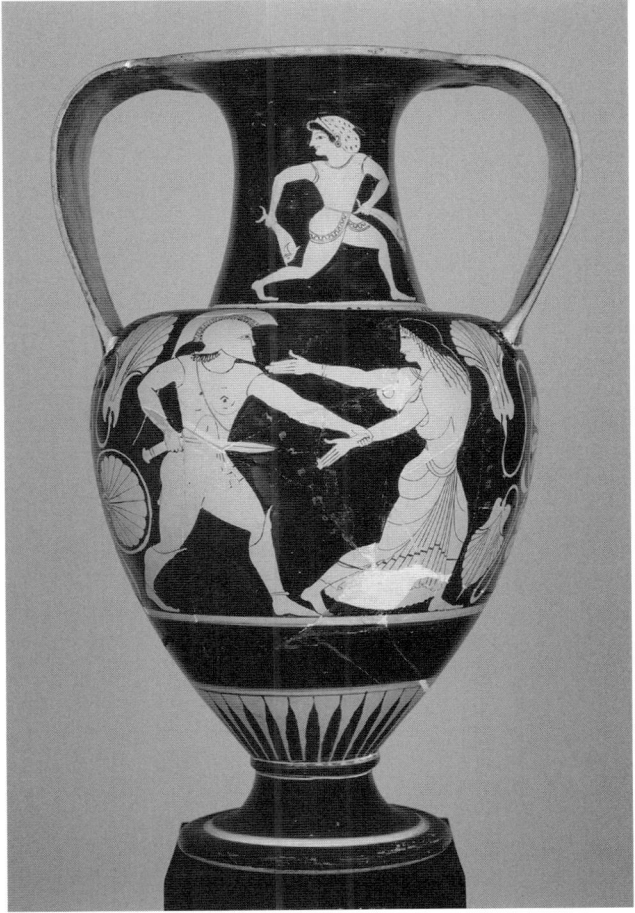

Fig. 5 Attic red-figure Nikosthenic amphora, Paris, Louvre G3. Photo: Hervé Lewandowski. © RMN-Grand Palais/Art Resource, NY.

can be seen in the large krater in Bologna attributed to the Niobid Painter (Fig. 6).[30] This composition includes Athena and a sanctuary of Apollo as indicated by the tripod, as well as other scenes from the Iliupersis, such as the recovery of Aithra to the left. There is also a second pursuit on the neck, a spear-bearing ephebe chasing a woman. Indeed, it is during the Early Classical period that the ephebic pursuit reaches its zenith of popularity in Attic vase-painting, and was equal to satyr pursuits in its frequency.[31] This interest in erotic pursuits is a significant development of subject matter in the first half of the fifth century, and I would suggest that rather than the influence of Aias pursuing Kassandra on the composition of Menelaos-Helen, that it is the popularity of youthful and divine pursuits that is a potential influence for the reformulation of the Menelaos-Helen scene and its subsequent increase in frequency in the Early Classical period.[32] This is perhaps clearer on a fragment of a kalpis that shows Eros with a phiale (Fig. 7).[33] His appearance, combined with Menelaos's sheathed sword and the anakalypsis gesture of Helen signifies that Menelaos's change of attitude from anger to lust is driven by the gods' agenda.

Once again, if we look at the patterns of shape and distribution in the fifth century, we can see other changes from the sixth century. Amphorae are no longer the dominant shape for the scene (Table 2). Cups account for a third of all scenes in the first quarter of the fifth century, and kraters are one-third of the production in the middle quarters. Amphorae are still common, but are always a secondary shape. Along with a broader range of shapes, there is a change in the pattern of distribution. Etruria, which was the findspot of three-quarters of all Menelaos-Helen vases in the last quarter of the sixth century, is the findspot of half of the vases with provenance during the fifth century (Table 3). Southern Italy and Sicily consistently account for about three-eighths of the vases, a pattern that reflects the broader markets that Athenian potters and painters were finding for their wares in the fifth century.[34] Even in Etruria there is a distinct shift in distribution, with a bit more than half of the Menelaos-Helen scenes going to Adriatic sites like Bologna and Spina, which had received none of the sixth-century imports.

I would suggest that the confrontation/recovery formulation of the Menelaos-Helen narrative had lost much of its interest as an export theme by the end of the sixth century and its decline was virtually complete by 475. Its reconfiguration into a pursuit formula extended its lifespan, building upon the interest among the painters in the Kerameikos in pursuit scenes generally, especially in the second quarter of the fifth century. As a pursuit scene, it did have some distinctiveness from other divine or ephebic pursuits in that it usually involved a bearded warrior, and so constituted a potentially interesting pursuit variation in the repertory of Athenian painters. It is also of narrative interest that the result of the pursuit,

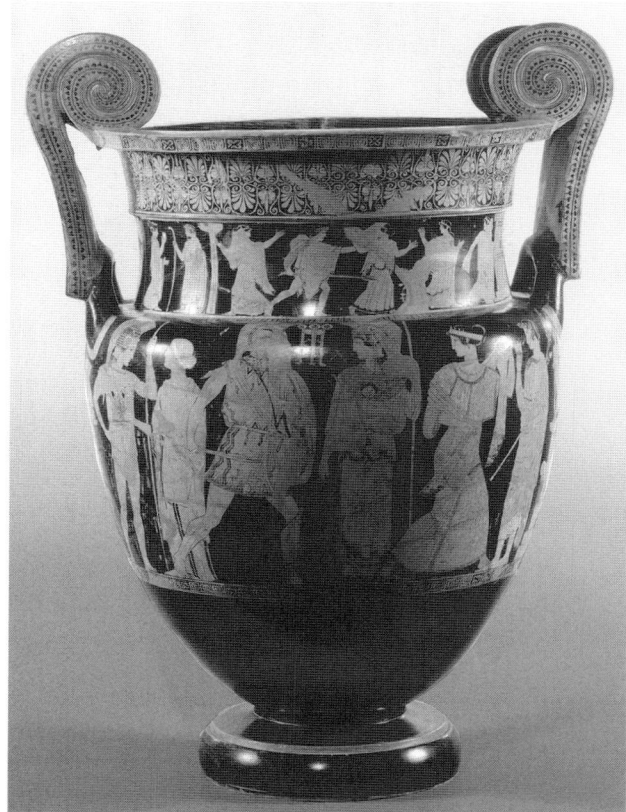

Fig. 6 Attic red-figure volute krater, Bologna 269. Photo: Alinari/Art Resource, NY.

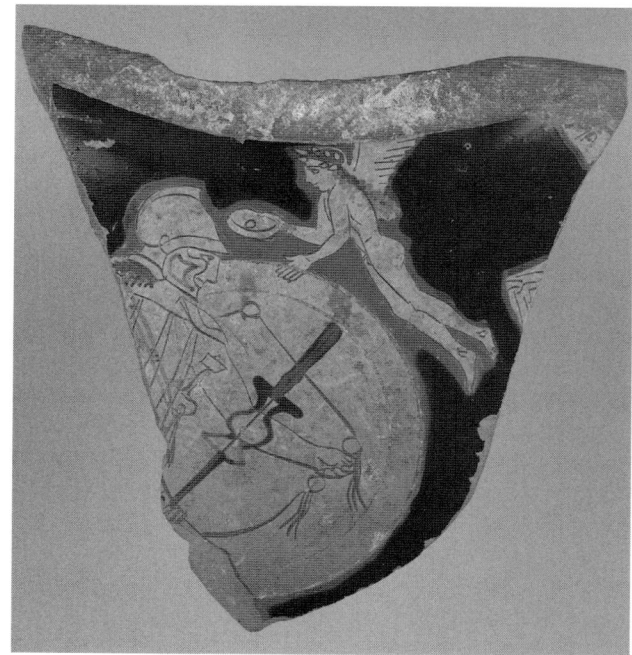

Fig. 7 Attic red-figure kalpis fragment, Princeton 2002-166. Photo: Courtesy Princeton University Art Museum. Gift in Memory of Emily Townsend Vermeule, Honorary Degree Holder of the Class of 1989 (2002-166).

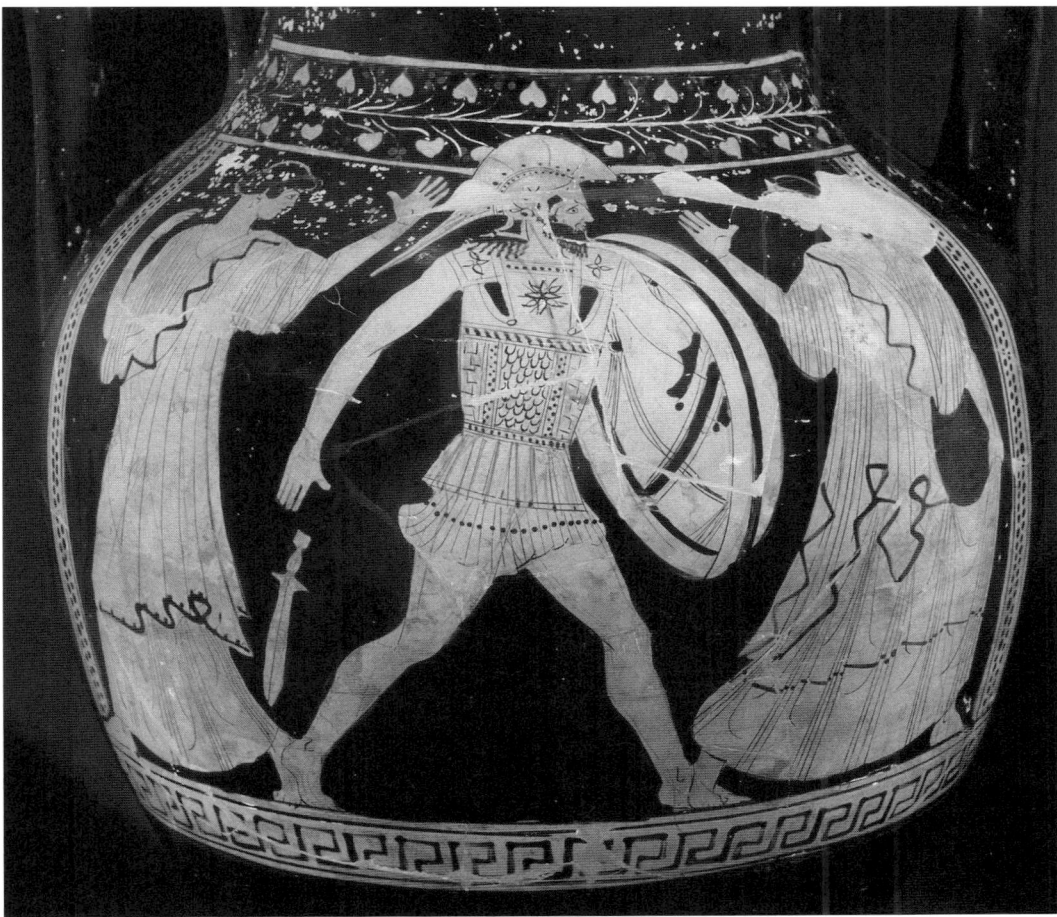

Fig. 8 Attic red-figure amphora, London E263. Photo: ©Trustees of the British Museum.

once identified as Menelaos-Helen by the viewer, would have been untypical of the erotic pursuit. There was no offspring from the resulting union, and rather than a forlorn existence as many of the victims of pursuit faced afterward, the viewer would know that Helen was reinstalled as the queen of Sparta.[35]

Narratologically, the pursuit version of Menelaos-Helen would be an example of a reversal of fortune from what one would normally expect in a pursuit scene, since the pursuer does not dominate the pursued in the end.[36] In this sense, there is still a narrative incongruity, as there was with the recovery of Helen in the sixth century, but there are significant structural differences. In the Archaic recovery scenes, Helen's reaction is not commensurate with Menelaos's action, and so sets up a visual incongruity regardless of whether the viewer knows the story. In the pursuit version, the incongruity and reversal exist not in the combination of action-reaction in the picture, but in the viewer's knowledge of the episode and its aftermath. If the viewer were not aware that the characters are Menelaos and Helen, the narrative picture would not be significantly distinguished from other pursuits for the viewer to realize this narrative is different from others and that the victim is restored to her position as wife and queen.

In this light, there is one final element within the pursuit formula that deserves attention, the motif of the dropped sword. This variation first appears on three vases in the first quarter of the fifth century, twice in the work of the Berlin Painter.[37] The number of examples doubles in the next quarter century, including an amphora by the Altamura Painter in the British Museum (Fig. 8; Color Pl. 30B).[38] Here, Menelaos's sword falls backwards as he has discarded it in his haste to catch Helen. The number of dropped-sword scenes nearly double again between 450 and 425, so that it is the single most common version of the Menelaos-Helen narrative in Attic vase painting during the last phase of its production, while all non-pursuit versions of the scene disappear, as can be seen in Table 6.

As an expression of Menelaos's change of intent and reaction to the sight of Helen, the motif is very effective, but the pattern of its use differs from the more typical pursuit formula. The third-quarter of the century is one of slightly declining interest in pursuit scenes generally and for Menelaos-Helen specifically. The increase, then, in the number of Menelaos-Helen scenes with a dropped sword is noteworthy as it suggests another shift in the interest for the narrative among Athenian pot painters. Indeed, five-eighths of the vases from 450–425 have a dropped sword, making it the most common narrative formula during the final phase of its production.

Most of the examples after 450 also feature a deity, either Aphrodite, Apollo, and/or Eros, as can be seen on a nestoris attributed to the Group of Polygnotos in the Getty Villa (Fig. 9).[39] Their appearance signifies divine oversight, but it is the motif of the dropped sword that once again creates an immediate visual incongruity that is absent from most pursuit scenes, in that pursuers usually keep hold of their weapons or attributes, even when gods are present. I would suggest that the dropped sword potentially signals a comic or parodic intent for the scene, based on recent studies of parody and humor by Steiner, Mitchell, and Walsh.[40]

In looking at the Getty nestoris, one can see that Menelaos has not only dropped his sword, but has thrown it aside as the handle has rotated 180° from its position when he held it, indicating that it is not just dropping but spinning as it falls. Menelaos is also sprinting rather than charging, oblivious to the full weight of the armor that he wears. In order words, he acts as though he has forgotten who he is: a warrior and king. All of the other figures act appropriately for their status and circumstances: Aphrodite stands overseeing the action, while Helen is dressed like a matron and flees in a position normal for that of erotic pursuit. Whereas in the sixth century, it was mostly the action of Helen that was incongruous, here it is the dominant figure of the warrior-king Menelaos. As Mitchell has argued from examples of Eurystheus, Iris, and other figures, his actions, and particularly the dropped sword, mock his status and identity.[41]

I would like to suggest that Menelaos's identity as the heroic King of Sparta is an object of ridicule or fun here. The visual language of the scene was well established and provided a normative expectation that he would take her back, whatever his initial feelings of anger. The dropped

Table 6 Menelaos-Helen Pursuit Scenes in the Fifth Century.

	500–475	475–450	450–425	Total
Total Scenes	23	37	16	76
All non-pursuits	7	3	0	10
Undetermined nucleus	2	1	0	3
Pursuit: Menelaos charges – Helen flees	**14**	**33**	**16**	**63**
Subset: Pursuit with dropped Sword	3	7	10	20
Subset: Anakalypsis	5	5	3	13

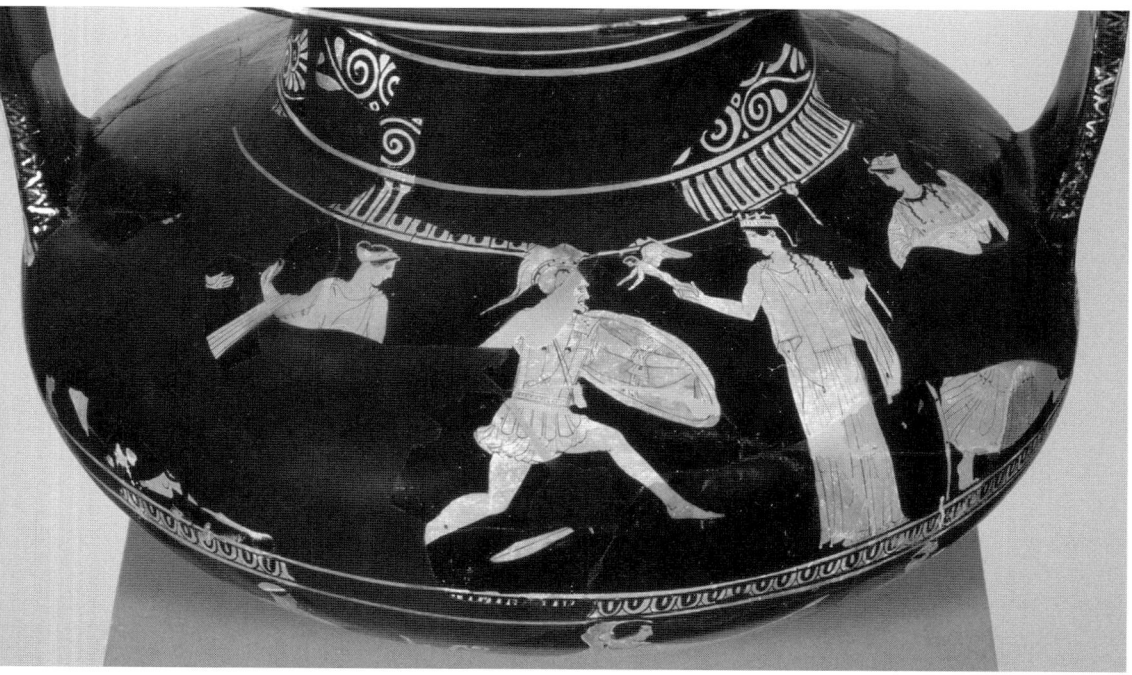

Fig. 9 Attic red-figure nestoris, Getty Villa 81.AE.183.2. Photo: The J. Paul Getty Museum, Villa Collection, Malibu, California, Anonymous gift.

sword exaggerates his change of mind into a loss of individual control and intent, and turns the subject into a scene of parody. The parody can be recognized and enjoyed by a viewer without recourse to the full story, but it is interesting that the surge in scenes with dropped swords takes place at a time when Athens and Sparta are strong rivals, first in the civil war of 462–451 and then during the time of peace under Perikles that ended with the Peloponnesian War. While humor and satire are notoriously difficult to translate and transmit, might the pursuit of Spartan Helen have been an opportunity for Athenian painters to parody Spartan men, and in a way that would resonate with a viewer not only in Athens, but also in Etruria, South Italy, and Sicily, wherever these vases were found? A satiric intent is impossible to prove, but can be considered and enjoyed to some extent still.

Acknowledgements

I would like to thank John Oakley for the invitation and the participants in the conference for comments and questions. For images and permissions, thanks to Irene Bosel (Staatliche Antikensammlung), Liz Kurtulik (Art Resources), Michael Padgett (Princeton), David Saunders (Getty Villa), and Christopher Sutherns and Charles Arnold (British Museum). All dates are BC.

Abbreviations

Hedreen 2001	G. Hedreen, Capturing Troy. The Narrative Functions of Landscape in Archaic and Early Classical Greek Art (2001)
Kahil	L. B. Ghali-Kahil, Les enlèvements et le retour d'Hélène dans les textes et les documents figurés (1955)
LIMC IV	LIMC IV (1988) 498–563 s.v. Helene (L. Kahil – N. Icard)
Recke 2002	M. Recke, Gewalt und Leid. Das Bild des Krieges bei den Athenern im 6. und 5. Jh. v. Chr. (2002)
Stelow 2005	A. Stelow, Not Quite the Best of the Achaians: Menelaos in Archaic Greek Poetry and Art, Ph.D. diss. (University of Minneosta, 2005)

Notes

1 Stelow 2005 222–228.
2 LIMC: LIMC IV 537–552 nos. 210–372; LIMC VIII (1997) 839–841 nos. 44–68 s.v. Menelaos (L. Kahil). M. L. Hart, Athens and Troy: The Narrative Treatment of the "Iliupersis" in Archaic Attic Vase-painting, Ph.D. diss. (University of California Los Angeles, 1992); Recke 2002; BAPD as accessed on November 4, 2012.
3 Kahil; LIMC IV, LIMC VIII (supra n. 2).
4 P. A. Clement, Hesperia 27, 1958, 47–73; Hedreen 2001 36–37. Hedreen 48 and Stelow 2005 223–224 note that the actions are part of the same basic scene.
5 Hart (supra n. 2).
6 H. A. Shapiro, ClAnt 9, 1990, 114–148.
7 Hart (supra n. 2) 216–217. 231. Berlin, Antikensammlung F1685: ABV 109,24; BAPD 310170; LIMC IV 537 no. 210.
8 Hedreen 2001 36–37; idem, ClAnt 15, 1996, 152–184.
9 Hedreen 2001 39. See C. Sourvinou-Inwood, "Reading" Greek Culture: Texts and Images, Rituals and Myths (1991) 29–57 on the distinction between spear and drawn sword in the intent of violence.
10 Recke 2002 20–52.
11 Stelow 2005 212–267, esp. 224–225.
12 On the gestures, see J. Oakley, in: E. Reeder (ed.), Pandora. Women in Classical Greece (1995) 63–73, esp. 65–66. More generally, see J. Oakley – R. Sinos, The Wedding in Ancient Athens (1993) 25–34.
13 Munich, Antikensammlungen 1383. ABV 150,7; BAPD 310434; LIMC IV 528–529 no. 157 pl. 320.
14 Vatican, Museo Gregoriano Etrusco Vaticano 16589. ABV 140,1; BAPD 310352; LIMC IV 537 no. 213 pl. 329.
15 M. D. Stansbury-O'Donnell, Pictorial Narrative in Ancient Greek Art (1999) 54–70.
16 Stelow 2005 223.
17 Oakley – Sinos (supra n. 12) 24–26. 32 on the gestures. I would agree with Hedreen 2001 45 that the *anakalypsis* gesture is more indicative of Helen's status as wife in the pictorial narrative, rather than an indication that the sight of her beauty changed Menelaos's resolve.
18 Stelow 2005 217–218.
19 London, British Museum B244. ABV 271,24; BAPD 320085; LIMC IV 548–549 no. 323. CVA British Museum 4 Great Britain 5 7–8 lists it as Demophon-Aithra, as does the British Museum website, while Kahil in LIMC IV, BAPD, and Recke 2002 273 no. 38 list it as the recovery of Helen. Another amphora in the manner of the Lysippides Painter in London has a similarly disputed identification of the scene as Menelaos-Helen or Demophon-Aithra (London B245, ABV 258,13; BAPD 302245; LIMC IV 538 no. 221 pl. 330). CVA British Museum 4 Great Britain 5 8: Demophon-Aithra; Kahil in LIMC IV; Recke 2002 274 no. 76: Menelaos-Helen; BAPD places a question mark after that subject. Given the drawn sword, *anakalypsis*, and grabbing gestures, this would seem less ambiguous as Menelaos-Helen than B244.
20 Sourvinou-Inwood (supra n. 9).
21 For example, Recke 2002 267–269 lists forty-one scenes of Aias-Kassandra before 500; 271–275 he lists ninety-two for Menelaos-Helen; 280–281, 18 for Neoptolemos-Priam.
22 The list of scenes showing the ambush, pursuit, or killing of Troilos in LIMC includes 110 examples from all of Attic vase painting (LIMC I [1981] 72–95 nos. 206–250. 265–268. 282–330. 337–348 s.v. Achilleus [A. Kossatz-Deismann]). Ninety-four of these are Attic black-figure. LIMC lists 139 Attic vase paintings with Menelaos and Helen.
23 A. Steiner, Reading Greek Vases (2007) 10–11.
24 Paris, Louvre Cp10268: ABV 189,6; BAPD 302487; LIMC IV 540 no. 235 pl. 333. Mykonos K31092: see Kahil pl. 47,1; LIMC IV 539–540 no. 236. Recke 2002 accepts the

cup (no. 49) but not the amphora (no. A5) as Menelaos-Helen, although neither is unambiguous and the warrior on the cup is without the armor typical for the standard set of scenes.

25   Paris, Louvre G3. ARV² 53,1; BAPD 200435; LIMC IV 540 no. 237 pl. 333.

26   See Stelow 2005 235 on the use of the inscription due to the novelty of Oltos's composition. Oltos did two other versions of the story that use the Menelaos leading-Helen standing formula, one with drawn sword and one with spears: 1) Menelaos leading with spears: Malibu, Getty 80.AE.154: BAPD 16676; LIMC IV 549 no. 336bis pl. 352; 2) Menelaos leading with sword: Odessa 21972: ARV² 67,137; BAPD 200577; LIMC IV 547 no. 310 pl. 348). The latter plate fragment was found in Kerch, and the names are also inscribed.

27   See Hedreen 2001 57–63. As Hedreen on page 61 points out, the setting is not crucial to the narrative, unlike Aias and Kassandra.

28   Kahil 77. 85–86.

29   On Attic vase production see F. Giudice, Vasi e frammenti "Beazley" da Locri Epizefiri (1989) 45 fig. 6; 59 fig. 9; 81 fig. 10; R. Panvini – F. Giudice (eds.), Ta Attika. Veder Greco a Gela ceramiche attiche figurate dall'antica colonia (2004) 75 fig. 1. For 525–500, Giudice counts 2015 vases, for 500–475, 3485 vases; for 475–450, 3496 vases.

30   Bologna, Museo Civico Archeologico 269. ARV² 599,8; BAPD 206936; LIMC IV 541 no. 250 pl. 336.

31   This is based on a forthcoming study on pursuits in Greek art based on a database of more than 2500 pursuit scenes.

32   On Aias-Kassandra as an influence see Recke 2001 41. On pursuit as a wedding reference see Oakley (supra n. 12) 65.

33   Princeton University Art Museum 2002.166. Attic red-figure kalpis fragment attributed to the Danae Painter.

34   G. Giudice, Il tornio, la nave, le terre lontane (2007) 426. Her Table A shows that for the period 450–425, findspots are most numerous in Athens (~500), followed by the Adriatic (~425), southern Italy (~350), western Etruria (~225), and Sicily (~210).

35   See comments of M. R. Lefkowitz, Hesperia 71, 2002, 338.

36   See Stansbury-O'Donnell (supra n. 15) 165–175.

37   Oakley (supra n. 12) 64–65.

38   London, British Museum E263. ARV² 594,54; BAPD 206878; LIMC IV 542 no. 264 pl. 337.

39   Malibu, Getty Villa 81.AE.183.2. BAPD 30684; LIMC IV 543–544 no. 276 pl. 341.

40   See, for example, Steiner (supra n. 23) 194–196. 258–262; D. Walsh, Distorted Ideals in Greek Vase-Painting: The World of Mythological Burlesque (2009) 134–143. 212–222; A. G. Mitchell, Greek Vase-Painting and the Origins of Visual Humour (2009) 95–149.

41   Mitchell (supra n. 40) 142.

26 Attic Black-figure and Red-figure Fragments from the Sanctuary of Apollo at Mandra on Despotiko

Robert F. Sutton and Yannos Kourayos

We present here a selection of figured Attic pottery from a newly discovered sanctuary of Apollo on Despotiko, a small, deserted island SW of Paros in the Cyclades (Fig. 1). The site Mandra, meaning animal-fold, takes its name from goat pens that occupied the site from at least the later nineteenth century until they were moved in 2004.[1] It runs along and overlooks a stubby peninsula that extends from the northern coast of Despotiko toward the southwest coast of Antiparos, to which it was still attached in Classical times together with the small intermediate islet Tsimintiri (Fig. 1).[2] The resulting isthmus created an attractive bay sheltered by the long southeastern tail of Antiparos, and a small altar on site inscribed ΕΣΤΙΑΣ ΙΣΘΜΙΑΣ (Of Hestia of the Isthmus) suggests that in antiquity the site was called Isthmia.[3] Pottery indicates that the cult dates probably from Late Geometric I, possibly earlier, and the site appears to be a textbook case of François Polignac's thesis that the emerging Greek *poleis* (Paros, in this case) established sanctuaries at their territorial limits in the course of ancient state formation.[4]

Kourayos's excavations over the past decade have revealed a rich complex of ancient and Late Antique structures spread along the crest of the Mandra peninsula (Fig. 2), including a roughly square Archaic temenos on a small plateau, another complex of buildings to the south, and more isolated structures extending to the northeast. Today the site is extremely vulnerable, with ancient walls emerging from the modern surface and abundant, fresh fragments of red-figure and other pottery lying on the surface. The architecture has been studied by a team from Munich led by Aenne Ohensorg.[5] The North Temenos is closed on the west by the five rooms and two porches of Building A, the northernmost section of which (Rooms A1 and A2) contains a double-cella temple with common porch erected in the second quarter of the sixth century BC. Not long after, three rooms for dining and a portico were added to the south. Over time other walls and rooms closed off the court, including a second temple structure Δ erected near Building A on the north and a large semi-circular altar in the center. Around 500 BC or a bit later, possibly just after the Athenian Miltiades' fatal invasion of Paros in 490 BC (Hdt. 6.132–136), the double-cella temple (Rooms A1–A2) was given a marble Doric façade. While much of the sanctuary was laid out in Archaic times, there was considerable later renovation; in the Southern Sector an earlier complex of rooms built on a slightly different orientation has recently been discovered below Classical structures. Pottery indicates that the sanctuary functioned through at least the Hellenistic period and probably into Roman Imperial times, when substantial activity is attested. Late Antiquity saw a major transformation, and marble architectural members of the Archaic sanctuary were incorporated into a warren of small rooms that were partly erected on the paved floors of Building A, cutting across the Archaic threshold of Room A5. Ceramic and documentary evidence indicates reoccupation in Venetian and Ottoman times before the modern goat fold attested by nineteenth-century travelers.[6]

The ascription to Apollo depends entirely on graffiti incised onto pottery in Archaic and Classical times.[7] Apollo's name, sometimes abbreviated in ΑΠ compendia, was incised on the rims of local versions of Archaic Laconian kraters and on other vase shapes; the common use of omicron for omega and vice versa is characteristic of the Parian alphabet and confirms Parian control of the site.[8] Other finds, including many female figurines, suggest that Apollo was worshipped with Artemis and Leto in the Delian triad, although a Delian sanctuary was excavated on Paros itself over a century ago near the polis center.[9]

The Attic pottery presented here should be considered in the context of other pottery and finds from the site. Despotiko Mandra has yielded a significant amount of sculpture, including the remarkably well-preserved upper half of a large-scale terracotta statuette painted in the style of the misnamed 'Melian' ware that was made on Paros, and especially marble sculpture, including many

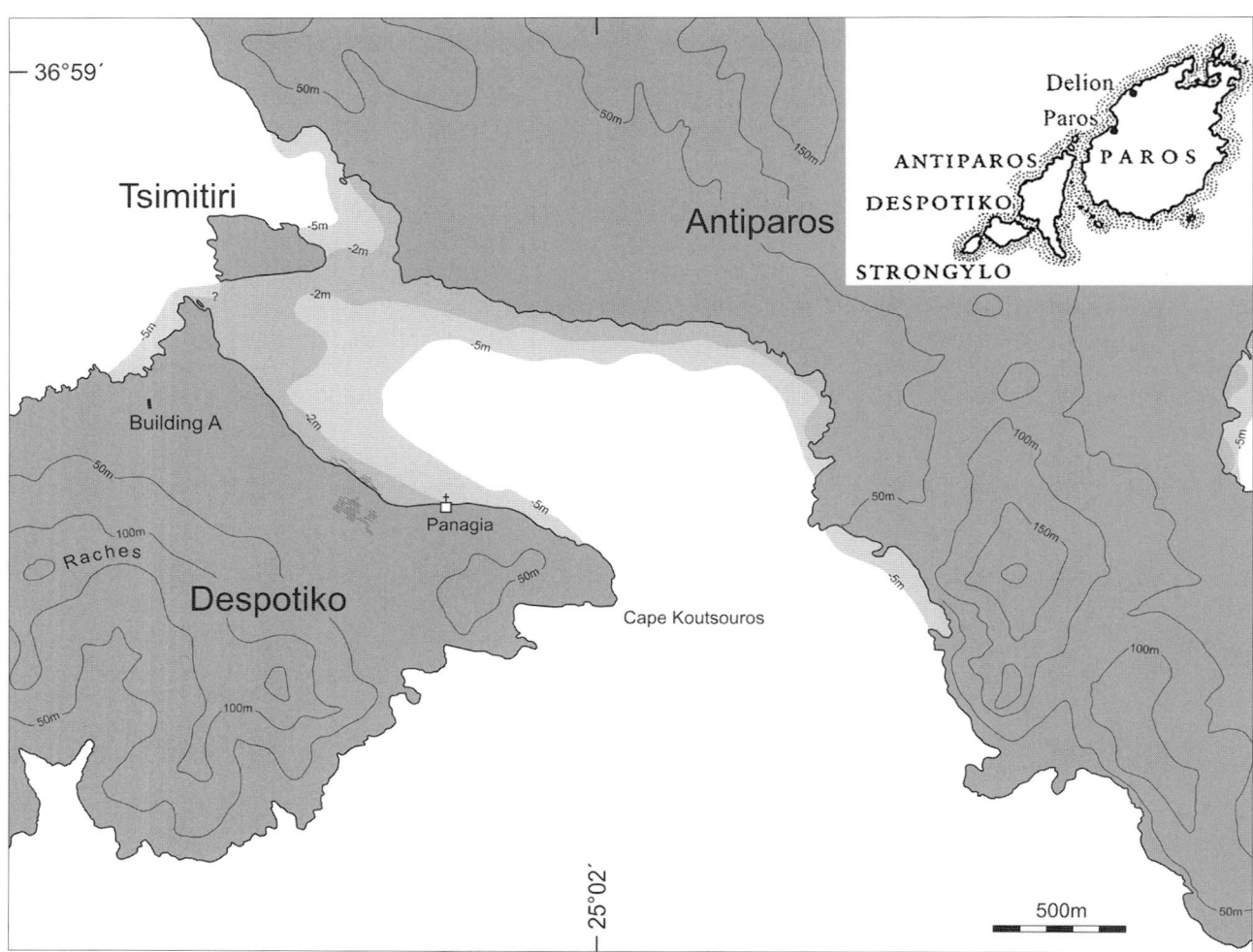

Fig. 1 Reconstruction of the isthmus that connected Despotiko to Antiparos in antiquity. Dark gray with black outline: modern shoreline. Medium gray: shoreline c. 2000 BP, sea level 2 m below present. Light gray, shoreline c. 5,000 BP, sea level 5 m below present. Courtesy E. Draganits; inset by R. Finnerty, after Hesperia 71, 2002, 176 fig. 20 (Papadopoulos and Smithson).

fragmentary kouroi that had been cut up and reused in constructions apparently of the Classical period.[10] In 2001 and 2002, one of the chambers of the double-cella temple, Room A1, yielded two substantial deposits of Archaic material.[11] We are currently completing study of the ceramics with Eleni Hasaki and briefly summarize some findings to provide a context for the Attic finds.[12]

The lower deposit, buried when the building was first constructed in the second quarter of the sixth century BC, includes metal tools and weapons, gems and other jewelry, faience and ivory imports, an ostrich egg, and the large 'Melian' terracotta statuette fragment just mentioned. The abundant pottery included many intact, small unguent vessels, mostly from Corinth with a few from East Greece, and fragmentary drinking vessels, mostly local. The Corinthian material dates from Transitional to Late Corinthian, the earliest of which had been preserved intact for roughly seventy-five years before their burial. These layers contained not one identifiable scrap of Attic pottery. The only Archaic Attic fragment from the room is a small fragment copying Exekias that was found in recent, disturbed levels.

Most of the Attic pottery recovered from this part of the site comes from Room A3, added in the third quarter of the sixth century BC, that was packed full of small fragments of drinking vessels and closed shapes, with very few unguent vessels. Indeed, the unguent vessels that were so prominent in the early deposit of room A1 drop out completely after the mid-sixth century; there are no later Attic or other lekythoi or alabastra to succeed the Corinthian and East Greek aryballoi, alabastra, etc., and one most conclude that their earlier presence does not reflect significant activity at the site. Instead, they were probably valued primarily for their fragrant contents and dedicated as minor luxuries beside the exotic faience, small jewelry, and ivory imports. In contrast, the Attic pottery of all periods consists almost entirely of fragmentary drinking vessels and kraters used

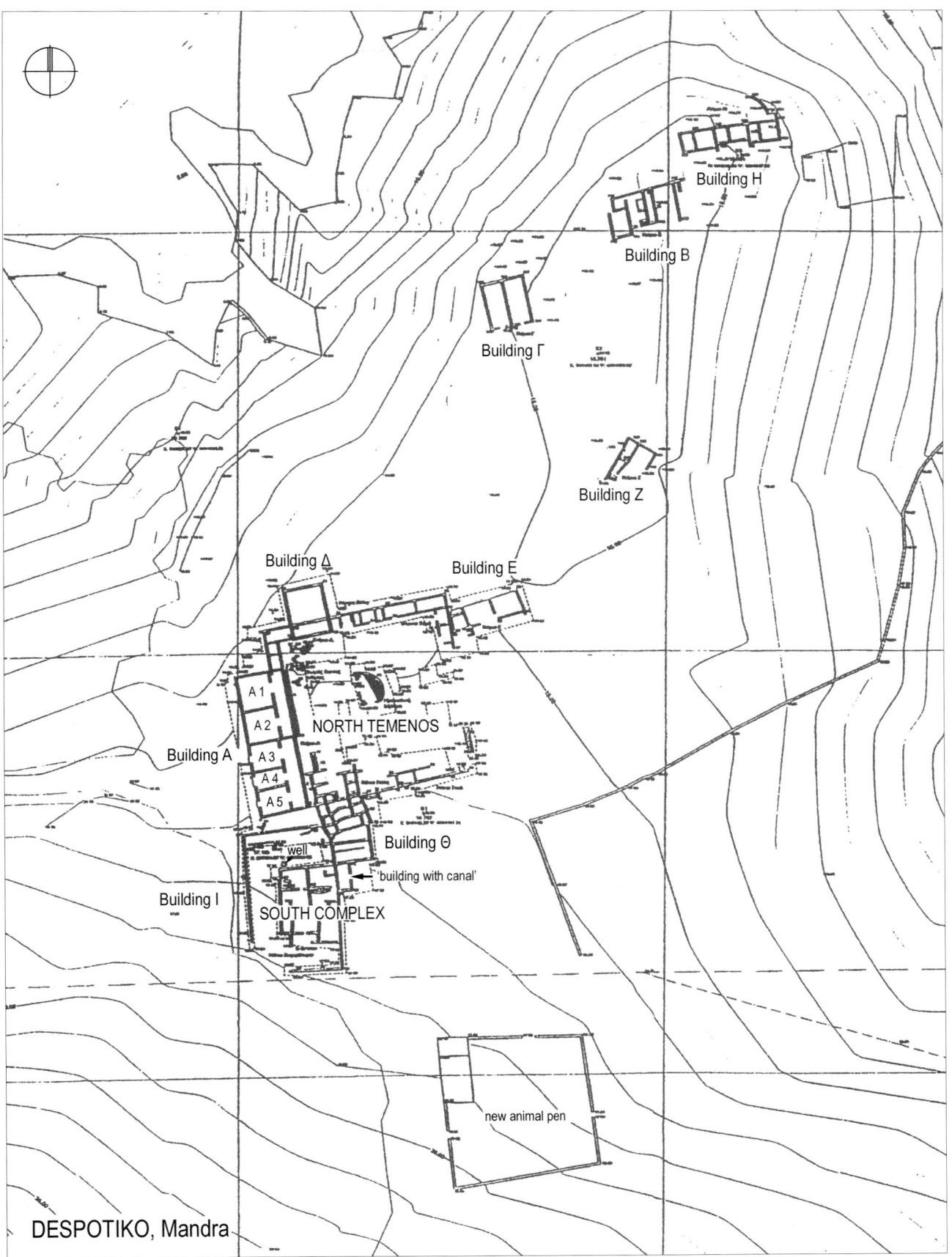

Fig. 2 Main cult area of the Sanctuary of Apollo at Despotiko Mandra. A. Ohnesorg.

by worshippers in communal ritual feasting and dedicated or discarded after use.

We present a selection of figured Attic pottery recovered after 2002, mostly from other parts of the site than Building A. Some were found on the surface, and the rest were removed from the rest of the context pottery after excavation and brought to the Paros Museum as "Significant Finds." Detailed study of the excavation pottery may yield further fragments and will certainly clarify their archaeological context. All is fragmentary, and we present here some of the better preserved, finer, or more interesting pieces.

The Attic black-figure recovered to date consists almost entirely of drinking shapes, a few closed shapes, and (as with Corinthian) no kraters. They date from the second quarter of the sixth century BC and into the fifth. Bowls for mixing wine were evidently supplied locally for the most part, although in the Archaic period they are not well represented, and we can cite only the fragmentary, inscribed imitations of Laconian kraters noted above with perhaps a small fragment from Laconia plus a unique 'Melian' dinos with inscribed figures and another worn dinos rim possibly imported from Chios.[13]

The earliest Attic pottery so far identified from Despotiko Mandra consists of two fragments of Siana cups dating from the second quarter of the sixth century. A small rim fragment of an overlap cup by the Heidelberg Painter, or possibly in his Manner, preserves part of a pair of battling hoplites (Figs. 3. 4; Color Pl. 31B).[14] Of the left-hand warrior only the tip of his raised spear and shield survive. The shield overlaps that of his opponent and is seen from inside to detail his incised left arm, arm brace (*porpax*), hand grip, and other fittings against the red interior. His opponent's shield has a border of red dots encircling a black disk with faded white facing panther-head blazon that seems to have stepped out of a Corinthian animal frieze. The hoplite wears a low-crested Corinthian helmet and belted nerbris over chitoniskos, an outfit that finds exact parallel in a wounded warrior on a cup by the Heidelberg Painter dated by Herman Brijder to the artist's Middle Period, c. 560–550;[15] that is probably when our fragment should be dated, even if some details are best paralleled in later work. Battle scenes are among the most popular subjects on the exterior of the Heidelberg Painter's cups, and our fragment fits in well with Brijder's detailed discussion.[16] The Heidelberg Painter's battles are more varied and detailed than those of the C Painter and also derive from Corinthian models going back to the Protocorinthian Chigi vase. He often shows three pairs of dueling warriors per side, although three cups show heroic duels with a central pair flanked by onlookers, and a few more-complex battles probably represent episodes from epic. The detailed depiction of this shield interior is particularly characteristic of the painter's more complex battles, while the panther device recurs on his cup in Vienna.[17]

A fragment from the handle zone of a double-decker Siana cup was found in the Archaic fill of Room A3 (Fig. 5).[18] It preserves the rump of a horse and much of a bird flying above, with the lower edge of the black handle; an odd detail is what appears to be the extended anus of the horse. The incision is sharp and crisp, and the added red on the horse tail and central band on the bird's wings is well preserved. The bird and full horse tail that narrows where it connects with the rump are similar to those found on the Middle and Late phases of Beazley's Shadow of the C Painter (570–550 BC), now conveniently renamed the Taras Painter by Brijder.[19]

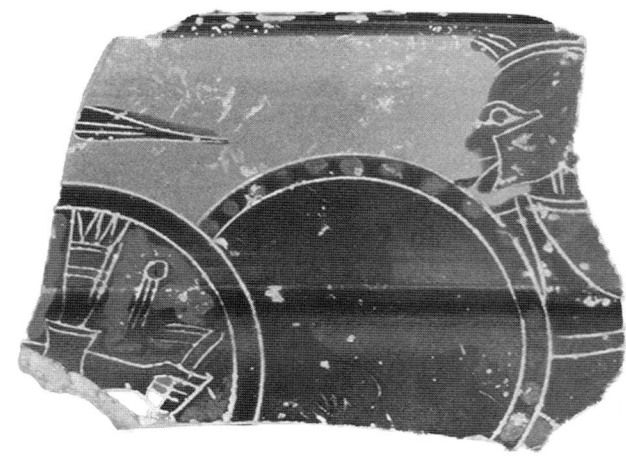

Fig. 3 Black-figure Siana cup fragment. Heidelberg Painter. Battling hoplites.

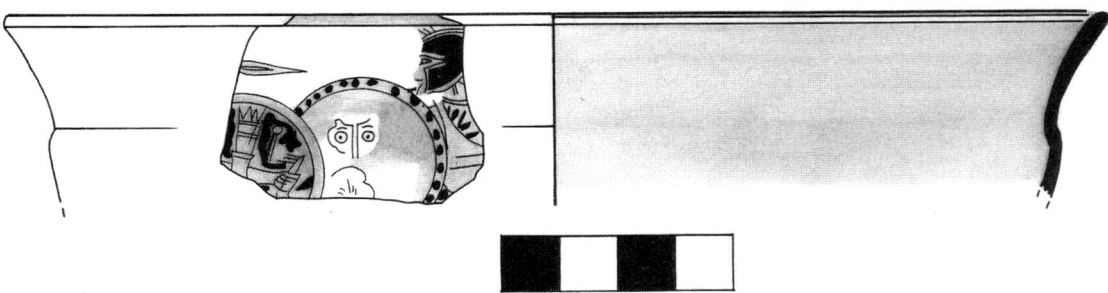

Fig. 4 Drawing of Siana cup fragment in Fig. 3. Drawing by Christina Kolb.

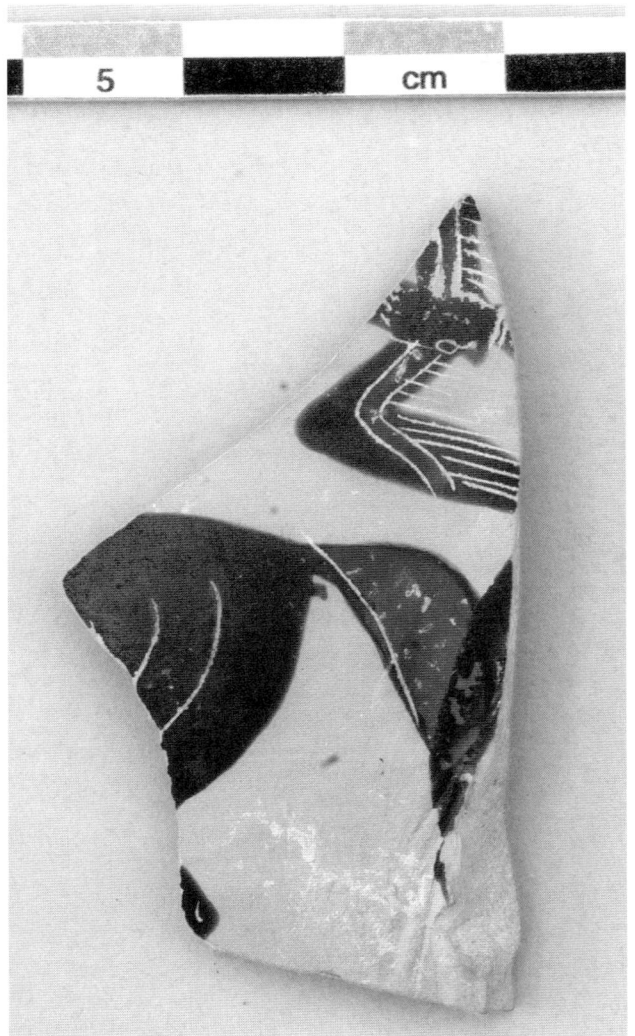

Fig. 5 Black-figure Siana cup fragment (AK 4170). Taras Painter (Shadow of the C Painter). Horse, bird.

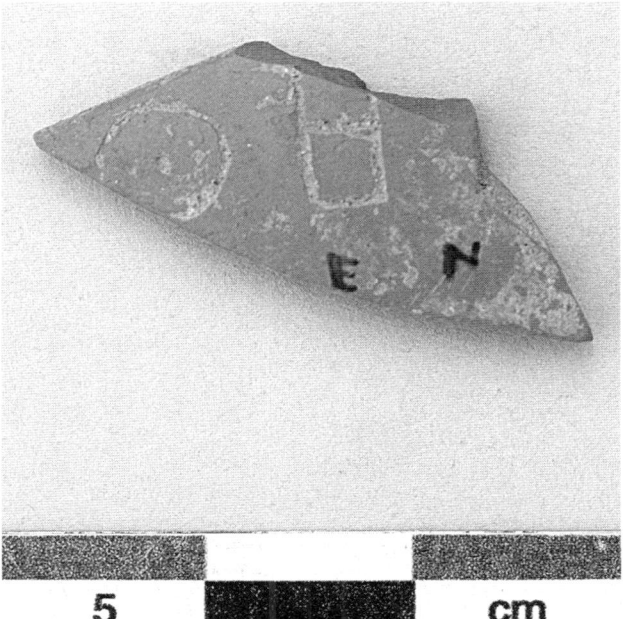

Fig. 6 Black-figure Little Master lip (?) cup fragment (AK 4171) with dipinto painted before firing (artist's signature?) and incised dedication.

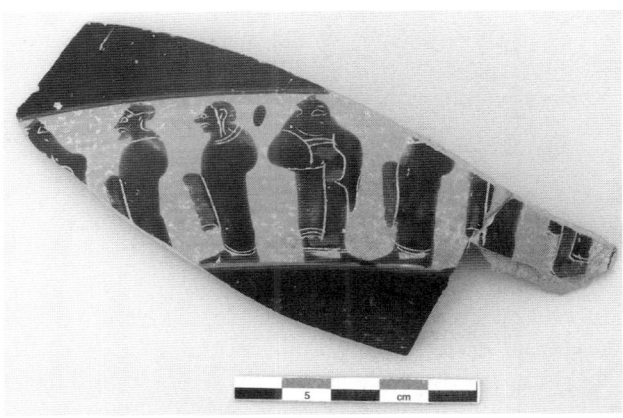

Fig. 7 Black-figure band cup fragment (AK 4166). Near BMN Painter. Two women (goddesses?) unveiling to approaching males.

A bit later, from the third quarter of the century, is a small, doubly inscribed fragment of a Little Master cup, most likely a lip cup, from Building Δ (Fig. 6).[20] Two letters painted before firing are likely from a potter's (or painter's) signature [. . . . εποιεσ]εν[. . . . ?], although other restorations are also possible, e.g. [Hερμογ]εν[ες . . . .].[21] With only two letters, it is impossible to identify the painter's hand, although many can be excluded. Later, after firing, a dedication was incised [. . . . ανε]θη[κε. . . .] using dotted theta and eta closed top and bottom. Both forms are attested on Paros, although the crossed theta is usual on stone until the fifth century.[22]

Better preserved is a band cup also from Building Δ, of which we illustrate the largest fragment (Fig. 7; Color Pl. 31A); there are another two or three non-joining pieces.[23] This fragment shows two groups of draped figures that each confront a standing female figure who unveils like a bride. The fully-preserved, central, female figure stands right as she unveils in the *anakalypsis* pose to greet three draped penguin figures who stand or slowly approach from the right with a trace probably of a fourth. To the left, separated from this group by a blob on the wall, likely intended for hanging drapery, two fully preserved penguin figures confront a second, partly preserved woman unveiling like the first. The leading penguin is a bearded male. His companion is beardless with long hair falling in front of the ear, but he has a male eye that is clearly different from the almond eyes of unveiling ladies, and is surely intended as a youth. No trace of added white survives on any of the figures. A substantial, non-joining fragment preserves the lower parts of four mantled figures facing left beside a handle stub on right; and a small piece has another unveiling woman to right confronting two draped figures. Both iconography and style are close to a finer cup in New York that Beazley placed Near the BMN Painter, who worked for Nikosthenes.[24] Given its discovery in Building Δ, provisionally identified as a second temple, the iconography of the Despotiko cup may be better understood in the context of cult and worship than as greeting a bride, as Richter suggested for the cup in New York, or as an early courting scene.[25]

A fragmentary skyphos of Class K2 shape (Figs. 8. 9) belongs to the diverse Haimonian Group (Manner of the Haimon Painter), as seen from the handle palmettes and wonderfully rubbery satyr; it is finer than most, uses incision, probably stands early in the series, and may be by the Haimon Painter himself.[26] One side shows seated Dionysos and satyr, probably complete; the maenad is from the other side of this or possibly another vessel and likely attended another seated divine figure. This is not a stock theme of the Haimonian Group, but is borrowed from cups of the Leafless Group and Group of Vatican G 57,[27] reinterpreted in an uncluttered, elegant composition that harks back to the simple clarity of Little Master design and allows us to recognize a neglected esthetic aspect of the Haemonian Group. The larger fragment was found to the west of Building A; the small, non-joining piece with maenad was found in the Southern Sector, whether from the same vessel or a companion piece. The date should be around 490 BC or later.

The excavations at Despotiko Mandra to date have produced more Attic red-figure than black-figure, including some high quality work that is now sadly battered. None is Archaic, and, indeed, most belongs to the second half of the fifth century. This significant period in the Aegean witnessed the height of the Athenian Empire and its protracted collapse during the Peloponnesian War. These fragments may demonstrate close economic ties within the Empire and probably a combination of local economic prosperity and redirection of high quality pieces closer to home as the western market for Attic pottery met competition from local production. While the Attic black-figure was mostly drinking shapes, the bulk of red-figure consists mostly of kraters, but also at least one skyphos and probably a kylix.

Probably the earliest is an Early Classical skyphos fragment showing a youth playing *auloi* by the Lewis Painter (Polygnotos II; Fig. 10).[28] Like his better High Classical successor the Penelope Painter, the Lewis Painter specialized in the simple Attic-type skyphos, more common in plain black, that provided a sturdy everyday alternative to the more elegant kylix and elaborated Archaic skyphoi. This slender youth with mantle draped over his left shoulder finds an exact counterpart in a komos scene on the painter's skyphos in Brussels, even down to the thick wreath with dilute inner markings that loops three-dimensionally around his head.[29] H. R. W. Smith placed the Brussels komos at the end of the artist's middle period, and saw the influence of the contemporary

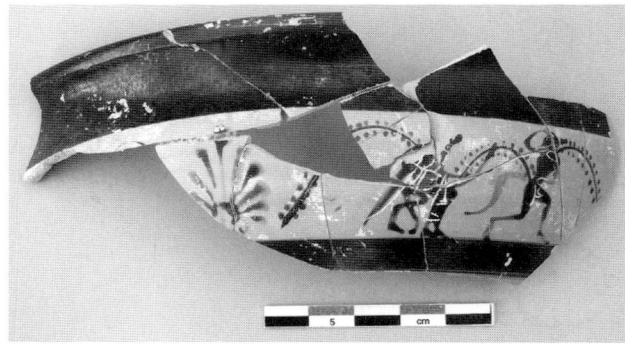

Fig. 8 Black-figure skyphos Type K2 fragment (AK 4389). Haimonian Group; Haimon Painter or his manner. A: Seated Dionysos with satyr.

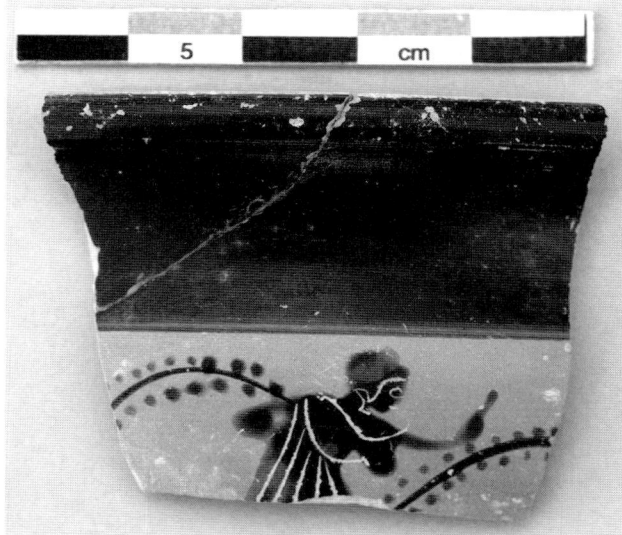

Fig. 9 Black-figure skyphos fragment (AK 4389, non-joining), probably from the reverse of the skyphos in Figure 8. B: maenad.

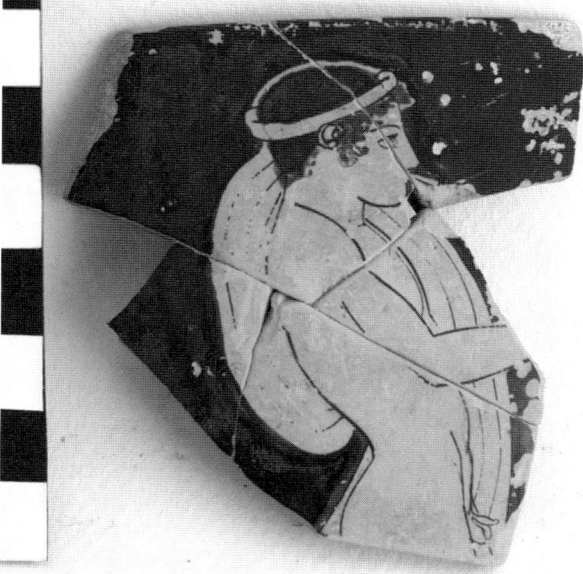

Fig. 10 Red-figure skyphos fragment. Lewis Painter. Flute player (auletes).

Euaion Painter, a cup painter who continued the tradition of Douris.[30]

The komos theme recurs with female *aulistriai* on later krater fragments. Just the upper part of a flute girl survives on a small fragment from Building Z that probably belongs in the larger Group of Polygnotos.[31] That tradition produced a long series of major painters of large vases who shared a common monumental vision that evolved from the Severe Style of the Early Classical Niobid Workshop through High Classical nobility and culminated in the lavish styles of the Dinos, Talos, and Pronomos Painters who led into the fourth century.[32] Even the narrow Polygnotan Group as defined by Beazley is large and diverse, and over time its individual painters often exhibit a variety of styles that make it difficult to distinguish or even to define them, as several scholars have noted, including Beazley himself, and significant works are often included in the manner of these artists.[33] Given the popularity of kraters at Despotiko Mandra, it may not be surprising to find its products so well represented there, but especially in the later years of the century one may wonder if there was a special commercial link. Several smaller fragments, in addition to the *aulistria* noted above, probably belong to this extended group, but two sets of high quality fragments stand out as products of the Dinos and Talos Painters or their closest associates.

The first is a late fifth-century komos on a fragmentary bell krater from the Southern Sector (Fig. 11; Color Pl. 31C).[34] The two fragments illustrated join at the base, revealing a tipsy reveler leaning against a flute girl, his arm around her shoulder, accompanied by torch-bearer. This is a warmer, more intimate version of a motif that reaches back at least to the Late Archaic komoi of the Brygos Painter, and seems to anticipate the type of the tipsy young Dionysos with Ariadne portrayed on the reverse of the Pronomos krater and elsewhere in the late fifth and early fourth century.[35] The reveler's torso is nude, with drapery that arches from behind in folds of subtly varying thickness to cover his groin and the right side of his torso. The *aulistria* is clothed in a transparent linen chiton whose fine lines reveal both legs and breasts, girt above the waist with a black belt, and similar dark lines reinforce the garment at her shoulders. The right forearm with torch and lower legs survive of the companion who lights their way, and on his legs we see yet another treatment of drapery; the heel of his trailing leg probably survives on the left edge of the large fragment of the handle palmette that survives almost entirely. This is likely a work of the Dinos Painter, a major artist of the late Rich Style, and looks forward to the Talos Painter in particular with connection also to the Pronomos Painter.[36] Without the heads precise attribution is uncertain, but the rich folds and male torso

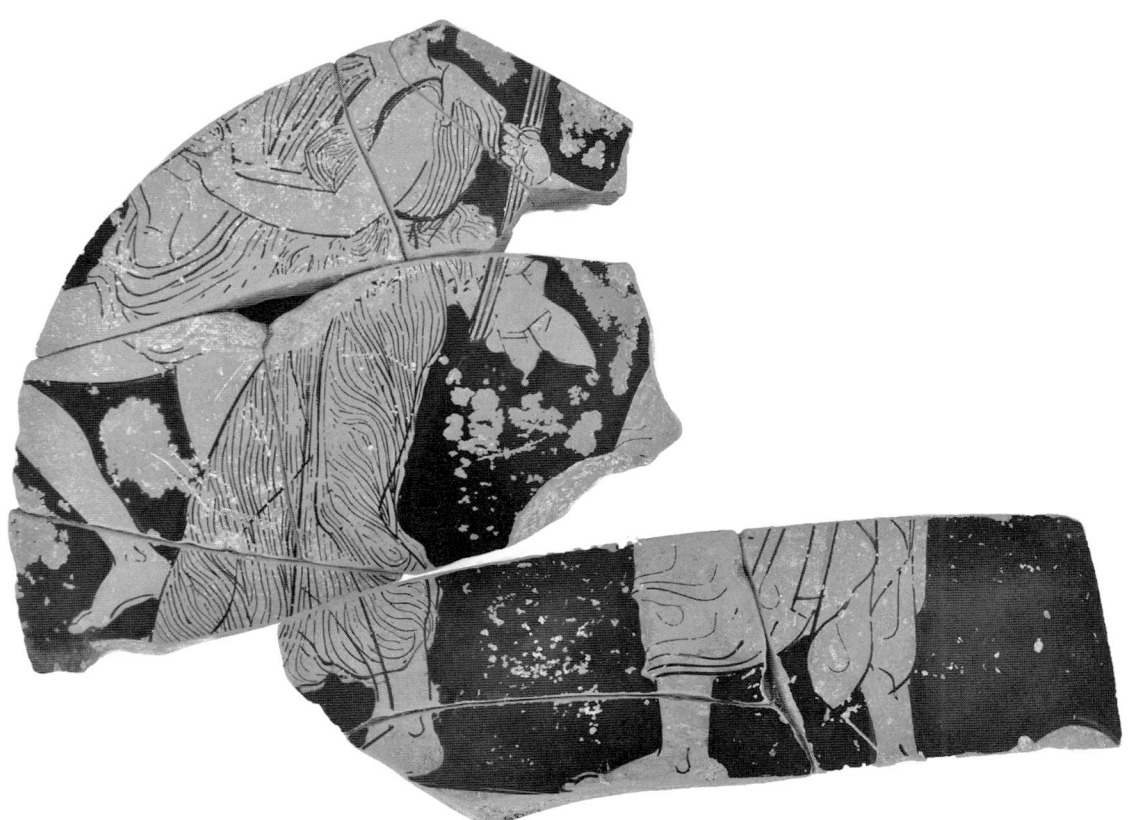

Fig. 11 Red-figure bell krater fragment (AK 5095. 5097). Dinos Painter. Komos.

with folds of varying width defined by thicker and thinner lines, the way the *aulistria's* neck articulates with her shoulders, and the dilute glaze curl on her neck, appear as early as the Kleophon and Dinos Painters, but these and other details also find later parallel in works by or near the Talos Painter.[37] The 'Meidian' drapery over her breasts finds earlier parallels in the work of the Christie and Kleophon Painters and is similar to that of the flautist on the Dinos Painter's masterpiece in Naples showing women worshipping Dionysos, of Hippodameia on the great neck amphora in Arezzo that Beazley attributed to the Manner of the Dinos Painter, and of Hera on the Talos krater.[38] The fine folds and fluidity of the skirt are late and closest in concept and detail to some figures by the Talos Painter.[39] The feet and other details find parallels in several of his works, including those in the Manner of the Dinos Painter.[40] In short, the drawing lies between the developed Dinos Painter and his successor the Talos Painter, and the intertwined revelers are similar to the reveling Dionysos and Ariadne type found on the Pronomos krater. Additional krater fragments with a symposium scene found in the same area in 2010 include heads that are certainly by the Dinos Painter, although it is not clear if they derive from the same vessel.[41] The Polygnotans often combine komos and symposium.[42]

Two non-joining fragments of an exceptionally fine calyx krater of the late fifth century are the work of the Talos Painter or extremely close (Figs. 12. 13).[43] As in other works of the Talos Painter and his closest colleagues, we find an assembly of gods, although here the occasion is not clear. One fragment (Fig. 12)[44] shows a woman in an elaborately decorated drapery seated on what appears to be a rock or other bit of landscape beside a second draped figure with a knobby staff, perhaps a thyrsus. The other fragment (Fig. 13)[45] preserves the upper, more recognizable end of the thyrsus, with a helmeted head, perhaps Athena's, and the wings either of Eros or Nike. The treatment of the feathers and elaborate drapery of the seated woman is close to details on a bell krater in the Villa Giulia Museum that Beazley placed near the Talos Painter.[46] Athena's helmet is similar in design to that of a hoplite on a loutrophoros in Amsterdam that Beazley assigned to the Talos Painter himself, and it appears, as Robertson indicates, that this artist and related groups may need reconfiguration.[47]

We close with an earlier mythological scene, an initially enigmatic krater fragment that eventually revealed itself as one of the oldest themes in Attic vase painting: Herakles battling the centaur Nessos (Fig. 14).[48] The hero can be recognized by the paws of his lion skin that hang down on either side of his left thigh; part of his genitals appear above, and the front of his extended right leg to his knee. Behind we see the tail and haunch of the centaur. A search of the subject in the BAPD reveals, that although the hero is more often shown behind the Centaur's body on vases of the Classical Period, a fourth-century pelike in Karlsruhe shows a similar scheme (also used earlier by the Berlin Painter) that confirms the identification.[49] Dating and attribution are less certain. The simple forms of the lion skin could belong to the later Archaic period, but the treatment of the genitals and extended relief line of the left thigh probably indicate an Early Classical date; given

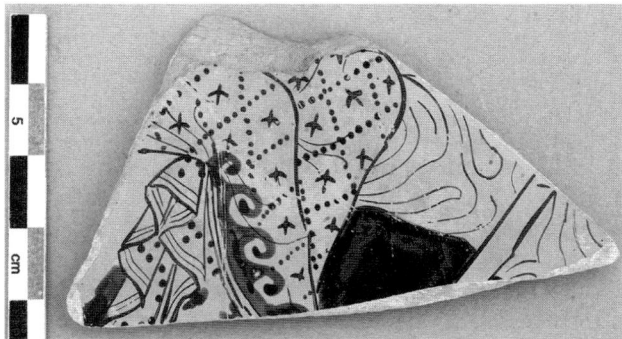

Fig. 12 Red-figure calyx krater fragment (AK 5103). Talos Painter (or in his manner). Assembly of gods: seated god and goddess, with thyrsus.

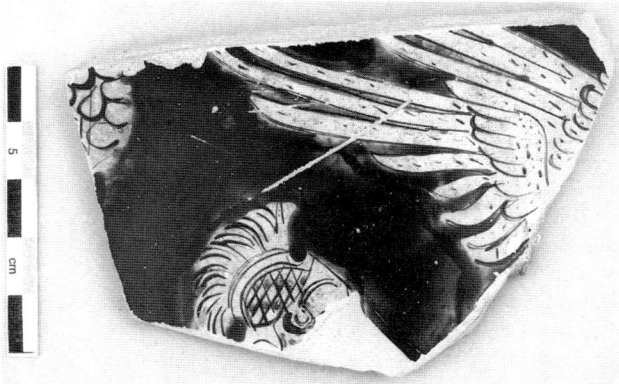

Fig.13 Red-figure calyx krater fragment (AK 4955). Talos Painter (or in his manner). Assembly of gods: head of Athena, wings of Eros or Nike, head of thyrsus.

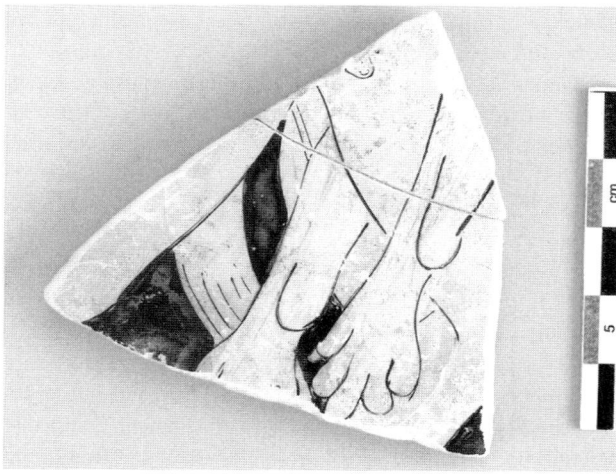

Fig. 14 Red-figure bell krater fragment (AK 4147). Herakles battling the Centaur Nessos. Probably Early Classical.

the high quality of the drawing, the lack of detail in the right knee seems to exclude a date much after 450 BC.

These fragments with others not included here, support the following summary.[50] The sanctuary at Despotiko Mandra has so far yielded only a small amount of Attic black-figure, mostly drinking vessels dating slightly before the mid-sixth century into the fifth. Attic red-figure is more abundant, all of it Classical, and most of it from the second half of the fifth century, including pieces of high quality. The presence of very high quality red-figure from the time of the Peloponnesian War probably reflects changing markets for Attic fine wares at this time with greater focus locally on Athenian trade under the Empire, and finds parallel in the presence of good quality Attic red-figure in unpublished graves on Paros, including a fragmentary tallboy lekythos by the Meidias Painter. By contrast, Otto Rubensohn found no Attic black-figure or red-figure in his tranches at the Delion on Paros; the little he reports, illustrating only an Archaic red-figure cup fragment, was recovered on the surface outside the excavation, and probably reflects the chances of preservation and the limited extent excavated.[51] When the graves and houses excavated on Paros over the past decades, often in rescue excavations, are published, comparison will doubtless show that the selection at Despotiko Mandra of black-figure cup shapes and mostly kraters with a few cups in red-figure was made specifically to support feasting in the sanctuary, and does not represent the range of shapes that was locally available.[52]

The fragments presented here may also indicate a degree of deliberate selection of subject matter on pottery that was used and dedicated at the sanctuary, including the band cup that may show worshippers approaching a pair of goddesses (Fig. 7), Dionysian subjects in black-figure (Figs. 7. 8, and at least one more), red figure komoi (Figs. 10–11, and another fragment with flute girl) and symposium,[53] and a few with mythological themes (Figs. 12–14). Other recognized subjects not discussed here include a rushing chariot (mythic abduction?), two standing hoplites, mantle figures, and perhaps an athletic scene and musical performance. This selection appears to be somewhat more focused than a random sample of the range of themes represented at any given time on Attic symposium ware.

Acknowledgements

R. F. Sutton is grateful to Y. Kourayos for the opportunity to study ceramics from Despotiko Mandra and to present a small portion here; to John Oakley for the invitation to participate in this conference and for organizing it and its two predecessors and the Schrader Fund of Indiana University for financial support. Thanks also to Kourayos' assistant Kornelia Daifa, John Pack and the Aegean Center of the Fine Arts on Paros, the ΚΑ˙ Ephorate of Prehistoric and Classical Antiquities, the guards at the Archaeological Museum of Paros, and the American School of Classical Studies at Athens. Photographs are by Sutton except as noted.

Abbreviations

Measurements: H = preserved height; W = preserved width; max. pres. dim. = maximum preserved dimension
c. = circa; esp. = especially; l. = left; r. = right

AK   Paros Archaeological Museum inventory number
Guide[2]   Y. Kourayos, Despotiko. The Sanctuary of Apollo (2012)
Robertson   M. Robertson, The Art of Vase-painting in Classical Athens (1992)

Notes

1. For detailed discussion of the site with bibliography see Guide[2]; Y. Kourayos – B. Burns, BCH 128–129, 2004–2005, 135–174; Y. Kourayos – A. Ohnesorg – K. Daifa Papayianni, The Sanctuary of Despotiko in the Cyclades. Excavations 2001–2012, AA 2012, 93–174; Y. Kourayos – R. F. Sutton – E. Hasaki, Ceramics, Contacts & Cult. Mandra on Despotiko, Paros, 2001–2002, in preparation.
2. E. Draganits, Austrian Journal of Earth Sciences, 102.1, 2009, 91–101.
3. Guide[2] 62; the letter forms are Late Classical or Early Hellenistic.
4. F. de Polignac, Cults, Territory, and the Origins of the Greek City-State, trans. J. Lloyd (1995).
5. Supra n. 1, revising M. Schuller, JdI 100, 1985, 319–398.
6. Guide[2] 72–75.
7. Full presentation in Kourayos – Sutton – Hasaki (supra n. 1); Guide[2] 18; Y. Kourayos, in: M. Yeroulanou – M. Stamatopoulou (eds.), Studies in Honour of J. J. Coulton (2005) 130 fig. 20.
8. L. H Jeffery, Local Scripts of Archaic Greece, rev. ed. by A. W. Johnston (1990) 289–290. 294; Y. Kourayos, in: J. de la Genière (ed.), Les clients de la céramique grecque, Cahiers du CVA 1 (2006) pl. 192, VI.2.
9. O. Rubensohn, Das Delion von Paros (1962).
10. Guide[2] 50–51. 53. 76–86; Y. Kourayos, in: G. Kokkorou-Alevras – W.-D. Niemeier (eds.), Neue Funde archaischer Plastik aus griechischen Heiligtümern und Nekropolen, Athenaia 3 (2012) 101–132.
11. Kourayos – Burns (supra n. 1) 139–156; Guide[2] 40–51; Y. Kourayos, An Archaic Votive Deposit from Despotiko Mandra: The Small Finds, AAA, forthcoming.
12. Supra n. 1. Some illustrated in Kourayos (supra n. 7) pls. 190–191.
13. Supra n. 7; 'Melian' dinos, Guide[2] 58.
14. Guide[2] 44, lower l.
15. H. Brijder, Siana Cups II. The Heidelberg Painter (1991) no 352 pl. 114a. c; BAPD 300577.
16. Brijder (supra n. 15) 386–389. 418–419; J. D. Beazley, The Development of Attic Black-figure, rev. ed. (1986) 21.

17 Brijder (supra n. 15) 386–387 fig. 95a. f no. 440 pl. 142g. h; for the interior cf. also no. 375 pl. 126 and no. 470 in the artist's manner, pl. 146,g–i, discussed on 427–433.
18 AK 4170 from Room A3, Grid 6, layer 3, Π2, SF1, 4/6/2004. H. 0.05.
19 H. Brijder, Siana Cups I and Komast Cups (1983) 151. 158. 164–165 no. 136 pl. 28a; no. 170 pl. 33, esp. f; no. 174 pl. 34c. d; idem, Siana Cups III (2000) add. no. 27 pl. 242; add. no. 28 pl. 243d; pl. 246.
20 AK 4071 from Building Δ, grid A6, layer 3, Π1, SF 1, 4/6/2004; max pres. dim. 0.028.
21 On Little Master cup inscriptions see H. R. Immerwahr, Attic Script (1990) 47–48 pls. 11–12.
22 Jeffery (supra n. 8) 289 reports that crossed forms of theta appear on Paros into the early fifth century BC; the dotted form appears earlier on Thasos, a Parian colony that maintained close ties with the metropolis. This fragmentary dedication may show an early advent of the form on Paros on *instrumenta*, or it may employ another script.
23 AK 4166 from grid A1:6, layer 3, Π1, SF1, 14/6/2004; H 0.123; illustrated, Guide[2] 59 below.
24 New York, MMA 14.147.3; BAPD 302856; CVA Metropolitan Museum of Art 2 USA 11 10 pls. 16,26A–D.
25 Ibid.; R. F. Sutton, in: A. Richlin (ed.), Pornography and Representation in Greece and Rome (1992) 14–20.
26 AK 4389 from grid Z1, layer 3, 26/6/2005; W 0.065; non-joining fragment from South Complex Room I, Trench NE of exterior space on SW of the room (T110–T112, foundation layer of T112, 2016/2012). See ABL 131–132 on the Haimon Painter's figures "like creatures in an aquarium"; 133 on his palmettes 264 no. 94; cf. Agora XXIII pls. 102. 103 nos. 1504–1532.
27 Leafless Group, cf. e.g. BAPD 6057. 6058. 331854. 331856; Group of Vatican G 57, cf. e.g. BAPD 306132. 306137.
28 From the South Complex; illustrated, Guide[2] 69. On the Lewis Painter see Robertson 167–169; on black skyphoi, Agora XII 81–87 nos. 303–377 fig. 4 pls. 14–17.
29 BAPD 213254; less close 213244. 213268; H. R. W. Smith, Der Lewismaler (1939) no. 19 pl. 12a.
30 Smith (supra n. 29) 16. 18.
31 AK 5234 from grid Θ2/15 προς I2/15, layer 3, Π3, 25/6/2003; illustrated, Guide[2] 22, upper r.; Kourayos 2006 (supra n. 7) pl. 192, IV.3.
32 Robertson 210–217. 221–223. 242–246. 255–259. The Washing Painter also derives from Polygnotos. S. B. Matheson, Polygnotos and Vase Painting in Classical Athens (1995) esp. 3–5, Chap. 2, goes no later than the Dinos Painter. For the final phase see T. Mannick (chapter 2) and L. Burn (chapter 3), in: O. Taplin – R. Wyles (eds.), The Pronomos Vase and its Context (2010) 5–31 citing recent work.
33 ARV[2] 1026–1064. See n. 32.
34 AK 5095 and AK 5097 from Grid Π1, layer 2, Π3 SF 2, 17/7/2008; illustrated in Guide[2] 68, lower l. with alien fragment on r.; AK 5096, two small fragments from this location, may also belong, preserving part of palmette; meander band; illustrated Guide[2] 69, lower l. with part of the palmette.
35 P. E. Arias – M. Hirmer, A History of 1000 Years of Greek Vase Painting, trans. and rev. B. Shefton [1961] 377–379. 382–383 pls. 219. 222; BAPD 217500. 218007; Taplin –Wyles (supra n. 32) figs. 0.0 [sic], nos. 11–15; fig. 0.2; 19–20 figs. 3.2–3.
36 Robertson 242–245.
37 BAPD 215288. 215220. 215758; compare the fluid torsos of the seated Argonauts on the Talos krater (BAPD 217518) and of Theseus on the krater BAPD 43429; G. Greco, RIA 8–9, 1985–1986, 1–35 fig. 3.
38 BAPD 215254. 215325; Christie Painter e.g. BAPD 213576. 213577. 213612. 213612; Kleophon Painter, BAPD 215146; the much touted 'Meidian' element here surely represents direct influence of contemporary monumental painters more than its transmission via the Meidias Painter and his colleagues.
39 The running woman on side A of the Talos krater and on the Theseus krater from Serra di Vaglio Greco (supra n. 37) 16 fig. 11.
40 BAPD 217555 (Painter of Louvre G 433); generally BAPD 215318. 215321, both Manner of the Dinos Painter; cf. also details on the Dinos Painter's Atalanta krater in Bologna (BAPD 215259) and the feet of the sailors on the Talos krater (supra n. 37).
41 AK 5273 from grid Π1, West T124, layer 2, Π3, 15/6/10.
42 Matheson (supra n. 32) 283–287.
43 On the relation of the Talos Painter to the Dinos Painter and Polygnotan Group see Robertson 259.
44 AK 103 found between Building A and the South complex, grid Λ5, layer 2, 25/5/08.
45 AK 4955, surface find South of Building E, Π3, SF2, 22/8/2007.
46 ARV[2] 1339,4. 5 (below); BAPD 217526. 217527; less close the drapery of Hephaistos on Palermo 2365, BAPD 217525. For the wings see also Taranto 143544, BAPD 41697, Manner of the Talos Painter.
47 ARV[2] 1338,4 (above), BAPD 217521; Robertson 259.
48 AK 4147 from Building Δ, grid A10 (N T4), layer 1, Π1, SF1, 23/6/2004.
49 Karlsruhe 75.36, BAPD 6195; Berlin Painter, neck amphora in Manchester, BAPD 201873.
50 Guide[2] 22. 60.
51 Rubensohn (supra n. 9) 128–129 pl. 22,13.
52 Cf. the range, mostly kraters, reported from Minoa on Amorgos, all from non-mortuary context, in M. Manoledakis, in: D. Paleothodoros (ed.), The Contexts of Painted Pottery in the Ancient Mediterranean World (Seventh – Fourth Centuries BCE) (2012), esp. 73–76.
53 Supra n. 41.

27 The Attic Phiale in Context. The Late Archaic Red-figure and Coral-red Workshops

Athena Tsingarida

The mesomphalic phiale in clay is a shape derived from Near-Eastern metalware. It was introduced into the Greek repertoire in the Geometric period and was soon copied in clay. Attic phialai in clay are occasionally known from the middle of the seventh century BC, but the shape becomes popular from the middle of the sixth century, most probably under the influence of the Nikosthenic workshop.[1] In a previous paper, I proposed relating two important groups of Six polychrome phialai to the ambit of the Nikosthenic workshop through the work of the Krokotos Group and the Theseus Painter, both known to have used this special technique on other shapes than phialai.[2]

In his study on the Phiale Painter, J. Oakley already noted that the shape was rare in red-figure.[3] This paper examines a small group of red-figure phialai, dating from the last quarter of the sixth century to the first quarter of the fifth century BC.[4] It further discusses the attribution of two pieces with ornamental patterns[5] and a group of undecorated coral-red phialai, which belong to the type of the so-called "Attic Achaemenid phialai",[6] all dated to the Late Archaic – Early Classical periods. The techniques and types of decoration associated with these vases might suggest unexpected workshop connections, and therefore, raise issues about the organization of Late Archaic Athenian workshops and the diversity of their production.

A Small Group of Oversized and Elaborate Products

Five pieces, three decorated with figures and two without, were first examined by M. Robertson in his publication of the oversized red-figure phiale, which is signed by Douris and now is at the Villa Giulia.[7] As noted by Robertson "they do not form a group in a stylistic sense but they stand apart from anything else and there are interrelationships between them".[8] These interrelationships might point to a common workshop.

Two of these phialai bear complex, multi-figured decoration on both the inside and the outside.[9] Such spectacular compositions, covering both the interior and the exterior of the vase, are rare on phialai since the shape usually displays decoration only in the interior zone and occasionally on some later examples on the omphalos.[10] It has been already noted that crowded compositions on either side of large-scaled, open drinking vessels, such as the phiale and the cup, seem to be closely associated with Euphronios the potter's workshop.[11] Although the three phialai decorated with figures cannot be attributed to one vase-painter, they might be further related on stylistic grounds to painters who have been associated with the workshop of the potter Euphronios at one stage of their careers.

The fragmentary phiale at the Getty (Fig. 1),[12] decorated with an Amazonomachy in the interior and with coral-red on the outside and on the interior side of the rim and tondo, was convincingly attributed to the Foundry Painter by M. Robertson,[13] a painter who decorated several cups made by the potter Euphronios.[14]

The large-sized phiale from the South terrace of the Etruscan sanctuary of Pyrgi[15] was attributed to Onesimos by D. Williams.[16] The distinctive ornamental border on the interior made of a frieze of addorsed palmettes with long pointed central fronts and lyre-formed surrounding tendrils is similar to that on several other cups by the painter.[17] Furthermore, the figures on the Pyrgi phiale seem to resemble most closely those on several other cups, surely works by Onesimos: the frontal face of the symposiast on the interior of the Pyrgi phiale finds parallels in other works,[18] and the distinctive rendering of straight strands and hair in dilute gloss on the beheaded youth on the outside are common with those of both the athlete on a cup at the Louvre[19] and those of the scalp on a warrior's helmet at the Getty, both pieces by Onesimos.[20] The latter decorated nine cups signed Euphronios *epoiesen* and is, therefore, closely associated to the potter.[21]

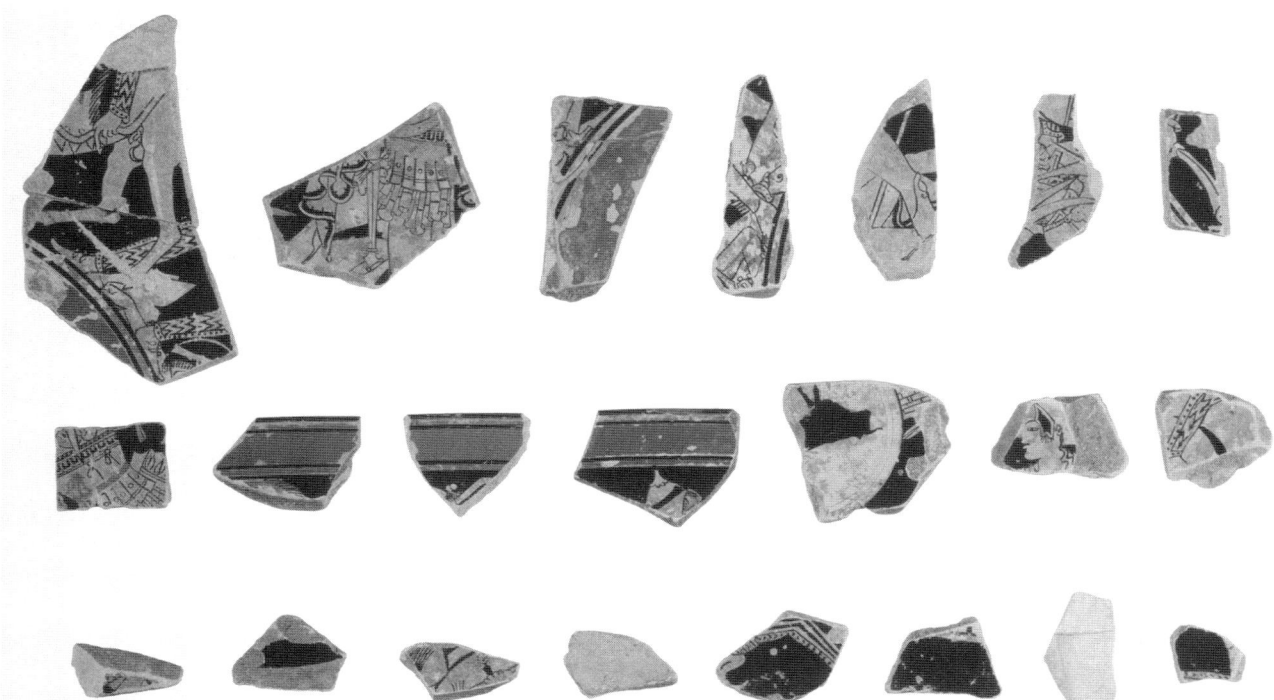

Fig. 1 Phiale (fragments) attributed to the Foundry Painter, Malibu, J. Paul Getty Museum 90.AE.38 (© The J. Paul Getty Museum, Villa Collection, Malibu, California).

The third phiale is signed by Douris as a painter and bears an incomplete *epoiesen* inscription.[22] Robertson suggested that the name ending in ...*kros* or ...*chros* might be that of Smikros, who is known as a painter. I noted elsewhere that if it is, indeed, Smikros who potted the Douris phiale, he most probably did it in the ambit of Euphronios' workshop.[23] Smikros and Euphronios have close ties, and according to Beazley, Smikros was Euphronios' imitator in the Pioneers' Group.[24] (See Hedreen in this volume) At the time when Euphronios regularly signed *epoiesen*, he made most of the contemporary oversized cups, which are the same kind of elaborate and exceptional products as the phiale signed by Smikros.[25] Moreover, Douris, who signed the figured phiale in his early period, is also known for the decoration of vases for Euphronios' workshop during the same period.[26]

The interiors of the bowls of two phialai without figural decoration are covered with deep coral-red gloss and are adorned with two decorative friezes around the now missing omphaloi (Figs. 2. 3; Color Pl. 32A).[27] On the basis of ornament, they were both associated either with the early work of the Berlin Painter (because of the distinctive lotus buds with double leaves)[28] or with the early work of Douris (because of the running spirals with drops).[29] Despite the slight difference noted in the profiles of their shape, 76.AE.96.1 being thicker and curving more than the flatter 76.AE.96.2,[30] C. Cardon compared the potter's work with that of the oversized coral-red cup in Munich, decorated by Euphronios and made by Chachrylion.[31] Stylistic links were acknowledged between Euphronios and the Berlin Painter, and Euphronios is further associated with the coral-red technique in his later career as a potter.[32] For both reasons, Cardon considered him as a likely candidate for the potter who made the two coral-red phialai.[33]

Both the painting and the potting of these phialai suggest a link with a single workshop, most probably that of the potter Euphronios. This association may be further reflected in the distinctive coral-red applied on three of these vases.[34] In a recent article, clay analysis of the coral-red applied on these vessels showed that the clay used to make the special gloss was the same as that used to make the rest of the vase, and that the potter used a single three-stage firing, two features that might be considered characteristic of the workshop.[35]

The Attic "Achaemenid phialai" in Clay and Cups of the Class of Agora P10359

I would like now to turn to another group of phialai that often used coral-red as part of their decoration, namely, the so-called Attic Achaemenid phialai in clay, a shape that has an offset high concave rim and often horizontal flutes on the bowl.[36] Some samples may be entirely black (Fig. 4), but most of them bear bichrome decoration made of coral-red on the bowl (inside and outside) and black gloss on the rim (Fig. 5). According to B. Sparkes who first

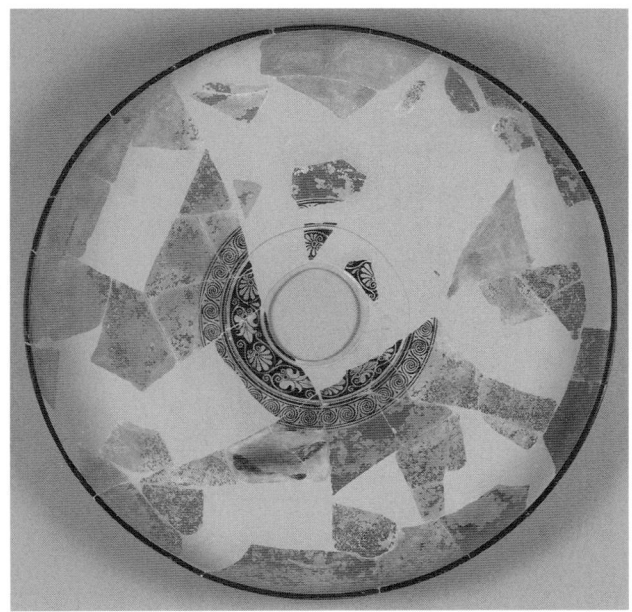

Fig. 2 Phiale attributed to the Berlin Painter, Malibu, J. Paul Getty Museum 76.AE.96.1 (© The J. Paul Getty Museum, Villa Collection, Malibu, California).

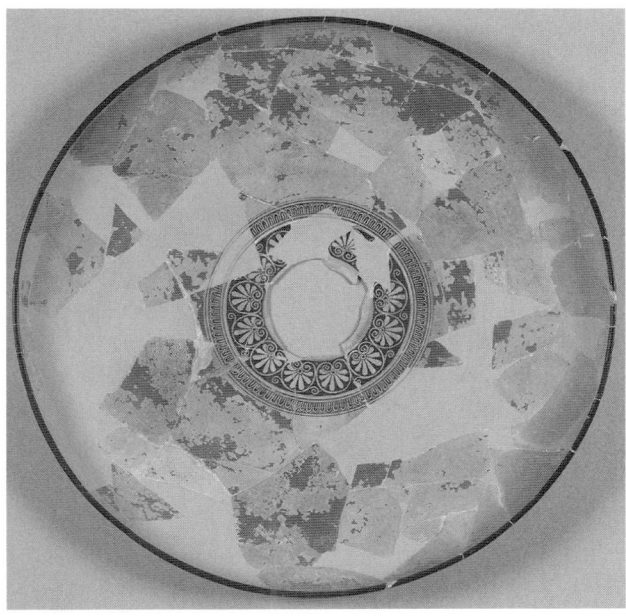

Fig. 3 Phiale attributed to the Berlin Painter, Malibu, J. Paul Getty Museum 76.AE.96.2 (© The J. Paul Getty Museum, Villa Collection, Malibu, California).

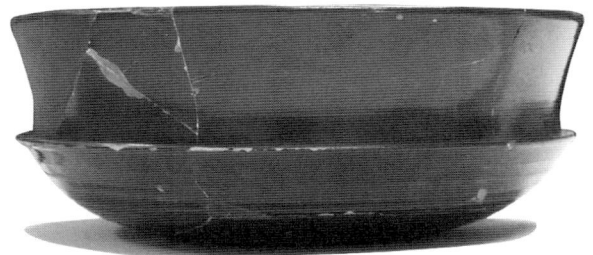

Fig. 4 Achaemenid phiale in clay, black-gloss, ca. 500–480, Athens, Agora Museum P 9274 (Photo: Author).

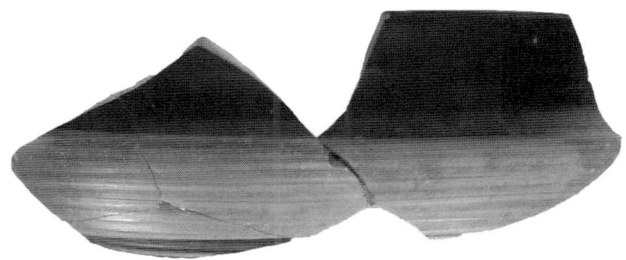

Fig. 5 Achaemenid phiale in clay, black-gloss and coral-red, ca. 500–480 BC, Athens, Agora Museum P 23118 (Photo: Author).

studied the group, the production started in the first quarter of the fifth century BC.[37] The date is provided for several phialai from the material assemblage of their context in well-deposits from the Agora[38] and in a tomb group from Valle Pegga in Spina.[39] Based on the similarity of shape, these early pieces may be grouped together and attributed to one workshop. They all display a similar shallow bowl decorated with horizontal shallow flutes made of slightly concave grooves and shallow edges, and they exhibit a sharply angled articulation of the bowl's rim. A few other phialai with similar features might be also attributed to the same workshop and dated to the same period (Fig. 6).[40]

Although previous scholarship compared these phialai to the fluted phiale by Sotades and dated them to the middle of the fifth century BC,[41] Sotades adopts a very different rendering of horizontal flutes, and does not use the distinctive, lustrous intentional coral-red gloss applied on the Late Archaic Achaemenid phialai. On the Sotadean phialai, the flutes join a more protruding edge and have distinctly curved mouldings (Fig. 7, London, British Museum 1894, 0719.2), while the red used on them is a matt colour applied after firing.[42] This distinctive rendering of the flutes might be considered as a transitional type between the early fifth-century Achaemenid phialai and a later and distant parallel, Agora P31465, from a "Public Dining Place" in the Athenian Agora (Fig. 7). This later phiale, dated to 420's, is grooved to create the effect of gadrooning. The wall composed of a series of convex flutes is rare in Attic pottery and is only known from a black-glossed pyxis from the Athenian Agora, also dated to the last quarter of the fifth century BC.[43] The grooves on the phiale from the "Public Dining Place" alternate black-gloss and dark red, but, as on the Sotades phiale and mastoi, the colour used here only superficially resembles the coral-red and is obtained by a matt gloss.[44]

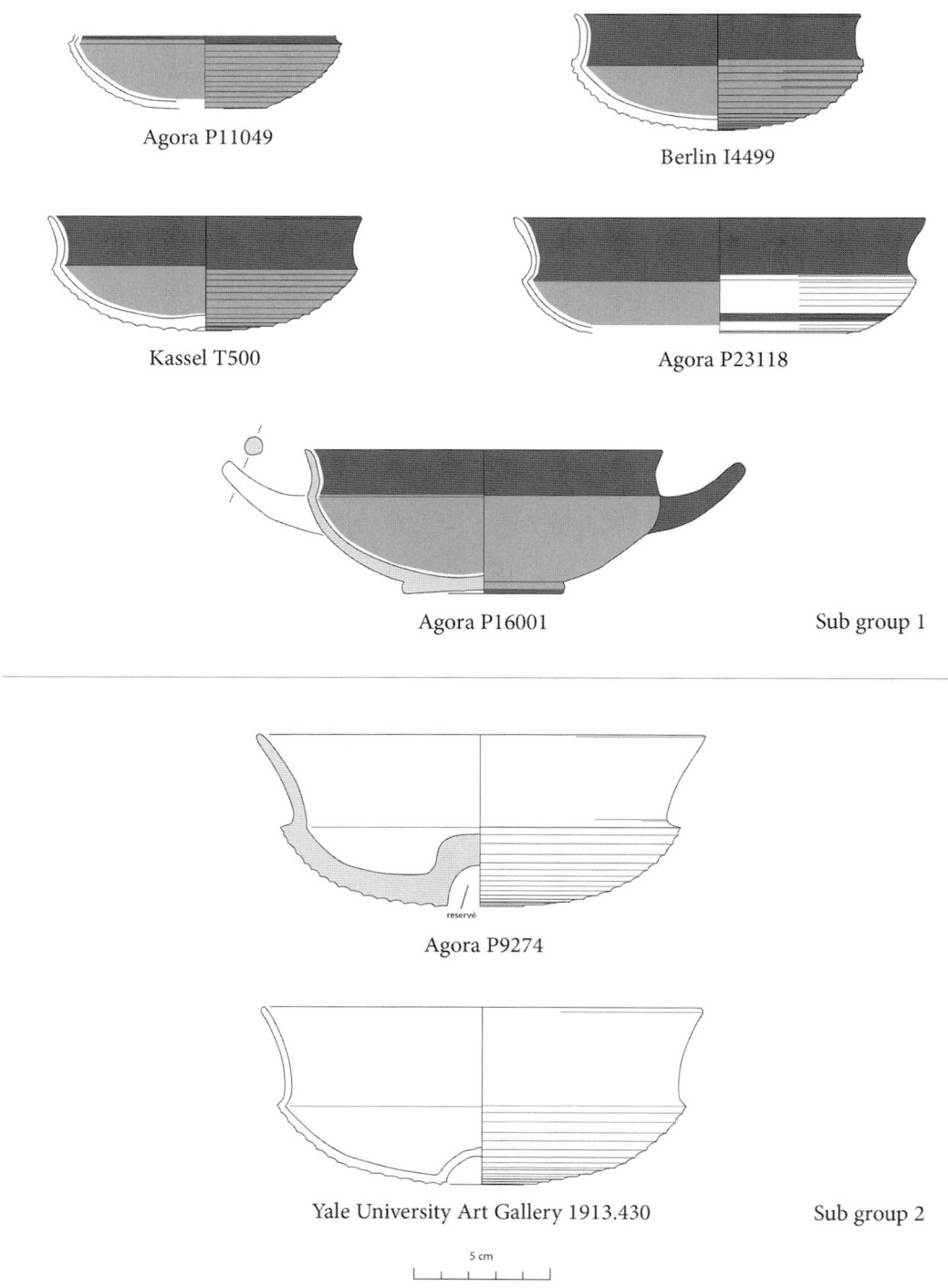

Fig. 6 Profile drawings of Achaemenid phialai in clay, dating to ca. 500–480 BC (Drawings: Author. Illustrator and plate: A. Stoll – N. Bloch, CReA-Patrimoine, ULB).

The phialai, attributed to the early fifth-century workshop, might be organized into two sub-groups (Fig. 6). Those, more numerous, in sub-group 1, are small-scaled, with an average diameter of 10–11 cm. They either lack the omphalos or display a very shallow central button, and are regularly decorated with coral red on the bowl.[45] Although clearly from the same workshop, since they display a similar profile of the fluted bowl and their rims are strongly offset, the phialai in sub-group 2 (Fig. 6) have a larger diameter of ca. 15–6 cm, a higher rim, and bear an omphalos.[46] They may be either entirely black or bichrome. In his study of the black-gloss pottery from

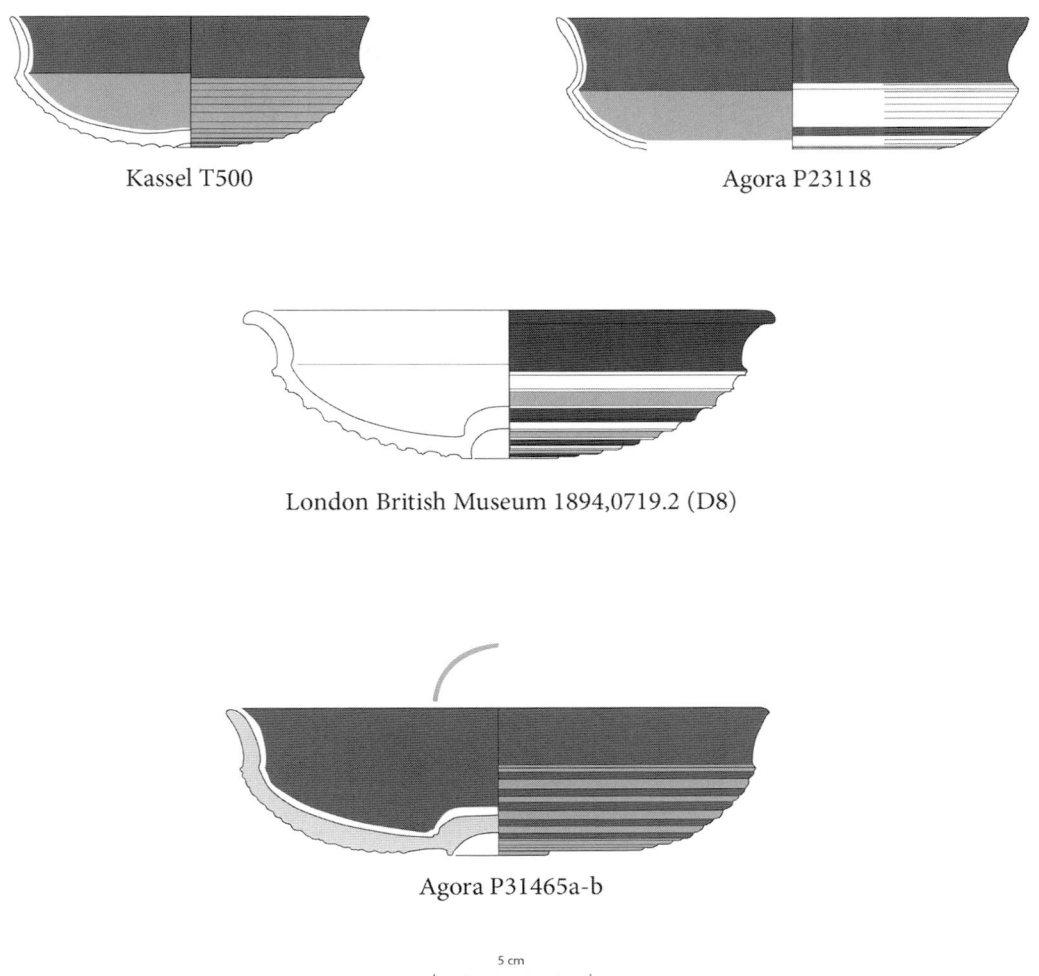

Fig. 7 Profile drawings of Achaemenid phialai in clay, Kassel T500 and Agora P23118 (ca. 500–480 BC), London British Museum 1894.0719.2 by Sotades (ca. 480–450 BC), Agora P 31465a–b (ca. 430–420 BC) (Drawings: Author. Illustrator and plate: A. Stoll – N. Bloch, CReA-Patrimoine, ULB).

the Athenian Agora, B. Sparkes related these Achaemenid phialai in clay with a contemporary Class of small and stemless cups, he named the Class of Agora P10359 (Fig. 6, Agora P16001). He attributed both products to the same workshop on the basis of the potter's work and the common use of coral-red.[47]

Figured and Non-figured Phialai

In her study of coral-red, B. Cohen notes that "throughout its history this glaze has been a function of potters rather than painters", and that "it [this glaze] is also strongly associated with artisans who might be called painters-potters".[48] Recent scientific investigation further confirmed that the elaborate technology used to make coral red was not commonly held knowledge.[49] If this special technique is the result of only a few skilled potters, are there any other elements that might suggest links between contemporary coral-red phialai decorated with figures, such as the oversized vessels attributed to the potter Euphronios, and the non-figured, coral-red, Achaemenid phialai and cups?

The name piece of the Class of Agora P10359 is the only known cup from the Class that is decorated with a figure on the inside. The black-figure Melitaean dog on the medallion, although difficult to attribute (Fig. 8; Color Pl. 32C),[50] may provide some evidence of connections with painters who worked in the Chachrylion/Euphronios workshop.

It is generally acknowledged that the Melitaean breed is more commonly depicted in Attic iconography from the 480s onwards,[51] while the few known representations of the dog on late sixth-, early fifth-century vases seem to concentrate on cups. From the 304 entries of dog representations on Attic vases listed in the BAPD, there are only a few examples of Melitaean dogs dated to the Late Archaic period. A significant part is attributed to cup-painters, such as Skythes,[52] Euphronios,[53] the Hegesiboulos Painter[54] and Onesimos[55], all vase-painters associated with either Chachrylion, Hegesiboulos or Euphronios the potter.

On technical and stylistic grounds, the dog on the cup from the Class of Agora P10350 recalls those seen on late sixth- and early fifth-century cups, attributed to the Hegesiboulos Painter, Euphronios or Onesimos.[56] The luxurious coat of the animal is indicated by the use of a few incisions and numerous relief lines, and its eye is incised. The combination of these two techniques, incision and relief line, suggests that the vase-painter was familiar with both black and red-figure, a characteristic of some pottery workshops active at the turn of the fifth century. The rendering of the dog resembles that of the dogs attributed to either the Hegesiboulos Painter or Euphronios. They share the large paws, the bushy tail and the alert ears. The almond-shaped eye with an elongated lachrymal canal of the Agora dog may be further paralleled with that of the dog on the coral-red cup from the 3rd Ephoria, attributed to Euphronios or the Hegesiboulos Painter (Fig. 9). The short ground line on which the animal stands on the Agora cup is indicated by a narrow black gloss band, a rather rare device, known from a few earlier cups and plates by Psiax,[57] or from single figures depicted on contemporary amphorae[58] or cups[59] attributed to Euphronios.[60]

Another possible link connecting Euphronios' workshop with the production of the early fifth-century Achaemenid phialai and cups of the Class of Agora 10350 may be found in the distinctive device used on the interior of the coral-red cups of the Class of Agora 10350. The interior of these vases is covered with coral-red and decorated with a black dotted circle within two larger glossed circles (Fig. 10; Color Pl. 32B). Two similar black circles border the interior coral-red band of the fragmentary phiale attributed to the Foundry Painter (Fig. 1), while, on the same vase, a smaller glossed circle frames the, now missing, omphalos.

The profiles of the few small coral-red cups of Type C with a concave lip, attributed to the workshop of Euphronios, are different from that of the coral red cups from the Class of Agora P10350: the former has an offset rim on the interior, while this feature is missing from the latter.[61] Yet, they share a similar display of coral-red and black gloss on the exterior: the bowl is covered with coral-red and the offset lip is black.

The evidence of the assemblage of pottery from an early fifth-century grave in Spina might also point to a connection with the workshop of Euphronios. The unspoiled grave T41D from the Valle Pegga at the Ferrara Museum[62] contains three Attic imports: an Achaemenid black-gloss phiale (sub-group 2 in our Class), a red-figure kylix attributed to the Antiphon Painter[63] and a rare early type of neck-pelike attributed to the Berlin Painter.[64] Although there are several known burials in Spina which yielded vases that had been kept by the deceased or his family for more than one generation, in grave T41D all the Attic vessels date to the early fifth century. The red-figure cup and the pelike were decorated by painters who were associated with Euphronios. The modelling of the cups decorated by the Antiphon Painter is generally attributed to Euphronios the potter,[65] while the red-figure neck-pelike of special shape is only known by another "replica" also from Spina, decorated by the Berlin Painter in an early stage of his career,[66] and by three unattributed

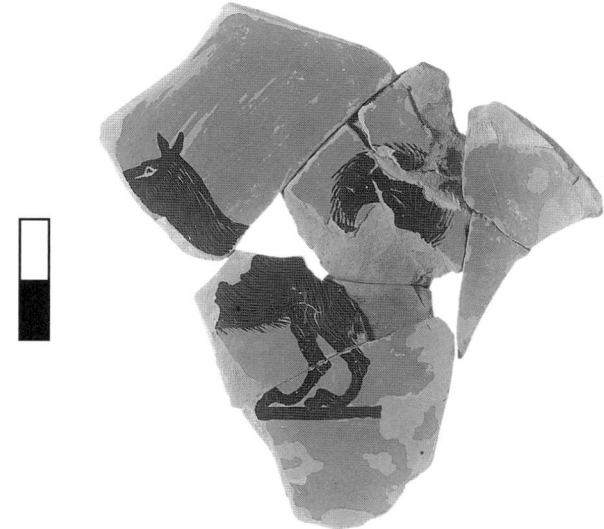

Fig. 8 Athens, Agora Museum P 10350: black-figure dog (© American School of Classical Studies at Athens, The Athenian Agora).

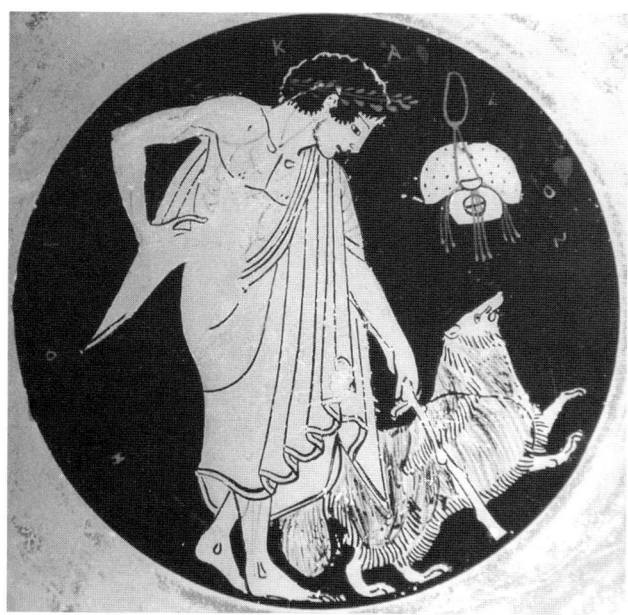

Fig. 9 Athens, 3rd Ephoria A5040 (Photo: after Stēlē: tomos eis mnēmēn Nikolaou Kontoleontos [1980] pl. 146).

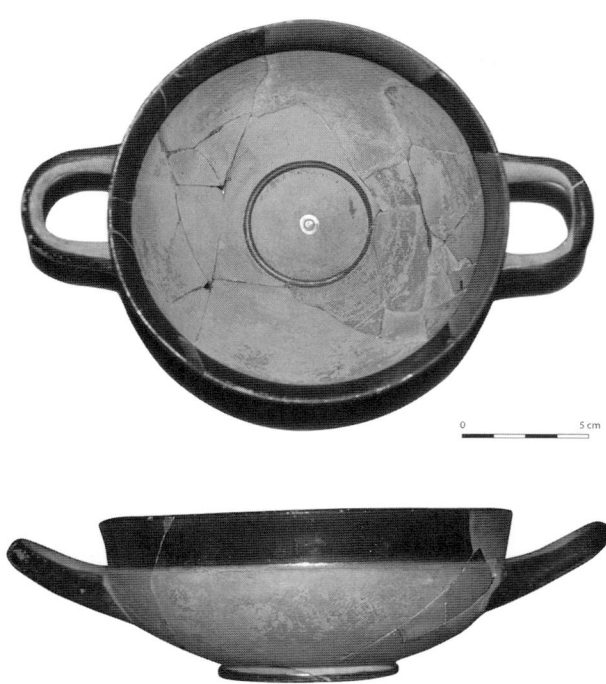

Fig. 10 Athens, Agora Museum P 16001 (Photos: Author).

black-figure examples.[67] In his seminal study on this shape, D. von Bothmer focused on the role of the Pioneers, and especially Euphronios, in the development of the neck-pelike from which stemmed the canonical black and red-figure pelikai.[68] Although arguments arose about the impact of the workshop on the marketing and distribution of pottery,[69] earlier studies suggest that middlemen might have played a role in the diffusion of products of certain pottery workshops in certain geographical areas.[70] If this relation between workshops and certain areas of distribution is valid, the presence in the Spina grave of two vases, related to Euphronios the potter, might further suggest that the contemporaneous Attic Achaemenid phiale found in the same grave was also a product of the workshop imported at the same time.

Some Concluding Remarks about the Organization of LA Workshops

Earlier scholarship acknowledges that workshop associations remain a complex matter, and there is a significant amount of literature discussing the size and organisation of workshops producing wares decorated with figures in the Athenian Kerameikos.[71] Although the works of B. Sparkes, L. Talcott,[72] and S. R. Roberts,[73] to name but a few, demonstrate that plain black-gloss and cups decorated with figures were made within the same workshops, this question is not often fully considered in studies of red-figure production. In this paper, the analysis of a range of products that goes from the fine and elaborate oversized phialai to the small undecorated fluted phialai and stemless cups, makes us wonder if the same large workshop was not responsible for their production.

Recent studies confirm the association of Chachrylion the potter and Euphronios the painter in the production of small coral-red cups bearing figural decoration in the tondo.[74] They further point to the expertise of the potter Hegesiboulos in coral-red through several signed vases and his association with Euphronios through similarities in the potter's work on cups.[75] In addition to the special technique, stylistic and iconographical features allow us to relate the black-figure dog on the stemless cup of the Class of Agora 10350 with the animals depicted on coral-red cups attributed to Euphronios or Hegesiboulos, and to point to a common workshop for the production of both of the vases decorated with figures and those without.

In an article published in APP II, M. Padgett already associated the production of the cups from the Class of Agora P10359, the Achaemenid phialai and the later Rheneia coral-red cups with the Sotades workshop.[76] We have seen that the main group of Achaemenid phialai and the cups from the Class of Agora P10359 must be dated to the first quarter of the fifth century, a generation earlier than Sotades' activity, and that it is, most probably, related to the contemporaneous workshop of Euphronios. Yet, the close study of the Attic Achaemenid phialai and the cups from the Class of Agora P 10359 sheds further light on a possible affiliation between the workshops of Euphronios and Sotades. While a first link between Euphronios and Sotades may be already seen through the potter Hegesiboulos and the coral-red production,[77] the present paper points to the transitional role played by Sotades in the making of fluted phialai and mastoids (Fig. 7). The analysis of the potter's work suggests that the Sotades workshop continued the production of Achaemenid phialai but changed the concave fluting into convex ribbing, developing the distinctive feature of the few later Achaemenid phialai, dated to the second half of the fifth century.

It is important to note that these different products seem to address different geographical and cultural areas. The elaborate, oversized phialai were found in Etruscan sanctuaries and graves, the small coral-red cups decorated with figures seems to have been made for a local Athenian clientele, while the fluted phialai and the coral-red cups of the Class of Agora P 10350 were mainly distributed to the eastern and western regions of the ancient Mediterranean world.[78] If this distinctive distribution pattern is valid, it might explain the association of these different products with one workshop for economic reasons. A diversified production caters to a wider variety of markets and demands, and helps the workshop to be profitable and remain a viable business.

Acknowledgements

I would like to thank John Oakley for inviting me to take part in APP III and for his great patience in collecting my paper. In particular, I also wish to thank J. Mertens (Metropolitan Museum of Art, New York), M. Padgett (Princeton, University Museum), S. Sarti (Soprintendenza per i Beni Archeologici della Toscana) and D. Saunders (J. Paul Getty Museum, Malibu) for sharing references and documents about the subject. I am deeply grateful to A. Stoll and N. Bloch (infographists at the CReA-Patrimoine, Université libre de Bruxelles) for preparing the plates and copying my profile drawings on Illustrator, and to S. Brook for improving my English. Many thanks are also due to the staff of the J. Paul Getty Museum for providing photographs and to Mrs J. Jordan (ASCSA, The Agora Excavations) for granting the permission to publish material from the Agora.

Notes

1 I. Wehgartner, Attsich weissgrundige Keramik. Maltechniken, Werkstätten, Formen, Verwendung (1983) 176 n. 47.
2 A. Tsingarida, in: D. Kurtz et al. (eds.), Essays in Classical Archaeology for Eleni Hatzivassiliou (1977–2007) (2008) 105–114.
3 J. H. Oakley, The Phiale Painter (1990) 54 and n. 368.
4 Pyrgi, Excavations of the southern area of the sanctuary; Gravisca, Excavations 73.10301; Malibu, Getty Museum 90.AE.38; Rome, Villa Giulia (ex-Getty Museum 81.AE.213; 85.AE.18).
5 Malibu, J.Paul Getty Museum 76.AE.96.1; 76.AE.96.2.
6 For this group, its distinctive features and chronology, see Agora XII 105–106. For the name see n. 36.
7 M. Robertson, in: Greek Vases in the J. Paul Getty Museum 5, 1991, 92–95.
8 Robertson (supra n. 7) 93.
9 Pyrgi, Excavations of the Southern area of the sanctuary; Rome, Villa Giulia (ex-Getty Museum 81.AE.213, 85.AE.18).
10 Dated to the second half of the fifth century BC: Museum of Fine Arts, Boston 97.371: Oakley (supra n. 3) pl. 120; Berlin, Antikenmuseum F2310: CVA Berlin 3 Germany 22 pl. 135,3.
11 A. Tsingarida, in: Tsingarida, Shapes 194, and more generally, on the attribution of large scaled cups and phialai to the workshop of the potter Euphronios, 188–193.
12 Malibu, J. Paul Getty Museum 90.AE.38, BAPD 24018.
13 Robertson (supra n. 7) 93.
14 See J. D. Beazley, in: D. C. Kurtz (ed.), Greek Vases: Lectures by J. D. Beazley (1989) 78; H. Bloesch, Formen attischen Schalen (1940) 71 no. 13; 73–74 nos. 18. 19. 20. 22; 79 no. 51.
15 M. P. Baglione, in: J. Christiansen – T. Melander (eds.), Proceedings of the 3rd Symposium on Ancient Greek and Related Pottery (1988) 17–24.
16 CVA British Museum 9 Great Britain 17 15. 23; the excavator, M. P. Baglione, initially attributed it to the Brygos Painter although she already pointed out the similar palmette border on the Medea cup by Onesimos: Malibu, J. Paul Getty Museum 79.AE.17, M. Ohly-Dumm, J. Paul Getty Museum Journal 9, 1981, 5–22.
17 E.g.: London, British Museum GR 1867.5-8.1061, ARV^2 455,9; 1654: CVA British Museum 9 Great Britain 17 23; Berlin F 2280–2281 and Vatican frr.: ARV^2 19,1–2: D. Williams, JbBerlMus 18, 1976, 9–23; Malibu, J. Paul Getty Museum 79.AE.17 & 19 (BAPD 7507).
18 E.g.: Rome, Villa Giulia (ex-Getty Museum 83.AE.362), BAPD 13363: the young Astyanax in the tondo; Paris, Musée du Louvre G291 and frr: the athlete in the tondo, ARV^2 322,36; BAPD 203286.
19 Paris, Musée du Louvre G297: ARV^2 322,35; 1706; BAPD 203285.
20 Malibu, J. Paul Getty Museum 86.AE.311: D. Williams, in: Greek Vases at the J. Paul Getty Museum 5, 1991, 47 fig. 7a.
21 ARV^2 313,2. 318,1; 318,2; 319,5; 319,6; 322,27; 325,79; 320,8; Rome, Villa Giulia (ex-Getty 83.AE.362), and probably ARV^2 330,4.
22 Rome, Villa Giulia (ex-Getty Museum 81.AE.213; 85.AE.18)
23 Tsingarida (supra n. 11) 192–193.
24 ARV^2 20.
25 Tsingarida (supra n. 11) 192–193.
26 D. Buitron-Oliver, Douris, a Master-Painter of Athenian Red-figure Vases (1995) 8–9. 67–68; see also for the potter's work typical of Euphronios: Bloesch (supra n. 14) nos. 2. 9.
27 Malibu, J. Paul Getty Museum 76.AE.96.1; 76.AE.96.2: BAPD 5732. 5733.
28 C. Cardon, GettyMusJ 6/7, 1978–1979, 135–137.
29 Robertson (supra n. 7) 94–95.
30 For a photo that shows the two phialai in side view, Cardon (supra n. 28) 132 figs. 3. 4.
31 Munich, Staatliche Antikensammlungen und Glyptothek 2620, ARV^2 16,17; 1619; Para 322. 379; $BAdd^2$ 153; BAPD 200080.
32 B. Cohen, The Colors of Clay. Special Techniques in Athenian Vases (2006) 49–50.
33 Cardon (supra n. 28) 137 and more recently Cohen (supra n. 32) 64–65 nos. 11. 12.
34 Malibu, J. Paul Getty Museum 90.AE.38; 76.AE.96.1; 76.AE.96.2.
35 M. S. Walton – E. Doehne – K. Trentelman – G. Chiari, in: K. Lapatin (ed.), Papers on Special Techniques in Athenian Vases (2008) 97–103.
36 The term was taken from Strong's typology of the phialai in metalware: D. E. Strong, Greek and Roman Gold and Silver Plates (1966) 76–77.
37 Agora XII 105–106. 272.
38 Athens, Agora Museum P11049, deposit D 15: 1, ca 525–480 BC (Agora XII 387); Agora Museum P23118, deposit H 12:15S, ca 520–480 BC (Agora XII 393); Agora Museum P9274, deposit M 17: 4, ca. 520–475 and shortly after (Agora XII 393).
39 Spina, Valle Pegga Tomb 41D.
40 In addition to the phialai reproduced in Fig. 6, one must add the following: Aigina, Archaeological Museum 1675 (I. Margreiter, Alt-Aegina II.3 [1988] no. 255); Aigina Archaeological Museum B51. B52 (D. Williams, AA 1987, 661 figs. 33. 35); two phialai from Olbia, Grave 30

(AA, 1914, 132 fig. 208); Phanagoria no. 335 (C. Morgan, Attic Fine Pottery of the Archaic and Hellenistic Periods in Phanagoria [2004] no. 335); Ruscino 0530 (J. J. July – P. Rouillard, La céramique attique de Ruscino, RANarb suppl 7 [1980] 174 no. 15) ; Ampurias no. 23 (E. Sanmarti-Grego – R. A. Santiago, RANarb 21, 1988, fig. 2 no. 23); Sardis, Att393 (J. S. Schaeffer – N. H. Ramage – C. H. Greenewalt, The Corinthian, Attic and Lakonian Pottery from Sardis [1997] pl. 52 Att393); Oria no. 663. no. 664 (G. Semerario, Ceramica greca e società nel archaico Lecce [1997] 209 nos. 663–664 fig. 186); Trachones, Geroulanos Collection (G. D. Weinberg, Hesperia 30, 1961, pl. 91a); Ferrara, Museo Nazional Archaeologico T41D, from Valle Pegga (ARV² 1669,772d).

41 See for instance, Berlin Antikenmuseum V.I. 4499: CVA Berlin 1 DDR 3 80 and Kassel Staatliche Museen T550, CVA Kassel 1 Germany 35 68 both dated to the middle of the fifth century BC.

42 For the difference between the coral-red and the matt red on the Sotadean fluted phialai and mastoi attested by stereomicroscope examination, Cohen (supra n. 32) 312.

43 Athens, Agora Museum P 16945, Agora XII no. 1303; see also M. Miller, Athens and Persia in the Fifth Century BC. A Study in Cultural Receptivity (1998) 140 figs. 45–46.

44 S. Rottroff – J. H. Oakley, Debris from a Public Dinning Place in the Athenian Agora, Hesperia Suppl. 25 (1992) 19 no. 201.

45 The following are part of the sub-group 1: Aigina, Archaeological Museum 1675 (Margreiter [supra n. 40] no. 255, black-glossed); two phialai from Olbia, coral-red and black-glossed, Grave 30 (AA 1914, 132 fig. 208); Phanagoria no. 335 (Morgan [supra n. 40] no. 335); Ruscino 0530 (July – Rouillard [supra n. 40] 174 no. 15); Ampurias n° 23 (Sanmarti-Grego – Santiago [supra n. 40] fig. 2 no. 23); Sardis, Att393 (Schaeffer – Ramage – Greenewalt [supra n. 40] pl. 52 Att393); Oria nos. 663. 664 (Semerario [supra n. 40] 209 n. 663–664 fig. 186).

46 Aigina Archaeological Museum B51. B52, black-glossed (Williams [supra n. 40] 661 figs. 33. 35); Trachones, Geroulanos collection (Weinberg [supra n. 40] pl. 91a); Ferrara, Museo Nazional Archaeologico T41D, from Valle Pegga (ARV² 1669,772d). The phialai from Trachones and Yale were considered by Beazley to be "replicas" and shaped from a different potter than Sotades (ARV² 1669,772d).

47 Agora XII 99. B. Sparkes dates the production of the cups to the first quarter of the fifth century BC/beginning of the second quarter.

48 Cohen (supra n. 32) 52.

49 Walton – Doehne – Trentelman – Chiari (supra n. 35) 103.

50 See recently, M. B. Moore, MetrMusJ 43, 2008, 17.

51 J. Busuttil, GaR 16, 1969, 205–208.

52 Former Basel Market, MM List, 1971, 53/70, circle of Skythes.

53 Athens, Third Ephoria, A5040: E. Papoutsaki-Serbeti, in: Stēlē: tomos eis mnēmēn Nikolaou Kontoleontos (1980) 321–327 pls. 146–147.

54 New York, Metropolitan Museum of Art 07.286.47: Moore (supra n. 50) 12 fig. 2.

55 Ex N. Hunt collection no. 8, attributed to Onesimos, Proto-Panaetian (current location unknown): Add² 393; BAPD 8839; Heidelberg, Ruprechts-Karl Universität 54: ARV² 328,116; Athens, Acropolis Museum 205: ARV² 329,133.

56 New York, Metropolitan Museum of Art 07.286.47 (The Hegesiboulos Painter); Athens, Third Ephoria, A5040 (Euphronios or the Hegesiboulos Painter); Ex N. Hunt collection no. 8 (current location unknown), attributed to Onesimos, Proto-Panaetian.

57 Psiax: St Petersburg, Hermitage B 9270, cup, ABV 294,22; BAPD 320368; Cohen (supra n. 32) 54–56 no. 7; Basel, Antikenmuseum Basel und Sammlung Ludwig Kä 421, plate, ABV 294,21; BAPD 320367; Cohen (supra n. 32) 199–200 no. 52.

58 Paris, Musée du Louvre G106, ARV² 18,3; Euphronios peintre à Athènes au VIe siècle avant J.-Chr (1990) 134–136 no. 18.

59 Paris, Musée du Louvre G106, ARV² 18,3; Euphronios (supra n. 58) 134–136 no. 18; in a tondo, London, British Museum GR 1837.6-9.58, ARV² 58,51; Euphronios (supra n. 58) 174–177 no. 36.

60 Although a single figure without patternwork is a distinctive feature of the Berlin Painter's compositions, when he adds a groundline the painter used short patterned strips to serve as a plinth for his images and not a simple reserved line as on the cup from the Class of Agora P 10350. For the development and use of single figures on open framed compositions, J. M. Hurwitt, AJA 81, 1977, 15–17.

61 For the profiles of two coral-red cups of Type C, Athens Agora Museum P32344 and Athens, Agora Museum P33221, attributed to Euphronios, see K. Lynch, The Symposium in Context. Pottery from a Late Archaic House near the Athenian Agora, Hesperia Suppl. 46 (2011) 228–229 figs. 84–85a.

62 Only the Attic figured vases were published. The complete material assemblage of the tomb may be seen on display at Ferrara, Museo Archeologico Nazionale, Room 1.

63 Ferrara, Museo Archeologico Nazionale 20508, ARV² 337,30bis, G. Riccioni, in: A. Cambitoglou (ed.), Studies in Honour of A. D. Trendall (1979) 125–128.

64 Ferrara, Museo Archeologico Nazionale T41, ARV² 205,114bis.

65 Bloesch (supra n. 14) 78–80 with one exception, Naples, Astarita 658, potted by Python, the regular potter of Douris, ARV² 340,71; BAdd² 1646; CVA British Museum 9 Great Britain 17 28.

66 Ferrara, Archaeological Museum T867, ARV² 205,114 (J. D. Beazley called T41 a replica of T867).

67 Eton College 16646, BAPD 16646; New York, Metropolitan Museum of Art 07.286.72, see Moore (supra n. 50) 39 fig. 28; Würzburg, Martin von Wagner Museum 233: for the group and further bibibliography, see D. von Bothmer, JHS 71, 1951, 46 nos. 4–6.

68 Von Bothmer (supra n. 67) 47.

69 R. Osborne, in S. Keay – S. Moser (eds.), Studies in Honour of B. Sparkes (2004) 78–94.

70 D. Palethodoros, MedHistR 22, 2007, 169.

71 Already by J. D. Beazley, in: Kurtz (supra n. 14) 39–59. "Workshop associations are still a complex matter, and in the relatively small area of the Kerameikos, shops must have been close together, movement between one and the next easy, and industrial espionage a daily occurrence": B. Sparkes, in: G. Boulter (ed.), Greek Art. Archaic into Classical (1985) 19.

72 E.g. for the Acrocups, Agora XII 96.
73 S. R. Roberts, Hesperia 55, 1986, especially 9–10.
74 Cohen (supra n. 32) 48–51; Lynch (supra n. 61) 93–95.
75 Cohen (supra n. 32) 50; D. Williams, in: Cohen (supra n. 32) 296.
76 M. Padgett, in: APP II 225–227.
77 Williams (supra n. 75) 296.
78 A. Tsingarida, in: Lapatin (supra n. 35) 193–199.

Color Plate 1

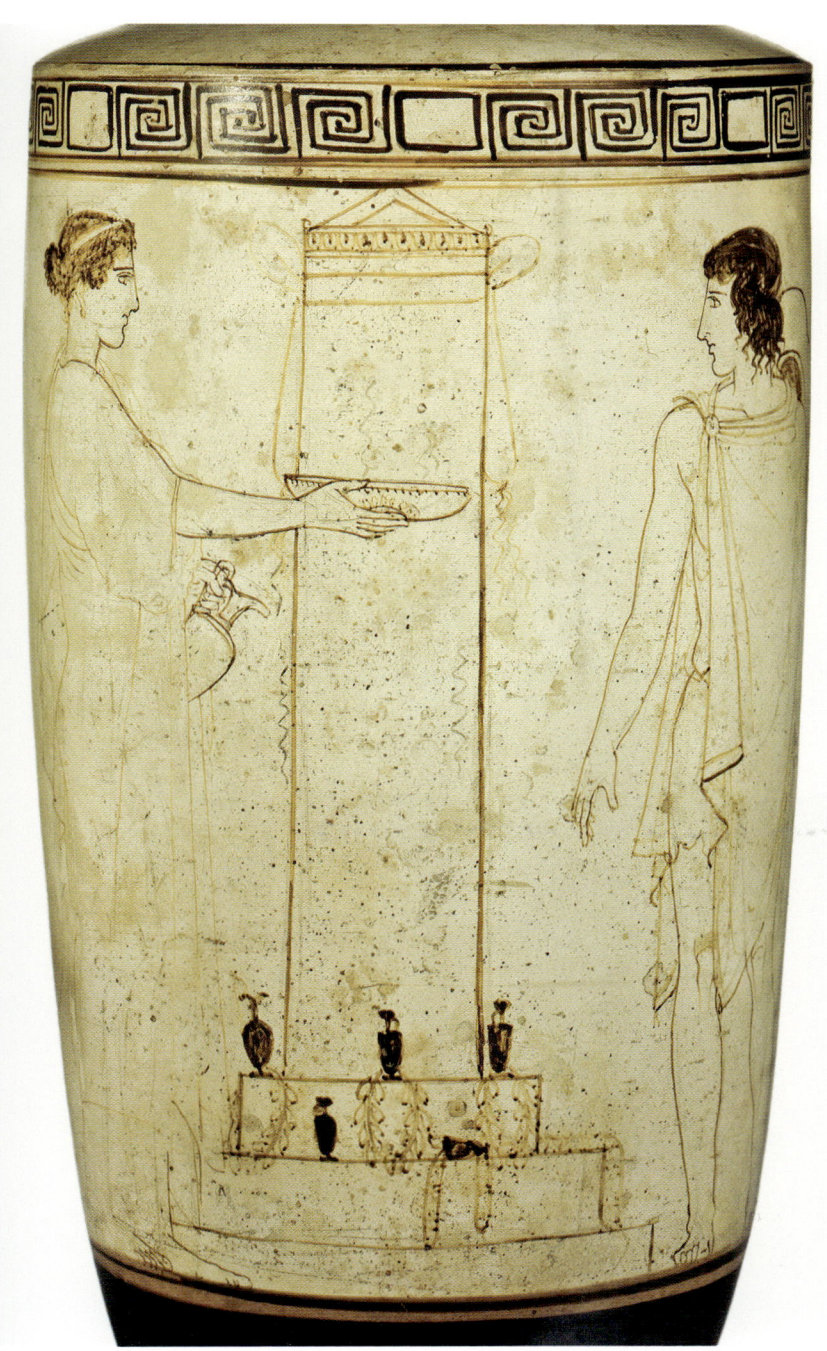

Pl. 1A. Attic white-ground lekythos attributed to the Bosanquet Painter. Basel, Antikenmuseum und Sammlung Ludwig, Kä 402. Photo: Antikenmuseum und Sammlung Ludwig/A. Voegelin.

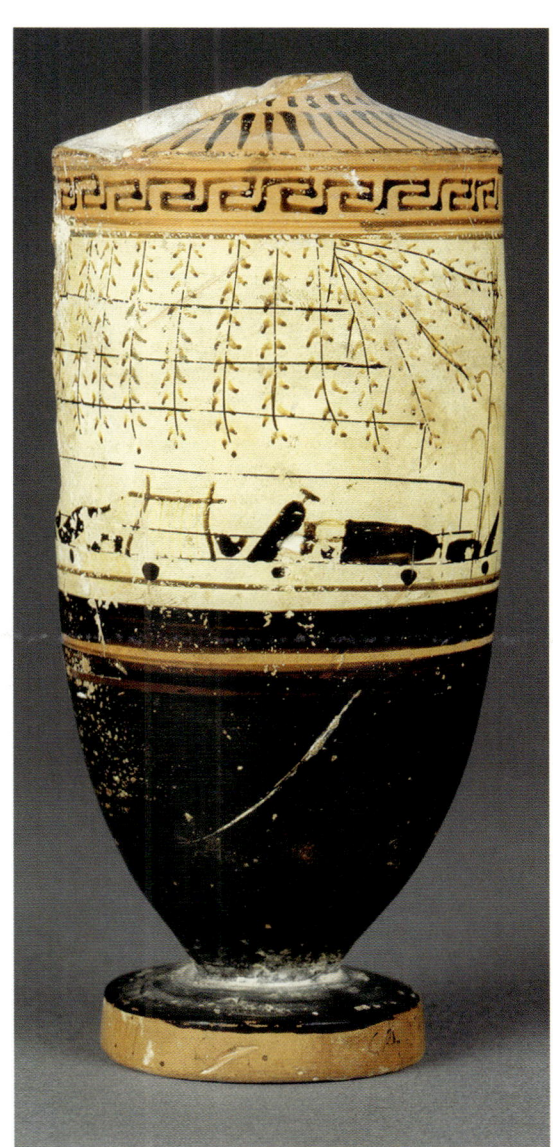

Pl. 1B. Unattributed Attic white-ground lekythos. Paris, Musée du Louvre CA 3758. Photo: Hervé Lewandowski, © RMN-Grand Palais/Art Resource, New York.

Color Plate 2

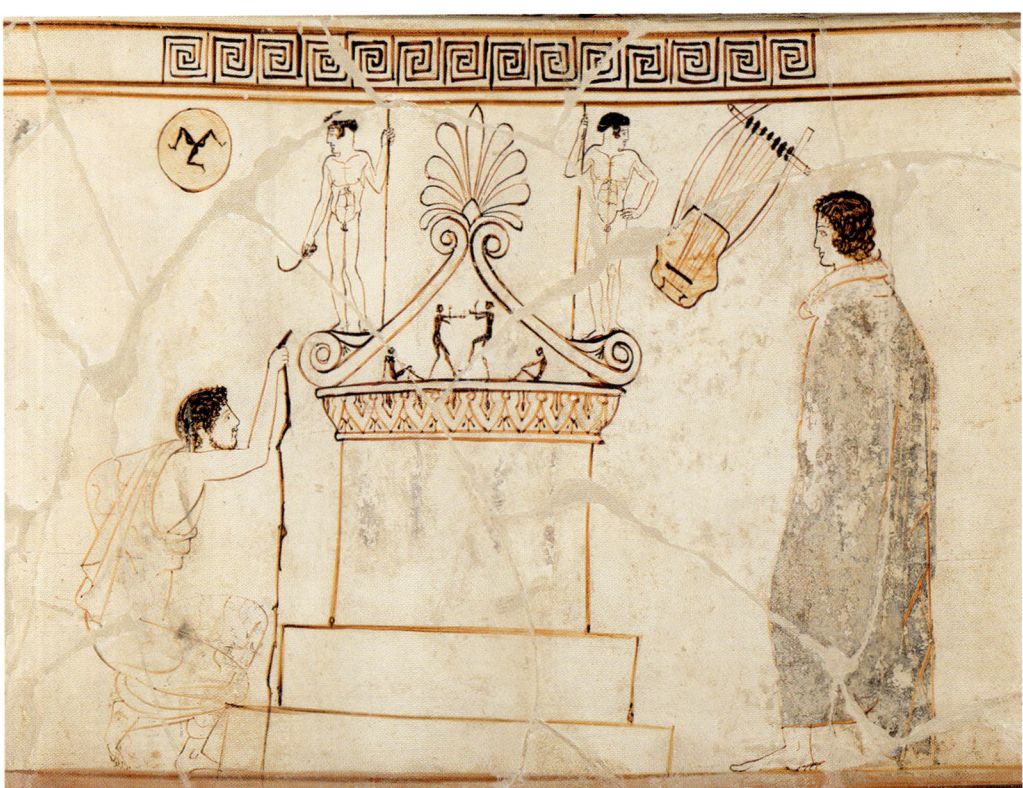

Pl. 2A. Attic white-ground lekythos attributed to the Thanatos Painter. Boston, Museum of Fine Arts 01.8080, Henry Lillie Pierce Fund. Photo: © 2013 Museum of Fine Arts, Boston.

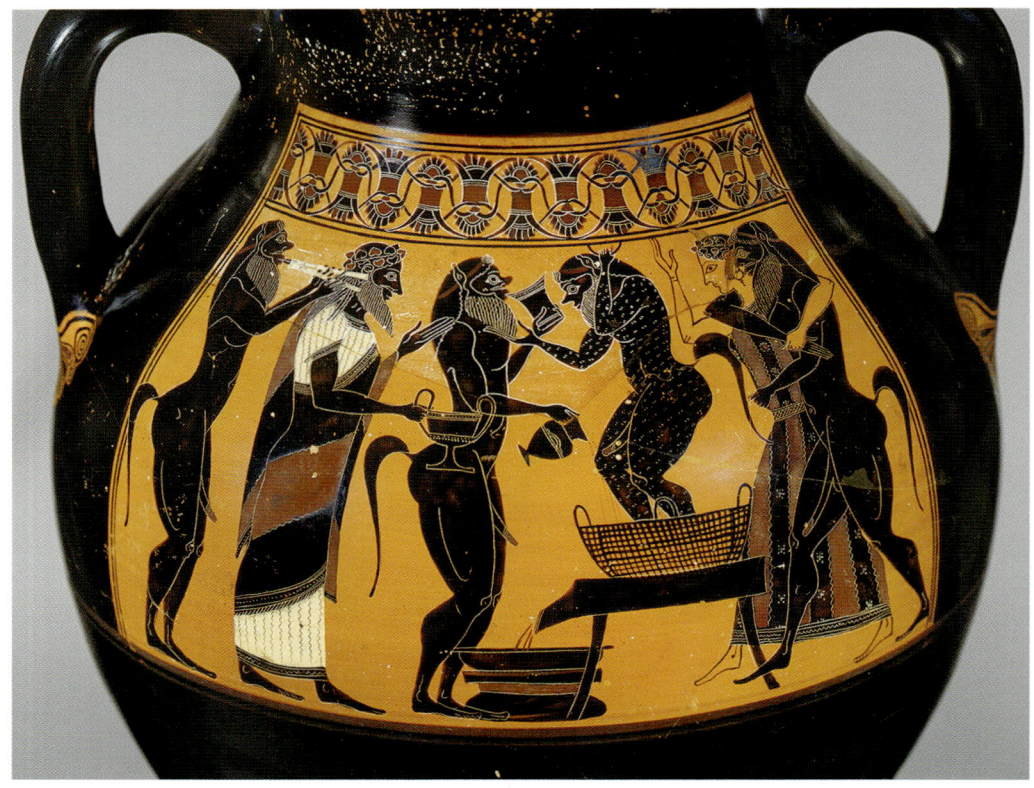

Pl. 2B. Dionysos with satyrs at the vintage: one satyr treads grapes in a basket, another dances with a maenad, panel on side A of Athenian black-figure amphora of type B, attributed to the Amasis Painter, ca. 540 BC, Basel, Antikenmuseum Basel und Sammlung Ludwig Kä 420 (Photo: Museum).

Color Plate 3

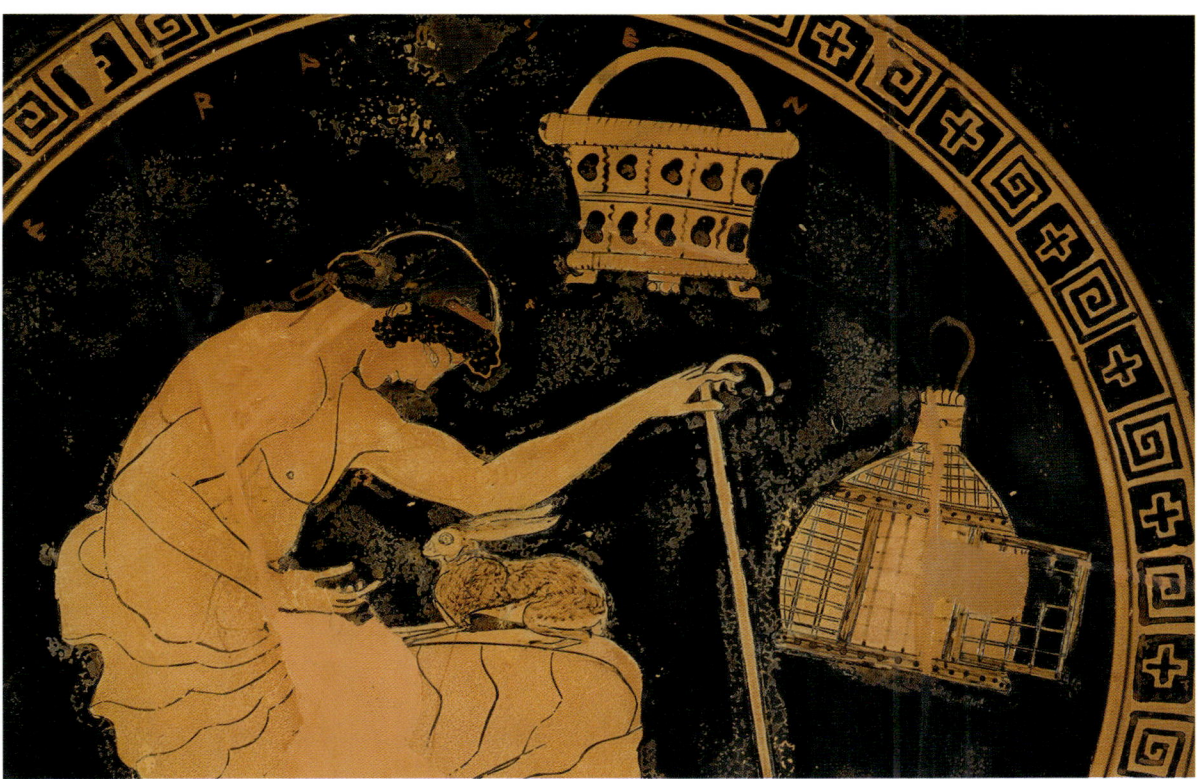

Pl. 3A. Youth with a hare on his lap and the animal's cage hanging at the right, detail, tondo of Athenian red-figure cup, by Douris, ca. 490 BC, private collection (Photo: private collection).

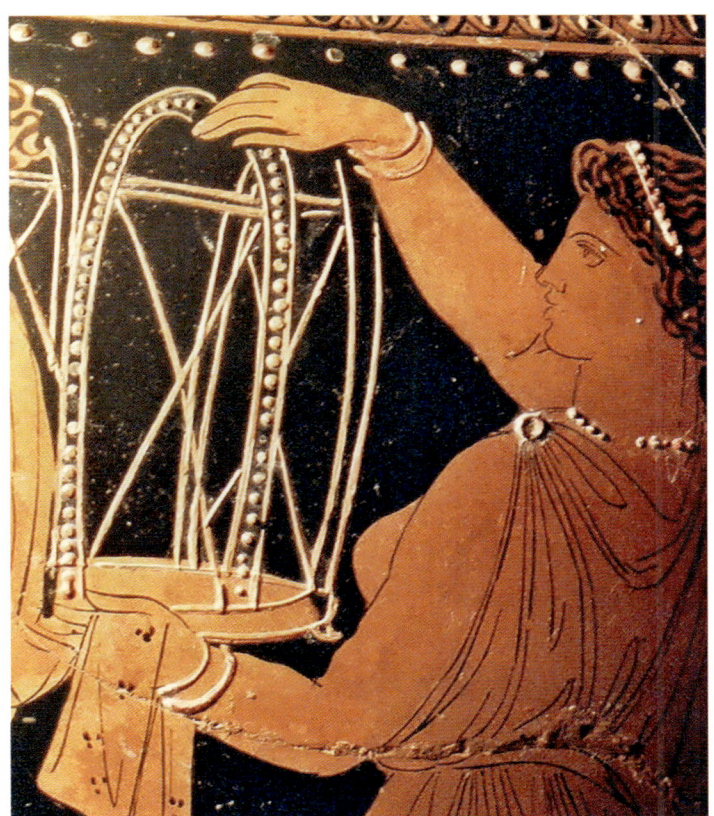

Pl. 3B. Woman carrying kaunon, detail, Athenian red-figure lebes gamikos (H. 46 cm), attributed to the Marsyas Painter, ca. 360 BC, The State Hermitage Museum, St. Petersburg, P 1906.175 (Photo: Author).

Color Plate 4

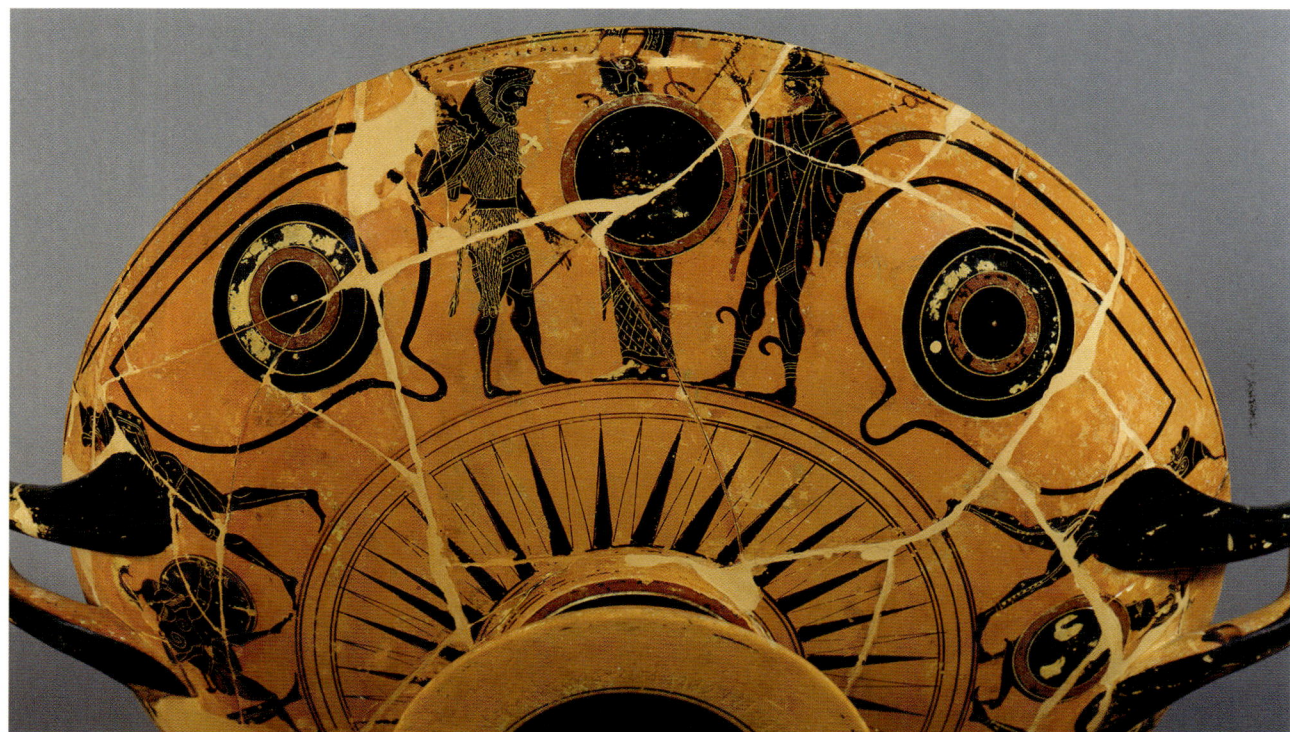

Pl. 4A. Eye cup attributed to the Lysippides Painter, Florence, Museo Archeologico Nazionale 74624, on loan to the Museo dell'Accademia Etrusca e della Città di Cortona. Photo courtesy of the Ministero per i Beni e le Attività Culturali – Soprintendenza per i Beni Archeologici della Toscana.

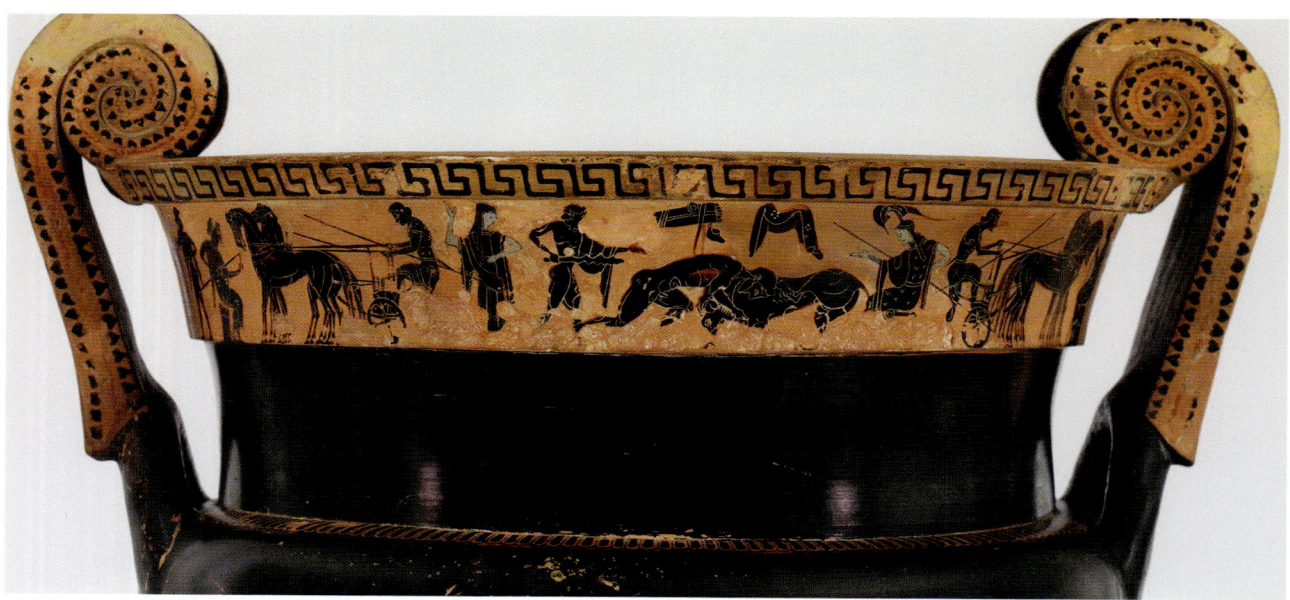

Pl. 4B. Black-figured volute krater, Baltimore, Walters Art Museum 48.29. Photo: © Walters Art Museum.

Color Plate 5

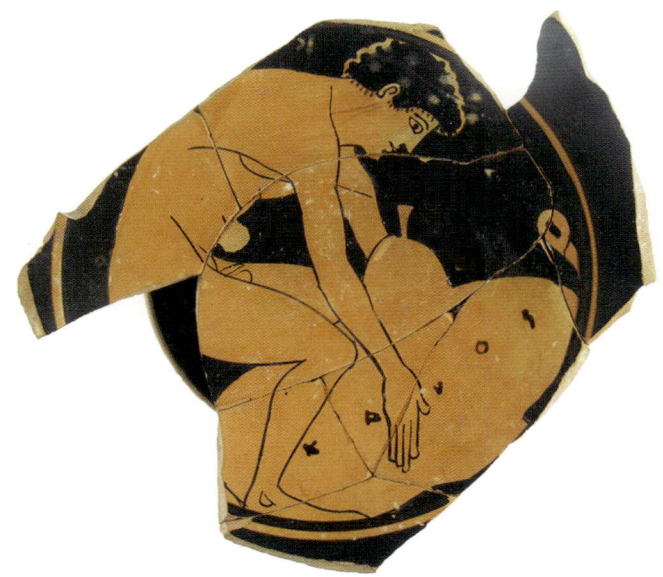

Pl. 5A. Kerameikos, Inv. 3193 (C. Graml).

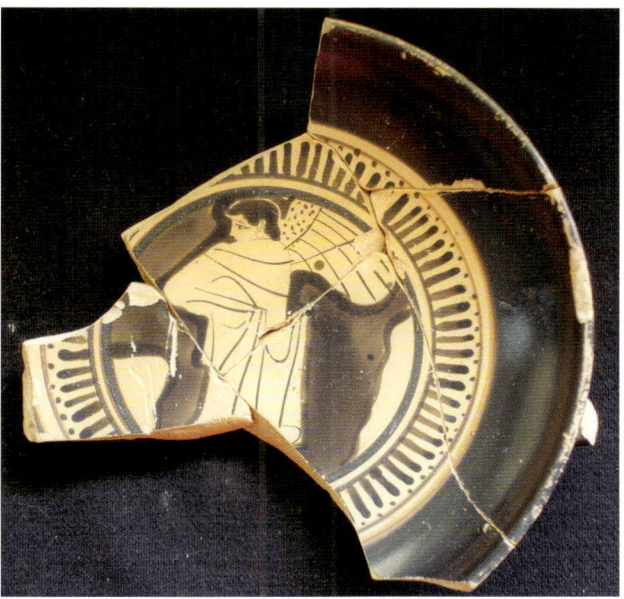

Pl. 5B. Kerameikos, Inv. 4847 (author).

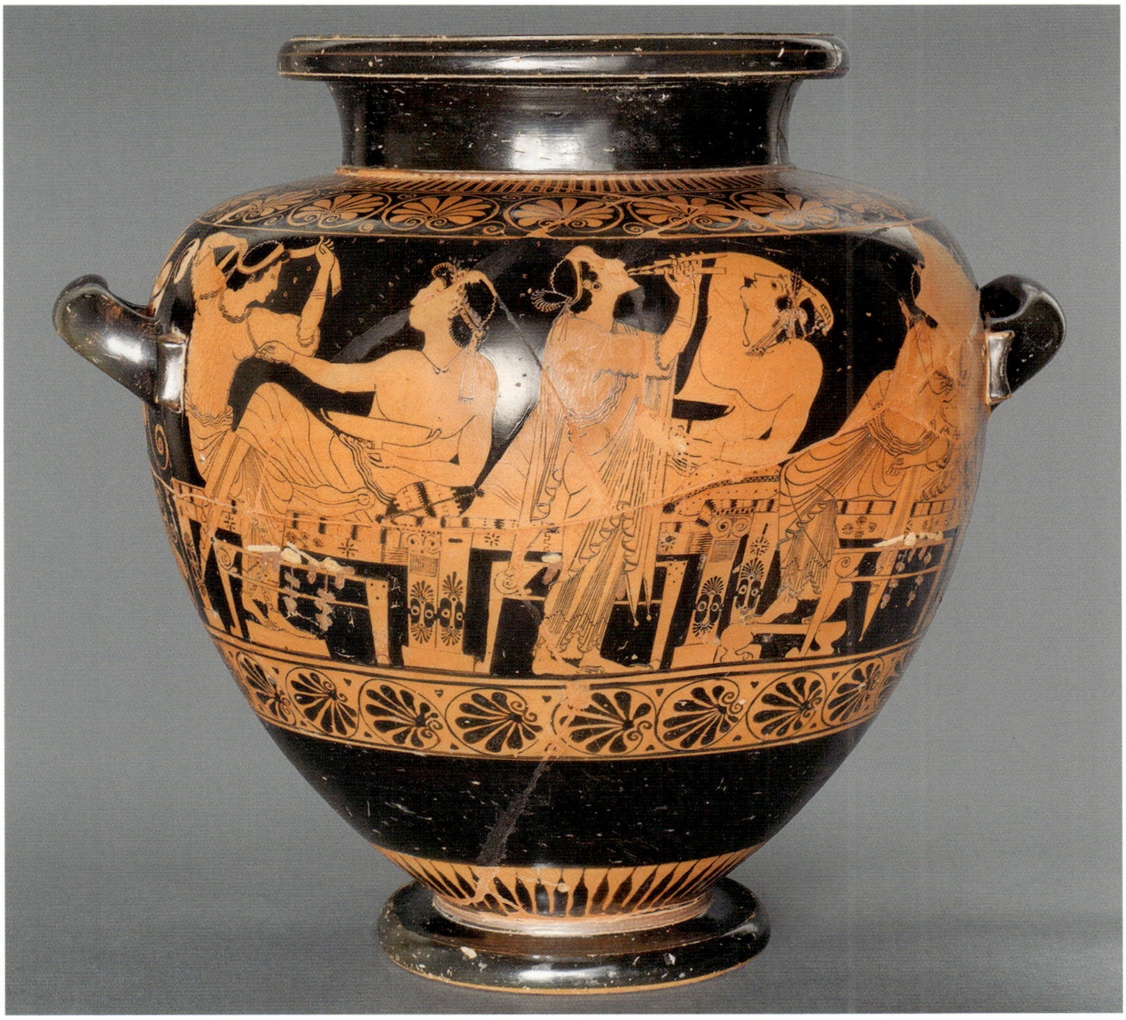

Pl. 5C. Brussels, Musées Royaux A717. Photo: Courtesy of the Musée Royaux, Brussels.

Color Plate 6

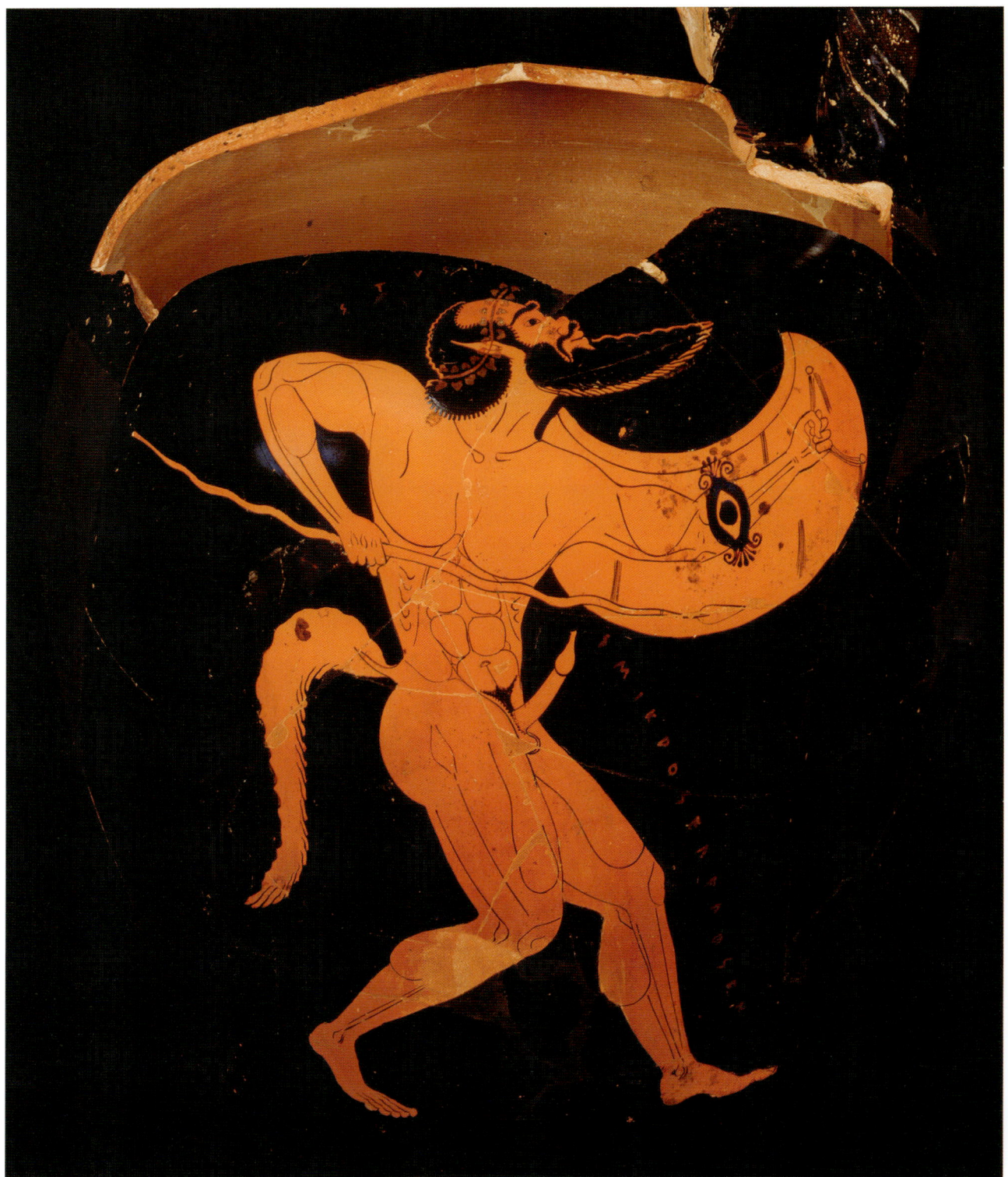

Pl. 6. Berlin, Antikensammlung 1966.19. Photo: Johannes Laurentius. Courtesy bpk, Berlin/Antikensammlung/Art Resource NY.

Color Plate 7

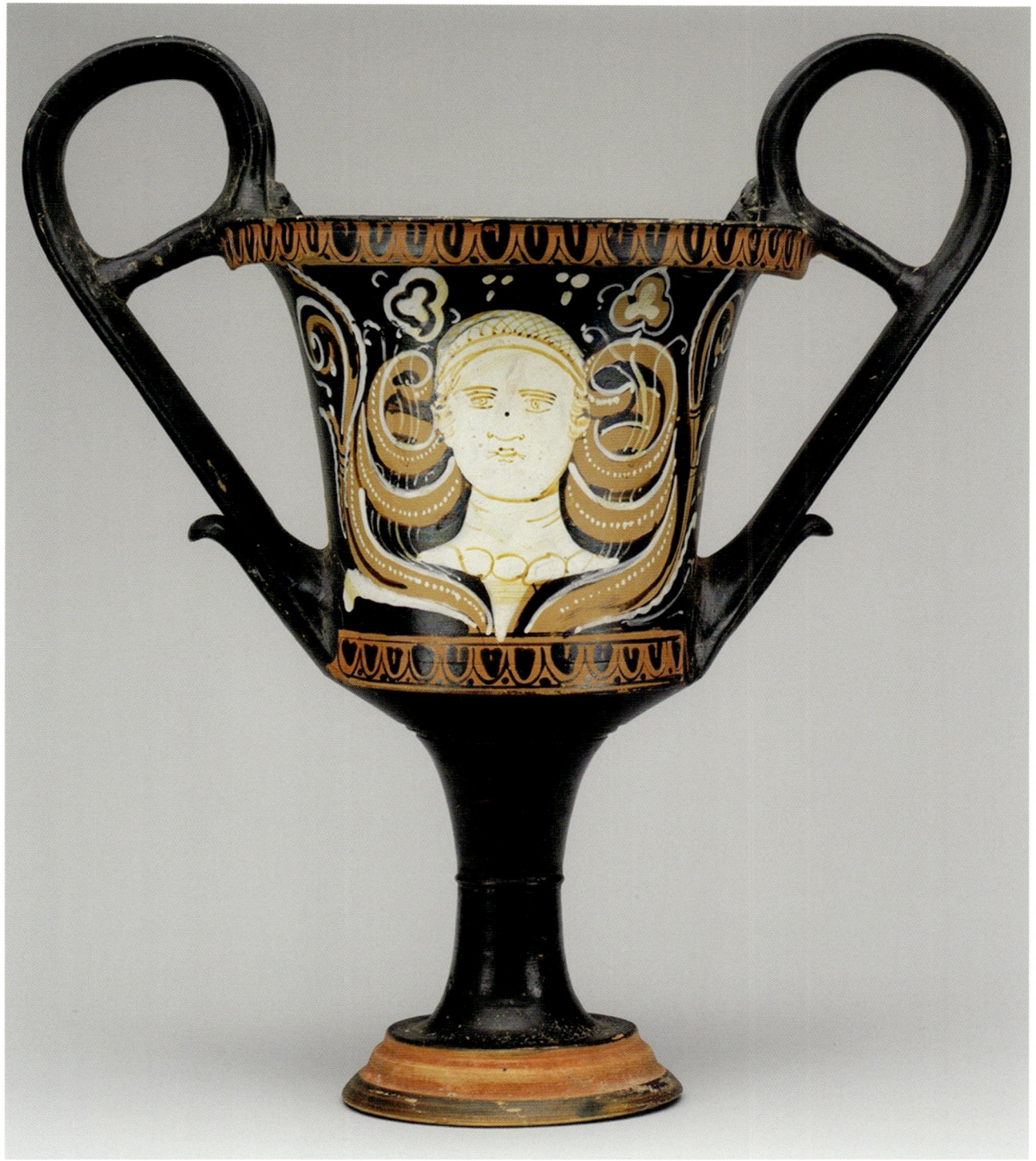

Pl. 7. New York, Metropolitan Museum of Art 06.1021.233, Apulian kantharos, Painter of Bari 5981, ca. 325–300 BC, from Canosa (Image © The Metropolitan Museum of Art).

Color Plate 8

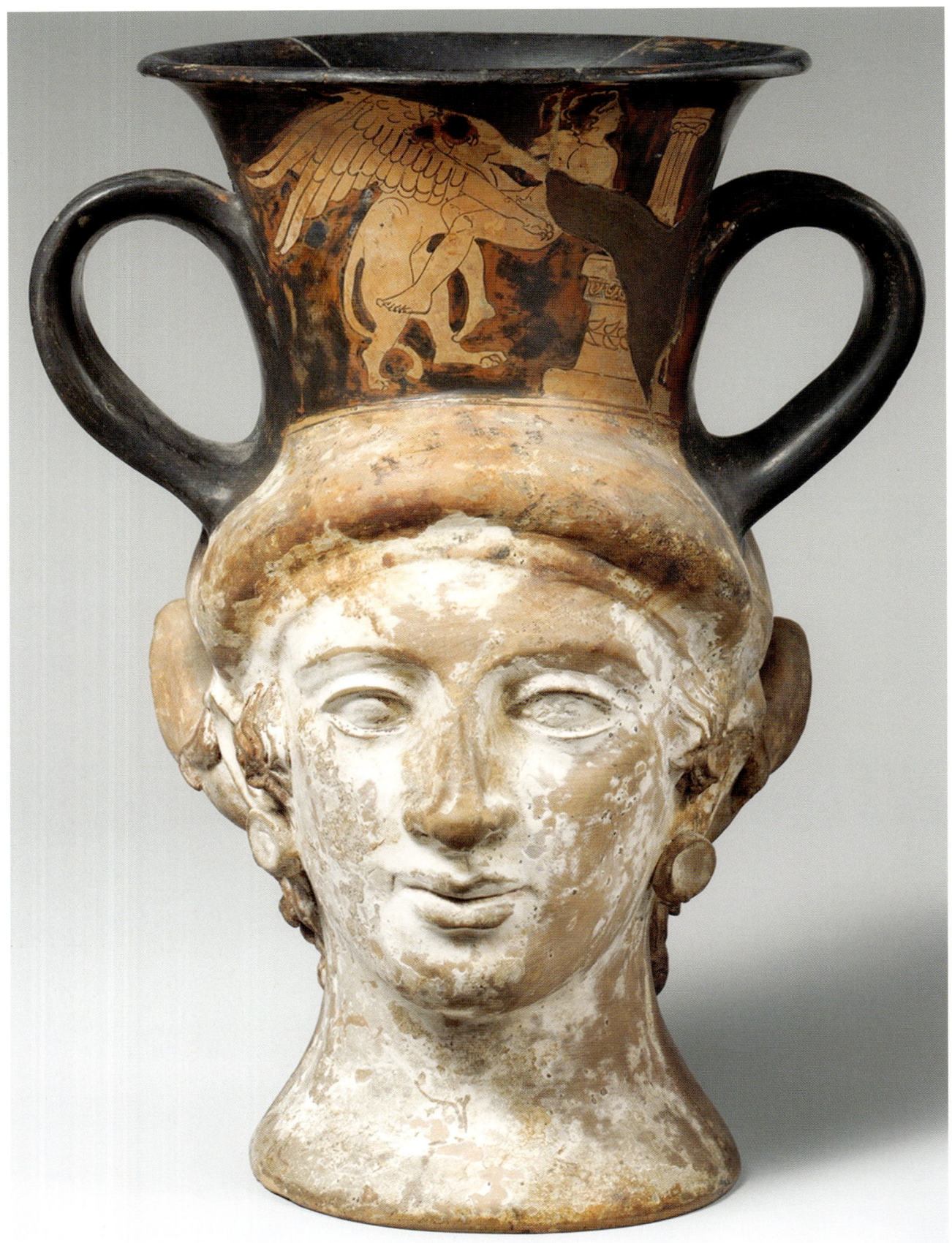

Pl. 8. New York, Metropolitan Museum of Art 21.88.64, Attic plastic janiform head kantharos of a satyr and woman, Class W (Persian Class) of Head Vases, late fifth century BC, said to be from Anzi, Basilicata (Image © The Metropolitan Museum of Art).

Color Plate 9

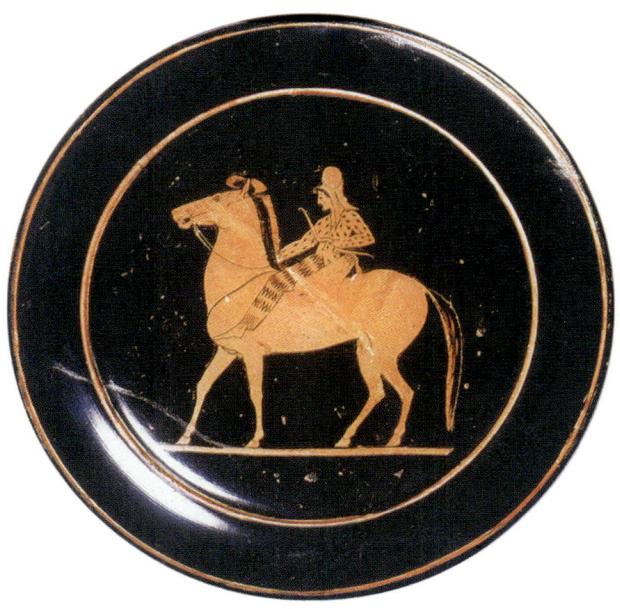

Pl. 9A. Plate attributed to Paseas: horseman in Scythian costume, inscription Miltiades kalos. Oxford, Ashmolean Museum 310. From Chiusi.

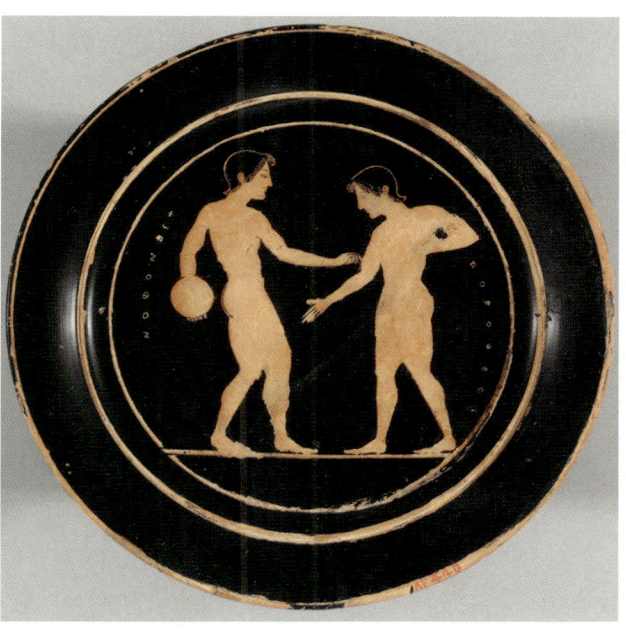

Pl. 9B. Plate attributed to Paseas: Dorotheos and Chsenophon with a discus. Museum of Fine Arts, Boston 03.785. From Chiusi.

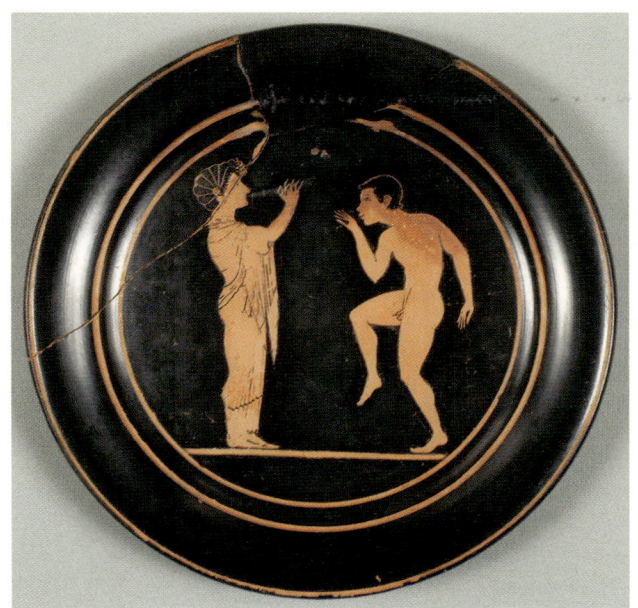

Pl. 9C. Plate attributed to Paseas: auletris and negro dancer. Chiusi, National Archaeological Museum 252138 (formerly Bettolle, Passerini Collection). From Bettolle.

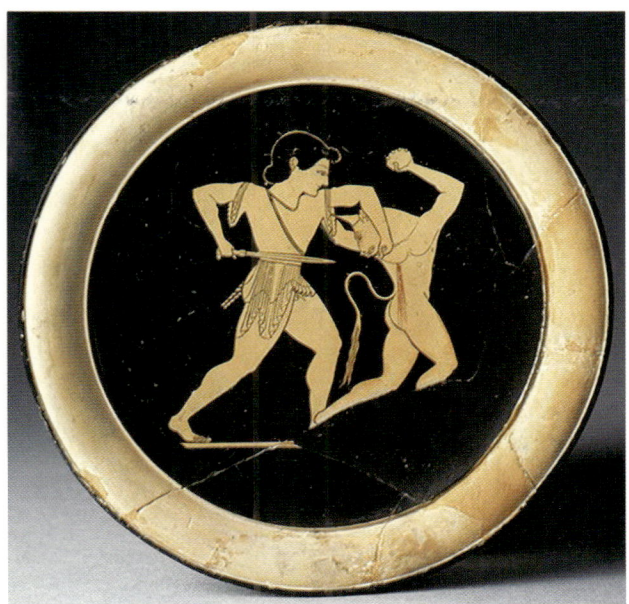

Pl. 9D. Plate attributed to Paseas: Theseus and the Minotaur. Paris, Louvre G 67.

Color Plate 10

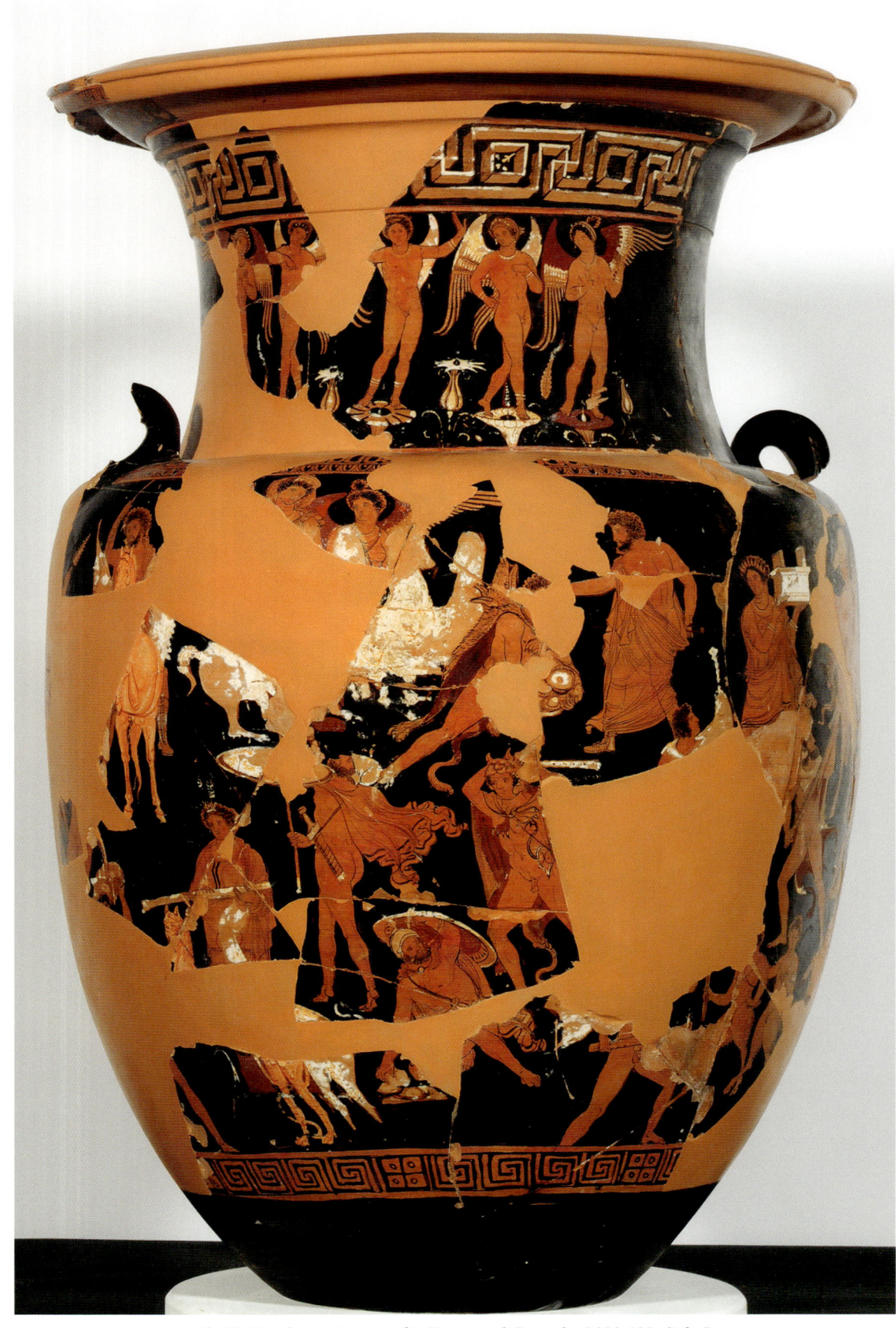

Pl. 10. Hamburg, Museum für Kunst und Gewerbe 2003.130, Side B.

Color Plate 11

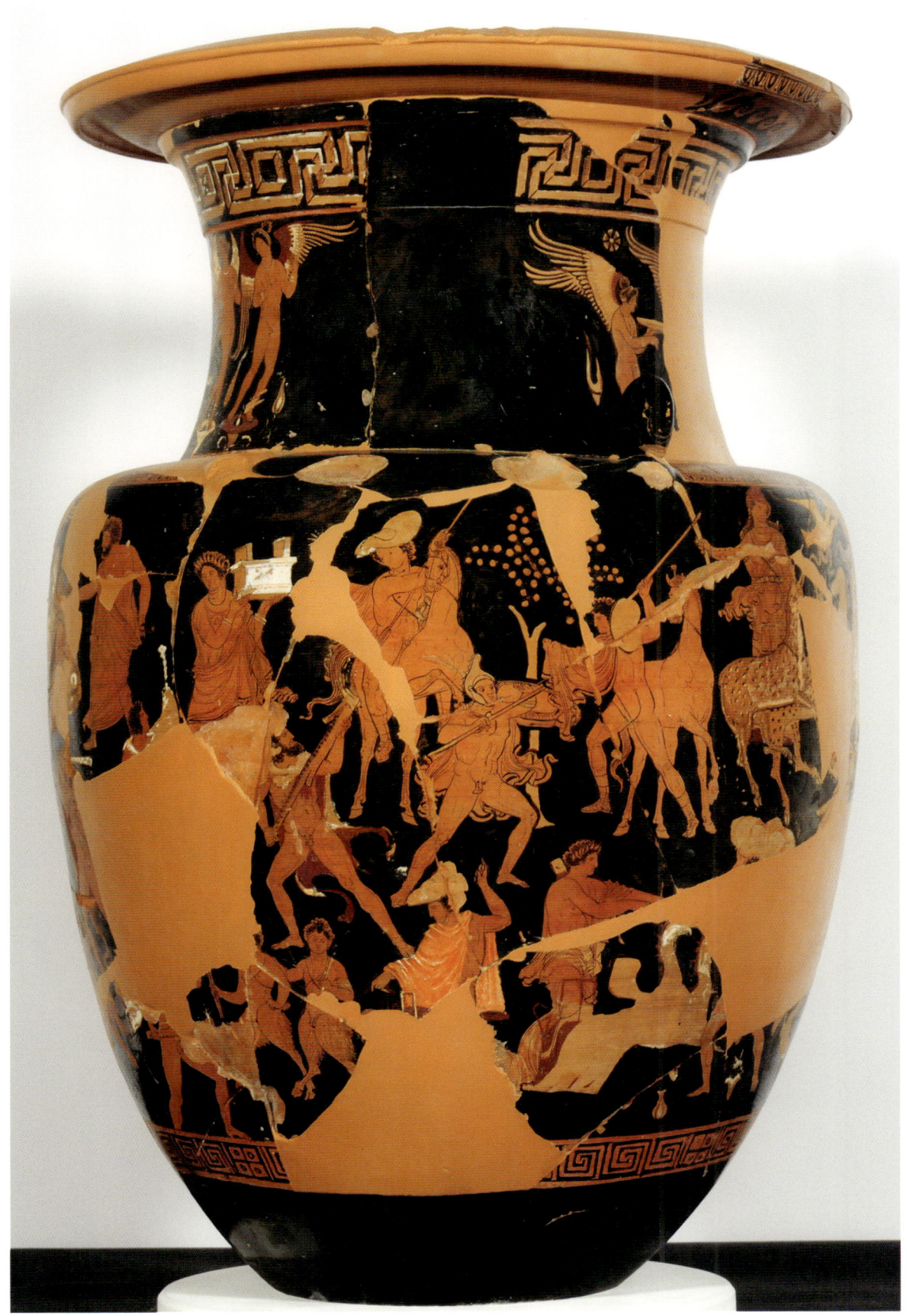

Pl. 11. Hamburg, Museum für Kunst und Gewerbe 2003.130, Side B/A.

Color Plate 12

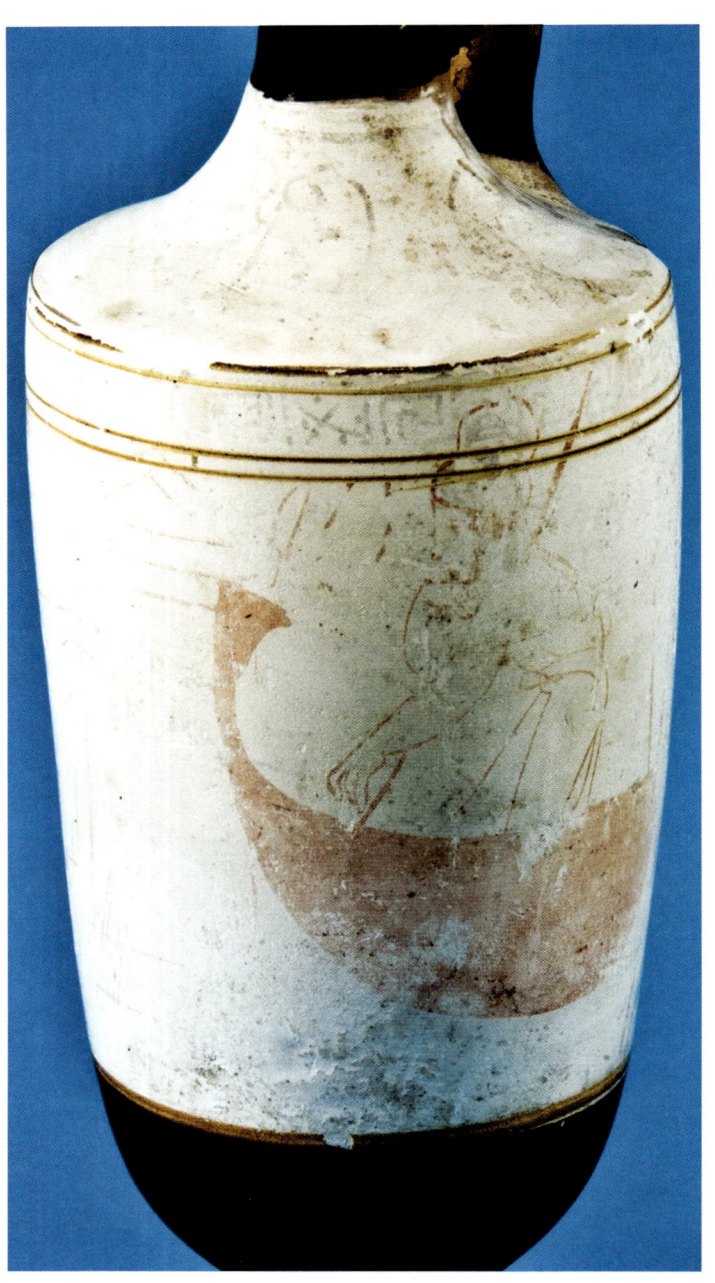

Pl. 12A. Attic White-ground Lekythos, Reed Painter, IAA, Inv. 72.5550.

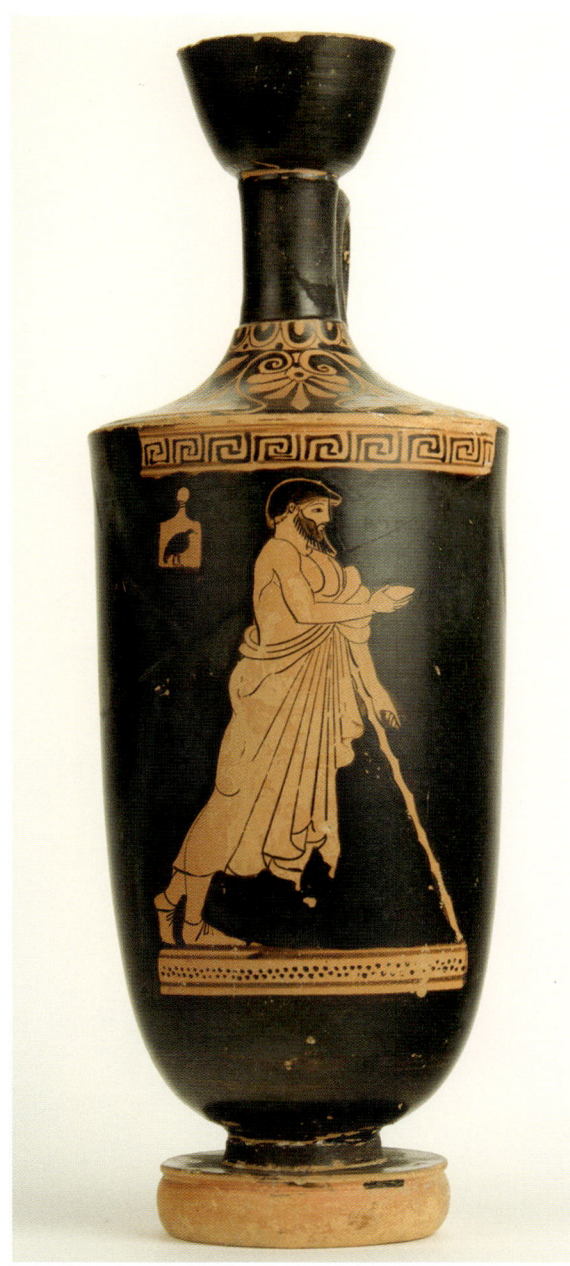

Pl. 12B. Oxford, Ashmolean 1888.1402, red-figure lekythos attributed to Near the Pan Painter.

Color Plate 13

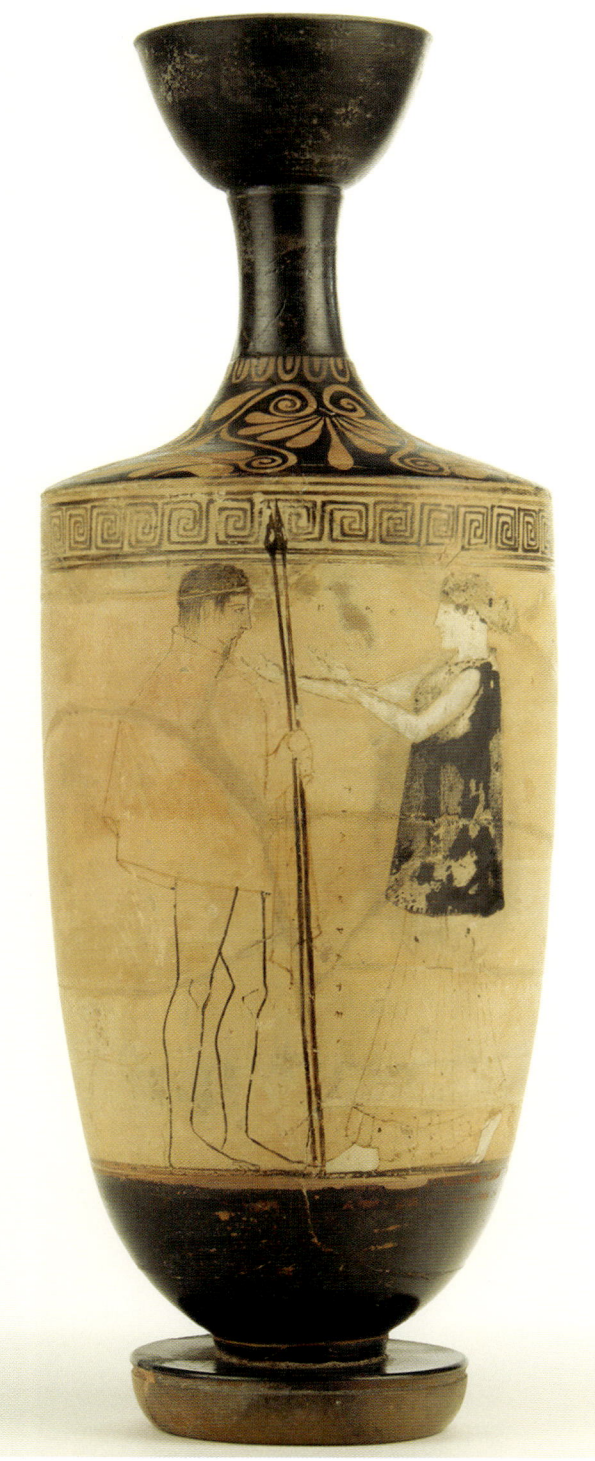

Pl. 13A. Oxford, Ashmolean 1891.686, white-ground lekythos by the Timokrates Painter.

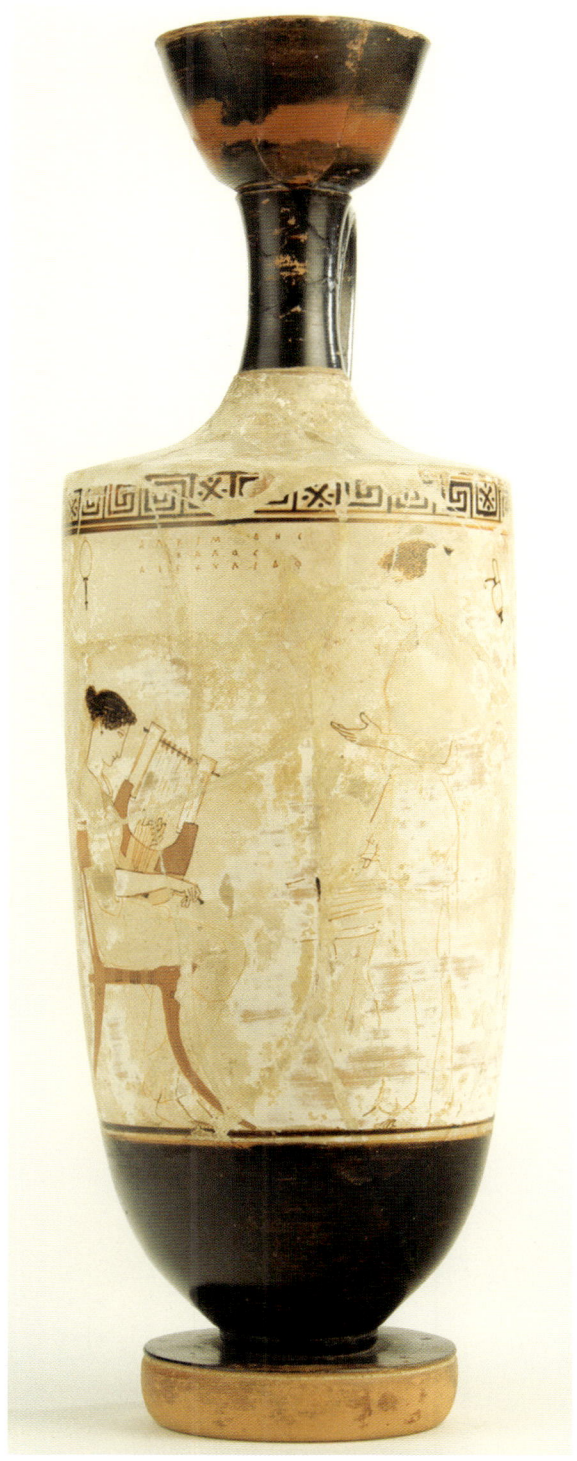

Pl. 13B. Oxford, Ashmolean 1889.1016, white-ground lekythos by the Achilles Painter.

Color Plate 14

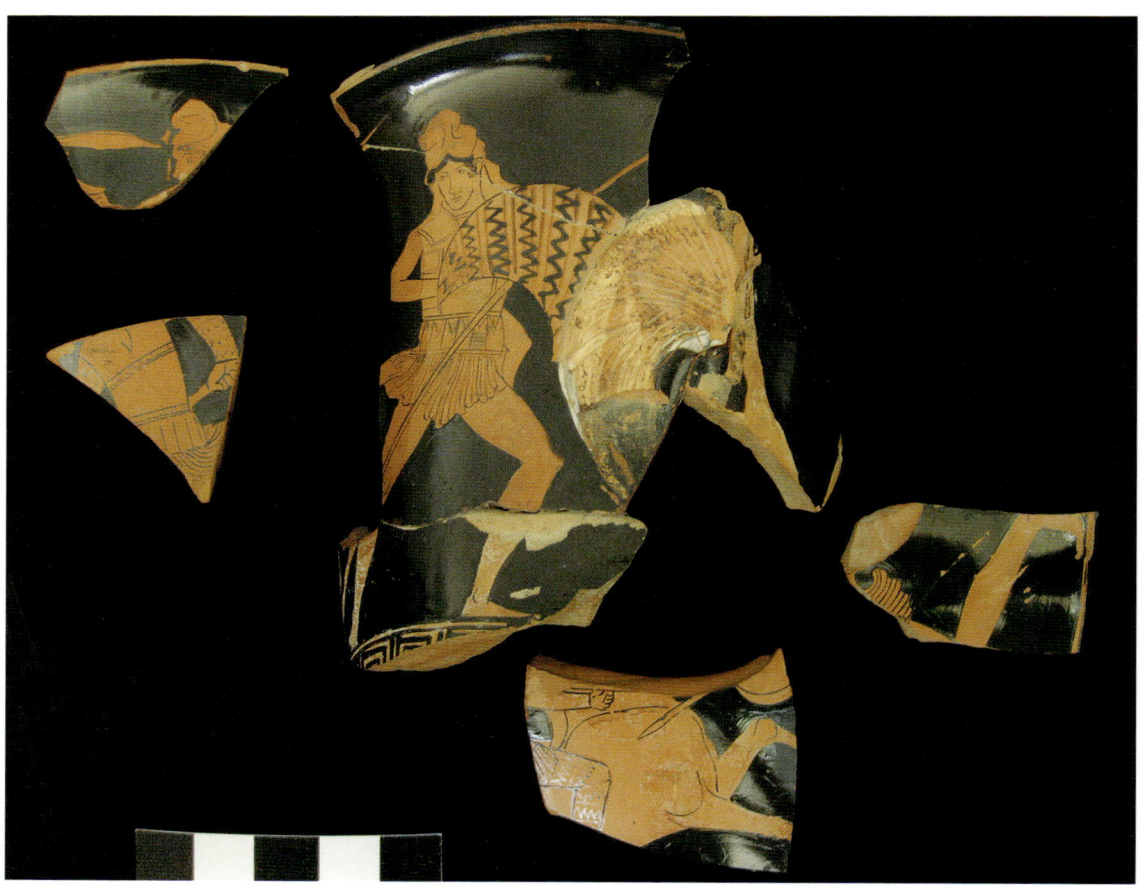

Pl. 14A. Gordion P 380 a, b + P 3356 + P 4688. Sotadaean rhyton in form of an Amazon on horseback (plastic figure largely missing); Amazonomachy on neck. Photo: Lynch with permission of the Gordion Excavations, University of Pennsylvania.

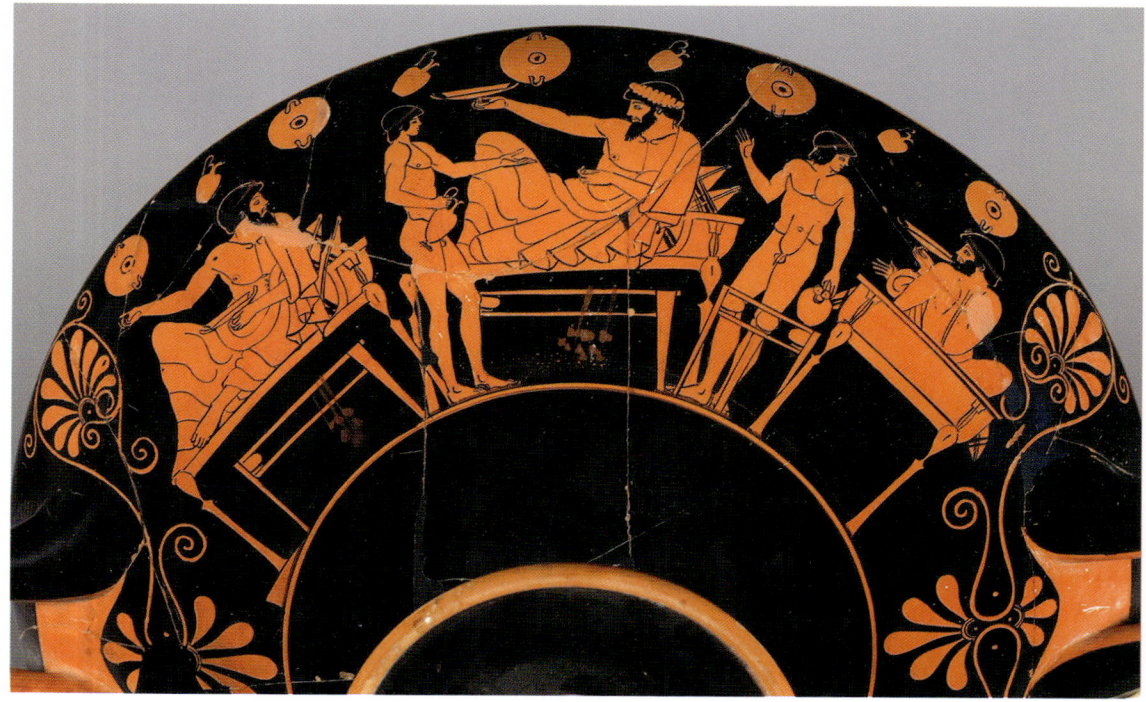

Pl. 14B. Athenian Red-figured Cup, attributed to Douris, 485–480 BC. London, British Museum 1843.11-3.15. © The Trustees of the British Museum. Photo: Museum.

Color Plate 15

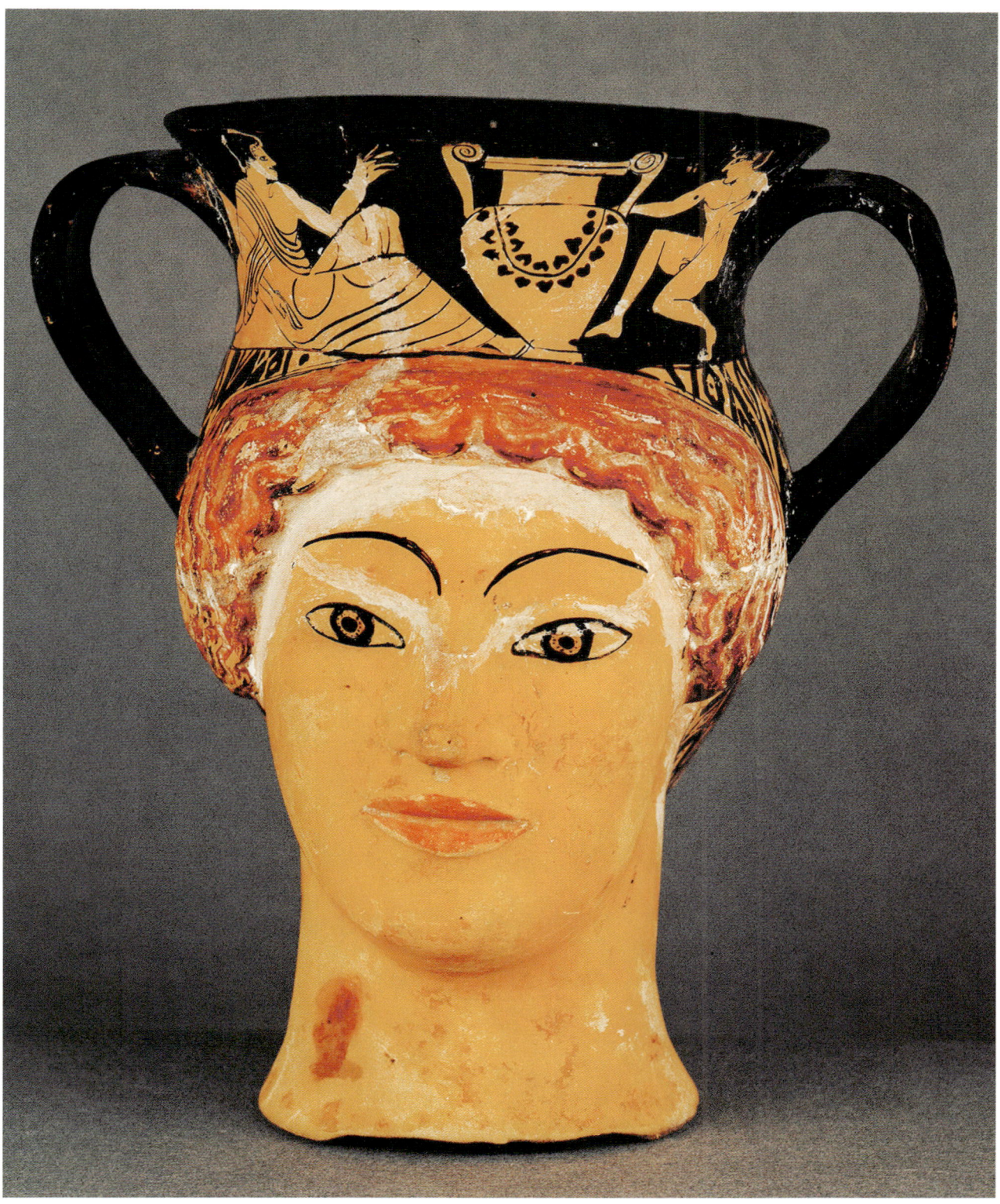

Pl. 15. Athenian Red-figured Kantharos, Recalling the Epeleios Painter, 510–500 BC. Paris, Louvre Museum H 46. Photo: Lessing.

Color Plate 16

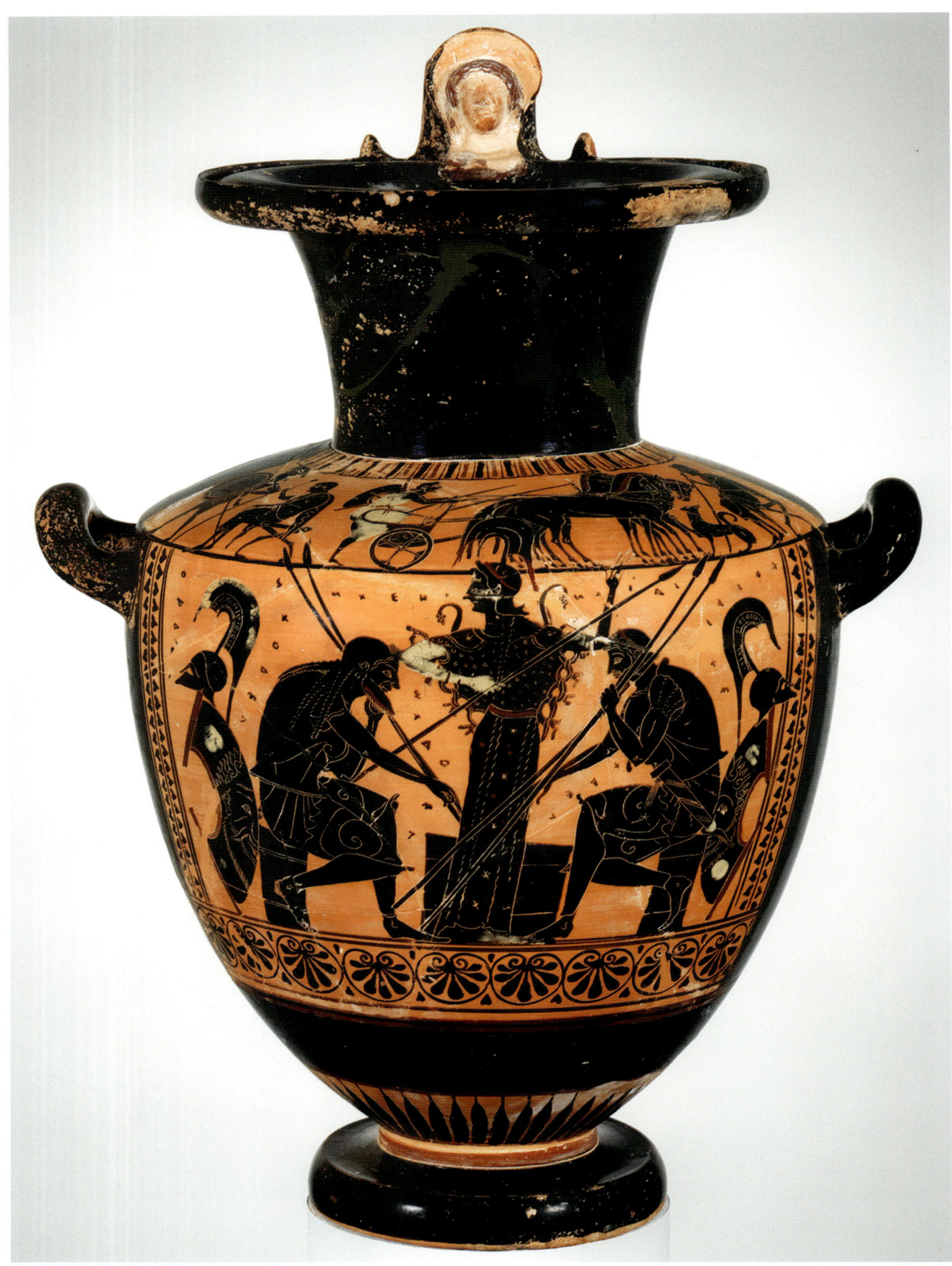

Pl. 16. Hydria attributed to the Leagros Group. Attic, ca. 510 BC. New York, The Metropolitan Museum of Art, 56.171.29. Fletcher Fund, 1956. Image © The Metropolitan Museum of Art.

Color Plate 17

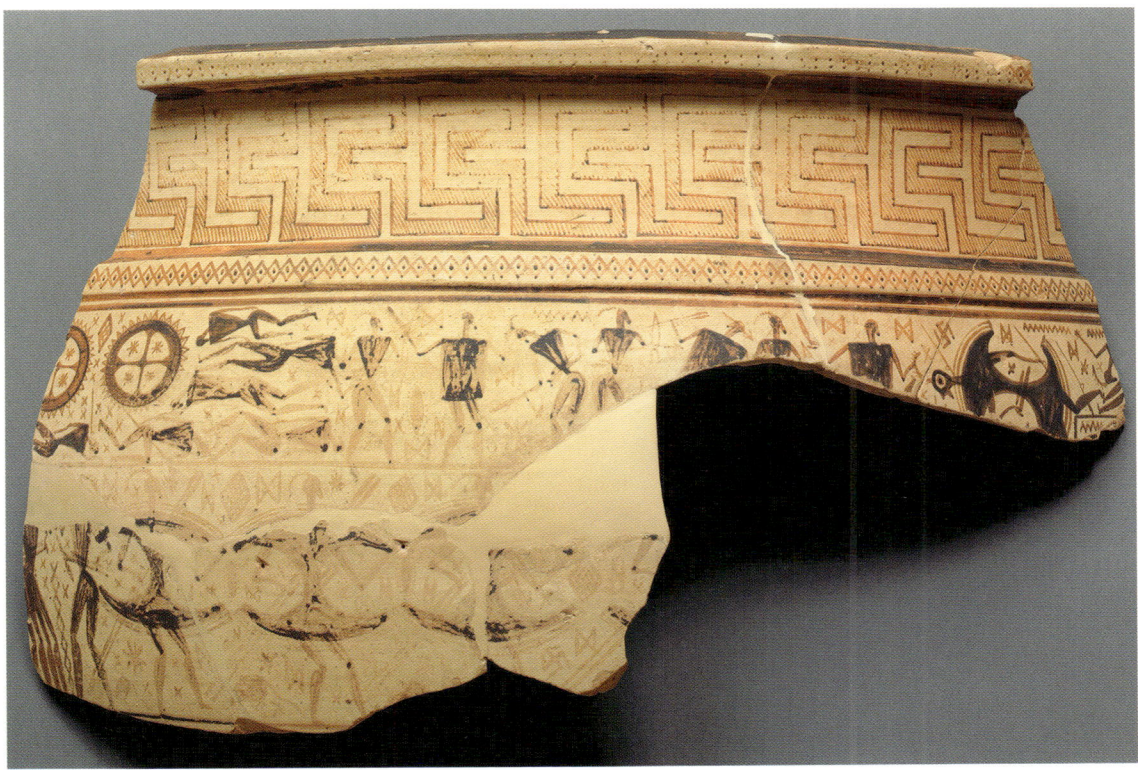
Pl. 17A. Krater, fragment. Attic, ca. 750 BC. Paris, Musée du Louvre A 519. Image © Musée du Louvre.

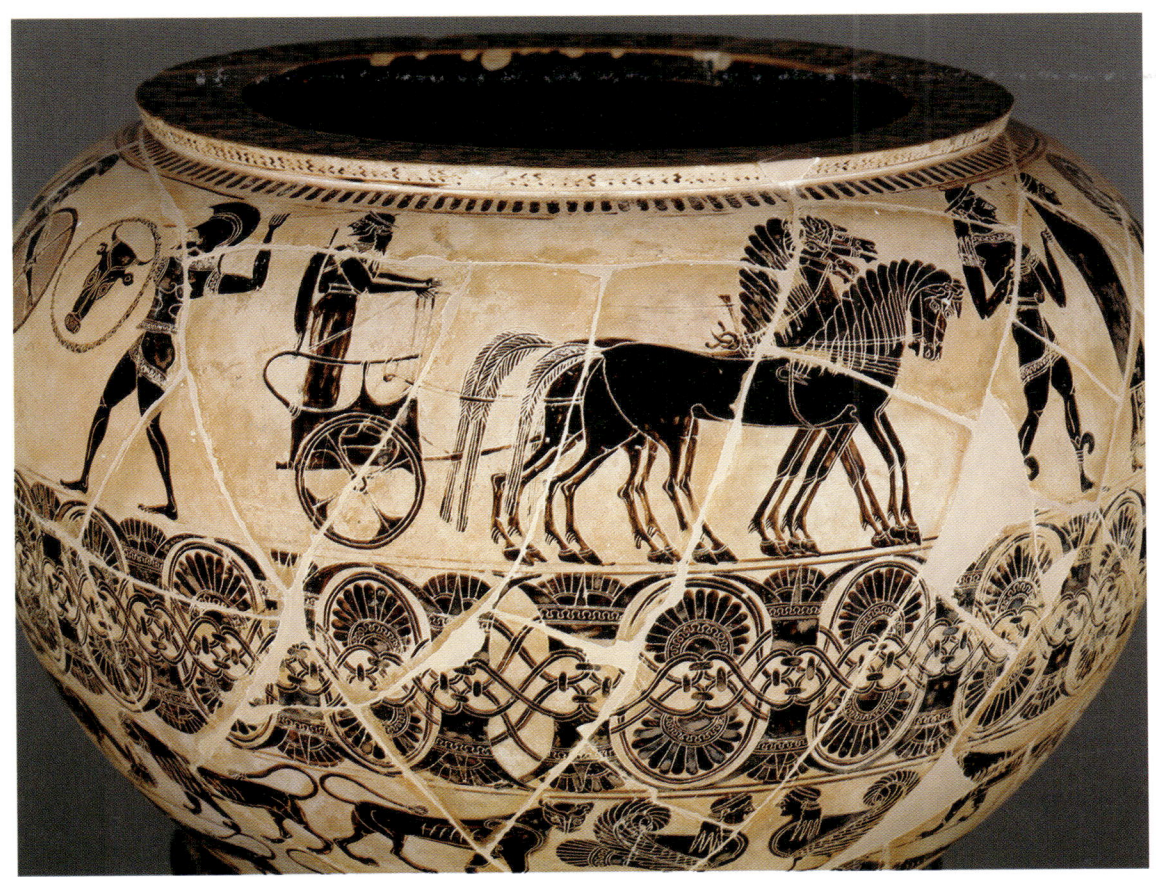
Pl. 17B. Dinos attributed to the Gorgon Painter. Attic, ca. 580 BC. Paris, Musée du Louvre E 874. Image © Musée du Louvre.

Color Plate 18

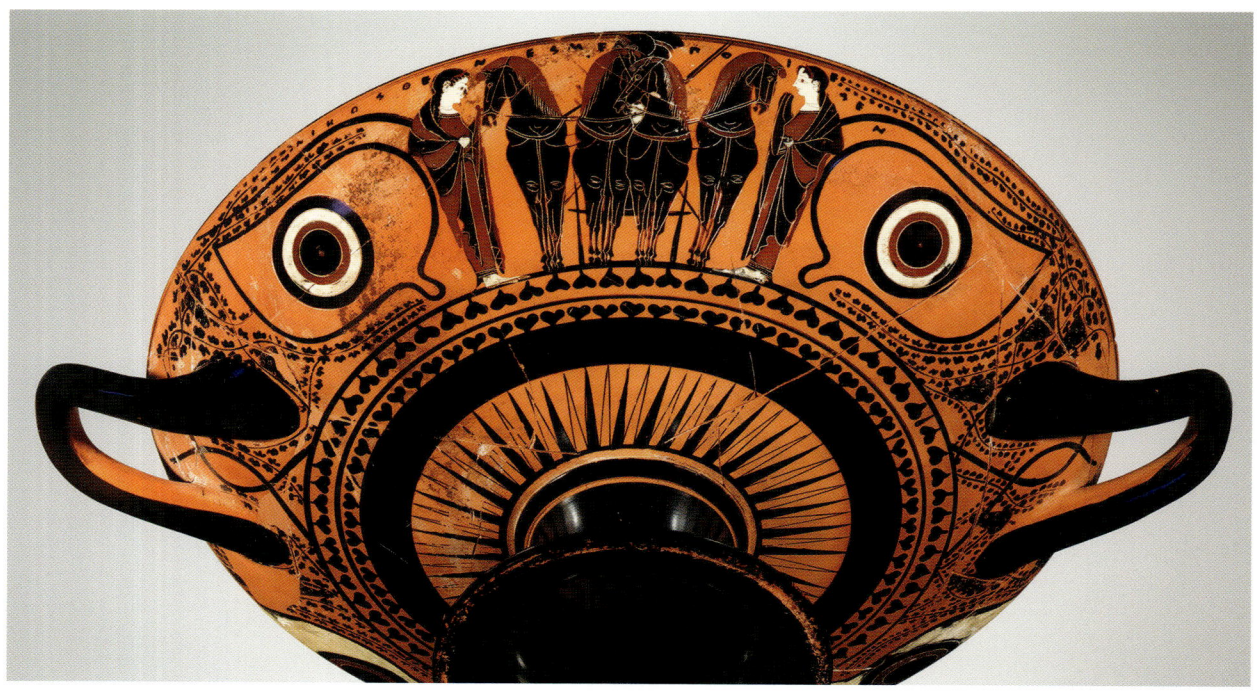

Pl. 18A. Kylix signed by Nikosthenes as potter. Attic, ca. 530 BC. New York, The Metropolitan Museum of Art, 14.136. Rogers Fund, 1914. Image © The Metropolitan Museum of Art.

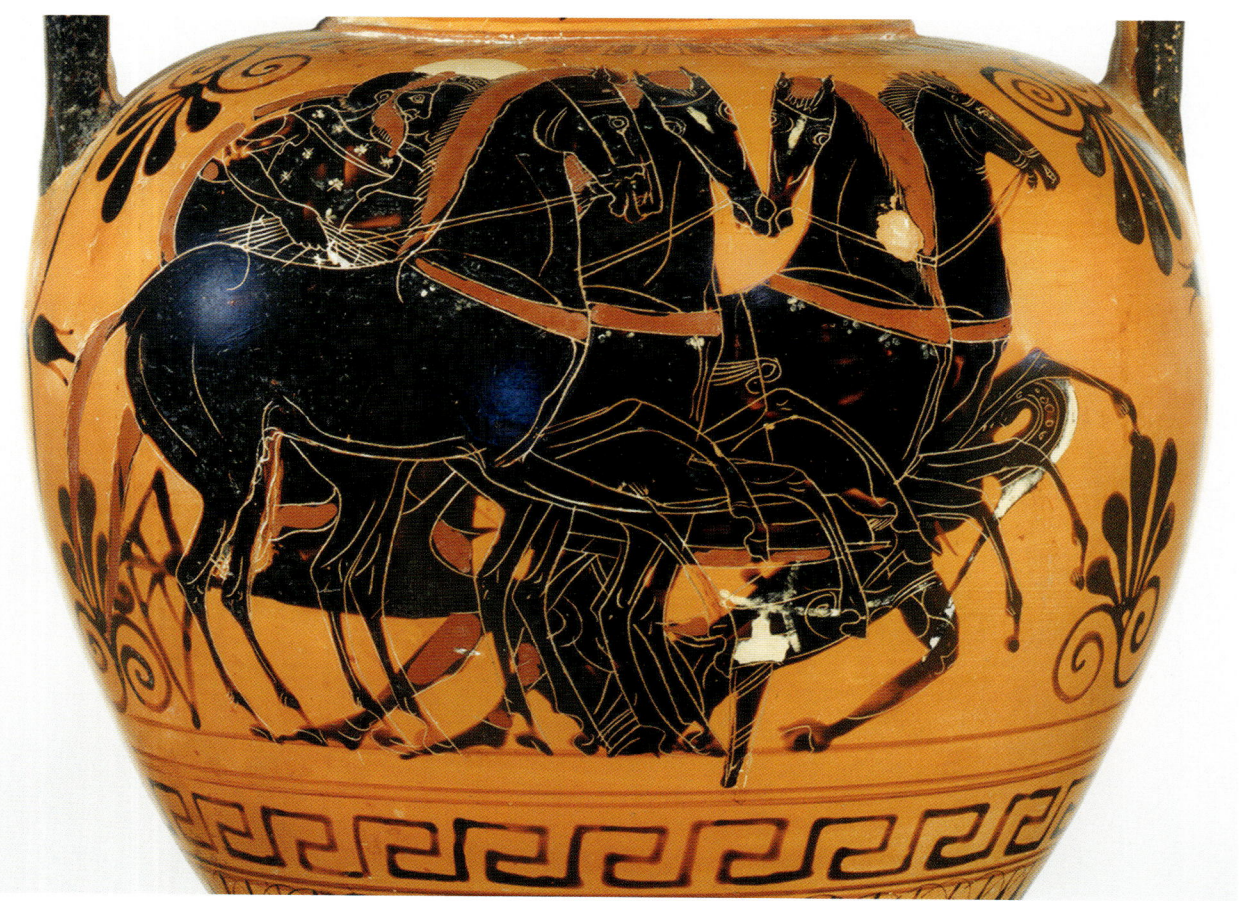

Pl. 18B. Neck-amphora attributed to the Manner of the Lysippides Painter. Attic, ca. 520 BC. New York, The Metropolitan Museum of Art, 23.160.60. Rogers Fund, 1923. Image © The Metropolitan Museum of Art.

Color Plate 19

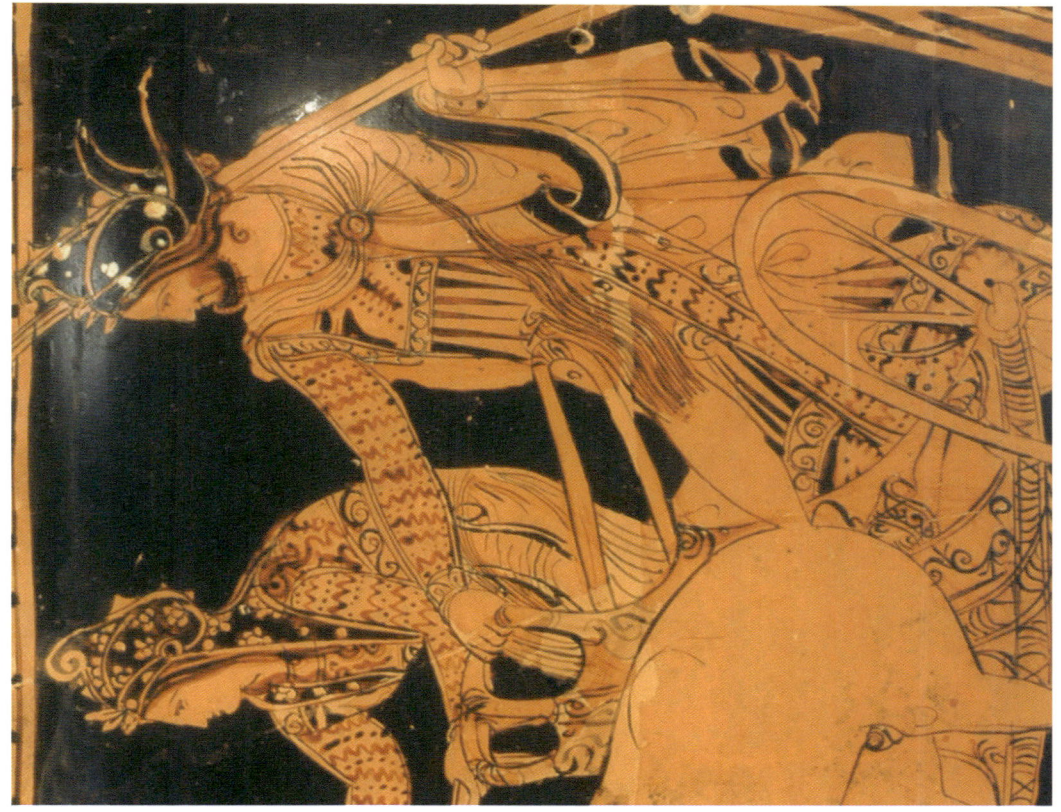

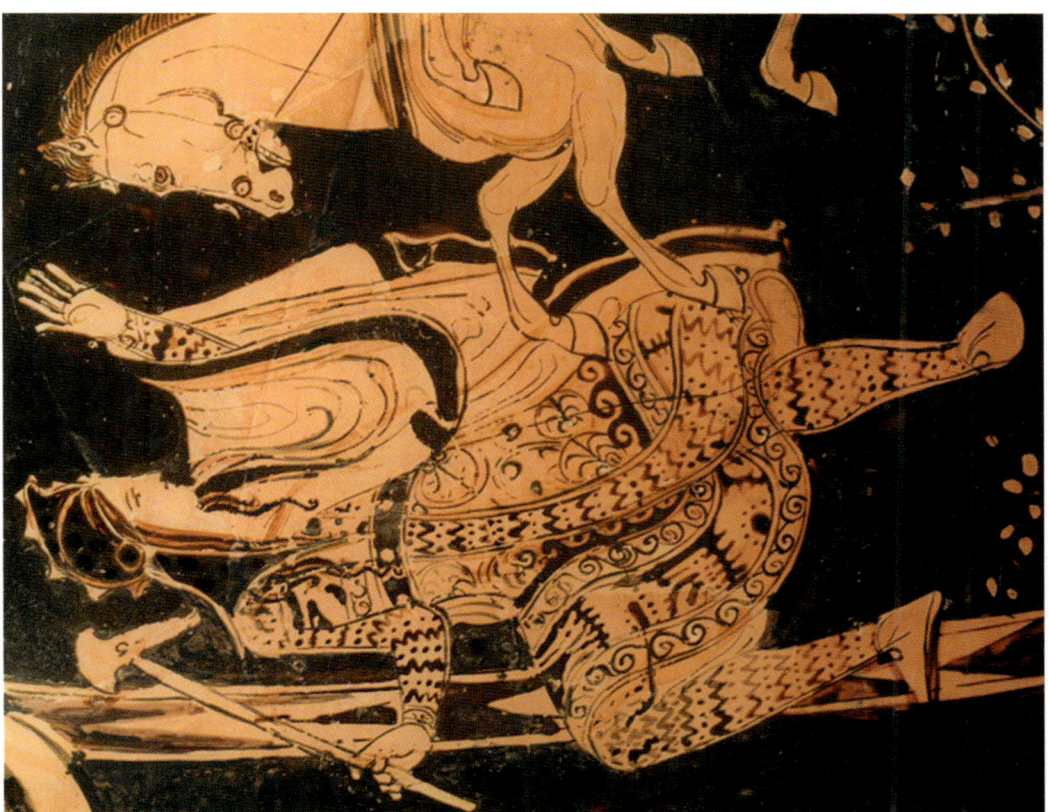

Pl. 19A–B. Attic red-figure column-krater, attributed to the Suessula Painter. Princeton University Art Museum. Museum purchase, Fowler McCormick, Class of 1921 Fund, Carl Otto von Kienbusch, Jr. Memorial Collection Fund, and Classical Purchase Fund, 2007–98.

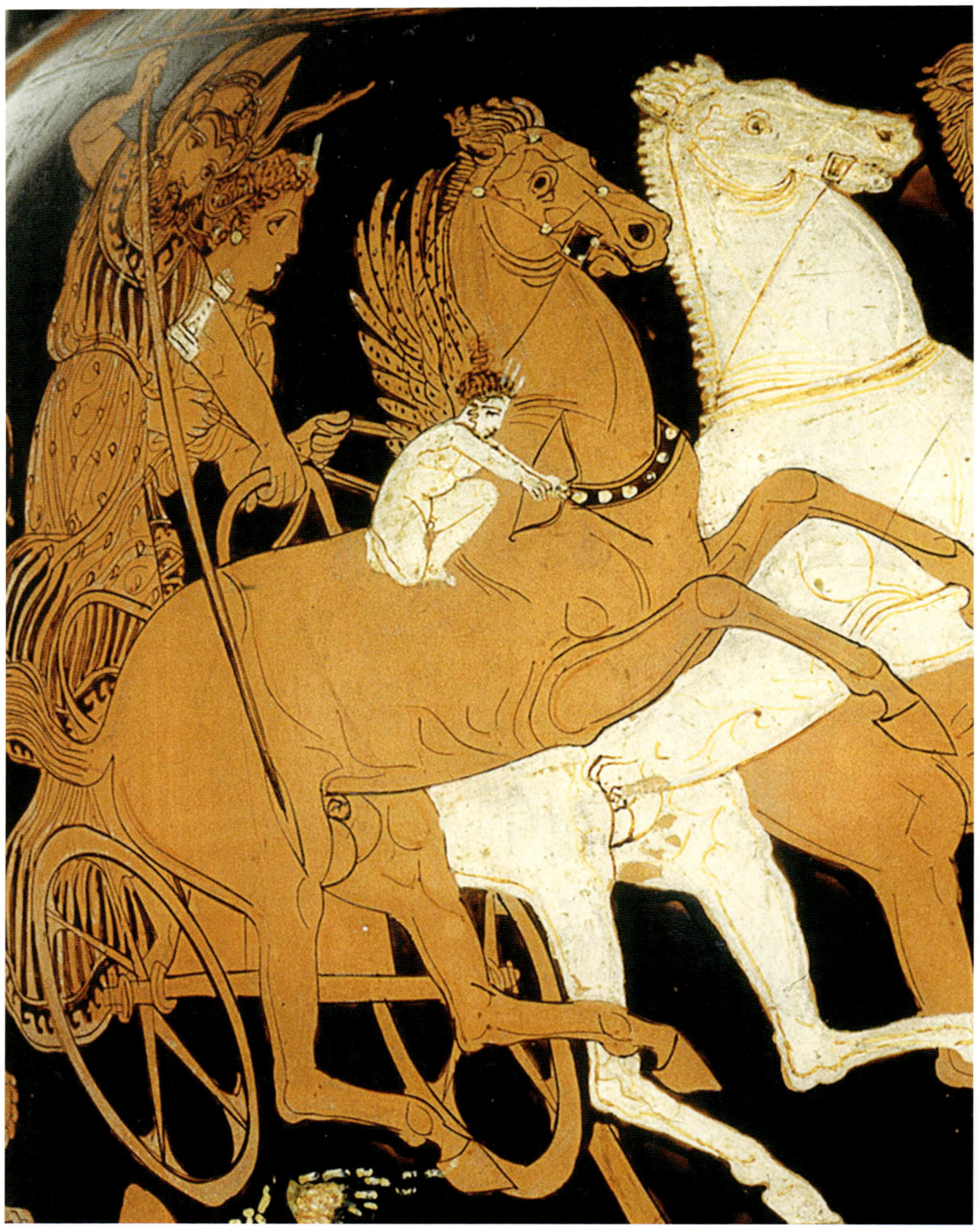

Pl. 20. Attic red-figure neck-amphora with twisted handles, attributed to the Suessula Painter. Paris, Musée du Louvre S 1677.

Color Plate 21

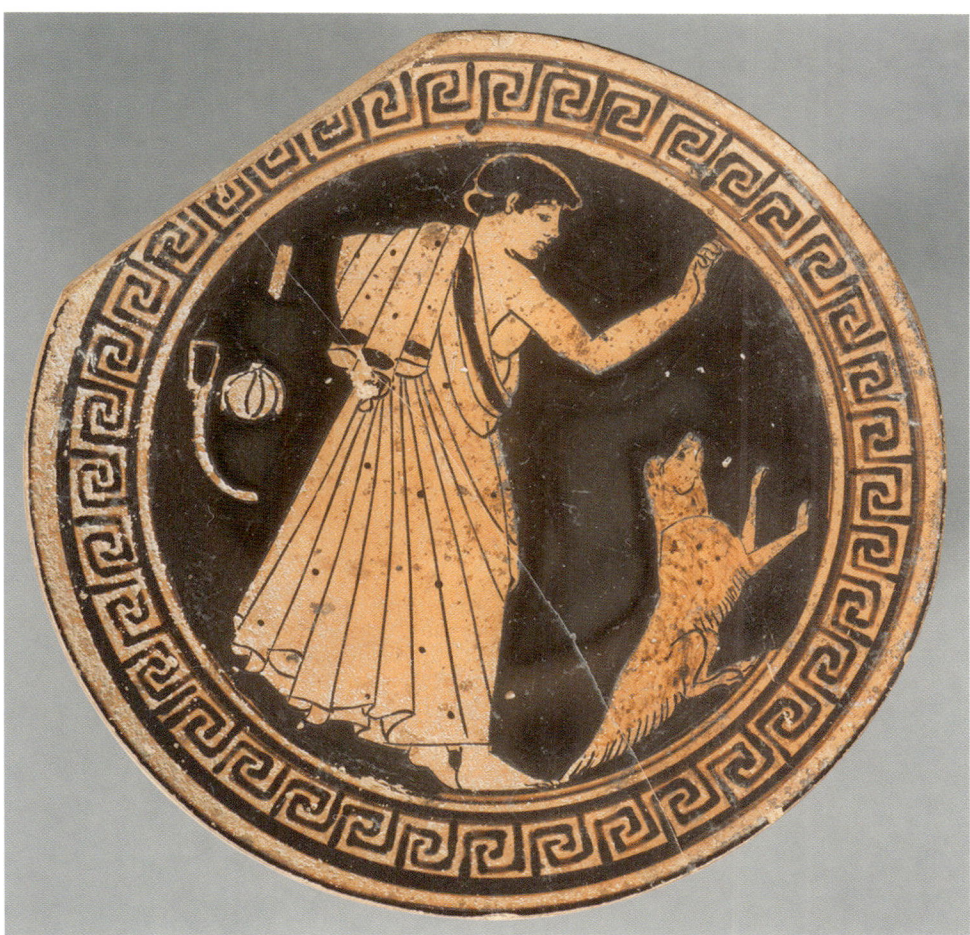

Pl. 21A. Tondo of an Attic red-figure kylix by the Brygos Painter. Musées Royaux d'Art et d'Histoire, Bruxelles R350. Photograph: Museum.

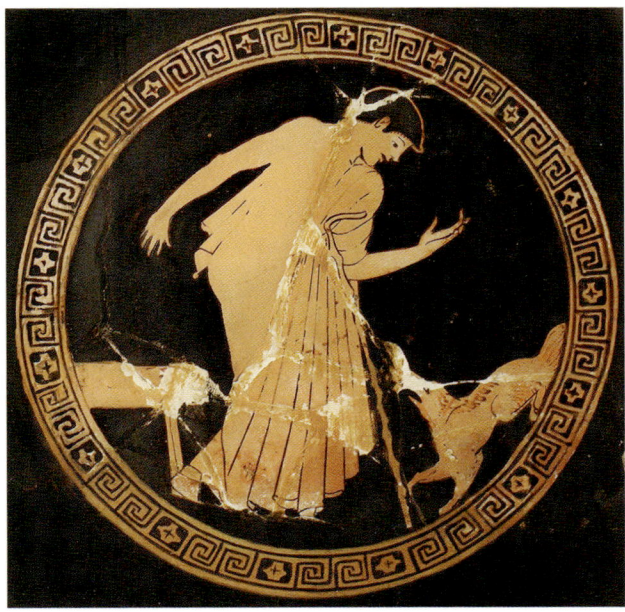

Pl. 21B. Attic red-figure Kylix by the Brygos Painter. © Phoebe A. Hearst Museum of Anthropology and the Regents of the University of California. Photography by Alicja Egbert, Catalogue No. 8-921.

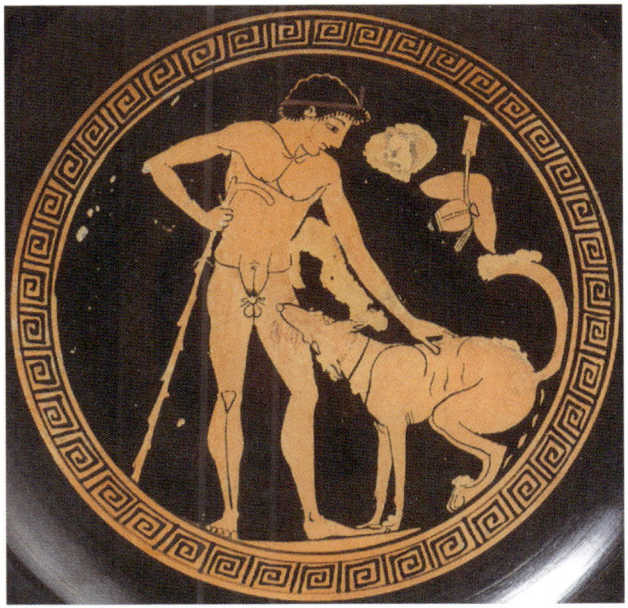

Pl. 21C. Attic red-figure kylix by the Triptolemos Painter. Side B (after Sotheby's [n. 3]).

Color Plate 22

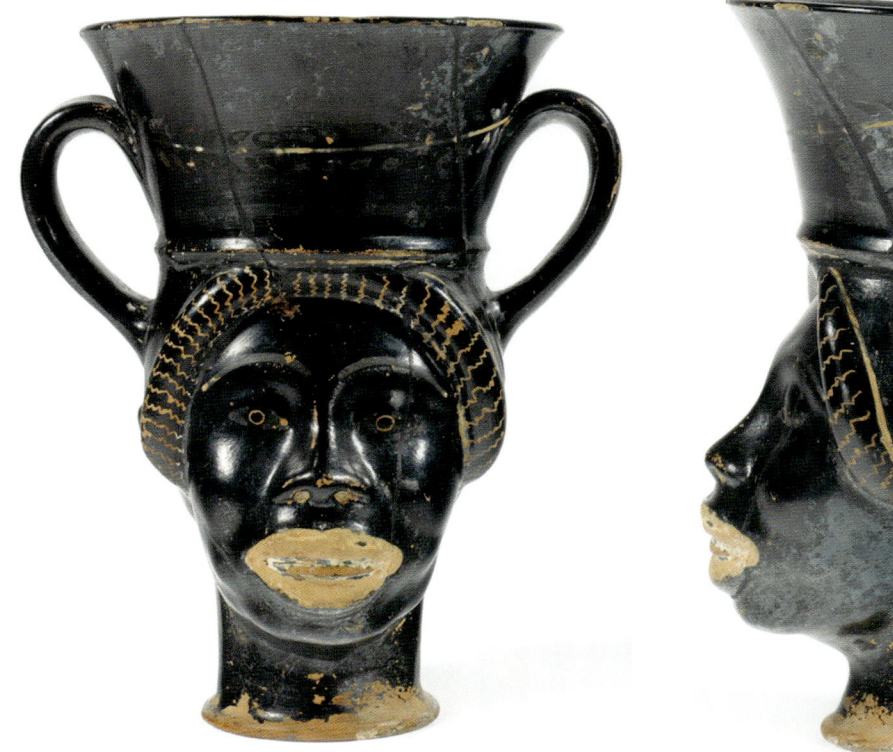

Pl. 22A–B. Head vase in the Kemper Museum of Art, St. Louis (WU 3284). Photograph: Douglas Gaubatz.

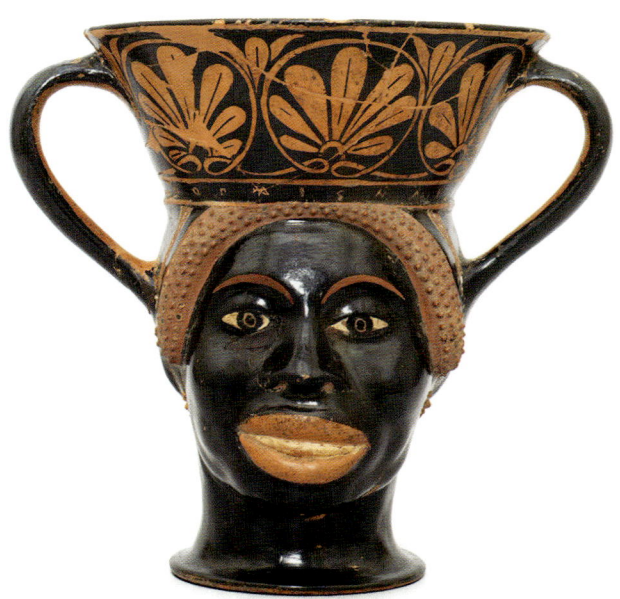

Pl. 22C. Head vase in Vienna Kunsthistorisches Museum 3714. Photograph: Kunsthistorisches Museum, Vienna.

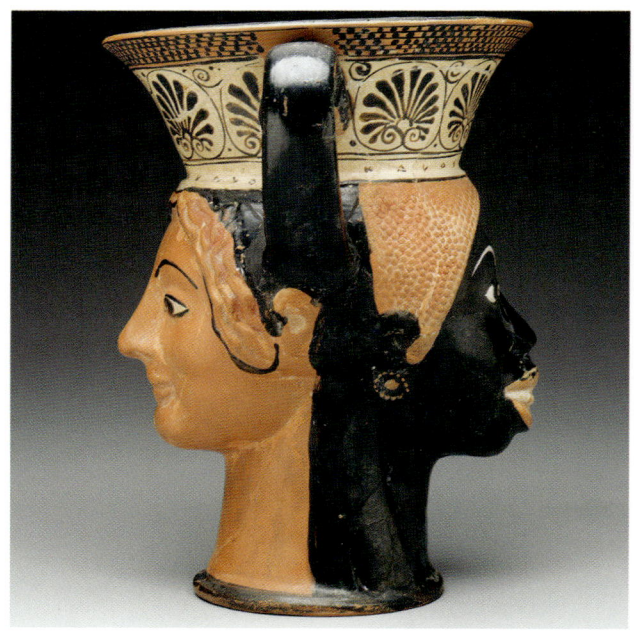

Pl. 22D. Janiform kantharos in the Museum of Fine Arts, Boston, 98.926. Photograph: Museum of Fine Arts, Boston.

Color Plate 23

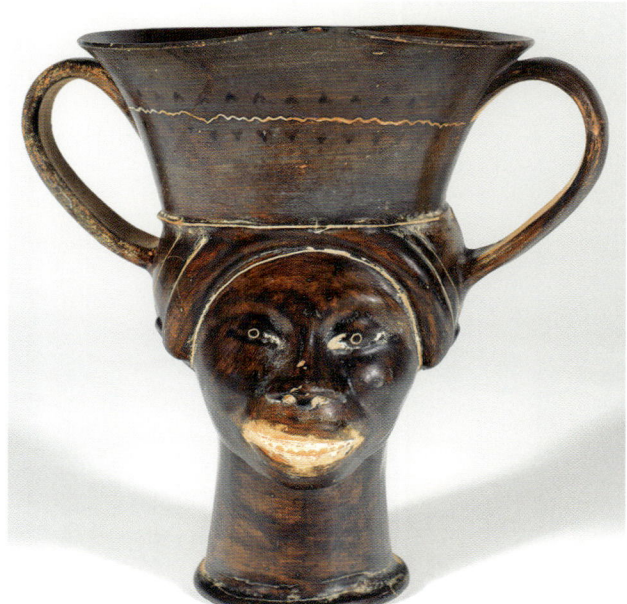
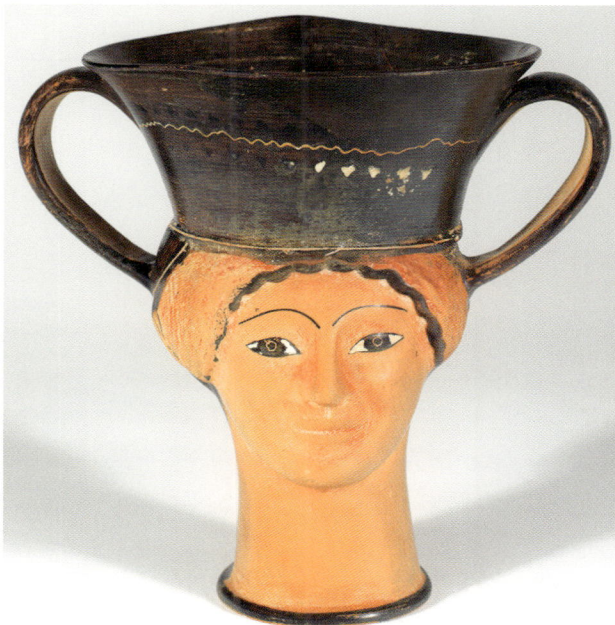

Pl. 23A–B. Janiform kantharos in Cambridge, Fitzwilliam Museum GR.2.1999. African woman. Photograph: © Fitzwilliam Museum, Cambridge.

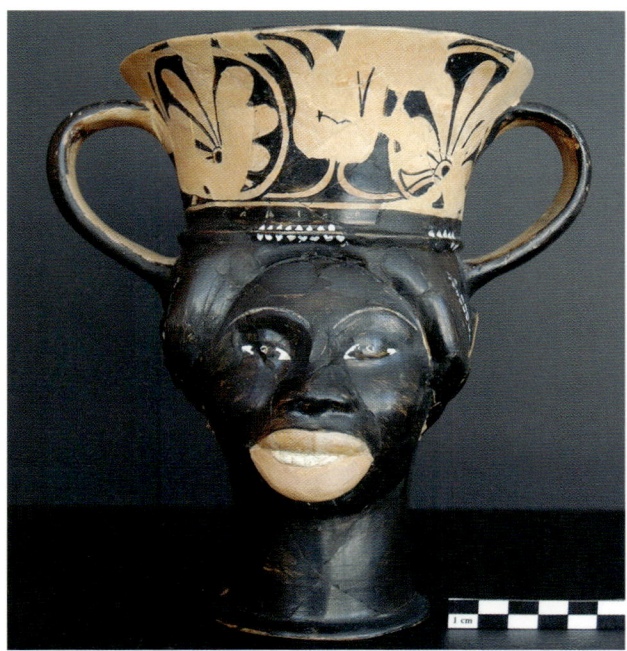
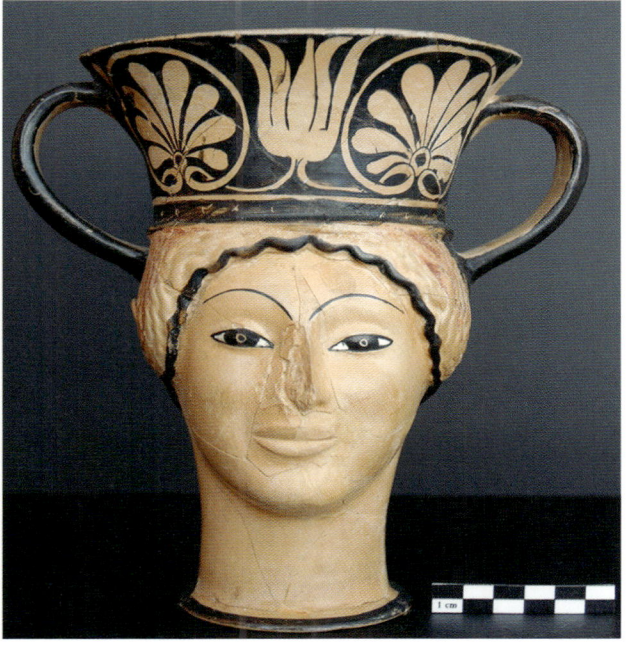

Pl. 23C–D. Janiform kantharos in the Archaeological Museum of Aiani. African woman and European woman. Photograph: Archaeological Museum of Aiani, reproduced by courtesy of Georgia Karamitrou-Mentessidi.

Color Plate 24

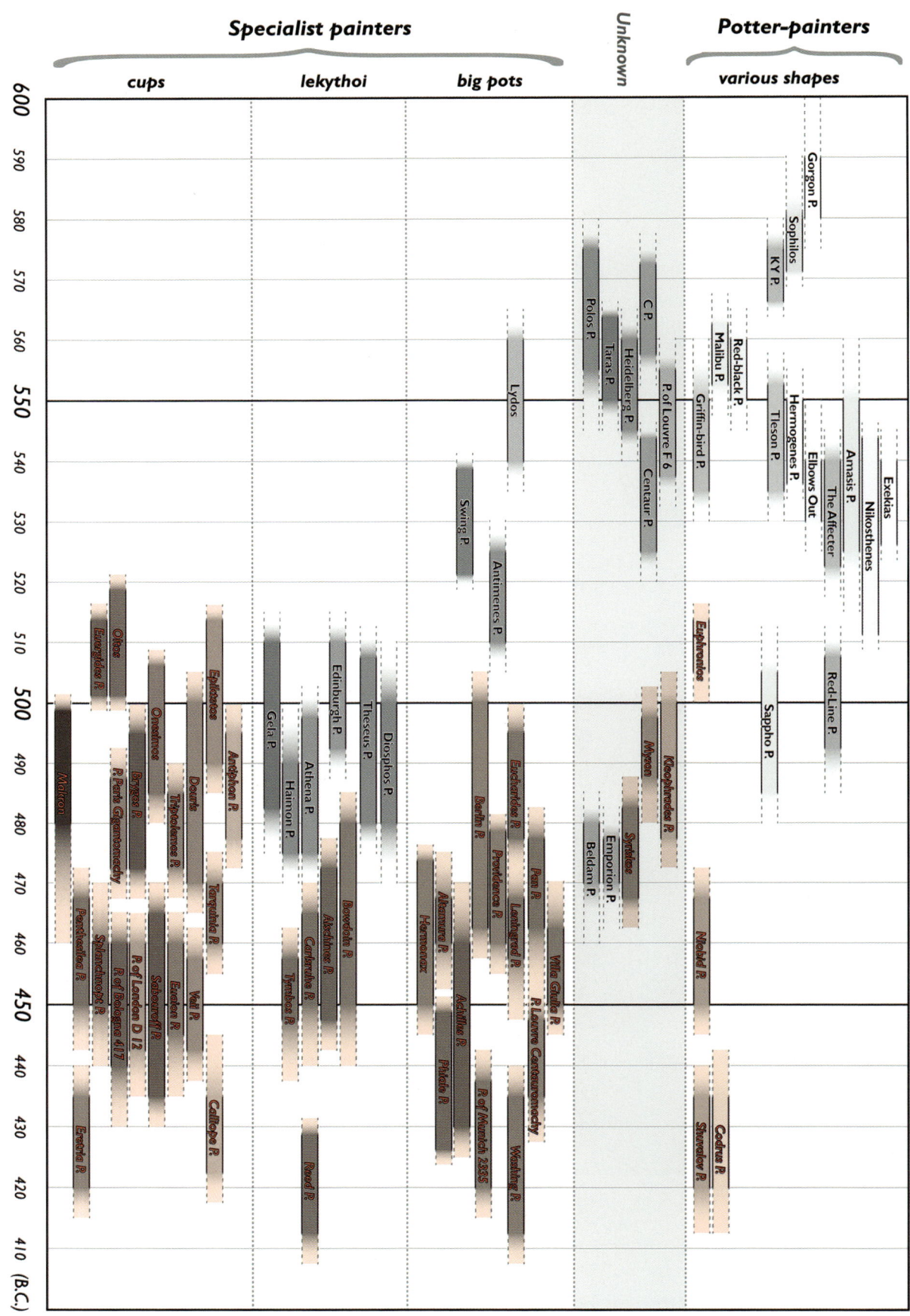

Pl. 24. Specialists and potter-painters in Archaic and Classical Athens.

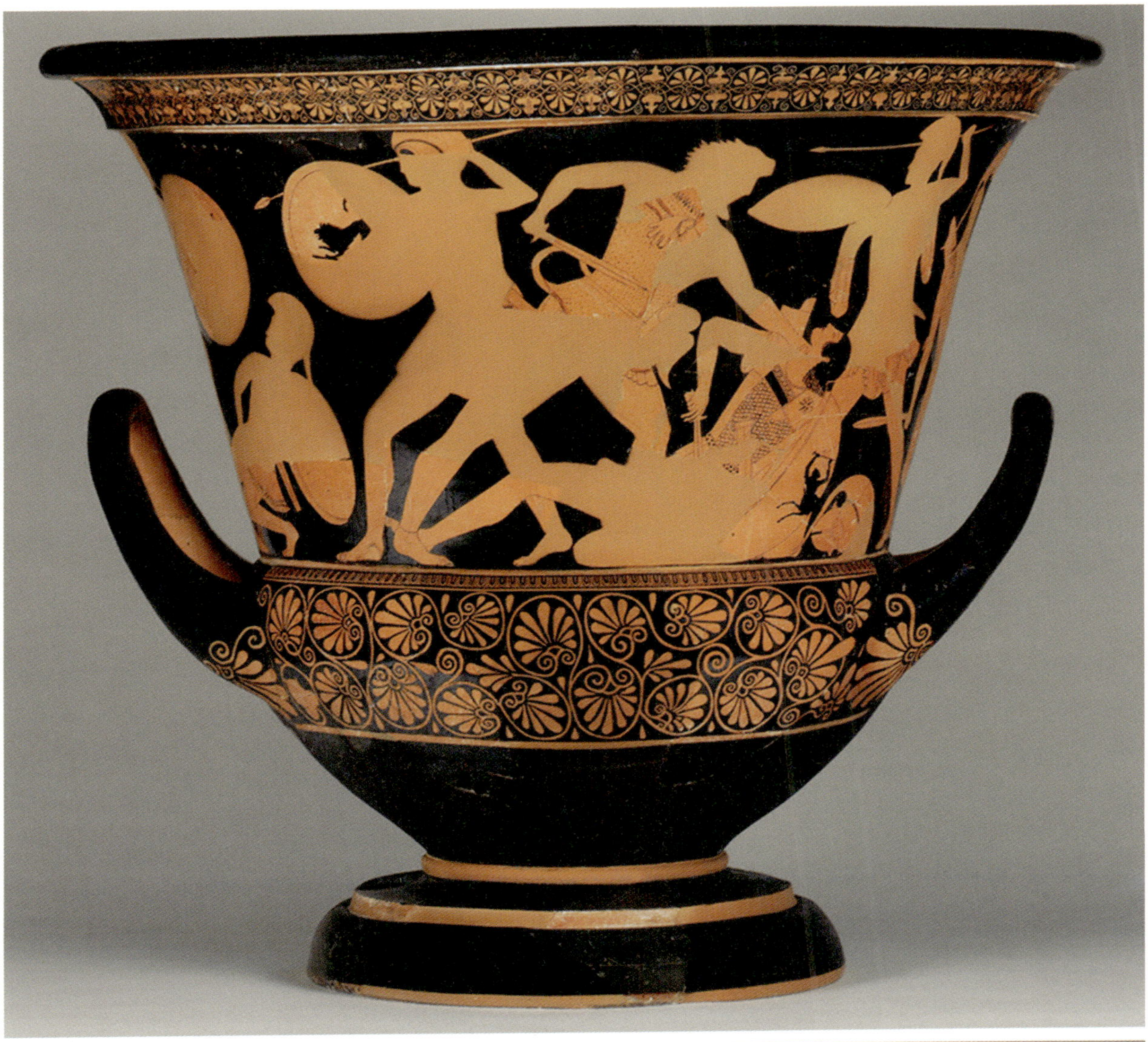

Color Plate 25

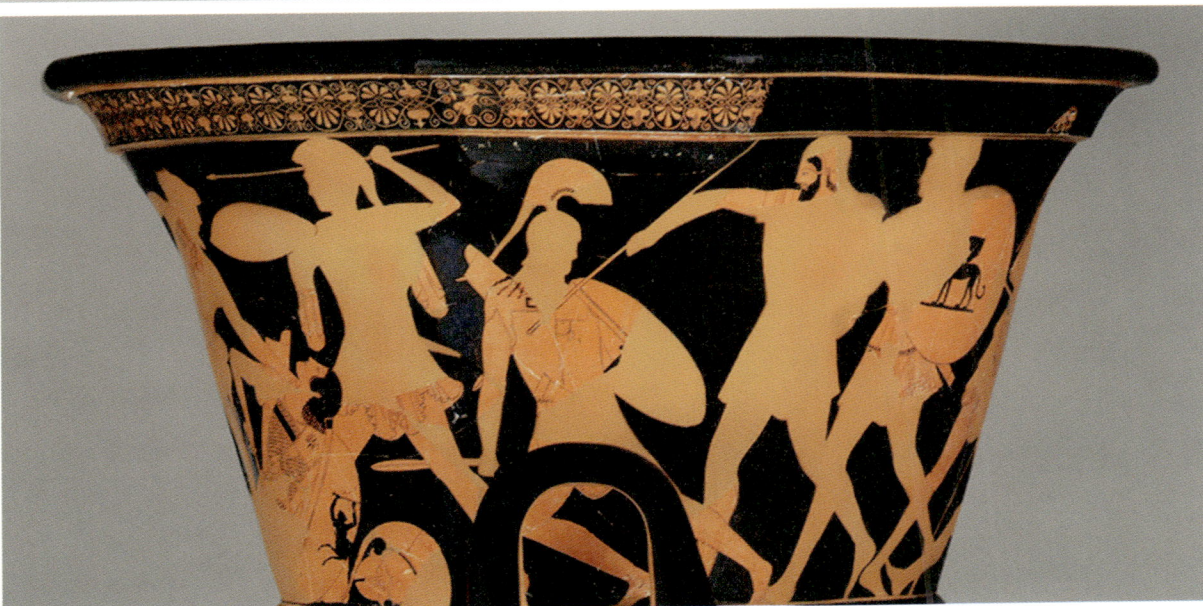

Pl. 25A–B. The J. Paul Getty Museum, Villa Collection, Malibu, California (81.AE. 219.2) Calyx krater attributed to the Syleus Painter. 480–470 BC. H. 64.5 × 68.9 cm (25 3/8 × 27 1/8 in).

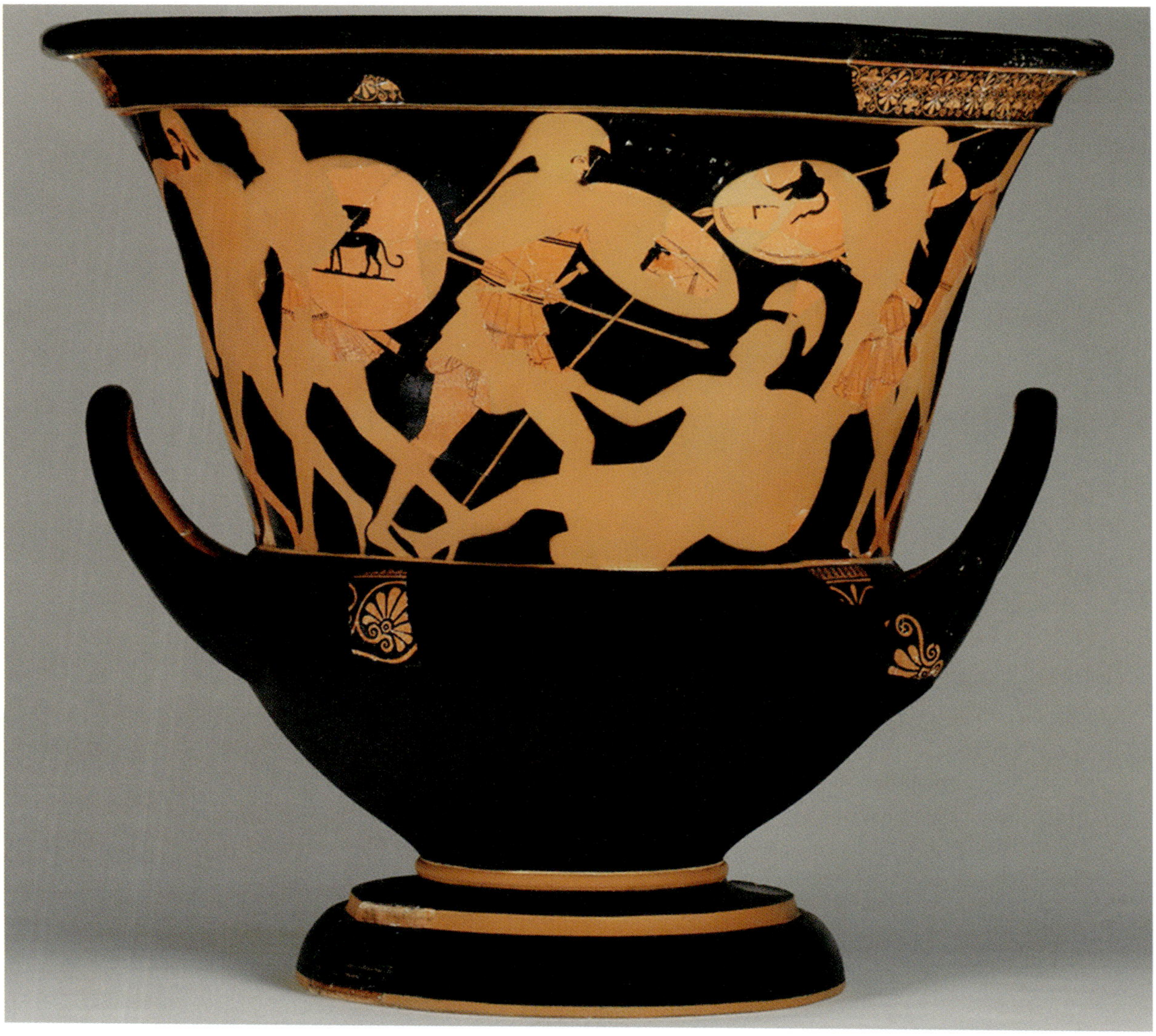

Color Plate 26

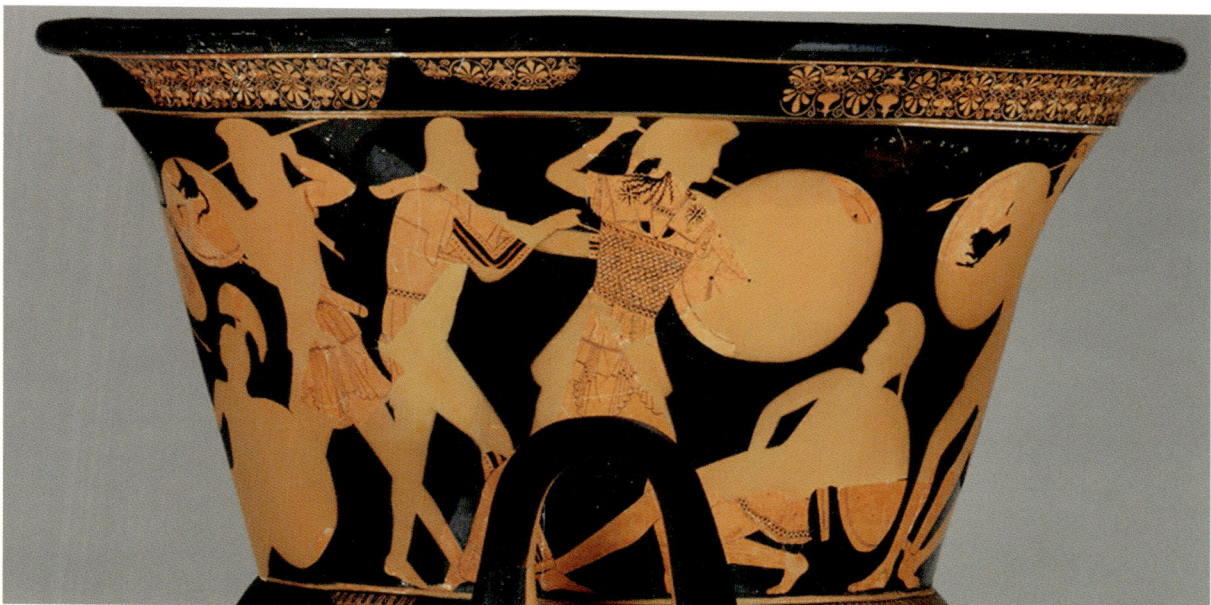

Pl. 26A–B. The J. Paul Getty Museum, Villa Collection, Malibu, California (81.AE. 219.2) Calyx krater attributed to the Syleus Painter. 480–470 BC. H. 64.5 × 68.9 cm (25 3/8 × 27 1/8 in).

Color Plate 27

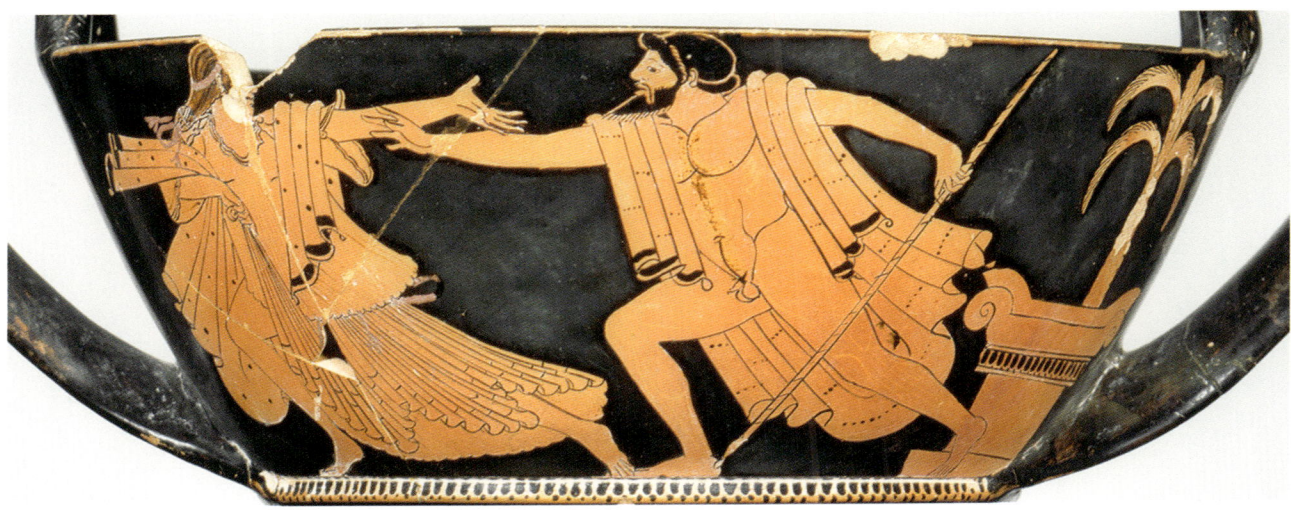

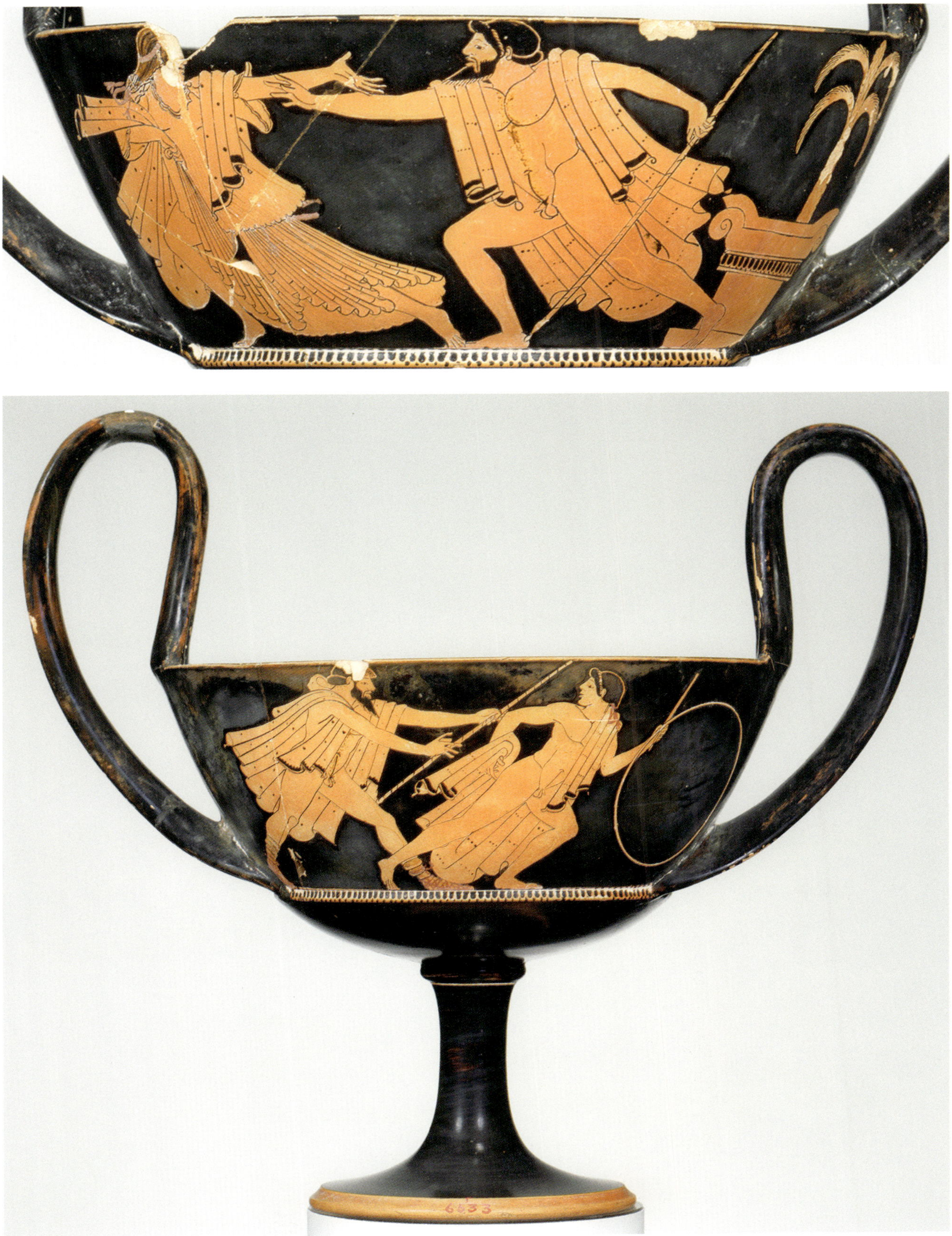

Pl. 27A–B. High-Handled cup (kantharos) with Zeus pursuing Aegina and Ganymede, attributed to the Brygos Painter, ceramic, red-figure, Greek Late Archaic period, about 490–480 BC, *Catharine Page Perkins Fund. (95.36) Photograph © 2013 Museum of Fine Arts, Boston.

Color Plate 28

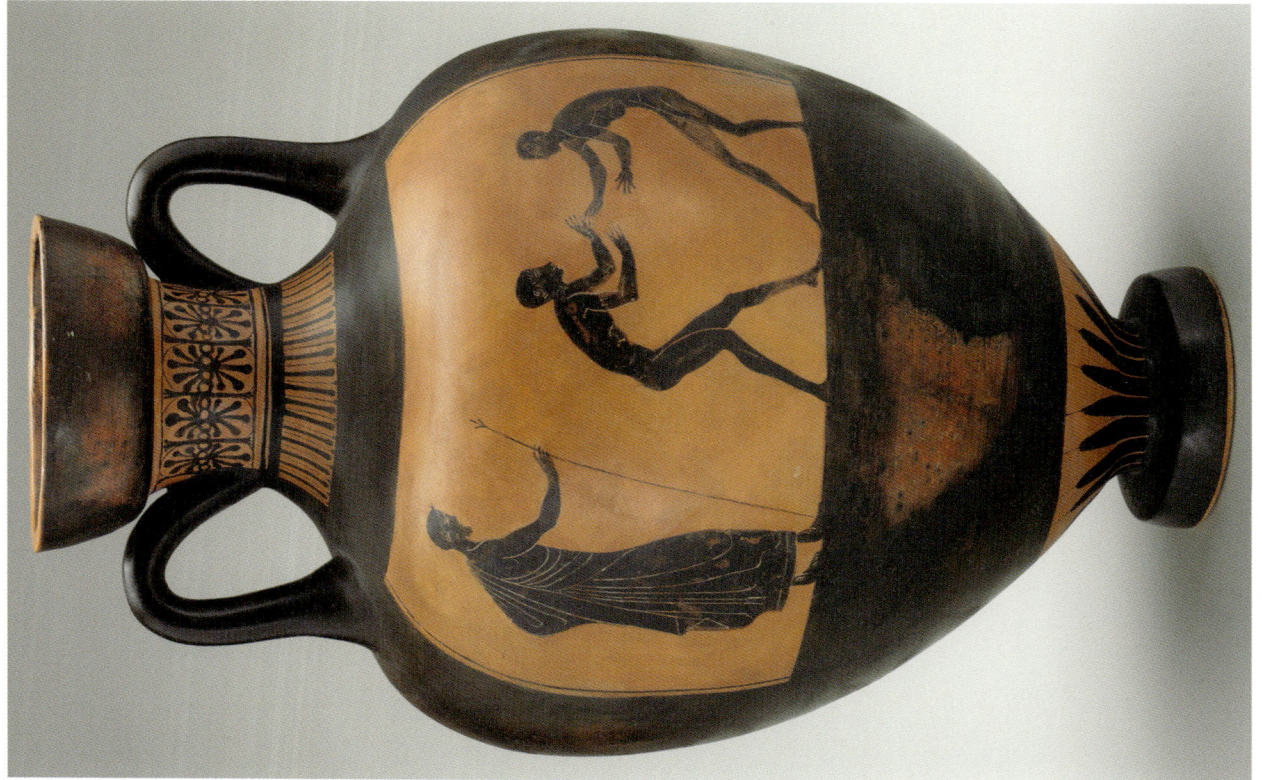

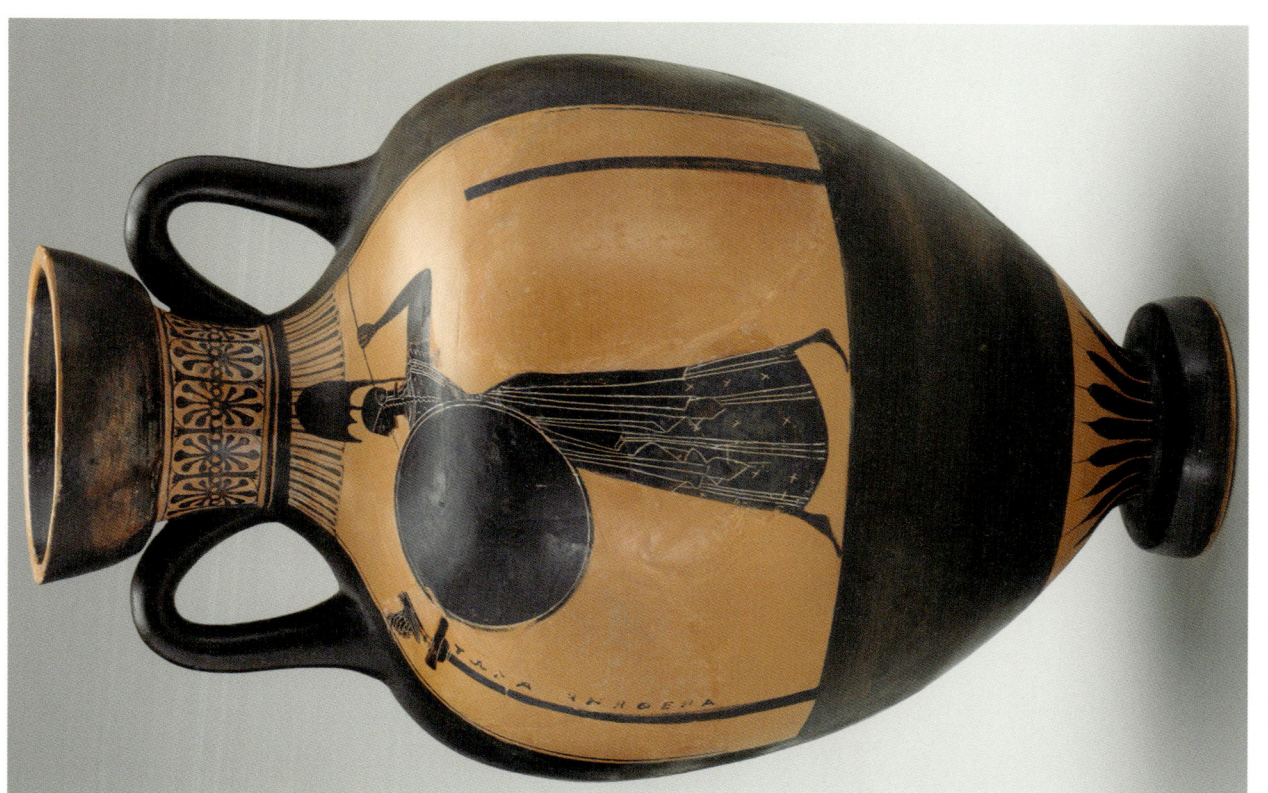

Pl. 28A. Baltimore Museum of Art 1960.55.3 (on loan to the Johns Hopkins University Archaeological Museum). Panathenaic prize amphora of the Robinson Group, Side A. Photo: Courtesy Baltimore Museum of Art.

Pl. 28B. Side B of the amphora in Color Pl. 28A: boy wrestlers. Photo: Courtesy Baltimore Museum of Art.

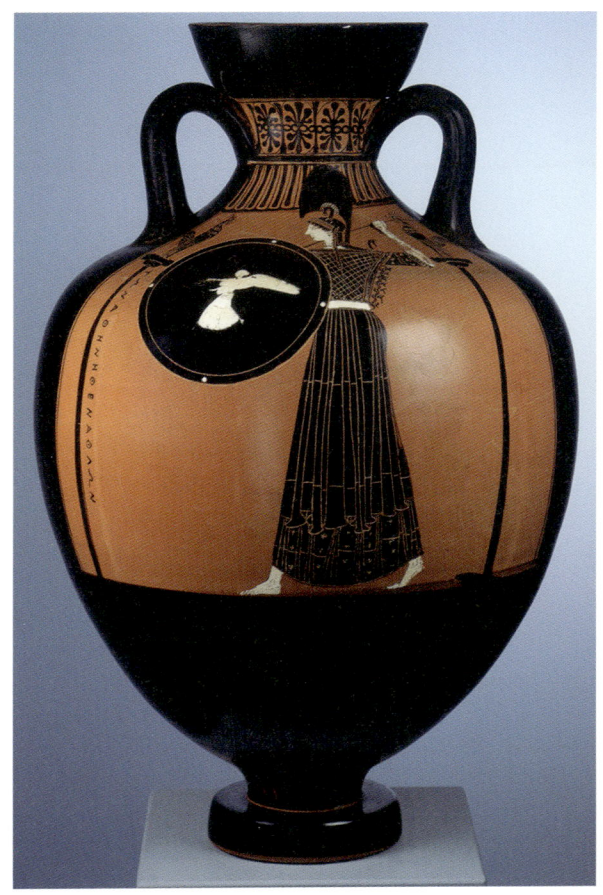

Pl. 29A. Copenhagen, Ny Carlsberg Glyptotek 3606. Panathenaic Prize amphora of the Robinson Group, Side A. Photo: Courtesy Museum.

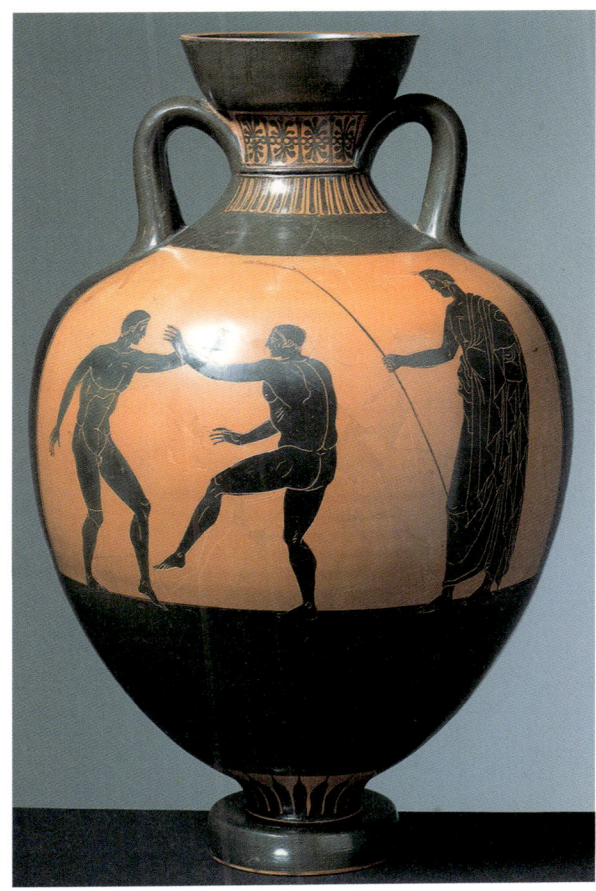

Pl. 29B. Side B of the amphora in Color Pl. 29A: youths wrestling. Photo: Courtesy Museum.

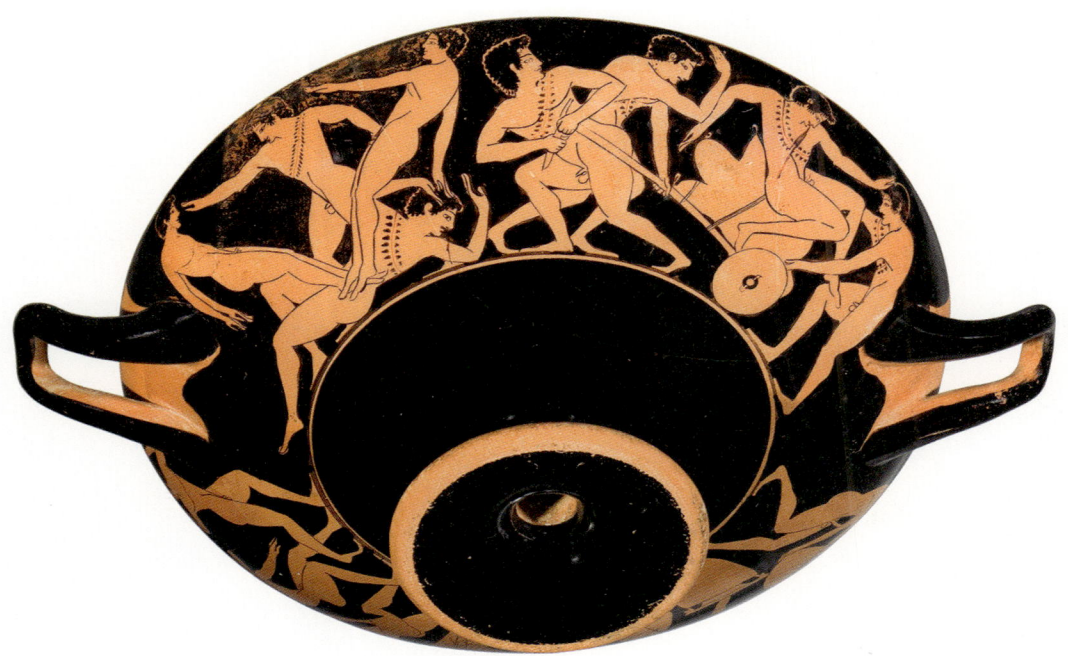

Pl. 29C. Basle, Antikenmuseum und Sammlung Ludwig BS463. Red-figure cup exterior. Epeleios Painter. Photo: Antikenmuseum Basel und Sammlung/A. Voegelin.

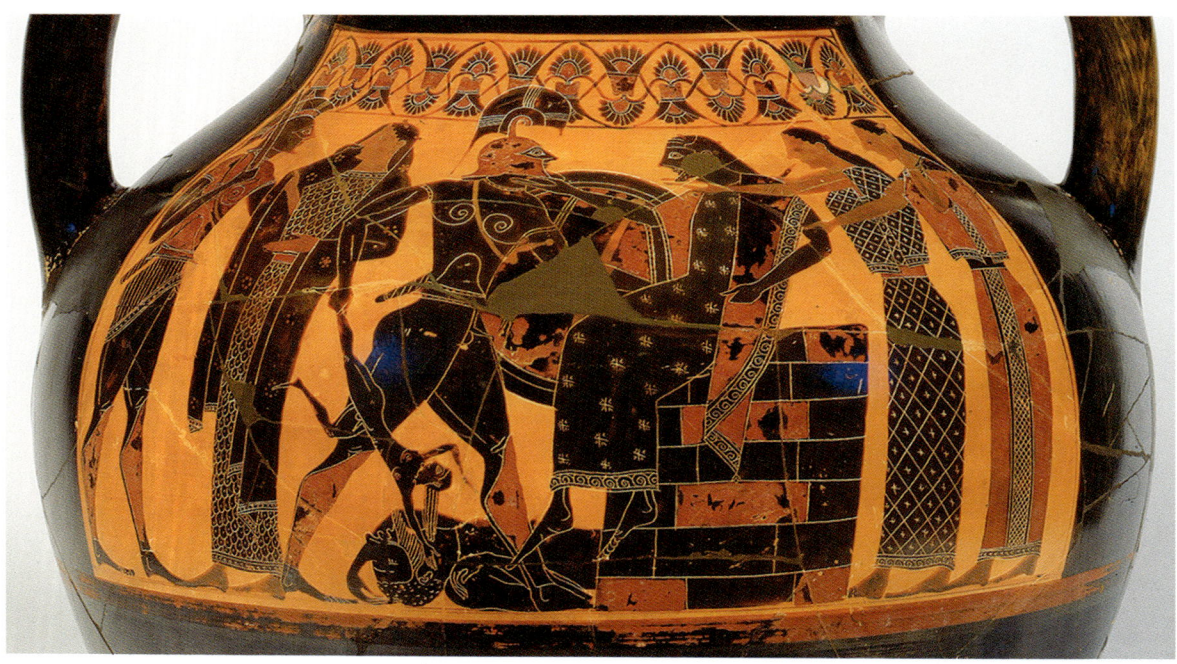

Pl. 30A. Attic black-figure amphora, Berlin F1685. Photo: bpk, Berlin/Antikensammlung, Staatliche Museen, Berlin, Germany/ Ingrid Gesk /Art Resource, NY.

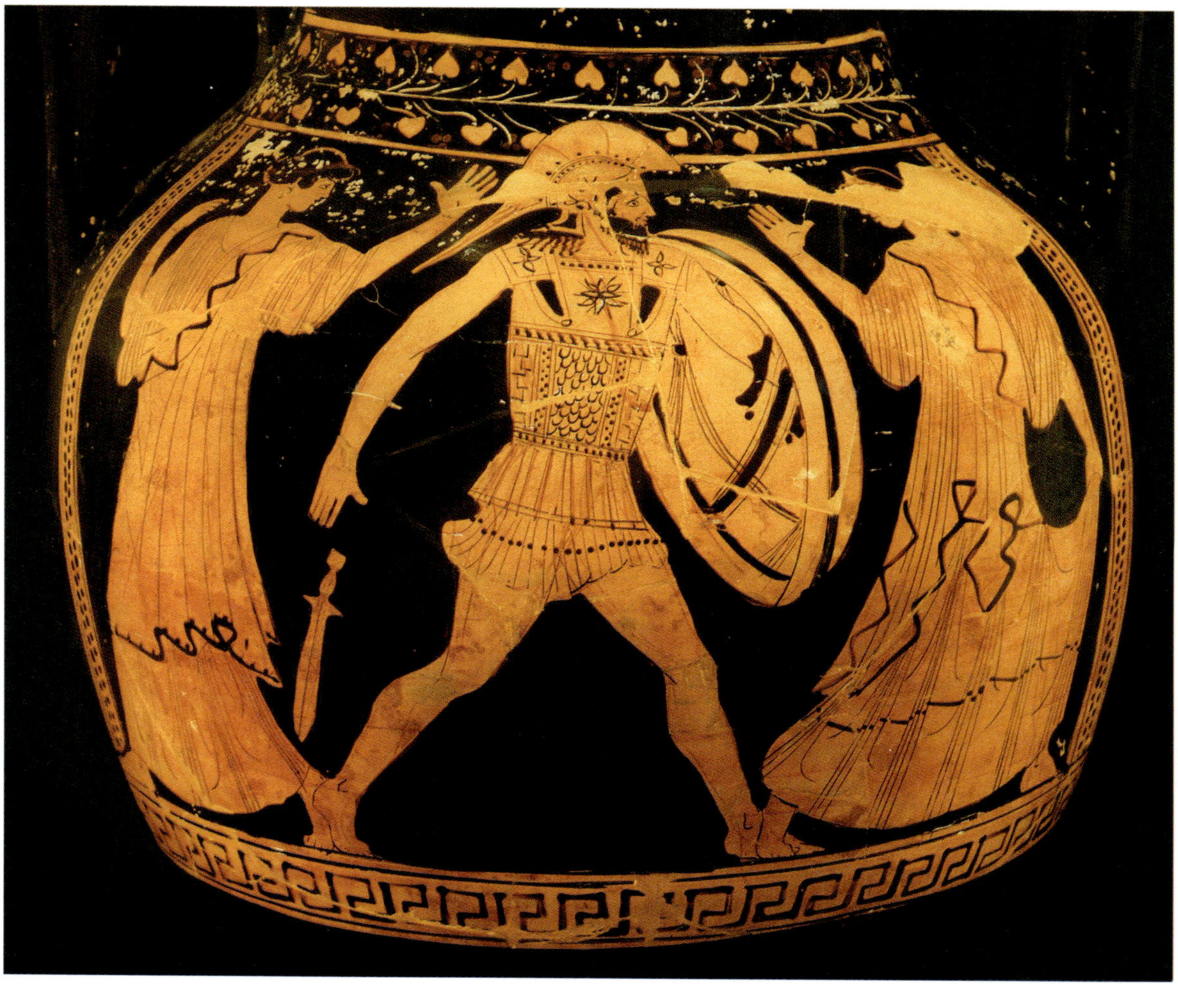

Pl. 30B. Attic red-figure amphora, London E263. Photo: ©Trustees of the British Museum.

Color Plate 31

Pl. 31A. Black-figure band cup fragment (AK 4166). Near BMN Painter. Two women (goddesses?) unveiling to approaching males.

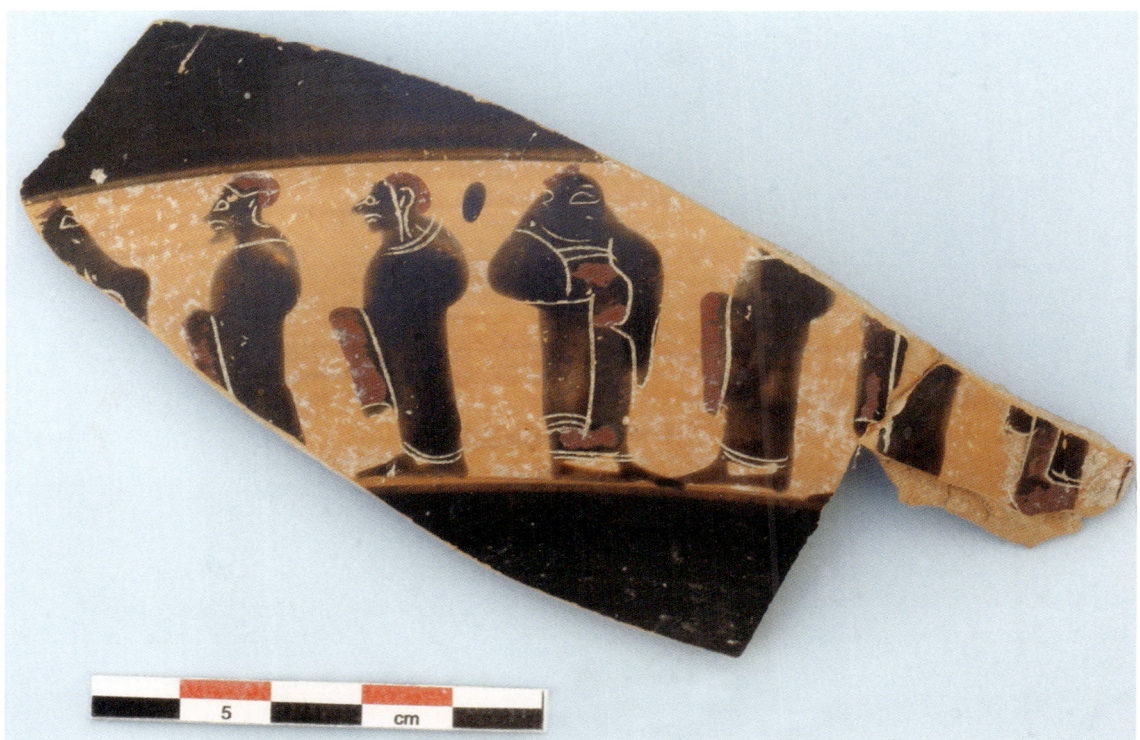

Pl. 31B. Black-figure Siana cup fragment. Heidelberg Painter. Battling hoplites.

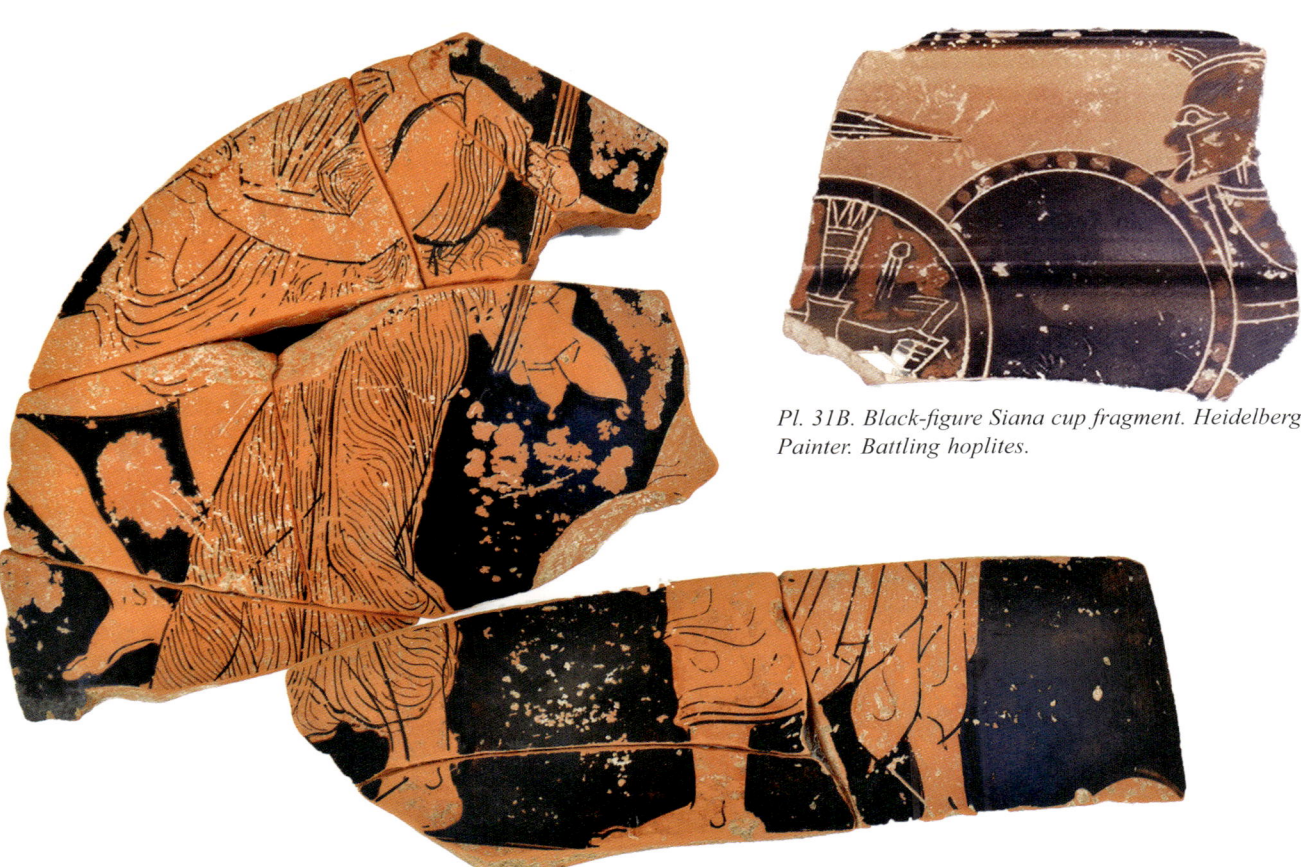

Pl. 31C. Red-figure bell krater fragment (AK 5095). Dinos Painter. Komos.

Color Plate 32

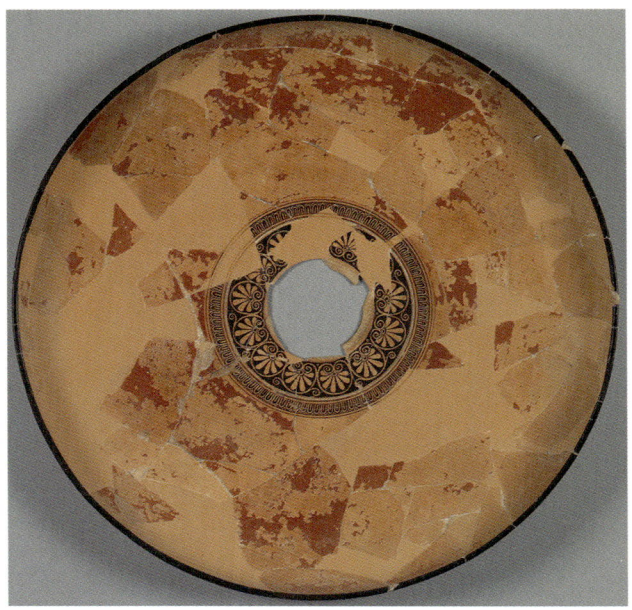

Pl. 32A. Phiale attributed to the Berlin Painter, Malibu, J. Paul Getty Museum 76.AE.96.2 (© The J. Paul Getty Museum, Villa Collection, Malibu, California).

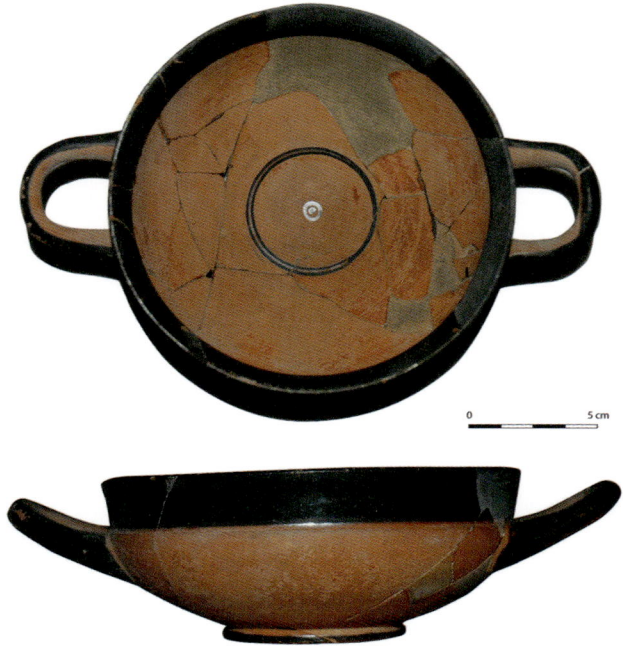

Pl. 32B. Athens, Agora Museum P 16001 (Photos: Author).

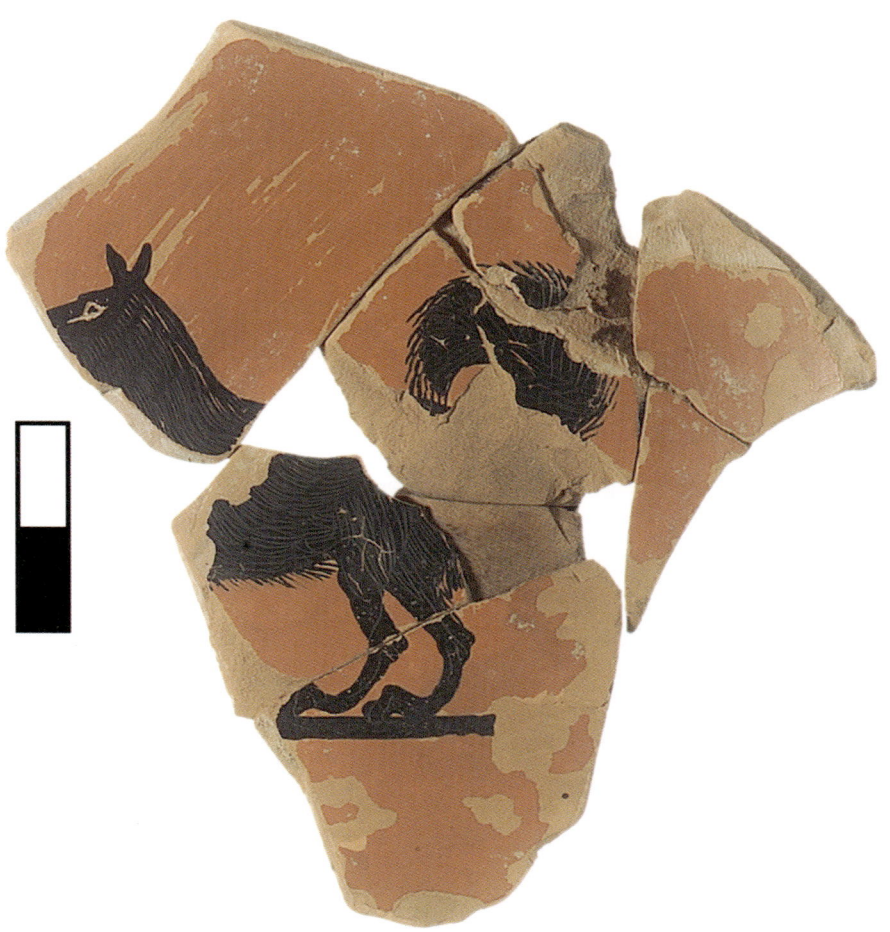

Pl. 32C. Athens, Agora Museum P 10350: black-figure dog (© American School of Classical Studies at Athens, The Athenian Agora).